# PROBLEM SOLVING AND PROGRAM DESIGN IN

second edition

# PROBLEM SOLVING AND PROGRAM DESIGN IN

second edition

## Jeri R. Hanly

UNIVERSITY OF WYOMING

## Elliot B. Koffman

TEMPLE UNIVERSITY

**Addison-Wesley Publishing Company**

Reading, Massachusetts • Menlo Park, California • New York • Don Mills, Ontario
Wokingham, England • Amsterdam • Bonn • Sydney • Singapore • Tokyo • Madrid
San Juan • Milan • Paris

**Lynne Doran Cote**  *Sponsoring Editor*
**Helen M. Wythe**  *Senior Production Editor*
**Maite Suarez-Rivas and Anita Devine**  *Assistant Editors*
**Lisa Delgado**  *Text Designer*
**Tech-Graphics**  *Illustrations*
**Eileen Hoff**  *Cover Design Supervisor*
**Diana Coe**  *Cover Design*
**Roy Logan**  *Senior Manufacturing Manager*
**Michael and Sigrid Wile**  *Composition*

**Library of Congress Cataloging-in-Publication Data**
Hanly, Jeri R.
    Problem solving and program design in C / Jeri R. Hanly, Elliot B.
Koffman. -- 2nd ed.
       p.    cm.
    Includes index.
    ISBN 0-201-59063-8
    1. C (Computer program language)    I. Koffman, Elliot B.
II. Title.
QA76.73.C15H363   1996
005.13'3--dc20                                95-7320
                                                  CIP

2 3 4 5 6 7 8 9 10–DOC–98979695

*To our families
Brian, Eric, and
Kevin Hanly;
Caryn, Richard,
Deborah, and
Robin Koffman*

This textbook teaches a disciplined approach to solving problems and to applying widely accepted software engineering methods to design program solutions as cohesive, readable, reusable modules. We present as an implementation vehicle for these modules a subset of ANSI C—a standardized, industrial-strength programming language known for its power and portability. This text can be used for a first course in programming methods: It assumes no prior knowledge of computers or programming. The text's broad selection of case studies and exercises allows an instructor to design an introductory programming course in C for computer science majors or for students from a wide range of other disciplines.

In preparing this new edition, we have made every effort to simplify the presentation wherever possible, striving for more focused chapters. For example, we have consolidated the coverage of relational, equality, and logical operators in Chapter 4 where conditions are first needed for selection structures. We have placed all three loop constructs in Chapter 5 along with the operators with side effects (++, +=, and so on).

This edition discusses user-defined functions with input parameters earlier than did Edition 1, presenting these functions in Chapter 3 and using them regularly thereafter. Besides expanding our coverage of ANSI C string library functions, we have added coverage of enumerated types, functions as parameters, stacks, and dynamic memory allocation. We also present several data structures composed of dynamically allocated nodes, including linked lists (used as stacks, as queues, and as ordered lists) and binary trees.

An important style change in this new edition is the early introduction of function prototypes. Consequently, our standard source file format in this edition is (1) preprocessor directives, (2) function prototypes, (3) function `main`, and (4) other function definitions.

## Using C to Teach Program Development

Two of our goals—teaching program design and teaching C—may be seen by some as contradictory. C is widely perceived as a language to be tackled only after one has learned the fundamentals of programming in some other, friendlier language. The perception that C is excessively difficult is traceable to the history of the language. Designed as a vehicle for programming the UNIX operating system, C found its original clientele among programmers who understood the complexities of the operating system and the underlying machine, and who considered it natural to exploit this knowledge in their programs. Therefore, it is not surprising that many textbooks whose primary goal is to teach C expose the student to program examples requiring an understanding of machine concepts that are not in the syllabus of a standard introductory programming course.

In this text we are able to teach both a rational approach to program development and an introduction to ANSI C because we have chosen the first goal as our primary one. One might fear that this choice would lead to a watered-down treatment of ANSI C. On the contrary, we find that the blended presentation of programming concepts and of the implementation of these concepts in C captures a focused picture of the power of ANSI C as a high-level programming language, a picture that is often blurred in texts whose foremost objective is the coverage of all of ANSI C. Even following this approach of giving program design precedence over discussion of C language features, we have arrived at a coverage of the essential constructs of C that is quite comprehensive.

## Pointers and the Organization of the Book

The order in which C language topics are presented is dictated by our view of the needs of the beginning programmer rather than by the structure of the C programming language. The reader may be surprised to discover that there is no chapter entitled "Pointers." This missing chapter title follows from our treatment of C as a high-level language, not from a lack of awareness of the critical role of pointers in C.

Whereas other high-level languages have separate language constructs for output parameters and arrays, C openly folds these concepts into its notion of a pointer, drastically increasing the complexity of learning the language. We simplify the learning process by discussing pointers from these separate perspectives where such topics normally arise when teaching other programming languages, thus allowing a student to absorb the intricacies of pointer usage a little at a time. Our approach makes possible the presentation of fundamental concepts using traditional high-level language terminology—output parameter, array, array subscript, string—and makes it easier for students without prior assembly language background to master the many facets of pointer usage.

Therefore, this text has not one, but four chapters that focus on pointers. Chapter 6 discusses the use of pointers as simple output and input/output parameters, Chapter 8 deals with arrays, Chapter 9 presents strings and arrays of pointers, and Chapter 14 describes dynamic memory allocation. In addition, Chapters 2 and 12 discuss file pointers.

## New to this Edition: Applications Written in C

A new feature of this edition is a collection of brief articles presenting applications written in C. Included are descriptions of Vivo320, a video-conferencing tool; LINEUP, a database system for criminal mug shots; and the Borland C/C++ compiler. In addition, one article traces the history of the joint development of UNIX and C.

## Software Engineering Concepts

The book presents many aspects of software engineering. Some are explicitly discussed and others are taught only by example. The connection between good problem-solving skills and effective software development is established early in Chapter 1 with a section that discusses the art and science of problem solving. The five-phase software development method presented in Chapter 1 is used to solve the first case study and is applied uniformly to case studies throughout the text. Major program style issues are highlighted in special displays, and the coding style used in examples is based on guidelines followed in segments of the C software industry. There are sections in several chapters that discuss algorithm tracing, program debugging, and testing.

Chapter 3 introduces procedural abstraction through selected C library functions, parameterless void functions, and functions that take input parameters and return a value. Chapters 4 and 5 include additional function examples, and Chapter 6 completes the study of functions that have simple parameters. The chapter discusses the use of pointers to represent output and input/output parameters, and Chapter 7 introduces the use of a function as a parameter.

Case studies and sample programs in Chapters 6, 8, and 11 introduce by example the concepts of data abstraction and of encapsulation of a data type and operators. Chapter 13 presents C's facilities for formalizing procedural and data abstraction in personal libraries defined by separate header and implementation files.

The use of visible function interfaces is emphasized throughout the text. We do not mention the possibility of using a global variable until Chapter 13, and then we carefully describe both the dangers and the value of global variable usage.

## Pedagogical Features

We employ several pedagogical features to enhance the usefulness of this book as a teaching tool. Some of these features are discussed below.

***End-of-Section Exercises***   Most sections end with a number of self-check exercises. These include exercises that require analysis of program fragments as well as short programming exercises. Answers to selected self-check exercises appear at the back of the book; answers to the rest of the exercises are provided in the instructor's manual.

***End-of-Chapter Exercises***   A set of quick-check exercises with answers follows each Chapter Review. There are also review exercises whose solutions appear in the instructor's manual.

***End-of-Chapter Projects***   Each chapter ends with a set of programming projects. Answers to selected projects appear in the instructor's manual.

*Examples and Case Studies*    The book contains a wide variety of programming examples. Whenever possible, examples contain complete programs or functions rather than incomplete program fragments. Each chapter contains one or more substantial case studies that are solved following the software development method. Numerous case studies give the student glimpses of important applications of computing, including database searching, business applications such as billing and sales analysis, word processing, environmental applications such as radiation level monitoring and water conservation.

*Syntax Display Boxes*    The syntax displays describe the syntax and semantics of new C features and provide examples.

*Program Style Displays*    The program style displays discuss major issues of good programming style.

*Error Discussions and Chapter Review*    Each chapter concludes with a section that discusses common programming errors. A chapter review includes a table of new C constructs.

## Appendixes and Supplement

A reference table of ANSI C constructs appears on the inside covers of the book, and the first appendix presents character set tables. Because this text covers only a subset of ANSI C, the remaining appendixes play an especially vital role in increasing the value of the book as a reference. Appendix B is an alphabetized table of ANSI C library facilities. Appendix C gives a table showing the precedence and associativity of all ANSI C operators; the operators not previously defined are explained in this appendix. Throughout the book, array referencing is done with subscript notation; Appendix D is the only coverage of pointer arithmetic. Appendix E lists all ANSI C reserved words.

*Source Code*

An on-line version of the source code figures is available at our anonymous ftp site. To access, set your ftp to `aw.com`. At the prompt, log in as `anonymous` and use your internet address as the password. From there, you change to the directory `cd cseng/authors/hanly/cs1.2e`.

*Instructor's Manual*

The Instructor's Manual includes chapter by chapter summaries and suggestions based on selected textbook figures. These are available via the `aw.com` ftp site. You will need to contact your sales rep for the password. Please see directions above under "Source Code" on how to access this site.

*Solutions and Test Questions*

Test questions and solutions to the internal self check, review questions and selected programming projects are available by contacting your local Addison-Wesley sales representative.

## Acknowledgments

Many people participated in the development of this book. We thank especially Cindy Johnson, who developed the articles on C applications, and Paul W. Abrahams, Kenneth Pugh of Pugh-Killeen Associates, Oliver Jones of Vivo Software Inc., and Michael R. Weisert of Borland International Inc., who provided the material for these articles. We thank Joan C. Horvath of the Jet Propulsion Laboratory, California Institute of Technology, for contributing several new programming exercises. We are grateful for the work of several Temple University and University of Wyoming students and former students who helped to verify the programming examples and who provided answer keys for the host of exercises. These include Mark Thoney, Lynne Doherty, Andrew Wrobel, Steve Babiak, Donna Chrupcala, Masoud Kermani, and Thayne Routh.

The principal reviewers were enormously helpful in suggesting improvements and in finding errors. They include: Steve Allan, Utah State University; Michael Beeson, San Jose State - Chico; John Lewis, Villanova University; James Schmolze, Tufts University; Larry Sells, Oklahoma City University; Travis Tull, University of Tulsa; Richard Weinand, Wayne State University; and Beth Weiss, University of Arizona.

It has been a pleasure to work with the Addison-Wesley team in this endeavor. The sponsoring editor, Lynne Doran Cote, provided much guidance and encouragement throughout all phases of manuscript revision. Her assistants, Maite Suarez-Rivas and Anita Devine, coordinated the review process and the preparation of the instructor's manual and handled a great variety of other details. Helen Wythe supervised the design and production of the book, while Tom Ziolkowski developed the marketing campaign.

J.R.H.
E.B.K.

# CONTENTS

# 6. Modular Programming 269

# 7. Simple Data Types                    315

# 8. Arrays                              355

# Appendixes

# Answers                                                        A1

# Index                                                          I1

# Overview of Computers and Programming

chapter

$S$ince the 1940s, the computer has dramatically changed the way we live and how we do business. Today computers provide instructional material in school, print transcripts, prepare bills and paychecks, reserve airline and concert tickets, allow us to bank and shop conveniently, and help us write term papers and even books.

The computer program's role in this technology is essential; without a list of instructions to follow, the computer is virtually useless. Programming languages allow us to write those programs and thus to communicate with computers.

You are about to begin the study of computer science using one of the most versatile programming languages available today: the C language. This chapter introduces you to the computer and its components and to the major categories of programming languages. It discusses how C programs are processed by a computer. It also describes a systematic approach to solving programming problems called the software development method and shows you how to apply it.

## 1.1 ELECTRONIC COMPUTERS THEN AND NOW

In our everyday life, we come in contact with computers frequently, some of us using computers for word processing or even having studied programming in high school. But it wasn't always this way. Not so long ago, most people considered computers to be mysterious devices whose secrets were known only by a few computer wizards.

The first electronic computer was built in the late 1930s by Dr. John Atanasoff and Clifford Berry at Iowa State University. Atanasoff designed his computer to assist graduate students in nuclear physics with their mathematical computations.

The first large-scale, general-purpose electronic digital computer, called the ENIAC, was completed in 1946 at the University of Pennsylvania with funding from the U.S. Army. Weighing 30 tons and occupying a 30-by-50-foot space, the ENIAC was used to compute ballistics tables, predict the weather, and make atomic energy calculations.

These early computers used vacuum tubes as their basic electronic component. Technological advances in the design and manufacture of electronic components led to new generations of computers that were considerably smaller, faster, and less expensive than previous ones.

**computer chip (micro-processor chip)** a silicon chip containing the circuitry for a computer processor

Using today's technology, the entire circuitry of a computer processor can be packaged in a single electronic component called a **computer chip** (Fig. 1.1), which is about the size of a postage stamp. Their affordability and small size

2

Mohammed ibn Musa al-Khowarizmi (mathamatision)

(a)                                                                    (b)

**Figure 1.1    Microprocessor Chip.** The Intel Pentium™ Processor chip (a) is an integrated circuit containing the full circuitry of a central processor unit (b). The Pentium™ executes 112 million instructions per second. (Courtesy Intel Corporation.)

enable computer chips to be installed in watches, pocket calculators, cameras, home appliances, automobiles, and, of course, computers.

Today, a common sight in offices and homes is a personal computer, which can cost less than $2000 and sit on a desk, and yet has as much computational power as one that 15 years ago cost more than $100,000 and filled a 9-by-12-foot room. Even smaller computers can fit inside a briefcase (Fig. 1.2a) or your hand (Fig. 1.2b).

Modern-day computers are categorized according to their size and performance. *Microcomputers,* shown in Fig. 1.2, are used by a single person at a time. The largest microcomputers are called *workstations* (Fig. 1.2c). Businesses and research laboratories also use larger and faster computers, called *minicomputers* and *mainframes,* which can be used by many people simultaneously. *Supercomputers,* the most powerful mainframe computers, can perform in seconds computations that might take hours or even days on other computers.

**hardware**
the actual computer equipment

The elements of a computer system fall into two major categories: hardware and software. **Hardware** is the equipment used to perform the necessary

(a)                                                            (b)

(c)

**Figure 1.2**   **(a) Notebook Computer.  (b) Palmtop Computer.  (c) Workstation.**

**software**
the set of programs associated with a computer

**program**
a list of instructions that enables a computer to perform a specific task

**binary number**
a number whose digits are 0 and 1

computations and includes the central processing unit (CPU), monitor, keyboard, and printer. **Software** consists of the **programs** that enable us to solve problems with a computer by providing it with lists of instructions to perform.

Programming a computer has undergone significant changes over the years. Initially, the task was very difficult, requiring programmers to write their program instructions as long **binary numbers** (sequences of 0s and 1s). Today's programming languages such as C make programming much easier.

**EXERCISES FOR SECTION 1.1**

Self-Check

1. Is a computer program a piece of hardware or is it software?
2. Which do you think is the major source of computer errors, faulty computer hardware or incorrect software?

# 1.2 INTRODUCTION TO COMPUTER HARDWARE

Despite significant variations in cost, size, and capabilities, modern computers resemble one another in many basic ways. Essentially, most consist of the following components:

- Main memory
- Secondary memory, which includes storage devices such as hard disks and floppy disks
- The central processor unit
- Input devices, such as keyboards and mouses
- Output devices, such as monitors and printers

Figure 1.3 shows how these components interact in a computer, with the arrows pointing in the direction of information flow. The program must first be transferred from *secondary storage* to *main memory* before it can be executed. Normally the person using a program (the *program user*) must supply some data to be processed. These data are entered through an *input device* and are stored in the computer's *main memory,* where they can be accessed and manipulated by the *central processor unit.* The results of this manipulation are then stored back in *main memory.* Finally, the information in main memory can be displayed through an *output device.* In the remainder of this section, we describe these components in more detail.

## Memory

Memory is an essential component in any computer. Let's look at what it consists of and how the computer works with it.

**Figure 1.3
Components of
a Computer**

Secondary
storage

**Input
devices**

Keyboard

Mouse

Main
memory

Central
processor
unit

Monitor

**Output
devices**

Printer

**memory cell**
an individual storage location
in memory

**address of a memory cell**
the relative position of a
memory cell in the computer's
main memory

**contents of a memory cell**
the information stored in a
memory cell, either a program
instruction or data

**stored program concept**
storing program instructions
in main memory prior to execution

**Anatomy of Memory**   Imagine the memory of a computer as an ordered
sequence of storage locations called **memory cells** (see Fig. 1.4). To store and
access information, the computer must have some way of identifying the individual memory cells. Therefore each memory cell has a unique **address** that
indicates its relative position in memory. Figure 1.4 shows a computer memory
consisting of 1000 memory cells with addresses 0 through 999. Most computers,
however, have millions of individual memory cells, each with its own address.

The data stored in a memory cell are called the **contents** of the cell. Every
memory cell always has some contents, although we may have no idea what they
are. In Fig. 1.4, the contents of memory cell 3 are the number −26 and the contents of memory cell 4 are the letter H.

Although not shown in Fig. 1.4, a memory cell can also contain a program
instruction. The ability to store programs as well as data is called the **stored
program concept**: A program's instructions must be stored in main memory
before they can be executed. We can change the computer's operation by storing
a different program in memory.

**Figure 1.4
1000 Memory
Cells in Main
Memory**

Memory

| Address | Contents |
|---------|----------|
| 0 | −27.2 |
| 1 | 354 |
| 2 | 0.005 |
| 3 | −26 |
| 4 | H |
| . | . |
| . | . |
| . | . |
| 998 | X |
| 999 | 75.62 |

**byte**
the amount of storage required
to store a single character
**bit**
a binary digit; a 0 or a 1

**Bytes and Bits**    A memory cell is actually a grouping of smaller units called bytes. A **byte** is the amount of storage required to store a single character, such as the letter H used in Fig. 1.4. The number of bytes a memory cell can contain varies from computer to computer. A byte is composed of even smaller units of storage called bits (see Fig. 1.5). The term **bit**, deriving from the words binary digit, is the smallest element a computer can deal with. Binary refers to a number system based on two numbers, 0 and 1, and so a bit is either a 0 or a 1. Generally there are eight bits to a byte.

**data storage**
setting the individual bits of a
memory cell to 0 or 1,
destroying its previous contents
**data retrieval**
copying the contents of a particular memory cell to another
storage area

**Storage and Retrieval of Information in Memory**    Each value in memory is represented by a particular pattern of 0s and 1s. A computer can either store a value or retrieve a value. To **store** a value, the computer sets each bit of a selected memory cell to either 0 or 1, destroying the previous contents of the cell in the process. To **retrieve** a value from a memory cell, the computer copies the pattern of 0s and 1s stored in that cell to another storage area for processing; the copy operation does not destroy the contents of the cell whose value is retrieved. This process is the same regardless of the kind of information—character, number, or program instruction—to be stored or retrieved.

**Figure 1.5
Relationship
Between a Byte
and a Bit**

```
                        ┌──────Bit
                        ↓
              |00101100|
              ←Byte→
```

**random access memory (RAM)**
the part of main memory that temporarily stores programs, data, and results
**read-only memory (ROM)**
the part of main memory that permanently stores programs or data
**volatile memory**
memory whose contents disappear when the computer is switched off

**Main Memory**    Main memory stores programs, data, and results. Most computers have two types of main memory: **random access memory (RAM)**, which offers temporary storage of programs and data, and **read-only memory (ROM)**, which stores programs or data permanently. RAM temporarily stores programs while they are being executed (carried out) by the computer. It also temporarily stores such data as numbers, names, and even pictures while a program is manipulating them. RAM is usually **volatile memory**, which means that everything in RAM will be lost when the computer is switched off.

ROM, on the other hand, stores information permanently within the computer. The computer can retrieve (or read), but cannot store (or write), information in ROM, hence its name, read-only. Because ROM is not volatile, the data stored there do not disappear when the computer is switched off. Startup instructions and other critical instructions are burned into ROM chips at the factory. When we refer to main memory in this text, we mean RAM because that is the part of main memory that is normally accessible to the programmer.

**Secondary Storage Devices**    Secondary storage devices provide semipermanent data storage capability. A common secondary storage device is a **disk drive**, which stores and retrieves data and programs on a storage medium called a **disk**. A disk is a circular sheet of plastic or metal that is coated with a magnetic material. The 0s and 1s of a byte of data are recorded as magnetic spots on the disk. A disk is considered semipermanent instead of permanent because its contents can be changed, rather like a cassette tape that contains music that can be played over and over, but that can be erased and recorded over.

**disk drive**
a device used to store and retrieve information on a disk
**disk**
a circular sheet of metal or plastic coated with a magnetic material used for secondary data storage in a computer

**hard disk**
a disk with drive that is built into the computer and normally cannot be removed
**floppy disk**
a personal, portable disk that can be used with different computers

There are two kinds of disks commonly used for secondary storage: **hard** (also called fixed) and **floppy**. Most computers contain one hard disk that cannot be removed from its disk drive and so provides a storage area to he shared by all users of the computer. Normally the programs that are needed to operate the computer system are stored on its hard disk. Each computer user can have one or more floppy disks that can be inserted into a computer's floppy disk drive. A floppy disk is a plastic sheet with a diameter of 3.5 or 5.25 inches housed in a thin square container. These floppy disks can store an individual user's programs and personal data.

A hard disk can store much more data, and can be accessed by the CPU much more quickly, than can a single floppy disk. Each user, however, can have an unlimited number of floppy disks. Unlike a hard disk, a floppy disk is portable, which means it can be used with many different computers as long as they are all compatible.

**file**
a collection of related information stored on a disk

Information stored on a disk is organized into separate collections called **files**. One file may contain a C program. Another file may contain the data to be processed by that program (a *data file*). A third file could contain the results generated by a program (an *output file*).

**directory**
a list of the names of files stored on a disk
**subdirectory**
a list of the names of files that relate to a particular topic

The names of all files stored on a disk are listed in the disk's **directory**. This directory may be broken into one or more levels of subdirectories, where each **subdirectory** stores the names of files that relate to the same general topic. For example, you might have separate subdirectories of files that contain homework assignments and programs for each course you are taking this semester. The details of how files are named and grouped in directories vary with each computer system. Follow the naming conventions that apply on your system.

**CD-ROM drive**
a device that accesses the data stored on a compact disk

An increasingly common secondary storage device is a **CD-ROM drive**. This drive accesses information stored on plastic disks that resemble the compact disks used in a CD player. Data on a compact disk are represented by sequences of tiny pits and smooth areas recorded by a laser. The ROM in CD-ROM indicates that currently most drives can only read the data stored on a CD and cannot write new information to the CD.

**Comparison of Main Memory and Secondary Storage**    Because the computer processor can manipulate data only in main memory, data stored in secondary storage, including program instructions, must be transferred into main memory before they can be processed. For this reason, the computer manipulates data and instructions already in main memory much faster than those in secondary storage.

A fixed disk has much more storage capacity than does main memory. On most computers, you can increase the size of main memory by installing additional memory chips. You can also increase the size of secondary storage, by purchasing additional floppy disks or installing another fixed disk. However, main memory is considerably more expensive than secondary storage. Furthermore, data in main memory are volatile and disappear when you switch off the computer, whereas data in secondary storage are semipermanent and do not disappear when the computer is switched off. Therefore store all your programs as files in secondary storage, and transfer a program file into main memory when you want it executed.

## Central Processor Unit

**central processor unit (CPU)**
coordinates all computer operations and performs arithmetic and logical operations on data

The **central processor unit (CPU)** has two roles: coordinating all computer operations and performing arithmetic and logical operations on data. The CPU follows the instructions contained in a computer program to determine which operations should be carried out and in what order. It then transmits coordinating control signals to the other computer components. For example, if the instruction requires scanning a data item, the CPU sends the necessary control signals to the input device.

**fetching an instruction**
retrieving an instruction from main memory

To process a program stored in main memory, the CPU retrieves each instruction in sequence (called **fetching an instruction**), interprets the instruction to determine what should be done, and then retrieves any data needed to carry out that instruction. Next, the CPU performs the actual manipulation, or processing, of the data it retrieved. The CPU stores the results in main memory.

The CPU can perform such arithmetic operations as addition, subtraction, multiplication, and division. The CPU also can compare the contents of two memory cells (for example, Which contains the larger value? Are the values equal?) and make decisions based on the results of that comparison.

## Input/Output Devices

We use *input/output (I/O) devices* to communicate with the computer. Specifically, they allow us to enter data for a computation and to observe the results of that computation.

**cursor**
a moving place marker that appears on the monitor

You will be using a *keyboard* (see Fig. 1.6) as an input device and a *monitor* (display screen) as an output device. When you press a letter or digit key on a keyboard, that character is sent to main memory and is also displayed on the monitor at the position of the **cursor,** a moving place marker (often a blinking line or rectangle). A computer keyboard resembles a typewriter keyboard except for some extra keys for performing special functions. For example, on the computer keyboard shown in Fig. 1.6, the 12 keys in the top row labeled F1 through F12 are **function keys.** The activity performed when you press a function key depends on the program currently being executed; that is, pressing F1 in one program will usually not produce the same results as pressing F1 in another program. Other special keys enable you to delete characters, move the cursor, and "enter" a line of data you typed at the keyboard (see the highlighted parts of Fig. 1.6).

**function keys**
special keyboard keys used to select a particular operation; the operation selected depends on the program being used

Another common input device is a mouse. A **mouse** is a hand-held device used to select an operation. When you move the mouse around on your desktop,

**mouse**
an input device that moves its cursor on the computer screen to select an operation

**Figure 1.6    Keyboard for IBM-Type Computers**

a rubber ball attached to the mouse rotates and simultaneously moves the *mouse cursor* (normally a small rectangle or an arrow) displayed on the monitor's screen. You select an operation by moving the mouse cursor to a word or **icon** (picture) that represents the computer operation you wish to perform and then pressing a mouse button to activate the operation selected.

**icon**
a picture representing a computer operation

**printer**
an output device that produces a hard copy of information sent to it

A monitor provides a temporary display of the information that appears on its screen. If you want *hard copy* (a printed version) of some information, you must send that information to an output device called a **printer**.

## Computer Networks

Until now we have talked about the components of individual computers. Often several computers are interconnected as a **computer network**, so each computer user can access a large hard disk and high-quality printers. The computer that controls access to the shared disk is called the **file server**. Each computer in the network also has its own keyboard, monitor, and disk drives. Many computer laboratories arrange their computer hardware in a network, called a Local Area Network or LAN.

**computer network**
a group of interconnected computers

**file server**
the computer in a network that controls access to the shared disk

Sharing computer resources is also a worldwide possibility: Millions of computer users around the world now share access to electronic mail systems and to a vast array of information services via the *wide area network* called Internet.

If you have a computer with a modem, you can connect to the information superhighway through a telephone line. A **modem** (**mo**dulator/**dem**odulator) converts binary computer data into audio tones that can be transmitted to another computer over a normal telephone circuit. At the computer on the receiving end, another modem converts the audio tones back to binary data. Early modems transmitted at only 300 baud (300 bits per second). Today's modems transmit over 25,000 bits per second.

**modem**
a device that converts binary data into audio signals that can be transmitted between computers over telephone lines

## EXERCISES FOR SECTION 1.2

Self-Check

1. If a computer executes instructions to sum the contents of memory cells 2 and 999 in Fig. 1.4 and store the result in cell 0, what would then be the contents of cells 0, 2, and 999?
2. One bit can have two values, 0 or 1. A combination of 2 bits can have 4 values: 00, 01, 10, 11. List all of the values you can form with a combination of 3 bits. Do the same for 4 bits.
3. List the following in order of smallest to largest: byte, bit, main memory, memory cell, secondary storage.

# 1.3 OVERVIEW OF PROGRAMMING LANGUAGES

We use programming languages to write computer programs. Although there are many different programming languages, the most commonly used today are called high-level languages. To understand the advantage of high-level languages, we must first understand how a computer communicates.

## Machine Language

**machine language**
a computer's native language with instructions that are binary numbers

The native tongue of a computer is **machine language**. Each machine language instruction is a binary string of 0s and 1s that specifies an operation and identifies the memory cells involved in that operation. For example, if we wanted to represent the algebraic formula

$$cost = price + tax$$

in a machine language program, we might need the sequence of instructions

```
0010 0000 0000 0100
0100 0000 0000 0101
0011 0000 0000 0110
```

In each machine language instruction, the operation to be performed and the address of the data to be manipulated are written as binary numbers. Although the computer would have no difficulty understanding the three preceding machine language instructions, they are unintelligible to most people.

## High-Level Languages

**high-level language**
a programming language whose instructions resemble everyday language

When writing programs in a **high-level language**, we use instructions that resemble everyday language. In C, we would use the statement

```
cost = price + tax;
```

which closely resembles the original formula. This statement means "Add the value of price to the value of tax and store the result as cost." When writing a program in a high-level language, we can reference data that are stored in memory using descriptive names—for example, price, cost, tax—rather than numeric memory cell addresses. We can also use familiar symbols (such as +) to describe operations we want performed.

**Table 1.1    Common High-Level Languages**

| High-Level Language | Original Purpose |
|---|---|
| C | For writing system software |
| C++ | Extension of C that supports object-oriented programming |
| Ada | U.S. Department of Defense language for real-time distributed systems |
| Lisp | For artificial intelligence applications |
| Pascal | For teaching students to program in a careful, disciplined way |
| Fortran (**For**mula **tran**slation) | For engineering and scientific applications |
| BASIC | Simple language intended for student use in schoolwork |
| COBOL | For performing business data processing |

**language standard**
a description of the syntax and meaning of each high-level language instruction

A high-level language has a **language standard** that describes the grammatical form (syntax) of the language. Every high-level language instruction must conform to the syntax rules specified in the language standard. These rules are very precise—they make no allowances for instructions that are *almost* correct. Programs that conform to these rules are *portable,* which means that they can be used without modification on many types of computers. A machine language program, on the other hand, can be used on only one type of computer.

**application software**
programs written to perform tasks for a computer user

**system software**
programs written to operate the computer system

Common high-level languages include C, C++, Ada, Lisp, Pascal, Fortran, BASIC, and COBOL. Although each of these languages was designed for a specific purpose (see Table 1.1), all are used to write a variety of **application software**—software that performs tasks for the computer user. Besides their use in writing application software, the languages C and C++ are frequently used to write **system software**—software that performs tasks required for the operation of the computer system.

## Relationship Between High-Level and Machine Language

**source program**
the high-level language program being translated

Because a computer understands only programs written in machine language, each instruction in a high-level language program must first be translated into machine language before it can be executed. The original high-level language program is called the **source program**; the machine-language translation is

**object program**
the machine-language translation of a source program

called the **object program**. The next section discusses the steps required to process a high-level language program.

**EXERCISES FOR SECTION 1.3**

Self-Check

1. What do you think these five high-level language statements mean?

   x = a + b + c;   x = y / z;   d = c - b + a;   z = z + 1;
   kelvin = celsius + 273.15;

2. List two reasons why it would be preferable to write a program in C rather than machine language.

# 1.4 PROCESSING A HIGH-LEVEL LANGUAGE PROGRAM

Before the computer can execute a high-level language program, the programmer must enter the source program into the computer and the computer must store it in executable form in memory. Several system programs assist with this task. We describe the role of these programs next and summarize the process in Fig. 1.7.

**editor (word-processor)**
a program used to create files containing lines of text

**compiler**
a program that translates a high-level language program into machine language

**syntax error**
an error in the grammatical form of a line in a high-level language program

**linker**
a program that combines (links) an object program with other object files

**executable file**
a disk file containing a ready-to-execute machine language program

**loader**
a program that places an executable file in memory

## Steps for Preparing a Program for Execution

1. Use an **editor** or a **word-processor** program to enter each line of the source program into memory and to save it on disk as a source file.
2. Use a **compiler** program to translate the source program into machine language. If there are any **syntax errors** (errors in grammar), the compiler displays these errors on the monitor. Use the editor program to correct the errors by editing and resaving the source program.
3. When the source program is free of syntax errors, the compiler saves its machine-language translation as an object program.
4. The **linker** program combines your object program with additional object files that may be needed for your program to execute (for example, programs for input and output) and saves the final machine language program as an **executable file** on disk.
5. The **loader** program places the executable file in memory, ready for execution.

**Figure 1.7
Preparing a
Program for
Execution**

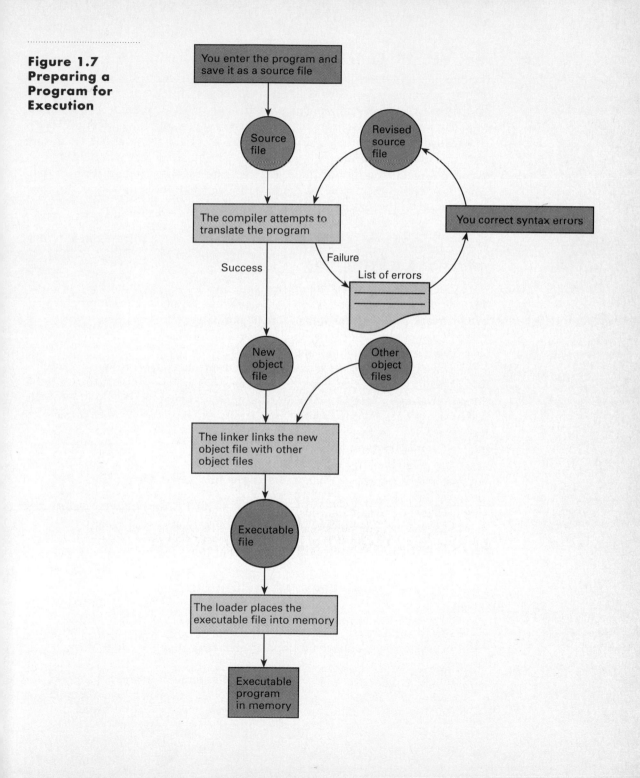

## The Operating System

**operating system**
the system program that controls the computer and with which the user interacts to initiate a system operation or an application program

The computer's operating system performs a key role in this process. When you first access a computer, you must interact with the **operating system** to specify the system operations you want the computer to perform. For example, you may want to access the editor to create a new program file, compile a C program, load and execute an object program, or copy a program file from your floppy disk to the computer's hard disk. You must use an operating system command to initiate any of these actions. The specific commands vary with each computer system; your instructor will give you information about the commands used with your computer's operating system.

## Executing a Program

To execute a machine language program, the CPU must examine each program instruction in memory and send out the command signals required to carry out the instruction. Although the instructions normally are executed in sequence, as we will discuss later, it is possible to have the CPU skip over some instructions or execute some instructions more than once.

**input data**
the data values that are scanned by a program

During execution, data can be entered into memory and manipulated in some specified way. Special program instructions are used for entering or scanning a program's data (called **input data**) into memory. After the input data have been processed, instructions for displaying or printing values in memory can be executed to display the program results. The lines displayed by a program are called the **program output**.

**program output**
the lines displayed by a program

Let's use the situation described in Fig. 1.8—executing a water bill program stored in memory—as an example. The first step of the program scans into memory data that describe the amount of water used. In step 2, the program manipulates the data and stores the results of the computations in memory. In the final step, the computational results are displayed as a water bill.

**EXERCISES FOR SECTION 1.4**

Self-Check

1. Would a syntax error be found in a source program or an object program? What system program would find a syntax error if one existed? What system program would you use to correct it?
2. Explain the differences among the source program, the object program, and an executable program. Which do you create, and which does the compiler create? Which does the linker or loader create?

**Figure 1.8    Flow of Information During Program Execution**

# 1.5 THE SOFTWARE DEVELOPMENT METHOD

Programming is a problem-solving activity. If you are a good problem solver, you have the potential to become a good programmer. Therefore, one goal of this book is to help you improve your problem-solving ability. Problem-solving methods are covered in many subject areas. Business students learn to solve problems with a *systems approach,* while engineering and science students use the *engineering and scientific method.* Programmers use the *software development method.*

## Software Development Method

1. Specify the problem requirements.
2. Analyze the problem.
3. Design the algorithm to solve the problem.

4. Implement the algorithm.
5. Test and verify the completed program.
6. Maintain and update the program.

### PROBLEM

*Specifying the problem requirements* forces you to state the problem clearly and unambiguously and to gain a clear understanding of what is required for its solution. Your objective is to eliminate unimportant aspects and zero in on the root problem. This goal may not be as easy to achieve as it sounds. You may find you need more information from the person who posed the problem.

### ANALYSIS

*Analyzing the problem* involves identifying the problem (a) *inputs*, that is, the data you have to work with; (b) *outputs*, that is, the desired results; and (c) any additional requirements or constraints on the solution. At this stage, you should also determine the required format in which the results should be displayed (for example, as a table with specific column headings) and develop a list of problem variables and their relationships. These relationships may be expressed as formulas.

   If steps 1 and 2 are not done properly, you will solve the wrong problem. Read the problem statement carefully, first, to obtain a clear idea of the problem and second, to determine the inputs and outputs. You may find it helpful to underline phrases in the problem statement that identify the inputs and outputs, as in the problem statement below.

Compute and display the <u>total cost of apples</u> given the number of <u>pounds of apples</u> purchased and the <u>cost per pound of apples</u>.

Next, summarize the information contained in the underlined phrases:

**Problem Inputs**
```
quantity of apples purchased (in pounds)
cost per pound of apples (in dollars per pound)
```

**Problem Output**
```
total cost of apples (in dollars)
```

Once you know the problem inputs and outputs, develop a list of formulas that specify relationships between them. The general formula

$$total\ cost = unit\ cost \times number\ of\ units$$

computes the total cost of any item purchased. Substituting the variables for our particular problem yields the formula

$$total\ cost\ of\ apples = cost\ per\ pound \times pounds\ of\ apples$$

In some situations, you may need to make certain assumptions or simplifications to derive these relationships. This process of modeling a problem by extracting the essential variables and their relationships is called **abstraction**.

**abstraction**
the process of modeling a problem by extracting the essential variables and their relationships

**algorithm**
a list of steps for solving a problem

**top-down design**
breaking a problem into its major subproblems and solving it by solving the subproblems

◀ **DESIGN** ▶

*Designing the algorithm to solve the problem* requires you to develop a list of steps called an **algorithm** to solve the problem and then verify that the algorithm solves the problem as intended. Writing the algorithm is often the most difficult part of the problem-solving process. Don't attempt to solve every detail of the problem at the beginning; instead, discipline yourself to use top-down design. In **top-down design** (also called *divide and conquer*), you first list the major steps, or subproblems, that need to be solved. Then you solve the original problem by solving each of its subproblems. Most computer algorithms consist of at least the following subproblems.

### Algorithm for a Programming Problem

1. Get the data.
2. Perform the computations.
3. Display the results.

**algorithm refinement**
development of a detailed list of steps to solve a particular step in the original algorithm

Once you know the subproblems, you can attack each one individually. For example, the perform-the-computations step may need to be broken down into a more detailed list of steps through a process called **algorithm refinement**.

You may be familiar with top-down design if you use an outline when writing a term-paper. Your first step is to create an outline of the major topics, which you then refine by filling in subtopics for each major topic. Once the outline is complete, you begin writing the text for each subtopic.

**desk checking**
the step-by-step simulation of the computer execution of an algorithm

Desk checking is an important part of algorithm design that is often overlooked. To **desk check** an algorithm, you must carefully perform each algorithm step (or its refinements) just as a computer would and verify that the algorithm works as intended. You'll save time and effort if you locate algorithm errors early in the problem-solving process.

◀ **IMPLEMENTATION** ▶

*Implementing the algorithm* (step 4 in the software development method) involves writing it as a program. You must convert each algorithm step into one or more statements in a programming language.

⬭ **TESTING**

*Testing and verifying the program* requires testing the completed program to verify that it works as desired. Don't rely on just one test case. Run the program several times using different sets of data, making sure that it works correctly for every situation provided for in the algorithm.

⬭ **MAINTENANCE**

*Maintaining and updating the program* involves modifying a program to remove previously undetected errors and to keep it up-to-date as government regulations or company policies change. Many organizations maintain a program for five years or more, often after the programmers who originally coded it have left or moved on to other positions.

A disciplined approach is essential if you want to create programs that are easy to read, understand, and maintain. You must follow accepted program style guidelines (which will be stressed in this book) and avoid tricks and programming shortcuts.

## Caution: Failure Is Part of the Process

Although having a step-by-step approach to problem solving is helpful, we must avoid jumping to the conclusion that if we follow these steps, we are *guaranteed* a correct solution the first time, every time. The fact that verification is so important implies an essential truth of problem solving: The first (also the second, the third, or the twentieth) attempt at a solution *may be wrong*. Probably the most important distinction between outstanding problem solvers and less proficient ones is that outstanding problem solvers are not discouraged by initial failures. Rather, they see the faulty and near-correct early solutions as a means of gaining a better understanding of the problem. One of the most inventive problem solvers of all time, Thomas Edison, is noted for his positive interpretation of the thousands of failed experiments that contributed to his incredible record of inventions. His friends report that he always saw those failures in terms of the helpful data they yielded about what did *not* work.

**EXERCISES FOR SECTION 1.5**

Self-Check

1. List the steps of the software development method.
2. In which phase is the algorithm developed? In which phase do you identify the problem inputs and outputs ?

# 1.6  APPLYING THE SOFTWARE DEVELOPMENT METHOD

Throughout this book, we use the first five steps of the software development method to solve programming problems. These example problems, presented as Case Studies, begin with a *problem statement.* As part of the problem *analysis,* we identify the data requirements for the problem, indicating the problem inputs and the desired outputs. Next, we *design* and refine the initial algorithm. Finally, we *implement* the algorithm as a C program. We also provide a sample run of the program and discuss how to *test* the program.

We walk you through a sample case study next. This example includes a running commentary on the process, which you can use as a model in solving other problems.

## Case Study: Converting Miles to Kilometers

### PROBLEM

Your summer surveying job requires you to study some maps that give distances in kilometers and some that use miles. You and your co-workers prefer to deal in metric measurements. Write a program that performs the necessary conversion.

### ANALYSIS

The first step in solving this problem is to determine what you are asked to do. You must convert from one system of measurement to another, but are you supposed to convert from kilometers to miles, or vice-versa? The problem states that you prefer to deal in metric measurements, so you must convert distance measurements in miles to kilometers. Therefore, the problem input is <u>distance in miles</u> and the problem output is <u>distance in kilometers</u>. To write the program, you need to know the relationship between miles and kilometers. Consulting a metric table shows that one mile equals 1.609 kilometers.

The data requirements and relevant formulas are listed below. `miles` identifies the memory cell that will contain the problem input and `kms` identifies the memory cell that will contain the program result, or the problem output.

**Data Requirements**

**Problem Input**
```
miles      /* the distance in miles*/
```

**Problem Output**
```
kms        /* the distance in kilometers */
```

**Relevant Formula**
*1 mile = 1.609 kilometers*

### DESIGN

Next, formulate the algorithm that solves the problem. Begin by listing the three major steps, or subproblems, of the algorithm.

## Algorithm

1. Get the distance in miles.
2. Convert the distance to kilometers.
3. Display the distance in kilometers.

Now decide whether any steps of the algorithm need further refinement or whether they are perfectly clear as stated. Step 1 (getting the data) and step 3 (displaying a value) are basic steps and require no further refinement. Step 2 is fairly straightforward, but some detail might help:

### Step 2 Refinement
2.1  The distance in kilometers is 1.609 times the distance in miles.

We list the complete algorithm with refinements below to show you how it all fits together. The algorithm resembles an outline for a term paper. The refinement of step 2 is numbered as step 2.1 and is indented under step 2.

## Algorithm with Refinements

1. Get the distance in miles.
2. Convert the distance to kilometers.
    2.1  The distance in kilometers is 1.609 times the distance in miles.
3. Display the distance in kilometers.

Let's desk check the algorithm before going further. If step 1 gets a distance of 10.0 miles, step 2.1 would convert it to $1.609 \times 10.00$ or 16.09 kilometers. This correct result would be displayed by step 3.

### IMPLEMENTATION

To implement the solution, you must write the algorithm as a C program. To do this, you must first tell the C compiler about the problem data requirements, that is, what memory cell names you are using and what kind of data will be stored in each memory cell. Next, convert each algorithm step into one or more C statements. If an algorithm step has been refined, you must convert the refinements, not the original step, into C statements.

Figure 1.9 shows the C program along with a sample execution. For easy identification, the program statements corresponding to algorithm steps are in color as is the input data typed in by the program user. Don't worry about understanding the details of this program yet. We explain the program in the next chapter.

### Figure 1.9  Miles-to-Kilometers Conversion Program

```
/*
 * Converts distance in miles to kilometers.
 */
#include <stdio.h>              /* printf, scanf definitions */
#define KMS_PER_MILE 1.609      /* conversion constant       */

int
main(void)
{
      double miles,   /* input - distance in miles.        */
             kms;     /* output - distance in kilometers   */

      /* Get the distance in miles. */
      printf("Enter the distance in miles> ");
      scanf("%lf", &miles);

      /* Convert the distance to kilometers. */
      kms = KMS_PER_MILE * miles;

      /* Display the distance in kilometers. */
      printf("That equals %f kilometers.\n", kms);

      return (0);
}
```

**Sample Run**
```
Enter the distance in miles> 10.00
That equals 16.090000 kilometers.
```

▬▬ **TESTING** ▬▬

How do you know the sample run is correct? You should always examine program results carefully to make sure that they make sense. In this run, a distance of 10.0 miles is converted to 16.09 kilometers, as it should be. To verify that the program works properly, enter a few more test values of miles. You don't need to try more than a few test cases to verify that a simple program like this is correct.

## EXERCISES FOR SECTION 1.6

Self-Check

1. Change the algorithm for the metric conversion program to convert distance in kilometers to miles.
2. List the data requirements, formulas, and algorithm for a program that converts a volume from quarts to liters.

# CHAPTER REVIEW

1. The basic components of a computer are main memory and secondary storage, the CPU, and input and output devices.
2. Main memory is organized into individual storage locations called memory cells.

   • Each memory cell has a unique address.
   • A memory cell is a collection of bytes; a byte is a collection of 8 bits.
   • A memory cell is never empty, but its initial contents may be meaningless to your program.
   • The current contents of a memory cell are destroyed whenever new information is stored in that cell.
   • Programs *must* be loaded into the memory of the computer before they can be executed.
   • Data cannot be manipulated by the computer until they are first stored in memory.

3. Information in secondary storage is organized into files: program files and data files. Secondary storage stores information in semipermanent form and is less expensive than main memory.
4. A computer cannot think for itself; you must use a programming language to instruct it in a precise and unambiguous manner to perform a task.
5. Programming a computer can be fun—if you are patient, organized, and careful.
6. Two categories of programming languages are machine language (meaningful to the computer) and high-level language (meaningful to the programmer).

Several system programs are used to prepare a high-level language program for execution. An editor enters a high-level language program into a file. A compiler translates a high-level language program (the source program) into machine language (the object program). The linker links this object program to other object files, creating an executable file, and the loader loads the executable file into memory.

7. Through the operating system, you can issue commands to the computer and manage files.

8. Follow the first five steps of the software development method to solve programming problems: (1) specify the problem, (2) analyze the problem, (3) design the algorithm, (4) implement the program, and (5) test and verify the solution. Write programs in a consistent style that is easy to read, understand, and maintain.

# QUICK-CHECK EXERCISES

1. The _____ translates a(n) _____ language program into _____.
2. A(n) _____ provides access to system programs for editing, compiling, and so on.
3. Specify the correct order for these operations: execution, translation, linking, loading.
4. A high-level language program is saved on disk as a(n) _____ file or a(n) _____ file.
5. The _____ finds syntax errors in the _____.
6. Before linking, a machine language program is saved on disk as a(n) _____ file.
7. After linking, a machine language program is saved on disk as a(n) _____ file.
8. Computer programs are _____ components of a computer system while a disk drive is _____.
9. In a high-level language, you can reference data using _____ rather than memory cell addresses.
10. Determine whether each of the following characteristics applies to main memory or secondary storage:

   a. Faster to access
   b. Volatile
   c. May be extended virtually without limit
   d. Less expensive
   e. Used to store files
   f. Central processor accesses it to obtain the next machine language instruction for execution
   g. Provides semipermanent data storage

11. A list of all files stored on a disk is stored in its _____ .
12. Give an example of a wide area network.

## ANSWERS TO QUICK-CHECK EXERCISES

1. compiler, high-level (or source program), machine language (or object program)
2. operating system
3. translation, linking, loading, execution
4. source, program
5. compiler, source program
6. object
7. executable
8. software, hardware
9. descriptive names
10. main (a, b, f), secondary (c, d, e, g)
11. directory
12. the Internet

## REVIEW QUESTIONS

1. List at least three kinds of information stored in a computer.
2. List two functions of the CPU.
3. List two input devices, two output devices, and two secondary storage devices.
4. Describe two categories of programming languages.
5. What is a syntax error?
6. What processes are needed to transform a C program to a machine language program that is ready for execution?
7. Explain the relationship between memory cells, bytes, and bits.
8. Name three high-level languages, and describe their original usage.
9. What are the differences between RAM and ROM?

# OVERVIEW OF C

chapter

This chapter introduces C—a high-level programming language developed in 1972 by Dennis Ritchie at AT&T Bell Laboratories. Because C was designed as a language in which to write the UNIX® operating system, it was originally used primarily for systems programming. Over the years, however, the power and flexibility of C, together with the availability of high-quality C compilers for computers of all sizes, have made it a popular language in industry for a wide variety of applications.

This chapter describes the elements of a C program and the types of data that can be processed by C. It also describes C statements for performing computations, for entering data, and for displaying results.

# 2.1 C LANGUAGE ELEMENTS

One advantage of C is that it lets you write programs that resemble everyday English. Even though you do not yet know how to write your own programs, you can probably read and understand the program in Fig. 1.9. Figure 2.1 repeats Fig. 1.9 with the basic features of C highlighted. We identify them briefly below, and explain them in detail in Sections 2.2 to 2.4.

## Preprocessor Directives

**preprocessor**
a system program that modifies a C program prior to its compilation

**preprocessor directive**
a C program line beginning with # that provides an instruction to the preprocessor

The C program in Fig. 2.1 has two parts: preprocessor directives and the main function. The **preprocessor directives** are commands that give instructions to the C **preprocessor**, whose job it is to modify the text of a C program *before* it is compiled. A preprocessor directive begins with a number symbol (#) as its first nonblank character. The two most common directives appear in Fig. 2.1: #include and #define.

**library**
a collection of useful functions and symbols that may be accessed by a program

The C language explicitly defines only a small number of operations: Many actions that are necessary in a computer program are not defined directly by C. Instead, every C implementation contains collections of useful functions and symbols called **libraries**. The ANSI (American National Standards Institute) standard for C requires that certain *standard libraries* be provided in every ANSI C implementation. A C system may expand the number of operations available by supplying additional libraries; an individual programmer can also create libraries of functions. Each library has a standard header file whose name ends with the symbols .h.

The #include directive gives a program access to a library. This directive causes the preprocessor to insert definitions from a standard header file into a program before compilation. The directive

```
#include <stdio.h>                      /* printf, scanf definitions */
```

**Figure 2.1    C Language Elements in Miles-to-Kilometers Conversion Program**

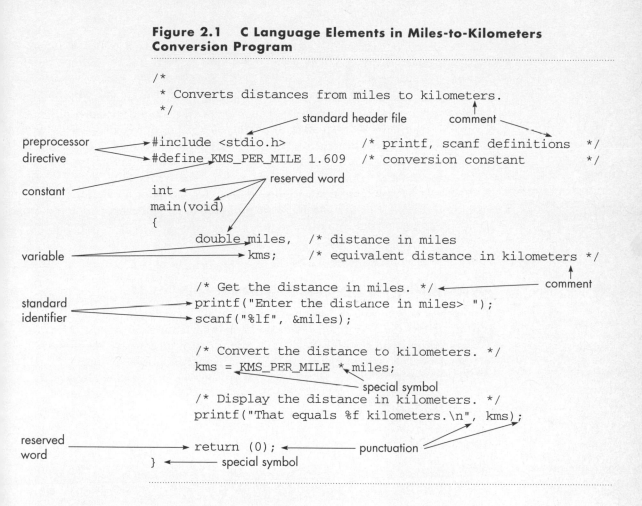

notifies the preprocessor that some names used in the program (such as scanf and printf) are found in the standard header file <stdio.h>.

The other preprocessor directive in Fig. 2.1

```
#define KMS_PER_MILE 1.609    /* conversion constant */
```

**constant macro**
a name that is replaced by a particular constant value before the program is sent to the compiler

associates the **constant macro** KMS_PER_MILE with the meaning 1.609. This directive instructs the preprocessor to replace each occurrence of KMS_PER_MILE in the text of the C program by 1.609 before compilation begins. As a result, the line

```
kms = KMS_PER_MILE * miles;
```

would read

```
kms = 1.609 * miles;
```

by the time it was sent to the C compiler. Only data values that never change (or change very rarely) should be given names using a #define, because an executing C program cannot change the value of a name defined as a constant macro. Using the constant macro KMS_PER_MILE in the text of a program for the value 1.609 makes it easier to understand and maintain the program.

    The text on the right of each preprocessor directive, starting with /* and ending with */, is a **comment.** Comments provide supplementary information making it easier for us to understand the program, but comments are ignored by the C preprocessor and compiler.

**comment**
text beginning with /* and ending with */ that provides supplementary information but is ignored by the preprocessor and compiler

## Syntax Displays for Preprocessor Directives

For each new C construct introduced in this book, we provide a syntax display that describes and explains its syntax and shows examples of its use. The following syntax displays describe the two preprocessor directives. The italicized elements in each construct are discussed in the interpretation section.

---

### #include Directive for Defining Identifiers from Standard Libraries

SYNTAX:    #include *<standard header file>*

EXAMPLES:  #include <stdio.h>
            #include <math.h>

INTERPRETATION: #include directives tell the preprocessor where to find the meanings of standard identifiers used in the program. These meanings are collected in files called *standard header files.* The header file stdio.h contains information about standard input and output functions such as scanf and printf. Descriptions of common mathematical functions are found in the header file math.h. We will investigate header files associated with other standard libraries in later chapters.

---

**#define Directive for Creating Constant Macros**

SYNTAX:      #define *NAME value*

EXAMPLES:  #define MILES_PER_KM 0.62137
                      #define PI 3.141593
                      #define MAX_LENGTH 100

INTERPRETATION: The C preprocessor is notified that it is to replace each use of the identifier *NAME* by *value*. C program statements cannot change the value associated with *NAME*.

## Function main

The two-line heading

```
int
main(void)
```

marks the beginning of the main function where program execution begins. Every C program has a main function. The remaining lines of the program form the *body* of the function which is enclosed in braces {, }.

    A function body has two parts: declarations and executable statements. The **declarations** tell the compiler what memory cells are needed in the function (for example, miles and kms in Fig. 2.1). To create this part of the function, the programmer uses the problem data requirements identified during problem analysis. The **executable statements** (derived from the algorithm) are translated into machine language and later executed.

    The main function contains *punctuation* and *special symbols* (*, =). Commas separate items in a list, a semicolon appears at the end of several lines, and braces ({, }) mark the beginning and end of the body of function main.

**declarations**
the part of a program that tells the compiler the names of memory cells in a program
**executable statements**
program lines that are converted to machine language instructions and executed by the computer

**main Function Definition**

SYNTAX:   int
                  main(void)
                  {
                      *function body*
                  }

*(continued)*

```
EXAMPLE: int
         main(void)
         {
             printf("Hello world\n");
             return (0);
         }
```

INTERPRETATION: Program execution begins with the main function. Braces enclose the main *function body* which contains declarations and executable statements. The line `int` indicates that the main function returns an integer value (0) to the operating system when it finishes normal execution. The symbols `(void)` indicate that the main function receives no data from the operating system before it begins execution.

## Reserved Words

**reserved word**
a word that has special meaning in C

Each line of Fig. 2.1 contains a number of different words classified as **reserved words**, identifiers from standard libraries, and names for memory cells. All the reserved words appear in lowercase; they have special meaning in C and cannot be used for other purposes. A complete list of ANSI C reserved words is found in Appendix E. Table 2.1 describes the reserved words in Fig 2.1.

**Table 2.1    Reserved Words in Fig. 2.1**

| Reserved word | Meaning |
| --- | --- |
| int | integer; indicates that the main function returns an integer value |
| void | indicates that the main function receives no data from the operating system |
| double | indicates that the memory cells store real numbers |
| return | returns control from the main function to the operating system |

## Standard Identifiers

**standard identifier**
a word having special meaning
but one that a programmer may
redefine (but redefinition is not
recommended!)

The other words in Fig. 2.1 are identifiers that come in two varieties: standard and user-defined. Like reserved words, **standard identifiers** have special meaning in C. In Fig. 2.1, the standard identifiers `printf` and `scanf` are names of operations defined in the standard input/output library. Unlike reserved words, standard identifiers can be redefined and used by the programmer for other purposes—however, we don't recommend this practice. If you redefine a standard identifier, C will no longer be able to use it for its original purpose.

## User-defined Identifiers

We choose our own identifiers (called *user-defined identifiers*) to name memory cells that will hold data and program results and to name operations that we define (more on this in Chapter 3). The first user-defined identifier in Fig. 2.1, `KMS_PER_MILE`, is the name of a constant macro.

You have some freedom in selecting identifiers. The syntax rules and some valid identifiers follow. Table 2.2 shows some invalid identifiers.

1. An identifier must consist only of letters, digits, and underscores.
2. An identifier cannot begin with a digit.
3. A C reserved word <u>cannot</u> be used as an identifier. *should Not*
4. An identifier defined in a C standard library should not be redefined.[†]

### Valid Identifiers

`letter_1`, `letter_2`, `inches`, `cent`, `CENT_PER_INCH`, `Hello`, `variable`

...........................................

[†]Rule 4 is actually advice from the authors rather than ANSI C syntax.

**Table 2.2   Invalid Identifiers**

| Invalid identifier | Reason invalid |
|---|---|
| `1Letter` | begins with a letter |
| `double` | reserved word |
| `int` | reserved word |
| `TWO*FOUR` | character * not allowed |
| `joe's` | character ' not allowed |

**Table 2.3** **Reserved Words and Identifiers in Fig. 2.1**

| Reserved Words | Standard Identifiers | User-defined Identifiers |
|---|---|---|
| `int`, `void`, `double`, `return` | `printf`, `scanf` | `KMS_PER_MILE`, `main`, `miles`, `kms` |

Although the syntax rules for identifiers do not place a limit on length, some ANSI C compilers do not consider two names to be different unless there is a variation within the first 31 characters. The two identifiers

```
per_capita_meat_consumption_in_1980
per_capita_meat_consumption_in_1995
```

would be viewed as identical by a C compiler that considered only the first 31 characters to be significant.

Table 2.3 lists the category of each identifier appearing in the main function of Fig. 2.1.

## Uppercase and Lowercase Letters

The C programmer must take great care in the use of uppercase and lowercase letters because the C compiler considers such usage significant. The names `Rate`, `rate`, and `RATE` are viewed by the compiler as *different* identifiers. Adopting a consistent pattern in the way you use uppercase and lowercase letters is helpful to the readers of your programs. You will see that all reserved words in C and the names of all standard library functions use only lowercase letters. One style that has been widely adopted in industry uses all uppercase letters in the names of constant macros. We follow this convention in this text; for other identifiers we use all lowercase letters.

## Program Style    *Choosing Identifier Names*

We discuss program style throughout the text in displays like this one. A program that "looks good" is easier to read and understand than one that is sloppy. Most programs will be examined or studied by someone other than the original programmers. In industry, programmers spend considerably more time on program maintenance (that is, updating and modifying the program) than they do on its original design or coding. A program that is neatly stated and whose meaning is clear makes everyone's job simpler.

Pick a meaningful name for a user-defined identifier, so its use is easy to understand. For example, the identifier `salary` would be a good name for a memory cell used to store a person's salary, whereas the identifier `s` or `bagel` would be a bad choice. If an identifier consists of two or more words, placing the underscore character (_) between words will improve the readability of the name (`dollars_per_hour` rather than `dollarsperhour`).

Choose identifiers long enough to convey your meaning, but avoid excessively long names because you are more likely to make a typing error in a longer name. For example, use the shorter identifier `lbs_per_sq_in` instead of the longer identifier `pounds_per_square_inch`.

If you mistype a name so that the identifier looks like the name of another memory cell, often the compiler cannot help you detect your error. For this reason and to avoid confusion, do not choose names that are similar to each other. Especially avoid selecting two names that are different only in their use of uppercase and lowercase letters, such as `LARGE` and `large`. Also try not to use two names that differ only in the presence or absence of an underscore (`xcoord` and `x_coord`).

---

**EXERCISES FOR SECTION 2.1**

Self-Check

1. Which of the following identifiers are (a) C reserved words, (b) standard identifiers, (c) conventionally used as constant macro names, (d) other valid identifiers, and (e) invalid identifiers?

```
void        MAX_ENTRIES    double      time      G        Sue's
return      printf         xyz123      part#2    "char"   #insert
this_is_a_long_one
```

2. Why shouldn't you use a standard identifier as the name of a memory cell in a program? Can you use a reserved word instead?
3. What part of a C implementation changes the text of a C program just before it is compiled? Name two directives that give instructions about these changes.
4. Why should `PI (3.14159)` be defined as a constant macro?

---

# 2.2 VARIABLE DECLARATIONS AND DATA TYPES

## Variable Declarations

**variable**
a name associated with a memory cell whose value can change

The memory cells used for storing a program's input data and its computational results are called **variables** because the values stored in variables can change

**variable declarations**
statements that communicate
to the compiler the names of
variables in the program and
the kind of information stored
in each variable

(and usually do) as the program executes. The **variable declarations** in a C program communicate to the C compiler the names of all variables used in a program. They also tell the compiler what kind of information will be stored in each variable and how that information will be represented in memory. The variable declarations

```
double miles; /* input - distance in miles.         */
double kms;   /* output - distance in kilometers    */
```

give the names of two variables (miles, kms) used to store real numbers. Note that C ignores the comments on the right of each line describing the usage of each variable.

A variable declaration begins with an identifier (for example, double) that tells the C compiler the type of data (such as a real number) stored in a particular variable. You can declare variables for any data type. C requires you to declare every variable used in a program.

### Syntax Display for Declarations

SYNTAX:    int *variable_list*;
           double *variable_list*;
           char *variable_list*;

EXAMPLES: int count,
              large;
           double x, y, z;
           char first_initial;
           char ans;

INTERPRETATION: A memory cell is allocated for each name in the *variable_list*. The type of data (double, int, char) to be stored in each variable is specified at the beginning of the statement. One statement may extend over multiple lines. A single data type can appear in more than one variable declaration, so the following two declaration sections are equally acceptable ways of declaring the variables rate, time, and age.

```
double rate, time;        double rate;
int age;                  int    age;
                          double time;
```

**data type**
a set of values and operations
that can be performed on
those values

## Data Types

A **data type** is a set of values and a set of operations on those values. A standard data type in C is a data type that is predefined such as char, double, and int. We use the standard data types double and int as abstractions for the real numbers and integers (in the mathematical sense). We introduce data types int, double, and char now and elaborate on them in Chapter 7.

Objects of a data type can be variables or constants. A positive numeric constant (or number) in a C program can be written with or without a + sign. A numeric constant cannot contain a comma.

Numeric constants in C are considered non-negative numbers. Although you can use a number like -10500 in a program, C views the minus sign as the negation operator (applied to the positive constant 10500) rather than as a part of the constant.

**Data Type int**    In mathematics, integers are whole numbers. The int data type is used to represent integers in C. Because of the finite size of a memory cell, not all integers can be represented by type int. ANSI C specifies that the range of data type int must include at least the values -32767 through 32767. You can store an integer in a type int variable, perform the common arithmetic operations (add, subtract, multiply, and divide), and compare two integers. Some values that you can store in a type int variable are

-10500    435    +15    -25    32767

**Data Type double**    A real number has an integral part and a fractional part which are separated by a decimal point. In C, the data type double is used to represent real numbers (for example, 3.14159, 0.0005, 150.0). You can store a real number in a type double variable, perform the common arithmetic operations (add, subtract, multiply, and divide), and compare them.

We can use scientific notation to represent real numbers (usually for very large or very small values). In normal scientific notation, the real number $1.23 \times 10^5$ is equivalent to 123000.0 where the exponent 5 means "move the decimal point 5 places to the right." In C scientific notation, we write this number as 1.23e5 or 1.23E5. Read the letter e or E as "times 10 to the power": 1.23e5 means 1.23 times 10 to the power 5. If the exponent has a minus sign, the decimal point is moved to the left (for example, 0.34e-4 is equivalent to 0.000034). Table 2.4 lists some real numbers and indicates which can be stored in a type double variable. The last line shows we can write a type double constant in C scientific notation without a decimal point.

Data type double is an abstraction for the real numbers because it does not include them all. Some real numbers are too large or too small, and some real numbers cannot be represented precisely because of the finite size of a memory cell. However, we can certainly represent enough of the real numbers in C to carry out most of the computations we wish to perform with sufficient accuracy.

**Table 2.4   Type double Constants  (real numbers)**

| Valid double constants | Invalid double constants |
| --- | --- |
| 3.14159 | 150 (no decimal point) |
| 0.005 | .12345e (missing exponent) |
| 12345.0 | 15e-0.3 (0.3 is invalid exponent) |
| 15.0e-04 (value is 0.0015) | |
| 2.34e2 (value is 234.5) | |
| 1.15e-3 (value is 0.00115) | 12.5e.3 (.3 is invalid exponent) |
| 12e+5 (value is 1200000.0) | 34,500.99 (comma is not allowed) |

**Data Type char**   Data type char represents an individual character value—a letter, a digit, or a special symbol. Each type char value is enclosed in apostrophes (single quotes) as shown here.

```
'A'  'z'  '2'  '9'  '*'  ':'  '"'  ' '
```

The next to last character value above represents the character "; the last one represents the blank character, which is typed by pressing the apostrophe key, the space bar, and the apostrophe key.

Although a type char value in a program requires apostrophes, a type char data value should not have them. Thus, for example, when entering the letter z as a character data item to be read by a program, press the z key instead of the sequence 'z'.

You can store a character in a type char variable and compare character data. C even allows you to perform arithmetic operations on type char data, but you should use this facility with care.

**EXERCISES FOR SECTION 2.2**

Self-Check

1. a. Write the following numbers in normal decimal notation:

   103e-4   1.2345e+6   123.45e+3

   b. Write the following numbers in C scientific notation:

   1300   123.45   0.00426

2. Indicate which of the following are valid type `int`, `double`, or `char` constants in C and which are not. Identify the data type of each valid constant.

```
15    'XYZ'    '*'    $    25.123    15.0    -999    .123    'x'
"X"   'True'   '-5'    32e-4
```

3. What would be the best variable type for the area of a circle in square inches? Which type for the number of cars passing through an intersection in an hour? The first letter of your last name?

## Programming

1. Write the `#define` preprocessor directive and declarations for a program that has a constant macro for `PI` (3.14159) and variables `radius`, `area`, and `circumf` declared as `double`, variable `num_circ` as an `int`, and variable `circ_name` as a `char`.

# 2.3 EXECUTABLE STATEMENTS

The executable statements follow the declarations in a function. They are the C statements used to write or code the algorithm and its refinements. The C compiler translates the executable statements into machine language; the computer executes the machine language version of these statements when we run the program.

## Programs in Memory

Before examining the executable statements in the miles-to-kilometers conversion program (Fig. 2.1), let's see what computer memory looks like before and after that program executes. Figure 2.2a shows the program loaded into memory and the program memory area before the program executes. The question marks in memory cells `miles` and `kms` indicate that the values of these cells are undefined before program execution begins. During program execution, the data value `10.00` is copied from the input device into the variable `miles`. After the program executes, the variables are defined as shown in Fig. 2.2b. We will see why next.

**Figure 2.2
Memory Before
(a) and After
(b) Execution of
a Program**

(a)                                    (b)

## Assignment Statements

**assignment statement**
an instruction that stores a
value or a computational
result in a variable

An **assignment statement** stores a value or a computational result in a variable, and is used to perform most arithmetic operations in a program. The assignment statement

```
kms = KMS_PER_MILE * miles;
```

assigns a value to the variable kms. The value assigned is the result of the multiplication (* means multiply) of the constant macro KMS_PER_MILE (1.609) by the variable miles. The memory cell for miles must contain valid information (in this case, a real number) before the assignment statement is executed. Fig. 2.3, shows the contents of memory before and after the assignment statement executes; only the value of kms is changed.

**Figure 2.3
Effect of** kms =
KMS_PER_MILE *
miles;

In C the symbol = is the assignment operator. Read it as "becomes," "gets," or "takes the value of" rather than "equals" because it is *not* equivalent to the "equal sign" of mathematics. In mathematics, this symbol states a relationship between two values, but in C it represents an action to be carried out by the computer.

---

## Assignment Statement

FORM:     *variable = expression;*

EXAMPLE: x = y + z + 2.0;

Interpretation: The *variable* before the assignment operator is assigned the value of the *expression* after it. The previous value of *variable* is destroyed. The *expression* can be a variable, a constant, or a combination of these connected by appropriate operators (for example, +, -, /, and *).

---

**EXAMPLE 2.1**    In C you can write assignment statements of the form

    sum = sum + item;

where the variable sum appears on both sides of the assignment operator. This is obviously not an algebraic equation, but it illustrates a common programming practice. This statement instructs the computer to add the current value of sum to the value of item; the result is then stored back into sum. The previous value of sum is destroyed in the process, as illustrated in Fig. 2.4. The value of item, however, is unchanged.

**Figure 2.4**
**Effect of** sum =
sum + item;

**EXAMPLE 2.2**

You can also write assignment statements that assign the value of a single variable or constant to a variable. If x and new_x are type double variables, the statement

```
new_x = x;
```

copies the value of variable x into variable new_x. The statement

```
new_x = -x;
```

instructs the computer to get the value of x, negate that value, and store the result in new_x. For example, if x is 3.5, new_x is -3.5. Neither of the assignment statements above changes the value of x.

Section 2.7 continues the discussion of type int and double expressions and operators.

## Input/Output Operations and Functions

Data can be stored in memory in two different ways: either by assignment to a variable or by copying the data from an input device into a variable using a function like scanf. You copy data into a variable if you want a program to manipulate different data each time it executes. This data transfer from the outside world into memory is called an **input operation**.

**input operation**
an instruction that copies data from an input device into memory

As it executes, a program performs computations and stores the results in memory. These program results can be displayed to the program user by an **output operation**.

**output operation**
an instruction that displays information stored in memory

All input/output operations in C are performed by special program units called **input/output functions**. The most common input/output functions are supplied as part of the C standard input/output library to which we gain access through the preprocessor directive

**input/output function**
a C function that performs an input or output operation

```
#include <stdio.h>
```

In this section we show how to use the input function scanf and the output function printf.

**function call**
calling or activating a function

In C a **function call** is used to call or activate a function. Calling a function is analogous to asking a friend to perform an urgent task. You tell your friend what to do (but not how to do it) and wait for your friend to report back that the task is finished. After hearing from your friend, you can go on and do something else.

## The printf Function

To see the results of a program execution, we must have a way to specify what variable values should be displayed. In Fig. 2.1 the statement

calls function `printf` (pronounced "print-eff") to display a line of program output. A function call consists of two parts: the function name and the **function arguments**, enclosed in parentheses. The arguments for `printf` consist of a **format string** (in quotes) and a **print list** (the variable kms). The function call above displays the line

```
That equals 16.090000 kilometers.
```

which is the result of displaying the format string `"That equals %f kilometers.\n"` after substituting the value of kms for its placeholder (`%f`) in the format string. A **placeholder** always begins with the symbol %. Here the placeholder `%f` marks the display position for a type `double` variable.

Table 2.5 shows placeholders for type `char`, `double`, and `int` variables. Each placeholder is an abbreviation for the type of data it represents. C uses `%f` (or `%lf`) and not `%d` with type `double` because programmers often refer to real numbers as *floating point numbers.*

The placeholders used with `scanf` are the same as those used with `printf` except for variables of type `double`. Type `double` variables use a `%f` placeholder in a `printf` format string and a `%lf` placeholder in a `scanf` format string.

The format string above also contains the **newline escape sequence** `\n`. Like all C escape sequences, `\n` begins with the backslash character.

**function argument**
enclosed in parentheses following the function name; provides information needed by the function

**format string**
in a call to `printf`, a string of characters enclosed in quotes ("), which specifies the form of the output line

**print list**
in a call to `printf`, the variables or expressions whose values are displayed

**placeholders**
symbols beginning with % in a format string that indicate where to display each ouput value

**newline escape sequence**
the character sequence \n which is used in a format string to terminate an output line

### Table 2.5 Placeholders in Format Strings

| placeholder | variable type | function use |
|---|---|---|
| %c | char | printf/scanf |
| %d | int | printf/scanf |
| %f | double | printf |
| %lf | double | scanf |

Including this sequence at the end of the format string terminates the current output line.

**Multiple Placeholders**   Format strings can have multiple placeholders. If the print list of a `printf` call has several variables, the format string should contain the same number of placeholders. C matches variables with placeholders in left-to-right order.

**EXAMPLE 2.3**

If `letter_1`, `letter_2`, and `letter_3` are type `char` variables and `age` is type `int`, the `printf` call

```
printf("Hi %c%c%c - your age is %d\n",
       letter_1, letter_2, letter_3, age);
```

displays a line such as

```
Hi EBK - your age is 35
```

The placeholders `%c%c%c` indicate the display position of the letters (E, B, and K) stored in the three type `char` variables, and the placeholder `%d` indicates the position of the value of `age` (35).  ←

---

### Syntax Display for printf Function Call

SYNTAX:      printf (*format string, print list*) ;
             printf (*format string*) ;

EXAMPLES:  printf("I am %d years old, and my gpa is %f\n",
                  age, gpa);
             printf("Enter the object mass in grams> ");

INTERPRETATION: The `printf` function displays the value of its *format string* after substituting in left-to-right order the values of the expressions in the *print list* for their placeholders in the *format string* and after replacing escape sequences such as \n by their meanings.

---

**More About \n**   The **cursor** is a moving place marker that indicates the next position on the screen where information will be displayed. When executing a `printf` function call, the cursor is advanced to the start of the next line on the screen if the \n escape sequence is encountered in the format string.

**cursor**
a moving place marker that indicates the next position on the screen where information will be displayed

We often end a `printf` format string with a `\n` (newline escape sequence) so that the call to `printf` produces a completed line of output. If no characters are printed on the next line before another newline character is printed, a blank line will appear in the output. For example, the calls

```
printf("Here is the first line\n");
printf("\nand this is the second.\n");
```

produce two lines of text with a blank line in between:

```
Here is the first line

and this is the second.
```

The blank line appears because the newline character terminates the first format string and begins the second. Notice that because the format strings of these calls to `printf` contain no placeholders, no print list of variables is needed.

If a `printf` format string contains a `\n` in the middle of the string

```
printf("This sentence appears \non two lines.\n");
```

the characters after the `\n` appear on a new output line:

```
This sentence appears
on two lines.
```

In the next section we will see examples where the newline escape sequence is omitted.

**Displaying Prompts**    When input data are needed in an interactive program, you should use the `printf` function to display a **prompting message,** or **prompt,** that tells the program user what data to enter. The `printf` statement below

**prompt**
**(prompting message)**
a message displayed to indicate what data to enter and in what form

```
printf("Enter the distance in miles> ");
scanf("%lf", &miles);
```

displays a prompt for square meters (a numeric value). The `printf` statement displays the format string and advances the cursor to the screen position following this string. The program user can then type in the data value requested which is processed by the `scanf` function as described next. The cursor is advanced to the next line when the user presses the <return> or <enter> key.

## The scanf Function

The statement

```
scanf("%lf", &miles);
```

calls function scanf (pronounced "scan-eff") to copy data into the variable miles. Where does function scanf get the data it stores in the variable miles? It copies the data from the standard input device. In most cases the standard input device is the keyboard; consequently, the computer will attempt to store in miles whatever data the program user types at the keyboard.

The format string "%lf" consists of a single placeholder that tells scanf what kind of data to copy into variable miles. Because the placeholder is %lf, the input operation will proceed without error only if the program user types in a number. Figure 2.5 shows the effect of the scanf operation.

Notice that in a call to scanf, the name of each variable that is to be given a value is preceded by the ampersand character (&). The & is the C *address-of* operator. In the context of this input operation, the & operator tells the scanf function *where* to find each variable into which it is to store a new value. If the ampersand were omitted, scanf would know only a variable's current value, not its location in memory, so scanf would be unable to store a new value in the variable.

When scanf executes, the program pauses until the required data are entered and the <return> or <enter> key is pressed. If an incorrect data character is typed, the program user can press the backspace key (←) to edit the data. However, once <return> or <enter> is pressed, the data are processed exactly as typed in and it is too late to correct any data entry errors.

The function call

```
scanf("%c%c%c", &letter_1, &letter_2, &letter_3);
```

causes the scanf function to copy data into each of the three variables, and the format string includes one %c placeholder for each variable. Assuming these variables are declared as type char, one character will be stored in each variable. The next three characters that are entered at the keyboard are stored in these variables. Note that case is important for character data, so the letters B and b have different representations in memory. Again, the program user should press the <return> or <enter> key after typing in three characters. Figure 2.6 shows the effect of this statement when the letters Bob are entered.

**Figure 2.5**
**Effect of**
`scanf("%lf", &miles);`

**Figure 2.6**
**Scanning Data**
**Line Bob**

The number of input characters consumed by the scanf function depends on the current format placeholder, which should reflect the type of the variable in which the data will be stored. Only one input character is used for a %c (type char variable). For a %lf or %d (type double or int variable), the program first skips any spaces and then scans characters until it reaches a character that cannot be part of the number. Usually the program user indicates the end of a number by pressing the space bar or by pressing the <return> or <enter> key. If you would like scanf to skip spaces before scanning a character, put a blank in the format string before the %c placeholder. If you type more data characters on a line than are needed by the current call to scanf, the extra characters will be processed by the next call to scanf.

---

### Syntax Display for scanf Function call

SYNTAX:   scanf (*format string*, *input list*) ;

EXAMPLE: scanf("%c%d", &first_initial, &age);

INTERPRETATION: The scanf function copies into memory data typed at the keyboard by the program user during program execution. The *format string* is a quoted string of place-holders, one placeholder for each variable in the *input list*. Each int, double, or char variable in the *input list* is preceded by an ampersand (&). Commas are used to separate variable names. The order of the placeholders must correspond to the order of the variables in the *input list*.

You must enter data in the same order as the variables in the *input list*. You should insert one or more blank characters or carriage returns between numeric items. If you plan to insert blanks or carriage returns between character data, you must include a blank in the format string before the %c placeholder.

## The return statement

The last line in the main function (Fig. 2.1)

```
return (0);
```

transfers control from your program to the operating system. The value in parentheses, 0, is considered the result of function `main`'s execution and it indicates that your program executed without error.

---

### Syntax Display for return statement

SYNTAX:   return *expression*;

EXAMPLE: return (0);

INTERPRETATION: The `return` statement transfers control from a function back to the activator of the function. For function `main`, control is transferred back to the operating system. The value of *expression* is returned as the result of the function execution.

---

**EXERCISES FOR SECTION 2.3**

Self-Check

1. Show the output displayed by the following program lines when the data entered are 5 and 7:

```
printf("Enter two integers> ");
scanf("%d%d", &m, &n);
m = m + 5;
n = 3 * n;
printf("m = %d\nn = %d\n", m, n);
```

2. Show the contents of memory before and after the execution of the program lines shown in Exercise 1.
3. Show the output displayed by the following lines if the value of exp is 11:

```
printf("My name is ");
printf("Jane Doe.");
printf("\n");
printf("I live in ");
printf("Ann Arbor, MI\n");
printf("and I have %d years ", exp);
printf("of programming experience.\n");
```

4. How could you modify the code in Exercise 3 so that a blank line would be displayed between the two sentences?

### Programming

1. Write a statement that asks the user to type three integers and another statement that stores the three user responses into `first`, `second`, and `third`.
2. a. Write a statement that displays the following line with the value of the type `double` variable `x` at the end.

   ```
   The value of x is _____
   ```

   b. Assuming `radius` and `area` are type `double` variables containing the radius and area of a circle, write a statement that will display this information in the form:

   ```
   The area of a circle with radius _____ is _____ .
   ```

3. Write a program that asks the user to enter the radius of a circle and then computes and displays the circle's area. Use the formula

$$area = PI \times radius \times radius$$

where *PI* is the constant macro `3.14159`.

## 2.4  GENERAL FORM OF A C PROGRAM

Now that we have discussed the individual statements that can appear in C programs, we review the rules for combining them into programs. We also discuss the use of punctuation, spacing, and comments in a program.

As shown in Fig. 2.7, each program begins with preprocessor directives that serve to provide information about functions from standard libraries and definitions of necessary program constants. Examples of such directives are `#include` and `#define`. Unlike the declarations and executable statements of the main function body, the preprocessor directives we have seen do not end in semicolons.

A simple C program defines the main function after the preprocessor directives. An open curly brace (`{`) signals the beginning of the main function body. Within this body, we first see the declarations of all the variables to be used by the main function. These variables are followed by the statements that are translated into machine language and are eventually executed. The statements we have looked at so far perform computations or input/output operations. The end of the main function body is marked by a closing curly brace (`}`).

**Figure 2.7**
**General Form**
**of a C Program**

*preprocessor directives*
*main function heading*
{
    *declarations*
    *executable statements*
}

C treats most line breaks like spaces so a C statement can extend over more than one line. (For example, the variable declaration in Fig. 2.1 extends over two lines.) You should not split a statement that extends over more than one line in the middle of an identifier, a reserved word, a constant, or a format string.

You can write more than one statement on a line. For example, the line

```
printf("Enter distance in miles> ");  scanf("%lf", &miles);
```

contains a statement that displays a prompt and a statement that gets the data requested. We recommend that you place only one statement on a line because it improves readability and makes it easier to maintain a program.

## Program Style   *Spaces in Programs*

The consistent and careful use of blank spaces can improve the style of a program. A blank space is required between consecutive words in a program line.

The compiler ignores extra blanks between words and symbols, but you may insert space to improve the readability and style of a program. You should always leave a blank space after a comma and before and after operators such as *, -, and =. You should indent the body of the main function and insert blank lines between sections of the program.

Although stylistic issues have no effect whatever on the meaning of the program as far as the computer is concerned, they can make it easier for people to read and understand the program. Take care, however, not to insert blank spaces where they do not belong. For example, there cannot be a space between the characters which surround a comment (/* and */). Also, you cannot write the identifier MAX_ITEMS as MAX ITEMS.

## Comments in Programs

**program documentation**
information (comments) that
enhances the readability of a
program

Programmers can make a program easier to understand by using comments to describe the purpose of the program, the use of identifiers, and the purpose of each program step. Comments are part of the **program documentation** because they help others read and understand the program. The compiler, however, ignores comments and they are not translated into machine language.

A comment can appear by itself on a program line, at the end of a line following a statement, or embedded in a statement. In the following variable declarations, the first comment is embedded in the declaration, while the second one follows the declaration.

```
double miles, /* input - distance in miles              */
       kms;   /* output - distance in kilometers         */
```

We document most variables in this way.

---

**Program Comment**

SYNTAX:     /* *comment text* */

EXAMPLES: /* This is a one-line or partial-line comment */
          /*
           * This is a multiple-line comment in which the stars
           * not immediately preceded or followed by slashes have
           * no special syntactic significance, but simply help
           * the comment to stand out as a block. This style is
           * often used to document the purpose of a program.
           */

INTERPRETATION: A slash-star indicates the start of a comment; a star-slash indicates the end of a comment. Comments are listed with the program but are otherwise ignored by the C compiler. A comment may be put in a C program anywhere a blank space would be valid.

*Note:* ANSI C does not permit the placement of one comment inside another.

---

## Program Style    *Using Comments*

Each program should begin with a header section that consists of a series of comments specifying

- the programmer's name
- the date of the current version
- a brief description of what the program does

If you write the program for a class assignment, you should also list the class identification and your instructor's name.

```
/*
 * Programmer: William Bell    Date completed: May 9, 1995
 * Instructor: Janet Smith     Class: CIS61
 *
 * Calculates and displays the area and circumference of a
 * circle
 */
```

Before you implement each step in the initial algorithm, you should write a comment that summarizes the purpose of the algorithm step. This comment should describe what the step does rather than simply restate the step in English. For example, the comment

```
/* Convert the distance to kilometers. */
kms = KMS_PER_MILE * miles;
```

is more descriptive and hence preferable to

```
/* Multiply KMS_PER_MILE by miles and store result in kms. */
kms = KMS_PER_MILE * miles;
```

**EXERCISES FOR SECTION 2.4**

Self-Check

1. Change these comments so they are syntactically correct.

   ```
   /* This is a comment? *\
   /* This one /* seems like a comment */ doesn't it */
   ```

2. Correct the syntax errors in the following program, and rewrite the program so that it follows our style conventions. What does each statement of your corrected program do? What output does it display?

   ```
   /*
    * Calculate and display the difference of two input values
    *)
   #include <stdio.h>
   int
   main(void) {int X, /* first input value */ x, /* second
     input value */
   sum; /* sum of inputs */
   scanf("%i%i";&X;&x); X + x = sum;
   printf("%d + %d = %d\n"; X; x; sum); return (0);}
   ```

Programming

1. Write a program that stores the values 'X' and 76.1 in separate memory cells. Your program should get the values as data items and display them again for the user when done.

# 2.5 ARITHMETIC EXPRESSIONS

To solve most programming problems, you will need to write arithmetic expressions that manipulate type int and double data. This section describes the operators used in arithmetic expressions and rules for writing and evaluating the expressions.

Table 2.6 shows all the arithmetic operators. Each operator manipulates two *operands* which may be constants, variables, or other arithmetic expressions. The operators +, -, *, and / may be used with type int or double operands. As shown in the last column, the data type of the result is the same as the data type of its operands. An additional operator, the remainder operator (%), can be used with integer operands to find the remainder of longhand division. We will discuss the division and remainder operators in the next subsection.

**Table 2.6    Arithmetic Operators**

| Arithmetic Operator | Meaning | Examples |
|---|---|---|
| + | addition | 5 + 2 is 7 |
| | | 5.0 + 2.0 is 7.0 |
| - | subtraction | 5 - 2 is 3 |
| | | 5.0 - 2.0 is 3.0 |
| * | multiplication | 5 * 2 is 10 |
| | | 5.0 * 2.0 is 10.0 |
| / | division | 5.0 / 2.0 is 2.5 |
| | | 5 / 2 is 2 |
| % | remainder | 5 % 2 is 1 |

## Operators / and %

When applied to two positive integers, the division operator (/) computes the integral part of the result of dividing its first operand by its second. For example, the value of 7.0 / 2.0 is 3.5, but the value of 7 / 2 is the integral part of this result, or 3. Similarly, the value of 299.0 / 100.0 is 2.99, but the value of 299 / 100 is the integral part of this result, or 2. If the / operator is used with a negative and a positive integer, the result may vary from one C implementation to another. For this reason, you should avoid using division with negative integers. The / operation is undefined when the divisor (the second operand) is 0. Table 2.7 shows some examples of integer division.

The remainder operator (%) returns the *integer remainder* of the result of dividing its first operand by its second. For example, the value of 7 % 2 is 1 because the integer remainder is 1.

You can use longhand division to determine the result of a / or % operation with integers. The calculation on the left shows the effect of dividing 7 by 2 by longhand division: we get a quotient of 3 (7 / 2) and a remainder of 1 (7 % 2). The calculation on the right shows that 299 % 100 is 99 because we get a remainder of 99 when we divide 299 by 100.

The magnitude of *m* % *n* must always be less than the divisor *n,* so if *m* is positive, the value of *m* % 100 must be between 0 and 99. The % operation is undefined when *n* is zero and varies from one implementation to another if *n* is negative. Table 2.8 shows some examples of the % operator.

**Table 2.7   Results of Integer Division**

| | |
|---|---|
| 3 / 15 = 0 | 18 / 3 = 6 |
| 15 / 3 = 5 | 16 / –3 varies |
| 16 / 3 = 5 | 0 / 4 = 0 |
| 17 / 3 = 5 | 4 / 0 is undefined |

**Table 2.8   Results of % Operation**

| | |
|---|---|
| 3 % 5 = 3 | 5 % 3 = 2 |
| 4 % 5 = 4 | 5 % 4 = 1 |
| 5 % 5 = 0 | 15 % 5 = 0 |
| 6 % 5 - 1 | 15 % 6 - 3 |
| 7 % 5 = 2 | 15 % -7 varies |
| 8 % 5 = 3 | 15 % 0 is undefined |

The formula

$$m \text{ equals } (m\ /\ n)\ *\ n + (m\ \%\ n)$$

defines the relationship between the operators / and % for an integer dividend of *m* and an integer divisor of *n*. We can see that this formula holds for the two problems discussed earlier by plugging in values for *m, n, m / n,* and *m % n*. In the first example that follows, *m* is 7 and *n* is 2; in the second, *m* is 299 and *n* is 100.

```
7    equals (7 / 2)   * 2 + (7 % 2)
     equals    3      * 2 + 1

299 equals (299 / 100) * 100 + (299 % 100)
     equals     2       * 100 +     99
```

**EXAMPLE 2.4**

If you have p pieces of candy and c children and want to distribute the candy equally, the expression

```
p / c
```

tells you how many pieces to give each child. For example, if p is 18 and c is 4, give each child 4 pieces. The expression

```
p % c
```

tells you how many pieces would be left over (18 % 4 is 2).

## Data Type of an Expression

The data type of each variable must be specified in its declaration, but how does C determine the data type of an expression? The data type of an expression depends on the type of its operands. Let's consider the types of expressions involving operands that are integers of type `int` or real numbers of type double.[†] For example, the expression

ace + bandage

is type `int` if both `ace` and `bandage` are type `int`; otherwise, it is type double. In general, an expression of the form

ace *arithmetic_operator* bandage

is of type `int` if *both* `ace` and `bandage` are of type `int`; otherwise, it is of type `double`.

    An expression that has operands of both type `int` and `double` is a **mixed-type expression**. The data type of such a mixed-type expression will be `double`.

**mixed-type expression**
an expression with operands of different types

## Mixed-type Assignment Statement

When an assignment statement is executed, the expression is first evaluated; then the result is assigned to the variable listed to the left of the assignment operator (=). Either a type `double` or a type `int` expression may be assigned to a type `double` variable, so if m and n are type `int` and p, x, and y are type `double`, the statements that follow assign the values shown in the boxes.

```
m = 3;
n = 2;
p = 2.0;
x = m / p;
y = m / n;
```

**mixed-type assignment**
the expression being evaluated and the variable to which it is assigned have different data types

    In a **mixed-type assignment** such as

y = m / n;

---

[†]C defines additional integer and real data types besides `int` and `double`, but these two types can represent most numbers used in programming applications.

the expression has a different data type from the variable getting its value. A common error is to assume that the type of y (the variable being assigned) causes the expression to be evaluated as if its operands were that type too. Remember, the expression is evaluated before the assignment is made, and the type of the variable being assigned has no effect whatsoever on the expression value. The expression m / n evaluates to the integer 1. This value is converted to type double (1.0) before it is stored in y.

Assignment of a type double expression to a type int variable causes the fractional part of the expression to be lost since it cannot be represented in a type int variable. The expression in the assignment statements

```
x = 9 * 0.5;
n = 9 * 0.5;
```

evaluates to the real number 4.5. If x is of type double, the number 4.5 is stored in x, as expected. If n is of type int, only the integral part of the expression value is stored in n, as shown.

## Expressions with Multiple Operators

In our programs so far, most expressions have involved a single arithmetic operator; however, expressions with multiple operators are common in C. Expressions can include both unary and binary operators. **Unary operators** take only one operand. In these expressions, we see the unary negation (−) and plus (+) operators.

**unary operator**
an operator with one operand

```
x = -y;
p = +x * y;
```

**binary operator**
an operator with two operands

**Binary operators** require two operands. When + and − are used to represent addition and subtraction, they are binary operators.

```
x = y + z;
z = y - x;
```

To understand and write expressions with multiple operators, we must know the C rules for evaluating expressions. For example, in the expression x + y / z, is + performed before / or is + performed after /? Is the expression x / y * z evaluated as (x / y) * z or as x / (y * z)? Verify for yourself that the order of evaluation does make a difference by substituting some simple values for x, y, and z. In both of these expressions, the / operator is evaluated first; the reasons are explained in the C rules for evaluation of arithmetic expressions which follow. These rules are based on familiar algebraic rules.

### Rules for Evaluating Expressions

a. *Parentheses rule:* All expressions in parentheses must be evaluated separately. Nested parenthesized expressions must be evaluated from the inside out, with the innermost expression evaluated first.

b. *Operator precedence rule:* Operators in the same expression are evaluated in the following order.

| | |
|---|---|
| unary +, – | first |
| *, /, % | next |
| binary +, – | last |

c. *Associativity rule:* Unary operators in the same subexpression and at the same precedence level (such as + and –) are evaluated right to left (*right associativity*). Binary operators in the same subexpression and at the same precedence level (such as + and –) are evaluated left to right (*left associativity*).

These rules will help you understand how C evaluates expressions. Use parentheses as needed to specify the order of evaluation. Often it is a good idea in complicated expressions to use extra parentheses to document clearly the order of operator evaluation. For example, the expression

```
x * y * z + a / b - c * d
```

can be written in a more readable form using parentheses:

```
(x * y * z ) + (a / b) - (c * d)
```

**EXAMPLE 2.5**

The formula for the area of a circle

$$a = \pi r^2$$

can be written in C as

```
area = PI * radius * radius;
```

where the meaning of the constant macro PI is 3.14159. Figure 2.8 shows the *evaluation tree* for this formula. In this tree, which you read from top to bottom, arrows connect each operand with its operator. The order of operator evaluation is shown by the number to the left of each operator; the letter to the right of the operator indicates which evaluation rule applies.

**Figure 2.8
Evaluation Tree
for** `area = PI *
radius * radius;`

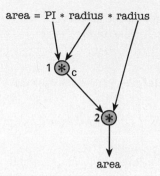

area = PI * radius * radius

In Fig. 2.9, we see a step-by-step evaluation of the same expression for a `radius` value of `2.0`. You may want to use a similar notation when computing by hand the value of an expression with multiple operators.

**Figure 2.9
Step-by-step
Expression
Evaluation**

```
area    =    PI    *    radius    *    radius
          3.14159      2.0              2.0
              6.28318
                             12.56636
```

**EXAMPLE 2.6** ▶ The formula for the average velocity, *v*, of a particle traveling on a line between points $p_1$ and $p_2$ in time $t_1$ to $t_2$ is

$$v = \frac{p_2 - p_1}{t_2 - t_1}$$

This formula can be written and evaluated in C as shown in Fig. 2.10. ◀

**Figure 2.10
Evaluation Tree
and Evaluation
for** `v = (p2 -
p1) / (t2 - t1);`

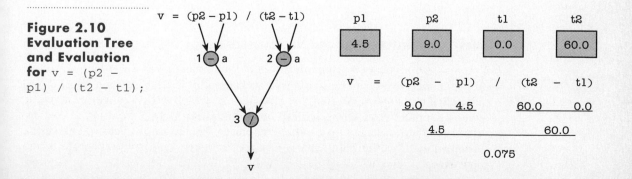

**EXAMPLE 2.7**  Consider the expression

```
z - (a + b / 2) + w * -y
```

containing type `int` variables only. The parenthesized expression

```
(a + b / 2)
```

is evaluated first (rule a) beginning with b / 2 (rule b). Once the value of b / 2 is determined, it can be added to a to obtain the value of (a + b / 2). Next, y is negated (rule b). The multiplication operation can now be performed (rule b) and the value for w * -y is determined. Then, the value of (a + b / 2) is subtracted from z (rule c). Finally, this result is added to w * -y. The evaluation tree and step-by-step evaluation for this expression are shown in Fig. 2.11.

**Figure 2.11 Evaluation Tree and Evaluation for** z – (a + b / 2) + w * –y

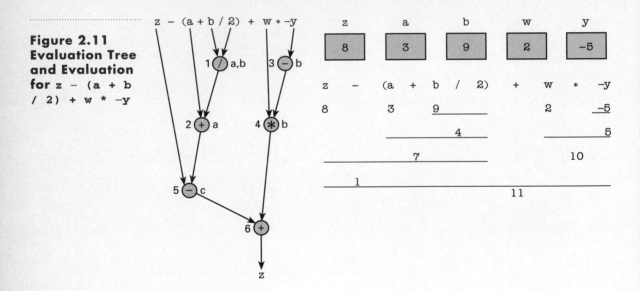

## Writing Mathematical Formulas in C

You may encounter two problems in writing a mathematical formula in C. First, multiplication often can be implied in a formula by writing the two items to be multiplied next to each other, for example, $a = bc$. In C, however, you must always use the * operator to indicate multiplication, as in

```
a = b * c;
```

The other difficulty arises in formulas with division. We normally write the numerator and the denominator on separate lines:

$$m = \frac{y - b}{x - a}$$

In C, however, the numerator and denominator are placed on the same line. Consequently, parentheses are often needed to separate the numerator from the denominator and to indicate clearly the order of evaluation of the operators in the expression. The above formula would be written in C as

```
m = (y - b) / (x - a);
```

Table 2.9 shows several mathematical formulas rewritten in C.
The points illustrated in these examples can be summarized as follows:

- Always specify multiplication explicitly by using the operator * where needed (formulas 1 and 4).
- Use parentheses when required to control the order of operator evaluation (formulas 3 and 4).
- Two arithmetic operators can be written in succession if the second is a unary operator (formula 5).

## Case Study: Evaluating a Collection of Coins

This case study demonstrates the manipulation of type `int` data (using / and %) and type `char` data.

### Table 2.9 Mathematical Formulas as C Expressions

| Mathematical Formula | C Expression |
| --- | --- |
| 1. $b^2 - 4ac$ | b * b - 4 * a * c |
| 2. $a + b - c$ | a + b - c |
| 3. $\frac{a + b}{c + d}$ | (a + b) / (c + d) |
| 4. $\frac{1}{1 + x^2}$ | 1 / (1 + x * x) |
| 5. $a \times -(b + c)$ | a * -(b + c) |

**◖ PROBLEM ◗**

Your local bank branch has many customers who save their change and periodically bring it in for deposit. Write a program to interact with their customers and determine the value of a collection of coins.

**◖ ANALYSIS ◗**

To solve this problem, you need to get the count of each type of coin (quarters, dimes, nickels, pennies) from a customer. From those counts, you can determine the total value of the coins in cents. Once you have that figure, you can do an integer division using 100 as the divisor to get the dollar value; the remainder of this division will be the left-over change. In the data requirements, list the total value in cents (`total_cents`) as a program variable, because it is needed as part of the computation process but is not a required problem output. To personalize the interaction, get each customer's initials before getting the coin counts.

**Data Requirements**

**Problem Inputs**
```
char first, middle, last   /* a customer's initials */
int quarters               /* the count of quarters */
int dimes                  /* the count of dimes    */
int nickels                /* the count of nickels  */
int pennies                /* the count of pennies  */
```

**Problem Outputs**
```
int dollars                /* value in dollars      */
int change                 /* left-over change      */
```

**Additional Program Variables**
```
int total_cents            /* total value in cents  */
```

**◖ DESIGN ◗**

**Initial Algorithm**

1. Get and display the customer's initials.
2. Get the count of each kind of coin.
3. Compute the total value in cents.
4. Find the value in dollars and change.
5. Display the value in dollars and change.

Steps 3 and 4 may need refinement. Their refinements are:

**Step 3 Refinement**
3.1 Find the equivalent value of each kind of coin in pennies and add these values.

**Step 4 Refinement**
4.1 `dollars` is the integer quotient of `total_cents` and 100.
4.2 `change` is the integer remainder of `total_cents` and 100.

**◀ IMPLEMENTATION ▶**

The program is shown in Fig. 2.12. The statements

```
scanf("%c%c%c", &first, &middle, &last);
printf("Hello %c%c%c, let's see what your coins are worth.\n",
       first, middle, last);
```

copy three data characters into `first`, `middle`, and `last` and display those characters as part of a welcoming message to the customer.
    The statement

```
total_cents = 25 * quarters + 10 * dimes +
              5 * nickels + pennies;
```

implements algorithm step 3.1. The statements

```
dollars = total_cents / 100;
change = total_cents % 100;
```

implement steps 4.1 and 4.2. The last call to `printf` displays the results.

**Figure 2.12 Finding the Value of Coins**

```
/*
 * Determines the value of a collection of coins.
 */
#include <stdio.h>
```

*(continued)*

**Figure 2.12**    *(continued)*

```
int
main(void)
{
      char first, middle, last; /* input - 3 initials            */
      int pennies, nickels;   /* input - count of each coin type */
      int dimes, quarters;    /* input - count of each coin type */
      int change;                /* output - change amount        */
      int dollars;               /* output - dollar amount        */
      int total_cents;           /* total cents                   */

      /* Get and display the customer's initials. */
      printf("Type in 3 initials and press return> ");
      scanf("%c%c%c", &first, &middle, &last);
      printf("Hello %c%c%c, let's see what your coins are worth.\n",
              first, middle, last);

      /* Get the count of each kind of coin. */
      printf("Number of quarters> ");
      scanf("%d", &quarters);
      printf("Number of dimes   > ");
      scanf("%d", &dimes);
      printf("Number of nickels > ");
      scanf("%d", &nickels);
      printf("Number of pennies > ");
      scanf("%d", &pennies);

      /* Compute the total value in cents. */
      total_cents = 25 * quarters + 10 * dimes +
                       5 * nickels + pennies;

      /* Find the value in dollars and change. */
      dollars = total_cents / 100;
      change = total_cents % 100;

      /* Display the value in dollars and change. */
      printf("\nYour coins are worth %d dollars and %d cents.\n",
              dollars, change);

      return (0);
}
```

*(continued)*

**Figure 2.12** *(continued)*

```
Type in 3 initials and press Return> BMC
Hello BMC, let's see what your coins are worth.
Number of quarters> 8
Number of dimes   > 20
Number of nickels > 30
Number of pennies > 77

Your coins are worth 6 dollars and 27 cents.
```

**TESTING**

To test this program, try running it with a combination of coins that yield an exact dollar amount with no left-over change. For example, 8 quarters, 0 dimes, 35 nickels, and 25 pennies should yield a value of 4 dollars and no cents. Then increase and decrease the amount of pennies by one (26 and 24 pennies) to make sure that these cases are also handled properly.

**EXERCISES FOR SECTION 2.5**

Self-Check

1. a. Evaluate the following expressions with 7 and 22 as operands.

   ```
   22 / 7       7 / 22       22 % 7       7 % 22
   ```

   Repeat this exercise for the following pairs of integers:
   b. 15, 16    c. 3, 23    d. −3, 16

2. Do a step-by-step evaluation of the expressions that follow if the value of celsius is 3 and salary is 12400.00.

   ```
   1.8 * celsius + 32.0
   (salary - 5000.00) * 0.20 + 1425.00
   ```

3. Given the constants and variable declarations

   ```
   #define PI 3.14159
   #define MAX_I 1000
   . . .
   double x, y;
   int a, b, i;
   ```

indicate which of the following statements are valid, and find the value stored by each valid statement. Also indicate which are invalid and why. Assume that a is 3, b is 4, and y is -1.0.

a. i = a % b;
b. i = (989 - MAX_I) / a;
c. i = b % a;
d. x = PI * y;
e. i = a / -b;
f. x = a / b;
g. x = a % (a / b);
h. i = b / 0;
i. i = a % (990 - MAX_I);
j. i = (MAX_I - 990) / a;
k. x = a / y;
l. i = PI * a;
m. x = PI / y;
n. x = b / a;
o. i = (MAX_I - 990) % a;
p. i = a % 0;
q. i = a % (MAX_I - 990);

4. What values are assigned by the legal statements in Exercise 3, assuming a is 5, b is 2, and y is 2.0?

5. Assume that you have the following variable declarations:

```
int color, lime, straw, red, orange;
double white, green, blue, purple, crayon;
```

Evaluate each of the statements below using the following values: color is 2, crayon is -1.3, straw is 1, red is 3, purple is 0.3E+1.

a. white = color * 2.5 / purple;
b. green = color / purple;
c. orange = color / red;
d. blue = (color + straw) / (crayon + 0.3);
e. lime = red / color + red % color;
f. purple = straw / red * color;

6. Let a, b, c, and x be the names of four type double variables, and let i, j, and k be the names of three type int variables. Each of the following statements contains one or more violations of the rules for forming arithmetic expressions. Rewrite each statement so that it is consistent with these rules.

a. x = 4.0 a * c;
b. a = ac;
c. i = 5j3;
d. k = 3(i + j);
e. x = 5a + bc;

## Programming

1. Write an assignment statement that might be used to implement the following equation in C.

$$q = \frac{kA(T_1 - T_2)}{L}$$

2. Write a program that stores the values 'X', 'O', 1.345E10, and 35 in separate memory cells. Your program should get the first three values as input
data, but use an assignment statement to store the last value.

# 2.6 FORMATTING NUMBERS IN PROGRAM OUTPUT

C displays all numbers in its default notation unless we instruct it to do otherwise.
This section explains how to specify the format or appearance of your output.

## Formatting Values of Type int

Specifying the format of an integer value displayed by a C program is fairly
easy. You simply add a number between the % and the d of the %d placeholder

**field width**
the number of columns used
to display a value

in the printf format string. This number specifies the **field width,** or number
of columns to use for the display of the value. The statement

```
printf("Results: %3d meters = %4d ft. %2d in.\n",
       meters, feet , inches);
```

indicates that 3 columns will be used to display the value of meters, 4
columns will be used for feet, and 2 columns will be used for inches (a
number between 0 and 11). If meters is 21, feet is 68, and inches is 11,
the program output will be

```
Results:  21 meters =   68 ft. 11 in.
```

In this line, notice that there is an extra space before the value of meters
(21) and two extra spaces before the value of feet (68). The reason is that the
placeholder for meters (%3d) allows space for 3 digits to be printed. Because
the value of meters is between 10 and 99, its two digits are displayed *right-
justified,* preceded by one blank space. Because the placeholder for feet (%4d)
allows room for 4 digits, printing its two-digit value right-justified leaves two
extra blank spaces. We can use the placeholder %2d to display any integer
value between -9 and 99. The placeholder %4d works for values in the range
-999 to 9999. For negative numbers, the minus sign is included in the count of
digits displayed.

Table 2.10 shows how two integer values are displayed using different
format string placeholders. The character □ represents a blank character. The
last line shows that C expands the field width if it is too small for the integer
value displayed.

**Table 2.10  Displaying 234 and –234 Using Different Placeholders**

| Value | Format | Displayed Output | Value | Format | Displayed Output |
|-------|--------|------------------|-------|--------|------------------|
| 234 | %4d | □234 | -234 | %4d | -234 |
| 234 | %5d | □□234 | -234 | %5d | □-234 |
| 234 | %6d | □□□234 | -234 | %6d | □□-234 |
| 234 | %1d | 234 | -234 | %2d | -234 |

## Formatting Values of Type double

To describe the format specification for a type double value, we must indicate both the total *field width* needed and the number of *decimal places* desired. The total field width should be large enough to accommodate all digits before and after the decimal point. There will be at least one digit before the decimal point because a zero is printed as the whole-number part of fractions that are less than 1.0 and greater than -1.0. We should also include a display column for the decimal point and for the minus sign if the number can be negative. The form of the format string placeholder is %*n*.*m*f where *n* is a number representing the total field width, and *m* is the desired number of decimal places.

If x is a type double variable whose value will be between -99.99 and 999.99, we could use the placeholder %6.2f to display the value of x to an accuracy of two decimal places. Table 2.11 shows different values of x displayed using this format specification. The values displayed are rounded to two decimal places and are displayed right-justified in 6 columns. When you round

**Table 2.11  Displaying x Using Format String Placeholder %6.2f**

| Value of x | Displayed Output | Value of x | Displayed Output |
|------------|------------------|------------|------------------|
| -99.42 | -99.42 | -25.554 | -25.55 |
| .123 | □□0.12 | 99.999 | 100.00 |
| -9.536 | □-9.54 | 999.4 | 999.40 |

**Table 2.12 Formatting Type double Values**

| Value | Format | Displayed Output | Value | Format | Displayed Output |
|-------|--------|------------------|-------|--------|------------------|
| 3.14159 | %5.2f | □3.14 | 3.14159 | %4.2f | 3.14 |
| 3.14159 | %3.2f | 3.14 | 3.14159 | %5.1f | □□3.1 |
| 3.14159 | %5.3f | 3.142 | 3.14159 | %8.5f | □3.14159 |
| .1234 | %4.2f | 0.12 | -.006 | %4.2f | -0.01 |
| -.006 | %8.3f | □□-0.006 | -.006 | %8.5f | -0.00600 |
| -.006 | %.3f | -0.006 | -3.14159 | %.4f | -3.1416 |

to two decimal places, if the third digit of the value's fractional part is 5 or greater, the second digit is incremented by 1 (-9.536 becomes -9.54). Otherwise, the digits after the second digit in the fraction are simply dropped (-25.554 becomes -25.55).

Table 2.12 shows some values that were displayed using other place-holders. The last line shows it is legal to omit the total field width in the format string placeholder. If you use a placeholder such as %.*m*f to specify only the number of decimal places, the value will be printed with no leading blanks.

## Program Style    *Eliminating Leading Blanks*

As shown in Tables 2.10 through 2.12, a value whose whole-number part requires fewer display columns than are specified by the format field width is displayed with leading blanks. To eliminate extra leading blanks, omit the field width from the format string placeholder. The simple placeholder %d will cause an integer value to be displayed with no leading blanks. A placeholder of the form %.*m*f has the same effect for values of type double, and this place-holder still allows you to choose the number of decimal places you wish.

**EXERCISES FOR SECTION 2.6**

Self-Check

1. Correct the statement

```
printf("Salary is %2.10f\n", salary);
```

2. Show how the value `-15.564` would be printed using the formats `%8.4f`, `%8.3f`, `%8.2f`, `%8.1f`, `%8.0f`, `%.2f`.

3. Assuming x (type `double`) is `12.335` and i (type `int`) is `100`, show the lines displayed by the following statements. For clarity, use the symbol ▮ to denote a blank space.

```
printf("x is %6.2f  i is %4d\n", x, i);
printf("i is %d\n", i);
printf ("x is %.1f\n", x);
```

Programming

1. If the variables a, b, and c are `504`, `302.558`, and `-12.31`, respectively, write a statement that will display the following line. (For clarity, a ▮ denotes a blank space.)

   ▮▮504▮▮▮▮▮302.56▮▮▮▮-12.3

## 2.7  INTERACTIVE MODE, BATCH MODE, AND DATA FILES

**interactive mode**
a mode of program execution in which the user responds to prompts by entering (typing in) data

**batch mode**
a mode of program execution in which the program scans its data from a previously prepared data file

There are two basic modes of computer operation: batch mode and interactive mode. The programs that we have written so far run in interactive mode. In **interactive mode,** the program user interacts with the program and types in data while it is running. We include prompts so the program user knows when to enter each data item. In **batch mode,** the program scans its data from a data file prepared beforehand instead of interacting with its user.

### Input Redirection

Figure 2.13 shows the miles-to-kilometers conversion program rewritten as a batch program. In Fig. 2.13, we assume that the standard input device is associated with a batch data file instead of with the keyboard. In most systems, this association can be accomplished relatively easily through *input-output redirection* using operating system commands. For example, in the UNIX® and MS-DOS® operating systems, you can instruct your program to take its input from file `mydata` instead of from the keyboard by placing the symbols `<mydata` at the end of the command line that causes your compiled and linked program to execute. If you normally used the command line

```
metric
```

**Figure 2.13   Batch Version of Miles-to-Kilometers Conversion Program**

```
/* Converts distances from miles to kilometers.     */

#include <stdio.h>     /* printf, scanf definitions */
#define KMS_PER_MILE 1.609 /* conversion constant   */

int
main(void)
{
      double miles,   /* distance in miles                        */
             kms;     /* equivalent distance in kilometers        */

      /* Get and echo the distance in miles. */
      scanf("%lf", &miles);
      printf("The distance in miles is %.2f.\n", miles);

      /* Convert the distance to kilometers. */
      kms = KMS_PER_MILE * miles;

      /* Display the distance in kilometers. */
      printf("That equals %.2f kilometers.\n", kms);

      return (0);
}
```

```
The distance in miles is 112.00.
That equals 180.21 kilometers.
```

to execute this program, your new command line would be

```
metric <mydata
```

### Program Style   *Echo Prints versus Prompts*

In Fig. 2.13, the statement

```
scanf("%lf", &miles);
```

gets a value for miles from the first (and only) line of the data file. Because the program input comes from a data file, there is no need to precede this statement with a prompting message. Instead, we follow the call to scanf with the statement

```
printf("The distance in miles is %.2f.\n", miles);
```

This statement *echo prints* or displays the value just stored in miles and provides a record of the data manipulated by the program. Without it, we would have no easy way of knowing what value scanf obtained for miles. Whenever you convert an interactive program to a batch program, make sure you replace each prompt with an echo print that follows the call to scanf.

## Output Redirection

You can also redirect program output to a disk file instead of to the screen. Then you can send the output file to the printer (using an operating system command) to obtain a hard copy of the program output. In UNIX or MS-DOS, use the symbols >myoutput to redirect output from the screen to file myoutput. These symbols should also be placed on the command line that causes your program to execute. The command line

```
metric >myoutput
```

executes the compiled and linked code for program metric, taking program input from the keyboard and writing program output to file myoutput. However, interacting with the running program will be difficult because all program output, including any prompting messages, will be sent to the output file. It would be better to use the command line

```
metric <mydata >myoutput
```

which takes program input from data file mydata and sends program output to output file myoutput.

## Program-Controlled Input and Output Files

As an alternative to input/output redirection, C allows a program to explicitly name a file from which the program will take input and a file to which the program will send output. Figure 2.14 shows a version of the distance conversion program that takes input data from a file named b:distance.dat and sends results to a file named b:distance.out.

**Figure 2.14  Miles-to-Kilometers Conversion Program with Named Files**

```c
/* Converts distances from miles to kilometers.     */

#include <stdio.h>      /* printf, scanf, fprint, fscanf, fopen, fclose
                           definitions                 */
#define KMS_PER_MILE 1.609 /* conversion constant   */

int
main(void)
{
      double miles, /* distance in miles                         */
             kms;   /* equivalent distance in kilometers         */
      FILE   *inp,  /* pointer to input file                     */
             *outp; /* pointer to output file                    */

      /* Open the input and output files.     */
      inp = fopen("b:distance.dat", "r");
      outp = fopen("b:distance.out", "w");

      /* Get and echo the distance in miles. */
      fscanf(inp, "%lf", &miles);
      fprintf(outp, "The distance in miles is %.2f.\n", miles);

      /* Convert the distance to kilometers. */
      kms = KMS_PER_MILE * miles;

      /* Display the distance in kilometers. */
      fprintf(outp, "That equals %.2f kilometers.\n", kms);

      /* Close files. */
      fclose(inp);
      fclose(outp);

      return (0);
}
```

Contents of input file `distance.dat`
112.0

Contents of output file `distance.out`
The distance in miles is 112.00.
That equals 180.21 kilometers.

A program that manipulates a specific file must first declare a *file pointer* variable in which to store the information necessary to permit access to a file. File pointer variables are of type FILE *. In Fig. 2.14, the statement

```
FILE    *inp,    /* pointer to input file              */
        *outp;   /* pointer to output file             */
```

declares that file pointer variables inp and outp will hold information allowing access to the program's input and output files, respectively. The operating system must prepare a file for input or output before permitting access. This preparation is the purpose of the calls to function fopen in the statements that follow:

```
inp = fopen("b:distance.dat", "r");
outp = fopen("b:distance.out", "w");
```

The first assignment statement *opens* (prepares for access) file b:distance.dat as a source of program input and stores the necessary access value in the file pointer variable inp. The "r" in the first call to fopen indicates that we wish to read (scan) data from the file opened. Because the second assignment statement includes a "w", indicating our desire to write to b:distance.out, outp is initialized as an output file pointer.

The next two statements demonstrate the use of the functions fscanf and fprintf, file equivalents of functions scanf and printf.

```
fscanf(inp, "%lf", &miles);
fprintf(outp, "The distance in miles is %.2f.\n", miles);
```

Function fscanf must first be given an input file pointer like inp. The remainder of a call to fscanf is identical to a call to scanf: It includes a format string and an input list. Similarly, function fprintf differs from function printf only in its requirement of an output file pointer like outp.

When a program has no further use for its input and output files, it *closes* them by calling function fclose with the file pointers:

```
fclose(inp);
fclose(outp);
```

**EXERCISES FOR
SECTION 2.7**

Self-Check

1. Explain the difference in placement of calls to printf used to display prompts and calls to printf used to echo data. Which calls are used in interactive programs, and which are used in batch programs?

2. How is input data provided to an interactive program? How is input data provided to a batch program?

Programming

1. Rewrite the program in Fig. 2.12 as two batch programs. In the first version, assume that the data file will be made accessible through input redirection. In the second version, use a program-controlled input file and a program-controlled output file.

# 2.8 COMMON PROGRAMMING ERRORS

**debugging**
removing errors from a program

As you begin to program, soon you will discover that a program rarely runs correctly the first time it executes. Murphy's Law, "If something can go wrong, it will," seems to have been written with the computer program in mind. In fact, errors are so common that they have their own special name—*bugs*—and the process of correcting them is called **debugging** a program. (According to computer folklore, computer pioneer Dr. Grace Murray Hopper diagnosed the first hardware error caused by a large insect found inside a computer component.) To alert you to potential problems, we will provide a section on common programming errors at the end of each chapter.

When the compiler detects an error, the computer displays an *error message,* which indicates that you have made a mistake and what the likely cause of the error might be. Unfortunately, error messages are often difficult to interpret and are sometimes misleading. As you gain experience, you will become more proficient at locating and correcting errors.

Three kinds of errors—syntax errors, run-time errors, and logic errors—can occur, as discussed in the following sections.

## Syntax Errors

**syntax error**
a violation of the C grammar rules, detected during program translation (compilation)

A **syntax error** occurs when your code violates one or more grammar rules of C and is detected by the compiler as it attempts to translate your program. If a statement has a syntax error, it cannot be translated and your program will not be executed.

Figure 2.15 shows a compiler listing of the miles-to-kilometers conversion program. A compiler listing is a listing created by the compiler during program translation that shows each line of the source program (preceded by a line number) and any syntax errors detected by the compiler. For this particular compiler, errors are indicated by lines that begin with five asterisks. The program contains the following syntax errors:

• missing semicolon at the end of the variable declaration (in line 271)

**Figure 2.15    Compiler Listing of a Program with Syntax Errors**

```
221 /* Converts distances from miles to kilometers. */
222
223 #include <stdio.h>          /* printf, scanf definitions   */
266 #define KMS_PER_MILE 1.609 /* conversion constant          */
267
268 int
269 main(void)
270 {
271      double kms
272
273      /* Get the distance in miles. */
274      printf("Enter the distance in miles> ");
***** Semicolon added at the end of the previous source line

275      scanf("%lf", &miles);
***** Identifier "miles" is not declared within this scope
***** Invalid operand of address-of operator

276
277      /* Convert the distance to kilometers. */
278      kms = KMS_PER_MILE * miles;
***** Identifier "miles" is not declared within this scope

279
280      /* Display the distance in kilometers. * /
281      printf("That equals %f kilometers.\n", kms);
282
283      return (0);
284 }
***** Unexpected end-of-file encountered in a comment
***** "}" inserted before end-of-file
```

- undeclared variable miles (detected in lines 275 and 278)
- last comment is not closed because of blank in * / close-comment sequence (in line 280)

The actual formats of the listing and the error messages produced by your compiler may differ from those in Fig. 2.15. Indeed, many C compilers do not produce a listing at all, but merely display error messages. In this listing, whenever an error is detected, the compiler displays a line starting with five asterisks followed by the error message. Notice that the line marked for an error is not always the line containing the programmer's mistake. (For example, the error occurring in line 271 is marked after line 274.)

The compiler attempts to correct errors wherever it can. Look at line 271 in the listing; it is missing a semicolon at the end. The compiler cannot be sure that this semicolon is missing until it processes the `printf` symbol on line 274. Because the `printf` is not a comma or a semicolon, the compiler then knows that the variable declaration statement begun on line 271 is not being continued to another line.

We see several cases in this listing where one mistake of the programmer leads to the generation of multiple error messages. For example, the missing declaration for variable `miles` causes an error message to be printed each time `miles` is used in the program. This message would also occur if we remembered to declare `miles` but mistyped it (perhaps as `milles`) in the declaration statement. The missing declaration for `miles` also causes the second error message on line 275. Because the address-of operator must have a variable as its operand, the fact that `miles` is not declared as a variable makes it an invalid operand.

The mistyped close-comment character sequence also causes multiple messages. Because any text is valid inside a comment, the compiler is unaware that there is a problem until it comes to the end of the source file without having encountered a } to end the program! After complaining about this unexpected turn of events (see line following line 284), it does what it can to correct the situation by closing the comment at the end of the source file text and adding a } to end the program properly.

Mistyping a close-comment sequence can cause errors that are very difficult to find. If the comment that is not correctly closed is in the middle of a program, the compiler will simply continue to treat program lines as comment text until it comes to the * / that closes the *next* comment. When you begin getting error messages that make you think your compiler isn't seeing part of your program, recheck your comments carefully. In the worst case, treating these executable statements as comments may not cause a syntax error—then the program will simply run incorrectly. Mistyping the open-comment sequence / * will make the compiler attempt to process the comment as a C statement, causing a syntax error.

Your strategy for correcting syntax errors should take into account the fact that one error can lead to many error messages. It is often a good idea to concentrate on correcting the errors in the declaration part of a program first. Then recompile the program before you attempt to fix other errors. Many of the other error messages will disappear once the declarations are correct.

Syntax errors are often caused by the improper use of quotation marks with format strings. Make sure that you always use a quote ( " ) to begin and end a string.

## Figure 2.16   A Program with a Run-time Error

```
111 #include <stdio.h>
262
263 int
264 main(void)
265 {
266       int    first, second;
267       double temp, ans;
268
269       printf("Enter two integers> ");
270       scanf("%d%d", &first, &second);
271       temp = second / first;
272       ans = first / temp;
273       printf("The result is %.3f\n", ans);
274
275       return (0);
276 }
```

```
Enter two integers> 14 3
Arithmetic fault, divide by zero at line 272 of routine main
```

## Run-time Errors

**run-time error**
an attempt to perform an invalid operation, detected during program execution

**Run-time errors** are detected and displayed by the computer during the execution of a program. A run-time error occurs when the program directs the computer to perform an illegal operation, such as dividing a number by zero. When a run-time error occurs, the computer will stop executing your program and will display a diagnostic message that indicates the line where the error was detected.

The program in Fig. 2.16 compiles successfully but cannot run to completion if the first integer entered is greater than the second. In this case, integer division causes the value assigned to `temp` in line 271 to be zero. Using `temp` as a divisor in line 272 causes the `divide by zero` error shown.

## Undetected Errors

Many execution errors may not prevent a C program from running to completion, but they may simply lead to incorrect results. Therefore it is essential that you predict the results your program should produce and verify that the actual output is correct.

A very common source of incorrect results in C programs is the input of a mixture of character and numeric data. Errors can be avoided if the programmer always keeps in mind scanf's different treatment of the %c placeholder on the one hand, and of the %d and %lf placeholders on the other. We noted that scanf first skips any blanks and carriage returns in the input when a numeric value is scanned. In contrast, scanf skips nothing when it scans a character unless the %c placeholder is preceded by a blank.

Figure 2.17 shows what appears to be a minor revision to the start of function main for the coin evaluation program from Fig. 2.12. We have added an integer variable year and we ask for a value of year before getting the user's initials. If the user types in 1995 and then the letters BMC, we would expect the second call to printf to display the message

Hello BMC, let's check your coins' value in 1995.

Instead, it displays the message

Hello
BM, let's check your coins' value in 1995.

---

**Figure 2.17    Revised Start of  main Function for Coin Evaluation**

```
int
main(void)
{
      char first, middle, last; /* input - 3 initials          */
      int pennies, nickels;   /* input - count of each coin type */
      int dimes, quarters;    /* input - count of each coin type */
      int change;                  /* output - change amount      */
      int dollars;                 /* output - dollar amount      */
      int total_cents;             /* total cents                 */
      int year;                    /* current year                */

      /* Get the current year.                                    */
      printf("Enter the current year and press return> ");
      scanf("%d", &year);

      /* Get the program user's initials.                         */
      printf("Type in 3 initials and press return> ");
      scanf("%c%c%c", &first, &middle, &last);
      printf("Hello %c%c%c, let's check your coins' value in %d.\n",
             first, middle, last, year);
      ...
```

To understand why, let's examine the status of memory at the time of the call to `printf`.

The value of `year` is correct, but the three characters stored are not `'B'`, `'M'`, `'C'`, but `'\n'`, `'B'`, and `'M'`. The `'\n'` in `first` is the character that results from the user pressing the <return> key after entering the number `1995`. The scan of `1995` stopped at this character, so it was the first character processed by the statement

```
scanf("%c%c%c", &first, &second, &third);
```

Because the letter `C` was not yet scanned, it will be scanned during the next `scanf` call. This will lead to further problems. The statement

```
scanf("%d", &quarters);
```

does not copy a value into `quarters` because the next character to scan is `C` which is not a digit character. Consequently, `quarters` will retain whatever value it happens to have. The same is true for variables `dimes`, `nickels`, and `pennies`. Consequently the results displayed by the program will be meaningless.

One simple way to repair the program would be to insert a space before the first `%c` placeholder. Then `scanf` will skip spaces (including carriage returns) before scanning a character.

```
scanf(" %c%c%c", &first, &second, &third);
```

Figure 2.18 shows another error that does not cause the program to abort with a run-time error message. The programmer has left out the `&` (address-of) operators on the variables in the call to `scanf`. Because `scanf` does not know where to find `first` and `second`, it is unable to store in them the values entered by the user. In this instance, the program runs to completion using whatever "garbage" values were originally in the memory locations named `first` and `second`.

**Figure 2.18    A Program That Produces Incorrect Results Due to & Omission**

```
#include <stdio.h>

int
main(void)
{
      int    first, second, sum;

      printf("Enter two integers> ");
      scanf("%d%d", first, second); /* ERROR!! should be  &first, &second */
      sum = first + second;
      printf("%d + %d = %d\n", first, second, sum);

      return (0);
}

Enter two integers> 14   3
5971289 + 5971297 = 11942586
```

### Logic Errors

**Logic errors** occur when a program follows a faulty algorithm. Because logic errors usually do not cause run-time errors and do not display error messages, they are very difficult to detect. The only sign of a logic error may be incorrect program output. You can detect logic errors by testing the program thoroughly, comparing its output to calculated results. You can prevent logic errors by carefully desk checking the algorithm and the program before you type it in.

Because debugging can be time-consuming, plan your program solutions carefully and desk check them to eliminate bugs early. If you are unsure of the syntax for a particular statement, look it up in the text or in the syntax guide printed on the inside back covers. Following this approach will save time and avoid trouble.

## CHAPTER REVIEW

1. Every C program has preprocessor directives and a main function. The main function contains variable declarations and executable statements.

2. Variable names must begin with a letter or an underscore (the latter not rec-ommended) and consist of letters, digits, and underscore symbols. A reserved word cannot be used as an identifier.

3. C's data types enable the compiler to determine how to store a particular value in memory and what operations can be performed on that value. Three standard data types are int, double, and char. The data type of each variable must be declared.

4. The executable statements are derived from the algorithm and are translated into machine language. Assignment statements are used to perform compu-tations and store results in memory. Function calls are used to get data (func-tions scanf and fscanf) and to display values stored in memory (functions printf and fprintf).

## New C Constructs

| Construct | Effect |
| --- | --- |
| **#include directive** | |
| `#include <stdio.h>` | Tells the preprocessor to give the program access to the header file for stan-dard I/O library. This includes information about the printf and scanf functions. |
| **#define directive for naming constant macros** | |
| `#define PI 3.14159` `#define STAR '*'` | Tells the preprocessor to use 3.14159 as the definition of the name PI and '*' as the meaning of the identifier STAR. |
| **main function heading** | |
| `int` `main(void)` | Marks the start of the function where program execution begins. |
| **variable declaration** | |
| `double pct, wt;` `int    high, mid, low;` `FILE  *inp, *outp;` | Allocates memory cells named pct and wt for storage of double-precision real numbers, cells named high, mid, and low for storage of integers, and cells named inp and outp for storage of file pointers. |
| **assignment statement** | |
| `distance = speed * time;` | Stores the product of speed and time as the value of the variable distance. |
| **file open** | |
| `inp = fopen("num.dat", "r");` `outp = fopen("num.out", "w");` | Opens num.dat as an input file, storing file pointer in inp. Opens num.out as an output file, storing file pointer in outp. |

*(continued)*

| Construct | Effect |
|---|---|
| **calls to input functions** | |
| `scanf("%lf%d", &pct, &high);` | Copies input data from the keyboard into the type `double` variable `pct` and the type `int` variable `high`. |
| `fscanf(inp, "%d%d", &mid,`<br>`        &low);` | Copies input data from file `num.dat` into the type `int` variables `mid` and `low`. |
| **calls to output functions** | |
| `printf("Percentage is %.3f\n", pct);` | Displays a line with the string `"Percentage is"` followed by the value of `pct` rounded to three decimal places. |
| `fprintf(outp, "%5d %5d %5d\n",`<br>`        high, mid, low);` | Stores in the file `num.out` a line containing the values of `high`, `mid`, and `low`. |
| **file close** | |
| `fclose(inp);`<br>`fclose(outp);` | Closes input file `num.dat` and newly created file `num.out`. |
| **return statement** | |
| `return (0);` | Final statement of function `main`. |

# QUICK-CHECK EXERCISES

1. What value is assigned to the type `double` variable x by the statement

   ```
   x = 25.0 * 3.0 / 2.5;
   ```

2. What value is assigned to x by the following statement, assuming x is `10.0`?

   ```
   x = x - 20.0;
   ```

3. Show the exact form of the output line displayed when x is `3.456`.

   ```
   printf("Three values of x are %4.1f*%5.2f*%.3f\n",
           x, x, x);
   ```

4. Show the exact form of the output line when n is `345`.

   ```
   printf("Three values of n are %4d*%5d*%d\n",
           n, n, n);
   ```

5. What data types would you use to represent the following items: number of children at school, a letter grade on an exam, the average number of school days a child is absent each year?
6. In which step of the software development method are the problem inputs and outputs identified?
7. If function `scanf` is getting two numbers from the same line of input, what characters should be used to separate them?
8. How does the computer determine how many data values to get from the input device when a `scanf` operation is performed?
9. In an interactive program, how does the program user know how many data values to enter when the `scanf` function is called?
10. The compiler listing shows which kind of errors (syntax or run-time)?

## ANSWERS TO QUICK-CHECK EXERCISES

1. `30.0`
2. `-10.0`
3. `Three values of x are #3.5*#3.46*3.456` (# = 1 blank)
4. `Three values of n are #345*##345*345`
5. `int, char, double`
6. analysis
7. blanks
8. It depends on the number of placeholders in the format string.
9. from reading the prompt
10. syntax errors

## REVIEW QUESTIONS

1. What type of information should be specified in the block comment at the very beginning of the program?
2. Which variables below are syntactically correct?

```
income        two fold
1time         c3po
int           income#1
Tom's         item
```

3. What is illegal about the following program fragment?

```
#include <stdio.h>
#define PI 3.14159

int
main(void)
{
      double c, r;

      scanf("%lf%lf", c, r);
      PI = c / (2 * r);
      . . .
}
```

4. Stylistically, which of the following identifiers would be good choices for names of constant macros?

```
gravity    G    MAX_SPEED    Sphere_Size
```

5. Write the data requirements, necessary formulas, and algorithm for Programming Project 6 in the next section.
6. The average pH of citrus fruits is 2.2, and this value has been stored in the variable avg_citrus_pH. Provide a statement to display this information in a readable way.
7. List three standard data types of C.
8. Convert the program statements below to take input data and echo it in batch mode.

```
printf("Enter two characters> ");
scanf("%c%c", &c1, &c2);
printf("Enter three integers separated by spaces> ");
scanf("%d%d%d", &n, &m, &p);
```

9. Write an algorithm that allows for the input of an integer value, doubles it, subtracts 10, and displays the result.

# PROGRAMMING PROJECTS

 1. Write a program to convert a temperature in degrees Fahrenheit to degrees Celsius.

$$C = \tfrac{5}{9}(F - 32)$$

**Data Requirements**

**Problem Input**
```
int fahrenheit /* temperature in degrees Fahrenheit    */
```

**Problem Output**
```
double celsius /* temperature in degrees Celsius       */
```

**Relevant Formula**
*celsius* = 5/9 (*fahrenheit* − 32)

2. Write a program to take two numbers as input data and display their sum, their difference, their product and their quotient.

**Data Requirements**

**Problem Inputs**
```
double x, y        /* two items */
```

**Problem Outputs**
```
double sum         /* sum of x and y             */
double difference  /* difference of x and y      */
double product     /* product of x and y         */
double quotient    /* quotient of x divided by y */
```

3. Write a program that predicts the score needed on a final exam to achieve a desired grade in a course. The program should interact with the user as follows:

```
Enter desired grade> B
Enter minimum average required> 79.5
Enter current average in course> 74.6
Enter how much the final counts
as a percentage of the course grade> 25

You need a score of 94.20 on the final to get a B.
```

In the example shown, the final counts 25% of the course grade.

4. Write a program that displays your first initial as a block letter. (*Hint:* Use a 6 × 6 grid for the letter and display six strings. Each string should consist of asterisks [*] interspersed with blanks.)

5. If a human heart beats on the average of once a second, how many times does the heart beat in a lifetime of 78 years? (Use 365.25 for days in a year.) Rerun your program for a heart rate of 75 beats per minute.

6. Write a program that takes the length and width of a rectangular yard and the length and width of a rectangular house situated in the yard. Your program should compute the time required to cut the grass at the rate of two square feet a second.

7. Write a program that takes as input the numerators and denominators of two fractions. Your program should display the numerator and denominator of the fraction that represents the product of the two fractions. Also, display the percent equivalent of the resulting product.

8. Redo Project 7; this time compute the sum of the two fractions.

9. The Pythagorean theorem states that the sum of the squares of the sides of a right triangle is equal to the square of the hypotenuse. For example, if two sides of a right triangle have lengths of 3 and 4, then the hypotenuse must have a length of 5. Together the integers 3, 4, and 5 form a *Pythagorean triple*. There are an infinite number of such triples. Given two positive integers, *m* and *n*, where $m > n$, a Pythagorean triple can be generated by the following formulas:

$$side1 = m^2 - n^2$$
$$side2 = 2mn$$
$$hypotenuse = m^2 + n^2$$

The triple (*side1* = 3, *side2* = 4, *hypotenuse* = 5) is generated by this formula when $m = 2$ and $n = 1$. Write a program that takes values for *m* and *n* as input and displays the values of the Pythagorean triple generated by the formulas above.

10. Write a program to compute the rate of growth, expressed as a percentage, of an insect population. Take as input the initial size of the population and its size one week later. Then predict the size of the population in yet another week, assuming that growth continues at the same rate.

# Top-down Design with Functions

chapter

Programmers who use the software development method to solve problems seldom tackle each new program as a unique event. Information contained in the problem statement and amassed during the analysis and design phases helps the programmer plan and complete the finished program. Programmers also use segments of earlier program solutions as building blocks to construct new programs.

In the first part of this chapter, we demonstrate how you can tap existing information and code in the form of predefined functions to write programs. In addition to using existing information, programmers can use top-down design techniques to simplify the development of algorithms and the structure of the resulting programs. To apply top-down design, the programmer starts with the broadest statement of the problem solution and works down to more detailed subproblems. In the second part of this chapter, we demonstrate top-down design and emphasize the role of modular programming using functions.

## 3.1 BUILDING PROGRAMS FROM EXISTING INFORMATION

Programmers seldom start off with a blank slate (or empty screen) when they develop a program. Often some—or all—of the solution can be developed from information that already exists or from the solution to another problem, as we demonstrate in this section.

Carefully following the software development method generates important system documentation before you even begin to code a program. This system documentation, consisting of a description of a problem's data requirements (developed during the Analysis phase) and its solution algorithm (developed during the Design phase), summarizes your intentions and thought processes.

You can use this documentation as a starting point in coding your program. For example, you can begin by editing the data requirements to conform to the C syntax for constant macro definitions and variable declarations as shown in Fig. 3.1 for the miles-to-kilometers conversion program. This approach is especially helpful if the documentation was created with a word processor and is in a file that you can edit.

To develop the executable statements in the main function, first use the initial algorithm and its refinements as program comments. The comments describe each algorithm step and provide program documentation that guides your C code. Figure 3.1 shows how the program will look at this point. After the comments are in place in the main function, you can begin to write the C statements. Place the C code for an unrefined step directly under that step. For a step that is refined, either edit the refinement to change it from English to C or replace it with C code. We illustrate this entire process in the next case study.

**Figure 3.1    Edited Data Requirements and Algorithm for Conversion Program**

```
/*
 * Converts distance in miles to kilometers.
 */

#include <stdio.h>               /* printf, scanf definitions */
#define KMS_PER_MILE 1.609       /* conversion constant */

int
main(void)
{
      double miles; /* input - distance in miles.      */
      double kms;   /* output - distance in kilometers */

      /* Get the distance in miles.                    */

      /* Convert the distance to kilometers.           */
         /* Distance in kilometers is
                1.609 * distance in miles.             */

      /* Display the distance in kilometers.           */

      return (0);
}
```

## Case Study: Finding the Area and Circumference of a Circle

**PROBLEM**

Get the radius of a circle. Compute and display the circle's area and circumference.

**ANALYSIS**

Clearly, the problem input is the circle's radius. Two outputs are requested: the circle's area and circumference. These variables should be type double because the inputs and outputs may contain fractional parts. The geometric relationships of a circle's radius to its area and circumference are listed below, along with the data requirements.

### Data Requirements

#### Problem Constant
```
PI      3.14159
```

#### Problem Input
```
radius      /* radius of a circle         */
```

#### Problem Outputs
```
area        /* area of a circle           */
circum      /* circumference of a circle  */
```

#### Relevant Formulas
*area of a circle* $= \pi \times radius^2$
*circumference of a circle* $= 2\pi \times radius$

**DESIGN**

After identifying the problem inputs and outputs, list the steps necessary to solve the problem. Pay close attention to the order of the steps.

### Initial Algorithm

1. Get the circle radius.
2. Calculate the area.
3. Calculate the circumference.
4. Display the area and the circumference.

### Algorithm Refinements

Next refine any steps that do not have an obvious solution (steps 2 and 3).

#### Step 2 Refinement
2.1 Assign `PI * radius * radius` to `area`.

#### Step 3 Refinement
3.1 Assign `2 * PI * radius` to `circum`.

**IMPLEMENTATION**

Figure 3.2 shows the C program so far. The main function lists the initial algorithm and its refinements as comments. To write the final program, convert the refinements (steps 2.1 and 3.1) to C and write C code for the unrefined steps (steps 1 and 4). Figure 3.3 shows the final program.

**Figure 3.2    Outline of Program Circle**

```
/*
 * Calculates and displays the area and circumference of a circle
 */

#include <stdio.h>
#define PI 3.14159

int
main(void)
{
      double radius;      /* input - radius of a circle  */
      double area;        /* output - area of a circle   */
      double circum;      /* output - circumference      */

      /* Get the circle radius */

      /* Calculate the area */
         /* Assign PI * radius * radius to area. */

      /* Calculate the circumference */
         /* Assign 2 * PI * radius to circum. */

      /* Display the area and circumference */

      return (0);
}
```

**Figure 3.3    Calculating the Area and the Circumference of a Circle**

```
/*
 * Calculates and displays the area and circumference of a circle
 */

#include <stdio.h>
#define PI 3.14159

int
main(void)
```

*(continued)*

**Figure 3.3** *(continued)*

```
{
        double radius; /* input - radius of a circle */
        double area;   /* output - area of a circle  */
        double circum; /* output - circumference     */

        /* Get the circle radius */
        printf("Enter radius> ");
        scanf("%lf", &radius);

        /* Calculate the area */
        area = PI * radius * radius;

        /* Calculate the circumference */
        circum = 2 * PI * radius;

        /* Display the area and circumference */
        printf("The area is %.4f\n", area);
        printf("The circumference is %.4f\n", circum);

        return (0);
}

Enter radius> 5.0
The area is 78.5397
The circumference is 31.4159
```

**TESTING**

The sample output in Fig. 3.3 provides a good test of the solution because it is relatively easy to compute by hand the area and the circumference for a radius value of 5.0. The radius squared is 25.0 and $\pi$ is approximately 3, so the value of the area appears to be correct. The circumference should be 10 times $\pi$, which is also an easy number to compute by hand.

## Case Study: Computing the Weight of a Batch of Flat Washers

Another way in which programmers use existing information is by *extending the solution for one problem to solve another*. For example, you can easily solve this problem by building on the solution to the previous one.

**PROBLEM**

You work for a hardware company that manufactures flat washers. To estimate shipping costs, your company needs a program that computes the weight of a specified quantity of flat washers.

**ANALYSIS**

A flat washer resembles a small donut. To compute the weight of a single flat washer, you need to know its rim area, its thickness, and the density of the material used in its construction. The last two quantities are problem inputs. However, the rim area (see Fig. 3.4) must be computed from two measurements that are provided as inputs: the washer's outer diameter and its inner diameter (diameter of the hole).

In the following data requirements, we list the washer's inner and outer radius (half the diameter) as program variables. We also list the rim area and weight of one washer (`unit_weight`) as program variables.

**Data Requirements**

> **Problem Constant**
> PI      3.14159

> **Problem Inputs**
> ```
> double hole_diameter /* diameter of hole */
> double edge_diameter /* diameter of outer edge */
> double thickness      /* thickness of washer */
> double density        /* density of material used */
> double quantity       /* number of washers made */
> ```

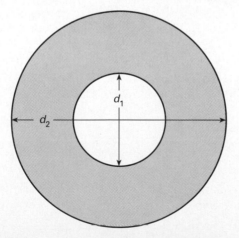

**Figure 3.4
Computing the
Rim Area of a
Flat Washer**

$$rim\ area = \pi(d_2/2)^2 - \pi(d_1/2)^2$$

**Problem Outputs**
```
double weight        /* weight of batch of washers */
```

**Program Variables**
```
double hole_radius   /* radius of hole */
double edge_radius   /* radius of outer edge */
double rim_area      /* area of rim */
double unit_weight   /* weight of 1 washer */
```

**Relevant Formulas**
*area of a circle = $\pi \times radius^2$*
*radius of a circle = diameter / 2*
*rim area = area of outer circle − area of hole*
*unit weight = rim area $\times$ thickness $\times$ density*

**DESIGN**

We list the algorithm next, followed by the refinement of Steps 3 and 4.

**Initial Algorithm**

1. Get the washer's inner diameter, outer diameter, and thickness.
2. Get the material density and quantity of washers manufactured.
3. Compute the rim area.
4. Compute the weight of one flat washer.
5. Compute the weight of the batch of washers.
6. Display the weight of the batch of washers.

**Step 3 Refinement**
3.1 Compute `hole_radius` and `edge_radius`.
3.2 `rim_area` is `PI * edge_radius * edge_radius - PI * hole_radius * hole_radius`

**Step 4 Refinement**
4.1 `unit_weight` is `rim_area * thickness * density`

**IMPLEMENTATION**

To write this program, edit the data requirements to write the variable declarations and use the initial algorithm with refinements as a starting point for the executable statements. Figure 3.5 shows the C program.

**Figure 3.5   Flat Washer Program**

```
/*
 * Computes the weight of a batch of flat washers.
 */

#include <stdio.h>
#define PI 3.14159

int
main(void)
{
      double hole_diameter;  /* input - diameter of hole          */
      double edge_diameter;  /* input - diameter of outer edge    */
      double thickness;      /* input - thickness of washer       */
      double density;        /* input - density of material used */
      double quantity;       /* input - number of washers made    */
      double weight;         /* output - weight of washer batch   */
      double hole_radius;    /* radius of hole                    */
      double edge_radius;    /* radius of outer edge              */
      double rim_area;       /* area of rim                       */
      double unit_weight;    /* weight of 1 washer                */

      /* Get the inner diameter, outer diameter, and thickness.*/
      printf("Inner diameter in centimeters> ");
      scanf("%lf", &hole_diameter);
      printf("Outer diameter in centimeters> ");
      scanf("%lf", &edge_diameter);
      printf("Thickness in centimeters> ");
      scanf("%lf", &thickness);

      /* Get the material density and quantity manufactured. */
      printf("Material density in grams per cubic centimeter> ");
      scanf("%lf", &density);
      printf("Quantity in batch> ");
      scanf("%lf", &quantity);

      /* Compute the rim area. */
      hole_radius = hole_diameter / 2.0;
      edge_radius = edge_diameter / 2.0;
      rim_area = PI * edge_radius * edge_radius -
                 PI * hole_radius * hole_radius;
```

*(continued)*

**Figure 3.5** *(continued)*

```
      /* Compute the weight of a flat washer. */
      unit_weight = rim_area * thickness * density;

      /* Compute the weight of the batch of washers. */
      weight = unit_weight * quantity;

      /* Display the weight of the batch of washers. */
      printf("\nThe expected weight of the batch is %.2f", weight);
      printf(" grams.\n");

      return (0);
}

Inner diameter in centimeters> 1.2
Outer diameter in centimeters> 2.4
Thickness in centimeters> 0.1
Material density in grams per cubic centimeter> 7.87
Quantity in batch> 1000

The expected weight of the batch is 2670.23 grams.
```

**TESTING**

To test this program, run it with inner and outer diameters such as 2 centimeters and 4 centimeters that lead to easy calculations for rim area (3 * PI square centimeters). You can verify that the program is computing the correct unit weight by entering 1 for quantity, and then verify that the batch weight is correct by running it for larger quantities.

**EXERCISES FOR SECTION 3.1**

Self-Check

1. Describe the problem inputs and outputs and write the algorithm for a program that computes an employee's gross salary given the hours worked and the hourly rate.
2. Write a preliminary version of the program from your solution to Self-Check Exercise 1. Show the declaration part of the program and the program comments corresponding to the algorithm and its refinements.
3. In computing gross salary, what changes should you make to extend the payroll algorithm in Self-Check Exercise 1 to include overtime hours to be paid at 1.5 times an employee's normal hourly rate? Assume that overtime hours are entered separately.

Programming

1. Add refinements to the program outline that follows and write the final C program.

```
/*
 * Compute the sum and average of two numbers.
 */

#include <stdio.h>

int
main(void)
{
        double one, two, /* input - numbers to process    */
               sum,      /* output - sum of one and two    */
               average;  /* output - average of one and two*/

        /* Get two numbers. */
        /* Compute sum of numbers. */
        /* Compute average of numbers. */
        /* Display sum and average. */

        return (0);
}
```

2. Write a complete C program for Self-Check Exercise 1.
3. Write complete C program for the revised payroll algorithm developed in Self-Check Exercise 3.
4. Assume that flat washers are manufactured by stamping them out from a rectangular piece of material of uniform thickness. Extend the washer program to compute (a) the number of square centimeters of material needed to manufacture a specified quantity of flat washers and (b) the weight of the left-over material.

# 3.2 LIBRARY FUNCTIONS

## Predefined Functions and Code Reuse

A primary goal of software engineering is to write error-free code. *Code reuse,* reusing program fragments that have already been written and tested whenever possible, is one way to accomplish this goal. Stated more simply, "Why reinvent the wheel?"

C promotes reuse by providing many predefined functions that can be used to perform mathematical computations. C's standard math library defines a function named `sqrt` that performs the square root computation. The function call in the assignment statement

activates the code for function `sqrt`, passing the argument x to the function. You activate a function by writing a function call. After the function executes, the function result is substituted for the function call. If x is 16.0, the assignment statement above is evaluated as follows:

1. x is 16.0, so function `sqrt` computes the $\sqrt{16.0}$, or 4.0.
2. The function result, 4.0, is assigned to y.

A function can be thought of as a "black box" that is passed one or more input values and automatically returns a single output value. Figure 3.6 illustrates this for the call to function `sqrt`. The value of x (16.0) is the function input, and the function result, or output, is $\sqrt{16.0}$ (result is 4.0).

If w is 9.0, the assignment statement

```
z = 5.7 + sqrt(w);
```

is evaluated as follows:

1. w is 9.0, so function `sqrt` computes the square root of 9.0, or 3.0.
2. The values 5.7 and 3.0 are added together.
3. The sum, 8.7, is stored in z.

**Figure 3.6
Function sqrt as
a "Black Box"**

**EXAMPLE 3.1**  The program in Fig. 3.7 displays the square root of two numbers provided as input data (`first` and `second`) and the square root of their sum. To do so, it must call the C function `sqrt` three times:

```
first_sqrt = sqrt(first);
second_sqrt = sqrt(second);
sum_sqrt = sqrt(first + second);
```

For the first two calls, the function arguments are variables (`first` and `second`). The third call shows that a function argument can also be an expression (`first + second`). For all three calls, the result returned by function `sqrt` is assigned to a variable. Because the definition of the standard `sqrt` function is found in the standard math library, the program begins with an additional `#include` directive.

If you look closely at the program in Fig. 3.7, you will see that each statement contains a call to a library function (`printf`, `scanf`, `sqrt`)—we have used C's predefined functions as building blocks to construct a new program.

**Figure 3.7    Square Root Program**

```
/*
 * Performs three square root computations
 */

#include <stdio.h> /* definitions of printf, scanf */
#include <math.h>  /* definition of sqrt */

int
main(void)
{
    double first, second,    /* input - two data values     */
           first_sqrt,       /* output - square root of first  */
           second_sqrt,      /* output - square root of second */
           sum_sqrt;         /* output - square root of sum    */

    /* Get first number and display its square root.  */
    printf("Enter the first number> ");
    scanf("%lf", &first);
    first_sqrt = sqrt(first);
    printf("The square root of the first number is %.2f\n", first_sqrt);
```

*(continued)*

**Figure 3.7**   *(continued)*

```
     /* Get second number and display its square root. */
     printf("Enter the second number> ");
     scanf("%lf", &second);
     second_sqrt = sqrt(second);
     printf("The square root of the second number is %.2f\n", second_sqrt);

     /* Display the square root of the sum of the two numbers. */
     sum_sqrt = sqrt(first + second);
     printf("The square root of the sum of the two numbers is %.2f\n",
            sum_sqrt);

     return (0);
}


Enter the first number> 9.0
The square root of the first number is 3.00
Enter the second number> 16.0
The square root of the second number is 4.00
The square root of the sum of the two numbers is 5.00
```

### Program Style   *Use of Color to Highlight New Constructs*

In Fig. 3.7, program lines that illustrate new constructs are in color, so that
you can find them easily. We will continue to use color for this purpose in figures that contain programs.

### C Library Functions

Table 3.1 lists the names and descriptions of some of the most commonly used
functions along with the name of the standard header file to #include in
order to have access to each function. A complete list of standard library functions appears in Appendix B.

 If one of the functions in Table 3.1 is called with a numeric argument
that is not of the argument type listed, the argument value is converted to the
required type before it is used. Conversions of type int to type double cause
no problems, but a conversion of type double to type int leads to the loss of
any fractional part, just as in a mixed-type assignment. For example, if we call
the abs function with the type double value -3.47, the result returned is the

type int value 3. For this reason, the library has a separate absolute value function (fabs) for type double arguments.

Most of the functions in Table 3.1 perform common mathematical computations. The arguments for log and log10 must be positive; the argument for sqrt cannot be negative. The arguments for sin, cos, and tan must be expressed in radians, not in degrees.

**Table 3.1    Some Mathematical Library Functions**

| Function | Standard Header File | Purpose: Example | Argument(s) | Result |
|----------|----------------------|------------------|-------------|--------|
| abs(x) | <stdlib.h> | Returns the absolute value of its integer argument: if x is −5, abs(x) is 5 | int | int |
| ceil(x) | <math.h> | Returns the smallest whole number that is not less than x: if x is 45.23, ceil(x) is 46.0 | double | double |
| cos(x) | <math.h> | Returns the cosine of angle x: if x is 0.0, cos(x) is 1.0 | double (radians) | double |
| exp(x) | <math.h> | Returns $e^x$ where $e = 2.71828...$: if x is 1.0, exp(x) is 2.71828 | double | double |
| fabs(x) | <math.h> | Returns the absolute value of its type double argument: if x is −8.432, fabs(x) is 8.432 | double | double |
| floor(x) | <math.h> | Returns the largest whole number that is not greater than x: if x is 45.23, floor(x) is 45.0 | double | double |
| log(x) | <math.h> | Returns the natural logarithm of x for x > 0.0: if x is 2.71828, log(x) is 1.0 | double | double |
| log10(x) | <math.h> | Returns the base-10 logarithm of x for x > 0.0: if x is 100.0, log10(x) is 2.0 | double | double |
| pow(x, y) | <math.h> | Returns $x^y$. If x is negative, y must be a whole number: if x is 0.16 and y is 0.5, pow(x, y) is 0.4 | double, double | double |
| sin(x) | <math.h> | Returns the sine of angle x: if x is 1.5708, sin(x) is 1.0 | double (radians) | double |
| sqrt(x) | <math.h> | Returns the non-negative square root of x ($\sqrt{x}$) for x ≥ 0.0: if x is 2.25, sqrt(x) is 1.5 | double | double |
| tan(x) | <math.h> | Returns the tangent of angle x: if x is 0.0, tan(x) is 0.0 | double (radians) | double |

**EXAMPLE 3.2**   We can use the C functions pow (power) and sqrt to compute the roots of a quadratic equation in $x$ of the form

$$ax^2 + bx + c = 0$$

The two roots are defined as

$$root_1 = \frac{-b + \sqrt{b^2 - 4ac}}{2a} \qquad root_2 = \frac{-b - \sqrt{b^2 - 4ac}}{2a}$$

when the *discriminant* ($b^2 - 4ac$) is greater than zero. If we assume that this is the case, we can use these assignment statements to assign values to root_1 and root_2.

```
/* Compute two roots, root_1 and root_2, for disc > 0.0 */
disc = pow(b,2) - 4 * a * c;
root_1 = (-b + sqrt(disc)) / (2 * a);
root_2 = (-b - sqrt(disc)) / (2 * a);
```

**EXAMPLE 3.3**  If we know the lengths of two sides ($b$ and $c$) of a triangle and the angle between them in degrees ($\alpha$), we can compute the length of the third side ($a$) using the following formula (see Fig. 3.8).

$$a^2 = b^2 + c^2 - 2bc \cos \alpha$$

To use the math library cosine function (cos), we must express its argument angle in radians instead of degrees. To convert an angle from degrees to radians, we multiply the angle by $\pi/180$. If we assume PI represents the constant $\pi$, the C assignment statement that follows computes the unknown side length.

```
a = sqrt(pow(b,2) + pow(c,2)
       - 2 * b * c * cos(alpha * PI / 180.0));
```

**Figure 3.8
Triangle with
Unknown Side _a_**

## A Look at Where We Are Heading

C also allows us to write our own functions. Let's assume that we have already written functions find_area and find_circum:

- Function find_area(r) returns the area of a circle with radius r.
- Function find_circum(r) returns the circumference of a circle with radius r.

We can reuse these functions in two programs shown earlier in this chapter (see Figs. 3.3 and 3.5). The program in Fig. 3.3 computes the area and the circumference of a circle. The statements

```
area = find_area(radius);
circum = find_circum(radius);
```

can be used to find these values. The expression part for each of the assignment statements is a function call with argument radius (the circle radius). The result returned by each function execution is stored in an output variable for the program (area or circum).

For the flat washer-program (Fig. 3.5), we can use the statement

```
rim_area = find_area(edge_radius) - find_area(hole_radius);
```

to compute the rim area for a washer. This statement is clearer than the one shown in the original program.

**EXERCISES FOR SECTION 3.2**

Self-Check

1. Rewrite the following mathematical expressions using C functions:
   a. $\sqrt{u+v} \times w^2$
   b. $\log_e (x^y)$
   c. $\sqrt{(x-y)^3}$
   d. $|xy - w/z|$

2. Evaluate the following:
   a. floor(15.8)
   b. floor(15.8 + 0.5)
   c. ceil(-7.2) * pow(4.0,2.0)
   d. sqrt(floor(fabs(-16.8)))
   e. log10(1000.0)

Programming

1. Write statements that compute and display the absolute difference of two type double variables, x and y ($|x-y|$).

2. Write a complete C program that prompts the user for the Cartesian coordinates of two points $(x_1, y_1)$ and $(x_2, y_2)$ and displays the distance between them computed using the following formula:

$$distance = \sqrt{(x_1 - x_2)^2 + (y_1 - y_2)^2}$$

# 3.3 TOP-DOWN DESIGN AND STRUCTURE CHARTS

**top-down design**
a problem-solving method in which you first break a problem up into its major subproblems and then solve the subproblems to derive the solution to the original problem

**structure chart**
a documentation tool that shows the relationships among the subproblems of a problem

Often the algorithm needed to solve a problem is more complex than those we have seen so far and the programmer must break up the problem into subproblems to develop the program solution. In attempting to solve a subproblem at one level, we introduce new subproblems at lower levels. This process, called **top-down design,** proceeds from the original problem at the top level to the subproblems at each lower level. The splitting of a problem into its related subproblems is analogous to the process of refining an algorithm. The case study below introduces a documentation tool—the **structure chart**—that will help you to keep track of the relationships among subproblems.

## Case Study: Drawing Simple Diagrams

### PROBLEM

You want to draw some simple diagrams on your printer or screen. Two examples are the house and female stick figure in Fig. 3.9.

### ANALYSIS

The house is formed by displaying a triangle without its base on top of a rectangle. The stick figure consists of a circular shape, a triangle, and a triangle without its base. We can draw both figures with these four basic components:

- a circle
- a base line

**Figure 3.9
House and Stick
Figure**

- parallel lines
- intersecting lines

**DESIGN**

To create the stick figure, you can divide the problem into three subproblems.

### Initial Algorithm

1. Draw a circle.
2. Draw a triangle.
3. Draw intersecting lines.

### Algorithm Refinements

Because a triangle is not a basic component, you must refine step 2, generating the following subproblems:

**Step 2 Refinement**
2.1  Draw intersecting lines.
2.2  Draw a base.

You can use a structure chart to show the relationship between the original problem and its subproblems, as in Fig. 3.10, where the original problem (level 0) is in the darker color and its three subordinate subproblems are shown at level 1. The subproblem *Draw a triangle* is also in color because it has its own subproblems (shown at level 2).

The subproblems appear in both the algorithm and the structure chart. The algorithm, not the structure chart, shows the order in which you carry out

**Figure 3.10
Structure Chart
for Drawing a
Stick Figure**

each step to solve the problem. The structure chart simply illustrates the subordination of subproblems to each other and to the original problem.

Self-Check

1. In which phase of the software development method do you apply top-down design to break the problem into suitable subproblems?
2. Draw the structure chart for the problem of drawing the house shown in Fig. 3.9.

# 3.4 FUNCTIONS WITHOUT ARGUMENTS

One way that programmers implement top-down design in their programs is by defining their own functions. Often, a programmer will write one function subprogram for each subproblem in the structure chart. In this section, we show how to use and define your own functions, focusing on simple functions that have no arguments and return no value.

As an example of top-down design with functions, you could use the main function in Fig. 3.11 to draw the stick figure of a person. In Fig. 3.11, the three algorithm steps are coded as calls to three function subprograms. For example, the statement

```
draw_circle();
```

calls a function (`draw_circle`) that implements the algorithm step *Draw a Circle*.

We call function `draw_circle` just like we call function `printf`. The empty parentheses after the function name indicate that `draw_circle` requires no arguments.

---

**Function Call Statement (Function without Arguments)**

SYNTAX:    *fname* ( ) ;

EXAMPLE: `draw_circle();`

INTERPRETATION: The function *fname* is called. After *fname* has finished execution, the program statement that follows the function call will be executed.

---

**Figure 3.11    Function Prototypes and Main Function for Stick Figure**

```
/*
 * Draws a stick figure
 */

#include <stdio.h>

/* function prototypes                                   */

void draw_circle(void);      /* Draws a circle           */

void draw_intersect(void);   /* Draws intersecting lines */

void draw_base(void);        /* Draws a base line        */

void draw_triangle(void);    /* Draws a triangle         */

int
main(void)
{
      /* Draw a circle.  */
      draw_circle();

      /* Draw a triangle.  */
      draw_triangle();

      /* Draw intersecting lines.  */
      draw_intersect();

      return (0);
}
```

## Function Prototypes

Just like other identifiers in C, a function must be declared before it can be referenced. One way to declare a function is to insert a function prototype before the main function. A **function prototype** tells the C compiler the data type of the function, the function name, and information about the arguments that the function expects. The data type of a function is determined by the type of value returned by the function. The functions declared in Fig. 3.11 are **void functions** (that is, their type is void) because they do not return a value. In the function prototype

**void function**
a function that does not return a
value

```
void draw_circle(void);   /* Draws a circle       */
```

the second void indicates that draw_circle expects no arguments.

---

### Function Prototype (Function without Arguments)

FORM:    *ftype fname*(void);

EXAMPLE: void draw_circle(void);

INTERPRETATION: The identifier *fname* is declared to be the name of a function. The identifier *ftype* specifies the data type of the function result.

*Note: ftype* is void if the function does not return a value. The argument list (void) indicates that the function has no arguments. The function prototype must appear before the first call to the function.

---

## Function Definitions

Although the prototype specifies the number of arguments a function takes, and the type of its result, it does not specify the function operation. To do this, you need to provide a definition for each function subprogram similar to the definition of the main function. Figure 3.12 shows the definition for function draw_circle.

The function heading is similar to the function prototype in Fig. 3.11 except that it is not ended by the symbol ;. We have adopted a style that places the function type on a separate line. (Industrial C developers often use this style to make function definitions easy to find in long source files.) The function body, enclosed in braces, consists of three calls to function printf that cause the computer to display a circular shape. We omit the return statement because draw_circle does not return a result.

The function call statement

```
draw_circle();
```

**Figure 3.12    Function draw_circle**

```
/*
 * Draws a circle
 */
void
draw_circle(void)
{
      printf("   *  \n");
      printf(" *    *\n");
      printf("  * * \n");
}
```

causes these `printf` statements to execute. Control returns to the main function after the circle shape is displayed.

**Function Definition (Function without Arguments)**

SYNTAX:    *ftype*
                *fname*(void)
                {
                        *local declarations*
                        *executable statements*
                }

EXAMPLE: /*
                 * Displays a block-letter H
                 */
                void
                print_h(void)
                {
                        printf("** **\n");
                        printf("** **\n");
                        printf("*****\n");
                        printf("** **\n");
                        printf("** **\n");
                }

*(continued)*

INTERPRETATION: The function *fname* is defined. In the function heading, the identifier *ftype* specifies the data type of the function result. Notice that there are no semicolons after the lines of the function heading. The braces enclose the function body. Any identifiers that are declared in the optional *local declarations* are defined only during the execution of the function and can be referenced only within the function. The *executable statements* of the function body describe the data manipulation to be performed by the function.

*Note: ftype* is void if the function does not return a value. The argument list (void) indicates that the function has no arguments. You can omit the void and write the argument list as ().

Each function body may contain declarations for its own variables. These variables are considered *local* to the function; in other words, they can be referenced only within the function. There will be more on this topic later.

The structure chart in Fig. 3.10 shows that the subproblem *Draw a triangle* (level 1) depends on the solutions to its subordinate subproblems *Draw intersecting lines* and *Draw a base* (both level 2). Figure 3.13 shows how you can use top-down design to code function draw_triangle. Instead of using printf statements to display a triangular pattern, the body of function draw_triangle calls functions draw_intersect and draw_base to draw a triangle.

**Figure 3.13    Function draw_triangle**

```
/*
 * Draws a triangle
 */
void
draw_triangle(void)
{
      draw_intersect();
      draw_base();
}
```

## Placement of Functions in a Program

Fig. 3.14 shows the complete program with function subprograms. The sub-program prototypes precede the main function (after any #include or #define directives) and the subprogram definitions follow the main function. The relative order of the function definitions does not affect their order of execution; that is determined by the order of execution of the function call statements.

**Figure 3.14  Program to Draw a Stick Figure**

```
/* Draws a stick figure */

#include <stdio.h>

/* Function prototypes */
void draw_circle(void);         /* Draws a circle             */

void draw_intersect(void);      /* Draws intersecting lines   */

void draw_base(void);           /* Draws a base line          */

void draw_triangle(void);       /* Draws a triangle           */

int
main(void)
{
      /* Draw a circle.           */
      draw_circle();

      /* Draw a triangle.         */
      draw_triangle();

      /* Draw intersecting lines. */
      draw_intersect();

      return (0);
}
```

*(continued)*

**Figure 3.14** *(continued)*

```c
/*
 * Draws a circle
 */
void
draw_circle(void)
{
      printf("    *    \n");
      printf(" *     * \n");
      printf("  * *   \n");
}

/*
 * Draws intersecting lines
 */
void
draw_intersect(void)
{
      printf("  / \\  \n"); /* Use 2 \'s to print 1 */
      printf(" /    \\ \n");
      printf("/      \\\n");
}

/*
 * Draws a base line
 */
void
draw_base(void)

{
      printf("-------\n");
}

/*
 * Draws a triangle
 */
void
draw_triangle(void)
{
      draw_intersect();
      draw_base();
}
```

If you look closely at function `draw_intersect`, you will notice that the symbol pair \ \ represents a single backslash character in a format string. This convention enables C to differentiate the backslash character from the escape symbol (just \ ).

### Program Style    *Use of Comments in a Program with Functions*

Figure 3.14 includes several comments. Each function begins with a comment that describes its purpose. If the function subprograms were more complex, we would include comments on each major algorithm step just as we do in function `main`. From now on throughout this text, the block comment and heading of each function definition are in color to help you locate functions in the program listing.

### Order of Execution of Function Subprograms and Main Function

Because the prototypes for the function subprograms appear before the main function, the compiler processes the function prototypes before it translates the main function. The information in each prototype enables the compiler to correctly translate a call to that function. The compiler translates a function call statement as a transfer of control to the function.

After compiling the main function, the compiler translates each function subprogram. During translation, when the compiler reaches the end of a function body, it inserts a machine-language statement that causes a *transfer of control* back from the function to the calling statement.

Figure 3.15 shows the main function and function `draw_circle` of the stick figure program in separate areas of memory. Although the C statements are

**Figure 3.15
Flow of Control
Between the
main Program
and a Function**

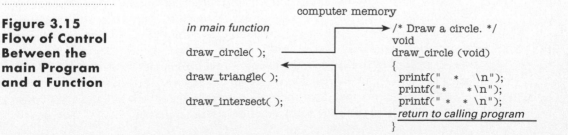

shown in Fig. 3.15, it is actually the object code corresponding to each statement that is stored in memory.

When we run the program, the first statement in the main function is the first statement executed (the call to `draw_circle` in Fig. 3.15). When the computer executes a function call statement, it transfers control to the function that is referenced (indicated by the colored line in Fig. 3.15). The computer allocates any memory that may be needed for variables declared in the function and then performs the statements in the function body. After the last statement in function `draw_circle` is executed, control returns to the main function (indicated by the black line in Fig. 3.15), and the computer releases any memory that was allocated to the function. After the return to the main function, the next statement is executed (the call to `draw_triangle`).

## Advantages of Using Function Subprograms

There are many advantages to using function subprograms. Their availability changes the way in which an individual programmer organizes the solution to a programming problem. For a team of programmers working together on a large program, subprograms make it easier to apportion programming tasks: Each programmer will be responsible for a particular set of functions. Finally, they simplify programming tasks because existing functions can be reused as the building blocks for new programs.

**procedural abstraction**
a programming technique in which a main function consists of a sequence of function calls and each function is implemented separately

**Procedural Abstraction**   Function subprograms allow us to remove from the main function the code that provides the detailed solution to a subproblem. Because these details are provided in the function subprograms and not in the main function, we can write the main function as a sequence of function call statements as soon as we have specified the initial algorithm and before we refine any of the steps. We should delay writing the function for an algorithm step until we have finished refining that step. With this approach to program design, called **procedural abstraction,** we defer implementation details until we are ready to write an individual function subprogram. Focusing on one function at a time is much easier than trying to write the complete program all at once.

**Reuse of Function Subprograms**   Another advantage of using function subprograms is that functions can be executed more than once in a program. For example, function `draw_intersect` is called twice in Fig. 3.14 (once by `draw_triangle` and once by the main function). Each time `draw_intersect` is called, the list of output statements shown in Fig. 3.14 is executed and a pair of intersecting lines is drawn. Without functions, the `printf` statements that draw the lines would be listed twice in the main function, thereby increasing the main function's length and the chance of error.

Finally, once you have written and tested a function, you can use it in other programs or functions. For example, the functions in the stick figure program could easily be reused in programs that draw other diagrams.

## Displaying User Instructions

The simple functions introduced in this section have limited capability. Without the ability to pass information into or out of a function, we can use functions only to display multiple lines of program output, such as instructions to a program user or a title page or a special message that precedes a program's results.

**EXAMPLE 3.4** ▶ Let's write a function (Fig. 3.16) that displays instructions to a user of the program that computes the area and the circumference of a circle (see Fig. 3.3). This simple function demonstrates one of the benefits of separating the statements that display user instructions from the main function body: Editing these instructions is simplified when they are separated from the code that performs the calculations.

If you place the prototype for function `instruct`

```
void instruct(void);
```

**Figure 3.16    Function instruct and the Output Produced by a Call**

```
/*
 * Displays instructions to a user of program to compute
 * the area and circumference of a circle.
 */
void
instruct(void)
{
      printf("This program computes the area\n");
      printf("and circumference of a circle.\n\n");
      printf("To use this program, enter the radius of\n");
      printf("the circle after the prompt: Enter radius>\n");
}


This program computes the area
and circumference of a circle.

To use this program, enter the radius of
the circle after the prompt: Enter radius>
```

just before the main function, you can insert the function call statement

```
instruct();
```

as the first executable statement in the main function. The rest of the main function consists of the executable statements shown earlier. Figure 3.16 shows the output displayed by calling function `instruct`.  ←

**EXERCISES FOR SECTION 3.4**

Self-Check

1. Assume that you have functions print_h, print_i, print_m, and print_o, each of which draws a large block letter (for example, print_o draws a block letter O). What is the effect of executing the following main function?

```
int
main(void)
{
        print_h();
        print_i();
        printf("\n\n\n");
        print_m();
        print_o();
        print_m();

        return (0);
}
```

2. Draw a structure chart for a program with three function subprograms that displays HI HO in a vertical column of block letters.

Programming

1. Write a function `draw_parallel` that draws parallel lines and a function `draw_rectangle` that uses `draw_parallel` and `draw_base` to draw a rectangle.
2. Write a complete program for the problem described in Self-Check Exercise 2.

3. Rewrite the miles-to-kilometers conversion program shown in Fig. 2.1, so that it includes a function that displays instructions to its user.
4. Show the revised program that calls function `instruct` for the circle area and circumference problem.

## 3.5 FUNCTIONS WITH INPUT ARGUMENTS

Programmers use functions like building blocks to construct large programs. Functions are more like Lego® blocks (Fig. 3.17) than the smooth-sided wooden blocks you might have used as a young child to demonstrate your potential as a budding architect. Your first blocks were big and did not link together, so buildings over a certain size would topple over. Legos, in contrast, have one surface with little protrusions and one surface with little cups. By placing the protrusions into the cups, you could build rather elaborate structures.

What does this have to do with programming? Simple functions like `draw_circle` and `instruct` are like wooden blocks. They can display information on the screen, but they are not particularly useful. To be able to construct more interesting programs, we must provide functions with "protrusions" and "cups" so they can be easily interconnected.

The arguments of a function are used to carry information into the function subprogram from the main function (or from another function subprogram) or to return multiple results computed by a function subprogram. Arguments that

**Figure 3.17
Lego® Blocks**

**input arguments**
arguments used to pass infor-mation into a function sub-program

**output arguments**
arguments used to return results to the calling function

carry information into the function subprogram are called **input arguments**; arguments that return results are called **output arguments**. We can also return a single result from a function by executing a `return` statement in the function body. We study functions with input arguments in this section and functions with output arguments in Chapter 6.

The use of arguments is a very important concept in programming. Arguments make function subprograms more versatile because they enable a function to manipulate different data each time it is called. For example, in the statement

```
rim_area = find_area(edge_radius) - find_area(hole_area);
```

each call to function `find_area` calculates the area of a circle with a different radius.

## void Functions with Input Arguments

In the last section, we used `void` functions like `instruct` and `draw_circle` to display several lines of program output. Recall that a `void` function does not return a result. We can use a `void` function with an argument to "dress up" our program output by having the function display its argument value in a more attrac-tive way.

**EXAMPLE 3.5** ▶

**actual argument**
an expression used inside the parentheses of a function call

**formal parameter**
an identifier that represents a corresponding actual argu-ment in a function definition

Function `print_rboxed` (Fig. 3.18) displays the value of its argument, a real number, in a box. The real number is displayed on the third line starting at the position of the placeholder `%7.2f`. When function `print_rboxed` is called, the value of its **actual argument** (135.68) is passed into the function and substituted for its **formal parameter** `rnum`. Because `rnum` appears only in the third call to `printf`, the real number 135.68 is displayed once inside the box. Figure 3.19 shows the effect of the function call

```
print_rboxed(135.68);
```
◀

**Figure 3.18    Function print_rboxed and Sample Run**

```
/*
 * Displays a real number in a box.
 */
```

*(continued)*

**Figure 3.18** *(continued)*

```
void
print_rboxed(double rnum)
{
      printf("***********\n");
      printf("*          *\n");
      printf("* %7.2f *\n", rnum);
      printf("*          *\n");
      printf("***********\n");
}


***********
*          *
*  135.68  *
*          *
***********
```

**Figure 3.19
Effect of
Executing**
`print_rboxed
(135.68);`

```
print_rboxed (135.68);
```

Call print_rboxed with rnum = 135.68

```
void
print_rboxed(double rnum)
{
      printf("***********\n");
      printf("*          *\n");
      printf("* %7.2f *\n", rnum);
      printf("*          *\n");
      printf("***********\n");
}
```

## Functions with Input Arguments and a Single Result

Next we show how to write functions with input arguments that return a single result, as diagrammed in Fig. 3.20. We can reference these functions in expressions just like the library functions described in Section 3.2.

Let's reconsider the problem of finding the area and circumference of a circle using functions with just one argument. Section 3.2 described functions `find_circum` and `find_area`, each of which has a single input argument (a circle radius) and returns a single result (the circle circumference or area). Fig. 3.21 shows these functions.

**Figure 3.20
Function with
Input
Arguments and
One Result**

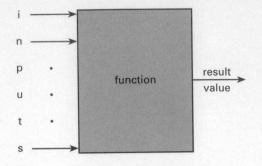

**Figure 3.21    Functions find_circum and find_area**

```
/*
 * Computes the circumference of a circle with radius r.
 * Pre:   r is defined and is > 0.
 *        PI is a constant macro representing an approximation of pi.
 */
double
find_circum(double r)
{
     return (2.0 * PI * r);
}



/*
 * Computes the area of a circle with radius r.
 * Pre:   r is defined and is > 0.
 *        PI is a constant macro representing an approximation of pi.
 *        Library math.h is included.
 */
double
find_area(double r)
{
     return (PI * pow(r, 2));
}
```

**Figure 3.22
Effect of
Executing**
`circum =
find_circum
(radius);`

Each function heading begins with the word `double`, indicating that the function result is a real number. Both function bodies consist of a single `return` statement. When either function executes, the expression in its `return` statement is evaluated and returned as the function result. If PI is the constant macro 3.14159, calling function `find_circum` causes the expression 2.0 * 3.14159 * r to be evaluated. To evaluate this expression, C substitutes the actual argument used in the function call for the formal parameter r.

For the function call below

```
radius = 10.0;
circum = find_circum(radius);
```

the actual argument, `radius`, has a value of 10.0 so the function result is 62.8318 (2.0 * 3.14159 * 10.0). The function result is assigned to `circum`. Figure 3.22 illustrates the function execution.

The function call to `find_area`

```
area = find_area(radius);
```

causes C to evaluate the expression 3.14159 * pow(r, 2) where pow is a library function (part of math.h) that raises its first argument to the power indicated by its second argument (pow(r, 2) computes $r^2$). When radius is 10.0, pow returns 100.0 and find_area returns a result of 314.59, which is assigned to area. This example shows that a user-defined function can call a C library function.

**Function Definition (Input Arguments and Single Result)**

SYNTAX: *function interface comment*
*ftype*
*fname (formal parameter declaration list)*
{
    *local variable declarations*
    *executable statements*
}

EXAMPLE:
```
/*
 * Finds the cube of its argument.
 * Pre: n is defined.
 */
int
cube(int n)
{
    return (n * n * n);
}
```

INTERPRETATION: The *function interface comment* is described in the next Program Style display. The next two lines are the function heading, which specifies the function name, *fname*, and the type of the result returned, *ftype*. It also indicates the names and types of the formal parameters in the *formal parameter declaration list*. Note that the lines of the heading do not end in semicolons. The braces enclose the function body. The type of any additional variables needed should be declared in the *local variable declarations*. The *executable statements* describe the data manipulation that the function performs on the parameters and local variables in order to compute the result value. Execution of a return statement causes the function to return control to the statement that called it. The function returns the value of the expression following return as its result.

*Note:* Use void as the *formal parameter declaration list* to indicate that a function has no arguments. The parentheses around the expression that follows return are not required.

**Program Style** *Function Interface Comment*

The block comment and heading that begin each function in Fig. 3.21 contain all the information required in order to use the function. The function interface block comment begins with a statement of what the function does. Then the line

```
* Pre: n is defined.
```

**precondition**
a condition assumed to be true
before a function call
**postcondition**
a condition assumed to be true
after a function executes

describes the condition that should be true before the function is called; this condition is known as the **precondition**. You will also want to include a statement describing the condition that must be true after the function completes execution, if some details of this **postcondition** are not included in the initial statement of the function's purpose.

We recommend that you begin all function definitions in this way. The function interface comment combined with the heading (or prototype) provide valuable documentation to other programmers who might want to reuse your functions in a new program without reading the function code.

## Functions with Multiple Arguments

Functions find_area and find_circum each have a single argument. We can also define functions with multiple arguments.

 **EXAMPLE 3.6**

Function scale (Fig. 3.23) multiplies its first argument (a real number) by 10 raised to the power indicated by its second argument (an integer). For example, the function call

scale(2.5, 2)

**Figure 3.23    Function scale**

```
/*
 * Multiplies its first argument by the power of 10 specified
 * by its second argument.
 * Pre : x and n are defined and math.h is included.
 */
double
scale(double x, int n)
{
     double scale_factor;      /* local variable */
     scale_factor = pow(10, n);

     return (x * scale_factor);
}
```

returns the value $250.0$ ($2.5 \times 10^2$). The function call

```
scale(2.5, -2)
```

returns the value $0.025$ ($2.5 \times 10^{-2}$).

In function scale, the statement

```
scale_factor = pow(10, n);
```

calls function pow to raise 10 to the power specified by the second formal parameter n. Local variable scale_factor, defined only during the execution of the function, stores this value. The return statement defines the function result as the product of the first formal parameter, x, and scale_factor.

Figure 3.24 shows a very simple main function written to test function scale. The printf statement calls function scale and displays the function result after it is returned. The arrows drawn in Fig. 3.24 show the information flow between the two actual arguments and formal parameters. To clarify the information flow, we omitted the function interface comment. The argument list correspondence is shown below.

| *Actual Argument* | corresponds to | *Formal Parameter* |
|---|---|---|
| num_1 | | x |
| num_2 | | n |

**Figure 3.24    Testing Function scale**

```
/*
 * Tests function scale.
 */

#include <math.h>

/* Function prototype */
double scale(double x, int n);

int
main(void)
```

*(continued)*

**Figure 3.24** **Testing Function Scale**

```
{
        double num_1;
        int num_2;

        /* Get values for num_1 and num 2 */
        printf("Enter a real number> ");
        scanf("%lf", &num_1);
        printf("Enter an integer> ");
        scanf("%d", &num_2);

        /* Call scale and display result. */
        printf("Result of call to function scale is %f\n",
                scale(num_1, num_2));        actual arguments

        return (0);
}


                                            information flow


double
scale(double x, int n)                      formal parameters
{
        double scale_factor;      /* local variable - 10 to power n */

        scale_factor = pow(10, n);

        return (x * scale_factor);
}


Enter a real number> 2.5
Enter an integer> -2
Result of call to function scale is 0.025
```

## Argument List Correspondence

When using multiple-argument functions, you must be careful to include the correct number of arguments in the function call. Also, the order of the actual arguments used in the function call must correspond to the order of the formal parameters listed in the function prototype or heading.

Finally, if the function is to return meaningful results, assignment of each actual argument to the corresponding formal parameter must not cause any loss of information. Usually, you should use an actual argument of the same data type as the corresponding formal parameter, although this is not always essential. For example, the `<math.h>` library description indicates that both parameters of the function `pow` are of type `double`. Function `scale` calls `pow` with two actual arguments of type `int`. This call does not cause a problem because there is no loss of information when an `int` is assigned to a type `double` variable. If you pass an actual argument of type `double` to a formal parameter of type `int`, loss of the fractional part of the actual argument would likely lead to an unexpected function result. Next, we summarize these constraints on the **n**umber, **o**rder, and **t**ype (**not**) of input arguments.

### Argument List Correspondence

- The **n**umber of actual arguments used in a call to a function must be the same as the number of formal parameters listed in the function prototype.
- The **o**rder of arguments in the lists determines correspondence. The first actual argument corresponds to the first formal parameter, the second actual argument corresponds to the second formal parameter, and so on.
- Each actual argument must be of a data **t**ype that can be assigned to the corresponding formal parameter with no unexpected loss of information.

## The Function Data Area

Each time a function call is executed, an area of memory is allocated for storage of that function's data. Included in the function data area are storage cells for its formal parameters and any local variables that may be declared in the function. The function data area is always lost when the function terminates; it is recreated empty (all values undefined) when the function is called again.

Figure 3.25 shows the main function data area and the data area for function `scale` after the function call `scale(num_1, num_2)` executes. The values `2.5` and `-2` are passed into the formal parameters `x` and `n`, respectively. The local variable, `scale_factor`, is initially undefined; the execution of the function body changes the value of this variable to `0.01`.

The local variable `scale_factor` can be accessed only in function `scale`. Similarly, the variables `num_1` and `num_2` declared in function `main` can be accessed only in function `main`. If you want a function subprogram to use the value stored in `num_1`, you must provide `num_1` as an actual argument when you call the function.

**Figure 3.25
Data Areas
After Call**
`scale(num_1,
num_2);`

## Testing Functions Using Drivers

**driver**
a short function written to test
another function by defining
its arguments, calling it, and
displaying its result

A function is an independent program module, and as such, it can be tested separately from the program that uses it. To run such a test, you should write a short **driver** function that defines the function arguments, calls the function, and displays the value returned. For example, the function `main` in Fig. 3.24 acts as a driver to test function `scale`.

**EXERCISES FOR
SECTION 3.5**

### Self-Check

1. Evaluate each of the following:
   a. `scale(3.14159, 3)`
   b. `find_circum(5.0)`
   c. `print_rboxed(find_circum(5.0))`
   d. `find_area(1.0)`
   e. `scale(find_area(10.0), -2)`
2. Explain the effect of reversing the function arguments in the call to `scale` shown in Example 3.6, that is, `scale(num_2, num_1)`.
3. How does the use of function arguments make it possible to write larger, more useful programs?

### Programming

1. Revise the flat-washer program (Fig. 3.5) to use function subprograms `find_area`, `find_rim_area`, `find_unit_weight`, and `instruct`. Show the complete program.

2. Write a function that computes the speed (km/h) one must average to reach a certain destination by a designated time. You need to deal only with arrivals occurring later on the same day as the departure. Function inputs include departure and arrival times as integers on a 24-hour clock (8:30 P.M. = 2030) and the distance to the destination in kilometers. Also write a driver program to test your function.

## 3.6 COMMON PROGRAMMING ERRORS

Remember to use a `#include` preprocessor directive for every standard library from which you are using functions. Place prototypes for your own function subprograms in the source file preceding the main function; place the actual function definitions after the main function.

Syntax or run-time errors may occur when you use functions. The acronym **not** summarizes the requirements for argument list correspondence. Provide the required **n**umber of arguments and make sure the **o**rder of arguments is correct. Make sure that each function argument is the correct **t**ype or that conversion to the correct type will lose no information. For user-defined functions, verify that each argument list is correct by comparing it to the formal parameter list in the function heading or prototype.

Also be careful in using functions that are undefined on some range of values. For example, if the argument for function `sqrt`, `log`, or `log10` is negative, a run-time error will occur.

## CHAPTER REVIEW

1. Develop your program solutions from existing information. Use the system documentation derived from applying the software development method as the initial framework for the program.

   - Edit the data requirements to obtain the main function declarations.
   - Use the refined algorithm as the starting point for the executable statements in the main function.

2. If a new problem is an extension of a previous one, modify the previous program rather than starting from scratch.

3. Use C's library functions to simplify mathematical computations through the reuse of code that has already been written and tested. Write a function call (consisting of the function name and arguments) to activate a library

function. After the function executes, the function result is substituted for the function call.

4. Use a structure chart to show subordinate relationships between subproblems.

5. Utilize modular programming by writing separate function subprograms to implement the different subproblems in a structure chart. Ideally, your main function will consist of a sequence of function call statements that activate the function subprograms.

6. You can write functions without arguments and results to display a list of instructions to a program user or to draw a diagram on the screen. Use a function call consisting of the function name followed by an empty pair of parentheses ( ) to activate such a function.

7. Write functions that have input arguments and that return a single result to perform computations similar to those performed by library functions. When you call such a function, each actual argument value is assigned to its corresponding formal parameter.

8. Place prototypes (similar to function headings) for each function subprogram before the main function, and place the function definitions after the main function in a source file. Use (void) to indicate that a function has no parameters.

## New C Constructs

| Construct | Effect |
| --- | --- |
| **Function Prototype (void function without arguments)** | |
| `void star_line(void);` | Describes `star_line` as a function with no result and no arguments |
| **Function Prototype (function with arguments and a result)** | |
| `double average(int n,`<br>`        double x);` | Describes `average` as a function with a type `double` result and two arguments, one type `int` and one type `double` |
| **Function Call Statement (void function without arguments)** | |
| `star_line();` | Calls function `star_line` and causes it to begin execution |
| **Function Call (function with arguments and a result)** | |
| `money = average(num_kids,`<br>`        funds);` | Calls function `average` to compute a result which is stored in `money` |

*(continued)*

**Function Definition (void function without arguments)**

```
void                                    Defines star_line as a function that prints a
star_line(void)                         vertical line of four asterisks
{
    printf("*\n*\n*\n*\n");
}
```

**Function Definition (function with arguments and a result)**

```
/*                                      Defines average as a function that returns the
 * Returns the average of               result of dividing its second argument by its
 * its 2 arguments.                     first argument
 * Pre : x and n are
 *       defined, x >= 0,
 *       n > 0.
 * Post: result is x / n
 */
double
average(int n, double x);
{
    return (x / n);
}
```

# QUICK-CHECK EXERCISES

1. Developing a program from its documentation means that every statement in the program has a comment. True or false?
2. The principle of code reuse states that every function in your program must be used more than once. True or false?
3. Write this equation as a C statement using functions exp, log, and pow:

$$y = (e^{n \ln b})^2$$

4. What is the purpose of a function argument?
5. Each function is executed in the order in which it is defined in the source file. True or false?
6. How is a function in a C program executed?
7. What is a formal parameter?
8. Explain how a structure chart differs from an algorithm.
9. What does the following function do?

```
void
nonsense(void)
```

```
    {
            printf("*****\n");
            printf("*   *\n");
            printf("*****\n");
    }
```

10. What does the following main function do?

```
int
main(void)
{
        nonsense();
        nonsense();
        nonsense();

        return (0);
}
```

11. If an actual argument of -35.7 is passed to a type `int` formal parameter, what will happen? If an actual argument of 17 is passed to a type `double` formal parameter, what will happen?

# ANSWERS TO QUICK-CHECK EXERCISES

1. False
2. False
3. `y = pow(exp(n * log(b)), 2);`
4. A function argument is used to pass information into a function.
5. False
6. It is called into execution by a function call, that is, the function name followed by its arguments in parentheses.
7. A formal parameter is used in a function definition to represent a corresponding actual argument.
8. A structure chart shows the subordinate relationships between subproblems; an algorithm lists the sequence in which subproblem solutions are carried out.
9. It displays a rectangle of asterisks.
10. It displays three rectangles of asterisks on top of each other.
11. The formal parameter's value will be -35. The formal parameter's value will be 17.0.

## REVIEW QUESTIONS

1. Define top-down design and structure charts.
2. What is a function prototype?
3. When is a function executed, and where should a function prototype and function definition appear in a source program?
4. What are three advantages of using functions?
5. Is the use of functions a more efficient use of the programmer's time or the computer's time? Explain your answer.
6. Write a program that prompts the user for the two legs of a right triangle and makes use of the `pow` and `sqrt` functions and the Pythagorean theorem to compute the length of the hypotenuse.
7. Write a program that draws a rectangle made of a double border of asterisks. Use two functions: `draw_sides` and `draw_line`.
8. Draw a structure chart for the program described in Review Question 7.
9. Write the prototype for a function called `script` that has three input parameters. The first parameter will be the number of spaces to display at the beginning of a line. The second parameter will be the character to display after the spaces, and the third parameter will be the number of times to display the second parameter on the same line.

## PROGRAMMING PROJECTS

1. Write two functions, one that displays a triangle and one that displays a rectangle. Use these functions to write a complete C program from the following outline:

```
int
main(void)
{
    /* Draw triangle. */
    /* Draw rectangle. */
    /* Display 2 blank lines. */
    /* Draw triangle. */
    /* Draw rectangle. */
}
```

2. Add the functions from Fig. 3.14 to the ones for Programming Project 1. Use these functions in a program that draws a rocket ship (triangle over rectangles over intersecting lines), a male stick-figure (circle over rectangle over intersecting lines), and a female stick-figure standing on the head of a

male stick-figure. Write function `skip_5_lines` and call it to place five blank lines between drawings.

3. Write a computer program that computes the duration of a projectile's flight and its height above the ground when it reaches the target. As part of your solution, write and call a function that displays instructions to the program user.

### Problem Constant

```
G 32.17 /* gravitational constant   */
```

### Problem Inputs

```
double theta /* input - angle (radians) of elevation    */
double distance /* input - distance (ft) to target       */
double velocity /* input - projectile velocity (ft/sec) */
```

### Problem Outputs

```
double time    /* output - time (sec) of flight           */
double height /* output - height at impact                */
```

### Relevant Formulas

$$time = \frac{distance}{velocity \times cos\,(theta)}$$

$$height = velocity \times sin(theta) \times time - \frac{g \times time^2}{2}$$

Try your program on these data sets.

| Inputs | Data Set 1 | Data Set 2 |
|---|---|---|
| angle of elevation | 0.3 radian | 0.71 radian |
| velocity | 800 ft/sec | 1,600 ft/sec |
| distance to target | 11,000 ft | 78,670 ft |

4. Write a program that takes a positive number with a fractional part and rounds it to two decimal places. For example, 32.4851 would round to 32.49, and 32.4431 would round to 32.44. (*Hint:* See problem 2b in the Self-Check Exercises for Section 3.2.)

5. Four track stars have entered the mile race at the Penn Relays. Write a program that scans in the race time in minutes (`minutes`) and seconds (`seconds`) for a runner and computes and displays the speed in feet per second (`fps`) and in meters per second (`mps`). (*Hints:* There are 5280 feet in one mile, and one kilometer equals 3282 feet.) Write and call a function that

displays instructions to the program user. Run the program for each star's data.

| Minutes | Seconds |
|---------|---------|
| 3 | 52.83 |
| 3 | 59.83 |
| 4 | 00.03 |
| 4 | 16.22 |

6. In shopping for a new house, you must consider several factors. In this problem the initial cost of the house, the estimated annual fuel costs, and the annual tax rate are available. Write a program that will determine the total cost of a house after a five-year period and run the program for each of the following sets of data.

| Initial House Cost | Annual Fuel Cost | Tax Rate |
|--------------------|------------------|----------|
| 67,000 | 2,300 | 0.025 |
| 62,000 | 2,500 | 0.025 |
| 75,000 | 1,850 | 0.020 |

To calculate the house cost, add the initial cost to the fuel cost for five years, then add the taxes for five years. Taxes for one year are computed by multiplying the tax rate by the initial cost. Write and call a function that displays instructions to the program user.

7. A cyclist coasting on a level road slows from a speed of 10 mi/hr to 2.5 mi/hr in one minute. Write a computer program that calculates the cyclist's constant rate of acceleration and determines how long the cyclist will take to come to rest, given an initial speed of 10 mi/hr. (*Hint:* Use the equation

$$a = \frac{v_f - v_i}{t}$$

where $a$ is acceleration, $t$ is time interval, $v_i$ is initial velocity, and $v_f$ is the final velocity.) Write and call a function that displays instructions to the program user and a function that computes $a$, given $t$, $v_f$, and $v_i$.

8. A manufacturer wishes to determine the cost of producing an open-top cylindrical container. The surface area of the container is the sum of the area of the circular base plus the area of the outside (the circumference of the base times the height of the container). Write a program to take the radius of the base, the height of the container, the cost per square centimeter of the

material (`cost`), and the number of containers to be produced (`quantity`). Calculate the cost of each container and the total cost of producing all the containers. Write and call a function that displays instructions to the user and a function that computes surface area.

9. Two positive integers *i* and *j* are considered to be *relatively prime* if there exists no integer greater than 1 that divides them both. Write a function `relprm` that has two input parameters, `i` and `j`, and returns a value of 1 if and only if `i` and `j` are relatively prime. Otherwise, `relprm` should return a value of 0.

10. Given the lengths *a, b, c* of the sides of a triangle, write a function to compute the area *A* of the triangle. The formula for computing *A* is given by

$$A = \sqrt{s(s-a)(s-b)(s-c)}$$

where *s* is the semiperimeter of the triangle. Write a driver program to get values for *a*, *b*, and *c* and call your function to compute *A*. The driver should print *A*, *a*, *b*, and *c*.

# Selection Structures: if and switch Statements

chapter

$T$his chapter begins your study of statements that control the flow of program execution. You will learn to use `if` and `switch` statements to select one statement group to execute from many alternatives. First, the chapter discusses conditions and logical expressions because the `if` statement relies on them.

The case studies in this chapter emphasize reusing solutions to prior problems to speed up the problem-solving process. You will also learn how to trace an algorithm or program to verify that it does what you expect.

# 4.1 CONTROL STRUCTURES

**control structure**
a combination of individual instructions into a single logical unit with one entry point and one exit point

**Control structures** control the flow of execution in a program or function. The C control structures enable you to combine individual instructions into a single logical unit with one entry point and one exit point.

Instructions are organized into three kinds of control structures to control execution flow: *sequence*, *selection*, and *repetition*. Until now we have been using only sequential flow. A **compound statement,** written as a group of statements bracketed by { and }, is used to specify sequential flow.

**compound statement**
a group of statements bracketed by { and } that are executed sequentially

```
{
    statement_1;
    statement_2;
        .
        .
        .
    statement_n;
}
```

Control flows from *statement*$_1$ to *statement*$_2$, and so on. You have been using compound statements all along—a function body consists of a single compound statement.

**selection control structure**
a control structure that chooses among alternative program statements

This chapter describes the C control structures for selection, and Chapter 5 covers the control structures for repetition. Some problem solutions require steps with two or more alternative courses of action. A **selection control structure** chooses which alternative to execute.

# 4.2 CONDITIONS

A program chooses among alternative statements by testing the value of key variables. For example, one indicator of the health of a person's heart is the resting heart rate. Generally a resting rate of 75 beats per minute or less indicates a healthy heart, but a resting heart rate over 75 indicates a potential problem. A program that gets a person's resting heart rate as data should compare that value to 75 and display a warning message if the rate is over 75.

If `rest_heart_rate` is a type `int` variable, the expression

```
rest_heart_rate > 75
```

performs the necessary comparison and evaluates to 1 (true) when `rest_heart_rate` is over 75; the expression evaluates to 0 (false) if `rest_heart_rate` is not greater than 75. Such an expression is called a **condition** because it establishes a criterion for either executing or skipping a group of statements.

**condition**
an expression that is either false (represented by 0) or true (usually represented by 1)

## Relational and Equality Operators

Most conditions that we use to perform comparisons will have one of these forms:

*variable*    *relational-operator*    *variable*
*variable*    *relational-operator*    *constant*
*variable*    *equality-operator*      *variable*
*variable*    *equality-operator*      *constant*

Table 4.1 lists the relational and equality operators.

**Table 4.1    Relational and Equality Operators**

| Operator | Meaning | Type |
|----------|---------|------|
| < | less than | relational |
| > | greater than | relational |
| <= | less than or equal to | relational |
| >= | greater than or equal to | relational |
| == | equal to | equality |
| ! = | not equal to | equality |

**EXAMPLE 4.1**

Table 4.2 shows some sample conditions in C. Each condition is evaluated assuming these variable and constant macro values:

| x | power | MAX_POW | y | item | MIN_ITEM | mom_or_dad | num | SENTINEL |
|---|-------|---------|---|------|----------|------------|-----|----------|
| -5 | 1024 | 1024 | 7 | 1.5 | -999.0 | 'M' | 999 | 999 |

**Table 4.2  Sample Conditions**

| Operator | Condition | English Meaning | Value |
|----------|-----------|-----------------|-------|
| <= | x <= 0 | x less than or equal to 0 | 1 (true) |
| < | power < MAX_POW | power less than MAX_POW | 0 (false) |
| >= | x >= y | x greater than or equal to y | 0 (false) |
| > | item > MIN_ITEM | item greater than MIN_ITEM | 1 (true) |
| == | mom_or_dad == 'M' | mom_or_dad equal to 'M' | 1 (true) |
| != | num != SENTINEL | num not equal to SENTINEL | 0 (false) |

## Logical Operators

**logical expression**
an expression that uses one or more of the logical operators && (and), || (or), ! (not)

With the three logical operators—&& (and), || (or), ! (not)—we can form more complicated conditions or **logical expressions.** Examples of logical expressions formed with these operators are

```
salary < MIN_SALARY  ||  dependents > 5
temperature > 90.0  &&  humidity > 0.90
n >= 0  &&  n <= 100
0 <= n  &&  n <= 100
```

The first logical expression determines whether an employee is eligible for special scholarship funds. It evaluates to 1 (true) if *either* the condition

```
salary < MIN_SALARY
```

or the condition

```
dependents > 5
```

is true. The second logical expression describes an unbearable summer day, with temperature and humidity both in the nineties. The expression evaluates to true only when *both* conditions are true. The last two expressions are equivalent and evaluate to true if n lies between 0 and 100 inclusive.

**logical complement (negation)**
the complement of a condition has the value 1 (true) when the condition's value is 0 (false); the complement of a condition has the value 0 (false) when the condition's value is nonzero (true)

  The third logical operator, ! (not), has a single operand and yields the **logical complement,** or **negation,** of its operand (that is, if the variable positive is nonzero (true), !positive is 0 (false) and vice versa). The logical expression

```
!(0 <= n  &&  n <= 100)
```

is the complement of the last expression in the list above. It evaluates to 1 (true) when n does not lie between 0 and 100 inclusive.

  Table 4.3 shows that the && operator (and) yields a true result only when both its operands are true. Table 4.4 shows that the || operator (or) yields a false result only when both its operands are false. Table 4.5 shows the ! operator (not).

**Table 4.3  The && Operator (and)**

| operand1 | operand2 | operand1 && operand2 |
|---|---|---|
| nonzero (true) | nonzero (true) | 1 (true) |
| nonzero (true) | 0 (false) | 0 (false) |
| 0 (false) | nonzero (true) | 0 (false) |
| 0 (false) | 0 (false) | 0 (false) |

**Table 4.4  The || Operator (or)**

| operand1 | operand2 | operand1 || operand2 |
|---|---|---|
| nonzero (true) | nonzero (true) | 1 (true) |
| nonzero (true) | 0 (false) | 1 (true) |
| 0 (false) | nonzero (true) | 1 (true) |
| 0 (false) | 0 (false) | 0 (false) |

**Table 4.5  The ! Operator (not)**

| operand1 | !operand1 |
|---|---|
| nonzero (true) | 0 (false) |
| 0 (false) | 1 (true) |

Tables 4.3 through 4.5 show that the result is always 0 or 1 when C evaluates a logical expression. However, C accepts *any nonzero value* as a representation of true. For now, we will always use the integer 1 when we need the value true, but knowing how C really views logical expressions will help you understand why some common mistakes that you may make will not be seen by the C compiler as syntax errors.

## Operator Precedence

An operator's precedence determines its order of evaluation. Table 4.6 lists the precedence of all C operators so far, from highest to lowest.

**unary operator**
an operator that has one
operand

The table shows that function calls are evaluated first. The **unary operators,** ! (not), + (plus sign), - (minus sign), and & (address of), which have a single operand are evaluated second. Next come all the binary operators in the sequence: arithmetic, relational, equality, and logical (&& and then ||). The assignment operator (=) is evaluated last. Notice that the precedence of operators + and - depends on whether they have one operand or two. In the expression

```
-x - y * z
```

the unary minus is evaluated first (-x), then *, and then the second -.

You can use parentheses to change the order of operator evaluation. If you remove the parentheses from the expression

```
(x < y  ||  x < z)  &&  x > 0.0
```

C would evaluate && before ||, thereby changing the meaning of the expression.

**Table 4.6   Operator Precedence**

| Operator | Precedence |
|---|---|
| function calls | highest |
| !  +  -  & (unary operators) | |
| *  /  % | |
| +  - | |
| <  <=  >=  > | |
| ==  != | |
| && | |
| \|\| | |
| = | lowest |

Also, you can use parentheses to clarify the meaning of expressions. If x, min, and max are type `double`, the C compiler interprets the expression

```
x + y < min + max
```

correctly as

```
(x + y) < (min + max)
```

because + has higher precedence than <, but the second expression is clearer.

**EXAMPLE 4.2**

Expressions 1 to 4 below contain different operands and operators. Each expression's value is given in the corresponding comment, assuming x, y, and z are type `double`, flag is type `int` and the variables have the values:

```
1. !flag                        /* !0 is 1 (true)          */
2. x + y / z  <=  3.5           /* 5.0 <= 3.5 is 0 (false) */
3. !flag || (y + z  >= x - z)   /* 1 || 1 is 1 (true)      */
4. !(flag || (y + z  >=  x - z))  /* !(0 || 1) is 0 (false) */
```

Fig. 4.1 shows the evaluation tree and step-by-step evaluation for expression 3.

**Figure 4.1
Evaluation Tree
and Step-by-
Step Evaluation
for `!flag ||
(y + z >= x
- z)`**

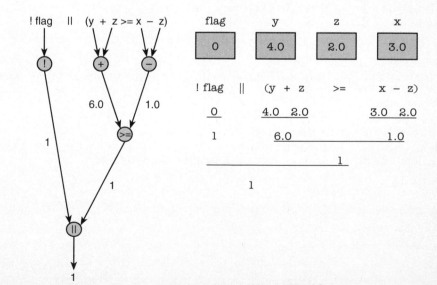

## Short-Circuit Evaluation

Although Fig. 4.1 shows the evaluation of the entire logical expression, C only evaluates part of the expression. An expression of the form $a \mid\mid b$ must be true if $a$ is true. Consequently, C stops evaluating the expression when it determines that the value of !flag is 1 (true). Similarly, an expression of the form $a$ && $b$ must be false if $a$ is false, so C would stop evaluating such an expression if its first operand evaluates to 0. This technique of stopping evaluation of a logical expression as soon as its value can be determined is called **short-circuit evaluation.**

**short-circuit evaluation**
stopping evaluation of a logical expression as soon as its value can be determined

## Writing English Conditions in C

To solve programming problems, you must convert conditions expressed in English to C. Many algorithm steps require testing to see if a variable's value is within a specified range of values. For example, if min represents the lower bound of a range of values and max represents the upper bound (min is less than max), the expression

```
min <= x  &&  x <= max
```

tests whether x lies within the range min through max, inclusive. In Fig. 4.2 this range is shaded. The expression is 1 (true) if x lies within this range and 0 (false) if x is outside the range.

**Figure 4.2
Range of True
Values for
min <= x  &&
x <= max**

**EXAMPLE 4.3**    Table 4.7 shows some English conditions and the corresponding C expressions. Each expression is evaluated assuming x is 3.0, y is 4.0, and z is 2.0.

**Table 4.7    English Conditions as C Expressions**

| English Condition | Logical Expression | Evaluation |
|---|---|---|
| x and y are greater than z | x > z  &&  y > z | 1 && 1 is 1 (true) |
| x is equal to 1.0 or 3.0 | x == 1.0  \|\|  x == 3.0 | 0 \|\| 1 is 1 (true) |
| x is in the range z to y, inclusive | z <= x  &&  x <= y | 1 && 1 is 1 (true) |
| x is outside the range z to y | !(z <= x  &&  x <= y) | !(1 && 1) is 0 (false) |
|  | z > x  \|\|  x > y | 0 \|\| 0 is 0 (false) |

**Figure 4.3
Range of True
Values for
z > x ||
x > y**

The first logical expression shows the C code for the English condition "x and y are greater than z". You may be tempted to write this as

```
x && y > z        /* invalid logical expression */
```

However, if we apply the precedence rules to this expression, we quickly see that it does not have the intended meaning. Also, the type `double` variable x is an invalid operand for the logical operator `&&`.

The third logical expression shows the C code for the mathematical relationship $z \leq x \leq y$. The boundary values, 2.0 and 4.0, are included in the range of $x$ values that yield a true result.

The last table entry shows a pair of logical expressions that are true when x is outside the range bounded by z and y. We get the first expression in the pair by complementing the expression just above it. The second expression states that x is outside the range if z is larger than x or x is larger than y. In Fig. 4.3 the shaded areas represent the values of x that yield a true result. Both y and z are excluded from the set of values that yield a true result.

## Comparing Characters

We can also compare characters in C using the relational and equality operators. Table 4.8 shows some examples of these comparisons.

**Table 4.8    Character Comparisons**

| Expression | Value |
| --- | --- |
| '9' >= '0' | 1 (true) |
| 'a' < 'e' | 1 (true) |
| 'B' <= 'A' | 0 (false) |
| 'Z' == 'z' | 0 (false) |
| 'a' <= 'A' | system dependent |
| 'a' <= ch  &&  ch <= 'z' | 1 (true) if ch is a lowercase letter |

The first three lines of Table 4.8 show that the digit characters and letters are ordered as expected (that is, `'0'<'1'<'2'< ... <'8'<'9'` and `'a'<'b'<'c'... <'y'<'z'`). The next two lines show that the lower-case and uppercase form of the same letter have different values and their order is system dependent. The last entry shows an expression that is true if `ch` is a lowercase letter. (On some systems, this expression also will be true for some characters that are not lowercase letters.)

## Logical Assignment

The simplest form of a logical expression in C is a single type `int` value or variable intended to represent the value true or false. We can use assignment statements to set such variables to true (a nonzero value) or false (0).

**EXAMPLE 4.4**

Given the declarations

```
int  age;           /* input - a person's age          */
char gender;        /* input - a person's gender        */
int  senior_citizen; /* logical - indicates senior status */
```

Assume that a value of 1 for `senior_citizen` indicates that the person is a senior citizen (65 years old or over). You can use the assignment statement

```
senior_citizen = 1;  /* Set senior status */
```

to set `senior_citizen` to true.

A more likely scenario is to set the value of `senior_citizen` based on the value scanned into `age`:

```
scanf("%d", &age);              /* Read the person's age */
senior_citizen = (age >= 65);   /* Set senior status     */
```

In the assignment above, the condition in parentheses evaluates first. Its value is 1 (true) if the value scanned into `age` is 65 or greater. Consequently, the value of `senior_citizen` is true when `age` satisfies the condition and false otherwise.

The logical operators `&&`, `||`, and `!` can be applied to `senior_citi-zen`. The expression

```
!senior_citizen
```

is 1 (true) if the value of age is less than 65. Finally, the logical expression

```
senior_citizen  &&  gender == 'M'
```

is 1 (true) if senior_citizen is 1 (true) and the character in gender is M.

**EXAMPLE 4.5** The following assignment statements assign values to two type int variables, in_range and is_letter. Variable in_range gets 1 (true) if the value of n is between −10 and 10 excluding the endpoints; is_letter gets 1 (true) if ch is an uppercase or a lowercase letter.

```
in_range = (n > -10  &&  n < 10);
is_letter = ('A' <= ch  &&  ch <= 'Z') ||
            ('a' <= ch  &&  ch <= 'z');
```

The expression in the first assignment statement is true if n satisfies both the conditions listed (n is greater than −10 and n is less than 10); otherwise, the expression is false.

The expression in the second assignment statement uses the logical operators &&, ||. The subexpression before || is true if ch is an uppercase letter; the subexpression after || is true if ch is a lowercase letter. Consequently, is_letter gets 1 (true) if either subexpression is true (that is, ch is a letter); otherwise, is_letter gets 0 (false). You can delete the parentheses without affecting the order of operator evaluation.

**EXAMPLE 4.6**  The statement below assigns the value 1 (true) to even (type int) if n is an even number:

```
even = (n % 2 == 0);
```

Because all even numbers are divisible by 2, the remainder of n divided by 2 (n % 2 in C) is 0 when n is an even number. The expression in parenthese is compares the remainder to 0, so its value is 1 (true) when the remainder is 0 and its value is 0 (false) when the remainder is nonzero.

## Complementing a Condition

You have seen how to complement a logical expression by preceding it with the symbol !. You can also complement a simple condition by just changing its operator.

EXAMPLE 4.7

Two forms of the complement of the condition

```
item == SENT
```

are

```
!(item == SENT)                          item != SENT
```

The form on the right is obtained by changing the equality operator (that is, changing == to !=).

Usually changing the equality or relational operator to complement a simple condition is easy to do. The relational operator <= should be changed to >, < should be changed to >=, and so on. Use the ! operator with more complicated expressions.

EXAMPLE 4.8

The condition

```
status == 'S'  &&   age > 25
```

is true for a single person over 25. The complement of this condition is

```
!(status == 'S'  &&   age > 25)
```

**DeMorgan's Theorem**    DeMorgan's theorem gives us a way of simplifying the logical expression above. DeMorgan's theorem states

- The complement of $expr_1$ && $expr_2$ is written as $comp_1$ || $comp_2$, where $comp_1$ is the complement of $expr_1$, and $comp_2$ is the complement of $expr_2$.
- The complement of $expr_1$ || $expr_2$ is written as $comp_1$ && $comp_2$, where $comp_1$ is the complement of $expr_1$, and $comp_2$ is the complement of $expr_2$.

Using DeMorgan's theorem, we can write the complement of

```
age > 25  &&   (status == 'S'  ||   status == 'D')
```

as

```
age <= 25  ||  (status != 'S'  &&  status != 'D')
```

The original condition is true for anyone who is over 25 and is either single or divorced. The complement would be true for anyone who is 25 or younger or for anyone who is currently married.

## EXERCISES FOR SECTION 4.2

### Self-Check

1. Assuming x is 15.0 and y is 25.0, what are the values of the following conditions?

```
x != y
x < x
x >= y - x
x == y + x - y
```

2. Evaluate each of the following expressions if a is 5, b is 10, c is 15, and flag is 1. Which parts of these expressions are not evaluated due to short-circuit evaluation?

```
a. c == a + b  ||  !flag
b. a != 7  &&  flag  ||  c >= 6
c. !(b <= 12)  &&  a % 2 == 0
d. !(a > 5  ||  c < a + b)
```

3. Show step-by-step evaluation of expression 4 in Example 4.2.
4. Complement each expression in Exercise 2. Use DeMorgan's theorem if applicable.
5. What value is assigned to the type int variable ans in this statement if the value of p is 100 and q is 50?

```
ans = (p > 95) + (q < 95);
```

This statement is not shown as an example of a reasonable assignment statement; rather, it is a sample of a statement that makes little sense to the reader. The statement is still legal and executable in C; however, because C uses integers to represent the logical values true and false.

### Programming

1. Write an expression to test for each of the following relationships.
   a. age is from 18 to 21 inclusive.
   b. water is less than 1.5 and also greater than 0.1.

c. year is divisible by 4. (*Hint:* Use %.)

d. speed is not greater than 55.

e. y is greater than x and less than z.

f. w is either equal to 6 or not greater than 3.

2. Write assignment statements for the following.

a. Assign a value of 1 to between if n is in the range −k through +k, inclusive; otherwise, assign a value of 0.

b. Assign a value of 1 to uppercase if ch is an uppercase letter; otherwise, assign a value of 0.

c. Assign a value of 1 to divisor if m is a divisor of n; otherwise, assign a value of 0.

# 4.3 THE if STATEMENT

You now know how to write a C expression that is the equivalent of a question such as "Is resting heart rate more than 56 beats per minute?" Next, we need to investigate a way to use the value of the expression to select a course of action. In C, the if statement is the primary selection control structure.

## if Statement with Two Alternatives

The if statement

```
if (rest_heart_rate > 56)
        printf("Keep up your exercise program!\n");
else
        printf("Your heart is in excellent health!\n");
```

selects one of the two calls to printf. It selects the statement following the parenthesized condition if the condition evaluates to 1 (true) (that is, if rest_heart_rate is greater than 56), or it selects the statement following else if the condition evaluates to 0 (false) (if rest_heart_rate is not greater than 56).

**flowchart**
a diagram that shows the step-by-step execution of a control structure

Figure 4.4(a) is a **flowchart** of the preceding if statement. A flowchart is a diagram that uses boxes and arrows to show the step-by-step execution of a control structure. A diamond-shaped box in a flowchart represents a decision. There is always one path into a decision and there are two paths out (labeled true and false). A rectangular box represents an assignment statement or a process.

Figure 4.4(a) shows that the condition (rest_heart_rate > 56) is evaluated first. If the condition is true, program control follows the arrow labeled true, and the assignment statement in the right rectangle is executed. If

**Figure 4.4**
**Flowchart of if**
**Statements with**
**(a) Two**
**Alternatives**
**and (b) One**
**Alternative**

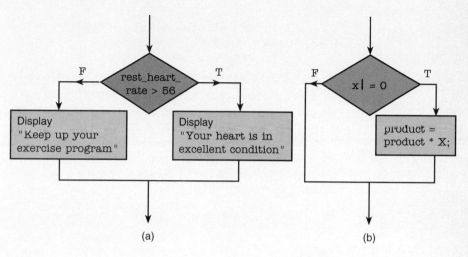

**Figure 4.4**
**Flowchart of if**
**Statements with**
**(a) Two**
**Alternatives**
**and (b) One**
**Alternative**

the condition is false, program control follows the arrow labeled false, and the assignment statement in the left rectangle is executed.

## if Statement with One Alternative

The `if` statement in the last section has two alternatives, but executes only one for a given value of `rest_heart_rate`. You also can write `if` statements with a single alternative that executes only when the condition is true.

The `if` statement diagrammed in Fig. 4.4(b)

```
/* Multiply Product by a nonzero X */
if (x != 0.0)
     product = product * x;
```

has one alternative, which is executed only when `x` is not equal to 0. It causes `product` to be multiplied by `x` and the new value to be saved in `product`, replacing the old value. If `x` is equal to 0, the multiplication is not performed.

## A Comparison of One and Two Alternative if Statements

**EXAMPLE 4.9**

The `if` statement below has two alternatives.

```
if (crsr_or_frgt == 'C')
     printf("Cruiser\n");
else
     printf("Frigate\n");
```

It displays either `Cruiser` or `Frigate`, depending on the character stored in the type `char` variable `crsr_or_frgt`. ◀

**EXAMPLE 4.10** ▶ The `if` statement that follows has one alternative; it displays the message `Cruiser` only when `crsr_or_frgt` has the value `'C'`. Regardless of whether `Cruiser` is displayed or not, the message `Combat ship` is displayed.

```
if (crsr_or_frgt == 'C')
     printf("Cruiser\n");
printf("Combat ship\n");
```
◀

**EXAMPLE 4.11** ▶ The program fragment

```
if crsr_or_frgt == 'C'        /* error - missing parentheses */
     printf("Cruiser\n");
printf("Combat ship\n");
```

is an incorrect version of the `if` statement in Example 4.10. The missing parentheses around the condition is a syntax error that will be detected (and possibly corrected) by the compiler.

The extra semicolon in the first line below

```
if (crsr_or_frgt == 'C');  /* error - improper placement of ;*/
     printf("Cruiser\n");
printf("Combat ship\n");
```

does not cause a violation of C syntax rules because the compiler translates the first line as a single-alternative `if` statement with an *empty statement* implying no action if the condition is true. The first `printf` loses its dependency on the value of the condition, so both calls to `printf` are executed unconditionally. ◀

---

**if Statement (One Alternative)**

FORM:     `if` (*condition*)
                    *statement_T*;

EXAMPLE: `if (x > 0.0)`
                    `pos_prod = pos_prod * x;`

INTERPRETATION: If *condition* evaluates to `true`, then *statement_T* is executed; otherwise, *statement_T* is skipped.

**if Statement (Two Alternatives)**

FORM:     if (condition)
                statement_T;
            else
                statement_F;

EXAMPLE: if (x >= 0.0)
                printf("positive\n");
            else
                printf("negative\n");

INTERPRETATION: If *condition* evaluates to true, then *statement_T* is executed and *statement_F* is skipped; otherwise, *statement_T* is skipped and *statement_F* is executed.

## Program Style    *Format of the if Statement*

All if statement examples in this text indent *statement_T* and *statement_F*. The word else is typed without indentation on a separate line. The format of the if statement makes its meaning apparent and is used solely to improve program readability; the format makes no difference to the compiler.

## EXERCISES FOR SECTION 4.3

Self-Check

1. What do these statements display?

   a. if (12 < 12)
           printf("less");
       else
           printf("not less");

   b. var1 = 25.12;
      var2 = 15.00;
      if (var1 <= var2)
              printf("less or equal");
      else
              printf("greater than");

2. What value is assigned to x when y is 15.0?

   a. x = 25.0;
      if (y != (x - 10.0))
          x = x - 10.0;
      else
          x = x / 2.0;

   b. if (y < 15.0)
          if (y >= 0.0)
              x = 5 * y;

```
         else
               x = 2 * y;
      else
         x = 3 * y;
   c. if (y < 15.0 && y >= 0.0)
         x = 5 * y;
      else
         x = 2 * y;
```

Programming

1. Write C statements to carry out the following steps.

   a. If item is nonzero, then multiply product by item and save the result in product; otherwise, skip the multiplication. In either case, print the value of product.

   b. Store the absolute difference of x and y in y, where the absolute difference is (x - y) or (y - x), whichever is positive. Do not use the abs or fabs function in your solution.

   c. If x is 0, add 1 to zero_count. If x is negative, add x to minus_sum. If x is greater than 0, add x to plus_sum.

## 4.4 if STATEMENTS WITH COMPOUND STATEMENTS

This section describes if statements having compound statements after the condition or the keyword else. When the symbol { follows the condition or else, the C compiler either executes or skips all statements through the matching }.

**EXAMPLE 4.12**   Suppose you are a biologist studying the growth rate of fruit flies. The if statement

```
if (pop_today > pop_yesterday) {
    growth = pop_today - pop_yesterday;
    growth_pct = 100.0 * growth / pop_yesterday;
    printf("The growth percentage is %.2f\n", growth_pct);
}
```

computes the population growth from yesterday to today as a percentage of yesterday's population. The compound statement after the condition executes only when today's population is larger than yesterday's. The first assignment

$$y = x?y \; ? \; x-y : y-x \; ;$$

computes the increase in the fruit fly population, and the second assignment converts it to a percentage of the original population, which is displayed. ◄

**EXAMPLE 4.13** ► As manager of a company's automobile fleet, you keep records of the safety ratings of the fleet cars. In the `if` statement that follows, the true task makes a record of an automobile (`auto_id`) whose crash test rating index (`ctri`) is at least as low (good) as the cutoff you have established for acceptably safe cars (`MAX_SAFE_CTRI`). The false task records an auto whose `ctri` does not meet your standard. In either case, an appropriate message is displayed, and one is added to the count of safe or unsafe cars. Both the true and false tasks are compound statements.

```c
if (ctri <= MAX_SAFE_CTRI) {
    printf("Car #%d: safe\n", auto_id);
    safe = safe + 1;
} else {
    printf("Car #%d: unsafe\n", auto_id);
    unsafe = unsafe + 1;
}
```

If you omit the braces enclosing the compound statements, the `if` statement would end after the first `printf` call. The assignment to `safe` would be translated as an unconditional statement (always executed), and the compiler would mark the keyword `else` as an error because a statement cannot begin with `else`. ◄

## Program Style   *Writing if Statements with Compound True or False Statements*

We enclose a compound statement that is a true task or a false task in braces. The placement of the braces is a matter of personal preference. We use the form shown in Example 4.13. Some programmers prefer to type each brace on its own line and to align the braces:

```c
if (condition)
{
    true task
}
else
{
    false task
}
```

Some programmers prefer to use braces around all true and false tasks whether compound or not, so that all if statements in a program have a consistent style. We recommend enclosing both the true and the false tasks in braces if either is a compound statement. Whichever style you choose, make sure you apply it consistently.

## Tracing an if Statement

A critical step in program design is to verify that an algorithm or C statement is correct before you spend extensive time coding or debugging it. Often a few extra minutes spent in verifying the correctness of an algorithm saves hours of coding and testing time.

**hand trace (desk check)**
step-by-step simulation of an
algorithm's execution

A **hand trace**, or **desk check**, is a careful, step-by-step simulation on paper of how the computer executes the algorithm or statement. The results of this simulation should show the effect of each step's execution using data that are relatively easy to process by hand.

 **EXAMPLE 4.14**

In many programming problems you must order a pair of data values in memory so that the smaller value is stored in one variable (say, x) and the larger value in another (say, y). The if statement in Fig. 4.5 rearranges any two values stored in x and y so that the smaller number is in x and the larger number is in y. If the two numbers are already in the proper order, the compound statement is not executed.

Variables x, y, and temp should all be the same data type. Although the values of x and y are being switched, an additional variable, temp, is needed to store a copy of one of these values.

## Figure 4.5   if Statement to Order x and y

```
if (x > y) {              /* Switch x and y */
    temp = x;             /* Store old x in temp */
    x = y;                /* Store old y in x */
    y = temp;             /* Store old x in y */
}
```

Table 4.9 traces the execution of this if statement when x is 12.5 and y is 5.0. The table shows that temp is initially undefined (indicated by ?). Each line of the table shows the part of the if statement that is being executed, followed by its effect. If any variable gets a new value, its new value is shown on

**Table 4.9   Trace of if Statement**

| Statement Part | x | y | temp | Effect |
|---|---|---|---|---|
| | 12.5 | 5.0 | ? | |
| if (x > y) { | | | | 12.5 > 5.0 is true. |
| temp = x; | | | 12.5 | Store old x in temp. |
| x = y; | 5.0 | | | Store old y in x. |
| y = temp; | | 12.5 | | Store old x in y. |

that line. If no new value is shown, the variable retains its previous value. The last value stored in x is 5.0, and the last value stored in y is 12.5.

The trace in Table 4.9 shows that 5.0 and 12.5 are correctly stored in x and y when the condition is true. To verify that the if statement is correct, you would need to select other data that cause the condition to evaluate to false. Also, you should verify that the statement is correct for special situations. For example, what would happen if x were equal to y? Would the statement still provide the correct result? To complete the hand trace, you would need to show that the algorithm handles this special situation properly.

In tracing each case, you must be careful to execute the statement step-by-step exactly as the computer would execute it. Often programmers assume how a particular step will be executed and don't explicitly test each condition and trace each step. A trace performed in this way is of little value.

**EXERCISES FOR SECTION 4.4**

Self-Check

1. Insert braces where they are needed so the meaning matches the indentation.

```
if (x > y)
        x = x + 10.0;
        printf("x Bigger\n");
else
        printf("x Smaller\n");
        printf("y is %.2f\n", y);
```

2. Correct the following if statement; assume the indentation is correct.

```
if (num1 < 0);
        product = num1 * num2 * num3;
        printf("Product is %d\n", product);
```

```
else;
      sum = num1 + num2 + num3;
      printf("Sum is %d\n", sum);
printf("Data: %d, %d, %d\n", num1, num2, num3);
```

3. Revise the style of the following if statement to improve its readability.

```
if (engine_type == 'J') {printf("Jet engine");
speed_category = 1;}
else{printf("Propellers"); speed_category
= 2;}
```

Programming

1. Write an if statement that might be used to compute and display the average of a set of *n* numbers whose sum is stored in variable total. This average should be found only if *n* is greater than 0; otherwise, an error message should be displayed.
2. Write an interactive program that contains an if statement that may be used to compute the area of a square (*area = side²*) or a triangle (*area = 1/2 × base × height*) after prompting the user to type the first character of the figure name (S or T).

# 4.5 DECISION STEPS IN ALGORITHMS

**decision step**
an algorithm step that selects
one of several actions

Algorithm steps that select from a choice of actions are called **decision steps.** The algorithm in the next problem contains decision steps to compute and display a customer's water bill based on usage. The decision steps are coded as if statements.

## Case Study: Water Bill Problem

◄ PROBLEM ►

Write a program that computes a customer's water bill. The bill includes a $35 water demand charge plus a consumption (use) charge of $1.10 for every thousand gallons used. Consumption is figured from meter readings (in thousands of gallons) taken recently and at the end of the previous quarter. If the customer's unpaid balance is greater than zero, a $2 late charge is assessed as well.

```
ANALYSIS
```

The total water bill is the sum of the demand and use charges, the unpaid balance, and a possible late charge. The demand charge is a program constant ($35), but the use charge must be computed. To do this, we must know the previous and current meter readings (the problem inputs). After obtaining these data, we can compute the use charge by multiplying the difference between the two meter readings by the charge for 1000 gallons, the problem constant $1.10. Next, we can determine the applicable late charge, if any, and finally compute the water bill by adding the four components. The data requirements and initial algorithm follow.

## Data Requirements

### Problem Constants
```
DEMAND_CHG 35.00    /* basic water demand charge        */
PER_1000_CHG 1.10   /* charge per thousand gallons used */
LATE_CHG 2.00       /* surcharge on an unpaid balance   */
```

### Problem Inputs
```
int previous  /* meter reading from previous quarter
                 in thousands of gallons            */
int current   /* meter reading from current quarter */
double unpaid /* unpaid balance of previous bill    */
```

### Problem Outputs
```
double bill         /* water bill                     */
double use_charge   /* charge for actual water use    */
double late_charge  /* charge for non-payment of part
                       of previous balance            */
```

### Relevant Formulas
*water bill = demand charge + use charge + unpaid balance*
*+ applicable late charge*

```
DESIGN
```

## Initial Algorithm

1. Display user instructions.
2. Get data: unpaid balance, previous and current meter readings.
3. Compute use charge.
4. Determine applicable late charge.
5. Figure bill amount.
6. Display the bill amount and charges.

**Figure 4.6    Structure Chart for Water Bill Problem**

The structure chart in Fig. 4.6 includes *data flow* information that shows the inputs and the outputs of each individual algorithm step. The structure chart shows that step 2 "Get data," provides values for unpaid, previous, and current as its outputs (data flow arrow points up). Similarly, step 3, "Compute use charge," uses previous and current as its inputs (data flow arrow points down) and provides use_charge as its output. We will discuss the relevance of the data flow information after we complete the problem solution.

As shown in the structure chart, we use functions to implement all but steps 2 and 5. Each function name appears below the subproblem it solves. Next, we turn our attention to the function subprograms. We will discuss each function except instruct_water, which is straightforward.

**ANALYSIS and DESIGN of comp_use_charge**

The structure chart shows that function comp_use_charge computes a value for use_charge based on data stored in previous and current. The data requirements and algorithm follow.

## Data Requirements for comp_use_charge

### Input Parameters
```
int previous  /* meter reading from previous quarter
                 in thousands of gallons          */
int current   /* meter reading from current quarter */
```

### Return Value
```
double use_charge  /* charge for actual water use*/
```

### Program Variable
```
int used /* thousands of gallons used this quarter */
```

### Relevant Formulas
*used = current meter reading − previous meter reading*
*use charge = used × charge per thousand gallons*

## Algorithm for comp_use_charge

1. used is current - previous
2. use_charge is used * PER_1000_CHG

### ANALYSIS and DESIGN of comp_late_charge

Function comp_late_charge returns a late charge of $2.00 or $0.00 depending on the unpaid balance. Consequently, it requires a decision step as shown in the algorithm that follows.

## Data Requirements for comp_late_charge

### Input Parameter
```
double unpaid /* unpaid balance of previous bill */
```

### Return Value
```
double late_charge /* charge for non-payment of part
                      of previous balance       */
```

## Algorithm for comp_late_charge

1. if unpaid > 0
        assess late charge
   else
        assess no late charge

**pseudocode**
a combination of English
phrases and C constructs to
describe algorithm steps

The decision step above is expressed in **pseudocode,** which is a mixture of English and C used to describe algorithm steps. The indentation and reserved words `if` and `else` show the logical structure of each decision step. Each decision step has a condition (following `if`) which can be written in English or C; similarly, the true and false tasks can be written in English or C.

### ANALYSIS and DESIGN of display_bill

The `void` function `display_bill` displays the bill amount and the `late_charge` and unpaid balance if any. The values of `bill`, `late_charge`, and `unpaid` are passed to the function as input arguments; `display_bill` displays these values on the screen.

### Data Requirements for display_bill

**Input Parameters**
```
double late_charge    /* charge for non-payment of
                         part of previous balance     */
double bill           /* bill amount                  */
double unpaid         /* unpaid balance               */
```

### Algorithm for display_bill

1. if `late_charge > 0`
        display late charge and unpaid balance
2. Display the bill amount.

### IMPLEMENTATION

Follow the approach described in Section 3.1 to write the program (Fig. 4.7). Begin by writing `#define` directives for the problem constants. In the main function, declare all variables from the problem data requirements that appear in the structure chart. Next write each step of the initial algorithm as a comment in the main function body. To complete the main function, code each algorithm step in-line (as part of the main function code) or as a function call. For each function call, refer to the structure chart to determine the names of the input arguments and the variable receiving the function result.

Follow a similar approach to write each function subprogram (Fig. 4.7). Declare all identifiers listed in the function data requirements as either formal parameters or local variables, depending on how the identifier is used by the function. Make sure that the order of parameters in the function heading corresponds to the order of arguments in the function call. After you write each function heading, copy it into the function prototype area preceding function `main`.

**Figure 4.7    Program for Water-Bill Problem**

```
/*
 * Computes and prints a water bill given an unpaid balance and previous and
 * current meter readings. Bill includes a demand charge of $35.00, a use
 * charge of $1.10 per thousand gallons, and a surcharge of $2.00 if there is
 * an unpaid balance.
 */

#include <stdio.h>

#define DEMAND_CHG   35.00  /* basic water demand charge                    */
#define PER_1000_CHG 1.10   /* charge per thousand gallons used             */
#define LATE_CHG      2.00  /* surcharge assessed on unpaid balance         */

/* Function prototypes                                                       */
void instruct_water(void);

double comp_use_charge(int previous, int current);

double comp_late_charge(double unpaid);

void display_bill(double late_charge, double bill, double unpaid);

int
main(void)
{
        int     previous;   /* input - meter reading from previous quarter
                               in thousands of gallons                       */
        int     current;    /* input - meter reading from current quarter   */
        double unpaid;      /* input - unpaid balance of previous bill      */
        double bill;        /* output - water bill                          */
        int     used;       /* thousands of gallons used this quarter       */
        double use_charge;  /* charge for actual water use                  */
        double late_charge; /* charge for non-payment of part of previous
                               balance                                       */

        /* Display user instructions.                                       */
        instruct_water();

        /* Get data: unpaid balance, previous and current meter
           readings.                                                        */
```

*(continued)*

**Figure 4.7**   *(continued)*

```
        printf("Enter unpaid balance> $");
        scanf("%lf", &unpaid);
        printf("Enter previous meter reading> ");
        scanf("%d", &previous);
        printf("Enter current meter reading> ");
        scanf("%d", &current);

        /* Compute use charge.                                          */
        use_charge = comp_use_charge(previous, current);

        /* Determine applicable late charge                             */
        late_charge = comp_late_charge(unpaid);

        /* Figure bill.                                                 */
        bill = DEMAND_CHG + use_charge + unpaid + late_charge;

        /* Print bill.                                                  */
        display_bill(late_charge, bill, unpaid);
        return (0);
}


/*
 * Displays user instructions
 */
void
instruct_water(void)
{
        printf("This program figures a water bill ");
        printf("based on the demand charge\n");
        printf("($%.2f) and a $%.2f per 1000 ", DEMAND_CHG, PER_1000_CHG);
        printf("gallons use charge.\n\n");
        printf("A $%.2f surcharge is added to ", LATE_CHG);
        printf("accounts with an unpaid balance.\n");
        printf("\nEnter unpaid balance, previous ");
        printf("and current meter readings\n");
        printf("on separate lines after the prompts.\n");
        printf("Press <return> or <enter> after ");
        printf("typing each number.\n\n");
}
```

*(continued)*

**Figure 4.7**    *(continued)*

```
/*
 * Computes use charge
 * Pre: previous and current are defined.
 */
double
comp_use_charge(int previous, int current)
{
      int used;   /* gallons of water used (in thousands)          */
      double use_charge;   /* charge for actual water use          */


      used = current - previous;
      use_charge = used * PER_1000_CHG;


      return (use_charge);
}



/*
 * Computes late charge.
 * Pre : unpaid is defined.
 */
double
comp_late_charge(double unpaid)
{
      double late_charge; /* charge for non-payment of part of previous
                              balance                                  */


      if (unpaid > 0)
            late_charge = LATE_CHG; /* Assess late charge on unpaid balance. */
      else
            late_charge = 0.0;


      return (late_charge);
}
```

*(continued)*

**Figure 4.7**   *(continued)*

```
/*
 * Displays late charge if any and bill.
 * Pre : late_charge, bill, and unpaid are defined.
 */
void
display_bill(double late_charge, double bill, double unpaid)
{
      if (late_charge > 0.0) {
            printf("\nBill includes $%.2f late charge", late_charge);
            printf(" on unpaid balance of $%.2f\n", unpaid);
      }
      printf("\nTotal due = $%.2f\n", bill);
}
```

▬▬◗ **TESTING** ◖▬▬

To test this program, run it with data sets that cause each branch of the two deci-sion steps to execute. For example, one data set should have a positive unpaid balance, and another should have an unpaid balance of zero. Figure 4.8 shows a sample run.

**Figure 4.8   Sample Run of Water-Bill Program**

```
This program figures a water bill based on the demand charge
($35.00) and a $1.10 per 1000 gallons use charge.

A $2.00 surcharge is added to accounts with an unpaid balance.

Enter unpaid balance, previous and current meter readings
on separate lines after the prompts.
Press <return> or <enter> after typing each number.

Enter unpaid balance> $71.50
Enter previous meter reading> 4198
Enter current meter reading> 4238

Bill includes $2.00 late charge on unpaid balance of $71.50

Total due = $152.50
```

## Program Style    *Consistent Use of Names in Functions*

Notice that we use the same identifier, `late_charge`, to refer to the customer's late charge in the main function and in two function subprograms. We declare `late_charge` as a local variable in functions `main` and `comp_late_charge` and as a formal parameter in function `display_bill`. Although C does not require that we use the same name for the customer's late charge in all three functions, it is perfectly permissible to do so. Using the same name avoids the confusion that would result from using different names to reference the same information.

## Program Style    *Cohesive Functions*

**cohesive function**
a function that performs a single operation

Function `comp_late_charge` only computes the late charge—it does not display it. That task is left to function `display_bill`. Functions that perform a single operation are called **cohesive functions.** Writing cohesive functions is good programming style, because cohesive functions are easier to read, write, debug, and maintain, and are more likely to be reusable.

## Program Style    *Using Constant Macros to Enhance Readability and Ease Maintenance*

The function subprograms in Fig. 4.7 reference the constant macros `DEMAND_CHG`, `PER_1000_CHG`, and `LATE_CHG`. It is perfectly permissible to reference such names in any function body that appears in the same source file as the constant macro definitions.

We could just as easily have placed the values that these names represent (`35.00`, `1.10`, and `2.00`) directly in the statements where they are needed. The resulting statements would be

```
printf("This program figures a water bill ");
printf("based on the demand charge\n");
printf("($%.2f) and a $%.2f per 1000 ";,
       35.00, 1.10);
printf("gallons use charge.\n\n");
printf("A $%.2f surcharge is added to ", 2.00);
printf("accounts with an unpaid balance.\n");
use_charge = used * 1.10;
late_charge = 2.00; /* Assess late charge on unpaid
                       balance. */
bill = 35.00 + use_charge + unpaid + late_charge;
```

However, use of constant macro names rather than actual values has two advantages. First, the original statements are easier to understand because they use the descriptive names `DEMAND_CHG`, `PER_1000_CHG`, and `LATE_CHG` rather than numbers, which have no intrinsic meaning. Second, a program written using constant macros is much easier to maintain than one written with constant values. For example, if we want to use different constant values in the water bill program in Fig. 4.7, we need to change only the constant macro definitions. However, if we inserted constant values directly in the statements, we would need to change any statements that manipulate the constant values.

Self-Check

1. Change the algorithm for function `comp_use_charge` assuming the fee is doubled for any gallons used in excess of 100,000. The basic fee is assessed for the first 100,000 gallons used.
2. Revise the flat-washer problem from Section 3.1 so that the user can compute the weight of a batch of circular or square washers. Give the algorithm with refinements. Draw a structure chart with data flow information for the new problem showing the relationship between the main program and its subproblems. Assume that the user can specify whether the washer type is circular or square.

Programming

1. Write function `comp_use_charge` described in Self-Check Exercise 1.

## 4.6 MORE PROBLEM SOLVING

### Data Flow Information in Structure Charts

In Fig. 4.6 the data flow information in the structure chart showed the inputs and outputs of each individual algorithm step. Data flow information is an important part of system documentation because it shows what program variables are processed by each step and the manner in which those variables are processed. If a step gives a new value to a variable, then the variable is considered an *output of the step*. If a step displays a variable's value or uses a variable in a computation without changing its value, the variable is considered an *input to the step*.

Figure 4.7 shows that a variable may have different roles for different subproblems in the algorithm. In the context of the original problem statement, `previous` and `current` are problem *inputs* (data supplied by the program user). However, in the context of the subproblem "Get data," the subproblem's task is to deliver values for `previous` and `current` to the main program; thus, `previous` and `current` are considered *outputs* from this step. In the context of the subproblem "Compute use charge," the subproblem's task is to use `previous` and `current` to compute `use_charge`, so they are *inputs* to this step. In the same way, the role of the other variables changes as we go from step to step in the problem.

## Modifying a Program with Function Subprograms

Often what appears to be a new problem will turn out to be a variation of one that you already solved. Consequently, an important skill in problem solving is the ability to recognize that one problem is similar to another solved earlier. As you progress through this course, you will start to build up your own personal library of programs and functions. Whenever possible, you should try to adapt or reuse parts of successful programs.

Writing programs that can be easily changed or modified to fit other situations is advisable; programmers and program users will often want to make slight improvements to a program after they use it. If the original program is well designed and modular, the programmer will be able to accommodate changing specifications with a minimum of effort. As you will find by working through the next problem, when changes are needed it may be possible to modify one or two functions rather than rewriting the entire program.

## Case Study: Water Bill with Conservation Requirements

**PROBLEM**

We need to modify the water-bill program so that customers who fail to meet conservation requirements are charged for all their water use at twice the rate of customers who meet the guidelines. Residents of this water district are required to use no more than 95% of the amount of water they used in the same quarter last year in order to qualify for the lower use rate of $1.10 per thousand gallons.

**ANALYSIS**

This problem is a modification of the water bill problem solved in the last section. Customers who meet the conservation guidelines should be charged the basic use rate of $1.10 per thousand gallons; those who do not should be charged at twice this rate. We can solve this problem by adding the use figure from last year to our problem inputs and modifying function `comp_use_charge`. The additions to the data requirements and revised algorithm for function `comp_use_charge` follow.

### Additions to Data Requirements

#### Problem Constants

```
OVERUSE_CHG_RATE 2.0    / * double use charge as non-
                              conservation penalty        */

CONSERV_RATE 95         /* percent of last year's use
                              allowed this year            */
```

#### Problem Inputs

```
int use_last_year       /* use for same quarter
                              last year                    */
```

### Algorithm for comp_use_charge

1. used is current - previous
2. if guidelines are met
        use_charge is used * PER_1000_CHARGE
   else
        notify customer of overuse
        use_charge is used * overuse_chg_rate *
            PER_1000_CHG

Figure 4.9 shows the revised function. If the condition

(used <= CONSERV_RATE / 100.0 * use_last_year)

is true, the conservation guidelines are met and the use charge is computed as before; otherwise, the customer is notified of the overuse, and the overuse charge rate is factored into the computation of the use charge.

### Figure 4.9    Function comp_use_charge Revised

```
/*
 * Computes use charge with conservation requirements
 * Pre: previous, current, and use_last_year are defined.
 */
double
comp_use_charge(int previous, int current, int use_last_year)
{
      int used;  /* gallons of water used (in thousands)       */
      double use_charge;  /* charge for actual water use        */
```

*(continued)*

**Figure 4.9**   *(continued)*

```
used = current - previous;
if (used <= CONSERV_RATE / 100.0 * use_last_year) {
        /* conservation guidelines met */
        use_charge = used * PER_1000_CHG;
} else {
        printf("Use charge is at %.2f times ", OVERUSE_CHG_RATE);
        printf("normal rate since use of\n");
        printf("%d units exceeds %d percent ", used, CONSERV_RATE);
        printf("of last year's %d-unit use.\n", use_last_year);
        use_charge = used * OVERUSE_CHG_RATE * PER_1000_CHG;
}

return (use_charge);
}
```

We must change the prototype for function `comp_use_charge` to match its heading and replace the call to function `comp_use_charge` in Fig. 4.7 with

```
use_charge = comp_use_charge(previous, current,
                             use_last_year);
```

To complete the program revision, change function `instruct_water` to display the new user instructions. Also, modify the main function to prompt for and get the value of `use_last_year`.

**EXERCISES FOR SECTION 4.6**

**Programming**

1. Provide the complete program for the water-bill problem with conservation requirements.

# 4.7  NESTED if STATEMENTS AND MULTIPLE-ALTERNATIVE DECISIONS

**nested if statement**
an if statement with another
if statement as its true task or
its false task

Until now we have used `if` statements to code decisions with one or two alternatives. In this section we use **nested if statements** (one `if` statement inside another) to code decisions with multiple alternatives.

**EXAMPLE 4.15** ▸

The following nested `if` statement has three alternatives. It increases one of three variables (`num_pos`, `num_neg`, or `num_zero`) by 1, depending on whether x is greater than zero, less than zero, or equal to zero, respectively. The boxes show the logical structure of the nested `if` statement: the second `if` statement is the false task (following `else`) of the first `if` statement.

```
/* increment num_pos, num_neg, or num_zero depending on x */

if (x > 0)
      num_pos = num_pos + 1;
else
      if (x < 0)
            num_neg = num_neg + 1;
      else /* x equals 0 */
            num_zero = num_zero + 1;
```

The execution of the nested `if` statement proceeds as follows: the first condition (x > 0) is tested; if it is true, `num_pos` is incremented and the rest of the `if` statement is skipped. If the first condition is false, the second condition (x < 0) is tested; if it is true, `num_neg` is incremented; otherwise, `num_zero` is incremented. It is important to realize that the second condition is tested *only* when the first condition is false. ◂

Table 4.10 traces the execution of this statement when x is −7. Because x > 0 is false, the second condition (x < 0) is tested.

## Comparison of Nested if and Sequence of ifs

Beginning programmers sometimes prefer to use a sequence of `if` statements rather than a single nested `if` statement. For example, the nested `if` statement in Example 4.15 is rewritten as a sequence of `if` statements.

**Table 4.10    Trace of if Statement in Example 4.15 for x = -7**

| Statement Part | Effect |
| --- | --- |
| `if (x > 0)` | −7 > 0 is false. |
| `if (x < 0)` | −7 < 0 is true. |
| `num_neg = num_neg + 1` | Add 1 to num_neg. |

```
if (x > 0)
    num_pos = num_pos + 1;
if (x < 0)
    num_neg = num_neg + 1;
if (x == 0)
    num_zero = num_zero + 1;
```

Although this sequence is logically equivalent to the original, it is neither as readable nor as efficient. Unlike the nested if statement, the sequence does not clearly show that exactly one of the three assignment statements is executed for a particular x. It is less efficient because all three of the conditions are always tested. In the nested if statement, only the first condition is tested when x is positive.

## Multiple-Alternative Decision Form of Nested if

Nested if statements can become quite complex. If there are more than three alternatives and indentation is not consistent, it may be difficult for you to determine the logical structure of the if statement. In situations like Example 4.15 in which each false task (except possibly the last) is followed by an if-then-else statement, you can code the nested if as the *multiple-alternative decision* described next.

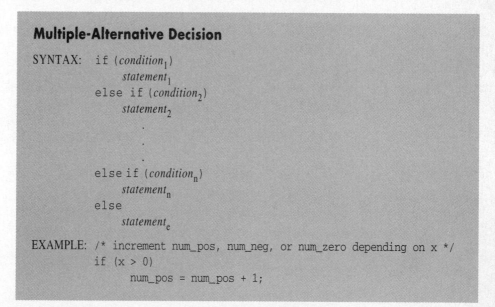

**Multiple-Alternative Decision**

SYNTAX:   if ($condition_1$)
               $statement_1$
          else if ($condition_2$)
               $statement_2$
                 .
                 .
                 .
          else if ($condition_n$)
               $statement_n$
          else
               $statement_e$

EXAMPLE: /* increment num_pos, num_neg, or num_zero depending on x */
         if (x > 0)
             num_pos = num_pos + 1;

*(continued)*

```
            else if (x < 0)
                num_neg = num_neg + 1;
            else /* x equals 0 */
                num_zero = num_zero + 1;
```

INTERPRETATION: The conditions in a multiple-alternative decision are evaluated in sequence until a true condition is reached. If a condition is true, the statement following it is executed, and the rest of the multiple-alternative decision is skipped. If a condition is false, the statement following it is skipped, and the next condition is tested. If all conditions are false, then *statement*$_e$ following the final `else` is executed.

*Notes:* In a multiple-alternative decision, the words `else` and `if` the next condition appear on the same line. All the words `else` align, and each dependent statement is indented under the condition that controls its execution.

**EXAMPLE 4.16**

Suppose you want to associate noise loudness measured in decibels with the effect of the noise. The following table shows the relationship between noise levels and human perceptions of noises.

| Loudness in Decibels (db) | Perception |
| --- | --- |
| 50 or lower | quiet |
| 51 – 70 | intrusive |
| 71 – 90 | annoying |
| 91 – 110 | very annoying |
| above 110 | uncomfortable |

The multiple-alternative decision in the following displays the perception of noise according to this table. If the noise were measured at 62 decibels, the last three conditions would be true if evaluated; however, the perception `62-decibel noise is intrusive.` would be displayed because the first true condition is `noise_db <= 70`.

```
/* Display perception of noise loudness */

if (noise_db <= 50)
    printf("%d-decibel noise is quiet.\n", noise_db);
else if (noise_db <= 70)
    printf("%d-decibel noise is intrusive.\n", noise_db);
```

```
else if (noise_db <= 90)
      printf("%d-decibel noise is annoying.\n", noise_db);
else if (noise_db <= 110)
      printf("%d-decibel noise is very annoying.\n",
            noise_db);
else
      printf("%d-decibel noise is uncomfortable.\n",
            noise_db);
```

## Order of Conditions in a Multiple-Alternative Decision

When more than one condition in a multiple alternative decision is true, only the task following the first true condition executes. Therefore, the order of the conditions can affect the outcome.

Writing the decision as follows would be incorrect. All but the loudest sounds (above 110 db) would be incorrectly categorized as "very annoying" because the first condition would be true and the rest would be skipped.

```
/* incorrect perception of noise loudness */

if (noise_db <= 110)
      printf("%d-decibel noise is very annoying.\n",
            noise_db);
else if (noise_db <= 90)
      printf("%d-decibel noise is annoying.\n",
            noise_db);
else if (noise_db <= 70)
      printf("%d-decibel noise is intrusive.\n",
            noise_db);
else if (noise_db <= 50)
      printf("%d-decibel noise is quiet.\n",
            noise_db);
else
      printf("%d-decibel noise is uncomfortable.\n",
            noise_db);
```

The order of conditions can also have an effect on program efficiency. If we know that loud noises are much more likely than soft ones, it would be more efficient to test first for noise levels above 110 db, next for levels between 91 and 110 db, and so on.

**EXAMPLE 4.17**  You could use a multiple-alternative `if` statement to implement a *decision table* that describes several alternatives. For instance, let's say you are an accountant setting up a payroll system based on Table 4.11 which shows five different ranges for salaries up to $150,000.00. Each table line shows the base tax amount (column 2) and tax percentage (column 3) for a particular salary range (column 1). Given a person's salary, you can calculate the tax due by adding the base tax to the product of the percentage times the excess salary over the minimum salary for that range.

For example, the second line of the table specifies that the tax due on a salary of $20,000.00 is $2,250.00 plus 18% of the excess salary over $15,000.00 (that is, 18% of $5000.00, or $900.00). Therefore, the total tax due is $2,250.00 plus $900.00, or $3,150.00.

The `if` statement in function `comp_tax` (Fig. 4.10) implements the tax table. If the value of `salary` is within the table range (0.00 to 150,000.00), exactly one of the statements assigning a value to `tax` will execute. Table 4.12 shows a trace of the `if` statement when `salary` is $25,000.00. You can see that the value assigned to `tax`, $4,050.00, is correct. ◄

**Table 4.11   Decision Table for Example 4.17**

| Salary Range ($) | Base Tax ($) | Percentage of Excess |
|---|---|---|
| 0.00– 14,999.99 | 0.00 | 15 |
| 15,000.00– 29,999.99 | 2,250.00 | 18 |
| 30,000.00– 49,999.99 | 5,400.00 | 22 |
| 50,000.00– 79,999.99 | 11,000.00 | 27 |
| 80,000.00–150,000.00 | 21,600.00 | 33 |

**Figure 4.10   Function comp_tax**

```
/*
 * Computes the tax due based on a tax table.
 * Pre : salary is defined.
 * Post: Returns the tax due for 0.0 <= salary <= 150,000.00;
 *       returns -1.0 if salary is outside the table range.
 */
double
comp_tax(double salary)
```

*(continued)*

**Figure 4.10**    *(continued)*

```
{
   if (salary < 0.0)
       tax = -1.0;
   else if (salary < 15000.00)                    /* first range      */
       tax = 0.15 * salary;
   else if (salary < 30000.00)                    /* second range     */
       tax = (salary - 15000.00) * 0.18 + 2250.00;
   else if (salary < 50000.00)                    /* third range      */
       tax = (salary - 30000.00) * 0.22 + 5400.00;
   else if (salary < 80000.00)                    /* fourth range     */
       tax = (salary - 50000.00) * 0.27 + 11000.00;
   else if (salary <= 150000.00)                  /* fifth range      */
       tax = (salary - 80000.00) * 0.33 + 21600.00;
   else
       tax = -1.0;

   return (tax);
}
```

**Table 4.12    Trace of if Statement in Fig. 4.10 for salary = $25000.00**

| Statement Part | salary | tax | Effect |
|---|---|---|---|
| | 25000.00 | ? | |
| if (salary < 0.0) | | | 25000.0 < 0.0 is false. |
| else if (salary < 15000.00) | | | 25000.0 < 15000.0 is false. |
| else if (salary < 30000.00) | | | 25000.0 < 30000.0 is true. |
| tax = (salary - 15000.00) | | | Evaluates to 10000.00. |
|          * 0.18 | | | Evaluates to 1800.00. |
|          + 2250.00; | | 4050.00 | Evaluates to 4050.00. |

## Program Style    *Validating the Value of Variables*

If you validate the value of a variable before using it in a computation, you can avoid processing invalid or meaningless data. Instead of computing an incorrect tax amount, function `comp_tax` returns `-1.0` (an impossible tax amount) if the value of `salary` is outside the range covered by the table (0.0 to 150,000.00). The first condition sets `tax` to `-1.0` if `salary` is negative. All conditions evaluate to false if `salary` is greater than 150,000.00, so the task following `else` also sets `tax` to `-1.0`. The function calling `comp_tax` should display an error message if the value returned to it is `-1.0`.

## Nested if Statements with More Than One Variable

In most of our examples, we have used nested `if` statements to test the value of a single variable; consequently, we have been able to write each nested `if` statement as a multiple-alternative decision. If several variables are involved in the decision, we cannot always use a multiple-alternative decision. Example 4.18 contains a situation in which we can use a nested `if` statement as a "filter" to select data that satisfy several different criteria.

 **EXAMPLE 4.18**

The Department of Defense would like a program that identifies single males between the ages of 18 and 26, inclusive. One way to do this is to use a nested `if` statement whose conditions test the next criterion only if all previous criteria tested were satisfied. In the following nested `if` statement, assume that all variables have values. The call to `printf` executes only when all conditions are true.

```
/* Print a message if all criteria are met. */
if (marital_status == 'S')
    if (gender == 'M')
        if (age >= 18  &&  age <= 26)
            printf("All criteria are met.\n");
```

An equivalent statement that uses a single `if` with a compound condition follows.

```
if (marital_status == 'S'  &&  gender == 'M'
    && age >= 18  &&  age <= 26)
        printf("All criteria are met.\n");
```

**EXAMPLE 4.19**  You are developing a program to control the warning signs at the exits of major tunnels. If roads are slick (road_status is 'S'), you want to advise drivers that stopping times are doubled or quadrupled, depending on whether the roads are wet or icy. Your program will also have access to the current temperature in degrees Celsius (temp), so a check as to whether the temperature is above or below freezing would allow you to choose the correct message. The nested if statement below summarizes the decision process you should follow; the flowchart in Fig. 4.11 diagrams the process.

```
if (road_status == 'S')
        if (temp > 0) {
                printf("Wet roads ahead\n");
                printf("Stopping time doubled\n");
        } else {
                printf("Icy roads ahead\n");
                printf("Stopping time quadrupled\n");
        }
else
        printf("Drive carefully!\n");
```

To verify that the nested if statement in Example 4.19 is correct, we trace its execution for all possible combinations of road-status values and temperatures.

**Figure 4.11
Flowchart of
Road Sign
Decision
Process**

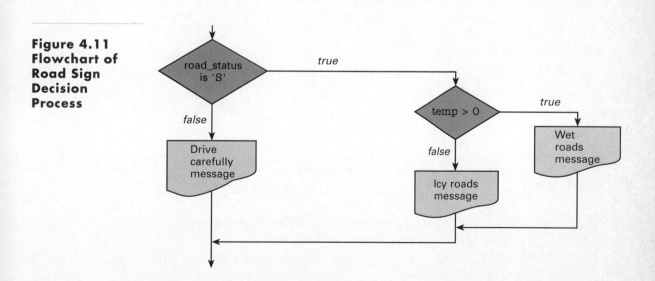

The flowchart's rightmost output is executed only when both conditions are true. The leftmost output is always executed when the condition involving `road_status` is false. The output in the middle occurs when the condition involving `road_status` is true, but the condition involving `temp` is false.

When you are writing a nested `if` statement, you should know that C associates an `else` with the most recent incomplete `if`. For example, if the first `else` of the road-sign decision were omitted, the following would be left:

```
/* incorrect interpretation of nested if */
if (road_status == 'S')
     if (temp > 0) {
          printf("Wet roads ahead\n");
          printf("Stopping time doubled\n");
     }
else
     printf("Drive carefully!\n");
```

Although the indentation would lead you to believe that the `else` remains the false branch of the first `if`, the C compiler actually sees it as the false branch of the second `if`. Indentation like this would match the actual meaning of the statement.

```
/* correct interpretation of nested if */

if (road_status == 'S')
      if (temp > 0) {
           printf("Wet roads ahead\n");
           printf("Stopping time doubled\n");
      } else
           printf("Drive carefully!\n");
```

To force the `else` to be the false branch of the first `if`, we place braces around the true task of this first decision.

```
/* interpretation with braces around first true task */

if (road_status == 'S') {
      if (temp > 0) {
           printf("Wet roads ahead\n");
           printf("Stopping time doubled\n");
      }
} else
      printf("Drive carefully!\n");
```

Note that we could not use a multiple-alternative decision statement to implement the flowchart in Fig. 4.11 because the second decision (temp > 0) falls on the true branch of the first decision. However, if we were to change the initial condition so the branches were switched, a multiple-alternative structure would work. We could do this simply by checking if the road is dry.

```
if (road_status == 'D') {
    printf("Drive carefully!\n");
} else if (temp > 0) {
    printf("Wet roads ahead\n");
    printf("Stopping time doubled\n");
} else {
    printf("Icy roads ahead\n");
    printf("Stopping time quadrupled\n");
}
```

The first condition is true only if the road is dry. The second condition is tested only when the first condition fails, so its dependent statement executes only when the road is not dry and the temperature is above freezing. Finally, the else clause executes only when the two conditions fail; then we know that the roads are not dry and the temperature is not above freezing.

**EXERCISES FOR SECTION 4.7**

Self-Check

1. Trace the execution of the nested if statement in Fig. 4.10 for a salary of $23,500.00.
2. What would be the effect of reversing the order of the first two conditions in the if statement in Fig. 4.10?
3. Write a nested if statement for the decision diagrammed in the accompanying flowchart. Use a multiple-alternative if for intermediate decisions where possible.

Programming

1. Rewrite the if statement for Example 4.16 using only the relational operator > in all conditions.
2. Implement the following decision table using a nested if statement. Assume that the grade point average is within the range 0.0 through 4.0.

| Grade Point Average | Transcript Message |
| --- | --- |
| 0.0 – 0.99 | Failed semester—registration suspended |
| 1.0 – 1.99 | On probation for next semester |
| 2.0 – 2.99 | (no message) |
| 3.0 – 3.49 | Dean's list for semester |
| 3.5 – 4.00 | Highest honors for semester |

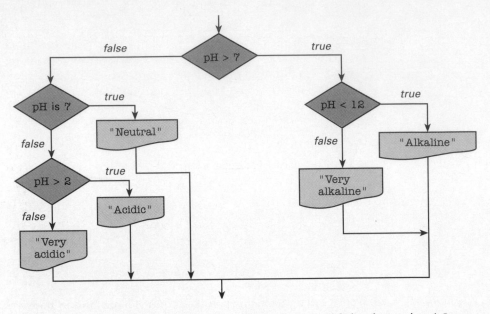

3. Implement the following decision table using a multiple-alternative if state-ment. Assume that the wind speed is given as an integer.

| Wind Speed (mph) | Category |
|---|---|
| below 25 | not a strong wind |
| 25 – 38 | strong wind |
| 39 – 54 | gale |
| 55 – 72 | whole gale |
| above 72 | hurricane |

4. The Air Force has asked you to write a program to label supersonic aircraft as military or civilian. Your program is to be given the plane's observed speed in km/h and its estimated length in meters. For planes traveling in excess of 1100 km/h, you will label those longer than 52 meters "civilian" and shorter aircraft as "military." For planes traveling at slower speeds, you will issue an "aircraft type unknown" message.

## 4.8 THE switch STATEMENT

*won't do strings*
*won't do comparison of ranges*
*strictly GO/NOGO*

The switch statement may also be used in C to select one of several alterna-tives. The switch statement is especially useful when the selection is based on the value of a single variable or of a simple expression (called the *controlling expression*). The value of this expression may be of type int or char, but not of type double.

**EXAMPLE 4.20**  The switch statement in Fig. 4.12 is one way of implementing the following decision table.

| Class ID | Ship Class |
| --- | --- |
| B or b | Battleship |
| C or c | Cruiser |
| D or d | Destroyer |
| F or f | Frigate |

The message displayed by the switch statement depends on the value of the controlling expression, that is, the value of the variable class (type char). First, this expression is evaluated; then, the list of case labels (case 'B':,

**Figure 4.12   Example of a switch Statement with Type char Case Labels**

```
switch (class) {
case 'B':
case 'b':
        printf("Battleship\n");
        break;

case 'C':
case 'c':
        printf("Cruiser\n");
        break;

case 'D':
case 'd':
        printf("Destroyer\n");
        break;

case 'F':
case 'f':
        printf("Frigate\n");
        break;          ← To stop evaluation
default:
        printf("Unknown ship class %c\n", class);
}
```

case `'b':`, case `'C':`, etc.) is searched until one label that matches the value of the controlling expression is found. Statements following the matching case label are executed until a break statement is encountered. The break causes an exit from the switch statement, and execution continues with the statement that follows the closing brace of the switch statement body. If no case label matches the value of the switch statement's controlling expression, the statements following the default label are executed, if there is a default label. If not, the entire switch statement body is skipped.  ⬅

Using a string such as "Cruiser" or "Frigate" as a case label is a common error. It is important to remember that type int and char values may be used as case labels, but strings and type double values cannot be used. Another common error is the omission of the break statement at the end of one alternative. In such a situation, execution "falls through" into the next alternative. We use a blank line after each break statement to emphasize the fact that there is no "fall-through."

Forgetting the closing brace of the switch statement body is also easy to do. If the brace is missing and the switch has a default label, the statements following the switch statement become part of the default case.

The following syntax display shows the form of the switch statement as a multiple-alternative decision structure.

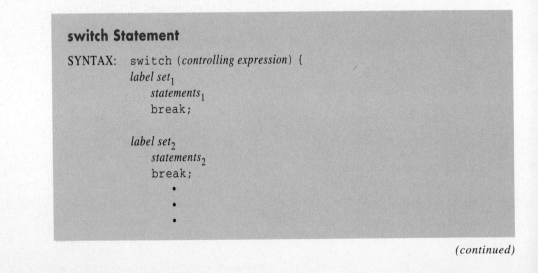

**switch Statement**

SYNTAX:    switch (*controlling expression*) {
      *label set*₁
        *statements*₁
      break;

      *label set*₂
        *statements*₂
      break;
        •
        •
        •

*(continued)*

```
            label set_n
                statements_n
                break;


        default:
            statements_d
        }
```

EXAMPLE: /* Determine life expectancy of a standard light
          bulb */
```
switch (watts) {
case 25:
        life = 2500;
        break;

case 40:
case 60:
        life = 1000;
        break;

case 75:
case 100:
        life = 750;
        break;

default:
        life = 0;
}
```

INTERPRETATION: The *controlling expression,* an expression with a value of type int or type char, is evaluated and compared to each of the case labels in the *label sets* until a match is found. A *label set* is made of one or more labels of the form case followed by a constant value and a colon. When a match between the value of the *controlling expression* and a case label value is found, the statements following the case label are executed until a break statement is encountered. Then the rest of the switch statement is skipped.

*Notes:* The *statements* following a case label may be one or more C statements, so you do not need to make multiple statements into a single compound statement using braces. If no case label value matches the controlling expression, the entire switch statement body is skipped unless it contains a default label. If so, the statements following the default label are executed when no other case label value matches the *controlling expression.*

## Comparison of Nested if Statements and the switch Statement

You can use a nested if statement, which is more general than the switch statement, to implement any multiple-alternative decision. The switch as described in the syntax display is more readable in many contexts, and should be used whenever practical. Case labels that contain type double values or strings are not permitted.

You should use the switch statement when each label set contains a reasonable number of case labels (a maximum of ten). However, if the number of values is large, use a nested if statement. You should include a default label in switch statements wherever possible. The discipline of trying to define a default will help you to consider what will happen if the value of your switch statement's controlling expression falls outside your set of case label values.

# C IN FOCUS

## UNIX

## THE SHARING OS

Accessing the Internet has introduced the UNIX operating system to a whole new generation of users. Because a large number of public access Internet sites run UNIX, you need at least a rudimentary knowledge of UNIX to use them.

How did UNIX come to be used by so many Internet hosts? The answer lies in its development history. Until the late 1960s, only large organizations had computers. These were large monolithic systems such as IBM's OS/360. These large systems were remote from individuals, and cared for and fed by professional programmers. The next generation of computers, minicomputers, introduced the concept of time-sharing. Time-sharing systems made it possible for users to connect to and use a computer interactively via terminals. This interactive computer usage, pioneered by operating systems such as UNIX, made computers far more accessible.

When Ken Thompson and Dennis Ritchie built the first UNIX system back in 1969, they weren't driven by sophisticated market research. They liked the interactive feel of the Multics system then being developed at MIT (as a joint project of MIT, General Electric, and Bell Laboratories) and had some ideas of their own that they wanted to try out.

As the UNIX developers worked to realize their ideas for the system, they created the C programming language in order to implement them. When Ritchie and Thompson rewrote the UNIX kernel, the heart of the operating system, in 1973, they used the C language to do it. Ever since then the UNIX system calls, which programs use to request services from the kernel, have been defined as C functions.

Self-Check

1. What will be printed by this carelessly constructed `switch` statement if the value of `color` is `'R'`?

```
switch (color) { /* break statements missing */
case 'R':
      printf("red\n");
case 'B':
      printf("blue\n");
case 'Y':
      printf("yellow\n");
}
```

2. Why can't we rewrite our multiple-alternative `if` statement code from Examples 4.16 and 4.17 using `switch` statements?

These system calls made it very natural to write application programs in C, and later in C++, and many UNIX user programs also follow C's syntactic conventions.

UNIX really began to spread in 1974 when Bell Labs licensed it to universities for educational purposes. Time-sharing was ideally suited to these institutions and was rapidly accepted. Another major milestone was Bell Lab's Seventh Edition of UNIX, released in 1976, which was the first release to have portability as a major goal. UNIX wasn't the first interactive system, but it was the first one that worked well and was easy to move to new computers.

UNIX's link to the Internet was predestined by its university base, but cemented by the development of the BSD (Berkeley Software Distribution) UNIX systems. Starting in 1979, BSD UNIX added networking capability using the TCP/IP protocol. This protocol is now standard for the Internet. In addition, a number of critical programs for accessing the Internet were developed at Berkeley. For example, the ftp program (file transfer protocol) for retrieving files from remote sites and the telnet program for logging into remote sites are UNIX programs that have become more or less standard even for other operating systems.

Although UNIX goes with C and the Internet, C and the Internet do not necessarily go with UNIX anymore. C and C++ have become the standard implementation languages for many different computer systems, notably Microsoft Windows and OS/2, and more Internet sites have front ends that eliminate the need to know UNIX commands. Nevertheless, UNIX continues to expand its user population.

Linux is a recent version of UNIX now available for personal computers. Until very recently there was still a major gap between the UNIX vision and the personal computer vision. Under UNIX, a computer system is shared; on a personal computer it is not. As sharing and connectivity become more important to personal computer users, UNIX's networking capabilities may position it for another generation of users. Many thanks to Paul Abrahams, a consulting computer scientist and a past president of the Association for Computing Machinery, for contributing his UNIX insights to this article. He runs Linux on his Pentium 90 computer and purchased the Linux CD-ROM for just $20. Linux is available at a number of ftp sites over the Internet, notably tsx-11.mit.edu, directory /pub/linux.

Programming

1. Write a `switch` statement that assigns to the variable `lumens` the expected brightness of a standard light bulb whose wattage has been stored in `watts`. Use this table:

| Watts | Brightness (in Lumens) |
|-------|------------------------|
| 15    | 125                    |
| 25    | 215                    |
| 40    | 500                    |
| 60    | 880                    |
| 75    | 1000                   |
| 100   | 1675                   |

Assign `-1` to `lumens` if the value of `watts` is not in the table.

2. Write a nested `if` statement equivalent to the `switch` statement described in the first programming exercise.

## 4.9 COMMON PROGRAMMING ERRORS

The fact that C relational and equality operators give a result of 1 for true and 0 for false means that C interprets some common mathematical expressions in a way that seems surprising at first. You would probably not anticipate the fact that the following `if` statement displays `Condition is true` for all non-negative values of x.

```
if (0 <= x <= 4)
      printf("Condition is true\n");
```

For example, let's consider the case when x is 5. The value of 0 <= 5 is 1, and 1 is certainly less than or equal to 4! In order to check if x is in the range 0 to 4, you should use the condition

```
(0 <= x  &&  x <= 4)
```

Remember that the C equality operator is ==. If you slip up and use =, the mathematical equal sign, the compiler can detect this error only if the first operand is not a variable. Otherwise, your code will simply produce incorrect results. For example, the code fragment that follows always prints x is 10, regardless of the value of x.

```
if (x = 10)
    printf("x is 10");
```

The assignment operator stores the value 10 in x. The value of an assignment expression is the value assigned, so in this case the value of the if condition of the statement is 10. Since 10 is nonzero, C views it as meaning true and executes the true task.

Don't forget to parenthesize the condition of an if statement and to enclose in braces a single-alternative if used as a true task within a double-alternative if. The braces will force the else to be associated with the correct if. Also enclose in braces a compound statement used as a true task or false task. If the braces are missing, only the first statement will be considered part of the task. This can lead to a syntax error if the braces are omitted from the true task of a double-alternative if. Leaving out the braces on the false task of a double-alternative if or on the true task of a single-alternative if will not usually generate a syntax error; the omission will simply lead to incorrect results. In the example that follows, the braces around the true task are missing. The compiler assumes that the semicolon at the end of the assignment statement terminates the if statement.

```
if (x > 0)
      sum = sum + x;
      printf("Greater than zero\n");
else
      printf("Less than zero\n");
```

The compiler may generate an unexpected symbol syntax error when it reaches the reserved word else.

When writing a nested if statement, try to select the conditions so that you can use the multiple-alternative format shown in Section 4.7. When possible, the logic should be constructed so each intermediate condition falls on the false branch of the previous decision. If more than one condition may be true at the same time, place the most restrictive condition first.

Remember that the C compiler matches each else with the closest unmatched if. If you are not careful, you may get a pairing that is different from what you expect. This may not cause a syntax error, but it will affect the outcome.

In switch statements, make sure the controlling expression and case labels are of the same permitted type (int or char but not double). Remember to include a default case; otherwise the entire body of the switch statement will be skipped if the controlling expression value is not listed in any of the case labels.

Don't forget that the body of the switch statement is a single compound statement, enclosed in one set of braces. However, the statements of each alternative within the switch are not enclosed in braces; instead, each alternative is ended by a break statement. If you omit a break statement, your program "falls through" and executes the statements for the next case.

## CHAPTER REVIEW

1. Use control structures to control the flow of statement execution in a program. The compound statement is a control structure for sequential execution.
2. Use selection control structures to represent decisions in an algorithm and use pseudocode to write them in algorithms. Use the if statement or switch statement to code decision steps in C.
3. Expressions whose values indicate whether certain conditions are true can be written

   - using the relational operators (<, <=, >, >=) and equality operators ( ==, ! =) to compare variables and constants
   - using the logical operators (&& (and), || (or), ! (not)) to form more complex conditions

4. Data flow information in a structure chart indicates whether a variable processed by a subproblem is used as an input or an output, or as both. An input provides data that are manipulated by the subproblem, and an output returns a value copied from an input device or computed by the subproblem. The same variable may be an input to one subproblem and an output from another.
5. Extending a solution is a problem-solving technique in which you solve a new problem by modifying the solution to an existing problem. Writing modular programs (with function subprograms) makes it easier to apply this technique.
6. A hand trace of an algorithm verifies whether it is correct. You can discover errors in logic by carefully hand tracing an algorithm. Hand tracing an algorithm before coding it as a program will save you time in the long run.
7. Nested if statements are common in C and are used to represent decisions with multiple alternatives. Programmers use indentation and the multiple-alternative decision form when applicable to enhance readability of nested if statements.
8. The switch statement implements decisions with several alternatives, where the alternative selected depends on the value of a variable or expression (the *controlling expression*). The controlling expression can be type int or char, but not type double.

## New C Constructs

| Construct | Effect |
|---|---|

### if Statement

*One Alternative*
```
if (x != 0.0)
    product = product * x;
```
Multiplies `product` by `x` only if `x` is nonzero.

*Double-Alternative*
```
if (temp > 32.0)
    printf("%.1f: above freezing",
           temp);
else
    printf("%.1f: freezing", temp);
```
If `temp` is greater than `32.0`, it is labeled as `above freezing`; otherwise, it is labeled as `freezing`.

*Multiple-Alternative*
```
if (x < 0.0) {
    printf("negative");
    absx = -x;
} else if (x == 0.0) {
    printf("zero");
    absx = 0.0;
} else {
    printf("positive");
    absx = x;
}
```
Displays one of three messages depending on whether `x` is negative, positive, or zero. Sets `absx` to represent the absolute value or magnitude of `x`.

### switch Statement

```
switch (next_ch) {
case 'A':
case 'a':
    printf("Excellent");
    break;

case 'B':
case 'b':
    printf("Good");
    break;

case 'C':
case 'c':
    printf("O.K.");
    break;
```
Displays one of five messages based on the value of `next_ch` (type char). If `next_ch` is `'D'`,`'d'`, or `'F'`, `'f'`, the student is put on probation. If `next_ch` is not listed in the case labels, displays an error message.

*(continued)*

**New C Constructs** *(continued)*

| Construct | Effect |
|---|---|

```
case 'D':
case 'd':
case 'F':
case 'f':
     printf("Poor, student is ");
     printf("on probation");
     break;

default:
    printf("Invalid letter grade");
}
```

# QUICK-CHECK EXERCISES

1. An if statement implements _____ execution.
2. What is a compound statement?
3. A switch statement is often used instead of _____.
4. What can be the values of an expression with a relational operator?
5. The relational operator <= means _____.
6. A hand trace is used to verify that a(n) _____ is correct.
7. List the three types of control structures.
8. Correct the syntax errors.

   ```
   if x > 25.0 {
           y = x
   else
           y = z;
   }
   ```

9. What value is assigned to fee by the if statement when speed is 75?

   ```
   if (speed > 35)
           fee = 20.0;
   else if (speed > 50)
           fee = 40.00;
   else if (speed > 75)
           fee = 60.00;
   ```

10. Answer Exercise 9 for the `if` statement that follows. Which `if` statement seems reasonable?

```
if (speed > 75)
      fee = 60.0;
else if (speed > 50)
      fee = 40.00;
else if (speed > 35)
      fee = 20.00;
```

11. What output line(s) are displayed by the statements that follow when grade is `'I'`? When grade is `'B'`? When grade is `'b'`?

```
switch (grade) {
case 'A':
      points = 4;
      break;

case 'B':
      points = 3;
      break;

case 'C':
      points = 2;
      break;

case 'D':
      points = 1;
      break;

case 'E':
case 'I':
case 'W':
      points = 0;
}

if (points > 0)
      printf("Passed, points earned = %d\n",
             points);
else
      printf("Failed, no points earned\n");
```

12. Explain the difference between the statements on the left and the statements on the right. For each group of statements, give the final value of x if the initial value of x is 1.

```
if (x >= 0)                if (x >= 0)
    x = x + 1;                 x = x + 1;
else if (x >= 1)           if (x >= 1)
    x = x + 2;                 x = x + 2;
```

13. a. Evaluate the expression

   1  &&  (30 % 10 >= 0)  &&  (30 % 10 <= 3)

   b. Is either set of parentheses required?
   c. Write the complement of the expression two ways. First, add one opera-
      tor and one set of parentheses. For the second version, use DeMorgan's
      theorem.

## ANSWERS TO QUICK-CHECK EXERCISES

1. conditional
2. one or more statements surrounded by braces
3. nested if statements or a multiple-alternative if statement
4. 0 and 1
5. less than or equal to
6. algorithm
7. sequence, selection, repetition
8. Parenthesize condition, remove braces (or add them around else:
   } else {), and add a semicolon to the first assignment statement.
9. 20.00, first condition is met
10. 40.00, the one in 10
11. when grade is 'I':
        Failed, no points earned
    when grade is 'B':
        Passed, points earned = 3
    when grade is 'b':
        The switch statement is skipped so the output printed depends on the
        previous value of points (which may be garbage).
12. A nested if statement is on the left; a sequence of if statements is on the
    right. On the left x becomes 2; on the right x becomes 4.
13. a. 1
    b. no
    c. !(1  &&  (30 % 10 >= 0)  &&  (30 % 10 <= 3))
       0  ||  (30 % 10 < 0)  ||  (30 % 10 > 3)

# REVIEW QUESTIONS

1. Making a decision between two alternative courses of action is usually implemented with a(n) _____ statement in C.
2. Trace the following program fragment; indicate which function will be called if a data value of 27.34 is entered.

```
printf("Enter a temperature> ");
scanf("%lf", &temp);
if (temp > 32.0)
      not_freezing();
else
      ice_forming();
```

3. Write a multiple-alternative `if` statement to display a message indicating the educational level of a student based on the student's number of years of schooling (0, none; 1–5, elementary school; 6–8, middle school; 9–12, high school; more than 12, college). Print a message to indicate bad data as well.
4. Write a `switch` statement to select an operation based on the value of `inventory`. Increment `total_paper` by `paper_order` if `inventory` is `'B'` or `'C'`; increment `total_ribbon` by `ribbon_order` if `inventory` is `'E'`, `'F'`, or `'D'`; increment `total_label` by `label_order` if `inventory` is `'A'` or `'X'`. Do nothing if `inventory` is `'M'`. Display an error message if the value of `inventory` is not one of these eight letters.
5. Write an `if` statement that displays an acceptance message for an astronaut candidate if the person's weight is between the values of `opt_min` and `opt_max` inclusive, the person's age is between `age_min` and `age_max` inclusive, and the person is a nonsmoker (`smoker` is false).
6. Implement the following flow diagram using a nested `if` structure.

# PROGRAMMING PROJECTS

1. Write a program that displays a message consisting of three block letters; each letter is either an X or an O. The program user's data determines whether a particular letter will be an X or O. For example, if the user enters the three letters XOX, the block letters X, O, and X will be displayed.
2. While spending the summer as a surveyor's assistant, you decide to write a program that transforms compass headings in degrees (0 to 360) to compass bearings. A compass bearing consists of three items: the direction you face (north or south), an angle between 0 and 90 degrees, and the direction you

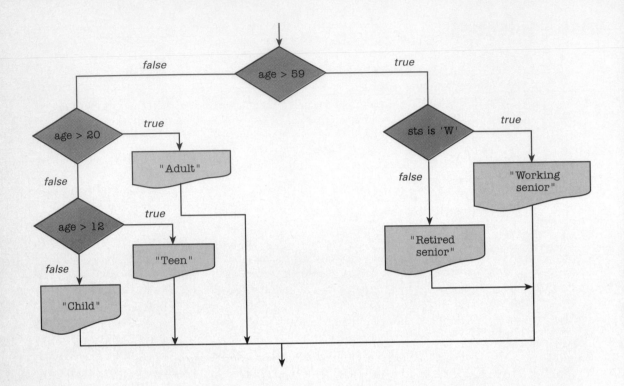

turn before walking (east or west). For example, to get the bearing for a compass heading of 110.0 degrees, you would first face due south (180 degrees) and then turn 70.0 degrees east (180.0 − 70.0 is 110.0). Therefore, the bearing is South 70.0 degrees East. Be sure to check the input for invalid compass headings.

3. The National Earthquake Information Center has asked you to write a program implementing the following decision table to characterize an earthquake based on its Richter scale number.

| Richter Scale Number (n) | Characterization |
| --- | --- |
| $n < 5.0$ | Little or no damage |
| $5.0 \leq n < 5.5$ | Some damage |
| $5.5 \leq n < 6.5$ | Serious damage: walls may crack or fall |
| $6.5 \leq n < 7.5$ | Disaster: houses and buildings may collapse |
| higher | Catastrophe: most buildings destroyed |

Could you handle this problem with a `switch` statement? If so, use a `switch` statement; if not, explain why.

4. Write a program that takes a classroom number, its capacity, and the size of the class enrolled so far and prints an <u>output</u> line showing the classroom number, the capacity, both the number of seats filled and the number available, and a message indicating whether the class is filled or not. Call a function to display the following heading before the requested output line.

Room    Capacity    Enrollment    Empty seats    Filled/Not Filled

Display each part of the output line under the appropriate column heading. Test your program four times using the following classroom data:

| Room | Capacity | Enrollment |
|------|----------|------------|
| 426 | 25 | 25 |
| 327 | 18 | 14 |
| 420 | 20 | 15 |
| 317 | 100 | 90 |

5. Write a program that takes the $x$–$y$ coordinates of a point in the Cartesian plane and prints a message telling either an axis on which the point lies or the quadrant in which it is found.

Sample lines of output:
```
(-1.0, -2.5) is in quadrant III
(0.0, 4.8) is on the y axis
```

6. Write a program that determines the day number (1 to 366) in a year for a date that is provided as input data. As an example, January 1, 1994 is day 1. December 31, 1993 is day 365. December 31, 1996 is day 366, since 1996 is a leap year. A year is a leap year if it is divisible by four, except that any year divisible by 100 is a leap year only if it is divisible by 400. Your program

should accept the <u>month, day, and year</u> as integers. Include a function `leap` that returns 1 if called with a leap year, 0 otherwise.

7. The New Telephone Company has the following rate structure for long-distance calls:

   a. The regular rate for a call is $0.40 per minute.
   b. Any call started after 6:00 P.M. (1800 hours) but before 8:00 A.M. (0800 hours) is discounted 50%.
   c. Any call longer than 60 minutes receives a 15% discount.
   d. All calls are subject to a 4% federal tax on the cost after any discounts.

   Write a program that takes the start time for a call based on a 24-hour clock and the length of the call in minutes. The gross cost (before any discounts or tax) should be displayed followed by the net cost (after discounts are deducted and tax is added). Use a function to display instructions to the program user, a function to compute the gross cost, and a separate function to compute each discount amount.

8. Write a program that will calculate and print bills for the city power company. The rates vary depending on whether the use is residential, commercial, or industrial. A code of R means residential use, a code of C means commercial use, and a code of I means industrial use. Any other code should be treated as an error.

   The rates are computed as follows:

   R: $6.00 plus $0.052 per kwh used
   C: $60.00 for the first 1000 kwh and $0.045 for each additional kwh
   I: Rate varies depending on time of usage:

   > Peak hours: $76.00 for first 1000 kwh
   >     and $0.065 for each additional kwh
   > Off-peak hours: $40.00 for first 1000 kwh
   >     and $0.028 for each additional kwh.

   Your program should prompt the user to enter an integer account number, the use code (type `char`), and the necessary consumption figures in whole numbers of kilowatt-hours. Your program should display the amount due from the user.

9. Write a program to control a bread machine. Allow the user to input the type of bread as W for White and S for Sweet. Ask the user if the loaf size is double and if the baking is manual. The following table details the time chart for the machine for each bread type. Display a statement for each step. If the loaf size is double, increase the baking time by 50%. If baking is manual, stop after the loaf-shaping cycle and instruct the user to remove the dough for manual baking. Use functions to display instructions to the user and to compute the baking time.

## Bread Time Chart

| Operation | White Bread | Sweet Bread |
|---|---|---|
| Primary kneading | 15 mins | 20 mins |
| Primary rising | 60 mins | 60 mins |
| Secondary kneading | 18 mins | 33 mins |
| Secondary rising | 20 mins | 30 mins |
| Loaf shaping | 2 seconds | 2 seconds |
| Final rising | 75 mins | 75 mins |
| Baking | 45 mins | 35 mins |
| Cooling | 30 mins | 30 mins |

# Repetition and Loop Statements

chapter 5

$\mathbf{I}$n your programs so far, the statements in the program body execute only once. However, in most commercial software that you use, you can repeat a process many times. For example when using an editor program or a word processor, you can move the cursor to a program line and perform as many edit operations as you need to.

Repetition, you'll recall, is the third type of program control structure (*sequence*, *selection*, *repetition*), and the repetition of steps in a program is called a **loop**. In this chapter we describe three C loop control statements: `while`, `for`, and `do-while`. In addition to describing how to write loops using each statement, we describe the advantages of each and explain when it is best to use each one. Like `if` statements, loops can be nested, and the chapter demonstrates how to write and use nested loops in your programs.

**loop**
a control stucture that repeats a group of steps in a program

## 5.1 REPETITION IN PROGRAMS AND THE while STATEMENT

Just as the ability to make decisions is an important programming tool, so is the ability to specify repetition of a group of operations. For example, a company that has seven employees will want to repeat the gross pay and net pay computations in its payroll program seven times, once for each employee. The **loop body** contains the statements to be repeated.

**loop body**
the statements that are repeated in the loop

Writing out a solution to a specific case of a problem can be helpful in preparing you to define an algorithm to solve the same problem in general. After you solve the sample case, ask yourself some of the following questions to determine whether loops will be required in the general algorithm:

1. Were there any steps I repeated as I solved the problem? If so, which ones?
2. If the answer to question 1 is yes, did I know in advance how many times to repeat the steps?
3. If the answer to question 2 is no, how did I know how long to keep repeating the steps?

Your answer to the first question indicates whether your algorithm needs a loop and what steps to include in the loop body if it does need one. Your answers to the other questions will help you determine which loop structure to choose for your solution. Keep these questions in mind as we explore the kinds of loops available in C. Later in the chapter, we will summarize the relationship between your answers to these questions and the design of a correct loop for your algorithm.

## The while Statement

Figure 5.1 shows a program fragment that computes and displays the gross pay for seven employees. The loop body is the compound statement that starts on the third line. The loop body gets an employee's payroll data and computes and displays that employee's pay. After seven weekly pay amounts are displayed, the statement following the loop body executes and displays the message All employees processed.

The three color lines in Fig. 5.1 control the looping process. The first statement

```
count_emp = 0;  /* no employees processed yet */
```

stores an initial value of 0 in the variable count_emp, which represents the count of employees processed so far. The next line evaluates the condition count_emp < 7. If the condition is true, the compound statement representing the loop body is executed, causing a new pair of data values to be scanned and a new pay amount to be computed and displayed. The last statement in the loop body

```
count_emp = count_emp + 1; /* increment count_emp */
```

adds 1 to the current value of count_emp. After executing the last step in the loop body, control returns to the line beginning with while and the condition is reevaluated for the next value of count_emp. The loop body is executed once for each value of count_emp from 0 to 6. Eventually, count_emp becomes 7, and the condition evaluates to false (0). When this happens, the loop body is not

### Figure 5.1    Program Fragment with a Loop

```
count_emp = 0;                  /* no employees processed yet */
while (count_emp < 7) {     /* test value of count_emp     */
    printf("Hours> ");
    scanf("%d", &hours);
    printf("Rate> ");
    scanf("%lf", &rate);
    pay = hours * rate;
    printf("Pay is $%6.2f\n", pay);
    count_emp = count_emp + 1; /* increment count_emp    */
}
printf("\nAll employees processed\n");
```

**Figure 5.2
Flowchart for
a while Loop**

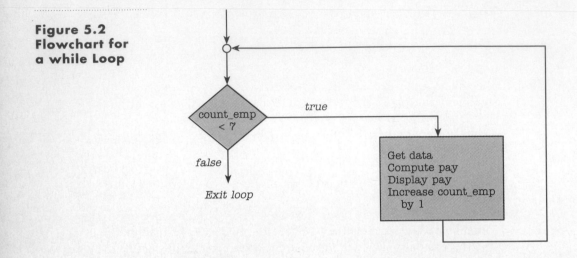

**loop repetition condition**
the condition that controls
loop repetition

executed and control passes to the display statement that follows the loop body. The expression following the reserved word while is called the **loop repetition condition.** The loop is repeated when this condition is true, that is, when its value is not 0. The *loop is exited* when this condition is false.

The flowchart in Fig. 5.2 summarizes what we have explained so far about while loops. In the flowchart, the expression in the diamond-shaped box is evaluated first. If that expression is true, the loop body is executed, and the process is repeated. The while loop is exited when the expression becomes false. If the loop repetition condition is false when it is first tested, then the loop body is not executed at all.

Make sure you understand the difference between the while statement in Fig. 5.2 and the following if statement:

```
if (count_emp < 7) {
        . . .
}
```

In an if statement, the compound statement after the parenthesized condition executes at most only once. In a while statement, the compound statement can execute more than once.

**loop control variable**
the variable whose value controls loop repetition

**Syntax of the while Statement**   In Fig. 5.1 the variable count_emp is called the **loop control variable** because its value determines whether the loop body is repeated. The loop control variable count_emp must be (1) initialized, (2) tested, and (3) updated for the loop to execute properly. Each step is summarized next.

- *Initialization.* `count_emp` is set to an initial value of 0 (*initialized to 0*) before the `while` statement is reached.
- *Testing.* `count_emp` is tested before the start of each loop repetition (called an *iteration* or a *pass*).
- *Updating.* `count_emp` is updated (its value increased by 1) during each iteration.

Similar steps must be performed for every `while` loop. Without the initialization, the initial test of `count_emp` is meaningless. The updating step ensures that the program progresses toward the final goal (`count_emp >= 7`) during each repetition of the loop. If the loop control variable is not updated, the loop will execute "forever." Such a loop is called an **infinite loop.**

**infinite loop**
a loop that executes forever

---

### while Statement

SYNTAX:   `while` (*loop repetition condition*)
      *statement*

EXAMPLE:
```
/* Display N asterisks. */
count_star = 0;
while (count_star < N) {
    printf("*");
    count_star = count_star + 1;
}
```

INTERPRETATION: The *loop repetition condition* (a condition to control the loop process) is tested; if it is true, the *statement* (loop body) is executed, and the *loop repetition condition* is retested. The *statement* is repeated as long as (`while`) the loop repetition condition is true. When this condition is tested and found to be false, the `while` loop is exited and the next program statement after the `while` statement is executed.

*Note:* If *loop repetition condition* evaluates to false the first time it is tested, *statement* is not executed.

---

**EXERCISES FOR SECTION 5.1**

Self-Check

1. Predict the output of this program fragment:

```
i = 0;
while (i <= 5) {
    printf("%3d %3d\n", i, 10 - i);
    i = i + 1;
}
```

| | |
|---|---|
| 0 | 10 |
| 1 | 9 |
| 2 | 8 |
| 3 | 7 |
| 4 | 6 |
| 5 | 5 |

2. What is displayed by this program fragment for an input of 10?

```
scanf("%d", &n);
ev = 0;
while (ev < n) {
    printf("%3d", ev);
    ev = ev + 2;
}
printf("\n");
```

*(handwritten: 10 above n; 0 2 4 6 8 in right margin)*

### Programming

1. Write a program fragment that produces this output:

```
0    1
1    2
2    4
3    8
4    16
5    32
6    64
```

## 5.2  COMPUTING A SUM OR A PRODUCT IN A LOOP

Loops often accumulate a sum or a product by repeating an addition or multiplication operation as demonstrated in Examples 5.1 and 5.2.

**EXAMPLE 5.1** The program in Fig. 5.3 has a `while` loop similar to the loop in Fig. 5.1. Besides displaying each employee's pay, it computes and displays the company's total payroll. Prior to loop execution, the statements

```
total_pay = 0.0;
count_emp = 0;
```

**accumulator**
a variable used to store a value being computed in increments during the execution of a loop

initialize both `total_pay` and `count_emp` to 0, where `count_emp` is the counter variable. Here `total_pay` is an **accumulator** variable and it accumulates the total payroll value. Initializing `total_pay` to 0 is critical; if you omit this step, your final total will be off by whatever value happens to be stored in `total_pay` when the program begins execution.  ◄

**Figure 5.3    Program to Compute Company Payroll**

```
/* Compute the payroll for a company */

#include <stdio.h>

int
main(void)
{
      double total_pay;           /* company payroll       */
      int    count_emp;           /* current employee      */
      int    number_emp;          /* number of employees   */
      double hours;               /* hours worked          */
      double rate;                /* hourly rate           */
      double pay;                 /* pay for this period   */

      /* Get number of employees. */
      printf("Enter number of employees> ");
      scanf("%d", &number_emp);

      /* Compute each employee's pay and add it to the payroll. */
      total_pay = 0.0;
      count_emp = 0;
      while (count_emp < number_emp) {
          printf("Hours> ");
          scanf("%lf", &hours);
          printf("Rate > $");
          scanf("%lf", &rate);
          pay = hours * rate;
          printf("Pay is $%6.2f\n\n", pay);
          total_pay = total_pay + pay;               /* Add next pay. */
          count_emp = count_emp + 1;
      }
      printf("All employees processed\n");
      printf("Total payroll is $%8.2f\n", total_pay);

      return (0);
}

Enter number of employees> 3
Hours> 50
Rate > $5.25
Pay is $262.50
```

*(continued)*

**Figure 5.3** *(continued)*

```
Hours> 6
Rate > $5.00
Pay is $ 30.00

Hours> 15
Rate > $7.00
Pay is $105.00

All employees processed
Total payroll is $  397.50
```

In the loop body, the assignment statement

```
total_pay = total_pay + pay;         /* Add next pay. */
```

adds the current value of pay to the sum being accumulated in total_pay. Consequently, the value of total_pay increases with each loop iteration. Table 5.1 traces the effect of repeating this statement for the three values of pay shown in the sample run. Recall that iteration means a pass through the loop.

**Table 5.1   Trace of Three Repetitions of Loop in Fig. 5.3**

| Statement | hours | rate | pay | total_pay | count_emp | Effect |
|---|---|---|---|---|---|---|
| | ? | ? | ? | 0.0 | 0 | |
| count_emp < number_emp | | | | | | true |
| scanf("%lf", &hours); | 50.0 | | | | | get hours |
| scanf("%lf", &rate); | | 5.25 | | | | get rate |
| pay = hours * rate; | | | 262.5 | | | find pay |
| total_pay = total_pay + pay; | | | | 262.5 | | add to total_pay |
| count_emp = count_emp + 1; | | | | | 1 | increment count_emp |

*(continued)*

**Table 5.1** *(continued)*

| Statement | hours | rate | pay | total_pay | count_emp | Effect |
|---|---|---|---|---|---|---|
| count_emp < number_emp | | | | | | true |
| scanf("%lf", &hours); | 6.0 | | | | | get hours |
| scanf("%lf", &rate); | | 5.0 | | | | get rate |
| pay = hours * rate; | | | 30.0 | | | find pay |
| total_pay = total_pay<br>    + pay; | | | | 292.5 | | add to<br>total_pay |
| count_emp = count_emp<br>    + 1; | | | | | 2 | increment<br>count_emp |
| count_emp < number_emp | | | | | | true |
| scanf("%lf", &hours); | 15.0 | | | | | get hours |
| scanf("%lf", &rate); | | 7.0 | | | | get rate |
| pay = hours * rate; | | | 105.0 | | | find pay |
| total_pay = total_pay<br>    + pay; | | | | 397.5 | | add pay to<br>total_pay |
| count_emp = count_emp<br>    + 1; | | | | | 3 | increment<br>count_emp |

## Program Style    *Writing General Loops*

Because the loop in Fig. 5.1 uses the loop repetition condition count_emp < 7, it processes exactly 7 employees. The loop in Fig. 5.3 is more general. It uses the loop repetition condition count_emp < number_emp so it can process any number of employees. The number of employees to be processed must be scanned into variable number_emp before the while statement executes. The loop repetition condition compares the number of employees processed so far (count_emp) to the total number of employees (number_emp).

## Multiplying a List of Numbers

In a similar way, we can use a loop to compute the product of a list of numbers as shown in the next example.

 **EXAMPLE 5.2**    The loop that follows multiplies data items together as long as the product remains less than 10,000. It displays the product calculated so far before asking

for the next data value. The product so far is updated on each iteration by executing the statement

```
product = product * item; /* Update product */
```

Loop exit occurs when the value of `product` is greater than or equal to 10,000. Consequently, the loop body does not display the last value assigned to `product`.

```
/* Multiply data while product remains less than 10000 */
product = 1;
while (product < 10000) {
    printf("%d\n", product); /* Display product so far */
    printf("Enter next item> ");
    scanf("%d", &item);
    product = product * item; /* Update product */
}
```

The loop in this example differs from other loops you have seen. Its repetition condition involves a test of the variable `product`. Besides controlling loop repetition, the variable `product` also holds the result of the computation that is performed in the loop. The other loops involve a test of `count_emp`, a variable that represents the count of loop repetitions. The computation being performed in the loop does not directly involve `count_emp`. We will discuss these differences further in Section 5.4.    ←

## Compound Assignment Operators

We have seen several instances of assignment statements of the form

$$variable = variable \; op \; expression;$$

where *op* is a C arithmetic operator. These include increments and decrements of loop counters

```
count_emp = count_emp + 1;
time = time - 1;
```

as well as statements accumulating a sum or computing a product in a loop, such as

```
total_pay = total_pay + pay;
product = product * item;
```

**Table 5.2    Compound Assignment Operators**

| Statement with Simple Assignment Operator | Equivalent Statement with Compound Assignment Operator |
|---|---|
| `count_emp = count_emp + 1;` | `count_emp += 1;` |
| `time = time - 1;` | `time -= 1;` |
| `total_time = total_time +`<br>`           time;` | `total_time += time;` |
| `product = product * item;` | `product *= item;` |
| `n = n * (x + 1);` | `n *= x + 1;` |

C provides special assignment operators that enable a more concise notation for statements of this type. For the operations +, -, *, /, and %, C defines the compound *op=* assignment operators +=, -=, *=, /=, and %=. A statement of the form

$$\textit{variable op= expression};$$

is an alternative way of writing the statement

$$\textit{variable = variable op (expression)};$$

Table 5.2 shows some examples using compound assignment operators. The last example demonstrates the relevance of the parentheses around *expression* in the definition of an assignment statement with a compound operator.

**EXERCISES FOR SECTION 5.2**

Self-Check

1. What output values are displayed by the following `while` loop for a data value of 5? Of 6? Of 7?

```
printf("Enter an integer> ");
scanf("%d", &x);
product = x;
count = 0;
while (count < 4) {
    printf("%d\n", product);
    product *= x;
    count += 1;
}
```

In general, for a data value of any number *n*, what does this loop display?

2. What values are displayed if the call to `printf` comes at the end of the loop instead of at the beginning?

3. The following segment needs some revision. Insert braces where they are needed and correct the errors. The corrected code should take five integers and display their sum.

```
count = 0;
while (count <= 5)
count += 1;
printf("Next number> ");
scanf("%d", &next_num);
next_num += sum;
printf("%d numbers were added; \n", count);
printf("their sum is %d.\n", sum);
```

4. Where possible, write equivalents for the following statements using compound assignment operators.

```
r = r / 10;
z = z * x + 1;
q = q + r * m;
m = m - (n + p);
```

### Programming

1. Write a program segment that computes 1 + 2 + 3 + . . . + (n – 1) + n, where n is a data value. Follow the loop body with an `if` statement that compares this value to `(n * (n + 1)) / 2` and displays a message that indicates whether the values are the same or different. What message do you think will be displayed?

## 5.3 COUNTING LOOPS AND THE for STATEMENT

**counting loop**
a loop whose required number of iterations can be determined before loop execution begins

The `while` loop shown in Fig. 5.3 is called a **counter-controlled loop** (or **counting loop**) because its repetition is managed by a loop control variable whose value represents a count. A counter-controlled loop follows this general format described in pseudocode:

Set *loop control variable* to an initial value of 0.
while *loop control variable* < *final value*
. . .
    Increase *loop control variable* by 1.

We use a counter-controlled loop when we can determine prior to loop execution exactly how many loop repetitions will be needed to solve the problem. This number should appear as the *final value* in the while condition.

## The for Statement

C provides the for statement as another form for implementing loops. The loops we have seen so far are typical of most repetition structures in that they have three loop control components in addition to the loop body:

- initialization of the *loop control variable,*
- test of the *loop repetition condition,* and
- change (update) of the *loop control variable.*

An important feature of the for statement in C is that it supplies a designated place for each of these three components. A for statement implementation of the loop from Fig. 5.3 is shown in Fig. 5.4.

The effect of this for statement is exactly equivalent to the execution of the comparable while loop section of the program in Fig. 5.3. Because the for statement's heading

```
for  (count_emp = 0;              /* initialization            */
         count_emp < number_emp; /* loop repetition condition */
         count_emp += 1) {        /* update                    */
```

**Figure 5.4    Using a for Statement in a Counting Loop**

```
/* Process payroll for all employees */
total_pay = 0.0;
for  (count_emp = 0;                /* initialization            */
        count_emp < number_emp;    /* loop repetition condition */
        count_emp += 1) {          /* update                    */
    printf("Hours> ");
    scanf("%lf", &hours);
    printf("Rate > $");
    scanf("%lf", &rate);
    pay = hours * rate;
    printf("Pay is $%6.2f\n\n", pay);
    total_pay = total_pay + pay;
}
printf("All employees processed\n");
printf("Total payroll is $%8.2f\n", total_pay);
```

combines the three loop control steps of initialization, testing, and update in one place, separate steps to initialize and update `count_emp` must not appear elsewhere. The `for` statement can be used to count up or down by any interval.

---

**for Statement**

SYNTAX:  for (*initialization expression*;
                *loop repetition condition*;
                *update expression*)
         *statement*

EXAMPLE: /* Display N asterisks. */
         for (count_star = 0;
              count_star < N;
              count_star += 1)
              printf("*");

INTERPRETATION: First, the *initialization expression* is executed. Then, the *loop repetition condition* is tested. If it is true, the *statement* is executed, and the *update expression* is evaluated. Then the *loop repetition condition* is retested. The *statement* is repeated as long as the *loop repetition condition* is true. When this condition is tested and found to be false, the `for` loop is exited, and the next program statement after the `for` statement is executed.

*Caution:* Although C permits the use of fractional values for counting loop control variables of type `double`, we strongly discourage this practice. Counting loops with type `double` control variables will not always execute the same number of times on different computers.

---

## Program Style    *Formatting the for Statement*

For clarity, we usually place each expression of the `for` heading on a separate line. If all three expressions are very short, we may place them together on one line. Here is an example:

```
/* Display nonnegative numbers < max */
for  (i = 0;  i < max;  i += 1)
     printf("%d\n", i);
```

The body of the `for` loop is indented. If the loop body is a compound statement or if we are using a style in which we bracket all loop bodies, we place the opening brace at the end of the `for` heading and terminate the statement by placing the closing brace on a separate line. This closing brace should be aligned with the "f" of the `for` that it is ending.

## Increment and Decrement Operators

The counting loops that you have seen have all included assignment expressions of the form

```
counter = counter + 1
```

or

```
counter += 1
```

**side effect**
a change in the value of a variable as a result of carrying out an operation

The increment operator `++` takes a single variable as its operand. The **side effect** of applying the `++` operator is that the value of its operand is incremented by one. Frequently, `++` is used just for this side effect, as in the following loop in which the variable `counter` is to run from 0 up to `limit`:

```
for (counter = 0;  counter < limit;  ++counter)
   . . .
```

The *value* of the expression in which the `++` operator is used depends on the position of the operator. When the `++` is placed immediately in front of its operand (*prefix increment*), the value of the expression is the variable's value *after* incrementing. When the `++` comes immediately after the operand (*postfix increment*), the expression's value is the value of the variable *before* it is incremented. Compare the action of the two code segments in Fig. 5.5, given an initial value of 2 in `i`.

**Figure 5.5
Comparison of
Prefix and
Postfix
Increments**

C also provides a decrement operator that can be used in either the prefix or postfix position. For example, if the initial value of n is 4, the code fragment on the left prints

   3   3

and the one on the right prints

   4   3

```
printf("%3d", --n);      printf("%3d", n--);
printf("%3d", n);        printf("%3d", n);
```

You should avoid using the increment and decrement operators in complex expressions in which the variables to which they are applied appear more than once. C compilers are expected to exploit the commutativity and associativity of various operators in order to produce efficient code. For example, this code fragment may assign y the value 13 (2 * 5 + 3) in one implementation and the value 18 (3 * 5 + 3) in another.

```
x = 5;
i = 2;
y = i * x + ++i;
```

A programmer must not depend on side effects that will vary from one compiler to another.

**EXAMPLE 5.3** ▶ Function `factorial` (Fig. 5.6) computes the factorial of an integer represented by the formal parameter n. The loop body executes for decreasing values of i from n through 2, and each value of i is incorporated in the accumulating product. Loop exit occurs when i is 1. ◀

**Figure 5.6    Function to Compute Factorial**

```
/*
 * Computes n!
 * Pre: n is greater than or equal to zero
 */
int
factorial(int n)
```

*(continued)*

**Figure 5.6** **(continued)**

```
{
      int i,           /* local variables */
         product;    /* accumulator for product computation */

      product = 1;
      /* Computes the product n x (n-1) x (n-2) x ... x 2 x 1 */
      for (i = n;  i > 1;  --i) {
           product = product * i;
      }

      /* Returns function result */
      return (product);
}
```

## Increments and Decrements Other than 1

We have seen for statement counting loops that count up by 1 and down by 1. Now we will use a loop that counts down by five to display a Celsius-to-Fahrenheit conversion table.

 **EXAMPLE 5.4**

The table displayed by the program in Fig. 5.7 shows temperature conversions from 10 degrees Celsius to −5 degrees Celsius because of the values of the constant macros named CBEGIN and CLIMIT. Since the loop update step subtracts CSTEP (5) from celsius, the value of the counter celsius decreases by five after each repetition. Loop exit occurs when celsius becomes less than CLIMIT, that is, when celsius is −10. Table 5.3 uses the small circled numbers to trace the execution of this counting for loop.

The trace in Table 5.3 shows that the loop control variable celsius is initialized to CBEGIN (10) when the for loop is reached. Since 10 is greater than or equal to CLIMIT (−5), the loop body is executed. After each loop repetition, CSTEP (5) is subtracted from celsius, and celsius is tested in the loop repetition condition to see whether its value is still greater than or equal to CLIMIT. If the condition is true, the loop body is executed again and the next value of fahrenheit is computed and displayed. If the condition is false, the loop is exited.

**Figure 5.7    Displaying a Celsius-to-Fahrenheit Conversion Table**

```
/* Conversion of Celsius to Fahrenheit temperatures */

#include <stdio.h>

/* Constant macros */
#define CBEGIN 10
#define CLIMIT -5
#define CSTEP 5

int
main(void)
{
      /* Variable declarations */
      int     celsius;
      double fahrenheit;

      /* Display the table heading */
      printf("   Celsius    Fahrenheit\n");

      /* Display the table */
1     for  (celsius = CBEGIN;
2           celsius >= CLIMIT;
3           celsius -= CSTEP) {
4         fahrenheit = 1.8 * celsius + 32.0;
5         printf("%6c%3d%8c%7.2f\n", ' ', celsius, ' ', fahrenheit);
      }

      return (0);
}
   Celsius    Fahrenheit
       10            50.00
        5            41.00
        0            32.00
       -5            23.00
```

**Table 5.3    Trace of Loop in Fig. 5.7**

| | Statement | celsius | fahrenheit | Effect |
|---|---|---|---|---|
| **1** | for    (celsius = CBEGIN; | 1 0 | ? | Initialize celsius to 1 0 |
| **2** | celsius >= CLIMIT; | | | 1 0 >= −5 is true |
| **4** | fahrenheit = 1.8 * celsius + 32.0; | | 50.0 | Assign 50.0 to fahrenheit |
| **5** | printf . . . | | | Display 1 0 and 50.0 |
| **3** | Update and test celsius<br>. . . celsius −= CSTEP | 5 | | Subtract 5 from celsius, giving 5 |
| **2** | celsius >= CLIMIT; | | | 5 >= −5 is true |
| **4** | fahrenheit = 1.8 * celsius + 32.0; | | 41.0 | Assign 41.0 to fahrenheit |
| **5** | printf . . . | | | Display 5 and 41.0 |
| **3** | Update and test celsius<br>. . . celsius −= CSTEP | 0 | | Subtract 5 from celsius, giving 0 |
| **2** | celsius >= CLIMIT; | | | 0 >= −5 is true |
| **4** | fahrenheit = 1.8 * celsius + 32.0; | | 32.0 | Assign 32.0 to fahrenheit |
| **5** | printf . . . | | | Display 0 and 32.0 |
| **3** | Update and test celsius<br>. . . celsius −= CSTEP | −5 | | Subtract 5 from celsius, giving −5 |
| **2** | celsius >= CLIMIT; | | | −5 >= −5 is true |
| **4** | fahrenheit = 1.8 * celsius + 32.0; | | 23.0 | Assign 23.0 to fahrenheit |
| **5** | printf . . . | | | Display −5 and 23.0 |
| **3** | Update and test celsius<br>. . . celsius −= CSTEP | −10 | | Subtract 5 from celsius, giving −1 0 |
| **2** | celsius >= CLIMIT; | | | −10 >= −5 is false, so exit loop |

Because the structure of the `for` statement makes it easy for the reader of a program to identify the major loop control elements, we will use it often in the remainder of our study of repetition when a loop requires simple initialization, testing, and updating of a loop control variable.

## Displaying a Table of Values

The program in Fig. 5.7 displays a table of output values. The `printf` call before the loop displays a string that forms the table heading. Within the loop body, the `printf` statement

```
printf("%6c%3d%8c%7.2f\n", ' ', celsius, ' ', fahrenheit);
```

displays a pair of output values each time it executes. Function `printf` substitutes the space character ' ' for the placeholders `%6c` and `%8c` in its format string, causing 6 blanks to precede the value of `celsius` and 8 blanks to separate the values of `celsius` and `fahrenheit`. The `\n` in the `printf` format string ends the line on which each pair of numbers appears, so the loop creates a table consisting of two columns of numbers.

**EXERCISES FOR SECTION 5.3**

Self-Check

1. Trace the execution of the loop that follows for n = 8. Show values of `odd` and `sum` after the update of the loop counter for each iteration.

```
sum = 0;
for  (odd = 1;
      odd < n;
      odd += 2)
   sum = sum + odd;

printf("Sum of positive odd numbers less than %d is %d.\n",
       n, sum);
```

2. Given the constant macro definitions of Fig. 5.7 (repeated here)

```
#define CBEGIN 10
#define CLIMIT -5
#define CSTEP   5
```

indicate what values of celsius would appear in the conversion table displayed if the for loop header of Fig. 5.7 were rewritten as shown:

```
a. for   (celsius = CLIMIT;
          celsius >= CBEGIN;
          celsius += CSTEP)
b. for   (celsius = CLIMIT;
          celsius <= CBEGIN;
          celsius += CSTEP)
c. for   (celsius = CLIMIT;
          celsius <= CSTEP;
          celsius += CBEGIN)
d. for   (celsius = CSTEP;
          celsius >= CBEGIN;
          celsius += CLIMIT)
```

3. What is the least number of times that the body of a while loop can be executed? The body of a for loop?

4. What values are assigned to n, m, and p, given these initial values?

5. Rewrite the code shown in Exercise 4 so the effect is equivalent but no increment/decrement operator appears in an expression with another arithmetic operator.

6. What errors do you see in the following fragment? Correct the code so it displays all multiples of 5 from 0 through 100.

```
for mult5 = 0;
mult5 < 100;
mult5 += 5;
printf("%d\n", mult5);
```

7. a. Trace the following program fragment:

```
j = 10;
for  (i = 1;  i <= 5;   ++i) {
    printf("%d   %d\n", i, j);
    j -= 2;
}
```

b. Rewrite the previous program fragment so that it produces the same output but uses 0 as the initial value of `i`.

Programming

1. Write a loop that displays a table of angle measures along with their sine and cosine values. Assume that the initial and final angle measures (in degrees) are available in `init_degree` and `final_degree` (type int variables), and that the change in angle measure between table entries is given by `step_degree` (also a type int variable). Remember that the math library's `sin` and `cos` functions take arguments that are in radians.
2. Write a program to display an inches-to-centimeters conversion table. The smallest and largest number of inches in the table are input values. Your table should give conversions in 6-inch intervals. One inch equals 2.54 cm.

# 5.4 CONDITIONAL LOOPS

In many programming situations, you will not be able to determine the exact number of loop repetitions before loop execution begins. When we multiplied a list of numbers in Example 5.2, the number of repetitions depended on the data entered. Although we did not know in advance how many times the loop would execute, we were still able to write a condition to control the loop. Here is another case of this type of repetition. You want to continue prompting the user for a data value as long as the response is unreasonable.

> Print an initial prompting message.
> Get the number of observed values.
> while the number of values is negative
>     Print a warning and another prompting message.
>     Get the number of observed values.

Like the counting loops we considered earlier, such a conditional loop typically has three parts that control repetition: initialization, testing of a loop repetition condition, and an update. Let's analyze the algorithm for ensuring valid input. Clearly, the loop repetition condition is

*number of values* < 0

Because it makes no sense to test this condition unless *number of values* has a meaning, getting this value must be the initialization step. The update action—

the statement that, if left out, would cause the loop to repeat infinitely—remains to be identified. Getting a new number of observed values within the loop body is just such a step. Since we have found these three essential loop parts, we can write this validating input loop in C by using a `while` statement:

```
printf("Enter number of observed values> ");
scanf("%d", &num_obs);                    /* initialization   */
while (num_obs < 0) {
    printf("Negative number invalid; try again> ");
    scanf("%d", &num_obs);                /* update           */
}
```

At first, it may seem odd that the initialization and update steps are identical. In fact, this is very often the case for loops performing input operations in situations where the number of input values is not known in advance.

**EXAMPLE 5.5**

The program in Fig. 5.8 is designed to assist in monitoring the gasoline supply in a storage tank at the Super Oil Company refinery. The program is to alert the supervisor when the supply of gasoline in the tank falls below 10% of the tank's 80,000-barrel storage capacity. Although the supervisor always deals with the contents of the tank in terms of a number of *barrels,* the pump that is used to fill tanker trucks gives its measurements in *gallons.* The barrel used in the petroleum industry equals 42 U.S. gallons.

The main function first prompts the operator for the amount of gasoline currently stored in the tank. Next, it calls function `monitor_gas` to monitor the removal of gasoline and to stop removals as soon as the current supply falls below the minimum supply level. After gasoline is pumped into each tanker, the operator enters the number of gallons removed and function `monitor_gas` updates the number of barrels still available (`current`). When the supply drops below the 10% limit, loop exit occurs and `monitor_gas` returns the value of `current` to the main function, which issues a warning.

A counting loop would not be appropriate in this program because we do not know in advance how many tanker deliveries will need to be processed before the warning is issued. However, the `for` statement is still a good choice because we do have initialization, testing, and update steps.

### Figure 5.8 Program to Monitor Gasoline Storage Tank

```c
/*
 * Monitor gasoline supply in storage tank. Issue warning when supply
 * falls below MIN_PCT % of tank capacity.
 */

#include <stdio.h>

/* constant macros */
#define CAPACITY     80000.0 /* number of barrels tank can hold       */
#define MIN_PCT      10       /* warn when supply falls below this
                                 percent of capacity                  */
#define GALS_PER_BRL 42.0    /* number of U.S. gallons in one barrel  */

/* Function prototype */
double monitor_gas(double min_supply, double start_supply);

int
main(void)
{
      double start_supply, /* input - initial supply in barrels        */
             min_supply,   /* minimum number of barrels left without
                              warning                                  */
             current;      /* output - current supply in barrels       */

      /* Compute minimum supply without warning  */
      min_supply = MIN_PCT / 100.0 * CAPACITY;

      /* Get initial supply */
      printf("Number of barrels currently in tank> ");
      scanf("%lf", &start_supply);

      /* Subtract amounts removed and display amount remaining
         as long as minimum supply remains.                            */
      current = monitor_gas(min_supply, start_supply);

      /* Issue warning                                                  */
      printf("only %.2f barrels are left.\n\n", current);
      printf("*** WARNING ***\n");
```

*(continued)*

**Figure 5.8**  *(continued)*

```
        printf("Available supply is less than %d percent of tank's\n",
               MIN_PCT);
        printf("%.2f-barrel capacity.\n", CAPACITY);

        return (0);
}

/*
 * Computes and displays amount of gas remaining after each delivery
 * Pre : min_supply and start_supply are defined.
 * Post: Returns the supply available (in barrels) after all permitted
 *       removals. The value returned is the first supply amount that is
 *       less than min_supply.
 */
double
monitor_gas(double min_supply, double start_supply)
{
        double remov_gals,    /* input - amount of current delivery      */
               remov_brls,    /*            in barrels and gallons        */
               current;       /* output - current supply in barrels      */

        for  (current = start_supply;
              current >= min_supply;
              current -= remov_brls) {
           printf("%.2f barrels are available.\n\n", current);
           printf("Enter number of gallons removed> ");
           scanf("%lf", &remov_gals);
           remov_brls = remov_gals / GALS_PER_BRL;

           printf("After removal of %.2f gallons (%.2f barrels),\n",
                  remov_gals, remov_brls);
        }

        return (current);
}


Number of barrels currently in tank> 8500.5
8500.50 barrels are available.
```

*(continued)*

**Figure 5.8** *(continued)*

```
Enter number of gallons removed> 5859.0
After removal of 5859.00 gallons (139.50 barrels),
8361.00 barrels are available.

Enter number of gallons removed> 7568.4
After removal of 7568.40 gallons (180.20 barrels),
8180.80 barrels are available.

Enter number of gallons removed> 8400.0
After removal of 8400.00 gallons (200.00 barrels),
only 7980.80 barrels are left.

*** WARNING ***
Available supply is less than 10 percent of tank's
80000.00-barrel capacity.
```

Let's take a close look at the loop in function monitor_gas. Logically, we want to continue to record amounts of gasoline removed as long as the supply in the tank does not fall below the minimum. The loop repetition condition, the second expression in the for loop heading, states that we stay in the loop as long as

```
current >= min_supply;
```

Since min_supply does not change, current is the variable that controls the loop. Therefore the first and third expressions of the for statement's heading handle the initialization and update of this variable's value.

Tracing this program with the data shown, we come first to the assignment statement that computes a value for min_supply of 8000.0, based on the tank capacity and minimum percentage. The call to printf just before the call to scanf generates the prompting message for entering the tank's initial supply. Next, the starting supply entered by the program operator is scanned into variable start_supply and the main function calls monitor_gas.

In monitor_gas, the initialization expression of the for statement copies the starting supply into current, the loop control variable, giving current the value 8500.5. When the loop repetition condition

```
current >= min_supply;
```

is first tested, it evaluates to true, causing the loop body (the compound statement in braces) to execute. The current supply is displayed followed by a prompting message. A value is obtained for gallons removed (5859.0), the value is converted to barrels, and this amount is displayed. When execution of the loop body is complete, the update expression of the `for` statement

```
current -= remov_brls
```

is executed, subtracting from the current supply the amount removed. The loop repetition condition is retested with the new value of current (8361.00). Since 8361.00 > 8000.0 is true, the loop body once again displays the current supply and processes a delivery of 7568.4 gallons, or 180.20 barrels. The value of current is then updated to 8180.80 barrels, which is still not below the minimum, so the loop body executes a third time, processing removal of 200.00 barrels. This time execution of the `for` statement update expression brings the value of current to 7980.80. The loop repetition condition is tested again: Since 7980.8 >= 8000.0 is false, loop exit occurs, and the statements following the closing brace of the loop body are executed.

Just as in the counting loop shown in Fig. 5.4, there are three critical steps in Fig. 5.8 that involve the loop control variable current.

- current is *initialized* to the starting supply in the `for` statement initialization expression.
- current is *tested* before each execution of the loop body.
- current is *updated* (by subtraction of the amount removed) during each iteration.

Remember that steps similar to these appear in virtually every loop you write. The C `for` statement heading provides you with a designated place for each of the three steps.

## Program Style    *Performing Loop Processing in a Function Subprogram*

In Fig. 5.8, function monitor_gas contains a `for` loop that performs the major program task—monitoring gasoline deliveries. The function result is the final value of the loop control variable, current. This program structure is fairly common and quite effective. Placing all loop processing in a function subprogram simplifies the main function.

**EXERCISES FOR
SECTION 5.4**

Self-Check

1. Give an example of data the user could enter for the storage tank monitoring program that would cause function monitor_gas to return without executing the body of the `for` loop.

2. Correct the syntax and logic of the code that follows so that it prints all multiples of 5 from 0 through 100:

```
for sum = 0;
    sum < 100;
    sum += 5;
printf("%d\n", sum);
```

3. What output is displayed if this list of data is used for the program in Fig. 5.8?

```
8350.8
7581.0
7984.2
```

4. How would you modify the program in Fig. 5.8 so that it also determines the number of deliveries (`count_deliv`) made before the gasoline supply drops below the minimum? Which is the loop control variable, `current` or `count_deliv`?

### Programming

1. There are 9870 people in a town whose population increases by 10 percent each year. Write a loop that displays the annual population and determines how many years (`count_years`) it will take for the population to surpass 30,000.
2. Rewrite the payroll program (Fig. 5.4), moving the loop processing into a function subprogram. Return the total payroll amount as the function result.

## 5.5 LOOP DESIGN

Being able to analyze the operation of a loop is one thing; designing your own loops is another. In this section, we will consider the latter. The comment that precedes the call to function `monitor_gas` in Fig. 5.8 is a good summary of the purpose of the loop in this function.

```
/* Subtract amounts removed and display amount remaining
   as long as minimum supply remains.                      */
```

Let's see how the problem-solving questions suggested in Sections 1.5 and 5.1 can help us formulate a valid loop structure. As always, the columns labeled "Answer" and "Implications . . ." in Table 5.3 represent an individual problem solver's thought processes and are not offered as the "one and only true path" to a solution.

**Table 5.4 Problem-Solving Questions for Loop Design**

| Question | Answer | Implications for the Algorithm |
|---|---|---|
| What are the inputs? | Initial supply of gasoline (barrels). Amounts removed (gallons). | Input variables needed:<br>`start_supply`<br>`remov_gals`<br>Value of `start_supply` must be input once, but amounts removed are entered many times. |
| What are the outputs? | Amounts removed in gallons and barrels, and the current supply of gasoline. | Values of `current` and `remov_gals` are echoed in the output. Output variable needed:<br>`remov_brls` |
| Is there any repetition? | Yes. One repeatedly<br>1. gets amount removed<br>2. converts the amount to barrels<br>3. subtracts the amount removed from the current supply<br>4. checks to see whether the supply has fallen below the minimum. | Program variable needed:<br>`min_supply` |
| Do I know in advance how many times steps will be repeated? | No. | Loop will not be controlled by a counter. |
| How do I know how long to keep repeating the steps? | As long as the current supply is not below the minimum. | The loop repetition condition is<br>`current >= min_supply` |

## Sentinel-Controlled Loops

Many programs with loops input one or more additional data items each time the loop body is repeated. Often we don't know how many data items the loop should process when it begins execution. Therefore, we must find some way to signal the program to stop reading and processing new data.

**sentinel value**
an end marker that follows the last item in a list of data

One way to do this is to instruct the user to enter a unique data value, called a **sentinel value,** after the last data item. The loop repetition condition tests each data item and causes loop exit when the sentinel value is read. Choose the sentinel value carefully; it must be a value that could not normally occur as data.

A loop that processes data until the sentinel value is entered has the form

1. Get a line of data.
2. while the sentinel value has not been encountered
     3. Process the data line.
     4. Get another line of data.

Note that this loop, like other loops we have studied, has an *initialization* (step 1), a *loop repetition condition* (step 2), and an update (step 4). Step 1 gets the first line of data; step 4 gets all the other data lines and then tries to obtain one more line. This attempted extra input permits entry (but not processing) of the sentinel value. For program readability, we usually name the sentinel by defining a constant macro.

**EXAMPLE 5.6**  A program that calculates the sum of a collection of exam scores is a candidate for using a sentinel value. If the class is large, the instructor may not know the exact number of students who took the exam being graded. The program should work regardless of class size. The loop below uses sum as an accumulator variable and score as an input variable.

***Sentinel Loop***

1. Initialize sum to zero.
2. Get first score.
3. while score is not the sentinel
     4. Add score to sum.
     5. Get next score.

One is tempted to try the following algorithm that reverses the order of steps 4 and 5 so as to be able to omit the duplication of step 5 in step 2.

***Incorrect Sentinel Loop***

1. Initialize sum to zero.
2. while score is not the sentinel
     3. Get score.
     4. Add score to sum.

There are two problems associated with this strategy. First, with no initializing input statement, you will have no value for score on which to judge the loop repetition condition when it is first tested. Second, consider the last two iterations of the loop. On the next-to-last iteration, the last data value is copied into score and added to the accumulating sum; on the last iteration, the attempt to get another score obtains the sentinel value. However, this fact will not cause the loop to exit until the loop repetition condition is tested again. Before exit occurs, the sentinel is added to sum. For these reasons, it is important to set up sentinel-controlled loops using the recommended structure: one input to get the loop going (the *initialization* input), and a second to keep it going (the *updating* input). The following program uses a while loop to implement the sentinel-controlled loop (Fig. 5.9). It also shows that the declaration of a variable may include an initialization.

The following sample dialogue would be used to enter the scores 55, 33, and 77:

```
Enter first score (or -99 to quit)> 55
Enter next score (-99 to quit)> 33
Enter next score (-99 to quit)> 77
Enter next score (-99 to quit)> -99

Sum of exam scores is 165
```

**Figure 5.9   Sentinel-Controlled while Loop**

```c
/* Compute the sum of a list of exam scores. */

#include <stdio.h>

#define SENTINEL -99

int
main(void)
{
      int sum = 0,    /* output - sum of scores input so far       */
          score;      /* input - current score                     */

      /* Accumulate sum of all scores.                             */
      printf("Enter first score (or %d to quit)> ", SENTINEL);
      scanf("%d", &score);        /* Get first score.              */
      while (score != SENTINEL) {
          sum += score;
          printf("Enter next score (%d to quit)> ", SENTINEL);
          scanf("%d", &score);    /* Get next score.               */
      }
      printf("\nSum of exam scores is %d\n", sum);

      return (0);
}
```

It is usually instructive (and often necessary) to question what happens when there are no data items to process. In this case, the sentinel value would be entered at the first prompt. Loop exit would occur right after the first and only test of the loop repetition condition, so the loop body would not be executed—that is, it is a loop with zero iterations. The variable sum would correctly retain its initial value of zero.                                   ←

## Using a for Statement to Implement a Sentinel Loop

Because the for statement combines the initialization, test, and update in one place, some programmers prefer to use it to implement sentinel-controlled loops. The for statement form of the while loop in Fig. 5.9 follows.

```
/* Accumulate sum of all scores.                    */
printf("Enter first score (or %d to quit)> ", SENTINEL);
for   (scanf("%d", &score);
       score != SENTINEL;
       scanf("%d", &score)) {
    sum += score;
    printf("Enter next score (%d to quit)> ", SENTINEL);
}
```

## Endfile-Controlled Loops

In Section 2.7, we discussed writing programs to run in batch mode using data files. A data file is always terminated by an endfile character that can be detected by the scanf and fscanf (file equivalent of scanf) functions. Therefore you can write a batch program that processes a list of data of any length without requiring a special sentinel value at the end of the data.

To write such a program, you must set up your input loop so it notices when scanf or fscanf encounters the endfile character. So far we have discussed only the effect scanf has on the variables passed to it as arguments. However, scanf also returns a result value just like the functions we studied in Section 3.2. When scanf is successfully able to fill its argument variables with values from the standard input device, the result value that it returns is the number of data items it actually obtained. For example, successful execution of the `scanf` in the following statement gets values for the variables in its input list, `part_id`, `num_avail`, and `cost`, and returns a result of 3, which is assigned to `input_status`:

```
input_status = scanf("%d%d%lf", &part_id, &num_avail, &cost);
```

However, if `scanf` runs into difficulty with invalid or insufficient data (for instance, if it comes across the letter `'o'` instead of a zero when trying to get a decimal integer), the function returns as its value the number of data items scanned before encountering the error or running out of data. This means that for the example shown, a nonnegative value less than 3 returned by `scanf` indicates an error. The third situation `scanf` can encounter is detecting the endfile character before getting input data for any of its arguments. In this case, `scanf` returns as its result the value of the standard constant EOF (a negative integer).

It is possible to design a repetition statement very similar to the sentinel-controlled loop that uses the status value returned by the scanning function to control repetition rather than using the values scanned. An example of such a loop is shown in Fig. 5.10, which is a batch version of the exam scores program in Fig. 5.9. The loop repetition condition

```
input_status != EOF
```

causes loop exit after the endfile character is reached.

**Figure 5.10    Batch Version of Sum of Exam Scores Program**

```
/*
 *  Compute the sum of the list of exam scores stored in the
 *  file scores.dat
 */

#include <stdio.h>          /* defines fopen, fclose, fscanf,
                                fprintf, and EOF                          */

int
main(void)
{
      FILE *inp;          /* input file pointer                           */
      int   sum = 0,      /* sum of scores input so far                   */
            score,        /* current score                                */
            input_status; /* status value returned by fscanf              */
```

*(continued)*

**Figure 5.10** **(continued)**

```
    inp = fopen("scores.dat", "r");

    printf("Scores\n");

    input_status = fscanf(inp, "%d", &score);
    while (input_status != EOF) {
        printf("%5d\n", score);
        sum += score;
        input_status = fscanf(inp, "%d", &score);
    }

    printf("\nSum of exam scores is %d\n", sum);
    fclose(inp);

    return (0);
}
```

```
Scores
   55
   33
   77

Sum of exam scores is 165
```

### Infinite Loops on Faulty Data

The behavior of the scanf and fscanf functions when they encounter faulty data can quickly make infinite loops of the while statements in Figs. 5.9 and 5.10. For example, let's assume the user responds to the prompt

```
Enter next score (-99 to quit)>
```

in Fig. 5.9 with the faulty data 7o (the second character is the letter 'o' rather than a zero). The function scanf would stop at the letter 'o', storing just the value 7 in score and leaving the letter 'o' unprocessed. On the next loop iteration, there would be no wait for the user to respond to the prompt, for scanf would find the letter 'o' awaiting processing. However, since this letter is not part of a valid integer, the scanf function would then leave the variable score unchanged and the letter 'o' unprocessed, returning a status value of zero as the result of the function call. Because the sentinel-controlled loop of Fig. 5.9 does not use the value returned by scanf, the printing of the prompt and the unsuccessful attempt to process the letter 'o' would repeat over and over.

Even though the loop of the batch program in Fig. 5.10 does use the status value returned by fscanf, it too would go into an infinite loop on faulty data. The only status value that causes this loop to exit is the negative integer meaning EOF. However, the endfile-controlled loop could be easily modified to exit when encountering end of file or faulty data. Changing the loop repetition condition to

```
input_status == 1
```

would cause the loop to exit on either end of file (input_status negative) or faulty data (input_status zero). We would also need to add an if statement after the loop to decide whether to simply print the results or to warn of bad input. The false task in the following if statement gets and displays the bad character when input_status is not EOF.

```
if (input_status == EOF) {
        printf("Sum of exam scores is %d\n", sum);
} else {
        fscanf(inp, "%c", &bad_char);
        printf("*** Error in input: %c ***\n", bad_char);
}
```

**EXERCISES FOR
SECTION 5.5**

Self-Check

1. Identify these three steps in the pseudocode that follows: the initialization of the loop control variable, the loop repetition condition, and the update of the loop control variable.

    a. Get a value for n.
    b. Give p the value 1.
    c. while n is positive
        d. Multiply p by n.
        e. Subtract 1 from n.
    f. Print p with a label.

2. What would be the behavior of the loop in Fig. 5.10 if the braces around the loop body were omitted?

### Programming

1. Translate the pseudocode from Exercise 1 using a `while` loop. Which of these three labels would it make sense to print along with the value of `p`?

   ```
   n*i =        n! =       n to the ith power =
   ```

2. Modify the loop in Fig. 5.3 so that it is a sentinel-controlled loop. Get an input value for `pay` as both the initialization and update steps of the loop. Use the value -99 as the sentinel.
3. Rewrite the program in Fig. 5.3 to run in batch mode with an endfile-controlled loop.
4. Write a program segment that allows the user to enter values and prints out the number of positive and the number of negative values entered. Design this segment as a sentinel-controlled loop using zero as the sentinel value.

## 5.6 NESTED LOOPS

Loops may be nested just like other control structures. Nested loops consist of an outer loop with one or more inner loops. Each time the outer loop is repeated, the inner loops are reentered, their loop control expressions are reevaluated, and all required iterations are performed.

**EXAMPLE 5.7**

The program in Fig. 5.11 contains a sentinel loop nested within a counting loop. This structure is being used to tally by month the local Audubon Club members' sightings of bald eagles for the past year. The data for this program consists of a group of integers followed by a zero, then a second group of integers followed by a zero, then a third group, and so on, for twelve groups of numbers. The first group of numbers represents sightings in January, the second represents sightings in February, and so on, for all twelve months.

The outer `for` loop repeats 12 times (value of NUM_MONTHS). The first statement in the outer loop sets the accumulator variable `sightings` to 0. The number of repetitions of the inner `while` loop depends on the data and may be zero (e.g., month 3 of the sample). The `if` statement nested in the inner loop adds a positive count of eagles to `sightings` and displays a warning message for negative counts. After exit from the inner loop, the outer loop displays the total sightings for the current month.

**Figure 5.11   Program to Process Bald Eagle Sightings for a Year**

```c
/*
 * Tally by month the bald eagle sightings for the year. Each month's
 * sightings are terminated by the sentinel zero.
 */

#include <stdio.h>

#define SENTINEL    0
#define NUM_MONTHS 12

int
main(void)
{

        int month,      /* number of month being processed              */
            mem_sight,  /* one member's sightings for this month        */
            sightings;  /* total sightings so far for this month        */

        printf("BALD EAGLE SIGHTINGS\n");
        for (month = 1;
             month <= NUM_MONTHS;
             ++month) {
            sightings = 0;
            scanf("%d", &mem_sight);
            while (mem_sight != SENTINEL) {
                if (mem_sight >= 0)
                    sightings += mem_sight;
                else
                    printf("Warning, negative count %d ignored",
                            mem_sight);
                scanf("%d", &mem_sight);
            }  /* inner while */

            printf("  month %2d: %2d\n", month, sightings);
        }  /* outer for */

        return (0);
}
```

*(continued)*

**Figure 5.11**    *(continued)*

```
Input data
2 1 4 3 0
1 2 0
0
5 4 -1 1 0
. . .

Results
BALD EAGLE SIGHTINGS
  month  1: 10
  month  2:  3
  month  3:  0
Warning, negative count -1 ignored
  month  4: 10
. . .
```

**EXAMPLE 5.8**    Figure 5.12 shows a sample run of a program with two nested counting loops. The outer loop is repeated three times (for i = 1, 2, 3). Each time the outer loop is repeated, the statement

```
printf("Outer %6d\n", i);
```

displays the string "Outer" and the value of i (the outer loop control variable). Next, the inner loop is entered, and its loop control variable j is reset to 0. The number of times the inner loop is repeated depends on the current value of i. Each time the inner loop is repeated, the statement

```
printf("  Inner %9d\n", j);
```

displays the string "Inner" and the value of j.

The outer loop control variable, i, appears in the condition that determines the number of repetitions of the inner loop. Although this is perfectly valid, you cannot use the same variable as the loop control variable of both an outer and an inner for loop in the same nest.    ◄

**Figure 5.12  Nested Counting Loop Program**

```
/*
 * Illustrates a pair of nested counting loops
 */

#include <stdio.h>

int
main(void)
{
      int i, j;   /* loop control variables */

      printf("              I     J\n");        /* prints column labels      */

      for  (i = 1;  i < 4;  ++i) {              /* heading of outer for loop  */
          printf("Outer %6d\n", i);
          for  (j = 0;  j < i;  ++j) {          /* heading of inner loop      */
              printf("  Inner%9d\n", j);
          }    /* end of inner loop */

      }    /*  end of outer loop */

      return (0);
}

              I   J
Outer         1
   Inner          0
Outer         2
   Inner          0
   Inner          1
Outer         3
   Inner          0
   Inner          1
   Inner          2
```

---

**EXERCISES FOR SECTION 5.6**

Self-Check

1. What is displayed by the following program segments, assuming m is 3 and n is 5?

```
a. for  (i = 1;  i <= n;  ++i) {
       for  (j = 0;  j < i;  ++j) {
          printf("*");
       }
       printf("\n");
   }
b. for  (i = n;  i > 0;  --i) {
       for  (j = m;  j > 0;  --j) {
          printf("*");
       }
       printf("\n");
   }
```

2. Show the output displayed by these nested loops:

```
for  (i = 0;  i < 2;  ++i) {
   printf("Outer %4d\n", i);
   for  (j = 0;  j < 3;  ++j) {
      printf("  Inner%3d%3d\n", i, j);
   }
   for  (k = 2;  k > 0;  --k) {
      printf("  Inner%3d%3d\n", i, k);
   }
}
```

Programming

1. Write a program that displays the multiplication table for numbers 0 to 9.
2. Write nests of loops that cause the following output to be displayed:

```
0
0 1
0 1 2
0 1 2 3
0 1 2 3 4
0 1 2 3
0 1 2
0 1
0
```

## 5.7 THE do-while STATEMENT AND FLAG-CONTROLLED LOOPS

Both the for statement and the while statement evaluate a loop repetition condition before the first execution of the loop body. In most cases, this pretest is desirable and prevents the loop from executing when there may be no data items to process or when the initial value of the loop control variable is outside its expected range. There are some situations, generally involving interactive input, when we know that a loop must execute at least one time. C provides the do-while statement to implement such loops as shown next.

**EXAMPLE 5.9**   The loop

```
do {
     printf("Enter a letter from A through E> ");
     scanf("%c", &letter_choice);
} while (letter_choice < 'A'  ||  letter_choice > 'E');
```

prompts the user to enter one of the letters A through E. After scanf gets a data character, the loop repetition condition tests to see whether letter_choice contains one of the letters requested. If so, the repetition condition is false, and the next statement after the loop executes. If letter_choice contains some other letter, the condition is true and the loop body is repeated. Since we know the program user must enter at least one data character, the do-while is an ideal statement to use to implement this loop.        ←

---

**do-while Statement**

SYNTAX:    do
                *statement*
            while (*loop repetition condition*);

EXAMPLE: /* Find first even number input */
            do
                 status = scanf("%d", &num);
            while (status > 0  &&  (num % 2) != 0);

INTERPRETATION: First, the *statement* is executed. Then, the *loop repetition condition* is tested, and if it is true, the *statement* is repeated and the *condition* retested. When this condition is tested and found to be false, the loop is exited and the next statement after the do-while is executed.

*Note:* If the loop body contains more than one statement, the group of statements must be surrounded by braces.

## Flag-Controlled Loops for Input Validation

Sometimes a loop repetition condition becomes so complex that placing the full expression in its usual spot is awkward. In many cases, the condition may be simplified by using a flag. A **flag** is a type int variable used to represent whether or not a certain event has occurred. A flag has one of two values: 1 (true) and 0 (false).

**flag**
a type int variable used to represent whether or not a certain event has occurred

**EXAMPLE 5.10** ▶ Function get_int (Fig. 5.13) returns an integer value that is in the range specified by its two arguments (n_min through n_max, inclusive). The loop repeatedly prompts the user for a value in the desired range. The outer do-while structure implements the stated purpose of the function. The type int variable error acts as a program flag to signal whether an error has been detected. It is initialized to 0 (false) at the beginning of the outer loop and is changed to 1 (true) when an error is detected by the if statement that validates the data scanned into in_val. Execution of the outer loop continues as long as error is true. The inner do-while skips any characters remaining on a data line by repeatedly scanning a character and checking to see whether it is the newline character '\n'.

Execution of the function call

```
next_int = get_int(10, 20);
```

proceeds as follows, assuming that the user responds to the first prompt by mistyping the number 20 as @20. Because the first character is @, scanf

**Figure 5.13    Validating Input Using do-while Statement**

```
/*
 * Returns the first integer between n_min and n_max entered as data.
 * Pre : n_min <= n_max
 * Post: Result is in the range n_min through n_max.
 */
int
get_int (int n_min, int n_max)
{
        int   in_val,                   /* input - number entered by user  */
              status;                   /* status value returned by scanf  */
        char skip_ch;                   /* character to skip               */
        int   error;                    /* error flag for bad input        */
```

*(continued)*

*constant Macro EOF*

**Figure 5.13** *(continued)*

```
/* Get data from user until in_val is in the range.              */
do {
    /* No errors detected yet. */
    error - 0;
    /* Get a number from the user. */
    printf("Enter an integer in the range from %d ", n_min);
    printf("to %d inclusive> ", n_max);
    status = scanf("%d", &in_val);

    /* Validate the number. */
    if (status != 1) {   /* in_val didn't get a number */
        error = 1;
        scanf("%c", &skip_ch);
        printf("Invalid character >>%c>>. ", skip_ch);
        printf("Skipping rest of line.\n");
    } else if (in_val < n_min  ||  in_val > n_max) {
        error = 1;
        printf("Number %d is not in range.\n", in_val);
    }

    /* Skip rest of data line. */
    do
        scanf("%c", &skip_ch);
    while (skip_ch != '\n');
```

*Skips the rest of the line*

```
} while (error);

    return (in_val);
}
```

returns 0 to status, error is set to 1, the first error message is displayed, and the inner do-while skips the rest of the data line. When the outer loop repeats, the user enters 2o. When scanf encounters the o, it stops scanning, stores the 2 in in_val, and returns the result 1 to status. Because the number 2 is less than n_min (10), error is set to 1, the second error message is displayed, and the inner do-while skips the rest of the data line. Because error is 1, the outer loop is repeated. After the user responds to the last prompt below by entering 20, the outer loop is exited and 20 is returned as the result and stored in `next_int`.

```
Enter an integer in the range from 10 to 20 inclusive> @20
Invalid character >>@>>. Skipping rest of line.
Enter an integer in the range from 10 to 20 inclusive> 2o
Number 2 is not in range.
Enter an integer in the range from 10 to 20 inclusive> 20    ←
```

The `do-while` is often the structure to choose when checking for valid input. As soon as the input loop of Fig. 5.13 receives a status code from `scanf` indicating an error, the loop body explicitly scans and echoes the bad character, skips the rest of the input line, and sets the error flag so the loop will execute again, permitting fresh (and hopefully valid) input. The `do-while` used in Fig. 5.13 also prevents an infinite input loop in the event the user types an invalid character.

## EXERCISES FOR SECTION 5.7

### Self-Check

1. Which of the following code segments is a better way to implement a sentinel-controlled loop? Why?

```
scanf("%d", &num);                    do {
while (num != SENT) {                      scanf("%d", &num);
    /* process num */                      if (num != SENT) {
    scanf("%d", &num);                          /* process num */}
}                                     } while (num != SENT);
```

2. Rewrite the following code using a `do-while` statement with no decisions in the loop body:

```
sum = 0;
for  (odd = 1;  odd < n;  odd = odd + 2)
    sum = sum + odd;
printf("Sum of the positive odd numbers less than %d is %d\n",
        n, sum);
```

In what situations will the rewritten code print an incorrect sum?

### Programming

1. Design an interactive input loop that scans pairs of integers until it reaches a pair in which the first integer evenly divides the second.

# 5.8 PROBLEM SOLVING ILLUSTRATED

In this section, we examine a programming problem that illustrates many of the concepts discussed in this chapter. The *top-down design* process will be demonstrated in solving this programming problem. The program will be implemented in a stepwise manner, starting with a list of major algorithm steps and continuing to add detail through refinement until the program and its function subprogram can be written.

## Case Study: Computing Radiation Levels

### PROBLEM

In a certain building at a top secret research lab, some yttrium-90 has leaked into the computer analysts' coffee room. The leak would currently expose personnel to 150 millirems of radiation a day. The half-life of the substance is about three days; that is, the radiation level is only half of what it was three days ago. The analysts want to know how long it will be before the radiation is down to a safe level of 0.466 millirem a day. They would like a chart that displays the radiation level for every three days with the message Unsafe or Safe after every line. The chart should stop just before the radiation level is one-tenth of the safe level, because the more cautious analysts will require a safety factor of 10. The program should also print the first day that the room can be entered.

### ANALYSIS

Each line of the chart will show a day number and a radiation level for that day. The last line in the chart should show the day and radiation just prior to safe entry. The data requirements and algorithm follow.

### Data Requirements

#### Problem Constants

```
SAFE_RAD  0.466     /* the safe radiation level in
                       millirems                     */
SAFETY_FACT  10.0   /* the safety factor             */
```

#### Problem Input

```
double init_radiation /* the initial radiation level  */
```

#### Problem Outputs

```
int day                /* the day number              */
double radiation_lev   /* the radiation level in millirems */
```

**DESIGN**

### Initial Algorithm

1. Compute the stopping level of radiation, that is, the safe level divided by the safety factor.
2. Prompt the user to enter the initial radiation level.
3. Compute and display the day number and the radiation level every three days that the radiation level exceeds the stopping radiation level. Also, indicate whether each level is safe or unsafe.
4. Display the day that the user can enter the room.

We will introduce a new variable (`min_radiation`) to hold the stopping level of radiation referred to in step 1 of our initial algorithm. As shown in the structure chart (Fig. 5.14), we will call a function, `rad_table`, to display the radiation table, and determine the day that the room can be entered.

### Additional Program Variable

```
double min_radiation  /* the stopping level
                              of radiation  */
```

**DESIGN and ANALYSIS of function rad_table**

Since it is clear that some steps of our solution will be repeated, we will use a `while` loop in our pseudocode for function `rad_table`.

**Figure 5.14
Structure Chart
for Computing
Radiation
Tables**

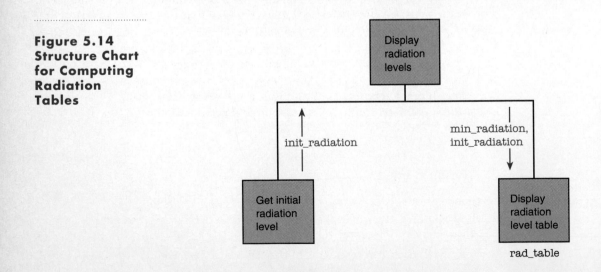

### Algorithm for rad_table

1. Initialize day to 0.
2. Initialize radiation_lev to init_radiation
3. while radiation_lev exceeds min_radiation
   4. Display the value of day, radiation_lev, and the string "Unsafe" or "Safe".
   5. Add 3 to the value of day.
   6. Compute radiation_lev for the next period.
7. Return the day number for safe entry.

Now we can further refine step 4 as shown next.

### Step 4 Refinement
4.     if radiation_lev exceeds SAFE_RAD
           Display day, radiation_lev, and "Unsafe".
    else
           Display day, radiation_lev, and "Safe".

**◄ IMPLEMENTATION ►**

The program appears in Fig. 5.15. Notice that we declare the loop control variable radiation_lev only in function rad_table because it is not needed in the main function. We use a for statement to implement the loop in function rad_table.

**◄ TESTING ►**

The only data item for this program is the initial radiation level. One run with a data value of 150.0 (millirems) will give you output that you can use to show correctness on valid, middle-of-the-road data. Check that each radiation value in the table displayed is one-half the previous value and that the number of days always increases by three. Also check that the first safe value is less than 0.466 millirem. Verify that your loop exited correctly by dividing the last radiation value displayed by 2.0. You must get a value that is less than or equal to 0.0466 (0.466/10.0 is 0.0466).

**EXERCISES FOR SECTION 5.8**

Self-Check

1. Replace the for statement in Fig. 5.15 with a while loop.
2. How would you modify the program in Fig. 5.15 to stop the table display *after,* instead of before, the radiation level becomes less than or equal to the safe level divided by the safety factor?

**Figure 5.15**    **Program to Compute Radiation Levels**

```
/*
 * Calculates and displays a table showing the safety level of a coffee room.
 */

#include <stdio.h>

#define SAFE_RAD    0.466  /* safe level of radiation                     */
#define SAFETY_FACT 10.0   /* safety factor                               */

int rad_table(double init_radiation, double min_radiation);

int
main(void)
{
      int    day;               /* day user can enter room               */
      double init_radiation,    /* radiation level right after leak      */
             min_radiation;     /* safe level divided by safety factor   */

      /* Compute stopping level of radiation.                            */
      min_radiation = SAFE_RAD / SAFETY_FACT;

      /* Prompts user to enter initial radiation level                   */
      printf("Enter the radiation level (in millirems)> ");
      scanf("%lf", &init_radiation);

      /* Displays table                                                  */
      day = rad_table(init_radiation, min_radiation);

      /* Display day the user can enter the room.                        */
      printf ("\nYou can enter the room on day %d.\n", day);

      return (0);
}

/*
 * Displays a table showing the radiation level and safety status every 3
 * days until the room is deemed safe to enter. Returns the day number for
 * the first safe day.
```

*(continued)*

**Figure 5.15** *(continued)*

```
 * Pre : min_radiation and init_radiation are defined.
 * Post: radiation_lev <= min_radiation
 */
int
rad_table(double init_radiation, double min_radiation)
{
      int    day;              /* days elapsed since substance leak      */
      double radiation_lev;    /* current radiation level                */

      day = 0;
      printf("\n   Day    Radiation   Status\n          (millirems)\n");
      for  (radiation_lev = init_radiation;
            radiation_lev > min_radiation;
            radiation_lev /= 2.0) {
       if   (radiation_lev > SAFE_RAD)
              printf("  %3d%5c%9.4f   Unsafe\n", day, ' ', radiation_lev);
       else
              printf("  %3d%5c%9.4f   Safe\n", day, ' ', radiation_lev);
       day += 3;
      }

      return (day);
}
```

```
Enter the radiation level (in millirems)> 150.0

   Day    Radiation   Status
          (millirems)
    0      150.0000   Unsafe
    3       75.0000   Unsafe
    6       37.5000   Unsafe
    9       18.7500   Unsafe
   12        9.3750   Unsafe
   15        4.6875   Unsafe
   18        2.3438   Unsafe
   21        1.1719   Unsafe
   24        0.5859   Unsafe
   27        0.2930   Safe
   30        0.1465   Safe
   33        0.0732   Safe

You can enter the room on day 36.
```

# 5.9 HOW TO DEBUG AND TEST PROGRAMS

In Section 2.8 we described the three general categories of errors: syntax errors, run-time errors, and logic errors. Sometimes the cause of a run-time error or the source of a logic error is apparent and the error can be fixed easily. Often, however, the error is not obvious and you may spend considerable time and energy locating it.

The first step in locating a hidden error is to examine the program output to determine which part of the program is generating incorrect results. Then you can focus on the statements in that section of the program to determine which are at fault. We describe two ways to do this next.

## Using Debugger Programs

A *debugger program* can help you debug a C program. The debugger program lets you execute your program one statement at a time (*single-step execution*). Through single-step execution, you can trace your program's execution and observe the effect of each C statement on variables you select. With single-step execution you can validate that loop control variables and other important variables (e.g., accumulators) are incremented as expected during each iteration of a loop. You can also check that input variables contain the correct data after each scan operation.

If your program is very long, you can separate your program into segments by setting *breakpoints* at selected statements. A breakpoint is like a fence between two segments of a program. You should set a breakpoint at the end of each major algorithm step. Then instruct the debugger to execute all statements from the last breakpoint up to the next breakpoint. When the program stops at a breakpoint, you can examine the values of selected variables to determine whether the program segment has executed correctly. If it has, you will want to execute through to the next breakpoint. If it has not, you may want to set more breakpoints in that segment or perhaps perform single-step execution through that segment.

## Debugging without a Debugger

If you cannot use a debugger, insert extra *diagnostic calls* to printf that display intermediate results at critical points in your program. For example, you should display the values of variables affected by each major algorithm step before and after the step executes. By comparing these results at the end of a run, you may be able to determine which segment of your program contains bugs.

Once you have determined the likely source of an error, you should insert additional diagnostic calls to `printf` to trace the values of critical variables in the "buggy" segment. For example, if the loop in Fig. 5.9 is not computing the correct sum, the call to `printf` in color below will display each value of `score` and `sum`. The asterisks highlight the diagnostic output in the debugging runs and the diagnostic calls to `printf` in the source program.

```
while (score != SENTINEL) {
    sum += score;
    printf("***** score is %d, sum is %d\n", score, sum);
    printf("Enter next score (%d to quit)> ", SENTINEL);
    scanf("%d", &score);     /* Get next score.          */
}
```

We usually include a `\n` at the end of every `printf` format string. It is especially critical that you do this in diagnostic calls to `printf` so that your output will be displayed immediately; otherwise, if a run-time error occurs before a `\n` is encountered in another format string, you may never see the diagnostic message.

Be careful when you insert diagnostic calls to `printf`. Sometimes you must add braces if a single statement inside an `if` or a `while` statement becomes a compound statement when you add a diagnostic `printf`.

Once it appears that you have located the error, you will want to take out the diagnostic statements. As a temporary measure, turn the diagnostic statements into comments by enclosing them in `/* */`. If the same errors crop up again in later testing, it is easier to remove the comment symbols than to retype the diagnostic statements.

## Off-by-One Loop Errors

A fairly common logic error in programs with loops is a loop that executes one more time or one less time than required. If a sentinel-controlled loop performs an extra repetition, it may erroneously process the sentinel value along with the regular data.

If a loop performs a counting operation, make sure that the initial and final values of the loop control variable are correct and that the loop repetition condition is right. For example, the following loop body executes $n + 1$ times instead of n times. If you want the loop body to execute exactly n times, change the loop repetition condition to count < n.

```
for  (count = 0;  count <= n;  ++count)
    sum += count;
```

loop boundaries
initial and final values of the
loop control variable

Often you can determine whether a loop is correct by checking the **loop boundaries**, that is, the initial and final values of the loop control variable. For a counting for loop, carefully evaluate the expression in the initialization step, substitute this value everywhere the counter variable appears in the loop body, and verify that it makes sense as a beginning value. Then choose a value for the counter that still causes the loop repetition condition to be true but that will make this condition false after one more evaluation of the update expression. Check the validity of this boundary value wherever the counter variable appears. As an example, in the for loop,

```
sum = 0;
k = 1;
for  (i = -n;  i < n - k;  ++i)
    sum += i * i;
```

check that the first value of the counter variable i is supposed to be −n and that the last value should be n − 2. Next, check that the assignment statement

```
sum += i * i;
```

is correct at these boundaries. When i is −n, sum gets the value of $n^2$. When i is n − 2, the value of $(n - 2)^2$ is added to the previous sum. As a final check, pick some small value of n (for example, 2) and trace the loop execution to see that it computes sum correctly for this case.

**TESTING**

After all errors have been corrected and the program appears to execute as expected, the program should be tested thoroughly to make sure that it works. For a simple program, make enough test runs to verify that the program works properly for representative samples of all possible data combinations.

**EXERCISES FOR
SECTION 5.9**

Self-Check

1. For the first counting loop in the subsection "Off-by-One Loop Errors," add debugging statements to show the value of the loop control variable at the start of each repetition. Also add debugging statements to show the value of sum at the end of each loop repetition.
2. Repeat Exercise 1 for the second loop in the same subsection.

# 5.10 COMMON PROGRAMMING ERRORS

Beginners sometimes confuse if and while statements because both statements contain a parenthesized condition. Always use an if statement to implement a decision step and a while or for statement to implement a loop.

The syntax of the for statement header is repeated.

```
for (initialization expression;
     loop repetition condition;
     update expression)
```

Remember to end the initialization expression and the loop repetition condition with semicolons. Be careful not to put a semicolon before or after the closing parenthesis of the for statement header. A semicolon after this parenthesis would have the effect of ending the for statement without making execution of the loop body dependent on its condition.

Another common mistake in using while and for statements is to forget that the structure assumes that the loop body is a single statement. Remember to use braces around a loop body consisting of multiple statements. Some C programmers always use braces around a loop body, whether it contains one or many statements. Keep in mind that your compiler ignores indentation, so a loop defined as shown (with braces around the loop body left out)

```
while (x > xbig)
        x -= 2;
        ++xbig;
/* end while */
```

really executes as

```
while (x > xbig)
        x -= 2; /* only this statement is repeated */

++xbig;
```

The C compiler can easily detect that there is something wrong with code in which a closing brace has been omitted on a compound statement. However, the error message noting the symbol's absence may be far from the spot where the brace belongs, and other error messages often appear as a side effect of the omission. When compound statements are nested, the compiler will associate the first closing brace encountered with the innermost structure. Even if it is the terminator for this inner structure that is left out, the compiler may complain about the outer structure. In the example that follows, the body of the `while` statement is missing a brace. However, the compiler will associate the closing brace before `else` with the body of the `while` loop and then proceed to mark the `else` as improper.

```
printf("Experiment successful? (Y/N)> ");
scanf("%c", &ans);
if (ans == 'Y') {
    printf("Enter one number per line (%d to quit)\n> ",
            SENT);
    scanf("%d", &data);
    while (data != SENT) {
        sum += data;
        printf("> ");
        scanf("%d", &data);
                            /* <- missing } */
} else {
    printf("Try it again tomorrow.\n");
    printf("Now follow correct shutdown procedure.\n");
}
```

Be careful when you use tests for inequality to control the repetition of a loop. The following loop is intended to process all transactions for a bank account while the balance is positive:

```
scanf("%d%lf", &code, &amount);
while (balance != 0.0) {
       . . .
        scanf("%d%lf", &code, &amount);
}
```

If the bank balance goes from a positive to a negative amount without being exactly 0.0, the loop will not terminate (an infinite loop). This loop is safer:

```
scanf("%d%lf", &code, &amount);
while (balance > 0.0) {
```

```
        . . .
    scanf("%d%lf", &code, &amount);
}
```

Be sure to verify that a loop's repetition condition will eventually become false (0); otherwise, an infinite loop may result. If you use a sentinel-controlled loop, remember to provide a prompt that tells the program's user what value to enter as the sentinel. Make sure that the sentinel value cannot be confused with a normal data item.

One common cause of a nonterminating loop is the use of a loop repetition condition in which an equality test is mistyped as an assignment operation. Consider the following loop that expects the user to type the number 0 (actually any integer other than 1) to exit:

```
do {
    . . .
    printf("One more time? (1 to continue/0 to quit)> ");
    scanf("%d", &again);
}   while (again = 1);  /* should be: again == 1 */
```

The value of the loop repetition condition will always be 1, never 0 (false), so this loop will not exit on an entry of zero or of any other number.

A do-while always executes at least once. Use a do-while only when there is no possibility of zero loop iterations. If you find yourself adding an if statement to patch your code with a result like this

```
if (condition₁)
    do {
        . . .
    } while (condition₁);
```

replace the segment with a while or for statement. Both these statements automatically test the loop repetition condition *before* executing the loop body.

Do not use increment, decrement, or compound assignment operators as subexpressions in complex expressions. At best, such usage leads to expressions that are difficult to read; at worst, to expressions that produce varying results in different implementations of C.

Remember the parentheses that are assumed to be around any expression that is the second operand of a compound assignment operator. Since the statement

```
a *= b + c;    is equivalent to    a = a * (b + c);
```

there is no shorter way to write

```
a = a * b + c;
```

Be sure that the operand of an increment or decrement operator is a variable and that this variable is referenced after executing the increment or decrement operation. Without a subsequent reference, the operator's side effect of changing the value of the variable is pointless. Do not use a variable twice in an expression in which it is incremented/decremented. Applying the increment/decrement operators to constants or expressions is illegal.

## CHAPTER REVIEW

1. Use a loop to repeat steps in a program. Two kinds of loops occur frequently in programming: counting loops and sentinel-controlled loops. For a counting loop, the number of iterations required can be determined before the loop is entered. For a sentinel-controlled loop, repetition continues until a special data value is scanned. The pseudocode for each loop form follows.

   **Counter-controlled loop**
   Set *loop control variable* to an initial value of 0.
   while *loop control variable < final value*
       . . .
       Increase *loop control variable* by 1.

   **Sentinel-controlled loop**
   Get a line of data.
   while the sentinel value has not been encountered
       Process the data line.
       Get another line of data.

2. C provides three statements for implementing loops: while, for, and do-while. Use the for to implement counting loops and the do-while to implement loops that must execute at least once such as data validation loops for interactive programs. Code other conditional loops using the for or while, using whichever implementation is clearer.

3. In designing a loop, focus on both loop control and loop processing. For loop processing, make sure that the loop body contains steps that perform the operation that must be repeated. For loop control, you must provide steps that initialize, test, and update the loop control variable. Make sure that the initialization step leads to correct program results when the loop body is not executed (zero-iteration loop).

## New C Constructs

| Construct | Effect |
|---|---|

### Counting for Loop

```
for (num = 0;
     num < 26;
     ++num) {
   square = num * num;
   printf("%5d %5d\n", num,
        square);
}
```

Displays 26 lines, each containing an integer from 0 to 25 and its square.

### Counting for Loop with a Negative Step

```
for (volts = 20;
     volts >= -20;
     volts -= 10) {
   current = volts / resistance;
   printf("%5d %8.3f\n", volts,
        current);
}
```

For values of volts equal to 20, 10, 0, -10, -20, computes value of current and displays volts and current.

### Sentinel-Controlled while Loop

```
product = 1;
printf("Enter %d to quit\n",
      SENVAL);
printf("Enter first number> ");
scanf("%d", &dat);
while (dat != SENVAL) {
    product *= dat;
    printf("Next number> ");
    scanf("%d", &dat);
}
```

Computes the product of a list of numbers. The product is complete when the user enters the sentinel value (SENVAL).

### Endfile-Controlled while Loop

```
sum = 0;
status = scanf("%d", &num);
while (status == 1) {
    sum += num;
    status = scanf("%d", &num);
}
```

Accumulates the sum of a list of numbers. The sum is complete when scanf detects the endfile character or encounters erroneous data.

*(continued)*

**New C Constructs** *(continued)*

| Construct | Effect |
|---|---|
| **do-while Loop**<br>```do {     printf("Positive number < 10> ");     scanf("d%, &num); } while (num < 1 || num >= 10);``` | Repeatedly displays prompt and stores a number in num until user enters a number that is in range. |
| **Increment / Decrement**<br>```z = ++j * k--;``` | Stores in z the product of the incremented value of j and the current value of k. Then k is decremented. |
| **Compound Assignment**<br>```ans *= a - b;``` | Assigns to ans the value of ans * (a - b). |

# QUICK-CHECK EXERCISES

1. A loop that continues to process input data until a special value is entered is called a _____-controlled loop.
2. Some for loops cannot be rewritten in C using a while loop. True or false?
3. It is an error if the body of a for loop never executes. True or false?
4. In an endfile-controlled while loop, the initialization and update expressions typically include calls to the function _____.
5. In a typical counter-controlled loop, the number of loop repetitions may not be known until the loop is executing. True or false?
6. During execution of the following program segment, how many lines of asterisks are displayed?

```
for  (i = 0;  i < 10;  ++i)
    for  (j = 0;  j < 5;  ++j)
        printf("**********\n");
```

7. During execution of the following program segment,
   a. How many times does the first call to printf execute?
   b. How many times does the second call to printf execute?

c. What is the last value displayed?

```
for (i = 0;  i < 7;  ++i) {
    for (j = 0;  j < i;  ++j)
        printf("%4d", i * j);
    printf("\n");
}
```

8. If the value of n is 4 and m is 5, is the value of the following expression 21?

```
++(n * m)
```

Explain your answer.

9. What are the values of n, m, and p after execution of this three-statement fragment?

```
j            k         n = j - ++k;
                       m = j-- + k--;
5            2         p = k + j;
```

10. What are the values of x, y, and z after execution of this three-statement fragment?

```
x         y         z         x *= y + z;
                              y /= 2 * z + 1;
3         5         2         z += x;
```

11. What does the following code segment display? Try each of these inputs: 345, 82, 6. Then, describe the action of the code.

```
printf("\nEnter a positive integer> ");
scanf("%d", &num);
do {
    printf("%d   ", num % 10);
    num /= 10;
} while (num > 0);
printf("\n");
```

*typedef char data -t;* *un*

# ANSWERS TO QUICK-CHECK EXERCISES

1. sentinel
2. false
3. false
4. fscanf

5. false
6. 50
7. a. 0 + 1 + 2 + 3 + 4 + 5 + 6 = 21
   b. 7
   c. 30
8. No. The expression is illegal. The increment operator cannot be applied to an expression such as (n * m).
9. n=2, m=8, p=6
10. x=21, y=1, z=23
11. Enter a positive integer> 345
    5   4   3
    Enter a positive integer> 82
    2   8
    Enter a positive integer> 6
    6

    The code displays the digits of an integer in reverse order and separated by spaces.

## REVIEW QUESTIONS

1. In what ways are the initialization, repetition test, and update steps alike for a sentinel-controlled loop and an endfile-controlled loop? How are they different?
2. Write a program that computes and displays the sum of a collection of Celsius temperatures entered at the terminal until a sentinel value of −275 is entered.
3. Hand-trace the program that follows given the following data:

```
4 2 8 4    1 4 2 1    9 3 3 1    -22 10 8 2    3 3 4 5
```

```c
#include <stdio.h>
#define SPECIAL_SLOPE  0.0

int
main(void)
{
        double slope, y2, y1, x2, x1;

        printf("Enter 4 numbers separated by spaces.");
        printf("\nThe last two numbers cannot be the ");
        printf("same, but\nthe program terminates if ");
        printf("the first two are.\n");
```

```
        printf("\nEnter four numbers> ");
        scanf("%lf%lf%lf%lf", &y2, &y1, &x2, &x1);

        for (slope = (y2 - y1) / (x2 - x1);
              slope != SPECIAL_SLOPE;
              slope = (y2 - y1) / (x2 - x1)) {
            printf("Slope is %5.2f.\n", slope);
            printf("\nEnter four more numbers> ");
            scanf("%lf%lf%lf%lf", &y2, &y1, &x2, &x1);
        }

        return (0);
    }
```

4. Rewrite the program in Review Question 3 so it uses a `while` loop.

5. Rewrite the program segment that follows, using a `for` loop:

```
count = 0;
i = 0;
while (i < n) {
    scanf("%d", &x);
    if (x == i)
            ++count;
    ++i;
}
```

6. Rewrite this `for` loop heading, omitting any invalid semicolons.

```
for (i = n;
      i < max;
      ++i;);
```

7. Write a `do-while` loop that repeatedly prompts for and takes input until a value in the range 0 through 15 inclusive is input. Include code that prevents the loop from cycling indefinitely on input of a wrong data type.

# PROGRAMMING PROJECTS

1. a. Write a program that will find the smallest, largest, and average values in a collection of N numbers. Get the value of N before scanning each value in the collection of N numbers.

   b. Modify your program to compute and display both the range of values in the data collection and the standard deviation of the data collection. To compute the standard deviation, accumulate the sum of the squares of the data values (`sum_squares`) in the main loop. After loop exit, use the formula

$$standard\ deviation = \sqrt{\frac{sum\_squares}{N} - average^2}$$

2. Write a program to generate a calendar for a year. The program should accept the year and the day of the week for January 1 of that year (1=Sunday, 7=Saturday). Remember, February has 29 days if the year is a leap year. (See Chapter 4, Programming Project 6). The calendar should be printed in the following form (for each month).

```
    January
                    1
  2  3  4  5  6  7  8
  9 10 11 12 13 14 15
 16 17 18 19 20 21 22
 23 24 25 26 27 28 29
 30 31
```

3. a. The Fibonacci sequence is a sequence of numbers beginning

$$1, 1, 2, 3, 5, 8, 13, 21, \ldots$$

The first two elements are defined to be 1. Each of the other elements is the sum of its two predecessors. Write a program that takes a value for $n$ in the range 1 to 30 and displays the first $n$ elements of the Fibonacci sequence.

   b. Modify your program so it displays the elements eight per line.

4. Let $n$ be a positive integer consisting of up to 10 digits, $d_{10}, d_9, \ldots, d_1$. Write a program to list in one column each of the digits in the number $n$. The rightmost digit, $d_1$, should be listed at the top of the column. *Hint:* If $n$ is 3704, what is the value of the digit when computed by using

```
digit = n % 10;
```

Test your program for values of $n$ equal to 6, 3704, and 170,498.

5. a. Write a program to process a collection of daily high temperatures. Your program should count and print the number of hot days (high temperature 85 or higher), the number of pleasant days (high temperature 60–84), and the number of cold days (high temperatures less than 60). It should also

display the category of each temperature. Test your program on the following data:

55  62  68  74  59  45  41  58  60  67  65  78  82  88  91
92  90  93  87  80  78  79  72  68  61  59

b. Modify your program to display the average temperature (a real number) at the end of the run.

6. Write a program to process weekly employee time cards for all employees of an organization. Each employee will have three data items: an identification number, the hourly wage rate, and the number of hours worked during a given week. Each employee is to be paid time-and-a-half for all hours worked over 40. A tax amount of 3.625 percent of gross salary will be deducted. The program output should show the employee's number and net pay. Display the total payroll and the average amount paid at the end of the run.

7. Suppose you own a beer distributorship that sells Piels (ID number 1), Coors (ID number 2), Bud (ID number 3), and Iron City (ID number 4) by the case. Write a program to

a. Get the case inventory for each brand for the start of the week.
b. Process all weekly sales and purchase records for each brand.
c. Display out the final inventory.

Each transaction will consist of two data items. The first item will be the brand identification number (an integer). The second will be the amount purchased (a positive integer value) or the amount sold (a negative integer value). For now you may assume that you always have sufficient foresight to prevent depletion of your inventory for any brand. (*Hint:* Your data entry should begin with four values representing the case inventory, followed by the transaction values.)

8. The pressure of a gas changes as the volume and temperature of the gas vary. Write a program that uses the Van der Waals equation of state for a gas

$$\left(P + \frac{an^2}{V^2}\right)(V - bn) = nRT$$

to display in tabular form the relationship between the pressure and the volume of $n$ moles of carbon dioxide at a constant absolute temperature ($T$). $P$ is the pressure in atmospheres and $V$ is the volume in liters. The Van der Waals constants for carbon dioxide are $a = 3.592$ L$^2 \cdot$ atm/mol$^2$ and $b = 0.0427$ L/mol. Use $0.08206$ L $\cdot$ atm/mol $\cdot$ K for the gas constant $R$. Inputs to the program include $n$, the Kelvin temperature, the initial and final volumes in milliliters, and the volume increment between lines of the table. Your program will display a table that varies the volume of the gas from the initial to the final volume in steps prescribed by the volume increment. Here is a sample run:

```
Please enter at the prompts the number of moles of carbon
dioxide, the absolute temperature, the initial volume in
milliliters, the final volume, and the increment volume
between lines of the table.

Quantity of carbon dioxide (moles)> 0.02
Temperature (kelvin)> 300
Initial volume (milliliters)> 400
Final volume (milliliters)> 600
Volume increment (milliliters)> 50

0.0200 moles of carbon dioxide at 300 kelvin

Volume (ml)       Pressure (atm)

    400               1.2246
    450               1.0891
    500               0.9807
    550               0.8918
    600               0.8178
```

9. A concrete channel to bring water to Crystal Lake is being designed. It will have vertical walls and be 15 feet wide. It will be 10 feet deep, have a slope of .0015 feet/foot, and a roughness coefficient of .014. How deep will the water be when 1000 cubic feet per second is flowing through the channel?

To solve this problem, we can use Manning's equation

$$Q = \frac{1.486}{N} AR^{2/3} S^{1/2}$$

where $Q$ is the flow of water (cubic feet per second), $N$ is the roughness coefficient (unitless), $A$ is the area (square feet), $S$ is the slope (feet/foot), and $R$ is the hydraulic radius (feet).

The hydraulic radius is the cross-sectional area divided by the wetted perimeter. For square channels like the one in this example,

*Hydraulic radius = depth × width / (2.0 × depth + width)*

To solve this problem, design a program that allows the user to guess a depth and then calculates the corresponding flow. If the flow is too little, the user should guess a depth a little higher; if the flow is too high, the user should guess a depth a little lower. The guessing is repeated until the computed flow is within 0.1 percent of the flow desired.

To help the user make an initial guess, the program should display the flow for half the channel depth. Note the example run:

```
At a depth of 5.0000 feet, the flow is 641.3255 cubic
feet per second.

Enter your initial guess for the channel depth
when the flow is 1000.0000 cubic feet per second
Enter guess> 6.0

Depth: 6.0000  Flow: 825.5906 cfs  Target: 1000.0000 cfs
Difference: 174.4094  Error: 17.4409 percent

Enter guess> 7.0

Depth: 7.0000  Flow: 1017.7784 cfs  Target: 1000.0000 cfs
Difference: -17.7784  Error: -1.7778 percent

Enter guess> 6.8
```

10. Bunyan Lumber Co. needs to create a table of the engineering properties of its lumber. The dimensions of the wood are given as the base and the height in inches. Engineers need to know the following information about lumber:

cross-sectional area: $base \times height$

moment of inertia: $\dfrac{base \times height^3}{12}$

section modulus: $\dfrac{base \times height^2}{6}$

The owner makes lumber with base sizes of 2, 4, 6, 8, and 10 inches. The height sizes are 2, 4, 6, 8, 10, and 12 inches. Produce a table with appropriate headings to show these values and the computed engineering properties. The first part of the table's outline is shown.

```
Lumber      Cross-sectional   Moment of    Section
Size             Area         Inertia      Modulus
  2 x   2
  2 x   4
  2 x   6
```

```
2 x  8
2 x 10
2 x 12
4 x  2
4 x  4
     .
     .
     .
```

11. Before high resolution graphics displays became common, computer termi-
    nals were often used to display graphs of equations using only text charac-
    ters. A typical technique was to create a vertical graph by spacing over on
    the screen, then displaying an *. Write a program that displays the graph of
    an increasing frequency sine wave this way. The program should ask the
    user for an initial step-size in degrees and the number of lines of the graph
    to display. A sample output begins as:

```
                            *
                                            *
                                               *
                                                 *
                                                  *
                                                    *
                                                     *
                                                      *
                                                     *
                                                   *
                                                 *
                                               *
                                             *
                                          *
                                       *
                                  *
                             *
                       *
                   *
             *
         *
       *
```

Turn the book 90° to see the sine-wave shape.

# Modular

# Programming

$\displaystyle \bf A$ carefully designed program constructed using functions has some properties of a stereo system. Each stereo component is an independent device that performs a specific operation. You might know the purpose of each component, but you certainly do not need to know what electronic parts each contains or how it functions to play or record music.

Electronic audio signals move back and forth over wires linking the stereo components. Plugs on the back of the stereo receiver are marked as inputs or outputs. Wires attached to the input plugs carry electronic signals into the receiver, where they are processed. These signals may come from the cassette deck, tuner, or CD player. The receiver sends new electronic signals through the output plugs to the speakers or back to the cassette deck for recording.

In Chapter 3 you learned how to write the separate components—functions—of a program. The functions correspond to the individual steps in a problem solution. You also learned how to provide inputs to a function and how to return a single output. In this chapter you complete your study of functions, learning how to connect the functions to create a program system—an arrangement of parts that makes your program operate like a stereo system as it passes information from one function to another.

## 6.1 FUNCTIONS WITH SIMPLE OUTPUT PARAMETERS

Argument lists provide the communication links between the main function and its function subprograms. Arguments make functions more versatile because they enable a function to manipulate different data each time it is called. So far, we know how to pass inputs into a function and how to use the `return` statement to send back one result value from a function. This section describes how programmers use output parameters to return multiple results from a function.

When a function call executes, the computer allocates memory space in the function data area for each formal parameter. The value of each actual parameter is stored in the memory cell allocated to its corresponding formal parameter. The function body can manipulate this value. Next, we will discuss how a function sends back multiple outputs to the function that calls it.

**EXAMPLE 6.1**  Function `separate` in Fig. 6.1 finds the sign, whole number magnitude, and fractional parts of its first parameter. In our previous examples, all the formal parameters of a function represent inputs to the function from the calling function. In function `separate`, however, only the first formal parameter, `num`, is an input; the other three formal parameters—`signp`, `wholep`, and `fracp`—are output parameters, used to carry multiple results from function `separate`

**Figure 6.1    Function separate**

```
/*
 * Separates a number into three parts: a sign (+, -, or  blank),
 * a whole number magnitude, and a fractional part.
 */
void
separate(double   num,     /* input - value to be split                  */
         char    *signp,   /* output - sign of num                       */
         int     *wholep,  /* output - whole number magnitude of num     */
         double *fracp)    /* output - fractional part of num            */
{
      double magnitude;   /* local variable - magnitude of num           */

      /* Determines sign of num */
      if (num < 0)
            *signp = '-';
      else if (num == 0)
            *signp = ' ';
      else
            *signp = '+';

      /* Finds magnitude of num (its absolute value) and
         separates it into whole and fractional parts                    */
      magnitude = fabs(num);
      *wholep = floor(magnitude);
      *fracp = magnitude - *wholep;
}
```

back to the function calling it. Figure 6.2 gives a diagram of the function as a box with one input and several outputs.

Let's focus for a moment on the heading of the function in Fig. 6.1.

```
void
separate(double   num,     /* input - value to be split       */
         char    *signp,   /* output - sign of num            */
         int     *wholep,  /* output - whole number magnitude
                                       of num                 */
         double *fracp)    /* output - fractional part of num */
```

The actual argument value passed to the formal parameter num is used to determine the values to be sent back through signp, wholep, and fracp.

**Figure 6.2
Diagram of
Function
separate with
Multiple Results**

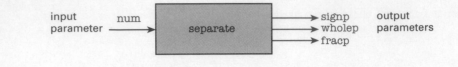

Notice that in Fig. 6.1 the declarations of these output parameters in the function heading have asterisks before the parameter names. In the assignment statements that use these parameters to send back the function results, there are also asterisks in front of the parameter names. The function type is void as it is for functions returning no result, and the function body does not include a return statement to send back a single value, as we saw in earlier functions.

A declaration of a simple output parameter such as char *signp tells the compiler that signp will contain the *address* of a type char variable. Another way to express the idea that signp is the address of a type char variable is to say that the parameter signp is a **pointer** to a type char variable. Similarly, the output parameters wholep and fracp are pointers to variables of types int and double. We have chosen names for these output parameters that end in the letter "p" because they are all pointers.

**pointer**
a memory cell whose content
is the address of another memory cell

Figure 6.3 shows a complete program including a brief function main that calls function separate. Function separate is defined as it was in Fig. 6.1, but pre- and postconditions have been added to its block comment. The calling function must declare variables in which function separate can store the multiple results it computes. Function main in our example declares three variables to receive these results—a type char variable sn, a type int variable whl, and a type double variable fr. Notice that no values are placed in these variables prior to the call to function separate, for it is the job of separate to define their values. This change of the values of memory cells in the data area of the calling function is considered a side effect of the call to function separate. This side effect is the intended outcome of the call to separate.

**Figure 6.3    Program That Calls a Function with Output Arguments**

```
/*
 * Demonstrates the use of a function with input and output parameters.
 */

#include <stdio.h>
#include <math.h>
```

*(continued)*

**Figure 6.3**    *(continued)*

```
void separate(double num, char *signp, int *wholep, double *fracp);

int
main(void)
{
      double value; /* input - number to analyze                        */
      char    sn;    /* output - sign of value                          */
      int     whl;   /* output - whole number magnitude of value        */
      double  fr;    /* output - fractional part of value               */

      /* Gets data                                                      */
      printf("Enter a value to analyze> ");
      scanf("%lf", &value);

      /* Separates data value into three parts                          */
      separate(value, &sn, &whl, &fr);

      /* Prints results                                                 */
      printf("Parts of %.4f\n  sign: %c\n", value, sn);
      printf("  whole number magnitude: %d\n", whl);
      printf("  fractional part:  %.4f\n", fr);

      return (0);
}

/*
 * Separates a number into three parts: a sign (+, -, or blank),
 * a whole number magnitude, and a fractional part.
 * Pre:  num is defined; signp, wholep, and fracp contain addresses of memory
 *       cells where results are to be stored
 * Post: function results are stored in cells pointed to by signp wholep, and
 *       fracp
 */
void
separate(double  num,      /* input - value to be split                */
         char    *signp,   /* output - sign of num                     */
         int     *wholep,  /* output - whole number magnitude of num   */
         double  *fracp)   /* output - fractional part of num          */
{
      double magnitude;  /* local variable - magnitude of num          */
```

*(continued)*

**Figure 6.3** *(continued)*

```
        /* Determines sign of num */
        if (num < 0)
                *signp = '-';
        else if (num == 0)
                *signp = ' ';
        else
                *signp = '+';

        /* Finds magnitude of num (its absolute value) and separates it into
            whole and fractional parts                                        */
        magnitude = fabs(num);
        *wholep = floor(magnitude);
        *fracp = magnitude - *wholep;
}


Enter a value to analyze> 35.817
Parts of 35.8170
  sign: +
  whole number magnitude: 35
  fractional part: 0.8170
```

Figure 6.4 shows the data areas of main and separate as they are set up by the function call statement

```
separate(value, &sn, &whl, &fr);
```

This statement causes the number stored in the actual argument value to be copied into the input parameter num and the addresses of the arguments sn, whl, and fr to be stored in the corresponding output parameters signp, wholep, and fracp. The small numbers in color represent possible actual addresses in memory. Since it makes no difference to our program which specific cells are used, we normally diagram an address stored in a memory cell simply as a pointer like the arrow from signp to sn. Note that the use of the address-of operator & on the actual arguments sn, whl, and fr is essential. If the operator & were omitted, we would be passing to separate the *values* of sn, whl, and fr, information that is worthless from the perspective of separate. The only way separate can store values in sn, whl, and fr is if it knows where to find

**Figure 6.4
Parameter
Correspondence
for**
`separate(value, &sn, &whl, &fr);`

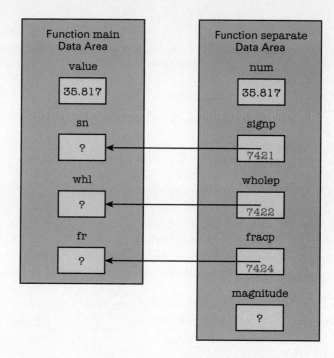

them in memory. The purpose of `separate` with regard to its second, third, and fourth arguments is comparable to the purpose of the library function `scanf` with regard to all of its arguments except the first (the format string).

In addition to the fact that the *values* of the actual output arguments in the call to `separate` are useless, these values are also of data types that do not match the types of the corresponding formal parameters. Table 6.1 shows the effect of the address-of operator `&` on the data type of a reference. You see that in general if a reference x is of type "whatever-type", the reference `&x` is of type "pointer to whatever-type", that is, "whatever-type *".

**Table 6.1    Effect of & Operator on the Data Type of a Reference**

| Declaration | Data Type of x | Data Type of &x |
|---|---|---|
| char   x | char | char * (pointer to char) |
| int   x | int | int * (pointer to int) |
| double x | double | double * (pointer to double) |

So far, we have examined how to declare simple output parameters in a function prototype and how to use the address-of operator & in a function call statement to pass pointers of appropriate types. Now we need to study how the function manipulates these pointers in order to send back multiple results. The statements in function separate that cause the return of results follow.

```
*signp = '-';
*signp = ' ';
*signp = '+';
*wholep = floor(magnitude);
*fracp = magnitude - *wholep;
```

In each case, the name of the formal parameter is preceded by the *indirection operator,* unary *. When the unary * operator is applied to a reference that is of some pointer type, it has the effect of following the pointer referenced by its operand. Figure 6.5 shows the difference between a *direct* reference to a variable of type "pointer to int" and an indirect or "pointer-following" reference to the same variable using the indirection operator.

For the data pictured in Fig. 6.4, the statement

```
*signp = '+';
```

follows the pointer in signp to the cell that function main calls sn and stores in it the character '+'. The statement

```
*wholep = floor(magnitude);
```

follows the pointer in wholep to the cell called whl by main and stores the integer 35 there. Similarly, the statement

```
*fracp = magnitude - *wholep;
```

**Figure 6.5
Comparison of
Direct and
Indirect
Reference**

| Reference | Cell meant | Value |
|-----------|------------|-------|
| nump | gray shaded cell | pointer |
| *nump | cell in color | 84 |

uses two indirect references: One accesses the value in main's local variable whl through the pointer in wholep, and another accesses fr of main through the pointer fracp to give the final output argument the value 0.817.

## Meanings of * Symbol

We have now seen three distinct meanings of the symbol *. In Chapter 2 we studied its use as the binary operator meaning multiplication. Function separate introduces two additional meanings. The *'s in the declarations of the function's formal parameters are part of the names of the parameters' data types. These *'s should be read as "pointer to." Thus the declaration

```
char *signp
```

tells the compiler that the type of parameter signp is "pointer to char."

The * has a completely different meaning when it is used as the unary indirection operator in the function body. Here it means "follow the pointer." Thus, *signp means follow the pointer in signp. Notice that the data type of the reference *signp is char; the data type of *wholep is int, and the data type of *fracp is double. Many students confuse the meaning of * in a reference with its meaning in a parameter declaration: They expect that all references with *'s will be of pointer data types. Remember that the unary operator * *does not* mean "pointer to."

**EXERCISES FOR SECTION 6.1**

Self-Check
1. Write a prototype for a function sum_n_avg that has three type double input parameters and two output parameters.

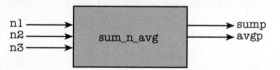

The function computes the sum and the average of its three input arguments and relays its results through two output parameters.
2. The following code fragment is from a function preparing to call sum_n_avg (see Exercise 1). Complete the function call statement.

```
{
        double one, two, three, sum_of_3, avg_of_3;
        printf("Enter three numbers> ");
```

```
scanf("%lf%lf%lf", &one, &two, &three);
sum_n_avg(_____);
. . .
}
```

3. Given the memory setup shown, fill in the chart by indicating the data type and value of each reference as well as the name of the function in which the reference would be legal.

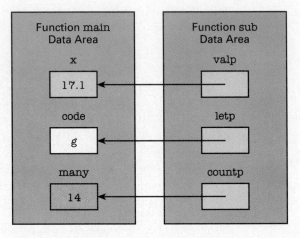

Give pointer values by referring to cell attributes. For example, the value of valp would be "pointer to color-shaded cell," and the value of &many would be "pointer to gray-shaded cell."

| Reference | Where Legal | Data Type | Value |
| --- | --- | --- | --- |
| valp | sub | double * | pointer to color-shaded cell |
| &many | | | |
| code | | | |
| &code | | | |
| countp | | | |
| *countp | | | |
| *valp | | | |
| letp | | | |
| &x | | | |

Programming

1. Define the function sum_n_avg whose prototype you wrote in Self-Check Exercise 1. The function should compute both the sum and the average of its three input parameters and relay these results through its output parameters.

# 6.2 MULTIPLE CALLS TO A FUNCTION WITH INPUT/OUTPUT PARAMETERS

In previous examples, we passed information into a function through its input parameters and returned results from a function through its output parameters. Our next example demonstrates the use of a single parameter both to bring a data value into a function and to carry a result value out of the function. It also demonstrates how a function may be called more than once in a given program and process different data in each call.

**EXAMPLE 6.2**

**sort**
a rearrangement of data in a particular sequence (increasing or decreasing)

The main function in Fig. 6.6 gets three data values, num1, num2, and num3, and rearranges the data so that they are in increasing sequence, with the smallest value in num1. The three calls to function order perform this **sorting** operation.

Each time function order executes, the smaller of its two argument values is stored in its first actual argument and the larger is stored in its second actual argument. Therefore, the function call

```
order(&num1, &num2);
```

stores the smaller of num1 and num2 in num1 and the larger in num2. In the sample run shown, num1 is 7.5 and num2 is 9.6, so these values are not changed by the function execution. However, the function call

```
order(&num1, &num3);
```

switches the values of num1 (initial value is 7.5) and num3 (initial value is 5.5). Table 6.2 traces the main function execution.

The body of function order is based on the if statement from Fig. 4.5. The function heading

```
void
order(double *smp, double *lgp)      /* input/output */
```

**Figure 6.6    Program to Sort Three Numbers**

```c
/*
 * Tests function order by ordering three numbers
 */
#include <stdio.h>

void order(double *smp, double *lgp);

int
main(void)
{
        double num1, num2, num3; /* three numbers to put in order    */

        /* Gets test data                                             */
        printf("Enter three numbers separated by blanks> ");

        scanf("%lf%lf%lf", &num1, &num2, &num3);
        /* Orders the three numbers                                   */
        order(&num1, &num2);
        order(&num1, &num3);
        order(&num2, &num3);

        /* Displays results                                           */
        printf("The numbers in ascending order are: %.2f %.2f %.2f\n",
                num1, num2, num3);

        return (0);
}

/*
 * Arranges arguments in ascending order.
 * Pre:  smp and lgp are addresses of defined type double variables
 * Post: variable pointed to by smp contains the smaller of the type
 *       double values; variable pointed to by lgp contains the larger
 */
void
order(double *smp, double *lgp)        /* input/output */
{
        double temp; /* temporary variable to hold one number during swap    */
        /* Compares values pointed to by smp and lgp and switches if necessary*/
        if (*smp > *lgp) {
                temp = *smp;
```

*(continued)*

**Figure 6.6** *(continued)*

```
            *smp = *lgp;
            *lgp = temp;
        }
}
```

```
Enter three numbers separated by blanks> 7.5 9.6 5.5
The numbers in ascending order are: 5.50 7.50 9.60
```

**Table 6.2  Trace of Program to Sort 3 Numbers**

| Statement | num1 | num2 | num3 | Effect |
|---|---|---|---|---|
| scanf("...", &num1, &num2, &num3); | 7.5 | 9.6 | 5.5 | Enters data |
| order(&num1, &num2); | | | | No change |
| order(&num1, &num3); | 5.5 | 9.6 | 7.5 | Switches num1 and num3 |
| order(&num2, &num3); | 5.5 | 7.5 | 9.6 | Switches num2 and num3 |
| printf("...", num1, num2, num3); | | | | Displays 5.5 7.5 9.6 |

identifies smp and lgp as *input/output parameters* because the function uses the current actual argument values as inputs and may return new values.

During the execution of the second call

```
order(&num1, &num3);
```

the formal parameter smp contains the address of the actual argument num1, and formal parameter lgp contains the address of the actual argument num3. Testing the condition

```
(*smp > *lgp)
```

causes both of these pointers to be followed, resulting in the condition

```
(7.5 > 5.5)
```

which evaluates to true. Executing the first assignment statement in the true task,

```
temp = *smp;
```

causes the 7.5 to be copied into the local variable temp. Figure 6.7 shows us a snapshot of the values in memory immediately after execution of this assignment statement.

Execution of the next assignment statement,

```
*smp = *lgp;
```

would cause the 7.5 in the variable pointed to by smp to be replaced by 5.5, the value of the variable pointer to by lgp. The final assignment statement,

```
*lgp = temp;
```

copies the contents of the temporary variable (7.5) into the variable pointed to by lgp. This completes the swap of values.

So far we have seen four kinds of functions, and we have studied how formal parameters are used in all of them. Table 6.3 compares the various kinds of functions and indicates the circumstances when each kind should be used.

**Figure 6.7
Data Areas
after**
`temp = *smp;`
**During Call**
`order(&num1,
&num3);`

**Table 6.3   Different Kinds of Function Subprograms**

| Purpose | Function Type | Parameters | To Return Result |
|---|---|---|---|
| To compute or obtain as input a single numeric or character value. | Same as type of value to be computed or obtained. | Input parameters hold copies of data provided by calling function. | Function code includes a `return` statement with an expression whose value is the result. |
| To produce printed output containing values of numeric or character arguments. | `void` | Input parameters hold copies of data provided by calling function. | No result is returned. |
| To compute multiple numeric or character results. | `void` | Input parameters hold copies of data provided by calling function.<br><br>Output parameters are pointers to actual arguments. | Results are stored in the calling function's data area by indirect assignment through output parameters. No `return` statement is required. |
| To modify argument values. | `void` | Input/output parameters are pointers to actual arguments. Input data is accessed by indirect reference through parameters. | Results are stored in the calling function's data area by indirect assignment through output parameters. No `return` statement is required. |

## Program Style   *Preferred Kinds of Functions*

Although all the kinds of functions in Table 6.3 are useful in developing program systems, we recommend that you use the first kind whenever it is possible to do so. Functions that return a single value are the easiest functions for a program reader to deal with. You will note that all the mathematical functions we discussed in Section 3.2 are of this variety. Since such functions take only input arguments, the programmer is not concerned with using such complexities as indirect referencing in the function definition or applying the address-of operator in the function call. If the value returned by the function is to be stored in a variable, the reader sees an assignment statement in the code of the calling function. If a function subprogram has a meaningful name, the reader can often get a good idea of what is happening in the calling function without reading the function subprogram's code.

**EXERCISES FOR SECTION 6.2**

Self-Check

1. What would be the effect of the following sequence of calls to function order? *Hint:* Trace the calls for num1 = 8, num2 = 12, num3 = 10.

    ```
    order(&num3, &num2);
    order(&num2, &num1);
    order(&num3, &num2);
    ```

2. Show the table of values for x, y, and z that is the output displayed by the following program. You will notice that the function sum does not follow the suggestion in the last Program Style segment of Section 6.2. You can improve this program in the programming exercise that follows.

    ```
    #include <stdio.h>

    void sum(int a, int b, int *cp);

    int
    main(void)
    {
            int x, y, z;

            x = 5; y = 3;

            printf("   x   y   z\n\n");

            sum(x, y, &z);
            printf("%4d%4d%4d\n", x, y, z);

            sum(y, x, &z);
            printf("%4d%4d%4d\n", x, y, z);

            sum(z, y, &x);
            printf("%4d%4d%4d\n", x, y, z);
    ```

```
            sum(z,  z,  &x);
            printf("%4d%4d%4d\n", x, y, z);

            sum(y,  y,  &y);
            printf("%4d%4d%4d\n", x, y, z);

            return (0);
      }

      void
      sum(int a, int b, int *cp)
      {
            *cp = a + b;
      }
```

Programming

1. Rewrite the sum function in Self-Check Exercise 2 as a function that takes just two input arguments. The sum computed should be returned as the function's type int result. Also, write an equivalent function main that calls your sum function.

# 6.3 SCOPE OF NAMES

**scope of a name**
the region in a program where a particular meaning of a name is visible

The **scope of a name** refers to the region of a program where a particular meaning of a name is visible or can be referenced. Let's consider the names in the program outline shown in Fig. 6.8. The names MAX and LIMIT are defined as constant macros and their scope begins at their definition and continues to the end of the source file. This means that all three functions can access MAX and LIMIT.

The scope of the function subprogram name fun_two begins with its prototype and continues to the end of the source file. This means that function fun_two can be called by functions one, main, and itself. The situation is different for function one because one is used as a formal parameter name in function fun_two. Therefore, function one can be called by the main function and itself but not by function fun_two.

All of the formal parameters and local variables in Fig. 6.8 are visible only from their declaration to the closing brace of the function in which they are declared. For example, from the line that is marked with the comment /* header 1 */ to the line marked /* end one */ the identifier anarg

**Figure 6.8**    **Outline of Program for Studying Scope of Names**

```
#define MAX   950
#define LIMIT 200

void one(int anarg, double second);        /* prototype 1 */

int fun_two(int one, char anarg);          /* prototype 2 */

int
main(void)
{
        int localvar;
        . . .
} /* end main */


void
one(int anarg, double second)              /* header 1    */
{
        int onelocal;                      /* local 1     */
        . . .
} /* end one */


int
fun_two(int one, char anarg)               /* header 2    */
{
        int localvar;                      /* local 2     */
        . . .
} /* end fun_two */
```

means an integer variable in the data area of function one. From the line with the comment /* header 2 */ through the line marked /* end fun_two */, this name refers to a character variable in the data area of fun_two. In the rest of the file, the name anarg is not visible.

Table 6.4 shows which identifiers are visible within each of the three functions.

**Table 6.4  Scope of Names in Fig. 6.8**

| Name | Visible in one | Visible in fun_two | Visible in main |
|------|----------------|--------------------|-----------------|
| MAX | yes | yes | yes |
| LIMIT | yes | yes | yes |
| main | no | no | yes |
| localvar (in main) | no | no | yes |
| one (the function) | yes | no | yes |
| anarg (int) | yes | no | no |
| second | yes | no | no |
| onelocal | yes | no | no |
| fun_two | yes | yes | yes |
| one (formal parameter) | no | yes | no |
| anarg (char) | no | yes | no |
| localvar (in fun_two) | no | yes | no |

# 6.4  FORMAL OUTPUT PARAMETERS AS ACTUAL ARGUMENTS

So far, all of our actual arguments in calls to functions have been either local variables or input parameters of the calling function. However, sometimes a function needs to pass its own output parameter as an argument when it calls another function. In Fig. 6.9, which we have left incomplete, we write a function which scans a data line representing a common fraction of the form

*numerator / denominator*

where *numerator* is an integer and *denominator* is a positive integer. The / symbol is a separator. The function is based on function get_int (see Fig. 5.13). Its outer loop repeats until a valid fraction is scanned and its inner loop skips any characters at the end of the data line.

Function scan_fraction has two output parameters, nump and denomp, through which it returns the numerator and denominator of the fraction scanned. Function scan_fraction needs to pass its output parameters to library function scanf which gets the needed numerator and denominator values. In all other calls to scanf, we applied the address-of operator & to each

**Figure 6.9    Function scan_fraction (incomplete)**

```
/*
 * Gets and returns a valid fraction as its result
 * A valid fraction is of this form: integer/positive integer
 * Pre : none
 */
void
scan_fraction(int *nump, int *denomp)
{
      char slash;    /* character between numerator and denominator      */
      int  status;   /* status code returned by scanf indicating
                        number of valid values obtained                  */
      int  error;    /* flag indicating presence of an error             */
      char discard;  /* unprocessed character from input line            */

      do {
          /* No errors detected yet                                      */
          error = 0;

          /* Get a fraction from the user                                */
          printf("Enter a common fraction as two integers separated ");
          printf("by a slash> ");
          status = scanf("%d %c%d",_____, _____, _____);

          /* Validate the fraction                                       */
          if (status < 3) {
                error = 1;
                printf("Invalid-please read directions carefully\n");
          } else if (slash != '/') {
                error = 1;
                printf("Invalid-separate numerator and denominator");
                printf(" by a slash (/)\n");
          } else if (*denomp <= 0) {
                error = 1;
                printf("Invalid—denominator must be positive\n");
          }
```

*(continued)*

**Figure 6.9**    *(continued)*

```
        /* Discard extra input characters                          */
        do {
            scanf("%c", &discard);
        } while (discard != '\n');
    } while (error);
}
```

variable to be filled. However, because nump and denomp store addresses, we can use them directly in the call to scanf:

```
scanf("%d %c%d", nump, &slash, denomp);
```

For this call, scanf stores the first number scanned in the variable whose address is in nump, the slash character (possibly preceded by blanks) in local variable slash, and the second number scanned in the variable whose address is in denomp. The if statement validates the fraction, setting the flag error to 1 (true) if the data entry was unsuccessful.

Figure 6.10 shows the data areas for scan_fraction and the function calling it. For the situation shown, scanf stores the two numbers scanned in variables numerator and denominator. The slash character is stored in local variable slash.

Passing a formal output parameter to another function requires careful consideration of its purpose in the function called. You may find it helpful to sketch the data areas as we did in Fig. 6.10. Table 6.5 gives you guidelines for function arguments of type int, double, and char.

**Figure 6.10
Data Areas for
scan_fraction
and Its Caller**

**Table 6.5    Passing an Argument x to Function some_fun**

| Actual Argument Type | Use in Calling Function | Purpose in Called Function (some_fun) | Formal Parameter Type | Call to some_fun | Example |
|---|---|---|---|---|---|
| int<br>char<br>double | local variable or input parameter | input parameter | int<br>char<br>double | some_fun(x) | Fig. 6.3, main: separate(value, &sn, &whl, &fr); (1st argument) |
| int<br>char<br>double | local variable | output or input/ output parameter | int   *<br>char  *<br>double *| some_fun(&x) | Fig. 6.3, main: separate(value, &sn, &whl, &fr); (2nd–4th arguments) |
| int   *<br>char  *<br>double * | output or input/ output parameter | output or input/ output parameter | int   *<br>char  *<br>double * | some_fun(x) | Fig. 6.9 completed, scanf(..., nump, &slash denomp); (2nd and 4th arguments) |
| int   *<br>char  *<br>double * | output or input/ output parameter | input parameter | int<br>char<br>double | some_fun(*x) | Self-Check Ex. 2 in 6.4, trouble: double_trouble (y, *x); (2nd argument) |

**EXERCISES FOR SECTION 6.4**

Self-Check

1. Box models of functions onef and twof follow. Do not try to define the complete functions; write only the portions described.

Assume that these functions are concerned only with integers, and write headings for onef and twof. Begin the body of function onef with a declaration of an integer local variable tmp. Show a call from onef to twof in which the input argument is dat, and tmp and out2p are the output arguments. Function onef intends for twof to store one integer result in tmp and one in the variable pointed to by out2p.

2. a. Classify each formal parameter of `double_trouble` and `trouble` as input, output, or input/output.
   b. What values of `x` and `y` are displayed by this program? *Hint:* Sketch the data areas of `main`, `trouble`, and `double_trouble` as the program executes.

```c
void double_trouble(int *p, int y);

void trouble(int *x, int *y);

int
main(void)
{
        int x, y;
        trouble(&x, &y);
        printf("x = %d, y = %d\n", x, y);
        return (0);
}

void
double_trouble(int *p, int y)
{
        int x;
        x = 14;
        *p = 2 * x - y;
}

void
trouble(int *x, int *y)
{
        double_trouble(x, 5);
        double_trouble(y, *x);
}
```

What naming convention introduced in Section 6.1 is violated in the formal parameter list of `trouble`?

# 6.5 A PROGRAM WITH MULTIPLE FUNCTIONS

In our next case study, we manipulate numeric data of a type not provided as one of C's base types. In order to do this, we must write our own functions to perform many operations that we take for granted when using types `int` and `double`.

## Case Study: Arithmetic with Common Fractions

**PROBLEM**

You are working problems in which you must display your results as integer ratios; therefore you need to be able to perform computations with common fractions and get results that are common fractions in reduced form. You want to write a program that will allow you to add, subtract, multiply, and divide several pairs of common fractions.

**ANALYSIS**

Because the problem specifies that results are to be in reduced form, we will need to include a fraction-reducing function in addition to the computational functions. If we break the problem into small enough chunks, there should be an opportunity to reuse code by calling the same function multiple times. The in-depth analysis of the problem is actually distributed through the development of these functions.

# C IN FOCUS

## Putting a Line-Up Online

Remember those police movie scenes where the witness is paging through stacks of bulky mug shot books? Today, the witness would use a pen pad and a video terminal to examine only those mug shots that fit the description of the perpetrator. The system that makes it all possible was the brain child of the Boston Police Department.

When two Boston Police officers started keeping a simple database of arrested persons on the department computer, they envisioned a larger system that would incorporate mug shots. They contacted International Optical Telecommunications (IOT), who agreed to develop a system for police departments everywhere. IOT hired MicroVisual Systems to provide the hardware for the sys-tem and to oversee its development. MVS hired two independent programmers to write the system: Kenneth Pugh to write the database, and Ted Kuklinski to write the hardware drivers.

Starting with general specifications from the police officers, police legal advisers added features to comply with law about police procedure. Ken Pugh then wrote a more detailed set of specifications that was ultimately approved by the police department. Pugh and Kuklinski jointly developed the interface specifications so that their two pieces would integrate easily, then worked independently to program the system.

The completed system keeps up to 400 attributes for each person, from height and weight to the location of scars

### Data Requirements

#### Problem Inputs

```
int n1, d1 /* numerator, denominator of first fraction  */
int n2, d2 /* numerator,denominator of second fraction  */
char op    /* arithmetic operator + - * or /            */
char again /* y or n depending on user's desire to
              continue                                   */
```

#### Problem Outputs

```
int n_ans  /* numerator of answer   */
int d_ans  /* denominator of answer */
```

**DESIGN**

As we develop an algorithm through stepwise refinement, we will look for instances in which a definition of a new function would simplify the design.

and tattoos. When a mug shot is taken, the video is translated and added to the database. To identify a perpetrator, a police officer first helps a victim or witness spell out the perpetrator's physical characteristics. The officer uses this information to search the database for arrested persons that match the description. The witness then reviews an electronic line up of suspects. (Mug shots are displayed in groups of four to satisfy legal requirements.) The witness uses a pen pad to move through the mug shots, zoom in on particular pictures, and can keep certain mug shots on the screen as more pictures are added. Once an identification is made, the officer can print out the personal information on the mug shot from the data base.

The system is divided into two functional parts: the data-entry subsystem and the line up system. The software, however, can be described by its logical parts. One is the database update and search portion. The second is the interface for the video cameras, video recorders/players, pen pads, and computers that make up the hardware portion of the system. C was used to program both parts of the system. For the hardware drivers, C was easier to use than assembly language. For the database, C could handle the large number of parameters better than PC-based database languages in use at that time. With the hundreds of attributes built into each entry, search speed was a key requirement. Pugh used a library of database routines written in C (called C-Tree) that provided ten to one hundred times the performance of contemporary database packages.

The interface was also written in C, using a library of user interface routines called Port Package. Port Package made it easy for a developer to create nice-looking programs that ported easily among the various computer systems.

Many thanks to Kenneth Pugh for providing the development story behind the mug shot program. Pugh is a principal in Pugh-Killeen Associates in Durham, NC, and consults for companies around the world in the areas of SystemArchitectronics, object-oriented design, operating systems, and information navigation. He holds a Bachelor of Science in electrical engineering from Duke University and a Master of Science degree from the University of Maryland.

### Initial Algorithm

1. Repeat as long as user wants to continue.
   2. Get a fraction problem.
   3. Compute the result.
   4. Display problem and result.
   5. Check if user wants to continue.

### Step 2 Refinement

2.1 Get first fraction.
2.2 Get operator.
2.3 Get second fraction.

### Step 3 Refinement

3.1 Select a task based on operator:
'+':      3.1.2 Add the fractions.
'−':      3.1.3 Add the first fraction and the negation of the second.
'*':      3.1.4 Multiply the fractions.
'/':      3.1.5 Multiply the first fraction and the reciprocal of the second.
3.2 Put the result fraction in reduced form.

### Step 3.2 Refinement

3.2.1 Find the greatest common divisor (gcd) of the numerator and denominator.
3.2.2 Divide the numerator and denominator by the gcd.

The structure chart in Fig. 6.11 shows the data flow among the steps we have identified.

### ◖ IMPLEMENTATION ◗

**stub**
a skeleton function that consists of a header and statements that display trace messages and assign values to output parameters; enables testing of the flow of control among functions before this function is completed

For Steps 2.1 and 2.3 we will use function scan_fraction from Fig. 6.9. We will write new function subprograms for get_operator (Step 2.2), add_fractions (Steps 3.1.2 and 3.1.3), multiply_fractions (Steps 3.1.4 and 3.1.5), reduce_fraction (Step 3.2), find_gcd (Step 3.2.1), and print_fraction part of Step 4). As a result, coding function main is quite straightforward. Figure 6.12 shows most of the program; however, the functions multiply_fractions and find_gcd have been left as exercises. In their places, we have inserted **stubs,** skeleton functions that have com-

**Figure 6.11
Structure Chart
for Common
Fraction
Problem**

plete comments and headers but merely assign values to their output parameters to allow testing of the partial system. Debugging and testing the system will be explained in Section 6.6.

**TESTING**

We have chosen to leave portions of our fraction system for you to write, but we would still like to test the functions that are complete. We have inserted a stub for each function not yet completed. Each stub prints an identification message and assigns values to its output parameters. For testing purposes, we made the find_gcd stub interactive so the program tester can enter a correct greatest common divisor and see if this leads to correct results.

Figure 6.13 shows a run of the program in its present form. Notice that when we choose operator + and enter a correct greatest common divisor interactively, the result is correct. However, when we choose operator *, although the program continues execution by calling the stubs, the result is incorrect because the stub for function `multiply_fractions` always returns a numerator and denominator value of 1.

**Figure 6.12    Program to Perform Arithmetic Operations on Common Fractions**

```
/*
 * Adds, subtracts, multiplies and divides common fractions, displaying
 * results in reduced form.
 */

#include <stdio.h>
#include <stdlib.h>    /* provides function abs */


/* Function prototypes */
void scan_fraction(int *nump, int *denomp);

char get_operator(void);

void add_fractions(int n1, int d1, int n2, int d2,
                   int *n_ansp, int *d_ansp);

void multiply_fractions(int n1, int d1, int n2, int d2,
                        int *n_ansp, int *d_ansp);

int find_gcd (int n1, int n2);

void reduce_fraction(int *nump, int *denomp);

void print_fraction(int num, int denom);

int
main(void)
{
      int  n1, d1;        /* numerator, denominator of first fraction    */
      int  n2, d2;        /* numerator, denominator of second fraction   */
      char op;            /* arithmetic operator + - * or /              */
      char again;         /* y or n depending on user's desire to continue */
      int  n_ans, d_ans;  /* numerator, denominator of answer            */
```

*(continued)*

**Figure 6.12**    *(continued)*

```
    /* While the user wants to continue, gets and solves arithmetic
       problems with common fractions                                   */
    do {
        /* Gets a fraction problem                                      */
        scan_fraction(&n1, &d1);
        op = get_operator();
        scan_fraction(&n2, &d2);

        /* Computes the result  */
        switch (op) {
        case '+':
                add_fractions(n1, d1, n2, d2, &n_ans, &d_ans);
                break;

        case '-':
                add_fractions(n1, d1, -n2, d2, &n_ans, &d_ans);
                break;

        case '*':
                multiply_fractions(n1, d1, n2, d2, &n_ans, &d_ans);
                break;

        case '/':
                multiply_fractions(n1, d1, d2, n2, &n_ans, &d_ans);
        }
        reduce_fraction(&n_ans, &d_ans);

        /* Displays problem and result                                  */
        printf("\n");
        print_fraction(n1, d1);
        printf(" %c ", op);
        print_fraction(n2, d2);
        printf(" = ");
        print_fraction(n_ans, d_ans);

        /* Asks user about doing another problem                        */
        printf("\nDo another problem? (y/n)> ");
        scanf(" %c", &again);
    } while (again == 'y'  ||  again == 'Y');
    return (0);
}
```

*(continued)*

**Figure 6.12**    *(continued)*

```c
/* Insert function scan_fraction from Fig. 6.9 here. */


/*
 * Gets and returns a valid arithmetic operator.  Skips over newline
 * characters and permits re-entry of operator in case of error.
 */
char
get_operator(void)
{
      char op;

      printf("Enter an arithmetic operator (+,-,*, or /)\n> ");
      for  (scanf("%c", &op);
            op != '+'  &&  op != '-'  &&
            op != '*'  &&  op != '/';
            scanf("%c", &op)) {
         if (op != '\n')
             printf("%c invalid, reenter operator (+,-, *,/)\n> ", op);
      }
      return (op);
}



/*
 * Adds fractions represented by pairs of integers.
 * Pre:  n1, d1, n2, d2 are defined;
 *       n_ansp and d_ansp are addresses of type int variables.
 * Post: sum of n1/d1 and n2/d2 is stored in variables pointed
 *       to by n_ansp and d_ansp.  Result is not reduced.
 */
void
add_fractions(int     n1, int      d1, /* input - first fraction   */
              int     n2, int      d2, /* input - second fraction  */
              int *n_ansp, int *d_ansp) /* output - sum of 2 fractions*/
{
      int denom,     /* common denominator used for sum (may not be least)   */
```

*(continued)*

**Figure 6.12**    *(continued)*

```
        numer,          /* numerator of sum                              */
        sign_factor;  /* -1 for a negative, 1 otherwise                  */

    /* Finds a common denominator                                        */
    denom = d1 * d2;

    /* Computes numerator                                                */
    numer = n1 * d2 + n2 * d1;

    /* Adjusts sign (at most, numerator should be negative)              */
    if (numer * denom >= 0)
        sign_factor = 1;
    else
        sign_factor = -1;

    numer = sign_factor * abs(numer);
    denom = abs(denom);

    /* Returns result                                                    */
    *n_ansp = numer;
    *d_ansp = denom;
}

/*
 ***** STUB *****
 * Multiplies fractions represented by pairs of integers.
 * Pre:  n1, d1, n2, d2 are defined;
 *       n_ansp and d_ansp are addresses of type int variables.
 * Post: product of n1/d1 and n2/d2 is stored in variables pointed
 *       to by n_ansp and d_ansp.  Result is not reduced.
 */
void
multiply_fractions(int     n1, int   d1, /*  input - first fraction      */
                   int     n2, int   d2, /*  input - second fraction     */
                   int *n_ansp,          /*  output -                    */
                   int *d_ansp)          /*      product of 2 fractions   */
{
    /* Displays trace message                                            */
    printf("\nEntering multiply_fractions with\n");
    printf("n1 = %d, d1 = %d, n2 = %d, d2 = %d\n", n1, d1, n2, d2);
```

*(continued)*

**Figure 6.12**   *(continued)*

```
        /* Defines output arguments                                     */
        *n_ansp = 1;
        *d_ansp = 1;
}

/*
 ***** STUB *****
 * Finds greatest common divisor of two integers
 */
int
find_gcd (int n1, int n2) /* input - two integers                       */
{
        int gcd;

        /* Displays trace message                                       */
        printf("\nEntering find_gcd with n1 = %d, n2 = %d\n", n1, n2);

        /* Asks user for gcd                                            */
        printf("gcd of %d and %d?> ", n1, n2);
        scanf("%d", &gcd);

        /* Displays exit trace message                                  */
        printf("find_gcd returning %d\n", gcd);
        return (gcd);
}


/*
 * Reduces a fraction by dividing its numerator and denominator by their
 * greatest common divisor.
 */
void
reduce_fraction(int *nump,    /* input/output -                         */
                int *denomp) /* numerator and denominator of fraction   */
{
        int gcd;    /* greatest common divisor of numerator & denominator */

        gcd = find_gcd(*nump, *denomp);
```

*(continued)*

**Figure 6.12**    *(continued)*

```
        *nump = *nump / gcd;
        *denomp = *denomp / gcd;
}


/*
 * Displays pair of integers as a fraction.
 */
void
print_fraction(int num, int denom)   /* input - numerator & denominator    */
{
        printf("%d/%d", num, denom);
}
```

**Figure 6.13    Sample Run of a Partially Complete Program Containing Stubs**

```
Enter a common fraction as two integers separated by a slash> 3/-4
Input invalid--denominator must be positive
Enter a common fraction as two integers separated by a slash> 3/4
Enter an arithmetic operator (+,-,*, or /)
> +
Enter a common fraction as two integers separated by a slash> 5/8
Entering find_gcd with n1 = 44, n2 = 32
gcd of 44 and 32?> 4
find_gcd returning 4

3/4 + 5/8 = 11/8
Do another problem? (y/n)> y
Enter a common fraction as two integers separated by a slash> 1/2
Enter an arithmetic operator (+,-,*, or /)
> 5
5 invalid, reenter operator (+,-,*,/)
> *
Enter a common fraction as two integers separated by a slash> 5/7
Entering multiply_fractions with
n1 = 1, d1 = 2, n2 = 5, d2 = 7
```

*(continued)*

**Figure 6.13** (continued)

```
Entering find_gcd with n1 = 1, n2 = 1
gcd of 1 and 1?> 1
find_gcd returning 1

1/2 * 5/7 = 1/1
Do another problem? (y/n)> n
```

**EXERCISES FOR SECTION 6.5**

Self-Check

1. Why are pointer types used for the parameters of scan_fraction?
2. Why was it not necessary to include a default case in the switch statement that calls add_fractions and multiply_fractions?

Programming

1. Implement the following algorithm as the find_gcd function needed in the common fraction system of Fig. 6.12. Your function will find the greatest common divisor (that is, the product of all common factors) of integers n1 and n2.

   1. Put the absolute value of n1 in q and of n2 in p.
   2. Store the remainder of q divided by p in r.
   3. while r is not zero
       4. Copy p into q and r into p.
       5. Store the remainder of q divided by p in r.
   6. p is the gcd.

2. Write the function multiply_fractions. If your result has a zero denominator, display an error message and change the denominator to 1.

## 6.6 DEBUGGING AND TESTING A PROGRAM SYSTEM

As the number of statements in a program system grows, the possibility of error also increases. If we keep each function to a manageable size, the likelihood of error increases much more slowly. It is also easier to read and test each function.

In the last case study, we inserted stubs in the program for functions that were not yet written. When a team of programmers is working on a problem, using stubs is a common practice. Obviously, not all functions will be ready at the same time, and the use of stubs enables us to test and debug the main program flow and those functions that are available.

Each stub displays an identification message and assigns values to its output parameters to prevent execution errors caused by undefined values. We show the stub for function `multiply_fractions` again in Fig. 6.14. If a program contains one or more stubs, the message printed by each stub when it is called provides a trace of the call sequence and allows the programmer to determine whether the flow of control within the program is correct. The process of testing a program in this way is called **top-down testing.**

**top-down testing**

the process of testing flow of control between a main function and its subordinate functions

**unit test**

a test of an individual function

When a function is completed, it can be substituted for its stub in the program. However, we often perform a preliminary test of a new function before substitution because it is easier to locate and correct errors when dealing with a single function rather than with a complete program system. We can perform such a **unit test** by writing a short driver function to call it.

## Figure 6.14 Stub for Function multiply_fractions

```
/*
 ***** STUB *****
 * Multiplies fractions represented by pairs of integers.
 * Pre:  n1, d1, n2, d2 are defined;
 *       n_ansp and d_ansp are addresses of type int variables.
 * Post: product of n1/d1 and n2/d2 is stored in variables pointed
 *       to by n_ansp and d_ansp.  Result is not reduced.
 */
void
multiply_fractions(int      n1, int    d1, /*  input - first fraction      */
                   int      n2, int    d2, /*  input - second fraction     */
                   int *n_ansp,            /*  output -                    */
                   int *d_ansp)            /*      product of 2 fractions   */
{
     /* Displays trace message                                             */
     printf("\nEntering multiply_fractions with\n");
     printf("n1 = %d, d1 = %d, n2 = %d, d2 = %d\n", n1, d1, n2, d2);

     /* Defines output arguments`                                          */
     *n_ansp = 1;
     *d_ansp = 1;
}
```

**Figure 6.15   Driver for Function scan_fraction**

```
/* Driver for scan_fraction */

int
main(void)
{
      int num, denom;
      printf("To quit, enter a fraction with a zero numerator\n");
      scan_fraction(&num, &denom);
      while (num != 0) {
            printf("Fraction is %d/%d\n", num, denom);
            scan_fraction(&num, &denom);
      }

      return (0);
}
```

Don't spend a lot of time creating an elegant driver because you will discard it as soon as the new function is tested. A driver function should contain only the declarations and executable statements necessary to perform a test of a single function. A driver function should begin by giving values to all input and input/output parameters. Next comes the call to the function being tested. After calling the function, the driver should display the function results. A driver for function scan_fraction is shown in Fig. 6.15.

Once you are confident that a function works properly, substitute it for its stub in the program system. The process of separately testing individual functions before inserting them in a program system is called **bottom-up testing.** Tests of the entire system are **system integration tests.**

By following a combination of top-down and bottom-up testing, a programming team can be fairly confident that the complete program system will be relatively free of errors when it is finally put together. Consequently, the final debugging sessions should proceed quickly and smoothly.

**bottom-up testing**
the process of separately testing individual functions of a program system
**system integration tests**
testing a system after replacing all its stubs with functions that have been pretested

## Debugging Tips for Program Systems

A list of suggestions for debugging a program system follows.

1. Carefully document each function parameter and local variable using comments as you write the code. Also describe the function's purpose using comments.

2. Create a trace of execution by displaying the function name as you enter it.
3. Trace or display the values of all input and input/output parameters upon entry to a function. Check that these values make sense.
4. Trace or display the values of all function outputs after returning from a function. Verify that these values are correct by hand computation. Make sure you declare all input/output and output parameters as pointer types.
5. Make sure that a function stub assigns a value to the variable pointed to by each output parameter.

If you are using a debugger, you may be able to specify whether you want to execute a function as if it were a single statement or whether you want to step through the individual statements of a function. Initially, execute the function as a single statement and trace the values of all input and output parameters (tips 3 and 4 above). If the function results are incorrect, step through its individual statements.

If you are not using a debugger, you should plan for debugging as you write each function rather than waiting until after you finish the whole program. Include the display statements (mentioned in debugging tips 2 through 4) in the original C code for the function. When you are satisfied that the function works correctly, remove the debugging statements. The simplest way is to change them to comments by enclosing them within the symbols / *, * /; if you have a problem later, you can remove these symbols, thereby changing the comments back to executable statements.

# 6.7 COMMON PROGRAMMING ERRORS

Many opportunities for error arise when you use functions with parameter lists, so be extremely careful. Proper use of parameters is difficult for beginning programmers to master, but it is an essential skill. One obvious pitfall is not ensuring that the actual argument list has the same number of items as the formal parameter list. Each actual input argument must be of a type that can be assigned to its corresponding formal parameter. An actual output argument must be of the same pointer data type as the corresponding formal parameter.

It is easy to introduce errors in a function that produces multiple results. If an output parameter is not of a pointer type or if the calling function neglects to send a correct variable address, the function results will be incorrect.

The C scope rules determine where a name is visible and can therefore be referenced. If an identifier is referenced outside its scope, an `undeclared symbol` syntax error will result.

# CHAPTER REVIEW

1. Parameters enable a programmer to pass data to functions and to return multiple results from functions. The parameter list provides a highly visible communication path between a function and its calling program. Using parameters enables a function to process different data each time it executes, thereby making it easier to reuse the function in other programs.

2. Parameters may be used for input to a function, for output or sending back results, and for both input and output. An input parameter is used only for passing data into a function. The parameter's declared type is the same as the type of the data. Output and input/output parameters must be able to access variables in the calling function's data area so they are declared as pointers to the result data types. The actual argument corresponding to an input parameter may be an expression or a constant; the actual argument corresponding to an output or input/output parameter must be the address of a variable.

3. The scope of an identifier dictates where it can be referenced. A parameter or local variable can be referenced anywhere in the function that declares it. A function name is visible from its declaration (the function prototype) to the end of the source file except within functions that have local variables of the same name. The same rule applies for a constant macro: it is visible from its #define directive.

## New C Constructs

| Function Example | Effect and Sample Call |
|---|---|

**Function That Returns Multiple Results**

```
void
make_change(double  change,      /* input  */
            double  token_val,   /* input  */
            int     *num_tokenp, /* output */
            double  *leftp)      /* output */
{
     *num_tokenp = floor(change /
                         token_val);
     *leftp = change - *num_tokenp *
                       token_val;
}
```

Determines how many of a certain bill or coin (token_val) should be included in change amount. This number is sent back through the output parameter num_tokenp. The amount of change remaining to be made is sent back through the output parameter leftp. The following call assigns a 3 to num_twenties and 11.50 to remaining_change.

*(continued)*

**New C Constructs** *(continued)*

| Function Example | Effect and Sample Call |
|---|---|

**Function Example**

**Effect and Sample Call**

```
int     num_twenties;
double remaining change;
    . . .
make_change(71.50, 20.00,
        &num_twenties,
        &remaining_change);
```

**Function with Input/Output Parameters**

```
void
correct_fraction(int *nump,      /* input/ */
                 int *denomp)  /* output */
{
    if ((*nump * *denomp) > 0)
        *nump = abs(*nump);
    else
        *nump = -abs(*nump);
    *denomp = abs(*denomp);
}
```

Corrects the form of a common
fraction so the denominator is
always positive (e.g., −5/3
rather than 5/−3).

```
int num, denom;

num = 5;
denom = -3;
correct_fraction(&num, &denom);
```

# QUICK-CHECK EXERCISES

1. The items passed in a function call are the _____ _____. The corresponding _____ _____ appear in the function prototype and heading.
2. Constants and expressions can be actual arguments corresponding to formal parameters that are _____ parameters.
3. Formal parameters that are output parameters must have actual arguments that are _____.
4. Which of the following is used to test a function: a driver or a stub?
5. Which of the following is used to test program flow in a partially complete system: a driver or a stub?
6. The part of a program where an identifier can be referenced is called the _____ of the identifier.
7. What are the values of main function variables x and y at the point marked /* values here */ in the following program?

```
/* nonsense */
void silly(int x);

int
main(void)
{
        int x, y;

        x = 10; y = 11;
        silly(x);
        silly(y);    /* values here */
                . . .

}


void
silly(int x)
{
        int y;

        y = x + 2;
        x *= 2;
}
```

8. Let's make some changes in our nonsense program. What are main's x and y at /* values here */ in the following version?

```
/* nonsense */
void silly(int *x);

int
main(void)
{
      int x, y;

      x = 10;   y = 11;
      silly(&x);
      silly(&y);   /* values here */
         . . .

}


void
silly(int *x)
{
```

```
        int y;

        y = *x + 2;
        *x = 2 * *x;
}
```

## ANSWERS TO QUICK-CHECK EXERCISES

1. actual arguments; formal parameters
2. input
3. addresses of variables/ pointers
4. driver
5. stub
6. scope
7. x is 10, y is 11
8. x is 20, y is 22

## REVIEW QUESTIONS

1. Write a function called `letter_grade` that has a type `int` input parameter called `points` and returns through an output parameter `gradep` the appropriate letter grade using a straight scale (90–100 is an A, 80–89 is a B, and so on). Return through a second output parameter (`just_missedp`) an indication of whether the student just missed the next higher grade (true for 89, 79, and so on).
2. Why would you choose to write a function that computes a single numeric or character value as a non `void` function that returns a result through a `return` statement rather than to write a `void` function with an output parameter?
3. Explain the allocation of memory cells when a function is called. What is stored in the function data area for an input parameter? Answer the same question for an output parameter.
4. Which of the functions in the following program outline *can* call the function `grumpy`? All function prototypes and declarations are shown; only executable statements are omitted.

```
int grumpy(int dopey);

char silly(double grumpy);

double happy(int goofy, char greedy);
```

```
int
main(void)
{
        double p, q, r;
        . . .
}

int
grumpy(int dopey)
{
        double silly;
        . . .
}

char
silly(double grumpy)
{
        double happy;
        . . .
}

double
happy(int goofy, char greedy)
{
        char grumpy;
        . . .
}
```

5. Sketch the data areas of functions main and silly as they appear immediately before the return from the first call to silly in Quick-Check Exercise 8.

6. Present arguments against these statements:

a. It is foolish to use function subprograms because a program written with functions has many more lines than the same program written without functions.

b. The use of function subprograms leads to more errors because of mistakes in using argument lists.

# PROGRAMMING PROJECTS

1. Write a program for an Automatic Teller Machine that dispenses money. The user should enter the amount desired (a multiple of 10 dollars) and the

machine dispenses this amount using the least number of bills. The bills dispensed are 50s, 20s and 10s. Write a function that determines how many of each kind of bill to dispense.

2. Write a program to dispense change. The user enters the amount paid and the amount due. The program determines how many dollars, quarters, dimes, nickels, and pennies should be given as change. Write a function with four output parameters that determines the quantity of each kind of coin.

3. Determine the following information about each value in a list of positive integers.

   a. Is the value a multiple of 7, 11, or 13?
   b. Is the sum of the digits odd or even?
   c. Is the value a prime number?

   You should write a function with three type int output parameters that send back the answers to these three questions. Some sample input data might be
   104   3773   13   121   77   30751.

4. To design a square timber column in a structure, three formulas must be satisfied:

   a. Buckling load:

   $$maximum\ load = (0.30 \times E \times area) / (length/width)^2$$

   b. Compressive stress:

   $$maximum\ load = area \times maximum\ compressive\ strength$$

   c. Slenderness limits:

   $$length/width \leq 50$$

   where E is the modulus of elasticity (1,700,000 psi), the area is the cross-sectional area in square inches, and

   $$maximum\ compressive\ strength = 445\ psi^2\ (Douglas\ fir).$$

   Write a program that uses these three formulas to give an initial design to a structural engineer. Assume the columns to be used are square and are available in intervals of 2 inches (i.e., 2 by 2, 4 by 4, and so on). Have the output look like the following:

```
Please enter the expected load in pounds> 9000
Please enter the length of the column in inches> 120
 . . .Testing a beam with width of 2.0 inches — failed the tests
 . . .Testing a beam with width of 4.0 inches — failed the tests
 . . .Testing a beam with width of 6.0 inches — OK
For a load of 9000.0 pounds and a length of 120.0 inches,
recommended square beam has sides of 6.0 inches.
```

Write a function for each of the three tests. Each function should return a 1 if the test is passed, a 0 otherwise.

5. The square root of a number $N$ can be approximated by repeated calculation using the formula

$$NG = 0.5(LG + N/LG)$$

where $NG$ stands for next guess and $LG$ stands for last guess. Write a function that calculates the square root of a number using this method.

The initial guess will be the starting value of $LG$. The program will compute a value for $NG$ using the formula given. The difference between $NG$ and $LG$ is checked to see whether these two guesses are almost identical. If they are, $NG$ is accepted as the square root; otherwise, the new guess ($NG$) becomes the last guess ($LG$) and the process is repeated (another value is computed for $NG$, the difference is checked, and so on). The loop should be repeated until the difference is less than 0.005. Use an initial guess of 1.0.

Write a driver function and test your square root function for the numbers 4, 120.5, 88, 36.01, 10000, and 0.25.

6. The electric company charges according to the following rate schedule:

9 cents per kilowatt-hour (kwh) for the first 300 kwh
8 cents per kwh for the next 300 kwh (up to 600 kwh)
6 cents per kwh for the next 400 kwh (up to 1000 kwh)
5 cents per kwh for all electricity used over 1000 kwh

Write a function to compute the total charge for each customer. Write a main function to call the charge calculation function using the following data:

| Customer Number | Kilowatt-hours Used |
|---|---|
| 123 | 725 |
| 205 | 115 |
| 464 | 600 |
| 596 | 327 |
| 601 | 915 |
| 613 | 1011 |
| 722 | 47 |

The program should print a three-column chart listing the customer number, the kilowatt-hours used, and the charge for each customer. The program should also compute and print the number of customers, the total kilowatt-hours used, and the total charges.

7. Write a function `ln_approx` that computes an approximation of the natural logarithm of a number between 1 and 2 by summing a given number of terms of this series:

$$\ln(1 + x) = \sum_{n=1}^{\infty} \frac{(-1)^{n+1} x^n}{n}$$

Also, write a driver that calls `ln_approx` twice with the same value, requesting first the sum of four terms of the series and then requesting seven terms. The program should print a message comparing the results of the two calls to the value returned by the math library function `log`.

8. Write a program to model a simple calculator. Each data line should consist of the next operation to be performed from the list below and the right operand. Assume the left operand is the accumulator value (initial value of 0). You need a function `scan_data` with two output parameters that returns the operator and right operand scanned from a data line. You need a function `do_next_op` that performs the required operation. `do_next_op` has two input parameters (the operator and operand) and one input/output parameter (the accumulator). The valid operators are:

| | |
|---|---|
| + | add |
| – | subtract |
| * | multiply |
| / | divide |
| ^ | power (raise left operand to power of right operand) |
| q | quit |

Your calculator should display the accumulator value after each operation. A sample run follows.

```
+ 5.0
result so far is 5.0
^ 2
result so far is 25.0
/ 2.0
result so far is 12.5
q 0
final result is 12.5
```

9. Write a function that computes and displays a table of negative powers of two ($2^{-1}$, $2^{-2}$, and so on) as both common fractions and decimals as shown next.

The range of powers printed should be determined by the function's input arguments. Test your function using a driver.

| Power of 2 | Fraction | Decimal Value |
|---|---|---|
| -1 | 1/2 | 0.5000 |
| -2 | 1/4 | 0.2500 |
| -3 | 1/8 | 0.1250 |

# SIMPLE DATA TYPES

c h a p t e r

**7**

$S$o far, we have used three standard data types: int, double, and char. We have seen how type int values are used in C to represent both the numeric concept of an integer and the logical concepts true and false. In this chapter, we take a closer look at these data types and at related standard types that represent different ranges of values.

No programming language can predefine all the data types that a programmer may need, so C allows a programmer to create new data types. In this chapter, you will learn how to define your own enumerated types. Both C's standard types and user-defined enumerated types are **simple**, or *scalar*, **data types** because only a single value can be stored in a variable of each type.

**simple data type**
a data type used to store a single value

This chapter also presents the notion of a function as a kind of data passed to a subprogram through a parameter. One type of analysis that you can perform on a function is finding a root of the function. The case study at the end of the chapter implements the bisection method for approximating a root.

# 7.1 REPRESENTATION AND CONVERSION OF NUMERIC TYPES

We have seen many examples of the representation of numeric information in C using the data types int and double. We used type int variables as loop counters and to represent data that were whole numbers, such as numbers of bald eagles. In most other instances, we used type double numeric data.

## Differences Between Numeric Types

You may wonder why having more than one numeric type is necessary. Can the data type double be used for all numbers? Yes, but on many computers, operations involving integers are faster than those involving numbers of type double. Less storage space is needed to store type int values. Also, operations with integers are always precise, whereas some loss of accuracy or *round-off error* may occur when dealing with type double numbers.

These differences result from the way numbers are represented in the computer's memory. All data are represented in memory as *binary strings,* strings of 0s and 1s. However, the binary string stored for the type int value 13 is not the same as the binary string stored for the type double number 13.0. The actual internal representation is computer dependent, and type double numbers usually require more bytes of computer memory than type int. Compare the sample int and double formats shown in Fig. 7.1.

**Figure 7.1
Internal
Formats of Type
int and Type
double**

type int format

| binary number |
| --- |

type double format

| mantissa | exponent |
| --- | --- |

Positive integers are represented by standard binary numbers. If you are familiar with the binary number system, you know that the integer 13 is represented as the binary number 01101.

The format of type double values (also called *floating-point format*) is analogous to scientific notation. The storage area occupied by the number is divided into two sections: the *mantissa* and the *exponent*. The mantissa is a binary fraction between 0.5 and 1.0 for positive numbers and between −0.5 and −1.0 for negative numbers. The exponent is an integer. The mantissa and exponent are chosen so that the following formula is correct.

$$real\ number = mantissa \times 2^{exponent}$$

Because of the finite size of a memory cell, not all real numbers in the range allowed can be represented precisely as type double values. We will discuss this concept later.

We have seen that type double values may include a fractional part, whereas type int values cannot. An additional advantage of the type double format is that a much larger range of numbers can be represented as compared to type int. Actual ranges vary from one implementation to another, but the ANSI standard for C specifies that the minimum range of positive values of type int is from 1 to 32,767 (approximately $3.3 \times 10^4$). The minimum range specified for positive values of type double is from $10^{-37}$ to $10^{37}$. To understand how small $10^{-37}$ is, consider the fact that the mass of one electron is approximately $10^{-27}$ grams, and $10^{-37}$ is one ten-billionth of $10^{-27}$. The enormity of $10^{37}$ may be clearer when you realize that if you multiply the diameter of the Milky Way galaxy in kilometers by a trillion, your numeric result is just one ten-thousandth of $10^{37}$.

You can determine the exact int and double ranges of the (ANSI-conforming) C implementation you are using by running the program in Fig. 7.2. The %c format specifier in the second call to printf calls for the values associated with the names DBL_MIN and DBL_MAX to be printed in scientific notation (see Section 2.2).

ANSI C provides several integer data types in addition to int. Table 7.1 lists these types along with their ranges in a typical microprocessor-based C implementation. Notice that the largest number represented by an unsigned type is

**Figure 7.2    Program to Print Implementation-Specific Ranges for Positive Numeric Data**

```
/*
 * Find implementation's ranges for positive numeric data
 */

#include <stdio.h>
#include <limits.h> /* definition of INT_MAX                    */
#include <float.h>  /* definitions of DBL_MIN, DBL_MAX          */

int
main(void)
{
      printf("Range of positive values of type int: 1 . . %d\n",
             INT_MAX);
      printf("Range of positive values of type double: %e . . %e\n",
             DBL_MIN, DBL_MAX);

      return (0);
}
```

about twice the magnitude of the largest value in the corresponding signed type. This results from using the sign bit as part of the number's magnitude.

Similarly, ANSI C defines three floating-point types that differ in their memory requirements: float, double, and long double. Values of type float must have at least six decimal digits of precision; both type double and long double values must have at least 10 decimal digits. Table 7.2 lists

**Table 7.1    Integer Types in C**

| Type | Range in Typical Microprocessor Implementation |
|---|---|
| short | −32,767 .. 32,767 |
| unsigned short | 0 .. 65,535 |
| int | −32,767 .. 32,767 |
| unsigned | 0 .. 65,535 |
| long | −2,147,483,647 .. 2,147,483,647 |
| unsigned long | 0 .. 4,294,967,295 |

**Table 7.2** **Floating-Point Types in C**

| Type | Approximate Range[*] | Significant Digits[*] |
|---|---|---|
| float | $10^{-37} .. 10^{38}$ | 6 |
| double | $10^{-307} .. 10^{308}$ | 15 |
| long double | $10^{-4931} .. 10^{4932}$ | 19 |

[*]In a typical microprocessor-based C implementation

the range of positive numbers representable by each of these types in a typical C microprocessor-based implementation.

## Numerical Inaccuracies

One of the problems in processing data of type double is that sometimes an error occurs in representing real numbers. Just as certain fractions cannot be represented exactly in the decimal number system (e.g., the fraction 1/3 is 0.333333...), so some fractions cannot be represented exactly as binary numbers in the mantissa of the type double format. The **representational error** (sometimes called *round-off error*) will depend on the number of binary digits (bits) used in the mantissa: the more bits, the smaller the error. Because of this kind of error, an equality comparison of two type double values can lead to surprising results.

**representational error**
an error due to coding a real number as a finite number of binary digits

The number 0.1 is an example of a number that has a representational error as a type double value. The effect of a small error is often magnified through repeated computations. Therefore the result of adding 0.1 one hundred times is not exactly 10.0, so the following loop may fail to terminate on some computers.

```
for (trial = 0.0;
     trial != 10.0;
     trial = trial + 0.1) {
   . . .
}
```

If the loop repetition test is changed to trial < 10.0, the loop may execute 100 times on one computer and 101 times on another. For this reason, it is best to use integer variables for loop control whenever you can predict the exact number of times a loop body should be repeated.

Other problems occur when manipulating very large and very small real numbers. When you add a large number and a small number, the larger number may "cancel out" the smaller number, resulting in a **cancellation error.** If $x$ is much larger than $y$, then $x + y$ may have the same value as $x$ (for example, 1000.0 + 0.0000001234 is equal to 1000.0 on some computers).

If two very small numbers are multiplied, the result may be too small to be represented accurately, so it will be represented as zero. This phenomenon is called **arithmetic underflow.** Similarly, if two very large numbers are multiplied, the result may be too large to be represented. This phenomenon, called **arithmetic overflow,** is handled in different ways by different C compilers. (Arithmetic overflow can occur when processing very large integer values as well.)

## Automatic Conversion of Data Types

In Chapter 2, we saw several cases in which data of one numeric type was automatically converted to another numeric type. Table 7.3 summarizes the automatic conversions we have seen. The variables in the table are declared and initialized as follows:

```
int    k = 5, m = 4, n;
double x = 1.5, y = 2.1, z;
```

**Table 7.3   Automatic Conversion of Numeric Data**

| Context of Conversion | Example | Explanation |
| --- | --- | --- |
| Expression with binary operator and operands of different numeric types | k + x<br><br>value is 6.5 | Value of int variable k is converted to type double format before operation is performed. |
| Assignment statement with type double target variable and type int expression | z = k / m;<br>expression value is 1;<br>value assigned to z is 1.0 | Expression is evaluated *first*. Then, the result is converted to type double format for assignment. |
| Assignment statement with type int target variable and type double expression | n = x * y;<br>expression value is 3.15;<br>value assigned to n is 3 | Expression is evaluated *first*. Then, the result is converted to type int format for assignment, and fractional part is lost. |

In Chapter 3 and Chapter 6, we studied what happens when an actual argument of one numeric data type is passed to a formal parameter of a different type. We saw that the actual argument value is converted to the format of the formal parameter just as if the assignment operator were used.

## Explicit Conversion of Data Types

**cast**
an explicit type-conversion
operation

In addition to automatic conversions, C also provides an explicit type conversion operation called a **cast.**

Function `main` in Fig. 6.12 uses the function call

```
scan_fraction(&n1, &d1);
```

to scan and return the numerator and denominator of a common fraction to the type `int` variables `n1` and `d1`, respectively. We can use the statement

```
frac = (double)n1 / (double)d1;
```

to compute and store in variable `frac` (type `double`) the decimal eqivalent of the fraction just scanned. For example, if `n1` is 2 and `d1` is 4, the value of `2.0 / 4.0` (value is `0.5`) would be assigned to `frac`. The expression above uses cast operations to prevent integer division. Without the cast operators, the expression `2 / 4` would evaluate to 0 and the statement

```
frac = n1 / d1;
```

would store `0.0` in `frac`.

Placing the name of the desired type in parentheses immediately before the value to be converted causes the value to be changed to the desired data format before it is used in computation. Because this explicit conversion is a very high-precedence operation, it is performed before the division.

Although we show explicit casts of both operands of the division operator in the first assignment above, explicitly converting only one would be sufficient, because the rules for evaluation of mixed-type expressions would then cause the other to be converted as well. However, we could *not* achieve our goal by writing the expression as

```
frac = (double)(n1 / d1);
```

In this case, the quotient `n1 / d1` is computed first, resulting in the loss of the fractional part. The cast to `double` simply converts this whole number quotient to type `double` format.

In addition to using casts to prevent the loss of a fractional part in integer division, we sometimes include casts that do not affect the result but simply make clear to the reader the conversions that would occur automatically. For example, evaluation of the following assignment statement causes two automatic conversions if m and sqrt_m are type int variables.

```
sqrt_m = sqrt(m);
```

The formal parameter of the sqrt library function is of type double, so a type int actual argument, such as the value of m, will automatically be converted to type double format for assignment to the formal parameter. The sqrt function also returns a value of type double that will automatically be converted to type int format for assignment to sqrt_m. One has the option of emphasizing to the reader the fact that these conversions are occurring by including explicit casts as in this statement:

```
sqrt_m = (int)sqrt((double)m);
```

When a cast operation is applied to a variable, the conversion carried out determines the value of the expression, but the conversion does not change what is stored in the variable. For example, if x is a type int variable whose value is 5, the following statements will first print 5.00 and then print 5. The value of the expression

```
(double)x
```

is 5.0, but the value stored in x is still the integer 5.

| Statements | Output |
| --- | --- |
| printf("%.2f\n", (double)x); | 5.00 |
| printf("%4d\n", x); | 5 |

In the next section, we study the representation of type char and see how we can convert from type char to type int and vice versa.

**EXERCISES FOR SECTION 7.1**

Self-Check

1. How does cancellation error differ from representational error?
2. If squaring $10^{-20}$ gives a result of zero, the type of error that has occurred is called _____ .
3. Evaluate the following expressions if x is 10.5, y is 7.2, m is 5, and n is 2.
   a. x / (double)m
   b. x / m
   c. (double)(n * m)
   d. (double)(n / m) + y
   e. (double)(n / m)

Programming

1. Run the program from Fig. 7.2 to determine the largest type int value and the largest type double value that can be used on your computer system's implementation of C.

# 7.2 REPRESENTATION AND CONVERSION OF TYPE char

We have seen C's data type char that allows us to store and manipulate individual characters such as those that comprise a person's name, address, and other personal data. We have declared variables of type char and have used type char constants consisting of a single character (for example, a letter, digit, or punctuation mark) enclosed in apostrophes. As shown below, we have assigned a character value to a character variable and have associated a character value with an identifier in a constant macro. We have also compared character values using the equality operators == and !=, and using the relational operators <, <=, >, and >=.

```
#define STAR '*'
      .
      .
      .
char next_letter;
next_letter = 'A';
if (next_letter < 'Z')
```

The character variable next_letter is assigned the character value 'A' by the assignment statement just shown. A single character variable or value may appear on the right-hand side of a character assignment statement. Character values may also be compared, scanned, printed, and converted to type int.

To understand the result of an order comparison, we must know something about the way characters are represented internally within your computer. Each character has its own unique numeric code; the binary form of this code is stored in a memory cell that has a character value. These binary numbers are compared by the relational operators in the normal way.

Three common character codes are shown in Appendix A. The digit characters are an increasing sequence of consecutive characters in all three codes. For example, in ASCII (American Standard Code for Information Interchange), the digit characters '0' through '9' have code values of 48 through 57 (decimal). The order relationship that follows holds for the digit characters (i.e., '0' < '1', '1' < '2', and so on).

```
'0'<'1'<'2'<'3'<'4'<'5'<'6'<'7'<'8'<'9'
```

The uppercase letters are also an increasing sequence of characters, but they are not necessarily consecutive. In ASCII, uppercase letters do have consecutive codes, namely the decimal code values 65 through 90. The order relationship that follows holds for uppercase letters.

```
'A'<'B'<'C'< ... <'X'<'Y'<'Z'
```

The lowercase letters are also an increasing, but not necessarily consecutive, sequence of characters. In ASCII, lowercase letters have the consecutive decimal code values 97 through 122, and the following order relationship holds.

```
'a'<'b'<'c'< ... <'x'<'y'<'z'
```

In our examples and programs, we will assume that the letters are consecutive characters.

In ASCII, the *printable characters* have codes from 32 (code for a blank or space) to 126 (code for the symbol ~). The other codes represent nonprintable *control characters*. Sending a control character to an output device causes the device to perform a special operation such as returning the cursor to column one, advancing the cursor to the next line, or ringing a bell.

Since characters are represented by integer codes, C permits conversion of type char to type int and vice versa. For example, you could use the following to find out the code your implementation uses for a question mark:

```
qmark_code = (int)'?';
printf("Code for ? = %d\n", qmark_code);
```

**EXAMPLE 7.1**

**collating sequence**
a sequence of characters
arranged by character-code
number

A **collating sequence** is a sequence of characters arranged by character code number. The program in Fig. 7.3 uses explicit conversion of type int to type char and char to int to print part of the C collating sequence. The program lists the portion of the sequence between the blank and the uppercase 'Z' inclusive. The sequence shown is for the ASCII code; the first character printed is a blank.

**Figure 7.3    Program to Print Part of the Collating Sequence**

```
/*
 * Prints part of the collating sequence
 */
```

*(continued)*

**Figure 7.3** *(continued)*

```
#include <stdio.h>

#define START_CHAR ' '
#define END_CHAR    'Z'

int
main(void)
{
        int char_code; /* numeric code of each character printed */

        for  (char_code = (int)START_CHAR;
              char_code <= (int)END_CHAR;
              char_code = char_code + 1)
           printf("%c", (char)char_code);
        printf("\n");

        return (0);
}

 !"#$%&'()*+,-./0123456789:;<=>?@ABCDEFGHIJKLMNOPQRSTUVWXYZ
```

**EXERCISES FOR SECTION 7.2**

Self-Check

1. Evaluate the following, assuming that letters have consecutive character codes.
   a. (int)'D' - (int)'A'
   b. (char)((int)'C' + 2)
   c. (int)'6' - (int)'7'
2. Write a for loop that would print the alphabet in lowercase letters, assuming that letters have consecutive codes.

Programming

1. Write a function next_char that returns as its type char value the character that follows in the collating sequence the value passed as the argument for next_char. (For now, ignore the possibility of a boundary error.)
2. Rewrite the loop from Self-Check Exercise 2 so it uses function next_char and has a type char loop control variable.

## 7.3 ENUMERATED TYPES

Good solutions to many programming problems require new data types. For example, in a budget program you might distinguish among the following categories of expenses: entertainment, rent, utilities, food, clothing, automobile, insurance, and miscellaneous. ANSI C allows you to associate a numeric code with each category by creating an **enumerated type** that has its own list of meaningful values.

**enumeration type**
a data type whose list of values is specified by the programmer in a type declaration

For example, the enumerated type expense_t has eight possible values:

```
typedef enum
        {entertainment, rent, utilities, food, clothing,
            automobile, insurance, miscellaneous}
expense_t;
```

Our new type name expense_t is used just as we would use a standard type such as int or double. Here is a declaration of variable expense_kind:

```
expense_t expense_kind;
```

**enumeration constant**
an identifier that is one of the values of an enumerated type

Defining type expense_t as shown causes the **enumeration constant** entertainment to be represented as the integer 0, constant rent to be represented as integer 1, utilities as 2, and so on. Variable expense_kind and the eight enumeration constants can be manipulated just as one would handle any other integers. Figure 7.4 shows a program that scans an integer representing an expense code and calls a function that uses a switch statement to display the code meaning.

**Figure 7.4** **Enumerated Type for Budget Expenses**

```
/*  Program demonstrating the use of an enumerated type */

#include <stdio.h>

typedef enum
      {entertainment, rent, utilities, food, clothing,
        automobile, insurance, miscellaneous}
expense_t;

void print_expense(expense_t expense_kind);
```

*(continued)*

**Figure 7.4**    *(continued)*

```
int
main(void)
{
      expense_t expense_kind;

      scanf("%d", &expense_kind);
      printf("Expense code represents ");
      print_expense(expense_kind);
      printf(".\n");

      return (0);
}

/*
 * Display string corresponding to a value of type expense_t
 */
void
print_expense(expense_t expense_kind)
{
      switch (expense_kind) {
      case entertainment:
            printf("entertainment");
            break;

      case rent:
            printf("rent");
            break;

      case utilities:
            printf("utilities");
            break;

      case food:
            printf("food");
            break;

      case clothing:
            printf("clothing");
            break;
```

*(continued)*

**Figure 7.4** *(continued)*

```
case automobile:
     printf("automobile");
     break;

case insurance:
     printf("insurance");
     break;

case miscellaneous:
     printf("miscellaneous");
     break;

default:
     printf("\n*** INVALID CODE ***\n");
}
}
```

The scope rules for identifiers (see Section 6.3) apply to enumerated types and enumeration constants. Enumeration constants must be identifiers; they cannot be numeric, character, or string literals (e.g. `"entertainment"` cannot be a value for an enumerated type.) We recommend that you place type definitions immediately after any `#define` and `#include` directives (see Fig. 7.4) so that you can use the types throughout all parts of your program. The reserved word `typedef` can be used to name many varieties of user-defined types. We will study some of these uses in Chapters 11 and 14.

---

**Enumerated Type Definition**

SYNTAX:  typedef enum
                 {*identifier_list*}
         *enum_type*;

EXAMPLE: typedef enum
                 {sunday, monday, tuesday, wednesday,
                  thursday, friday, saturday}
         day_t;

---

*(continued)*

INTERPRETATION: A new data type named *enum_type* is defined. The valid values of this type are the identifiers of *identifier_list*. The first identifier is represented by the integer 0, the second by the integer 1, and so on.

*Note:* A particular identifier can appear in only one *identifier_list* in a given scope.

An identifier cannot appear in more than one enumerated type definition. For example, the definition

```
typedef enum
        {monday, tuesday, wednesday, thursday, friday}
weekday_t;
```

could not be used with the type `day_t` shown in the Syntax Display.

Relational, assignment, and even arithmetic operators can be used with enumerated types, just as with other integers. For type `day_t`, the following relations are true:

```
sunday < monday
wednesday != friday
tuesday >= sunday
```

We can combine the use of arithmetic operators and casts to find enumeration constants that follow and precede a current value.

**EXAMPLE 7.2**

If `today` and `tomorrow` are type `day_t` variables, the following `if` statement assigns the value of `tomorrow` based on the value of `today`:

```
if (today == saturday)
        tomorrow = sunday;
else
        tomorrow = (day_t)(today + 1);
```

Because the days of a week are cyclical, `tomorrow` should be set to `sunday` when `today` is `saturday`. The last value (`saturday`) in type `day_t` is treated separately, because adding 1 to its integer representation yields a result not associated with a valid `day_t` value.

Because C handles enumerated type values just as it handles other integers, C provides no range checking to verify that the value stored in an enumerated-type variable is valid. For example, this assignment statement will not cause a run-time error even though it is clearly invalid.

```
today = saturday + 3;
```

We have seen that an enumerated-type variable can be used as the controlling expression of a switch statement. Such a variable can also be used as a loop counter, as is demonstrated in the next example.

**EXAMPLE 7.3**

The for loop in Fig. 7.5 scans the hours worked each weekday for an employee and accumulates the sum of these hours in week_hours. Again, today is a variable of type day_t, so the loop executes for today equal to monday through friday. During each iteration, the calls to printf and print_day display a prompt where print_day (see Programming Exercise 2 at the end of this section) displays the day name. When today has the value monday, the prompt is

```
Enter hours for Monday>
```

Next, each value scanned into day_hours is added to week_hours. After loop exit, the final value of week_hours is displayed. We explain why we need function print_day next.

**Figure 7.5   Accumulating Weekday Hours Worked**

```
/* Program to demonstrate an enum type loop counter */

#include <stdio.h>

typedef enum
     {monday, tuesday, wednesday, thursday, friday,
      saturday, sunday}
day_t;

void print_day(day_t day);


int
main(void)
```

*(continued)*

**Figure 7.5**    *(continued)*

```
{
    double week_hours = 0.0, day_hours;
    day_t today;

    for  (today = monday;  today <= friday;  ++today) {
        printf("Enter hours for ");
        print_day(today);
        printf("> ");
        scanf("%lf", &day_hours);
        week_hours += day_hours;
    }

    printf("\nTotal weekly hours are %.2f\n", week_hours);

    return (0);
}
```

Because different enumerated types can be used in each program, C's input/output library functions scan and display enumerated type values only as integers. However, you can code your own functions to display the meaning of enumeration constants. Like `print_expense` in Fig. 7.4, such a function typically uses a `switch` statement.

**EXERCISES FOR SECTION 7.3**

Self-Check

1. Evaluate each of the following expressions, assuming before each operation that the value of variable `today` (type `day_t`) is `thursday`.

   a. `(int)monday`                d. `(day_t)(today + 1)`
   b. `(int)today`                 e. `(day_t)(today - 1)`
   c. `today < tuesday`            f. `today >= thursday`

2. Indicate whether each of the following type definition groups is valid or invalid. Explain the flaws in invalid definitions.

   a. `typedef enum`
      `      {'A', 'B', 'C'}`
      `   letters_t;`

b. typedef enum
       {a, b, c}
   letters_t;
   typedef enum
       {c, d}
   twolet_t;
c. typedef enum
       {while, for, if, switch}
   stmt_t;

Programming

1. Declare an enumerated type month_t and rewrite the following if statement, assuming that cur_month is type month_t instead of type int.
   Also, write the equivalent switch statement.

```
if (cur_month == 1)
        printf("Happy New Year\n");
else if (cur_month == 6)
        printf("Summer begins\n");
else if (cur_month == 9)
        printf("Back to school\n");
else if (cur_month == 12)
        printf("Happy Holidays\n");
```

2. Write function print_day for enumerated type day_t.

# 7.4 ITERATIVE APPROXIMATIONS

Numerical analysis is the branch of mathematics and computer science that
develops algorithms for solving computational problems. Problems from numerical analysis include finding solutions to sets of equations, performing operations on matrices, finding roots of equations, and performing mathematical
integration. The next case study illustrates a method for iteratively approximating a root of an equation.

**root (zero of a function)**
a function argument value that
causes the function result to
be zero

Many real-world problems can be solved by finding roots of equations. A
value $k$ is a **root** of an equation, $f(x) = 0$, if $f(k)$ equals zero. If we graph the
function $f(x)$, as shown in Fig. 7.6, the roots of the equation are those points
where the $x$-axis and the graph of the function intersect. The roots of the equation $f(x) = 0$ are also called the *zeros* of the function $f(x)$.

The *bisection method* is one way of approximating a root of the equation
$f(x) = 0$. This method repeatedly generates approximate roots until a true root is

**Figure 7.6
Six Roots for
the Equation
f(x) = 0**

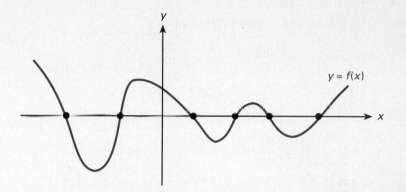

discovered or until an approximation is found that differs from a true root by less than *epsilon,* where *epsilon* is a very small constant (for example, 0.0001). The approximation can be found if we can isolate the true root and the approximate root within the same interval whose length is less than *epsilon.* In our next case study, we develop a function to implement this method of iterative approximation.

## Function Parameters

Although we could develop a bisection function to find roots of one specified function, our bisection routine would be far more useful if we could call it to find a root of any function, just by specifying the name of the function in the call. To do this we must be able to include a function in the parameter list of another function. Declaring a function parameter is accomplished by simply including a prototype of the function in the parameter list. For example, if you want to write a function `evaluate` that evaluates another function at three dif-

**Table 7.4    Calls to Function evaluate and the Output Produced**

| Call to evaluate | Output Produced |
|---|---|
| evaluate(sqrt, 0.25, 25.0, 100.0); | f(0.25000) = 0.50000<br>f(25.00000) = 5.00000<br>f(100.00000) = 10.00000 |
| evaluate(sin, 0.0, 3.14159,<br>        0.5 * 3.14159); | f(0.00000) = 0.00000<br>f(3.14159) = 0.00000<br>f(1.57079) = 1.00000 |

**Figure 7.7** **Using a Function Parameter**

```
/*
 * Evaluate a function at three points, displaying results.
 */
void
evaluate(double f(double f_arg), double pt1, double pt2, double pt3)
{
      printf("f(%.5f) = %.5f\n", pt1, f(pt1));
      printf("f(%.5f) = %.5f\n", pt2, f(pt2));
      printf("f(%.5f) = %.5f\n", pt3, f(pt3));
}
```

ferent points and displays the results, write `evaluate` as shown in Fig. 7.7. Then you can call `evaluate` either with library functions that take a type `double` argument and return a type `double` result or with your own function that meets these criteria. Table 7.4 shows two calls to `evaluate` along with the output generated.

## Case Study: Bisection Method for Finding Roots

**PROBLEM**

Develop a function `bisect` that approximates a root of a function `f` on an interval that contains an odd number of roots.

**ANALYSIS**

A program that is to call function `bisect` should first tabulate function values to find an appropriate interval in which to search for a root. If a change of sign occurs on an interval, that interval must contain an odd number of roots. Figure 7.8 shows two such intervals. If there is no change of sign, the interval may contain no roots.

Let us assume that $[x_{left}, x_{right}]$ (x_left to x_right) is an interval on which a change of sign does occur and in which there is exactly one root. Furthermore, assume that the function $f(x)$ is continuous on this interval. If we bisect this interval by computing its midpoint $x_{mid}$, using the formula

$$x_{mid} = \frac{x_{left} + x_{right}}{2.0}$$

**Figure 7.8
Change of Sign
Implies an Odd
Number of
Roots**

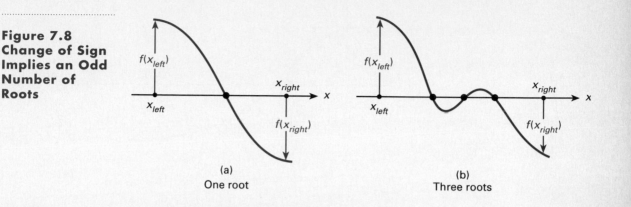

(a)
One root

(b)
Three roots

there are three possible outcomes: the root is in the lower half of the interval, $[x_{left}, x_{mid}]$; the root is in the upper half of the interval, $[x_{mid}, x_{right}]$; or $f(x_{mid})$ is zero. Figure 7.9 shows these three possibilities graphically.

A fourth possibility is that the length of the interval is less than *epsilon*. In this case, any point in the interval is an acceptable root approximation.

### Data Requirements

**Problem Inputs**
```
double x_left          /* left endpoint of interval   */
double x_right         /* right endpoint of interval  */
double epsilon         /* error tolerance             */
double f(double farg)  /* function whose root is sought*/
```

**Problem Outputs**
```
double  root    /* approximate root of f               */
int     *errp   /* indicates whether error detected
                   during root search                  */
```

**DESIGN**

The initial interval on which to search for a root is defined by the input parameters x_left and x_right. Before searching this interval, we must verify that it contains an odd number of roots. If it does, we need to repeatedly bisect the interval, searching the half containing an odd number of roots until we find a true root or until the length of the interval to search is less than epsilon.

**Figure 7.9
Three
Possibilities
That Arise
When the
Interval [$x_{left}$,
$x_{right}$] Is
Bisected**

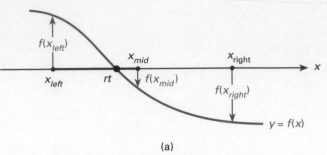

(a)

The root *rt* is in the half interval [$x_{left}$, $x_{mid}$].

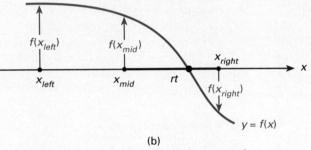

(b)

The root *rt* is in the half interval [$x_{mid}$, $x_{right}$].

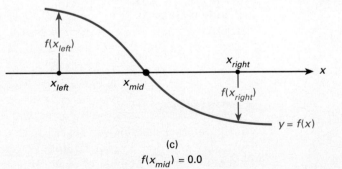

(c)

$f(x_{mid}) = 0.0$

## Initial Algorithm

1. if the interval contains an even number of roots
    2. Set error flag.
    3. Display error message.
  else
    4 Clear error flag
    5. repeat as long as interval size is greater than `epsilon` and root is not found
        6. Compute the function value at the midpoint of the interval.
        7. if the function value is zero, the midpoint is a root.
        8. else choose the left or right half of the interval in which to continue the search.
9. Return the midpoint of the final interval as the root.

## Program Variables

```
int root_found   /* whether or not root is found */
double x_mid     /* interval midpoint */
double f_left,   /* values of function at left and */
       f_mid,    /* right endpoints and at midpoint */
       f_right   /* of interval */
```

## Refinement of Step 1

1.1 `f_left = f(x_left)`
1.2 `f_right = f(x_right)`
1.3 if signs of `f_left` and `f_right` are the same (i.e., if their product is nonnegative)

## Refinement of Step 5

5.1 while `x_right - x_left > epsilon` and `!root_found`

## Refinement of Step 8

8.1 if root is in left half of interval (`f_left * f_mid < 0.0`)
    8.2 Change right end to midpoint
  else
    8.3 Change left end to midpoint

**◀ IMPLEMENTATION ▶**

Figure 7.10 shows an implementation of this algorithm. We have added some calls to `printf` to make function `bisect` self-tracing.

## Figure 7.10    Finding a Function Root Using the Bisection Method

```c
/*
 *  Finds roots of the equations
 *       g(x) = 0    and     h(x) = 0
 *  on a specified interval [x_left, x_right] using the bisection method.
 */

#include <stdio.h>
#include <math.h>

double bisect(double x_left, double x_right, double epsilon,
              double f(double farg), int *errp);
double g(double x);
double h(double x);


int
main(void)
{
      double x_left, x_right, /* left, right endpoints of interval  */
             epsilon,          /* error tolerance        */
             root;
      int    error;

      /*  Get endpoints and error tolerance from user            */
      printf("\nEnter interval endpoints> ");
      scanf("%lf%lf", &x_left, &x_right);
      printf("\nEnter tolerance> ");
      scanf("%lf", &epsilon);

      /*  Use bisect function to look for roots of g and h        */
      printf("\n\nFunction g");
      root = bisect(x_left, x_right, epsilon, g, &error);
      if (!error)
            printf("\n   g(%.7f) = %e\n", root, g(root));

      printf("\n\nFunction h");
      root = bisect(x_left, x_right, epsilon, h, &error);
      if (!error)
            printf("\n   h(%.7f) = %e\n", root, h(root));
```

*(continued)*

**Figure 7.10** *(continued)*

```
      return (0);
}

/*
 *  Implements the bisection method for finding a root of a function f.
 *  Finds a root (and sets output parameter error flag to FALSE) if
 *  signs of fp(x_left) and fp(x_right) are different. Otherwise sets
 *  output parameter error flag to TRUE.
 */
double
bisect(double x_left,           /* input  - endpoints of interval in */
       double x_right,          /*           which to look for a root */
       double epsilon,          /* input  - error tolerance          */
       double f(double farg),   /* input  - the function             */
       int    *errp)            /* output - error flag               */
{
      double x_mid,      /* midpoint of interval */
             f_left,     /* f(x_left)            */
             f_mid,      /* f(x_mid)             */
             f_right;    /* f(x_right)           */
      int    root_found = FALSE;

      /* Computes function values at initial endpoints of interval  */
      f_left = f(x_left);
      f_right = f(x_right);

      /* If no change of sign occurs on the interval there is not a
         unique root. Searches for the unique root if there is one.*/
      if (f_left * f_right > 0) {   /* same sign */
            *errp = TRUE;
            printf("\nMay be no root in [%.7f, %.7f]", x_left, x_right);
      } else {
            *errp = FALSE;

            /*  Searches as long as interval size is large enough
                and no root has been found                          */
            while (fabs(x_right - x_left) > epsilon  &&  !root_found) {

                  /* Computes midpoint and function value at midpoint */
                  x_mid = (x_left + x_right) / 2.0;
                  f_mid = f(x_mid);
```

*(continued)*

**Figure 7.10**    *(continued)*

```
                if (f_mid == 0.0)  {                /* Here's the root    */
                    root_found = TRUE;
                } else if (f_left * f_mid < 0.0) {/* Root in [x_left,x_mid]*/
                    x_right = x_mid;
                } else {                           /* Root in [x_mid,x_right]*/
                    x_left = x_mid;
                    f_left = f_mid;
                }

                /* Prints root and interval or new interval */
                if (root_found)
                    printf("\nRoot found at x = %.7f, midpoint of [%.7f, %.7f]",
                           x_mid, x_left, x_right);
                else
                    printf("\nNew interval is [%.7f, %.7f]",
                           x_left, x_right);
            }
        }

    /*  If there is a root, it is the midpoint of [x_left, x_right]     */
    return ((x_left + x_right) / 2.0);
}

/*  Functions for which roots are sought                              */

/*      3      2
 *  5x   - 2x  + 3
 */
double
g(double x)
{
    return (5 * pow(x, 3.0) - 2 * pow(x, 2.0) + 3);
}

/*    4     2
 *  x   - 3x  - 8
 */
double
h(double x)
{
    return (pow(x, 4.0) - 3 * pow(x, 2.0) - 8);
}
```

TESTING

The C program shown in Figure 7.10 looks for approximate roots for the equations $g(x) = 0$ and $h(x) = 0$ on the interval [x_left, x_right]. The left and right endpoints, x_left and x_right, and the tolerance, epsilon, are inputs from the user. The main function gets these three inputs, calls function bisect, and displays the results. Each call to bisect passes a function name as the fourth argument. Because the bisection method as implemented in Fig. 7.10 can be applied to any function that both returns a type double value and takes a single type double argument, we can test bisect on multiple functions in a single program run. When bisect is executing as a result of function main's statement

```
root = bisect(x_left, x_right, epsilon, g, &error);
```

the statement

```
f_left = f(x_left);
```

is equivalent to

```
f_left = g(x_left);
```

However, when bisect executes as a result of the call statement

```
root = bisect(x_left, x_right, epsilon, h, &error);
```

the same statement means

```
f_left = h(x_left);
```

Fig. 7.11 shows the results of one run of the program in Fig. 7.10.

**Figure 7.11    Sample Run of Bisection Program with Trace Code Included**

```
Enter interval endpoints> -1.0  1.0
Enter tolerance> 0.001

Function g
New interval is [-1.0000000, 0.0000000]
New interval is [-1.0000000, -0.5000000]
New interval is [-0.7500000, -0.5000000]
```

*(continued)*

```
New interval is [-0.7500000, -0.6250000]
New interval is [-0.7500000, -0.6875000]
New interval is [-0.7500000, -0.7187500]
New interval is [-0.7343750, -0.7187500]
New interval is [-0.7343750, -0.7265625]
New interval is [-0.7304688, -0.7265625]
New interval is [-0.7304688, -0.7285156]
New interval is [-0.7294922, -0.7285156]
   g(-0.7290039) = -2.697494e-05

Function h
May be no root in [-1.0000000, 1.0000000]
```

**EXERCISES FOR SECTION 7.4**

Self-Check

1. Find endpoints of an interval one unit long in which a root of $h(x) = 0$ is found for function h from Fig. 7.10.
2. It is unusual for a program to use equality comparison of two type double values as in

   ```
   if (f_mid == 0.0)
   ```

   Find a function and an interval that would cause this test to evaluate to 1 (true).

Programming

1. Revise the program in Fig. 7.10 so that if the user enters an interval longer than one unit, the program checks one-unit segments of the interval until a subinterval is found with different signs for the values of function g. The program should then call bisect with this subinterval and function g.

## 7.5 COMMON PROGRAMMING ERRORS

Predicting and hand-checking the results of every program is especially important because of the way C represents the various data types. Arithmetic underflow and overflow resulting from a poor choice of variable type are common causes of erroneous results. Programs that approximate solutions to numerical problems by repeated calculations often magnify small representational errors.

To defend against such errors, a C programmer should check the ranges of values represented by each type in the C implementation used, and should consider the likely values of every variable before choosing a data type.

When you define enumerated types, remember that only identifiers can appear in the list of values (enumeration constants) for the type. Be careful not to reuse one of these identifiers in another type or as a variable name in a function that needs your type definition. Keep in mind that there is no built-in facility for input/output of the identifiers that are the valid values of an enumerated type. You must either scan and display the underlying integer representation or write your own input/output functions. Remember that C does not verify the validity of integers stored in enumerated-type variables.

# CHAPTER REVIEW

1. Type `int` and `double` data have different internal representations. Type `int` values are represented as binary numbers with the leftmost bit containing the sign of the number. Type `double` data are represented by a binary exponent and mantissa.
2. Additional integer types are `short`, `unsigned short`, `unsigned`, `long`, and `unsigned long`. Type `short` typically represents a smaller range of integers than type `int`; `long` represents a larger range. An `unsigned` type uses the sign bit in its representation of the magnitude of a positive number.
3. Additional floating point types are `float`, which typically represents a smaller range than type `double`, and `long double`, which may represent a larger range.
4. Arithmetic with floating point data may not be precise, because not all real numbers can be represented exactly. Other types of numerical errors include cancellation error, and arithmetic overflow and underflow.
5. Type `char` data are represented by storing a binary code value for each symbol. ASCII is a commonly used character code.
6. You can declare your own data types in C using the reserved word `typedef`.
7. Defining an enumerated type requires listing the identifiers that are the values of the type. Each value is represented by an integer. Using enumerated types makes programs more readable because the type's values are meaningful for a particular application.
8. A variable or expression can be explicitly converted to another type by writing the new type's name in parentheses before the value to convert. Such a cast is a very high-precedence operation.
9. A function can take another function as a parameter.

10. Numerical analysis is the branch of mathematics and computer science that develops algorithms for mathematical computation. We demonstrated how to use the bisection method, a technique for iterative approximation of a root of a function.

## New C Constructs

| Construct | Effect |
|---|---|
| **Enumerated Type Definition**<br>```typedef enum<br>    {keyboard, mouse, dot_matrix,<br>     laser, scanner, synthesizer}<br>periph_t;``` | An enumerated type `periph_t` is defined with values `keyboard`, `mouse`, `dot_matrix`, `laser`, `scanner`, and `synthesizer`. Values will be represented by integers 0 (`keyboard`) through 5 (`synthesizer`). |
| **Enumeration Variable Declaration and Assignment**<br>```periph_t peripheral;```<br><br>```peripheral = scanner;``` | Variable `peripheral` can represent any of the `periph_t` enumeration constants. Integer 4 is stored in `peripheral`, representing value `scanner`. |
| **Declaration of Variables of Additional Standard Types**<br>```unsigned   n;<br>long double x;``` | Variable n can represent twice as many positive integers as can a variable of type `int`. Variable x may accommodate a larger range of floating-point values than a variable of type `double`. |

# QUICK-CHECK EXERCISES

1. Assuming an ASCII character set, evaluate these expressions.
   a. `(char)((int)'z' - 2)`
   b. `(int)'F' - (int)'A'`
   c. `(char)(5 + (int)'M')`

2. What does this segment print?

```
for  (ch = (int)'d';
        ch < (int)'n';
        ch += 3)
     printf("%c", (char)ch);
  printf("\u");
```

3. Which of the following can be an enumeration constant?

   a. an integer    b. a floating-point number    c. an identifier
   d. a string value

4. Why is it possible that the following C expression will not evaluate to 1 (true)?

```
(0.1 + 0.1 + 0.1 + 0.1 + 0.1 == 0.5)
```

5. What is wrong with the following enumerated type definition?

```
typedef enum
     {2, 3, 5, 7, 11, 13}
prime_t;
```

6. Consider the enumerated type definition:

```
typedef enum
     {frosh, soph, jr, sr}
class_t;
```

What is the value of each of the following?

   a. (int)sr    b. (class_t)0    c. (class_t)((int)soph + 1)
   d. What is displayed by this code fragment?

```
   for  (class = frosh;  class <= sr;  ++class)
        printf("%d  ", class);
   printf("\n");
```

7. If this condition is true, what kind of error has occurred?

```
87654321.0 + 0.000123 == 87654321.0
```

8. If the value of the expression

```
32120 + 1000
```

is a negative number, what kind of error has occurred?

9. Consider this enumerated type definition

```
typedef enum
        {jan, feb, mar, apr, may, jun, jul,
         aug, sep, oct, nov, dec}
month_t;
```

Write a function `next_month` that takes a `month_t` parameter and returns the type `month_t` abbreviation that follows. Let `jan` follow `dec`.

# ANSWERS TO QUICK-CHECK EXERCISES

1. a. `'x'`
   b. 5
   c. `'R'`
2. `dgjm`
3. c. an identifier
4. Because of representational error, the fraction 0.1 cannot be represented exactly in binary.
5. Integers cannot be enumerated type values.
6. a. 3     b. `frosh`     c. `jr`     d. 0  1  2  3
7. cancellation error
8. arithmetic overflow
9. ```
   month_t
   next_month(month_t this_month)
   {
         month_t next;

         if (this_month == dec)
               next = jan;
         else
               next = (month_t)((int)this_month + 1);

         return (next);
   }
   ```

# REVIEW QUESTIONS

1. What are the advantages of data type `int` over data type `double`? What are the advantages of type `double` over type `int`?
   ```

2. List and explain three computational errors that may occur in type `double` expressions.

3. Assume you are using the ASCII character set, and write a `for` loop that runs from the code for `'Z'` down to the code for `'A'` and prints only the consonants. Define a function `is_vowel` that returns a `1` if its character argument is a vowel and a `0` otherwise. Call this function from your loop.

4. Write a C function with type `int` argument n and type `double` argument x that returns as its value the sum of the first n terms of the series

$$x + \frac{x^2}{2} + \frac{x^3}{3} + \frac{x^4}{4} + \cdots + \frac{x^n}{n}$$

5. Write a function for displaying (as a string) a value of enumerated type `season_t`:

```
typedef enum
      {winter, spring, summer, fall}
season_t;
```

6. Define an enumerated type `fiscal_t` as the months from July through June. Declare a variable named `month` of type `fiscal_t`, and write a `switch` statement controlled by `month` that displays `"summer"` for `june`, `july`, and `august`; `"fall"` for `september`, `october`, `november`; `"winter"` for `december`, `january`, `february`; `"spring"` for `march`, `april`, `may`; and `"invalid month"` for other values.

7. Write a `for` loop that would display

```
0.1   0.2   0.3   0.4   0.5   0.6   0.7   0.8   0.9   1.0
```

for *all* C implementations.

8. If the maximum value representable as an `int` were 32,767, which of the following values would likely be the maximum value representable as type `unsigned` in the same implementation?

a. 32,767        b. 45,000        c. 65,534        d. 75,767

9. An explicit conversion from one data type to another is called a _____ .

# PROGRAMMING PROJECTS

1. Write a program that computes the sum

$$s = \sum_{i=1}^{1000} x \qquad \text{where } x = 0.1$$

Compute this sum twice: once with the variables for *s* and *x* declared `float`, once with the variables declared `double`. Calculate the error in each sum (100.0 − *s*). You may wish to use these declarations:

```
float  sf, xf = 0.1f;
double sd, xd = 0.1;
```

2. Experiments that are either too expensive or too dangerous to perform are often simulated on a computer when the computer is able to provide a good representation of the experiment. Write a program that uses a random number generator to simulate the dropping of glass rods that break into three pieces.

   The purpose of the experiment is to estimate the probability that the lengths of the three pieces are such that they might form the sides of a triangle. For the purposes of this experiment, you may assume that the glass rod always breaks into three pieces and that a break is equally likely to occur at any point along the rod. If you use the line segment 0 to 1 on the real number line as a mathematical model of the glass rod, a random number generator function can be used to generate two numbers between 0 and 1 to represent the coordinates of the breaks. The triangle inequality—that is, the sum of the lengths of two sides of a triangle is always greater than the length of the third side—may be used to test the length of each piece against the lengths of the other two pieces.

   To estimate the probability that the pieces of the rod form a triangle, you will need to repeat the experiment many times and count the number of times a triangle can be formed from the pieces. The probability estimate is the number of successes divided by the total number of rods dropped. Your program should prompt the user for the number of rods to drop and allow the experiment to be repeated. Use a sentinel value of −1 to halt execution of the program.

   ANSI C has a function `rand` defined in `<stdlib.h>`. This function returns an integer between 0 and the value associated with `RAND_MAX`, a constant macro that is defined in the same library. You can use this function in defining your own pseudorandom number generator that will return values in the range 0 to 1.

3. The rate of decay of a radioactive isotope is given in terms of its half-life *H*, the time lapse required for the isotope to decay to one-half of its original mass. The isotope strontium-90 ($^{90}$Sr) has a half-life of 28 years. Compute and print in table form the amount of this isotope that remains after each year for *n* years, given the initial presence of an amount in grams. The values of *n* and *amount* should be provided interactively. The amount of $^{90}$Sr remaining can be computed by using the following formula:

$$r = amount \times C^{(y/H)}$$

where *amount* is the initial amount in grams, $C$ is expressed as $e^{-0.693}$ ($e$ = 2.71828), $y$ is the number of years elapsed, and $H$ is the half-life of the isotope in years.

4. The value for $\pi$ can be determined by the series equation

$$\pi = 4 \times \left( 1 - \frac{1}{3} + \frac{1}{5} + \frac{1}{7} + \frac{1}{9} - \frac{1}{11} + \frac{1}{13} - \ldots \right)$$

   Write a program to calculate the value of $\pi$ using the formula given including terms up through 1/99.

5. In this chapter we studied the bisection method for finding a root of an equation. Another method for finding a root, Newton's method, usually converges to a solution even faster than the bisection method, if it converges at all. Newton's method starts with an initial guess for a root, $x_0$, and then generates successive approximate roots $x_1, x_2, \ldots, x_j, x_{j+1}, \ldots$, using the iterative formula

$$x_{j+1} = x_j - \frac{f(x_j)}{f'(x_j)}$$

   where $f'(x_j)$ is the derivative of function $f$ evaluated at $x = x_j$. The formula generates a new guess, $x_{j+1}$, from a previous one, $x_j$. Sometimes Newton's method will fail to converge to a root. In this case, the program should terminate after many trials, perhaps 100.

   Figure 7.12 shows the geometric interpretation of Newton's method where $x_0$, $x_1$, and $x_2$ represent successive guesses for the root. At each point $x_j$, the derivative, $f'(x_j)$, is the slope of the tangent to the curve, $f(x)$. The next guess for the root, $x_{j+1}$, is the point at which the tangent crosses the $x$ axis.

   From geometry, we get the equation

$$\frac{y_{j+1} - y_j}{x_{j+1} - x_j} = m$$

   where $m$ is the slope of the line between points $(x_{j+1}, y_{j+1})$ and $(x_j, y_j)$. In Fig. 7.12, we see that $y_{j+1}$ is zero, $y_j$ is $f(x_j)$, and $m$ is $f'(x_j)$; therefore by substituting and rearranging terms, we get

$$-f(x_j) = f'(x_j) \times (x_{j+1} - x_j)$$

   leading to the formula shown at the beginning of this problem.

   Write a program that uses Newton's method to approximate the $n$th root of a number to six decimal places. If $x^n = c$, then $x^n - c = 0$. Finding a root of

**Figure 7.12
Geometric
Interpretation
of Newton's
Method**

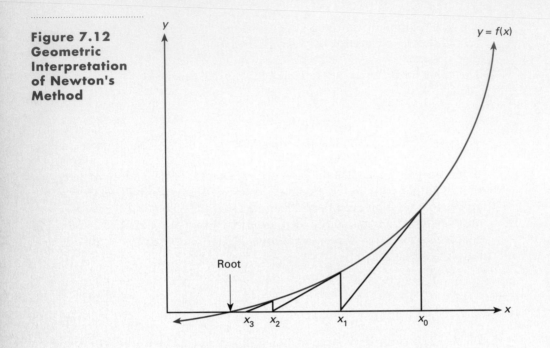

the second equation will give you $\sqrt[n]{c}$. Test your program on $\sqrt{2}$, $\sqrt[3]{7}$, and $\sqrt[3]{-1}$. Your program could use $c/2$ as its initial guess.

6. You would like to find the area under the curve

$$y = f(x)$$

between the lines $x = a$ and $x = b$. One way to approximate this area is to use line segments as approximations of small pieces of the curve and then to sum the areas of trapezoids created by drawing perpendiculars from the line segment endpoints to the $x$-axis, as shown in Fig. 7.13. We will assume that $f(x)$ is nonnegative over the interval $[a,b]$. The trapezoidal rule approximates this area $T$ as

$$T = \frac{h}{2}\left(f(a) + f(b) + 2\sum_{i=1}^{n-1} f(x_i)\right)$$

**Figure 7.13**
**Approximating**
**the Area Under**
**a Curve with**
**Trapezoids**

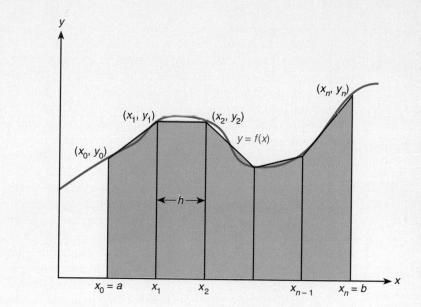

for *n* subintervals of length *h:*

$$h = \frac{b - a}{n}$$

Write a function `trap` with input parameters a, b, n, and f that implements the trapezoidal rule. Call `trap` with values for n of 2, 4, 8, 16, 32, 64, and 128 on functions

$$g(x) = x^2 \sin x \qquad (a = 0, b = 3.14159)$$

and

$$h(x) = \sqrt{4 - x^2} \qquad (a = -2, b = 2)$$

Function *h* defines a half-circle of radius 2. Compare your approximation to the actual area of this half-circle.

*Note:* If you have studied calculus, you will observe that the trapezoidal rule is approximating

$$\int_a^b f(x)dx$$

7. Since communications channels are often noisy, numerous ways have been devised to ensure reliable data transmission. One successful method uses a checksum. A checksum for a message can be computed by summing the integer codes of the characters in the message and finding the remainder of this sum divided by 64. The integer code for a space character is added to this result to obtain the checksum. Since this value is within the range of the displayable characters, it is displayed as a character as well. Write a program that accepts single-line messages ending with a period and displays the checksum character for each message. Your program should continue displaying checksums until the user enters a line with only a period.

8. A finite state machine (FSM) consists of a set of states, a set of transitions, and a string of input data. In the FSM of Fig. 7.14, the named ovals represent states, and the arrows connecting the states represent transitions. The FSM is designed to recognize a list of C identifiers and nonnegative integers, assuming that the items are ended by one or more blanks, and that a period marks the end of all the data. Table 7.5 traces how the diagrammed machine would process a string composed of one blank, the digits 9 and 5, two blanks, the letter K, the digit 9, one blank, and a period. The machine begins in the start state.

**Figure 7.14
Finite State
Machine for
Numbers and
Identifiers**

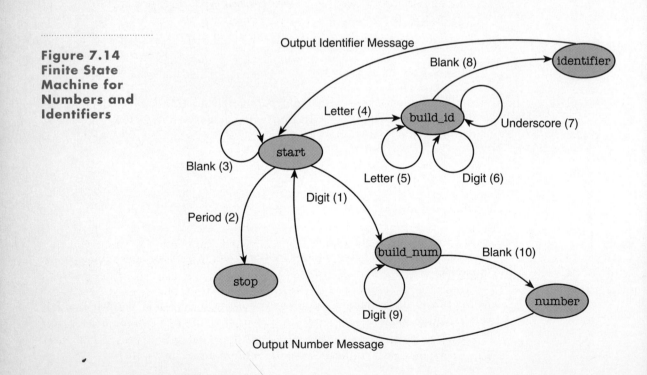

**Table 7.5 Trace of Fig. 7.12 FSM on data " 95    K9 ."**

| State | Next Character | Transition |
|---|---|---|
| start | ' ' | 3 |
| start | '9' | 1 |
| build_num | '5' | 9 |
| build_num | ' ' | 10 |
| number | | Output number message |
| start | ' ' | 3 |
| start | 'K' | 4 |
| build_id | '9' | 6 |
| build_id | ' ' | 8 |
| identifier | | Output identifier message |
| start | '.' | 2 |
| stop | | |

Write a program that uses an enumerated type to represent the names of the states. Your program should process a correctly formatted line of data, identifying each data item. Here is a sample of correct input and output.

*Input*:
```
rate  R2D2 48   2 time   555666 .
```

*Output*:
```
rate — Identifier
R2D2 — Identifier
48 — Number
2 — Number
time — Identifier
555666 — Number
```

Use the following code fragment in main, and design function transition to return the next state for all the numbered transitions of the finite state machine. If you include the header file ctype.h, you can use the library function isdigit which returns 1 if called with a digit character, 0 otherwise. Similarly, the function isalpha checks whether a character is a letter. When your program correctly models the behavior of the FSM shown, extend the FSM and your program to allow optional signs and optional fractional parts (i.e., a decimal point followed by zero or more digits) in numbers.

```
current_state = start;
do {
    if (current_state == identifier) {
        printf(" - Identifier\n");
        current_state = start;
    } else if (current_state == number) {
        printf(" - Number\n");
        current_state = start;
    }
    scanf("%c", &transition_char);
    if (transition_char != ' ')
        printf("%c", transition_char);
    current_state = transition(current_state,
                               transition_char);
} while (current_state != stop);
```

# ARRAYS

c h a p t e r

$S$imple data types use a single memory cell to store a variable. To solve many programming problems, it is more efficient to group data items together in main memory than to allocate an individual memory cell for each variable. A program that processes exam scores for a class, for example, would be easier to write if all the scores were stored in one area of memory and were able to be accessed as a group. C allows a programmer to group such related data items together into a single composite **data structure**. In this chapter, we look at one such data structure: the **array.**

**data structure**
a composite of related data items stored under the same name
**array**
a collection of data items of the same type

## 8.1 DECLARING AND REFERENCING ARRAYS

**array element**
a data item that is part of an array

An array is a collection of two or more adjacent memory cells, called **array elements**, that are associated with a particular symbolic name. To set up an array in memory, we must declare both the name of the array and the number of cells associated with it.

The declaration

```
double x[8];
```

instructs the compiler to associate eight memory cells with the name x; these memory cells will be adjacent to each other in memory. Each element of array x may contain a single type `double` value, so a total of eight such numbers may be stored and referenced using the array name x.

**subscripted variable**
a variable followed by a subscript in brackets, designating an array element
**array subscript**
a value or expression enclosed in brackets after the array name, specifying which array element to access

To process the data stored in an array, we reference each individual element by specifying the array name and identifying the element desired (for example, element 3 of array x). The **subscripted variable** x[0] (read as x sub zero) may be used to reference the initial or 0th element of the array x, x[1] the next element, and x[7] the last element. The integer enclosed in brackets is the **array subscript**, and its value must be in the range from zero to one less than the number of memory cells in the array.

**EXAMPLE 8.1**

Let x be the array shown in Fig. 8.1. Notice that x[1] is the second array element and x[7], not x[8], is the last array element. A sequence of statements that manipulate this array is shown in Table 8.1. The contents of array x after execution of these statements are shown after Table 8.1. Only x[2] and x[3] are changed.

**Figure 8.1 The Eight Elements of Array x**

```
double x[8];
```

Array x

| x[0] | x[1] | x[2] | x[3] | x[4] | x[5] | x[6] | x[7] |
|------|------|------|------|------|------|------|------|
| 16.0 | 12.0 | 6.0 | 8.0 | 2.5 | 12.0 | 14.0 | -54.5 |

**Table 8.1  Statements That Manipulate Array x**

| Statement | Explanation |
|-----------|-------------|
| `printf("%.1f", x[0]);` | Displays the value of `x[0]`, which is `16.0`. |
| `x[3] = 25.0;` | Stores the value `25.0` in `x[3]`. |
| `sum = x[0] + x[1];` | Stores the sum of `x[0]` and `x[1]`, which is `28.0` in the variable `sum`. |
| `sum += x[2];` | Adds `x[2]` to `sum`. The new `sum` is `34.0`. |
| `x[3] += 1.0;` | Adds `1.0` to `x[3]`. The new `x[3]` is `26.0`. |
| `x[2] = x[0] + x[1];` | Stores the sum of `x[0]` and `x[1]` in `x[2]`. The new `x[2]` is `28.0`. |

Array x

| x[0] | x[1] | x[2] | x[3] | x[4] | x[5] | x[6] | x[7] |
|------|------|------|------|------|------|------|------|
| 16.0 | 12.0 | 28.0 | 26.0 | 2.5 | 12.0 | 14.0 | -54.5 |

**EXAMPLE 8.2**  We declare two arrays for a student records program as follows:

```
int    id[NUM_STUDENTS];
double gpa[NUM_STUDENTS];
```

Here we assume that NUM_STUDENTS has already appeared in a #define directive such as

```
#define NUM_STUDENTS 50
```

The arrays id and gpa each have 50 elements. Each element of array id can be used to store an integer value; each element of array gpa can be used to store a

**parallel arrays**
two or more arrays with the same number of elements used for storing related information about a collection of data objects

value of type double. If you use these declarations in a problem to assess the range and distribution of grade point averages, you can store the first student's i.d. in id[0], and store the same student's gpa in gpa[0]. Because the data stored in id[i] and gpa[i] relate to the ith student, the two arrays are called **parallel arrays.** Samples of these arrays are shown next.

| id[0] | 5503 | | gpa[0] | 2.71 |
| id[1] | 4556 | | gpa[1] | 3.09 |
| id[2] | 5691 | | gpa[2] | 2.98 |
| | ... | | | ... |
| id[49] | 9146 | | gpa[49] | 1.92 |

**EXAMPLE 8.3** We show the #define directives and type and variable declaration sections for a grading program next.

```
#define NUM_QUEST     10   /* number of questions on daily
                                quiz */
#define NUM_CLASS_DAYS 5   /* number of days in a week of
                                class */


typedef enum
        {monday, tuesday, wednesday, thursday, friday}
class_days_t;


    . . .


char answer[NUM_QUEST];   /* correct answers for one quiz */
int  score[NUM_CLASS_DAYS]; /* one student's quiz scores for
                                each day */
```

Array answer is declared with 10 elements; each element can store a single character. We can use this array to store the 10 answers for a true-false quiz (e.g., answer[0] is 'T', answer[1] is 'F'). Array score has five elements corresponding to the five class days listed in the class_days_t type declaration. Since the enumeration constants monday through friday are

**Figure 8.2
Arrays answer
and score**

represented by the integers 0 through 4, we can use them as subscripts on array score. Sample arrays are illustrated in Fig. 8.2.

 **EXAMPLE 8.4** You can declare more than one array in a single type declaration. The statements

```
double cactus[5], needle, pins[6];
int    factor[12], n, index;
```

declare cactus and pins to be arrays with five and six type double elements, respectively. The variable factor is an array with 12 type int elements. In addition, individual memory cells will be allocated for storage of the simple variables needle, n, and index.

## Array Initialization

We can initialize a simple variable when we declare it:

```
int sum = 0;
```

We can also initialize an array in its declaration. We can omit the size of an array that is being fully initialized since the size can be deduced from the initialization list. For example, in the following statement, we initialize a 25-element array with the prime numbers less than 100.

```
int prime_lt_100[] = {2, 3, 5, 7, 11, 13, 17, 19, 23, 29, 31,
                 37, 41, 43, 47, 53, 59, 61, 67, 71,
                 73, 79, 83, 89, 97};
```

## Array Declaration

SYNTAX:    *element-type aname* [*size*];                    /* uninitialized */
           *element-type aname* [*size*] = {*initialization list*};/* initialized */

EXAMPLE:   #define A_SIZE 5
           . . .
           double a[A_SIZE];
           char vowels[] = {'A', 'E', 'I', 'O', 'U'};

INTERPRETATION: The general uninitialized array declaration just given allocates storage space for array *aname* consisting of *size* memory cells. Each memory cell can store one data item whose data type is specified by *element-type* (i.e., double, int, or char). The individual array elements are referenced by the subscripted variables *aname* [0], *aname* [1], ..., *aname* [*size*-1]. A constant expression of type int is used to specify an array's *size*.

In the initialized array declaration shown, the *size* shown in brackets is optional since the array's size can also be indicated by the length of the *initialization list*. The *initialization list* consists of constant expressions of the appropriate *element-type* separated by commas. Element 0 of the array being initialized is set to the first entry in the *initialization list*, element 1 to the second, and so forth.

**EXERCISES FOR
SECTION 8.1**

Self-Check

1. What is the difference in meaning between x3 and x[3]?
2. For the declaration

   char grades[5];

   how many memory cells are allocated for data storage? What type of data can be stored there? How does one refer to the initial array element? To the final array element?
3. Declare one array for storing the square roots of the integers from 0 through 10 and a second array for storing the cubes of the same integers.

## 8.2 ARRAY SUBSCRIPTS

We use a subscript to differentiate between the individual array elements and to specify which array element is to be manipulated. We can use any expression of type int as an array subscript. However, to create a valid reference, the value of this subscript must lie between 0 and one less than the declared size of the array.

Understanding the distinction between an array subscript value and an array element value is essential. The original array x from Fig. 8.1 follows. The subscripted variable x[i] references a particular element of this array. If i has the value 0, the subscript value is 0, and x[0] is referenced. The value of x[0] in this case is 16.0. If i has the value 2, the subscript value is 2, and the value of x[i] is 6.0. If i has the value 8, the subscript value is 8, and we cannot predict the value of x[i] because the subscript value is out of the allowable range.

Array x

| x[0] | x[1] | x[2] | x[3] | x[4] | x[5] | x[6] | x[7] |
|------|------|------|------|------|------|------|------|
| 16.0 | 12.0 | 6.0 | 8.0 | 2.5 | 12.0 | 14.0 | -54.5 |

**EXAMPLE 8.6**  Table 8.2 lists some sample statements involving the array x above. The variable i is assumed to be of type int with value 5. Make sure you understand each statement.

**Table 8.2   Code Fragment That Manipulates Array x**

| Statement | Explanation |
|-----------|-------------|
| `i = 5;` | |
| `printf("%d  %.1f", 4, x[4]);` | Displays 4 and 2.5 (value of x[4]) |
| `printf("%d  %.1f", i, x[i]);` | Displays 5 and 12.0 (value of x[5]) |
| `printf("%.1f", x[i] + 1);` | Displays 13.0 (value of x[5] plus 1) |
| `printf("%.1f", x[i] + i);` | Displays 17.0 (value of x[5] plus 5) |
| `printf("%.1f", x[i + 1]);` | Displays 14.0 (value of x[6]) |
| `printf("%.1f", x[i + i]);` | Invalid. Attempt to display x[10] |
| `printf("%.1f", x[2 * i]);` | Invalid. Attempt to display x[10] |
| `printf("%.1f", x[2 * i - 3]);` | Displays -54.5 (value of x[7]) |
| `printf("%.1f", x[(int)x[4]]);` | Displays 6.0 (value of x[2]) |
| `printf("%.1f", x[i++]);` | Displays 12.0 (value of x[5]); then assigns 6 to i |
| `printf("%.1f", x[--i]);` | Assigns 5 (6 - 1) to i and then displays 12.0 (value of x[5]) |
| `x[i - 1] = x[i];` | Assigns 12.0 (value of x[5]) to x[4] |
| `x[i] = x[i + 1];` | Assigns 14.0 (value of x[6]) to x[5] |
| `x[i] - 1 = x[i];` | Illegal assignment statement |

The two attempts to display element x[10], which is not in the array, may result in a run-time error, but they are more likely to print incorrect results. Consider the call to printf that uses (int)x[4] as a subscript expression. Since this expression evaluates to 2, the value of x[2] (*not* x[4]) is printed. If the value of (int)x[4] were outside the range 0 through 7, its use as a subscript expression would not reference a valid array element. ⬅

---

**Array Subscripts**

SYNTAX: *aname* [*subscript*]

EXAMPLE: b[i + 1]

INTERPRETATION: The *subscript* may be any expression of type int. Each time a subscripted variable is encountered in a program the subscript is evaluated and its value determines which element of array *aname* is referenced.

*Note:* It is the programmer's responsibility to verify that the *subscript* is within the declared range. If the subscript is in error, an invalid reference will be made. Although occasionally a run-time error message will be printed, more often an invalid reference will cause a side effect whose origin is difficult for the programmer to pinpoint. The side effect can also lead to incorrect program results.

---

**EXERCISES FOR SECTION 8.2**

Self-Check

1. Show the contents of array x after executing the valid statements in Table 8.2.
2. For the new array derived in Exercise 1, describe what happens when the valid statements in Table 8.2 are executed for i = 3.

## 8.3 USING for LOOPS FOR SEQUENTIAL ACCESS

Very often, we wish to process the elements of an array in sequence, starting with element zero. An example would be scanning data into the array or printing its contents. In C, we can accomplish this processing easily using an *indexed* for loop, a counting loop whose loop control variable runs from zero to one less than the array size. Using the loop counter as an array *index* (subscript) gives access to each array element in turn.

 The following array `square` will be used to store the squares of the integers 0 through 10 (e.g., `square[0]` is 0, `square[10]` is 100). We assume that the name `SIZE` has been defined to be 11.

```
int square[SIZE], i;
```

The `for` loop

```
for  (i = 0;  i < SIZE;  ++i)
    square[i] = i * i;
```

initializes this array, as shown.

Array square

| [0] | [1] | [2] | [3] | [4] | [5] | [6] | [7] | [8] | [9] | [10] |
|-----|-----|-----|-----|-----|-----|-----|-----|-----|-----|------|
| 0 | 1 | 4 | 9 | 16 | 25 | 36 | 49 | 64 | 81 | 100 |

 For array `score` (see Example 8.3), the assignment statements

```
score[monday] = 9;
score[tuesday] = 7;
score[wednesday] = 5;
score[thursday] = 3;
score[friday] = 1;
```

assign the values shown in Fig. 8.2 to `score`. Assuming that `today` is type `class_day_t` and `ascore` is type `int`, the following statements have the same effect.

```
ascore = 9;
for  (today = monday; today <= friday; ++today) {
    score[today] = ascore;
    ascore -= 2;
}
```

## Statistical Computations Using Arrays

One common use of arrays is for storage of a collection of related data values. Once the values are stored, we can perform some simple statistical computations. In Fig. 8.3, we use the array x for this purpose.

The program in Fig. 8.3 uses three for loops to process the array x. The constant macro MAX_ITEM determines the size of the array. The variable i is used as the loop control variable and array subscript in each loop.

The first for loop,

```
for  (i = 0;  i < MAX_ITEM;  ++i)
     scanf("%lf", &x[i]);
```

stores one input value into each element of array x (the first item is placed in x[0], the next in x[1], and so on). The call to scanf is repeated for each

**Figure 8.3  Program to Print a Table of Differences**

```
/*
 * Computes the mean and standard deviation of an array of data and displays
 * the difference between each value and the mean.
 */

#include <stdio.h>
#include <math.h>

#define MAX_ITEM  8  /* maximum number of items in list of data           */

int
main(void)
{
     double x[MAX_ITEM], /* data list                                     */
            mean,        /* mean (average) of the data                    */
            st_dev,      /* standard deviation of the data                */
            sum,         /* sum of the data                               */
            sum_sqr;     /* sum of the squares of the data                */
     int    i;

     /* Gets the data                                                     */
     printf("Enter %d numbers separated by blanks or <return>s\n> ",
            MAX_ITEM);
     for  (i = 0;  i < MAX_ITEM;  ++i)
         scanf("%lf", &x[i]);
```

*(continued)*

**Figure 8.3** *(continued)*

```
        /* Computes the sum and the sum of the squares of all data      */
        sum = 0;
        sum_sqr = 0;
        for   (i = 0;  i < MAX_ITEM;  ++i) {
            sum += x[i];
            sum_sqr += x[i] * x[i];
        }


        /* Computes and prints the mean and standard deviation          */
        mean = sum / MAX_ITEM;
        st_dev = sqrt(sum_sqr / MAX_ITEM - mean * mean);
        printf("The mean is %.2f.\n", mean);
        printf("The standard deviation is %.2f.\n", st_dev);


        /* Displays the difference between each item and the mean        */
        printf("\nTable of differences between data values and mean\n");
        printf("Index       Item       Difference\n");
        for   (i = 0;  i < MAX_ITEM;  ++i)
            printf("%3d%4c%9.2f%5c%9.2f\n", i, ' ', x[i], ' ', x[i] - mean);

        return (0);
}


Enter 8 numbers separated by blanks or <return>s
> 16   12   6   8   2.5   12   14   -54.5
The mean is 2.00.
The standard deviation is 21.75.


Table of differences between data values and mean
Index        Item        Difference
  0          16.00          14.00
  1          12.00          10.00
  2           6.00           4.00
  3           8.00           6.00
  4           2.50           0.50
  5          12.00          10.00
  6          14.00          12.00
  7         -54.50         -56.50
```

value of i from 0 to 7; each repetition gets a new data value and stores it in x[i]. The subscript i determines which array element receives the next data value.

The second for loop accumulates (in sum) the sum of all values stored in the array. The loop also accumulates (in sum_sqr) the sum of the squares of all element values. This loop implements the formulas

$$sum = x[0] + x[1] + \cdots + x[6] + x[7] = \sum_{i=0}^{MAX\_ITEM\,-1} x[i]$$

$$sum\_sqr = x[0]^2 + x[1]^2 + \cdots + x[6]^2 + x[7]^2 = \sum_{i=0}^{MAX\_ITEM\,-1} x[i]^2$$

This loop will be discussed in detail later.

The last for loop,

```
for  (i = 0;  i < MAX_ITEM;  ++i)
    printf("%3d%4c%9.2f%5c%9.2f\n", i, ' ', x[i], ' ',
           x[i] - mean);
```

displays a table. Each line of the table displays an array subscript, an array element, and the difference between that element and the mean, x[i] − mean. Notice that the placeholders in the format string of the call to printf cause each column of values in the output table to be lined up under its respective column heading.

Now that we have seen the entire program, we will take a closer look at the computation for loop:

```
/* Computes the sum and the sum of the squares of all data */
sum = 0;
sum_sqr = 0;
for  (i = 0;  i < MAX_ITEM;  ++i) {
    sum += x[i];
    sum_sqr += x[i] * x[i];
}
```

This loop accumulates the sum of all eight elements of array x in the variable sum. Each time the loop body executes, the next element of array x is added to sum. Then this array element value is squared, and its square is added to the sum being accumulated in sum_sqr. We trace the execution of this program fragment in Table 8.3 for the first three repetitions of the loop.

The *standard deviation* of a set of data is a measure of the spread of the data values around the mean. A small standard deviation indicates that the data

**Table 8.3   Partial Trace of Computing for Loop**

| Statement | i | x[i] | sum | sum_sqr | Effect |
|---|---|---|---|---|---|
| `sum = 0;` | | | 0.0 | | Initializes `sum` |
| `sum_sqr = 0;` | | | | 0.0 | Initializes `sum_sqr` |
| | | | | | |
| `for (i = 0;` | 0 | 16.0 | | | Initializes `i` to 0 |
| `    i < MAX_ITEM;` | | | | | which is less than 8 |
| `      ...` | | | | | |
| `  sum += x[i];` | | | 16.0 | | Adds `x[0]` to `sum` |
| `  sum_sqr +=` | | | | | |
| `    x[i] * x[i];` | | | | 256.0 | Adds `256.0` to `sum_sqr` |
| | | | | | |
| increment and test `i` | 1 | 12.0 | | | `1 < 8` is true |
| `  sum += x[i];` | | | 28.0 | | Adds `x[1]` to `sum` |
| `  sum_sqr +=` | | | | | |
| `    x[i] * x[i];` | | | | 400.0 | Adds `144.0` to `sum_sqr` |
| | | | | | |
| increment and test `i` | 2 | 6.0 | | | `2 < 8` is true |
| `  sum += x[i];` | | | 34.0 | | Adds `x[2]` to `sum` |
| `  sum_sqr +=` | | | | | |
| `    x[i] * x[i];` | | | | 436.0 | Adds `36.0` to `sum_sqr` |

values are all relatively close to the average value. For MAX_ITEM data items, if we assume that x is an array whose lowest subscript is 0, the standard deviation is given by the formula

$$standard\ deviation = \sqrt{\frac{\sum_{i=0}^{MAX\_ITEM-1} x[i]^2}{MAX\_ITEM} - mean^2}$$

In Fig. 8.3, this formula is implemented by the statement

`st dev = sqrt (sum_sqr / MAX_ITEM - mean * mean);`     ←

## Program Style   *Using Loop Control Variables as Array Subscripts*

In Fig. 8.3, the variable i, which is the counter of each indexed for loop, determines which array element is manipulated during each loop repetition. The use of the loop control variable as an array subscript is common, because it allows the programmer to specify easily the sequence in which the elements of an array are to be manipulated. Each time the value of the loop control variable is increased, the next array element is automatically selected. Note that the same loop control variable is used in all three loops. This reuse is not necessary but is permitted since the loop control variable is always initialized at loop entry. Thus, i is reset to 0 when each loop is entered.

**EXERCISES FOR SECTION 8.3**

Self-Check

1. Write an indexed for loop to fill the arrays described in Exercise 3 at the end of Section 8.1. Each array element should be assigned the value specified for it.

## 8.4 USING ARRAY ELEMENTS AS FUNCTION ARGUMENTS

Figure 8.3 uses x[i] as an argument for functions scanf and printf. The actual array element referenced depends on the value of i. The call

```
printf("%3d%4c%9.2f%5c%9.2f\n", i, ' ', x[i], ' ',
       x[i] - mean);
```

uses array element x[i] as an input argument to function printf. When i is 3, the value of x[3] or 8.0 is passed to printf and displayed.

The call

```
scanf("%lf", &x[i]);
```

uses array element x[i] as an output argument of scanf. When i is 4, the address of array element x[4] is passed to scanf, and scanf stores the next value scanned (2.5) in element x[4].

You can also pass array elements as arguments to functions that you write. Each array element must correspond to a formal parameter that is the same simple type as the array element.

 **EXAMPLE 8.9**

The function prototype below shows one type double input parameter (arg_1) and two type double output parameters (*arg2_p and *arg3_p).

```
void do_it (double arg_1, double *arg2_p, double *arg3_p);
```

If p, q, and r are declared as type `double` variables in the calling module, the statement

```
do_it (p, &q, &r);
```

passes the value of p to function `do_it` and returns the function results to variables q and r. If x is declared as an array of type `double` elements in the calling module, the statement

```
do_it(x[0], &x[1], &x[2]);
```

uses the first three elements of array x as actual arguments. Array element x[0] is an input argument and x[1] and x[2] are output arguments (see Fig. 8.4). In function `do_it`, you can use statements like

```
*arg2_p = ...
*arg3_p = ...
```

to return values to the calling module. These statements use indirection to follow the pointers arg2_p and arg3_p to send the function results back to the calling module. Because the function parameters arg2_p and arg3_p contain addresses of array elements x[1] and x[2], the function execution changes the values of those elements.

**Figure 8.4
Data Area for
Calling Module
and Function
do_it**

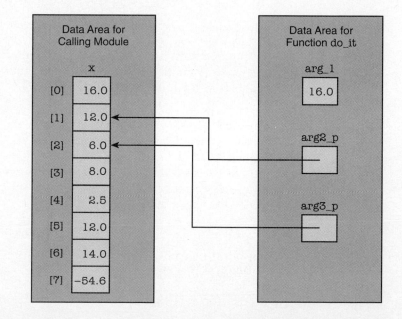

Self-Check

1. Write a statement that assigns to `seg_len` the length of a line segment from $x_i y_i$ to $x_{i+1} y_{i+1}$ using the formula

$$\sqrt{(x_{i+1} - x_i)^2 + (y_{i+1} - y_i)^2}$$

Assume that $x_i$ represents the $i$th element of array x, that $y_i$ represents the $i$th element of array y, and that the minimum i is 0.

2. Write a `for` loop that sums the even values from the `LIST_SIZE`-element array `list`. For example, the sum for this list would be 104 (30 + 12 + 62).

Array list

| list[0] | list[1] | list[2] | list[3] | list[4] | list[5] |
|---------|---------|---------|---------|---------|---------|
| 30 | 12 | 51 | 17 | 45 | 62 |

3. Write a `for` loop that sums the even-numbered elements (elements 0, 2, and 4) from array `list`. For the list shown in Exercise 2, the sum would be 126 (30 + 51 + 45).

Programming

1. Write a program to store an input list of 10 integers in an array; then display a table similar to the following showing each data value and what percentage each value is of the total of all 10 values.

| n | % of total |
|-----|-----------|
| 8 | 4.00 |
| 12 | 6.00 |
| 18 | 9.00 |
| 25 | 12.50 |
| 24 | 12.00 |
| 30 | 15.00 |
| 28 | 14.00 |
| 22 | 11.00 |
| 23 | 11.50 |
| 10 | 5.00 |

# 8.5 ARRAY ARGUMENTS

Besides passing individual array elements to functions, we can write functions that have arrays as arguments. Such functions can manipulate some, or all, of the elements corresponding to an actual array argument.

## Formal Array Parameters

When an array name with no subscript appears in the argument list of a function call, what is actually stored in the function's corresponding formal parameter is the address of the initial array element. In the function body, we can use subscripts with the formal parameter to access the array's elements. However, the function manipulates the original array, not its own personal copy, so an assignment to one of the array elements by a statement in the function changes the contents of the original array.

**EXAMPLE 8.10**  Figure 8.5 shows a function that stores the same value (in_value) in all elements of the array corresponding to its formal array parameter list. The statement

```
list[i] = in_value;
```

stores in_value in element i of its actual array argument. ◀

In function fill_array, the array parameter is declared as

```
int list[]
```

Notice that the argument declaration does not indicate how many elements are in list. Because C does not allocate space in memory for a copy of the actual array, the compiler does not need to know the size of the array parameter. In fact, since we do not provide the size, we have the flexibility to pass to the function an array of any number of integers.

**Figure 8.5    Function fill_array**

```
/*
 * Sets all elements of its array parameter to in_value.
 * Pre:  n and in_value are defined.
 * Post: list[i] = in_value, for 0 <= i < n.
 */
void
fill_array (int list[],     /* output - list of n integers            */
            int n,          /* input - number of list elements        */
            int in_value)   /* input - initial value                  */
{

     int i;                 /* array subscript and loop control        */

     for  (i = 0;  i < n;  ++i)
         list[i] = in_value;
}
```

## Argument Correspondence for Array Parameters

To call function `fill_array`, you must specify the actual array argument, the number of array elements, and the value to be stored in the array. If `y` is an array with 10 type `int` elements, the function call

```
fill_array(y, 10, num);
```

stores the value of `num` in the 10 elements of array `y`. If `x` is a five-element array of type `int` values, the statement

```
fill_array(x, 5, 1);
```

causes function `fill_array` to store 1 in all elements of array `x`.
    Figure 8.6 shows the data areas just before the return from the function call

```
fill_array(x, 5, 1);
```

Notice that C stores the address of the type `int` variable `x[0]` in `list`. In fact, the call

```
fill_array(&x[0], 5, 1);
```

**Figure 8.6
Data Areas
Before Return
from** fill_array
(x, 5, 1);

would execute exactly like the call above. However, this call may lead the reader of the code to expect that fill_array may be using only the array element x[0] as an output argument. For readability, you should use the name of an array (with no subscript) when you call a function that processes the list the array represents.

**Use of *list Instead of list[] in a Formal Parameter List**
In the declaration for function fill_array, we can use either parameter declaration:

```
int  list[]
int *list
```

The first tells us that the actual argument is an array. However, because C passes an array argument by passing the address of its initial element, the second declaration would be equally valid for an integer array parameter. In this text, we will usually use the first form to declare a parameter representing an array, saving the second form to represent simple output parameters. You should take care, however, to remember that a formal parameter of the form

$type_1$ *param

is compatible with an actual argument that is an array of $type_1$ values.

## Arrays as Input Arguments

ANSI C provides a qualifier that we can include in the declaration of the array formal parameter in order to notify the C compiler that the array is only an input to the function and that the function does not intend to modify the array. This qualifier allows the compiler to mark as an error any attempt to change an array element within the function.

**EXAMPLE 8.11**

Function get_max in Fig. 8.7 can be called to find the largest value in an array. It uses the variable list as an array input parameter. If x is a five-element array of type int values, the statement

```
x_large = get_max(x, 5);
```

## Figure 8.7    Function to Find the Largest Element in an Array

```
/*
 *  Returns the largest of the first n values in array list
 *  Pre:  First n elements of array list are defined and n > 0
 */
int
get_max(const int list[], /* input - list of n integers            */
        int         n)     /* input - number of list elements to examine   */
{
      int i,
          cur_large;        /* largest value so far                */

      /*  Initial array element is largest so far.                 */
      cur_large = list[0];

      /*  Compare each remaining list element to the largest so far;
          save the larger                                          */
      for  (i = 1;  i < n;  ++i)
          if (list[i] > cur_large)
                cur_large = list[i];

      return (cur_large);
}
```

 — limits ability of program to change of the area area of the array causes function `get_max` to search array x for its largest element; this value is returned and stored in `x_large`. As in the call to function `fill_array` shown in Fig. 8.6, formal argument `list` actually contains the address of the type int variable `x[0]`.  ←

---

### Array Input Parameter

SYNTAX: const *element-type array-name* [ ]
    or
    const *element-type *array-name*

EXAMPLE: int
    get_min_sub(const double data[], /* input - array

```
                                     of numbers */
        int          data_size)  /* input -
                                 number of elements */
{
    int    i,
           small_sub;  /* subscript of smallest
                          value so far            */
    small_sub = 0;     /* Assume first element is
                          smallest.                */
    for (i = 1; i < data_size; ++i)
        if (data[i] < data[small_sub])
            small_sub = i;

    return (small_sub);
}
```

INTERPRETATION: In a formal parameter list, the reserved word const indicates that the array variable declared is strictly an input parameter and will not be modified by the function. This fact is important because the value of the declared formal parameter will be the address of the actual argument array; if const were omitted, modification of the argument would be possible. The data type of an array element is indicated by *element-type*. The [ ] after *array_name* means that the corresponding actual argument will be an array. What is actually stored in the formal parameter when the function is called is the address of the initial element of the actual argument array. Since this value is a pointer to a location used to store a value of type *element-type*, the second syntax option is equivalent to the first.

## Returning an Array Result

In C, it is not legal for a function's return type to be an array; therefore, defining a function of the variety modeled in Fig. 8.8 requires use of an output argument to send the result array back to the calling module.

In Section 6.1, we saw that when we use simple output parameters, the calling function must declare variables into which the function subprogram will store its results. Similarly, a function returning an array result depends on its caller to provide an array variable into which the result can be stored. We have already seen an example of a function with an array output parameter (function `fill_array` in Fig. 8.5). The next example shows a function with two input array parameters and an output array parameter that returns an array result.

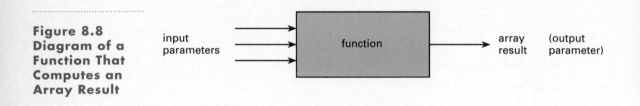

**Figure 8.8
Diagram of a
Function That
Computes an
Array Result**

**EXAMPLE 8.12**

Function `add_arrays` in Fig. 8.9 adds two arrays. The sum of arrays `ar1` and `ar2` is defined as `arsum` such that `arsum[i]` is equal to `ar1[i]` + `ar2[i]` for each subscript `i`. The last parameter, `n`, specifies how many corresponding elements are summed.

The formal parameter list declaration

```
const double ar1[],
const double ar2[],
double      arsum[],
int         n
```

indicates that formal parameters `ar1`, `ar2`, and `arsum` stand for actual argument arrays whose elements are of type `double` and that `ar1` and `ar2` are strictly input parameters, as is `n`. The function can process type `double` arrays of any size as long as the preconditions stated in the initial block comment are met.

**Figure 8.9   Function to Add Two Arrays**

```
/*
 *  Adds corresponding elements of arrays ar1 and ar2, storing  the result in
 *  arsum. Processes first n elements only.
 *  Pre:  First n elements of ar1 and ar2 are defined. arsum's corresponding
 *        actual argument has a declared size >= n (n >= 0)
 */
void
add_arrays(const double ar1[],    /* input -                                */
           const double ar2[],    /*     arrays being added                 */
           double       arsum[], /* output - sum of corresponding           */
                                  /*          elements of ar1 and ar2        */
           int          n)        /* input -  number of element             */
                                  /*          pairs summed                   */
{
     int i;

     /* Adds corresponding elements of ar1 and ar2                          */
     for  (i = 0;  i < n;  ++i)
          arsum[i] = ar1[i] + ar2[i];
}
```

If we assume that a calling function has declared three five-element arrays x, y, and x_plus_y and has filled x and y with data, the call

```
add_arrays(x, y, x_plus_y, 5);
```

would lead to the memory setup pictured in Fig. 8.10.

After execution of the function, x_plus_y[0] will contain the sum of x[0] and y[0], or 3.5; x_plus_y[1] will contain the sum of x[1] and y[1], or 6.7; and so on. Input argument arrays x and y will be unchanged; output argument array x_plus_y will have these new contents:

x_plus_y after call to add_arrays

| 3.5 | 6.7 | 4.7 | 9.1 | 12.2 |
|-----|-----|-----|-----|------|

**Figure 8.10
Function Data
Areas for**
`add_arrays(x,
y, x_plus_y,
5);`

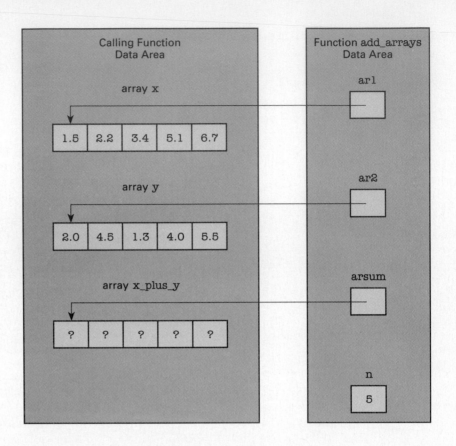

### Address-of Operator Not Used

Note carefully that in the *call* to `add_arrays` there is no notational difference between the references to input argument arrays `x` and `y` and the reference to output argument array `x_plus_y`. Specifically, the & (address-of) operator is *not* applied to the name of the output array argument. We discussed earlier the fact that C always passes whole arrays used as arguments by storing the *address* of the initial array element in the corresponding formal parameter. Since the output parameter `arsum` is declared with no `const` qualifier, function `add_arrays` automatically has access and authority to change the corresponding actual array argument.

## Partially Filled Arrays

Frequently, a program will need to process many lists of similar data; these lists may not all be the same length. In order to reuse an array for processing more than one data set, the programmer often declares an array large enough to hold the largest data set anticipated. This array can be used for processing shorter lists as well, provided that the program keeps track of how many array elements are actually in use.

**EXAMPLE 8.13**

The purpose of function `fill_to_sentinel` is to fill a type `double` array with data until the designated sentinel value is encountered in the input data. Figure 8.11 shows both the input parameters that `fill_to_sentinel` requires and the results that are communicated through its output parameters.

**Figure 8.11 Diagram of Function fill_to_sentinel**

When we use an array that may be only partially filled (such as `dbl_arr` in Fig. 8.11), we must deal with *two* array sizes. One size is the array's declared size, represented by the input parameter `dbl_max`, shown in Fig. 8.11. The other is the size counting only the elements in use, represented by the output parameter `dbl_sizep`. The declared size is only of interest at the point in a program where the array is being filled, for it is important not to try to store values beyond the array's bounds. However, once this input step is complete, the array size relevant in the rest of the processing is the number of elements actually filled. Figure 8.12 shows an implementation of function `fill_to_sentinel`.

Figure 8.13 shows a main function that calls `fill_to_sentinel`. The main function is using batch mode; it issues no prompting message, but it does echo print its input data. Notice that after the call to `fill_to_sentinel`, the expression used as the upper bound on the subscripting variable in the loop that echo prints the data is not the array's declared size, `A_SIZE`. Rather, it is the variable `in_use` that designates how many elements of `arr` are currently filled.

In the call to `fill_to_sentinel` in Fig. 8.13, we see another example of the difference between the way an array output argument is passed to a function and the way a simple output argument is passed. Both `arr` and `in_use` are output arguments, but the address-of operator & is applied only to the simple variable `in_use`. Since `arr` is an array name with no subscript, it already represents an address, the address of the initial array element.

```
/*
 *  Gets data to place in dbl_arr until value of sentinel is encountered in
 *  the input.
 *  Returns number of values stored through dbl_sizep.
 *  Stops input prematurely if there are more than dbl_max data values before
 *  the sentinel or if invalid data is encountered.
 *  Pre:  sentinel and dbl_max are defined and dbl_max is the declared size of
 *        dbl_arr
 */
void
fill_to_sentinel(int     dbl_max,     /* input - declared size of dbl_arr    */
                 double  sentinel,    /* input - end of data value in
                                                 input list                  */
                 double  dbl_arr[],   /* output - array of data              */
                 int     *dbl_sizep)  /* output - number of data values
                                                 stored in dbl_arr           */
{
    double data;
    int    i, status;

    /* Sentinel input loop                                                   */
    i = 0;
    status = scanf("%lf", &data);
    while (status == 1  &&  data != sentinel  &&  i < dbl_max) {
        dbl_arr[i] = data;
        ++i;
        status = scanf("%lf", &data);
    }

    /* Issues error message on premature exit                                */
    if (status != 1) {
        printf("\n*** Error in data format ***\n");
        printf("*** Using first %d data values ***\n", i);
    } else if (data != sentinel) {
        printf("\n*** Error: too much data before sentinel ***\n");
        printf("*** Using first %d data values ***\n", i);
    }

    /* Sends back size of used portion of array                              */
    *dbl_sizep = i;
}
```

**Figure 8.13   Driver for Testing fill_to_sentinel**

```
/* Driver to test fill_to_sentinel function */

#define A_SIZE  20
#define SENT    -1.0

int
main(void)
{
      double arr[A_SIZE];
      int    in_use,      /* number of elements of arr in use */
             i;

      fill_to_sentinel(A_SIZE, SENT, arr, &in_use);

      printf("List of data values\n");
      for  (i = 0;  i < in_use;  ++i)
          printf("%13.3f\n", arr[i]);

      return (0);
}
```

## Stacks

A stack is a data structure in which only the top element can be accessed. To illustrate, the plates stored in the spring-loaded device in a buffet line perform like a stack. A customer always takes the top plate; when a plate is removed, the plate beneath it moves to the top.

**pop**
remove the top element of a stack

**push**
insert a new element at the top of the stack

The following diagram shows a stack of three characters. The letter C, the character at the top of the stack, is the only one we can access. We must remove C from the stack in order to access the symbol +. Removing a value from a stack is called **popping the stack**, and storing an item in a stack is called **pushing it onto the stack.**

```
┌─┐
│C│
│+│
│2│
└─┘
```

Figure 8.14 shows functions pop and push. The formal parameter *top points to the variable that stores the subscript of the element at the top of the stack. Each push operation increments the value pointed to by top before storing the new item at the top of the stack (i.e., in element stack[*top]). Each pop operation returns the item currently at the top of the stack and then decrements the value pointed to by top. The if condition in push checks that there is room on the stack before storing a new item. The if condition in pop checks that the stack is not empty before popping it. If the stack is empty, STACK_EMPTY (a previously defined constant macro) is returned instead.

We can use the array s declared next to store a stack of up to STACK_SIZE characters where s_top stores the subscript of the element at the top of the stack. Giving s_top an initial value of -1 ensures that the first item pushed onto the stack will be stored in the stack element s[0].

```
char s[STACK_SIZE];   /* a stack of characters */
int  s_top = -1;      /* stack s is empty       */
```

The statements

```
push(s, '2', &s_top, STACK_SIZE);
push(s, '+', &s_top, STACK_SIZE);
push(s, 'C', &s_top, STACK_SIZE);
```

create the stack shown earlier where the last character pushed (C) is at the top of the stack (array element s[2]).

**Figure 8.14    Functions push and pop**

```
void
push(char stack[],    /* input/output - the stack */
     char item,       /* input - data being pushed onto the stack */
     int  *top,       /* input/output - pointer to top of stack */
     int  max_size)   /* input - maximum size of stack */
{
     if (*top < max_size-1) {
         ++(*top);
         stack[*top] = item;
     }
}
```

*(continued)*

**Figure 8.14**   *(continued)*

```
char
pop(char stack[],    /* input/output - the stack */
    int  *top)       /* input/output - pointer to top of stack */
{
    char item;       /* value popped off the stack */

    if (*top >= 0) {
        item = stack[*top];
        --(*top);
    } else {
        item = STACK_EMPTY;
    }

    return (item);
}
```

**EXERCISES FOR SECTION 8.5**

Self-Check

1. When is it better to pass an entire array of data to a function rather than individual elements?

2. Assume a main function contains declarations for three type double arrays—c, d, and e, each with six elements. Also assume that values have been stored in all array elements. Explain the effect of each valid call to add_arrays (see Fig. 8.9). Explain why each invalid call is invalid.

   a. add_arrays(ar1, ar2, c, 6);
   b. add_arrays(c[6], d[6], e[6], 6);
   c. add_arrays(c, d, e, 6);
   d. add_arrays(c, d, e, 7);
   e. add_arrays(c, d, e, 5);
   f. add_arrays(c, d, 6, 3);
   g. add_arrays(e, d, c, 6);
   h. add_arrays(c, c, c, 6);
   i. add_arrays(c, d, e, c[1]); (if c[1] is 4.3?
       if c[1] is 91.7?)
   j. add_arrays(&c[2], &d[2], &e[2], 4);

3. Modify function fill_to_sentinel from Fig. 8.12 so its return type is int rather than void. Have the function return the value 1 if no error

conditions occur and 0 if there is an error. In all other respects, leave the function's purpose unchanged.

4. Can you think of a way to combine the following two statements from the body of the `while` loop of function `fill_to_sentinel` into just one statement?

```
dbl_arr[i] = data;
++i;
```

5. Assume stack `s` is a stack of `MAX_SIZE` characters and `s_top` is the subscript of the element at the top of stack `s`. Perform the following sequence of operations. Indicate the result of each operation and the new stack if it is changed. Rather than draw the stack each time, use the notation $|2+C/$ to represent a stack of four characters, where the last symbol on the right ($/$) is at the top of the stack.

```
/* Start with an empty stack. */
s_top = -1;
push(s, '$', &s_top, MAXSIZE);
push(s, '-', &s_top, MAXSIZE);
ch = pop(s, &s_top);
```

### Programming

1. Define a function `multiply` that computes and returns the product of the type `int` elements of its array input argument. The function should have a second input argument telling the number of array elements to use.

2. Define a function `abs_table` that takes an input array argument with type `double` values and displays a table of the data and their absolute values like the table shown.

| x | \|x\| |
|------:|------:|
| 38.4 | 38.4 |
| -101.7 | 101.7 |
| -2.1 | 2.1 |
| . . . | |

3. Write a function that negates the type `double` values stored in an array. The first argument should be the array (an input/output parameter) and the second should be the number of elements to negate.

4. Write a function that takes two type `int` array input arguments and their effective size and produces a result array containing the absolute differences between corresponding elements. For example, for the three-element input arrays 5 -1  7 and 2  4 -2, the result would be an array containing 3 5 9.

5. Rewrite operators `push` and `pop` for a stack of integers. Also, write a new function `retrieve` that accesses the element at the top of the stack without removing it.

# 8.6 SEARCHING AND SORTING AN ARRAY

This section discusses two common problems in processing arrays: *searching* an array to determine the location of a particular value and *sorting* an array to rearrange the array elements in numerical order. As an example of an array search, we might want to search an array of student exam scores to determine which student, if any, got a particular score. An example of an array sort would be rearranging the array elements so that they are in increasing order by score. Sorting an array would be helpful if we wanted to display the list in order by score or if we needed to locate several different scores in the array.

## Array Search

In order to search an array, we need we know the array element value we are seeking, or the search *target*. Then, we can perform the search by examining in turn each array element using a loop and by testing whether the element matches the target. The search loop should be exited when the target value is found; this process is called a *linear search*. The following algorithm for linear search sets a flag (for loop control) when the element being tested matches the target.

### Algorithm

1. Assume the target has not been found.
2. Start with the initial array element.
3. Repeat while the target is not found and there are more array elements
    4. if the current element matches the target
        5. Set a flag to indicate that the target has been found.
    else
        6. Advance to the next array element.
7. if the target was found
    8. Return the target index as the search result.
else
    9. Return $-1$ as the search result.

Figure 8.15 shows a function that implements this algorithm. This function returns the index of the target if it is present in the array; otherwise, it returns $-1$. The local variable `i` (initial value 0) selects the array element that is compared to the target value.

### Figure 8.15    Function That Searches for a Target Value in an Array

```c
#define NOT_FOUND -1   /* Value returned by search function if target not
                          found                                          */

/*
 *  Searches for target item in first n elements of array arr
 *  Returns index of target or NOT_FOUND
 *  Pre:  target and first n elements of array arr are defined and n>=0
 */
int
search(const int arr[],  /* input - array to search                     */
       int         target, /* input - value searched for                */
       int         n)      /* input - number of elements to search      */
{
      int i,
          found = 0,     /*  whether or not target has been found        */
          where;         /*  index where target found or NOT_FOUND       */

      /*  Compares each element to target                                */
      i = 0;
      while (!found && i < n) {
          if (arr[i] == target)
                found = 1;
          else
                ++i;
      }

      /* Returns index of element matching target or NOT_FOUND           */
      if (found)
            where = i;
      else
            where = NOT_FOUND;

      return (where);
}
```

The type int variable found is used to represent the logical concept of
whether the target has been found yet and is tested in the loop repetition condition. The variable is initially set to 0 for false (the target is certainly not found

before we begin searching for it) and is reset to 1 for true only if the target is found. After found becomes true or the entire array has been searched, the loop is exited, and the decision statement following the loop defines the value returned.

If array ids is declared in the calling function, the assignment statement

```
index = search(ids, 4902, ID_SIZE);
```

calls function search to search the first ID_SIZE elements of array ids for the target ID 4902. The subscript of the first occurrence of 4902 is saved in index. If 4902 is not found, then index is set to -1.

## Sorting an Array

Many programs execute more efficiently if the data they process are sorted before processing begins. For example, a check-processing program executes more quickly if all checks are in order by checking-account number. Other programs produce more understandable output if the information is sorted before it is displayed. For example, your university might want your instructor's grade report sorted by student ID number. In this section, we describe one simple sorting algorithm from among the many that have been studied by computer scientists.

The *selection sort* is a fairly intuitive (but not very efficient) sorting algorithm. To perform a selection sort of an array with n elements (subscripts 0 through n-1), we locate the smallest element in the array and then switch the smallest element with the element at subscript 0, thereby placing the smallest element in the first position. Then we locate the smallest element remaining in the subarray with subscripts 1 through n-1 and switch it with the element at subscript 1, thereby placing the second smallest element in the second position. Then we locate the smallest element remaining in the subarray with subscripts 3 through n-1 and switch it with the element at subscript 3, and so on.

### Algorithm for Selection Sort

1. for each value of fill from 0 to n-2
    2. Find index_of_min, the index of the smallest element in the unsorted subarray list[fill] through list[n-1].
    3. if fill is not the position of the smallest element (index_of_min)
        4. Exchange the smallest element with the one at position fill

Figure 8.16 traces the operation of the selection sort algorithm on an array of length 4. The first array shown is the original array. Then we show each step as the next smallest element is moved to its correct position. Each array diagram

**Figure 8.16
Trace of
Selection Sort**

|  | [0] | [1] | [2] | [3] |
|---|---|---|---|---|
|  | 74 | 45 | 83 | 16 |

fill is 0. Find the smallest element in subarray
list[0] through list[3] and swap it with list[0].

|  | [0] | [1] | [2] | [3] |
|---|---|---|---|---|
|  | 16 | 45 | 83 | 74 |

fill is 1. Find the smallest element in subarray
list[1] through list[3] — no exchange needed.

|  | [0] | [1] | [2] | [3] |
|---|---|---|---|---|
|  | 16 | 45 | 83 | 74 |

fill is 2. Find the smallest element in subarray
list[2] through list[3] and swap it with list[2].

|  | [0] | [1] | [2] | [3] |
|---|---|---|---|---|
|  | 16 | 45 | 74 | 83 |

has two parts: a subarray that is sorted (in color) and a subarray that has not yet
been sorted. After each pass through the array, the sorted subarray contains an
additional element. Notice that, at most, n-1 exchanges will be required to
sort an array with n elements.

We will use function get_min_range to perform step 2. Function
select_sort in Fig. 8.17 performs a selection sort on the array represented
by parameter list, which is an input/output parameter. Notice that its declaration is of the same form as the output parameter arrays discussed in the
previous section. Local variable index_of_min holds the index of the smallest value found so far in the current subarray. At the end of each pass, if
index_of_min and fill are not equal, the statements

```
temp = list[index_of_min];
list[index_of_min] = list[fill];
list[fill] = temp;
```

exchange the array elements with subscripts fill and index_of_min. After
function select_sort executes, the values in its corresponding array argument will form an increasing sequence. See Programming Exercise 1 for a
description of function get_min_range.

**Figure 8.17 Function select_sort**

```
/*
 *  Finds the position of the smallest element in the subarray
 *  list[first] through list[last].
 *  Pre:  first < last and elements 0 through last of array list are defined.
 *  Post: Returns the subscript k of the smallest element in the subarray;
 *        i.e., list[k] <= list[i] for all i in the subarray
 */
int get_min_range(int list[], int first, int last);

/*
 *  Sorts the data in array list
 *  Pre:  first n elements of list are defined and n >= 0
 */
void
select_sort(int list[],     /* input/output - array being sorted          */
            int n)          /* input - number of elements to sort         */
{
      int fill,             /* first element in unsorted subarray          */
          temp,             /* temporary storage                           */
          index_of_min;     /* subscript of next smallest element          */

      for (fill = 0; fill < n-1; ++fill) {
          /* Find position of smallest element in unsorted subarray */
          index_of_min = get_min_range(list, fill, n-1);

          /* Exchange elements at fill and index_of_min */
          if (fill != index_of_min) {
              temp = list[index_of_min];
              list[index_of_min] = list[fill];
              list[fill] = temp;
          }
      }
}
```

**EXERCISES FOR SECTION 8.6**

Self-Check

1. For the search function in Fig. 8.15, what happens if:
    a. the last id stored matches the target?
    b. several id's match the target?

2. Trace the execution of the selection sort on the following two lists:

```
10  55  34  56  76  5          5  15  25  35  45  45
```

Show the arrays after each exchange occurs. How many exchanges are required to sort each list? How many comparisons?

3. How could you modify the selection-sort algorithm to get the scores in descending order (largest score first)?

Programming

1. Write function `get_min_range` based on function `get_min_sub` in the syntax display for array input parameter. Function `get_min_range` returns the subscript of the smallest value in a portion of an array containing type `int` values. It has three arguments: an array, the first subscript in the subarray, and the last subscript in the subarray.

2. Another method of performing the selection sort is to place the largest value in position $n-1$, the next largest in position $n-2$, and so on. Write this version.

3. Modify the heading and declarations of function `select_sort` so it would sort an array of type `double` values. Be careful—some variables should still be of type `int`!

## 8.7 MULTIDIMENSIONAL ARRAYS

**multidimensional array**
an array with two or more dimensions

In this section, we introduce **multidimensional arrays**, that is, arrays with two or more dimensions. We will use two-dimensional arrays to represent tables of data, matrices, and other two-dimensional objects. A two-dimensional object that many are familiar with is a tic-tac-toe board. The array declaration

```
char tictac[3][3];
```

allocates storage for a two-dimensional array (`tictac`) with three rows and three columns. This array has nine elements, each of which must be referenced by specifying a row subscript (0, 1, or 2) and a column subscript (0, 1, or 2). Each array element contains a character value. The array element `tictac[1][2]` marked in Fig. 8.18 is in row 1, column 2 of the array; the element contains the character O. The diagonal line consisting of array elements `tictac[0][0]`, `tictac[1][1]`, and `tictac[2][2]` represents a win for player X because each cell contains the character X.

A function that takes a tic-tac-toe board as a parameter will have a declaration similar to this in its prototype:

```
char tictac[][3]
```

**Figure 8.18
A Tic-tac-toe
Board Stored as
Array tictac**

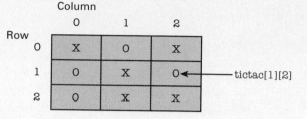

In the declaration of a multidimensional array parameter, only the first dimension, the number of rows, can be omitted. Including both dimensions is also permissible. Because tic-tac-toe boards do not vary in size, using the declaration that follows would probably make more sense.

```
char tictac[3][3]
```

**Multidimensional Array Declaration**

SYNTAX:  *element-type aname* [*size₁*] [*size₂*] ... [*sizeₙ*] ;   /* storage
                                                                      allocation    */
         *element-type aname* [ ] [*size₂*] ... [*sizeₙ*]      /* parameter in
                                                                  prototype     */

EXAMPLES: `double table[NROWS][NCOLS];`  /* storage allocation   */

```
          void
          process_matrix(int in[][4],   /* input parameter      */
                         int out[][4],  /* output parameter     */
                         int nrows)     /* input - number of
                                           rows                 */
```

INTERPRETATION:  The first form shown allocates storage space for an array *aname* consisting of $size_1 \times size_2 \times \ldots \times size_n$ memory cells. Each memory cell can store one data item whose data type is specified by *element-type*. The individual array elements are referenced by the subscripted variables *aname*[0][0]...[0] through *aname*[$size_1-1$][$size_2-1$]... [$size_n-1$]. An integer constant expression is used to specify each $size_i$.

The second declaration form shown is valid when declaring a multidimensional array parameter in a function prototype. The size of the first dimension (the number of rows) is the only size that can be omitted. As for one-dimensional arrays, the value actually stored in an array formal parameter is the address of the initial element of the actual argument.

*Note:* ANSI C requires that an implementation allow multidimensional arrays of at least six dimensions.

**EXAMPLE 8.14**     The array `table`

```
double table[7][5][6];
```

consists of three dimensions: The first subscript may take on values from 0 to 6; the second, from 0 to 4; and the third, from 0 to 5. A total of 7 × 5 × 6, or 210, type `double` values may be stored in the array `table`. All three subscripts must be specified in each reference to array `table` in order to access a single number (e.g., `table[2][3][4]`).    ←

**EXAMPLE 8.15** ▶    Function `filled` checks whether a tic-tac-toe board is completely filled (see Fig. 8.19). If the board contains no cells with the value ' ', the function returns 1 for true; otherwise, it returns 0 for false.    ←

**Figure 8.19    Function to Check Whether Tic-tac-toe Board is Filled**

```
/* Checks whether a tic-tac-toe board is completely filled. */
int
filled(char ttt_brd[3][3])  /*  input - tic-tac-toe board              */
{
      int r, c,   /* row and column subscripts   */
          ans;    /* whether or not board filled */

      /*  Assumes board is filled until blank is found               */
      ans = 1;

      /*  Resets ans to zero if a blank is found                     */
      for  (r = 0;  r < 3;  ++r)
          for  (c = 0;  c < 3;  ++c)
              if (ttt_brd[r][c] == ' ')
                    ans = 0;

      return (ans);
}
```

## Initialization of Multidimensional Arrays

You can initialize multidimensional arrays in their declarations just like you initialize one-dimensional arrays. However, instead of listing all table values in one list, the values are usually grouped by rows. For example, the following statement would declare a tic-tac-toe board and initialize its contents to blanks.

```
char tictac[3][3] = { {' ', ' ', ' '}, {' ', ' ', ' '},
                      {' ', ' ', ' '} };
```

## Arrays with Several Dimensions

The array `enroll` declared here

```
int enroll[MAXCRS][5][4];
```

*course* / *year*
*campus*

and pictured in Fig. 8.20 is a three-dimensional array that may be used to store the enrollment data for a college. We will assume that the college offers 100 (MAXCRS) courses at five different campuses. In keeping with C's practice of starting array subscripts with zero, we will number the freshman year 0, the sophomore year 1, and so on. Thus `enroll[1][4][3]` represents the number of seniors taking course 1 at campus 4.

Array `enroll` is composed of a total of 2000 (100 × 5 × 4) elements. A potential pitfall exists when you are dealing with multidimensional arrays: Memory space can be used up rapidly if several multidimensional arrays are declared in the same program. You should be aware of the amount of memory space required by each large array in a program.

We can answer many different questions by processing the data in Fig. 8.20. We can determine the total number of students taking a particular course, the number of juniors in course 2 at all campuses, and so on. The type of information desired determines the order in which we must reference the array elements.

**EXAMPLE 8.16**

The program fragment that follows Fig. 8.20 finds and displays the total number of students in each course.

**Figure 8.20
Three-
Dimensional
Array enroll**

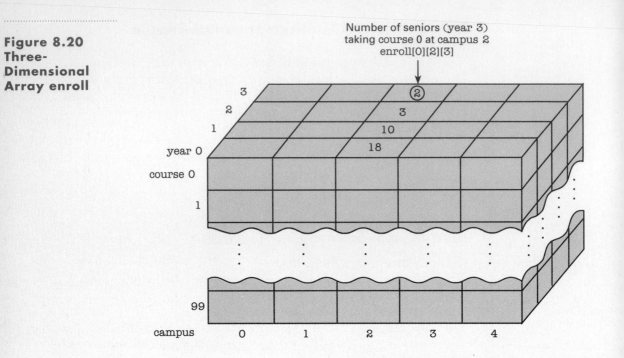

```
/*  Finds and displays number of students in each course  */
for  (course = 0;  course < MAXCRS;  ++course) {
    crs_sum = 0;
    for  (campus = 0;  campus < 5;  ++campus) {
        for  (cls_rank = 0;  cls_rank < 4;  ++cls_rank) {
            crs_sum += enroll[course][campus][cls_rank];
        }
    }
    printf("Number of students in course %d is %d\n",
           course, crs_sum);
}
```

Since we are displaying the number of students in each course, the loop control variable for the outermost indexed loop is the subscript that denotes the course.

The program fragment that follows displays the number of students at each campus. This time the loop control variable for the outermost indexed loop is the subscript that denotes the campus.

```
/* Finds and displays number of students at each campus    */
for  (campus = 0;  campus < 5;  ++campus) {
    campus_sum = 0;

    for  (course = 0;  course < MAXCRS;  ++course) {
        for  (cls_rank = 0;  cls_rank < 4;  ++cls_rank) {
            campus_sum += cnroll[course][campus][cls_rank];
        }
    }

    printf("Number of students at campus %d is %d\n",
            campus, campus_sum);
}
```

**EXERCISES FOR
SECTION 8.7**

Self-Check

1. Redefine MAXCRS as 5, and write and test program segments that perform the following operations:
   a. Enter the enrollment data.
   b. Find the number of juniors in all classes at all campuses. Students will be counted once for each course in which they are enrolled.
   c. Write a function that has three input parameters: the enrollment array, a class rank, and a course number. The function is to find the number of students of the given rank who are enrolled in the given course on all campuses. Try using your function to find the number of sophomores (rank = 1) on all campuses who are enrolled in course 2.
   d. Compute and display the number of upperclass students in all courses at each campus, as well as the total number of upperclass students enrolled on all campuses. (Upperclass students are juniors and seniors—ranks 2 and 3.) Again, students will be counted once for each course in which they are enrolled.

Programming

1. Write a function that displays the values on the diagonal of its $10 \times 10$ matrix parameter.

## 8.8 ARRAY PROCESSING ILLUSTRATED

The next problem illustrates two common ways of selecting array elements for processing. Sometimes we need to manipulate many or all elements of a table in some uniform manner (for example, display them all). In such situations, it makes sense to process the table rows or columns in sequence (*sequential access*), starting with the first and ending with the last.

At other times, the order in which the array elements are accessed depends either on the order of the problem data or the nature of the formula that is the basis of the processing. In these situations, access to element i+1 of an array does not necessarily occur right after access to element i. Thus, we are not using sequential access, but rather *random access*.

## Case Study: Analysis of Sales Data

**PROBLEM**

The sales manager of your company needs a sales analysis program to track sales performance by salesperson and by quarter. The program will read all sales transactions from a text file. The data for each transaction will be the salesperson's number, the quarter in which the sale took place, and the sales amount. The sales transactions are in no particular order. After scanning all sales transactions, the program should display a table in the form shown in Fig. 8.21, which includes totals by person and by quarter.

**ANALYSIS**

You will need separate arrays to hold the sales table, the personal totals (row sums), and the quarterly totals (column sums).

**Figure 8.21   Sales Analysis Output**

```
                          Sales Summary
                          ----- -------


Salesperson      Fall        Winter        Spring        Summer        TOTAL
-------------------------------------------------------------------------------
    0          2785.00      2282.00       5720.00       6330.00      17117.00
    1          4715.00      1676.00       6067.00        929.00      13387.00
    2          1253.00      1495.00       2884.00       4173.00       9805.00
    3          3946.00      1508.00       2844.00       2969.00      11267.00
    4          3558.00      3481.00       2608.00       5590.00      15237.00
-------------------------------------------------------------------------------
QUARTER TOTALS 16257.00     10442.00      20123.00      19991.00
```

### Data Requirements

#### New Type
```
quarter_t  {fall, winter, spring, summer}
```

#### Problem Constants
```
NUM_SALES_PEOPLE  5
NUM_QUARTERS      4
```

#### Problem Inputs
```
Sales transactions file
double sales[NUM_SALES_PEOPLE][NUM_QUARTERS] /* sales
        data array: first dimension subscript is
        an int, second is a quarter_t value */
```

#### Problem Outputs
```
double person_totals[NUM_SALES_PEOPLE]  /* Totals for
        each salesperson; for each row of table */
double quarter_totals[NUM_QUARTERS]     /* Totals for
        each quarter; for each column of table */
```

### DESIGN

### Initial Algorithm

1. Scan sales data, posting by salesperson and quarter, and returning a value to show success or failure of the data scan.
2. if the data scan proceeded without error
    3. Compute salesperson totals (row sums).
    4. Compute quarterly totals (column sums).
    5. Display the sales table along with the row and column sums.

### IMPLEMENTATION

#### Coding Function main

We will call functions for steps 1, 3, 4, and 5. After introducing a program variable status to record the success or failure of the data scan, we can code function main directly from our initial algorithm pseudocode. Figure 8.22 shows the main function along with the necessary preprocessor directives and type definition.

## Figure 8.22   Sales Analysis Main Function

```
/*
 *  Scans sales figures for one year and stores them in a table organized
 *  by salesperson and quarter. Displays the table and the annual totals
 *  for each person and the sales totals for each quarter
 */

#include <stdio.h>

#define SALES_FILE       "sales.dat"   /* name of sales data file */
#define NUM_QUARTERS      4
#define NUM_SALES_PEOPLE 5

typedef enum
      {fall, winter, spring, summer}
quarter_t;

int  scan_table(double sales[][NUM_QUARTERS], int num_rows);
void sum_rows(double row_sum[], double sales[][NUM_QUARTERS], int num_rows);
void sum_columns(double col_sum[], double sales[][NUM_QUARTERS],
                int num_rows);
void display_table(double sales[][NUM_QUARTERS], const double
                  person_totals[], const double quarter_totals[],
                  int num_rows);
{  Insert function prototypes for any helper functions. }

int
main(void)
{
      double sales[NUM_SALES_PEOPLE][NUM_QUARTERS]; /* table of sales */
      double person_totals[NUM_SALES_PEOPLE];       /* row totals */
      double quarter_totals[NUM_QUARTERS];          /* column totals */
      int    status;

      status = scan_table(sales, NUM_SALES_PEOPLE);
      if (status == 1) {
            sum_rows(person_totals, sales, NUM_SALES_PEOPLE);
            sum_columns(quarter_totals, sales, NUM_SALES_PEOPLE);
            display_table(sales, person_totals, quarter_totals,
                        NUM_SALES_PEOPLE);
      }
      return (0);
}
```

### Coding function scan_table

Function `scan_table` (Fig. 8.23) scans in the data from the files `sales.dat` one line at a time until end-of-file or an error is encountered. Within the loop body, `scan_table` checks the range of both the salesperson and the quarter of the current transaction. If the data is valid, the statement

```
sales[trans_person][quarter] += trans_amt;
```

adds the current sales amount to the total being accumulated for the salesperson indicated by `trans_person` (row subscript) and `quarter` (column sub-script). Because the data are in no particular order, the elements of array `sales` are accessed randomly. Before beginning the data scan, the function must initialize all the elements of the `sales` array to zero. This is the purpose of the call to `initialize`. The implementation of function `initialize` is also shown in Fig. 8.23. Because `initialize` must change the value of every element of `sales`, it accesses the elements sequentially, using nested `for` loops. The outer `for` loop provides row subscripts running from zero to one less than the number of rows, and the inner loop provides column subscripts of type `quarter_t` running from `fall` through `summer`.

**Figure 8.23   Function scan_table and Helper Function initialize**

```
/*
 *  Scans the sales data from SALES_FILE and computes and stores the sales
 *  results in the sales table. Flags out-of-range data and data format
 *  errors.
 *  Post:  Each entry of sales represents the sales total for a particular
 *         salesperson and quarter.
 *            Returns 1 for successful table scan, 0 for error in scan.
 *  Calls: initialize to initialize table to all zeros
 */
int
scan_table(double sales[][NUM_QUARTERS], /* output */
           int num_rows)                 /* input  */
{
      double    trans_amt;       /* transaction amount */
      int       trans_person;    /* salesperson number */
      quarter_t quarter;         /* sales quarter      */
      FILE      *sales_filep;     /* file pointer to sales file */
      int       valid_table = 1;  /* data valid so far  */
```

*(continued)*

**Figure 8.23** *(continued)*

```
int      status;              /* input status          */
char     ch;                  /* one character in bad line */

/*  Initialize table to all zeros */
initialize(sales, num_rows, 0.0);

/*  Scan and store the valid sales data */
sales_filep = fopen(SALES_FILE, "r");
for  (status = fscanf(sales_filep, "%d%d%lf", &trans_person,
                      &quarter, &trans_amt);
      status == 3  &&  valid_table;
      status = fscanf(sales_filep, "%d%d%lf", &trans_person,
                      &quarter, &trans_amt)) {
    if (fall <= quarter  &&  quarter <= summer  &&
        trans_person >= 0  &&  trans_person < num_rows) {
        sales[trans_person][quarter] += trans_amt;
    } else {
        printf("Invalid salesperson or quarter -- \n");
        printf("  person is %d, quarter is ", trans_person);
        display_quarter(quarter);
        printf("\n\n");
        valid_table = 0;
    }
}

if (!valid_table) {            /* error already processed */
    status = 0;
} else if (status == EOF) {  /* end of data without error */
    status = 1;
} else {                       /* data format error */
    printf("Error in sales data format. Revise data.\n");
    printf("ERROR HERE >>> ");
    for  (status = fscanf(sales_filep, "%c", &ch);
          status == 1  &&  ch != '\n';
          status = fscanf(sales_filep, "%c", &ch))
        printf("%c", ch);
    printf(" <<<\n");
    status = 0;
}
return (status);
}
```

*(continued)*

**Figure 8.23**   *(continued)*

```
/*
 *  Stores value in all elements of sales.
 *  Pre:   value is defined and num_rows is the number of rows in
 *         sales.
 *  Post: All elements of sales have the desired value.
 */
void
initialize(double sales[][NUM_QUARTERS], /* output */
           int     num_rows,             /* input  */
           double value)                 /* input  */
{
      int       row;
      quarter_t quarter;

      for  (row = 0;  row < num_rows;  ++row)
          for  (quarter = fall;  quarter <= summer;  ++quarter)
              sales[row][quarter] = value;
}
```

### Coding Functions sum_rows and sum_columns

The design and implementation of functions `sum_rows` and `sum_columns` are left as an exercise for you. Function `sum_rows` will need nested loops similar to those in function `initialize`. Full execution of the inner loop should add up the values in one row of `sales`. After exiting the inner loop, the accumulated sum should be stored in the element of `row_sum` corresponding to the current row. Function `sum_columns` will need a revision of the nested loops that allows the column subscript to remain constant while the row subscript varies.

### Coding Function display_table

You should display the information in a two-dimensional array in the same way that humans visualize it: as a table whose rows correspond to the array's first dimension and whose columns correspond to the array's second dimension. To accomplish this, access and display the array elements row by row.

Function `display_table` (Fig. 8.24) displays the data in the sales table in the form shown in Fig. 8.21. In addition to the array data (first parameter), the function also displays the salesperson totals (second parameter) and the quarterly totals (third parameter).

**Figure 8.24** **Function display_table and Helper Function display_quarter**

```
/*
 *  Displays the sales table data in table form along with the row and column
 *  sums.
 *  Pre:  sales, person_totals, quarter_totals, and num_rows are defined.
 *  Post: Values stored in the three arrays are displayed.
 */
void
display_table(double       sales[][NUM_QUARTERS], /* input */
              const double person_totals[],       /* input */
              const double quarter_totals[],       /* input */
              int          num_rows)               /* input */
{
      int       person;
      quarter_t quarter;

      /* Display heading */
      printf("%34cSales Summary\n%34c----- -------\n\n", ' ', ' ');
      printf("%12s%5c", "Salesperson", ' ');
      for  (quarter = fall;  quarter <= summer;  ++quarter){
            display_quarter(quarter);
            printf("%8c", ' ');
      }
      printf("TOTAL\n");
      printf("----------------------------------------");
      printf("----------------------------------------\n");

      /* Display table */
      for  (person = 0;  person < num_rows;  ++person) {
          printf("%6d%4c", person, ' ');
          for  (quarter = fall;  quarter <= summer;  ++quarter)
              printf("%6c%8.2f", ' ', sales[person][quarter]);
          printf("%6c%8.2f\n", ' ', person_totals[person]);
      }
      printf("---------------------------------------");
      printf("----------------------------------------\n");
      printf("QUARTER TOTALS ");
      for  (quarter = fall;  quarter <= summer;  ++quarter)
          printf("%9.2f%5c", quarter_totals[quarter], ' ');
      printf("\n");
}
```

*(continued)*

**Figure 8.24**    *(continued)*

```
/*
 *  Display an enumeration constant of type quarter_t
 */
void
display_quarter (quarter_t quarter)
{
      switch (quarter) {
      case fall:     printf("Fall ");
                     break;

      case winter:   printf("Winter");
                     break;

      case spring:   printf("Spring");
                     break;

      case summer:   printf("Summer");
                     break;

      default:       printf("Invalid quarter %d", quarter);
      }
}
```

---

◀ **TESTING** ▶

To test the sales analysis program, create four sample data files. In one, place only correct data. In the second, include a salesperson number $>=$ NUM_SALES_PEOPLE. In the third, include a quarter number greater than 3 (summer). In the fourth file, place a data format error such as a letter where a number belongs. Check that your correct file produces reasonable results:  the sum of the salesperson totals should match the sum of the quarterly totals. Verify that each erroneous file brings forth the correct error message.

Self-Check

1. For each fragment, which array locations are displayed and in which order?

```
a. for  (next_quarter = fall;
          next_quarter <= summer;
          ++next_quarter)
      printf("%12.2f", sales[1][next_quarter]);
b. for  (next_person = 0;
          next_person < 5;
          ++next_person)
      printf("%12.2f", sales[next_person][spring]);
c. for  (next_quarter = fall;
          next_quarter <= summer;
          ++next_quarter) {
      for  (next_person = 0;
            next_person < 5;
            ++next_person)
         printf("%12.2f",
                sales[next_person][next_quarter]);
      printf("\n");
   }
```

Programming

1. Write functions sum_rows and sum_columns called from function main in Fig. 8.22.
2. Write a function that determines who has won a game of tic-tac-toe. The function should first check all rows to see whether one player occupies all the cells in one row, next check all columns, and then check the two diagonals. The function should return a value from the enumerated type {no_winner, x_wins, o_wins}.

## 8.9 COMMON PROGRAMMING ERRORS

The most common error in using arrays is a subscript-range error. An out-of-range reference occurs when the subscript value used is outside the range specified by the array declaration. For the array celsius,

```
int celsius[100];
```

a subscript-range error occurs when `celsius` is used with a subscript that has a value less than 0 or greater than 99. If the value of `i` is 150, a reference to the subscripted variable `celsius[i]` may cause an error message such as

```
access violation at line no. 28
```

In many situations, however, no run time error message will be produced—the program will simply produce incorrect results. In ANSI C, the prevention of subscript-range errors is entirely the responsibility of the programmer. Subscript-range errors are not syntax errors; consequently, they will not be detected until program execution, and often not even then. They are most often caused by an incorrect subscript expression, a loop counter error, or a nonterminating loop. Before spending considerable time in debugging, you should check all suspect subscript calculations carefully for out-of-range errors. View the successive values of a subscripting variable in a debugger program, or insert diagnostic output statements that print subscript values that are of concern.

If a subscript-range error occurs inside an indexed loop, verify that the subscript is in range for both the initial and the final values of the loop control variable. If these values are in range, it is likely that all other subscript references in the loop are in range as well.

If a subscript-range error occurs in a loop controlled by a variable other than the array subscript, check that the loop control variable is being updated as required. If it is not, the loop may be repeated more often than expected, causing the subscript-range error. This error could happen if the control-variable update step was inside a condition or was inadvertently omitted.

When using arrays as arguments to functions, be careful not to apply the address-of operator to the array name even if the array is an output argument. However, do remember to use the & on an array *element* that is being passed as an output argument.

Be sure to use the correct forms for declaring array input and output parameters in function prototypes. Remember when reading C code that a parameter declared as

```
int *z
```

could represent a single integer output parameter or an integer array parameter. Comment your own prototypes carefully and use the alternate declaration form

```
int z[]
```

for array parameters to assist readers of your code.

If you are working on a computer system with very limited memory, you may find that some correct C programs generate run-time error messages indicating an access violation. The use of arrays can cause a program to require large amounts of memory for function data areas. The portion of memory set aside for function data areas is called the *stack*. You may need to tell your operating system that an increased stack size is necessary in order to be able to run programs using large arrays.

## CHAPTER REVIEW

1. A data structure is a grouping of related data items in memory.
2. An array is a data structure used to store a collection of data items of the same type.
3. An individual array element is referenced by placing immediately after the array name a square-bracketed subscript for each dimension.
4. The initial element of a one-dimensional array x is referenced as x[0]. If x has n elements, the final element is referenced as x[n-1].
5. An indexed for loop whose counter runs from 0 to one less than an array's size enables us to reference all the elements of a one-dimensional array in sequence by using the loop counter as the array subscript. Nested for loops provide sequential access to multidimensional array elements.
6. For an array declared as a local variable, space is allocated in the function data area for all the array elements.
7. For an array declared as a function parameter, space is allocated in the function data area for only the address of the initial element of the actual argument passed.
8. The name of an array with no subscript always refers to the address of the initial array element.
9. A function that creates an array result should require the calling module to pass an output argument array in which to store the result.

### New C Constructs

| Example | Effect |
|---|---|

**Array Declarations**

**Local Variables**

| | |
|---|---|
| `double data[30];`<br>`int    matrix[2][3];` | Allocates storage for 30 type `double` items in array `data` (`data[0]`, `data[1]`, ..., `data[29]`), and six type `int` items (2 rows of 3 columns) in two-dimensional array `matrix` (`matrix[0][0]`, `matrix[0][1]`, `matrix[0][2]`, `matrix[1][0]`, `matrix[1][1]`, `matrix[1][2]`). |

*(continued)*

**New C Constructs**    *(continued)*

| Example | Effect |
|---|---|
| **Initialization** | |
| `char vowels[5] =`<br>`     {'A', 'E', 'I', 'O', 'U'};` | Allocates storage for five type `char` items in array `vowels` and initializes the array contents: `vowels[0]='A'`, `vowels[1]='E'`,... `vowels[4]='U'`. |
| `int  id[2][2] =`<br>`     { {1, 0}, {0, 1} };` | Allocates four locations for the $2 \times 2$ matrix `id`, initializing the storage so `id[0][0]=1`, `id[0][1]=0`, `id[1][0]=0`, and `id[1][1]=1`. |
| **Input Parameter** | |
| `void`<br>`print_alpha(const char alpha[],`<br>`            const int   m[],`<br>`            int         a_size,`<br>`            int         m_size)`<br>`     or`<br>`... (const char *alpha, ...` | States that function `print_alpha` uses arrays `alpha` and `m` as input parameters only— `print_alpha` will not change their contents. |
| **Output or Input/Output Parameter** | |
| `void`<br>`fill(int nums[], int n)`<br>`     or`<br>`... (int *nums,...` | States that function `fill` can both look at and modify the actual argument array passed to `nums`. |
| **Array References** | |
| `if (data[0] < 39.8)` | Compares value of initial element of array `data` to `39.8`. |
| `for  (i = 0;  i < 30;  ++i)`<br>`    data[i] /= 2.0;` | Divides each element of array `data` by 2, changing the array contents. |
| `for  (i = 0;  i < 2;  ++i) {`<br>`    for  (j = 0;  j < 3;  ++j)`<br>`      printf("%6d", matrix[i][j]);`<br>`    printf("\n");`<br>`  }` | Displays contents of `matrix` in 2 rows with 3 columns. |

# QUICK-CHECK EXERCISES

1. What is a data structure?
2. Of what data type are array subscripting expressions?
3. Can two elements of the same array be of different data types?

4. If an array is declared to have 10 elements, must the program use all ten?
5. The two methods of array access are called _____ and _____ .
6. An _____ loop allows us to access easily the elements of an array in _____ order.
7. What is the difference in the use of array b that is implied by these two prototypes?

```
int fun_one(int b[], n);
int fun_two(const int b[], n);
```

8. Look again at the prototypes in Exercise 7. Why does neither array declaration indicate a size?
9. Let nums be an array of 12 type int locations. Describe how the following loop works.

```
i = 0;
for  (status = scanf("%d", &n);
         status == 1  &&  i < 12;
         status = scanf("%d", &n))
      nums[i++] = n;
```

10. How many elements does array m have? Show how you would reference each one.

```
double m[2][4];
```

11. If x is an array declared

```
int x[10];
```

and you see a function call such as

```
some_fun(x, n);
```

how can you tell whether x is an input or an output argument?

# ANSWERS TO QUICK-CHECK EXERCISES

1. A data structure is a grouping of related values in main memory.
2. type int
3. no

4. no
5. sequential, random
6. indexed, sequential
7. In `fun_one`, `b` can be used as an output parameter or as an input/output parameter. In `fun_two`, `b` is strictly an input parameter array.
8. The size of `b` is not needed because the function does not allocate storage for copying parameter arrays. Only the starting address of the actual argument array will be stored in the formal parameter.
9. As long as `scanf` continues to return a value of 1 meaning a valid integer has been obtained for n, unless the subscript `i` is ≥ 12, the loop body will store the input in the next element of `nums` and will increment the loop counter. The loop exits on EOF (`scanf` returns a negative value), on invalid data (`scanf` returns zero), or on `i` no longer being less than 12.
10. `m` has 8 elements: `m[0][0]`, `m[0][1]`, `m[0][2]`, `m[0][3]`, `m[1][0]`, `m[1][1]`, `m[1][2]`, `m[1][3]`
11. You can't tell by looking at the function call, nor can you rely on the prototype of `some_fun` to tell you either unless the corresponding formal parameter declaration has a `const` qualifier. If it does, `x` must be an input argument.

# REVIEW QUESTIONS

1. Identify an error in the following C statements:

```
int x[8], i;
for  (i = 0;  i <= 8;  ++i)
     x[i] = i;
```

Will the error be detected? If so, when?
2. Declare an array of type `double` values called `exper` that can be referenced by using any day of the week as a subscript, where 0 represents Sunday, 1 represents Monday, and so on.
3. The statement marked `/*  this  one  */` in the following code is valid. True or false?

```
int counts[10], i;
double x[5];
printf("Enter an integer between 0 and 4> ");
i = 0;
scanf("%d", &counts[i]);
x[counts[i]] = 8.384;  /* this one */
```

4. What are the two common ways of selecting array elements for processing?
5. Write a C program segment to display the index of the smallest and the largest numbers in an array x of 20 integers. Assume array x already has values assigned to each element.
6. Write a C function called reverse that takes an array named x as an input parameter and an array named y as an output parameter. A third function parameter is n, the number of values in x. The function should copy the integers in x into y but in reverse order (i.e., y[0] gets x[n - 1], ... y[n - 1] gets x[0]).
7. Write a program segment to display the sum of the values in each row of a 5 × 3 type double array named table. How many row sums will be displayed? How many elements are included in each sum?
8. Answer Review Question 7 for the column sums.

# PROGRAMMING PROJECTS

1. Write a program to take two numerical lists of the same length ended by a sentinel value and store the lists in arrays x and y, each of which has 20 elements. Let n be the actual number of data values in each list. Store the product of corresponding elements of x and y in a third array, z, also of size 20. Display the arrays x, y, and z in a three-column table. Then compute and display the square root of the sum of the items in z. Make up your own data, and be sure to test your program on at least one data set with number lists of exactly 20 items. One data set should have lists of 21 numbers, and one set should have significantly shorter lists.
2. Let arr be an array of 20 integers. Write a program that first fills the array with up to 20 input values and then finds and displays both the *subscript* of the largest item in arr and the value of the largest item.
3. Each year the Department of Traffic Accidents receives accident-count reports from a number of cities and towns across the country. To summarize these reports, the department provides a frequency-distribution printout that gives the number of cities reporting accident counts in the following ranges: 0–99, 100–199, 200–299, 300–399, 400–499, and 500 or above. The department needs a computer program to take the number of accidents for each reporting city or town and add one to the count for the appropriate accident range. After all the data have been processed, the resulting frequency counts are to be displayed.
4. A normalized vector $X$ is defined as

$$x_i = \frac{v_i}{\sqrt{\sum_{i=1}^{n} v_i^2}} ; \quad i = 1, 2, \dots, n$$

Each element of the normalized vector $X$ is computed by dividing the corresponding element $(v_i)$ of the original vector by the square root of the sum of the squares of all the original vector's elements. Design and test a program that repeatedly scans and normalizes vectors of different lengths. Define functions `scan_vector`, `normalize_vector`, and `print_vector`.

5. Generate a table that indicates the rainfall for the city of Plainview and compares the current year's rainfall for the city with the rainfall from the previous year. Display some summary statistics that will indicate both the annual rainfall for each year and the average monthly rainfall for each year. The input data will consist of twelve pairs of numbers. The first number in each pair will be the current year's rainfall for a month, and the second number will be what fell during the same month the previous year. The first data pair will represent January, the second will be February, and so forth. If you assume the data begin

```
3.2    4      (for January)
2.2    1.6    (for February)
```

the output should resemble the following:

```
                   Table of monthly rainfall

                   January     February    March . . .
       This year     3.2          2.2
       Last year     4.0          1.6


Total rainfall this year:  35.7
Total rainfall last year:  42.8
Average monthly rainfall for this year:  3.6
Average monthly rainfall for last year:  4.0
```

6. Write an interactive program that plays a game of Hangman. Store the word to be guessed in successive elements of an array of individual characters called `word`. The player must guess the letters belonging to `word`. The program should terminate when either all letters have been guessed correctly (the player wins) or a specified number of incorrect guesses have been made (the computer wins). *Hint:* Use another array, `guessed`, to keep track of the solution so far. Initialize all elements of `guessed` to the `'*'` symbol. Each time a letter in `word` is guessed, replace the corresponding `'*'` in `guessed` with that letter.

7. The results from the mayor's race have been reported by each precinct as follows:

| Precinct | Candidate A | Candidate B | Candidate C | Candidate D |
|----------|-------------|-------------|-------------|-------------|
| 1 | 192 | 48 | 206 | 37 |
| 2 | 147 | 90 | 312 | 21 |
| 3 | 186 | 12 | 121 | 38 |
| 4 | 114 | 21 | 408 | 39 |
| 5 | 267 | 13 | 382 | 29 |

Write a program to do the following:

a. Display the table with appropriate labels for the rows and columns.
b. Compute and display the total number of votes received by each candidate and the percentage of the total votes cast.
c. If any one candidate received over 50 percent of the votes, the program should display a message declaring that candidate the winner.
d. If no candidate received 50 percent of the votes, the program should display a message declaring a runoff between the two candidates receiving the highest number of votes; the two candidates should be identified by their letter names.
e. Run the program once with the data shown and once with candidate C receiving only 108 votes in Precinct 4.

8. Write a function that will merge the contents of two sorted (ascending order) arrays of type `double` values, storing the result in an array output parameter (still in ascending order). The function should not assume that both its input parameter arrays are the same length but can assume that one array does not contain two copies of the same value. The result array should also contain no duplicate values.

*Hint:* When one of the input arrays has been exhausted, do not forget to copy the remaining data in the other array into the result array. Test your function with cases in which (1) the first array is exhausted first, (2) the second array is exhausted first, and (3) the two arrays are exhausted at the same time (i.e., they end with the same value). Remember that the arrays input to this function *must already be sorted.*

9. The binary search algorithm that follows may be used to search an array when the elements are in order. This algorithm is analogous to the following approach for finding a name in a telephone book.

   a. Open the book in the middle, and look at the middle name on the page.
   b. If the middle name isn't the one you're looking for, decide whether it comes before or after the name you want.
   c. Take the appropriate half of the section of the book you were looking in and repeat these steps until you land on the name.

**Algorithm for Binary Search**

1. Let bottom be the subscript of the initial array element.
2. Let top be the subscript of the last array element.
3. Let found be false.
4. Repeat as long as bottom isn't greater than top and the target has not been found
    5. Let middle be the subscript of the element halfway between bottom and top.
    6. if the element at middle is the target
        7. Set found to true and index to middle.
    else if the element at middle is larger than the target
        8. Let top be middle − 1.
    else
        9. Let bottom be middle + 1.

Write and test a function binary_srch that implements this algorithm for an array of integers. When there is a large number of array elements, which function do you think is faster: binary_srch or the linear search function of Fig. 8.15?

10. The *bubble sort* is another technique for sorting an array. A bubble sort compares adjacent array elements and exchanges their values if they are out of order. In this way, the smaller values "bubble" to the top of the array (toward element 0), while the larger values sink to the bottom of the array. After the first pass of a bubble sort, the last array element is in the correct position; after the second pass the last two elements are correct, and so

on. Thus, after each pass, the unsorted portion of the array contains one less element. Write and test a function that implements this sorting method.

11. Write a program that simulates the movement of radioactive particles in a two-dimensional shield around a reactor. A particle in the shield can move in one of four directions. The direction for the next second of travel is determined by generation of a random number between 1 and 4 (forward, backward, left, right). A change in direction is interpreted as a collision with another particle resulting in a dissipation of energy. Each particle can have only a limited number of collisions before it dies. For each particle that enters the shield, determine whether that particle exits the shield before it dies. A particle exits the shield if its net forward travel time is $n$ seconds before $k$ collisions occur (i.e., it takes $n$ more forward steps than backward steps). Determine the percentage of particles that exit the shield where $n$, $k$, and the number of particles are data items. See Programming Project 2 at the end of Chapter 7 for information about the library function `rand`.

12. Statistical analysis of data makes heavy use of arrays. One such analysis, called cross-tabulation, is used to help decide whether a relationship exists between two or more variables. For example, the following data might represent opinions from a survey concerning an amendment to the U.S. Constitution making it illegal to destroy or damage the U.S. flag in any way.

| Opinion | Male | Female | Total |
|---------|------|--------|-------|
| In Favor | 63 | 27 | 90 |
| Opposed | 19 | 42 | 61 |
| No Opinion | 6 | 39 | 45 |
| Totals | 88 | 108 | 196 |

Write a C program that will take pairs of male/female response totals (one pair per line)

```
63   27
19   42
 6   39
```

and display the cross-tabulation matrix including the row totals and the column totals.

13. The *Game of Life,* invented by John H. Conway, is supposed to model the genetic laws for birth, survival, and death (see *Scientific American,* October 1970, p. 120). We will play the game on a board that consists of 25 squares in the horizontal and vertical directions (a total of 625 squares). Each square can be empty, or it can contain an X indicating the presence of an organism. Each square (except for the border squares) has eight neighbors.

The color shading shown in the following segment of the board marks the neighbors of the organism named X*:

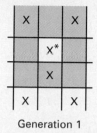

Generation 1

The next generation of organisms is determined according to the following criteria:

a. Birth—an organism will be born in each empty location that has exactly three neighbors.

b. Death—an organism with four or more organisms as neighbors will die from overcrowding. An organism with fewer than two neighbors will die from loneliness.

c. Survival—an organism with two or three neighbors will survive to the next generation. Possible generations 2 and 3 for the sample follow:

Generation 2        Generation 3

Take an initial configuration of organisms as input data. Display the original game array, calculate the next generation of organisms in a new array, copy the new array into the original game array, and repeat the cycle for as many generations as you wish. *Hint:* Assume that the borders of the game array are infertile regions where organisms can neither survive nor be born; you will not have to process the border squares.

# STRINGS

chapter

$S$o far, we have seen limited use of character data because most applications that process character data deal with a grouping of characters, a data structure called a *string*. Because C implements the string data structure using arrays of type `char`, we could not explore strings until we had a foundational understanding of arrays.

Strings are important in computer science because many computer applications are concerned with the manipulation of textual data rather than numerical data. Computer-based *word processing systems* enable a user to compose letters, term papers, newspaper articles, and even books at a computer terminal instead of at a typewriter. Storing the text in the computer's memory allows us to modify the text, check the spelling electronically, move whole paragraphs, and then print a fresh copy without mistakes or erasures.

Strings play an important role in science as well. The chemist works with elements and compounds whose names often combine alphabetic and numeric characters (e.g., $C_{12}H_{22}O_{11}$)—data easily represented by a string. Molecular biologists identify amino acids by name and map our DNA with strings of amino acid abbreviations. Many mathematicians, physicists, and engineers spend more time modeling our world with equations (strings of character and numeric data) than they do crunching numbers. In subsequent chapters, we will meet other representations of some of these concepts that are more easily manipulated than the string model; however, we will still need strings as the vehicle for communication between the computer system and the human user.

In the sections that follow, we will introduce some fundamental operations that can be performed on character data. We will investigate selected functions from the standard string and ctype libraries that provide most of C's facilities for working with character strings.

## 9.1 STRING BASICS

We have already used string constants extensively in our earlier work. Indeed, every one of our calls to `scanf` or `printf` used a string constant as the first argument. Consider this call:

```
printf("Average = %.2f", avg);
```

The first argument is the string constant `"Average = %.2f"`, a string of 14 characters. Notice that the blanks in the string are characters just as valid as those requiring ink! Like other constant values, a string constant can be associated with a symbolic name using the `#define` directive.

```
#define ERR_PREFIX    "*****Error - "
#define INSUFF_DATA   "Insufficient Data"
```

## Declaring and Initializing String Variables

As we mentioned earlier, a string in C is implemented as an array, so declaring a string variable is the same as declaring an array of type `char`. In

```
char string_var[30];
```

the variable `string_var` will hold strings from 0 to 29 characters long. It is C's handling of this varying length characteristic that distinguishes the string data structure from other arrays. C permits initialization of string variables using either a brace-enclosed character list as shown in Chapter 8 or a string constant as shown in the following declaration of `str`.

```
char str[20] = "Initial value";
```

Let's look at `str` in memory after this declaration with initialization.

| [0] | | | | [4] | | | | | [9] | | | | | [14] | | | | | [19] |
|-----|---|---|---|-----|---|---|---|---|-----|---|---|---|---|------|---|---|---|---|------|
| I | n | i | t | i | a | l | | v | a | l | u | e | \0 | ? | ? | ? | ? | ? | ? |

**null character**
character `'\0'` that marks the end of a string in C

Notice that `str[13]` contains the character `'\0'`, the **null character** that marks the end of a string. Using this marker allows the string's length within the character array to vary from 0 to one less than the array's declared size. All of C's string-handling functions simply ignore whatever is stored in the cells following the null character. The following diagram shows `str` holding a string that is the longest it can represent—19 characters plus the null character.

| [0] | | | | [4] | | | | | [9] | | | | | [14] | | | | | [19] |
|-----|---|---|---|-----|---|---|---|---|-----|---|---|---|---|------|---|---|---|---|------|
| n | u | m | b | e | r | s | | a | n | d | | s | t | r | i | n | g | s | \0 |

## Arrays of Strings

Because one string is an array of characters, an array of strings is a two-dimensional array of characters in which each row is one string. The following are statements to declare an array to store up to 30 names, each of which is less than 25 characters long.

```
#define NUM_PEOPLE 30
#define NAME_LEN   25
    . . .
char names[NUM_PEOPLE][NAME_LEN];
```

We can initialize an array of strings at declaration in the following manner:

```
char month[12][10] = {"January", "February", "March", "April",
                      "May", "June", "July", "August",
                      "September", "October", "November",
                      "December"};
```

## Input/Output with printf and scanf

Both `printf` and `scanf` can handle string arguments as long as the place-holder `%s` is used in the format string:

```
printf("Topic: %s\n", string_var);
```

The `printf` function, like other standard library functions that take string arguments, depends on finding a null character in the character array to mark the end of the string. If `printf` were passed a character array that contained no `'\0'`, the function would first interpret the contents of each array element as a character and display it. Then `printf` would continue to display as characters the contents of memory locations following the array argument until it encountered a null character or until it attempted to access a memory cell that was not assigned to the program, causing a run-time error. When we write our own string-building functions, we must be sure that a null character is inserted at the end of every string. This inclusion of the null character is automatic for constant strings.

The `%s` placeholder in a `printf` format string can be used with a minimum field width as shown.

```
printf("***%8s***%3s***\n", "Short", "Strings");
```

The first string is displayed right-justified in a field of eight columns. The second string is longer than the specified field width, so the field is expanded to accommodate it exactly with no padding. We are more accustomed to seeing lists of strings printed left-justified rather than right-justified. Consider the two lists in Fig. 9.1.

Placing a minus sign prefix on a placeholder's field width causes left justification of the value displayed. If `president` is a string variable, repeated execution of this call to `printf` will produce a left-justified list.

```
printf("%-20s\n", president);
```

The `scanf` function can be used for input of a string. However, when we call `scanf` with a string variable as an argument, we must remember that array

**Figure 9.1
Right and Left
Justification of
Strings**

| Right-justified | Left-justified |
|---:|:---|
| George Washington | George Washington |
| John Adams | John Adams |
| Thomas Jefferson | Thomas Jefferson |
| James Madison | James Madison |

output arguments are *always* passed to functions by sending the address of the initial array element. Therefore we do not apply the address-of operator to a string argument passed to scanf or to any other function. In Fig. 9.2, we see a brief main function performing string I/O with scanf and printf. In this program, the user is expected to type in a string representing an academic

**Figure 9.2    String Input/Output with scanf and printf**

```
#include <stdio.h>

#define STRING_LEN   10

int
main(void)
{
      char dept[STRING_LEN];
      int  course_num;
      char days[STRING_LEN];
      int  time;

      printf("Enter department code, course number, days and ");
      printf("time like this:\n> COSC 2060 MWF 1410\n> ");
      scanf("%s%d%s%d", dept, &course_num, days, &time);
      printf("%s %d meets %s at %d\n", dept, course_num, days, time);

      return (0);
}

Enter department code, course number, days and time like this:
> COSC 2060 MWF 1410
> MATH 1270 TR 800
MATH 1270 meets TR at 800
```

department, an integer course code, a string abbreviation for the days of the week the course meets, and an integer that gives the meeting time of the class.

The approach scanf takes to string input is very similar to its processing of numeric input. As shown in Fig. 9.3, when it scans a string, scanf skips leading whitespace characters such as blanks, newlines, and tabs. Starting with the first nonwhitespace character, scanf copies the characters it encounters into successive memory cells of its character array argument. When it comes across a whitespace character, scanning stops, and scanf places the null character at the end of the string in its array argument.

Because of the way scanf treats whitespace, the values could be spaced on the data lines in many ways that would result in variables dept, course_num, days, and time receiving correct values upon execution of the scanf call in Fig. 9.2. For example, the data could have been entered one value per line with extra whitespace:

```
>       MATH
  1270
     TR
                1800
```

or two values per line:

```
> MATH 1270
  TR 1800
```

Function scanf would have difficulty if some essential whitespace between values were omitted or if a nonwhitespace separator were substituted. For example, if the data were entered as

```
> MATH1270 TR 1800
```

scanf would store the eight-character string "MATH1270" in dept and would then be unable to convert T to an integer for storage using the next parameter.

**Figure 9.4    Execution of** `scanf("%s%d%s%d", dept, &course_num,`
`days, &time);` **on Entry of Invalid Data**

```
                       dept
     [0]               [4]              [9]    space not allocated for dept
    ┌───┬───┬───┬───┬───┬───┬───┬───┬───┬───┬───┬───┬───┬───┬───┬───┬───┬───┐
    │ M │ A │ T │ H │ , │ 1 │ 2 │ 7 │ 0 │ , │ T │ R │ , │ 1 │ 8 │ 0 │ 0 │\0 │
    └───┴───┴───┴───┴───┴───┴───┴───┴───┴───┴───┴───┴───┴───┴───┴───┴───┴───┘
```

The situation would be worse if the data were entered as

> MATH,1270,TR,1800

Then the `scanf` function would store the entire 17-character string plus `'\0'`
in the `dept` array, causing characters to be stored in eight locations not allocated to `dept`, as shown in Fig. 9.4.

For easy input of predictable-length strings that have no internal blanks,
`scanf` with the `%s` placeholder works well. However, in an environment in
which the proper data entry format may not be observed or where even an occa-
sional program fault is critical, a more robust string input function should be
used. We will write one such function in Section 9.3.

**EXAMPLE 9.1**

Earlier in this chapter, we declared an array of strings suitable for holding 30
names (a two-dimensional array of type `char` values). Let's see how to use
`scanf` and `printf` to fill this array and echo print it.

You will recall from our study of arrays that no address-of operator is
needed when an array is passed as an output argument. Because each element
`names[i]` of an array of strings represents a kind of array, it is passed as an
output argument without using the `&` operator. The following code segment
fills parallel arrays `names` and `ages` with data. In the call to `scanf`, note the
contrasting application of the `&` operator to elements of the `ages` array since
these elements are simple output arguments of type `int`.

```
#define NUM_PEOPLE 30
#define NAME_LEN   25
  . . .
char names[NUM_PEOPLE][NAME_LEN];

for  (i = 0;  i < NUM_PEOPLE;  ++i) {
    scanf("%s%d", names[i], &ages[i]);
    printf("%-35s %3d\n", names[i], ages[i]);
}
```

Self-Check

1. When the scanf function is scanning a string, if there is more input data (with no blanks) than will fit in the array output argument, scanf _____ (choose one).
   a. copies in only the characters that will fit and ignores the rest.
   b. copies in the whole string overflowing the output argument because scanf has no way of knowing the array's declared size.
   c. scans all the characters but stores only the ones that fit, discarding the rest.
2. When printf is given a string argument to print using a %s placeholder, how does it know how many characters to print?
3. Declare a 30-character array, and initialize it at declaration to a string of 29 blanks.

Programming

1. Write a program that takes a word less than 25 characters long and prints a statement like this:

   ```
   fractal starts with the letter f
   ```

   Have the program process words until it encounters a "word" beginning with the character '9'.

## 9.2 STRING LIBRARY FUNCTIONS: ASSIGNMENT AND SUBSTRINGS

We have become accustomed to using the assignment operator = to copy data into a variable. Although we do use the assignment symbol in a declaration of a string variable with initialization, this context is the *only* one in which the operator means to copy the string that is the right operand into the variable that is the left operand. We have seen that an array name with no subscript represents the address of the initial array element. This address is constant and cannot be changed through assignment, so the following code fragment will cause a compiler error message such as Invalid target of assignment:

```
char one_str[20];
one_str = "Test string";   /* Does not work */
```

C provides the string assignment operation in the same way that it provides square root and absolute value operations—through library functions. Along with assignment functions, the library `string.h` provides functions for substring, concatenation, string length, string comparison, and whole line input operations, to name a few. Table 9.1 summarizes selected functions from `string.h`, and Appendix B presents the complete library. Notice that the data type of the value returned by each string-building function is the pointer type `char *`. As always, an array is being represented by the address of its initial value.

**Table 9.1    Some String Library Functions from string.h**

| Function | Purpose: Example | Parameters | Result Type |
|---|---|---|---|
| strcpy | Makes a copy of source, a string, in the character array accessed by dest: `strcpy(s1, "hello");` | char *dest<br>const char *source | char * |
| strncpy | Makes a copy of up to n characters from source in dest: `strncpy(s1, "inevitable", 5)` stores the first five characters of the source in s1, and does NOT add a null character. | char *dest<br>const char *source<br>size_t† n | char * |
| strcat | Appends source to the end of dest: `strcat(s1, "and more");` | char *dest<br>const char *source | char * |
| strncat | Appends up to n characters of source to the end of dest, adding the null character if necessary: `strncat(s1, "and more", 10);` | char *dest<br>const char *source<br>size_t† n | char * |
| strcmp | Compares s1 and s2 alphabetically; returns a negative value if s1 should precede s2, a zero if the strings are equal, and a positive value if s2 should precede s1 in an alphabetized list: `if (strcmp(name1, name2) == 0) ...` | const char *s1<br>const char *s2 | int |
| strncmp | Compares the first n characters of s1 and s2 returning positive, zero, and negative values as does strcmp: `if (strncmp(n1, n2, 12) == 0) ...` | const char *s1<br>const char *s2<br>size_t† n | int |
| strlen | Returns the number of characters in s, not counting the terminating null: `strlen("What")` returns 4. | const char *s | size_t |

†`size_t` is an unsigned integer

## String Assignment

Function `strcpy` copies the string that is its second argument into its first argument. To carry out the desired assignment shown in our faulty code above, we would write

```
strcpy(one_str, "Test String");
```

Like a call to `scanf` with a `%s` placeholder, a call to `strcpy` can easily overflow the space allocated for the destination variable (`one_str` in the example given). Variable `one_str` has room for up to 19 characters plus the null character. This call to `strcpy`

```
strcpy(one_str, "A very long test string");
```

would overflow `one_str`, storing the final characters `'i'`, `'n'`, `'g'`, and `'\0'` in memory allocated for other variables. The values of these other variables would seem to change spontaneously. On rare occasions, such overflow would generate a run-time error message.

The string library provides another string-copying function named `strncpy` that takes an argument specifying the number of characters to copy (call this number *n*). If the string to be copied (the source string) is shorter than *n* characters, the remaining characters stored are null. For example,

```
strncpy(one_str, "Test string", 20);
```

would give `one_str` the value:

| [0] | | | | [4] | | | | | [9] | | | | | [14] | | | | | [19] |
|---|---|---|---|---|---|---|---|---|---|---|---|---|---|---|---|---|---|---|---|---|
| T | e | s | t | | s | t | r | i | n | g | \0 | \0 | \0 | \0 | \0 | \0 | \0 | \0 | \0 | \0 |

The net effect is the same as the call

```
strcpy(one_str, "Test string");
```

since any characters after the first null are ignored. However, when the source string is longer than *n* characters, only the first *n* characters are copied.

```
strncpy(one_str, "A very long test string", 20);
```

| [0] | | | | [4] | | | | | [9] | | | | | [14] | | | | | [19] |
|---|---|---|---|---|---|---|---|---|---|---|---|---|---|---|---|---|---|---|---|---|
| A | | v | e | r | y | | l | o | n | g | | t | e | s | t | | s | t | r | |

Notice that although this call to strncpy has prevented overflow of destination string one_str, it has not stored a valid string in one_str: There is no terminating '\0'. In general, one can assign as much as will fit of a source string (source) to a destination (dest) of length dest_len by using these two statements:

```
strncpy(dest, source, dest_len - 1);
dest[dest_len - 1] = '\0';
```

Both strcpy and strncpy mimic the assignment operator in that the value they return is the string assigned (specifically, the copy that is in the destination variable). The calling function actually has two ways of referencing the results: It can either use the first argument from the call or use the function result. This characteristic is typical of string-building functions in the string library.

## Substrings

**substring**
a fragment of a longer string

We frequently need to reference a **substring** of a longer character string. For example, we might want to examine the "Cl" in the string "NaCl", or the "30" in the string "Jan. 30, 1996". We have already seen that function strncpy can be used to extract the first *n* characters of a string. Considering how strncpy works will give us insight into how we could also use this function to copy a middle or an ending portion of a string. Assuming that the prototype of strncpy is

```
char *strncpy(char *dest, const char *source, size_t n);
```

Fig. 9.5 depicts the data areas of strncpy and the calling function just before the return from the call to strncpy in this code fragment:

```
char result[10], s1[15] = "Jan. 30, 1996";
strncpy(result, s1, 9);
result[9] = '\0';
```

This figure reminds us that an array reference with no subscript (such as result and s1) actually represents the address of the initial array element. If we wish to use strncpy to extract a middle substring, we must call the function with the address of the first character to copy. For example, given the same value of s1, this code fragment would extract the substring "30"

```
strncpy(result, &s1[5], 2);
result[2] = '\0';
```

**Figure 9.5**
**Execution of**
`strncpy(result, s1, 9);`

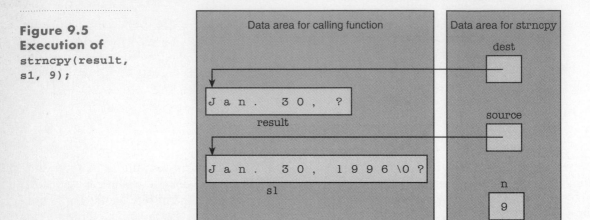

as shown in Fig. 9.6.

To extract the final characters of a source string, we can use `strcpy` as in this call to copy the `1996` at the end of `s1`.

```
strcpy(result, &s1[9]);
```

Function `strcpy` always copies characters beginning with the initial character of a source string and continuing until a `'\0'` has been encountered (and copied).

**Figure 9.6**
**Execution of**
`strncpy(result, &s1[5], 2);`

Calls to string library copy functions that extract three substrings of the string stored in `pres` are shown. Notice the only case in which a programmer need not explicitly assign a `'\0'` to end a substring—when the substring extracted includes the end of the source string. We see this case in the extraction of `"Quincy"`. Of course, if the space allocated for `middle` were insufficient to accommodate the copied substring, `strcpy` would overflow `middle`.

The program in Fig. 9.7 breaks compounds into their elemental components, assuming that each element name begins with a capital letter and that our implementation is using the ASCII character set. For example, this program would break `"NaCl"` into `"Na"` and `"Cl"`. The `if` statement in the `for` loop tests whether the character at position `next` is uppercase. If so, `strncpy` copies into `elem` all characters from the last capital letter (at position `first`) up to (but not including) the capital letter at position `next`.

The statement

```
printf("%s\n", strcpy(elem, &compound[first]));
```

following the loop is used to display the last component. Notice that this final call to `printf` takes advantage of the fact that `strcpy` returns as its value the starting address of the string it has just stored in `elem`. Because this final call to `strcpy` has extracted a complete string (i.e., a string ending in `'\0'`), we can avoid writing two statements

```
strcpy(elem, &compound[first]);
printf("%s\n", elem);
```

by simply calling `strcpy` right at the spot where the value it computes is needed—that is, in the argument list for `printf`.

**Figure 9.7  Program Using strncpy and strcpy Functions to Separate Compounds into Elemental Components**

```
/*
 *  Displays each elemental component of a compound
 */

#include <stdio.h>
#include <string.h>

#define CMP_LEN  30  /* size of string to hold a compound  */
#define ELEM_LEN 10  /* size of string to hold a component */

int
main(void)
{
    char compound[CMP_LEN];  /* string representing a compound */
    char elem[ELEM_LEN];     /* one elemental component        */
    int  first, next;

    /*  Gets data string representing compound                 */
    printf("Enter a compound> ");
    scanf("%s", compound);

    /*  Displays each elemental component.  These are identified
        by an initial capital letter.                          */
    first = 0;
    for  (next = 1;  next < strlen(compound);  ++next)
        if (compound[next] >= 'A'  &&  compound[next] <= 'Z') {
                strncpy(elem, &compound[first], next - first);
                elem[next - first] = '\0';
                printf("%s\n", elem);
                first = next;
        }

    /*  Displays the last component                            */
    printf("%s\n", strcpy(elem, &compound[first]));

    return (0);
}
```

*(continued)*

**Figure 9.7    (continued)**

```
Enter a compound> H2SO4
H2
S
O4
```

Also check carefully the use of CMP_LEN and strlen(compound). In this program, we see again the use of part of an array. As we studied in Chapter 8, in situations like this, the declared size of the array is no longer the effective size once data have been stored in the array. The **string length** as found by the strlen function is the number of characters in the string up to (but not including) the null character. This length may be less or greater than the array's declared size, but the only valid lengths are from zero to one less than the declared size. We call a string of length zero the **empty string**. The type of the value returned by strlen is size_t, an unsigned integer type.

**string length**
in a character array, the number of characters before the first null character

**empty string**
a string of length zero: the first character of the string is the null character

## EXERCISES FOR SECTION 9.2

Self-Check

1. Given the string variables pres, first, and last as defined in Example 9.2, show what would be displayed by this code fragment.

```
strncpy(first, pres, 2);
first[2] = '\0';
printf("%s", first);
printf(" %s", strcpy(last, &pres[7]));

strncpy(first, &pres[7], 2);
first[2] = '\0';
strncpy(last, &pres[14], 2);
last[2] = '\0';
printf(" %s%s\n", first, last);
```

2. Given these declarations,

```
char socsec[12] = "123-45-6789";
char ssnshort[7], ssn1[4], ssn2[3], ssn3[5];
```

write statements to accomplish the following:

a. Store in ssnshort as much of socsec as will fit.
b. Store in ssn1 the first three characters of socsec.

c. Store in `ssn2` the middle two-digit portion of `socsec`.

d. Store in `ssn3` the final four digits of `socsec`.

Be sure your statements store valid strings in each variable.

Programming

1. Write a program to take a product code from Millie's Mail-Order Catalog and separate it into its component parts. A MMOC product code begins with one or more letters identifying the warehouse where the product is stored. Next come the one or more digits that are the product ID. The final field of the string starts with a capital letter and represents qualifiers such as size, color, and so on. For example, ATL1203S14 stands for product 1203, size 14, in the Atlanta warehouse. Write a program that takes a code, finds the position of the first digit and of the first letter after the digits, and uses `strcpy` and `strncpy` to display a report such as the following:

```
Warehouse:  ATL
Product:    1203
Qualifiers: S14
```

2. Complete function `trim_blanks` whose purpose is to take a single string input parameter (`to_trim`) and return a copy of the string with leading and trailing blanks removed. Use `strncpy` in `trim_blanks`.

a_string (before)

n_string (after the call: trim_blanks(n_string, a_string);)

```
char *
trim_blanks(char       *trimmed, /* output */
            const char *to_trim) /* input  */
{

    /* Find subscript of first nonblank in to_trim */

    /* Find subscript of last nonblank in to_trim  */

    /* Use strncpy to store trimmed string in trimmed */

}
```

# 9.3 LONGER STRINGS: CONCATENATION AND WHOLE-LINE INPUT

**concatenation**
joining of two strings

In this section we will study two library functions that let us join (**concatenate**) two strings to form a longer string. We also present functions that allow us to scan a full line of character data from the keyboard or from a file.

## Concatenation

String library functions `strcat` and `strncat` modify their first string argument by adding all or part of their second string argument at the end of the first argument. Both functions assume that sufficient space is allocated for the first argument to allow addition of the extra characters.

**EXAMPLE 9.4**

Consider this code fragment:

```
#define STRSIZ 15
char f1[STRSIZ] = "John ", f2[STRSIZ] = "Jacqueline ",
     last[STRSIZ] = "Kennedy";

strcat(f1, last);
strcat(f2, last);        /* invalid overflow of f2 */
```

The first call to `strcat` copies the string `"Kennedy"` at the end of `f1`, creating the string `"John Kennedy"` which has 12 characters plus the null character, a string that fits in the 15-character array `f1`. However, the second call to `strcat` creates the 19-character (including `'\0'`) string `"Jacqueline Kennedy"`, a string that overflows `f2` and could have the side effect of changing `last` if `last` is allocated immediately after `f2`. As an alternative to the second call to `strcat`, we could write

```
strncat(f2, last, 3);
f2[STRSIZ - 1] = '\0';
```

These statements add onto `"Jacqueline "` the portion of `"Kennedy"` that will fit at the end of `f2` without overflow, creating the string `"Jacqueline Ken"`. Just as `strcpy` always copies a complete string ended by a null character, so `strcat` always joins a complete string at the end of its first argument. In contrast, function `strncat`, like function `strncpy`, builds a string ending in `'\0'` only if there is a null character among the *n* characters copied.

When writing a string-manipulating program, one usually does not know in advance the sizes of the strings used as data. Fortunately, the string library provides function `strlen`, which returns the length of the value of its string argument, not counting the `'\0'` character. For example, this code fragment displays the numbers 8 and 16 followed by the phrase `Jupiter Symphony`.

```
#define STRSIZ 20

char s1[STRSIZ] = "Jupiter ",
     s2[STRSIZ] = "Symphony";
printf("%d %d\n", strlen(s1), strlen(strcat(s1, s2)));
printf("%s\n", s1);
```

Notice that the blank at the end of the initial value of `s1` is counted in `s1`'s length. Also take note that the call to `strcat` modifies the value of `s1` even when embedded in other function calls. Both `strcat` and `strncat` return as the function value the modified first argument. If `s1` and `s2` are both character strings declared to hold `STRSIZ` characters, the following decision statement would concatenate the full strings, if possible without overflow, and would concatenate only as much of the second string as would fit otherwise.

```
if (strlen(s1) + strlen(s2) < STRSIZ) {
    strcat(s1, s2);
} else {
    strncat(s1, s2, STRSIZ - strlen(s1) - 1);
    s1[STRSIZ - 1] = '\0';
}
```

The condition correctly verifies that the sum of the lengths of `s1` and `s2` is strictly *less than* `STRSIZ`; if the sum *equaled* `STRSIZ`, then the `'\0'` that `strcat` places at the end of its result would overflow `s1`.

You can see from our examples of the use of `strcpy`, `strncpy`, `strcat`, and `strncat` that there are two critical questions that must always be in the mind of a C programmer who is manipulating strings:

- Is there enough space in the output parameter for the entire string being created?
- Does the created string end in `'\0'`?

## Distinction between Characters and Strings

When using `strcat`, one may be tempted to supply a single character as one of the two strings to join. A type `char` value is *not* a valid argument for a function with a corresponding parameter of type `char *`. Note the difference internally between the representations of the character `'Q'` and the string `"Q"`.

character `'Q'`         string `"Q"` (represented by its initial address)

If you wish to add a single character at the end of a string, you should view the string as an array and use assignment to subscripted elements for access. Be sure to include the null character at the end of the string.

## Scanning a Full Line

Although blanks are natural separators to place between numeric data values, viewing them as delimiters (as do functions `scanf` and `fscanf`) when processing strings may not make sense since a blank is a perfectly valid character element of a string. For interactive input of one complete line of data, the stdio library provides the function `gets`. Consider this code fragment:

```
char line[80];
printf("Type in a line of data.\n"> ");
```

If the user responds to the prompt as follows,

```
Type in a line of data.
> Here is a short sentence.
```

the value stored in `line` would be

```
Here is a short sentence.\0...
```

The `\n` character representing the <return> or <enter> key pressed at the end of the sentence is *not* stored. Like `scanf`, `gets` can overflow its string argument if the user enters a longer data line than will fit.

The stdio library's file version of `gets`, `fgets`, behaves somewhat differently. Function `fgets` takes three arguments—the output parameter string, a maximum number of characters to store ($n$), and the file pointer to the data source. Function `fgets` will never store more than $n - 1$ characters from the data file, and the final character stored will always be `'\0'`. However, the next to last character may or may not be `'\n'`. If `fgets` has room to store the entire line of data, it will include `'\n'` before `'\0'`. If the line is truncated, no `'\n'` is stored. Like other string-building functions we have studied, `fgets` stores the string created in its first argument and returns this string argument (i.e., its address) as its value. When a call to fgets encounters the end of file, the value returned is the address 0, which is considered the *null pointer*. Figure 9.8 shows a program that scans a data file one line at a time and creates a new double-spaced version with the lines numbered.

## Figure 9.8  Demonstration of Whole-Line Input

```
/*
 *  Numbers and double spaces lines of a document. Lines longer than
 *  LINE_LEN - 1 characters are split on two lines.
 */

#include <stdio.h>
#include <string.h>

#define LINE_LEN 80
#define NAME_LEN 40

int
main(void)
{
      char line[LINE_LEN], inname[NAME_LEN], outname[NAME_LEN];
      FILE *inp, *outp;
      char *status;
      int i = 0;

      printf("Name of input file> ");
      scanf("%s", inname);
      printf("Name of output file> ");
      scanf("%s", outname);

      inp = fopen(inname, "r");
      outp = fopen(outname, "w");

      for  (status = fgets(line, LINE_LEN, inp);
            status != 0;
            status = fgets(line, LINE_LEN, inp)) {
         if (line[strlen(line) - 1] == '\n')
               line[strlen(line) - 1] = '\0';
         fprintf(outp, "%3d>> %s\n\n", ++i, line);
      }
```

*(continued)*

**Figure 9.8**   *(continued)*

```
        return (0);
}
```

File used as input

In the early 1960s, designers and implementers of operating
systems were faced with a significant dilemma. As people's
expectations of modern operating systems escalated, so did
the complexity of the systems themselves. Like other
programmers solving difficult problems, the systems
programmers desperately needed the readability and
modularity of a powerful high-level programming language.

Output file

1>> In the early 1960s, designers and implementers of operating

2>> systems were faced with a significant dilemma. As people's

3>> expectations of modern operating systems escalated, so did

4>> the complexity of the systems themselves. Like other

5>> programmers solving difficult problems, the systems

6>> programmers desperately needed the readability and

7>> modularity of a powerful high-level programming language.

**EXERCISES FOR
SECTION 9.3**

Self-Check

1. Given the string pres (value is "Adams, John Quincy") and the 40-
   character temporary variables tmp1 and tmp2, what string is displayed by
   the following code fragment?

   ```
   strncpy(tmp1, &pres[7], 4);
   tmp1[4] = '\0';
   strcat(tmp1, " ");
   strncpy(tmp2, pres, 5);
   tmp2[5] = '\0';
   printf("%s\n", strcat(tmp1, tmp2));
   ```

2. There is an error in the last line of the following code fragment. What is the error? Why is it wrong? How would you correctly achieve the intent of this call?

```
strcpy(tmp1, &pres[12]);
strcat(tmp1, " ");
strcat(tmp1, pres[7]);
```

Programming

1. Write a function `bracket_by_len` that takes a word as an input argument and returns the word bracketed to indicate its length. Words less than 5 characters long are bracketed with << >>, words 5 to 10 letters long are bracketed with (* *), and words over 10 characters long are bracketed with /+ +/. Your function should require the calling function to provide as the first argument, space for the result, and as the third argument, the amount of space available. Consider the expected results of these calls to the function.

```
bracket_by_len(tmp, "insufficiently", 20)        →
        "/+insufficiently+/"
bracket_by_len(tmp, "the", 20)           →        "<<the>>"
```

# 9.4 STRING COMPARISON

In earlier chapters, we studied the fact that characters are represented by numeric codes, and we used relational and equality operators to compare characters. For example, the conditions

```
crsr_or_frgt == 'C'
```

and

```
ch1 < ch2
```

were used to test character variables in decision statements. Unfortunately, these operators cannot be used for comparison of strings because of C's representation of strings as arrays.

Because an array name used with no subscript represents the address of the initial array element, if `str1` and `str2` are string variables, the condition

```
str1 < str2
```

is *not* checking whether `str1` precedes `str2` alphabetically. However, the comparison *is* legal, for it determines whether the place in memory where storage of `str1` begins precedes the place in memory where `str2` begins.

The standard string library provides the `int` function `strcmp` for comparison of two strings that we will refer to as `str1` and `str2`. Function `strcmp` separates its argument pairs into three categories as shown in Table 9.2.

In this table, we are using the expression "less than" as a string generalization of the "less than" comparison of characters. We have seen that for character variables `ch1` and `ch2`, `ch1 < ch2` is true if the numeric character code value of `ch1` is less than the code in `ch2`. ANSI C extends this concept to strings by stating the following two conditions to define "less than."

1. If the first n characters of `str1` and `str2` match and `str1[n]`, `str2[n]` are the first nonmatching corresponding characters, `str1` is less than `str2` if `str1[n] < str2[n]`.

```
str1 t h r i l l          str1 e n e r g y
str2 t h r o w            str2 f o r c e
            *                    *
First 3 letters match.    First 0 letters match.
str1[3] < str2[3]         str1[0] < str2[0]
   'i' < 'o'                 'e' < 'f'
```

2. If `str1` is shorter than `str2` and all the characters of `str1` match the corresponding characters of `str2`, `str1` is less than `str2`.

```
str1  j o y
str2  j o y o u s
```

**Table 9.2   Possible Results of strcmp(str1, str2)**

| Relationship | Value Returned | Example |
| --- | --- | --- |
| `str1` is less than `str2` | negative integer | `str1` is `"marigold"` `str2` is `"tulip"` |
| `str1` equals `str2` | zero | `str1` and `str2` are both `"end"` |
| `str1` is greater than `str2` | positive integer | `str1` is `"shrimp"` `str2` is `"crab"` |

The string library also provides an analogous function strncmp that bases its comparison on only the first *n* characters of the two strings, where *n* is the third argument. For example, if str1 is "joyful" and str2 is "joyous", the function calls strncmp(str1, str2, 1), strncmp(str1, str2, 2), and strncmp(str1, str2, 3) all return the value 0 because "j" matches "j", "jo" matches "jo", and "joy" matches "joy". However, strncmp(str1, str2, 4) would return a negative integer, indicating that "joyf" precedes "joyo" alphabetically.

**EXAMPLE 9.5** String comparisons are essential when alphabetizing a list. To alphabetize a list of words made up of either all uppercase or all lowercase letters, we could use the selection sort algorithm we developed in Section 8.6. Figure 9.9 compares the numeric and string versions of code that compares list elements in the search for the index of the smallest (or alphabetically first). It also shows the numeric and string versions of a code fragment that exchanges two array elements. In the string versions we see the use of the string library functions strcmp and strcpy. The string exchange code assumes that temp is a local string variable with sufficient space to hold a copy of any string in list.

**Figure 9.9   Numeric and String Versions of Portions of Selection Sort That Compare and Exchange Elements**

........................................................................................

*Comparison* (in function that finds index of "smallest" remaining element)

| Numeric | String |
|---|---|
| `if (list[i] < list[first])` | `if (strcmp(list[i], list[first]) < 0)` |
| `    first = i;` | `        first = i;` |

*Exchange of elements*

```
temp = list[index_of_min];        strcpy(temp, list[index_of_min]);
list[index_of_min] =              strcpy(list[index_of_min], list[fill]);
             list[fill];          strcpy(list[fill], temp);
list[fill] = temp;
```

_____

**EXAMPLE 9.6** When we process a list of string data interactively, we often do not know in advance how much data will be entered. In this situation, we can use a sentinel-controlled loop, prompting the user to type in the sentinel value when entry of the data is complete. Figure 9.10 outlines such a loop, using strcmp to check for entry of the sentinel (represented by the constant macro SENT).

**Figure 9.10    Sentinel-Controlled Loop for String Input**

```
printf("Enter list of words on as many lines as you like.\n");
printf("Separate words by at least one blank.\n");
printf("When done, enter %s to quit.\n", SENT);

for  (scanf("%s", word);
      strcmp(word, SENT) != 0;
      scanf("%s", word)) {
   /* process word */
   ...
}
```

**EXERCISES FOR
SECTION 9.4**

Self-Check

1. Write C code to accomplish each of the following goals.
   a. Write a message indicating whether name1 and name2 match.
   b. Store in the string variable word either the value of w1 or of w2. Choose the value that comes first alphabetically.
   c. Store in mtch matching initial portions of s1 and s2. For example, if s1 is "placozoa" and s2 is "placement", mtch becomes "plac". If s1 is "joy" and s2 is "sorrow", mtch becomes the empty string.

Programming

1. Write the string selection sort function described in Example 9.5.

# 9.5  ARRAYS OF POINTERS

In Section 9.4, we discussed how we might modify our numeric selection sort code to create a program that would alphabetize a list of strings composed of uppercase or lowercase letters. Let's look closely at the code that exchanges two strings in Fig. 9.11.

**Figure 9.11    Exchanging String Elements of an Array**

```
strcpy(temp, list[index_of_min]);
strcpy(list[index_of_min], list[fill]);
strcpy(list[fill], temp);
```

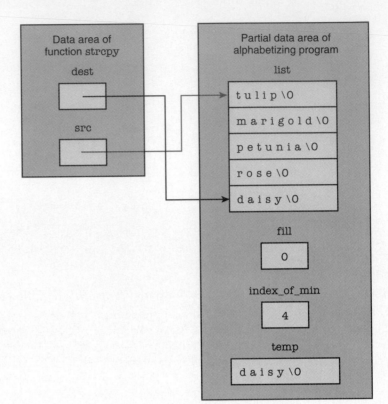

**Figure 9.12
Executing**
`strcpy (list
[index_of_min],
list[fill]);`

Figure 9.12 pictures the data area of strcpy and the data area of the calling function as the second call to strcpy begins. This figure reminds us that C represents every array by its starting address. Since each element of list is a reference to an array of characters, it is passed to a function as a pointer, that is, as the address of the array's element 0. When we consider sorting a list of strings, we see a lot of copying of characters from one memory cell to another. We have three operations that copy an entire string for every exchange that the sort requires, and when the sort is complete, our original list is lost.

In fact, C's use of pointers to represent arrays presents us with an opportunity to develop an alternate approach to our sorting problem. Study the two arrays in Fig. 9.13.

Listing the values of the elements of alphap

| | | |
|---|---|---|
| alphap[0] | address of | "daisy" |
| alphap[1] | address of | "marigold" |
| alphap[2] | address of | "petunia" |
| alphap[3] | address of | "rose" |
| alphap[4] | address of | "tulip" |

**Figure 9.13
An Array
of Pointers**

alphap                                    original

| | | |
|---|---|
| | tulip \0 |
| | marigold \0 |
| | petunia \0 |
| | rose \0 |
| | daisy \0 |

calls to our attention that daisy, marigold, petunia, rose, tulip form an alphabetized list. Therefore, if we were to execute this loop,

```
for  (i = 0;  i < 5;  ++i)
    printf("%s\n", alphap[i]);
```

we would see displayed the contents of original in alphabetical order, just as if we had copied the strings into a new array and sorted them. When printf sees a %s specifier, it *always* expects to receive the starting address of a string as the corresponding input argument, so alphap[i] is just as legitimate an argument as original[i].

How would we declare the array of pointers alphap? Each element is the address of a character string, and there are five elements, so the appropriate declaration is

```
char *alphap[5];
```

In our next example, we explore how to use an array of pointers to maintain two orderings of a list of strings while keeping only one copy of each string.

**EXAMPLE 9.7**  The Open School admits children to its kindergarten in the order in which they apply. However, most of the staff's use of the list of applicants is made easier if the list is alphabetized. The program in Fig. 9.14 takes an input list of names reflecting the order in which applications were received and creates an array of pointers through which the list can be accessed in alphabetical order.

The array of pointers is initialized by assigning to each element the starting address of one of the strings in the applicants array. Then a selection sort is applied to the array of pointers. Although strcmp looks at the actual strings whose starting addresses are in the array of pointers, the element exchange code moves only the pointers.

**Figure 9.14    Two Orderings of One List Using an Array of Pointers**

```
/*
 *  Maintains two orderings of a list of applicants:  the original
 *  ordering of the data, and an alphabetical ordering accessed through an
 *  array of pointers.
 */

#include <stdio.h>
#define STRSIZ 30  /*  maximum string length */
#define MAXAPP 50  /*  maximum number of applications accepted */

int alpha_first(char *list[], int min_sub, int max_sub);
void select_sort_str(char *list[], int n);

int
main(void)
{
    char   applicants[MAXAPP][STRSIZ]; /* list of applicants in the
                                          order in which they applied  */
    char *alpha[MAXAPP];               /* list of pointers to
                                          applicants                    */
    int    num_app,                    /* actual number of applicants   */
           i;
    char   one_char;

    /*  Gets applicant list                                             */
    printf("Enter number of applicants (0 . . %d)\n> ", MAXAPP);
    scanf("%d", &num_app);
    do    /* skips rest of line after number */
        scanf("%c", &one_char);
    while (one_char != '\n');

    printf("Enter names of applicants on separate lines\n");
    printf("in the order in which they applied\n");
    for  (i = 0;  i < num_app; ++i)
        gets(applicants[i]);

    /*  Fills array of pointers and sorts                               */
    for  (i = 0;  i < num_app;  ++i)
        alpha[i] = applicants[i];  /* copies ONLY address */
    select_sort_str(alpha, num_app);
```

*(continued)*

**Figure 9.14**    *(continued)*

```
        /*  Displays both lists                                                    */
        printf("\n\n%-30s%5c%-30s\n\n", "Application Order", ' ',
              "Alphabetical Order");
        for  (i = 0;  i < num_app;  ++i)
            printf("%-30s%5c%-30s\n", applicants[i], ' ', alpha[i]);


        return(0);
}


/*
 *  Finds the index of the string that comes first alphabetically in
 *  elements min_sub..max_sub of list
 *  Pre:  list[min_sub] through list[max_sub] are of uniform case;
 *        max_sub >= min_sub
 */
int
alpha_first(char *list[],       /* input - array of pointers to strings      */
            int    min_sub,     /* input - minimum and maximum subscripts    */
            int    max_sub)     /*   of portion of list to consider          */
{
    int first, i;

    first = min_sub;
    for  (i = min_sub + 1;  i <= max_sub;  ++i)
        if (strcmp(list[i], list[first]) < 0)
            first = i;

    return (first);
}


/*
 *  Orders the pointers in array list so they access strings
 *  in alphabetical order
 *  Pre:  first n elements of list reference strings of uniform case;
 *        n >= 0
 */
```

*(continued)*

**Figure 9.14** *(continued)*

```
void
select_sort_str(char *list[], /* input/output - array of pointers being
                                  ordered to access strings alphabetically */
             int   n)       /* input - number of elements to sort        */
{
     int   fill,            /* index of element to contain next string in order */
           index_of_min; /* index of next string in order */
     char *temp;

     for  (fill = 0;  fill < n - 1;  ++fill) {
          index_of_min = alpha_first(list, fill, n - 1);

          if (index_of_min != fill) {
                  temp = list[index_of_min];
                  list[index_of_min] = list[fill];
                  list[fill] = temp;
          }
     }
}

Enter number of applicants (0 . . 50)
> 5
Enter names of applicants on separate lines
in the order in which they applied
SADDLER, MARGARET
INGRAM, RICHARD
FAATZ, SUSAN
GONZALES, LORI
KEITH, CHARLES
```

Application Order                    Alphabetical Order

SADDLER, MARGARET                    FAATZ, SUSAN
INGRAM, RICHARD                      GONZALES, LORI
FAATZ, SUSAN                         INGRAM, RICHARD
GONZALES, LORI                       KEITH, CHARLES
KEITH, CHARLES                       SADDLER, MARGARET

---

Using an array of pointers to represent a second or third or fourth ordering
of a list of strings has several benefits. First, a pointer (an integer address)
requires less storage space than a full copy of a character string. Second, our

sorting function executes faster when it copies only pointers and not complete arrays of characters. Finally, because the strings themselves are stored only once, a spelling correction made in the original list would automatically be reflected in the other orderings as well.

### Arrays of String Constants

C also permits the use of an array of pointers to represent a list of string constants. Two alternatives for representing the list of month names we saw in Section 9.1 follow.

```
char month[12][10] = {"January", "February", "March", "April",
                      "May", "June", "July","August",
                      "September", "October", "November",
                      "December"};
char *month[12] = {"January", "February", "March", "April",
                   "May", "June", "July", "August",
                   "September", "October", "November",
                   "December"};
```

**EXERCISES FOR SECTION 9.5**

Actually, the number of rows (12) is optional in both of these declarations since the initialization list also implies this value.

#### Self-Check

1. Write two prototypes for a function that orders a list of strings according to string length—shortest to longest. In the first, the function should expect an input/output argument that is a two-dimensional array of characters in which strings have at most STRSIZ characters. In the second, the function should expect an input/output argument that is an array of pointers.
2. Consider the following valid call to printf. Is strs a two-dimensional array of characters or an array of pointers to strings?

   ```
   printf("%s\n", strs[4]);
   ```

#### Programming

1. Write the function described in Exercise 1 using an array of pointers.

## 9.6 CHARACTER OPERATIONS

When we develop programs that involve string processing, often we must work with the individual characters that make up the string. C provides character input/output routines as part of the stdio library, and an extensive collection of facilities for character analysis and conversion is available in the library we #include as <ctype.h>.

## Character Input/Output

The stdio library includes a routine named getchar that is used to get the next character from the standard input source, the same input source that scanf uses. Unlike scanf, getchar does not expect the calling module to pass as an argument the address of a variable in which to store the input character. Rather, getchar takes no arguments and returns the character as its result. Either of the following two expressions can be used to store the next available input character in ch.

```
scanf("%c", &ch)                 ch = getchar()
```

There is, however, a difference between the two fragments, because the *values* of the expressions themselves are different. You will recall that scanf returns as its value an integer representing the number of values it took from the input stream for storage through its output parameters. When scanf encounters the end of the input file, it returns the value associated with EOF. In the expression that calls getchar, we have an assignment operator, so the value of the expression is the value assigned, namely the character that getchar found in standard input. What if there were no characters for getchar to take? What if getchar came across the end of the data? When we look up a full description of the getchar facility, we discover that the type of the value it returns is not char but int. We have already seen that in a computer, characters are represented by integer codes, and in Chapter 7 we used character codes that we cast as type int as the initial and ending values of a type int loop control variable.

Although character codes are, in fact, integers, in most C implementations the char data type is allotted only enough space to store the range of integers actually used by the implementation's character set. This range does not include the negative value associated with the name EOF. The data type int must be able to represent a much larger range of integers that includes both the full range of character codes and the EOF value. For this reason, we use a type int variable to store the result of a call to getchar, at least until we verify that getchar did not return EOF.

To get a single character from a file, use the facility getc. The call

```
getc(inp)
```

is comparable to a call to getchar, except that the character returned is obtained from the file accessed by file pointer inp.

**EXAMPLE 9.8**

In Fig. 9.15 we write a scanline function that uses getchar. Like the library function gets, our scanline function takes as its first argument the

**Figure 9.15    Implementation of scanline Function Using getchar**

```
/*
 *  Gets one line of data from standard input.  Returns an empty string on
 *  end of file.  If data line will not fit in allotted space, stores
 *  portion that does fit and discards rest of input line.
 */
char *
scanline(char *dest,      /* output - destination string               */
         int  dest_len) /* input  - space available in dest           */
{
      int i, ch;
      /*  Gets next line one character at a time.                      */
      i = 0;
      for  (ch = getchar();
            ch != '\n'  &&  ch != EOF   &&  i < dest_len - 1;
            ch = getchar())
          dest[i++] = ch;
      dest[i] = '\0';

      /*  Discards any characters that remain on input line            */
      while (ch != '\n'  &&  ch != EOF)
          ch = getchar();

      return (dest);
}
```

string variable in which to store the input line. Unlike gets, scanline also takes a second argument indicating the amount of space available. It stores in the output argument either the full input line or as much as will fit. Then it discards any characters remaining on the line until '\n' or EOF is encountered. We could declare scanline's first parameter as

char dest[]

since dest is an array of characters. We have chosen the notation shown so as to be consistent with declarations in the C standard string library.

The standard library's single-character output facilities are putchar (for display on the standard output device) and putc (for files). Both take as their first argument a type int character code. Because type char can always be converted to type int with no loss of information, we frequently call putchar and putc with arguments of type char:

putchar('a');                          putc('a', outp);

## Character Analysis and Conversion

In many string-processing applications, we need to know if a character belongs to a particular subset of the overall character set. Is this character a letter? a digit? a punctuation mark? The library we #include as <ctype.h> defines facilities for answering questions like these and also provides routines to do common character conversions like uppercase to lowercase or lowercase to uppercase. Table 9.3 lists a number of these routines; each takes a single type int argument representing a character code. The *classification* routines (those whose names begin with "is") return a nonzero value (not necessarily 1) if the condition checked is true. The example given for the isspace routine is a loop that can be used to advance to the next nonblank input character.

**Table 9.3** **Character Classification and Conversion Facilities in ctype Library**

| Facility | Checks | Example |
|---|---|---|
| isalpha | if argument is a letter of the alphabet | `if (isalpha(ch))`<br>`    printf("%c is a letter\n", ch);` |
| isdigit | if argument is one of the ten decimal digits | `dec_digit = isdigit(ch);` |
| islower (isupper) | if argument is a lowercase (or uppercase) letter of the alphabet | `if (islower(fst_let)) {`<br>`    printf("\nError: sentence ");`<br>`    printf("should begin with a ");`<br>`    printf("capital letter.\n");`<br>`}` |
| ispunct | if argument is a punctuation character, that is, a noncontrol character that is not a space, a letter of the alphabet, or a digit | `if (ispunct(ch))`<br>`    printf("Punctuation mark: %c\n",`<br>`            ch);` |
| isspace | if argument is a whitespace character such as a space, a newline, or a tab | `c = getchar();`<br>`while (isspace(c)  &&  c != EOF)`<br>`    c = getchar();` |

| Facility | Converts | Example |
|---|---|---|
| tolower (toupper) | its lowercase (or uppercase) letter argument to the uppercase (or lowercase) equivalent and returns this equivalent as the value of the call | `if (islower(ch))`<br>`    printf("Capital %c = %c\n",`<br>`            ch, toupper(ch));` |

**EXAMPLE 9.9** When we alphabetize a list of strings, we must frequently deal with words containing a mixture of uppercase and lowercase letters. In this situation, we cannot rely on `strcmp` to give useful results. This call to `strcmp`

```
strcmp("Ziegler", "aardvark")
```

will return a negative value indicating that `"Ziegler"` is less than `"aard-vark"` if our system is using the ASCII character codes, since all capital letters have lower ASCII character codes than the lowercase letters. On computers that use the EBCDIC character set, we also have difficulty handling a mixture of uppercase and lowercase letters because all *lowercase* letters have smaller character codes than uppercase letters (see Appendix A). Figure 9.16 shows a function `string_greater` that could be used to find out-of-order elements when alphabetizing a list of strings in a situation where the case of the letters should be ignored. The function converts each of its arguments to all capital letters using `string_toupper` before comparing them. Since `str1` and `str2` are strictly input parameters of `string_greater`, their values must not be changed. However, `string_toupper` does change its parameter, so we first make copies of `str1` and `str2` in `s1` and `s2` and then send these copies to `string_toupper`. ◀

**Figure 9.16  String Function for a Greater-Than Operator That Ignores Case**

```
#include <string.h>
#include <ctype.h>

#define STRSIZ 80

/*
 *  Converts the lowercase letters of its string argument to uppercase
 *  leaving other characters unchanged.
 */
char *
string_toupper(char *str) /* input/output - string whose lowercase
                             letters are to be replaced by uppercase   */
{
      int i;
```

*(continued)*

**Figure 9.16**   *(continued)*

```
      for  (i = 0;  i < strlen(str);  ++i)
          if (islower(str[i]))
                str[i] = toupper(str[i]);

      return (str);
}

/*
 *  Compares two strings of up to STRSIZ characters ignoring the case of
 *  the letters.  Returns the value 1 if str1 should follow str2 in an
 *  alphabetized list; otherwise returns 0
 */
int
string_greater(const char *str1,   /* input -                         */
              const char *str2)   /*    strings to compare           */
{
      char s1[STRSIZ], s2[STRSIZ];

      /*  Copies str1 and str2 so string_toupper can modify copies       */
      strcpy(s1, str1);
      strcpy(s2, str2);

      return (strcmp(string_toupper(s1), string_toupper(s2)) > 0);
}
```

**EXERCISES FOR SECTION 9.6**

Self-Check

1. What is wrong with the following statement? How would you rewrite it to accomplish its apparent purpose?

```
if (isupper(strncpy(tmp, str, 1)))
    printf("%s begins with a capital letter\n", str);
```

Programming

1. Write a function scanstring that works basically like scanf with a %s placeholder—that is, it skips leading whitespace and then copies a string up to the next whitespace character—except that it uses getchar and takes an extra argument stating the amount of space available in the first argument. Unlike scanf, function scanstring should prevent overflow of its string argument.

2. Write a batch program that takes and echoes input data one character at a time until `EOF` is encountered and then prints a summary such as

```
The 14 lines of text processed contained 20 capital
letters, 607 lowercase letters, and 32 punctuation
marks.
```

# 9.7 STRING-TO-NUMBER AND NUMBER-TO-STRING CONVERSIONS

Some of the most common operations in a computer program are the conversion of a string like `"3.14159"` to the type `double` numeric value it represents and the conversion of a number like `-36` from its internal representation in computer memory to the three-character string `"-36"` that is our usual picture of this number. Such conversions are constantly being carried out by the library functions `scanf` and `printf`. Table 9.4 and Table 9.5 review some of the format string placeholders that we have used in earlier chapters to guide the conversion process. The characters that were scanned are in color. Table 9.5 also presents some new placeholders. The last example in Table 9.5 shows the use of a maximum field width. The `%3.3s` placeholder indicates output of a string using a minimum field width of 3 (`3.3`) and a maximum field width of 3 (`3.3`). As a result, only the first three characters of the string are printed.

**Table 9.4   Review of Use of scanf**

| Declaration | Statement | Data (▮ Means Blank) | Value Stored |
|---|---|---|---|
| char t | scanf("%c", &t); | ▮g | ▮ |
|  |  | \n | \n |
|  |  | A | A |
| int n | scanf("%d", &n); | ▮32▮ | 32 |
|  |  | ▮▮-8.6 | -8 |
|  |  | ▮+19▮ | 19 |
| double x | scanf("%lf", &x); | ▮▮▮4.32▮ | 4.32 |
|  |  | ▮-8▮ | -8.0 |
|  |  | ▮1.76e-3▮ | .00176 |
| char str[10] | scanf("%s", str); | ▮▮hello\n | hello\0 |
|  |  | overlengthy▮ | overlengthy\0 |
|  |  |  | (overruns length of str) |

**Table 9.5   Placeholders Used with printf**

| Value | Placeholder | Output (▊ Means Blank) |
|---|---|---|
| 'a' | %c | a |
|  | %3c | ▊▊a |
|  | %-3c | a▊▊ |
| -10 | %d | -10 |
|  | %2d | -10 |
|  | %4d | ▊-10 |
|  | %-5d | -10▊▊ |
| 49.76 | %.3f | 49.760 |
|  | %.1f | 49.8 |
|  | %10.2f | ▊▊▊▊▊49.76 |
|  | %10.3e | ▊4.976e+01 |
| "fantastic" | %s | fantastic |
|  | %6s | fantastic |
|  | %12s | ▊▊▊fantastic |
|  | %-12s | fantastic▊▊▊ |
|  | %3.3s | fan |

The functions printf and scanf are such powerful string manipulators that sometimes we would like to directly control the strings on which they work. The stdio library gives us this ability through similar functions named sprintf and sscanf. The sprintf function requires space for a string as its first argument. Consider this call to sprintf; assume that s has been declared as char s[100], and the values of type int variables mon, day, and year are as shown.

sprintf(s, "%d/%d/%d", mon, day, year);

Function sprintf substitutes values for placeholders just as printf does, but instead of printing the result, sprintf stores it in the character array accessed by its initial argument.

s

The sscanf function works exactly like scanf except that instead of taking the data values for its output parameters from the standard input device, it takes data from the string that is its first argument. For example, the illustration that follows shows how

```
sscanf(" 85   96.2   hello", "%d%lf%s", &num, &val, word);
```

stores values from the first string.

| num | val | word |
|-----|-----|------|
| 85 | 96.2 | hello \0 |

**EXAMPLE 9.10**  Because `sscanf` is available, we have the option of taking an entire data line as input and verifying that it conforms to the expected format before attempting to convert and store the line's values in memory. For example, if one line of data is expected to contain two nonnegative integers and then a string of up to 15 characters, one could write a validation function that would take the entire data line as an input argument and check the line one character at a time. The validation routine would look for optional whitespace characters followed by a group of digits, more whitespace, another group of digits, more whitespace, and then up to 15 nonwhitespace characters. If the validation function discovered an error, it could print a message and return the position of the character where the error was detected. Otherwise, it could return a negative value. Figure 9.17 shows a program segment that assumes the availability of such a validation function and also of the `scanline` function defined in Fig. 9.15.

**Figure 9.17  Program Segment That Validates Input Line before Storing Data Values**

```c
char data_line[STRSIZ], str[STRSIZ];
int n1, n2, error_mark, i;

scanline(data_line, STRSIZ);
error_mark = validate(data_line);

if (error_mark < 0) {
    /*  Stores in memory values from correct data line    */
    sscanf(data_line, "%d%d%s", &n1, &n2, str);
} else {
    /*  Displays line and marks spot where error detected */
    printf("\n%s\n", data_line);
    for  (i = 0;  i < error_mark;  ++i)
        putchar(' ');
    putchar('/');
}
```

In our next example, we combine the power of sprintf/sscanf with the ability to directly access an array element to produce convenient functions for the conversion of one representation of a date to another.

**EXAMPLE 9.11**  The conversion of a date from a representation including a month name to a list of three numbers (12 January 1941 → 1 12 1941) and the reverse conversion are very common in everyday life. The program in Fig. 9.18 shows functions for both conversions and a driver program to test them. Arrays of pointers to strings are extremely useful for storing the constants needed in this type of conversion. Note that we could change the representation of the date string to use an abbreviation (12 JAN 1941) or a different language (12 janvier 1941) merely by using a different initialization of our array. The conversion from a string including the month name to a group of three numbers involves a search of the list of month names using a function that is a string adaptation of the numeric linear search function we developed in Chapter 8.

**Figure 9.18   Functions That Convert Representations of Dates**

```c
/*
 *  Functions to change the representation of a date from a string containing
 *  day, month name and year to three integers (month day year) and vice versa
 */

#include <stdio.h>
#include <string.h>

#define STRSIZ 40
char *nums_to_string_date(char *date_string, int month, int day,
                          int year, const char *month_names[]);
int search(const char *arr[], const char *target, int n);
void string_date_to_nums(const char *date_string, int *monthp,
                         int *dayp, int *yearp, const char *month_names[]);

/*  Tests date conversion functions                                          */
int
main(void)
{
        char *month_names[12] = {"January", "February", "March", "April", "May",
                                 "June", "July", "August", "September",
                                 "October", "November", "December"};
```

*(continued)*

**Figure 9.18** *(continued)*

```
        int m, y, mon, day, year;
        char date_string[STRSIZ];
        for  (y = 1993;  y < 2010;  y += 10)
            for  (m = 1;  m <= 12;  ++m) {
                printf("%s", nums_to_string_date(date_string,
                                                 m, 15, y, month_names));
                string_date_to_nums(date_string, &mon, &day, &year,
                                    month_names);
                printf(" = %d/%d/%d\n", mon, day, year);
            }

        return (0);
}

/*
 *  Takes integers representing a month, day and year and produces a
 *  string representation of the same date.
 */
char *
nums_to_string_date(char       *date_string,    /* output - string
                                                    representation        */
                    int         month,          /* input  -              */
                    int         day,            /*    representation      */
                    int         year,           /*    as three numbers    */
                    const char *month_names[])   /* input  - string represen-
                                                    tations of months     */
{
    sprintf(date_string, "%d %s %d", day, month_names[month - 1], year);
    return (date_string);
}

#define NOT_FOUND -1    /*  Value returned by search function if target
                            not found                                     */

/*
 *  Searches for target item in first n elements of array arr
 *  Returns index of target or NOT_FOUND
 *  Pre:  target and first n elements of array arr are defined and n>0
 */
```

*(continued)*

**Figure 9.18** *(continued)*

```
int
search(const char *arr[],       /*  array to search                    */
       const char *target,      /*  value searched for                 */
        int        n)           /*  number of array elements to search  */
{
    int i,
        found = 0,      /*  whether or not target has been found */
        where;          /*  index where target found or NOT_FOUND*/

    /*  Compares each element to target                        */
    i = 0;
    while (!found && i < n) {
        if (strcmp(arr[i], target) == 0)
            found = 1;
        else
            ++i;
    }

    /* Returns index of element matching target or NOT_FOUND    */
    if (found)
        where = i;
    else
        where = NOT_FOUND;
    return (where);
}


/*
 *  Converts date represented as a string containing a month name to
 *  three integers representing month, day, and year
 */
void
string_date_to_nums(const char *date_string,    /* input - date to convert */
                    int        *monthp,         /* output - month number */
                    int        *dayp,           /* output - day number   */
                    int        *yearp,          /* output - year number  */
                    const char *month_names[])  /* input - names used in
                                                        date string       */
{
```

*(continued)*

**Figure 9.18    *(continued)***

```
        char mth_nam[STRSIZ];
        int  month_index;

        sscanf(date_string, "%d%s%d", dayp, mth_nam, yearp);

        /*  Finds array index (range 0..11) of month name.           */
        month_index = search(month_names, mth_nam, 12);
        *monthp = month_index + 1;
}

15 January 1993 = 1/15/1993
15 February 1993 = 2/15/1993
.  .  .
15 December 2003 = 12/15/2003
```

This date conversion application is one instance where C's required use of zero as the subscript of an initial array element is rather annoying. If we could have an array with row subscripts 1...12, the conversion from month number to name would be more direct. We have chosen to use a 12-string array and to correct the off-by-one error in the conversion functions. In `nums_to_string_date` we have

```
sprintf(date_string, "%d %s %d", day,
        month_names[month - 1], year);
```

and in `string_date_to_nums` we find the reference

```
*monthp = month_index + 1;
```

⬅

**EXERCISES FOR SECTION 9.7**

Self-Check

1. Consider the following call to `sscanf` from the `string_date_to_nums` function.

   ```
   sscanf(date_string, "%d%s%d", dayp, mth_name, yearp);
   ```

   Why is the address-of operator not applied to any of the arguments?

2. Write a code segment that uses an array of pointers to strings and `sprintf` to convert a type `double` monetary value less than `10.00` to a string for use on a check. For example, `4.83` would be converted to `"Four and 83/100 dollars"`.

Programming

1. Write a type `int` function `strtoint` and a type `double` function `strtodouble` that convert string representations of numbers to their numeric equivalents.

```
strtoint("-8")  →  -8
strtodouble("-75.812")  →  -75.812
```

# 9.8 STRING PROCESSING ILLUSTRATED

You have been using a text editor to create and edit C programs. This is probably a fairly sophisticated program that uses special commands to move the cursor around the screen and to specify edit operations. Although you cannot develop such an editor yet, you can write a less sophisticated one that processes a single line of text.

## Case Study: Text Editor

### PROBLEM

Design and implement a program to perform editing operations on a line of text. Your editor should be able to locate a specified target substring, delete a substring, and insert a substring at a specified location. The editor should expect source strings of less than 80 characters.

### ANALYSIS

The editor's main function must get the source line to edit and then repeatedly scan and process editor commands until it receives the Q (Quit) command. We will allow strings of up to 99 characters, but we will not check for overflow.

### Data Requirements

#### Problem Constant
```
MAX_LEN      100     /* maximum size of a string */
```

#### Problem Inputs
```
char souce[MAX_LEN]      /* source string */
char command             /* edit command */
```

#### Problem Output
```
char source[MAX_LEN]     /* modified source string */
```

**DESIGN**

### Initial Algorithm

1. Scan the string to be edited into source.
2. Get an edit command.
3. while command isn't Q
      4. Perform edit operation.
      5. Get an edit command.

### Refinements and Program Structure

Step 4 is performed by function do_edit. A structure chart for the text editor is shown in Fig. 9.19; the local variables and algorithms for function do_edit follow.

#### Local Variables
```
char str[MAX_LEN]        /* string to find, delete, or
                            insert */
int  index               /* position in source */
```

### Algorithm for do_edit

1. switch command
      'D' : 2. Get the substring to be deleted (str).
           3. Find the position of str in source.
           4. if str is found, delete it.

      'I' : 5. Get the substring to insert (str).
           6. Get position of insertion (index).
           7. Perform insertion of str at index position of source.

**Figure 9.19   Structure Chart for Text Editor Program**

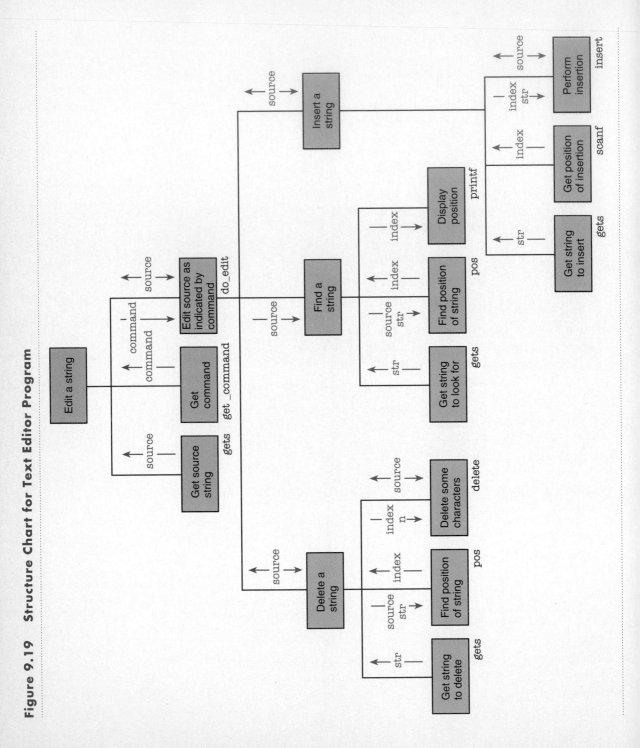

'F': 8. Get the substring to search for (`str`).
9. Find the position of `str` in `source`.
10. Report position.
Otherwise:
11. Display error message.

Function `do_edit` uses a function that finds the position of one string in another (`pos`) for Steps 3 and 9, a function that deletes a certain number of characters from a string (`delete`) for Step 4, and a function that inserts one string in another (`insert`) for step 7.

**◀ IMPLEMENTATION ▶**

Figure 9.20 shows a complete implementation of the text editor and Fig. 9.21 shows a sample run. Read the helper functions `pos`, `insert`, and `delete` carefully as examples of functions that use C string library functions.

**Figure 9.20    Text Editor Program**
......................................................................................................................................................

```
/*
 *   Performs text editing operations on a source string
 */

#include <stdio.h>
#include <string.h>
#include <ctype.h>

#define MAX_LEN    100
#define NOT_FOUND -1

char *delete(char *source, int index, int n);
char *do_edit(char *source, char command);
char  get_command(void);
char *insert(char *source, const char *to_insert, int index);
int   pos(const char *source, const char *to_find);

int
main(void)
{
      char source[MAX_LEN], command;
```

*(continued)*

**Figure 9.20**   *(continued)*

```
    printf("Enter the source string:\n> ");
    gets(source);

    for (command = get_command();
         command != 'Q';
         command = get_command()) {
        do_edit(source, command);
        printf("New source: %s\n\n", source);
    }

    printf("String after editing: %s\n", source);
    return (0);
}


/*
 *  Returns source after deleting n characters beginning with source[index].
 *  If source is too short for full deletion, as many characters are
 *  deleted as possible.
 *  Pre:  All parameters are defined and
 *        strlen(source) - index - n < MAX_LEN
 *  Post:  source is modified and returned
 */
char *
delete(char *source,   /* input/output - string from which to delete part */
       int   index,    /* input - index of first char to delete          */
       int   n)        /* input - number of chars to delete              */
{
    char rest_str[MAX_LEN];   /* copy of source substring following
                                 characters to delete */

    /*  If there are no characters in source following portion to
        delete, delete rest of string */
    if (strlen(source) <= index + n) {
        source[index] = '\0';

    /*  Otherwise, copy the portion following the portion to delete
        and place it in source beginning at the index position        */
    } else {
        strcpy(rest_str, &source[index + n]);
```

*(continued)*

**Figure 9.20** *(continued)*

```
            strcpy(&source[index], rest_str);
      }

      return (source);
}

/*
 *  Performs the edit operation specified by command
 *  Pre:  command and source are defined.
 *  Post: After scanning additional information needed, performs a
 *        deletion (command = 'D') or insertion (command = 'I') or
 *        finds a substring ('F') and displays result; returns
 *        (possibly modified) source.
 */
char *
do_edit(char *source,  /* input/output - string to modify or search */
        char  command) /* input - character indicating operation    */
{
      char str[MAX_LEN];  /* work string */
      int  index;

      switch (command) {
      case 'D':
            printf("String to delete> ");
            gets(str);
            index = pos(source, str);
            if (index == NOT_FOUND)
                  printf("'%s' not found\n", str);
            else
                  delete(source, index, strlen(str));
            break;

      case 'I':
            printf("String to insert> ");
            gets(str);
            printf("Position of insertion> ");
            scanf("%d", &index);
            insert(source, str, index);
            break;
```

*(continued)*

**Figure 9.20** *(continued)*

```
        case 'F':
                printf("String to find> ");
                gets(str);
                index = pos(source, str);
                if (index == NOT_FOUND)
                        printf("'%s' not found\n", str);
                else
                        printf("'%s' found at position %d\n", str, index);
                break;

        default:
                printf("Invalid edit command '%c'\n", command);
        }

        return (source);
}

/*
 * Prompt for and get a character representing an edit command and
 * convert it to uppercase. Return the uppercase character and ignore
 * rest of input line.
 */
char
get_command(void)
{
        char command, ignore;

        printf("Enter D(Delete), I(Insert), F(Find), or Q(Quit)> ");
        scanf(" %c", &command);

        do
            ignore = getchar();
        while (ignore != '\n');

        return (toupper(command));
}

/*
 * Returns source after inserting to_insert at position index of
 * source. If source[index] doesn't exist, adds to_insert at end of
 * source.
```

*(continued)*

**Figure 9.20**    *(continued)*

```
 *  Pre:  all parameters are defined, space available for source is
 *        enough to accommodate insertion, and
 *        strlen(source) - index - n < MAX_LEN
 *  Post: source is modified and returned
 */
char *
insert(char       *source,     /* input/output - target of insertion */
       const char *to_insert, /* input - string to insert           */
       int        index)      /* input - position where to_insert
                                         is to be inserted           */
{
     char rest_str[MAX_LEN]; /* copy of rest of source beginning
                                with source[index] */

     if (strlen(source) <= index) {
          strcat(source, to_insert);
     } else {
          strcpy(rest_str, &source[index]);
          strcpy(&source[index], to_insert);
          strcat(source, rest_str);
     }

     return (source);
}

/*
 *  Returns index of first occurrence of to_find in source or
 *  value of NOT_FOUND if to_find is not in source.
 *  Pre:  both parameters are defined
 */
int
pos(const char *source,   /* input - string in which to look for to_find */
    const char *to_find)  /* input - string to find                      */

{
     int  i = 0, find_len, found = 0, position;
     char substring[MAX_LEN];

     find_len = strlen(to_find);
```

*(continued)*

**Figure 9.20** *(continued)*

```
    while (!found  &&  i <= strlen(source) - find_len) {
        strncpy(substring, &source[i], find_len);
        substring[find_len] = '\0';

        if (strcmp(substring, to_find) == 0)
            found = 1;
        else
            ++i;
    }

    if (found)
        position = i;
    else
        position = NOT_FOUND;

    return (position);
}
```

**Figure 9.21** **Sample Run of Text Editor Program**

```
Enter the source string:
> Internet use is growing rapidly.
Enter D(Delete), I(Insert), F(Find), or Q(Quit)> d
String to delete> growing█
New source: Internet use is rapidly.

Enter D(Delete), I(Insert), F(Find), or Q(Quit)> F
String to find> .
'.' found at position 23
New source: Internet use is rapidly.

Enter D(Delete), I(Insert), F(Find), or Q(Quit)> I
String to insert>  █expanding
Position of insertion> 23
New source: Internet use is rapidly expanding.

Enter D(Delete), I(Insert), F(Find), or Q(Quit)> q
String after editing: Internet use is rapidly expanding.
```

> **TESTING**

Choose test cases that check various boundary conditions as well as middle-of-the-road data. For example, to check the Delete command, try to delete the first few characters of source, the last few, and a substring in the middle of source. Also try a substring that appears more than once to verify that only the first occurrence is deleted. Attempt two impossible deletions, one of a substring that does not resemble any part of source, and one of a substring that matches a part of source except for its last character. Also test insertions at the beginning of source, exactly at the end of source, at a position several characters beyond the end of source, and in the middle of source. Use the Find command to look for all of source, single-letter pieces of source from the beginning, middle, and end, and multiple-character substrings from the beginning, middle and end of the source string. Be sure to look for a substring not present in source, too.

# 9.9 COMMON PROGRAMMING ERRORS

When manipulating string variables, the programmer must use great care in the allocation and management of memory. When we work with numeric values or single characters, we commonly compute a value of interest in a function, storing the result value temporarily in a local variable of the function until it is returned to the calling module using the return statement. One cannot use this approach in string functions, for such functions do not actually return a string *value* in the same way that an int function returns an integer value. Rather a string function returns the *address* of the initial character of a string. If we were to use the same strategy in a string function as we do in many numeric functions, we would build our result string in a local variable and return the address of the new string as the function value. The problem with this approach is that the function's data area is deallocated as soon as the return statement is executed, so it is not valid to access from the calling module the string the function constructed in its own local variable. Figure 9.22 shows a poor rewrite of the scanline function from Fig. 9.15. Rather than requiring the calling function to provide space in which to construct the function result as the earlier scanline did (and as is the practice of the functions in the C string library), this faulty scanline returns a string built in local storage. As a consequence, the string that the printf function tries to print is in a section of memory that neither main nor printf has any legitimate right to access and that may be overwritten with new values at any moment. What makes this type of error particularly grievous is that on some C implementations it will compile and pass unit testing without creating any error in the output.

　To avoid creation of such "time-bomb" functions that do not "blow up" until system integration tests, follow the pattern of the C string library and

**Figure 9.22** **Flawed scanline Returns Address of Deallocated Space**

```
/*
 * Gets one line of data from standard input.  Returns an empty string on end
 * of file.  If data line will not fit in allotted space, stores portion that
 * does fit and discards rest of input line.
 **** Error:  returns address of space that is immediately deallocated.
 */
char *
scanline(void)
{
     char dest[MAX_STR_LEN];
     int  i, ch;

     /*  Get next line one character at a time.                          */
     i = 0;
     for  (ch = getchar();
           ch != '\n'  && ch != EOF  &&  i < MAX_STR_LEN - 1;
           ch = getchar())
         dest[i++] = ch;
     dest[i] = '\0';

     /*  Discard any characters that remain on input line                */
     while (ch != '\n"  &&  ch != EOF)
         ch = getchar();

     return (dest);
}
```

have any string functions you write require the calling module to provide as the
first argument a variable in which to build the string result. Some ANSI C compilers will flag the error illustrated in Fig. 9.22.

A second error that creeps into C programs with string use is the misuse or
neglect of the & operator. The fact that this operator is *not* applied to strings or
to any other whole arrays used as output arguments often leads beginning users
of C to forget that the address-of operator must still be used on simple output
arguments such as variables of type int, char, or double, as well as on
single array elements of these types when used as output arguments. You may
want to review the use of the & on simple variables as shown in Table 6.5.

Another problem that is common with string use is the overflow of character arrays allocated for strings. Since many string library functions just assume

that the calling module has provided adequate space for whatever may need to be stored, calling these functions with inadequate storage causes errors that are really difficult to find. In Fig. 9.4, which is repeated here, we see such a situation.

Execution of scanf("%s%d%s%d", dept, &course_num, days, &time);
on Entry of Invalid Data

Whatever was stored in the cells following array dept has just been overwritten. If that memory was being used for other program variables, their values will appear to change spontaneously.

The scanline function that we wrote as an example protects the calling function from string overflow by requiring an input argument telling how much space is available for the string result. This function takes care to prevent storage of a string that is too long. We encourage you to use protective functions like this in your string programs.

A relatively minor error that can lead to difficult bugs is forgetting that all strings end with the null character. The programmer must remember the null character both when allocating space for a string and when building a string one character at a time.

It is easy to slip and use equality or relational operators when comparing strings or the assignment operator for copying them. Remember to use strcmp or strncmp for comparisons and library functions such as strcpy or strncpy for copying strings.

# CHAPTER REVIEW

1. Strings in C are arrays of characters ended by the null character '\0'.
2. String input is done using scanf and fscanf with %s descriptors for strings separated by whitespace, using gets and fgets for input of whole lines, and using getchar and getc for single character input.
3. String output is done using printf and fprintf with %s descriptors; putchar and putc do single character output.
4. The string library provides functions for string assignment and extraction of substrings (strcpy and strncpy), for string length (strlen), for concatenation (strcat and strncat), and for alphabetic comparison (strcmp and strncmp).

5. The standard I/O library includes functions for string-to-number (`sscanf`) and number-to-string (`sprintf`) conversion.
6. String-building functions typically require the calling module to provide space for the new string as an output parameter and they return the address of this parameter as the function result.
7. String manipulation in C requires the programmer to take great care to avoid overflow of string variables and creation of strings not ending in `'\0'`.
8. Multiple orderings of a list of strings can be maintained by storing the strings once and creating arrays of pointers for additional orderings.
9. The ctype library provides functions for classification and conversion of single characters.

## New C Constructs

| Statement | Effect |
|---|---|
| **Declarations** | |
| `char str[100];` | Allocates space for a string of up to 99 characters plus the null character. |
| `char str[11] = "          ";` | Allocates space for a string of up to 10 characters plus the null and initializes it to all blanks. |
| `char *abbrevs[10];` | Declares an array of 10 pointers to character strings. |
| `const char *arg1`<br>or<br>`const char arg1[]` | Declares a string input parameter. |
| `char *out`<br>or<br>`char out[]` | Declares a string output or input/output parameter. |
| `char names[10][20];` | Allocates space for an array of 10 strings, each of which has up to 19 characters plus the null character. |
| `char *weekdays[] =`<br>`  {"Mon", "Tue", "Wed",`<br>`   "Thu", "Fri"};` | Declares and initializes an array of pointers to five strings. |
| `char list[][20]` | Declares an output or input/output parameter that is an array of strings in which each string has up to 19 characters plus the null. |
| `char *strs[]` | Declares an output or input/output parameter that is an array of pointers to strings. |
| **Calls to I/O and Conversion Functions** | |
| `gets(str1);` | Gets a line of data from the keyboard and stores it as a string in `str1` (without `'\n'`). |
| `c1 = getchar();` | Gets a character from the keyboard and stores its `int` character code in `c1`, or stores EOF in `c1` on end of file. |

## New C Constructs    *(continued)*

| Statement | Effect |
|---|---|

### Calls to I/O and Conversion Functions *(continued)*

```
putchar(c1);
```
Displays character value of c1.

```
sprintf(s, "%d + %d = %d", x,
        y, x + y);
```
If x is 3 and y is 4, builds and returns the string "3 + 4 = 7".

```
sscanf("14.3 -5", "%lf%d",
        &p, &n);
```
Stores 14.3 in p and −5 in n.

### Calls to Character Functions

```
if (islower(c1))
    c1 = toupper(c1);
```
If c1's value is 'q', stores 'Q' in c1.

```
isdigit(c2)
```
Returns 1 (true) if c2 is one of the characters '0', '1', '2', '3', '4', '5', '6', '7', '8', '9'.

### Calls to String Library

```
strlen(a_string)
```
Returns the number of characters in the string a_string up to but not including the null character.

```
strcmp(str1, str2)
```
Returns a negative integer if str1 precedes str2 alphabetically, a positive integer if str2 precedes str1, and zero if str1 and str2 are equal.

```
strncmp(str1, str2, 4)
```
Compares first 4 characters of str1 to first 4 characters of str2, returning a negative integer if the str1 substring precedes the str2 substring alphabetically, a positive integer if it follows, and zero if the substrings are equal.

```
strcpy(str_result, str_src)
```
Copies all the characters of str_src including the null character into str_result. Assumption is that str_result has enough room for all these characters.

```
strncpy (str_result,
        str_src, 10)
```
Copies first 10 characters of str_src into str_result. Assumption is that str_result has room for all ten. Characters stored include '\0' *only* if strlen(str_src) < 10.

```
strcat(str_result, new)
```
Concatenates the complete value of new on the end of str_result. Assumption is that str_result has room enough for its own current value plus the added characters of new.

```
strncat(str_result, new, 10)
```
Concatenates the value of new at the end of str_result providing new's length (not counting the null character) is less than or equal to 10. Otherwise, it concatenates the first 10 characters of new on the end of str_result. It always adds a null character at the end, so at most 11 characters are added to str_result.

## QUICK-CHECK EXERCISES

1. For each of the following functions, explain its purpose, the type(s) of its output parameters, and the type(s) of its input parameter(s). Also indicate if it is user-defined or if it is from the string library or from the ctype library.

   | | | |
   |---|---|---|
   | strcpy | strncpy | strncat |
   | islower | strcat | scanline |
   | isalpha | strlen | strcmp |

2. Look at Appendix A, which lists three character sets. Which of the following expressions may yield different results on different computers?

   a. `(char)45`
   b. `'a' < 'A'`
   c. `'A' < 'Z'`
   d. `('A' <= ch && ch <= 'Z') && isalpha(ch)`
   e. `(int)'A'`
   f. `(int)'B' - (int)'A'`

3. Which of the following strings could represent space allocated for a local variable? Which could represent a formal parameter of any length?

   ```
   char str1[50]     char str2[]
   ```

4. A program you have written is producing incorrect results on your second data set, although it runs fine on the first. As you debug, you discover that the value of one of your strings is spontaneously changing from "blue" to "al" in the following code segment. What could be wrong?

   ```
   . . .
   printf("%s\n", s1);   /*  displays "blue" */
   scanf("%s", s2);
   printf("%s\n", s1);   /*  displays "al"   */
   . . .
   ```

5. Declare a variable `str` with as little space as would be reasonable given that `str` will hold each of the values below in turn.

   ```
   carbon    uranium    tungsten    bauxite
   ```

6. What is the value of `t1` after execution of these statements if the value of `t2` is `"Merry Christmas"`?

   ```
   strncpy(t1, &t2[3], 5);   t1[5] = '\0';
   ```

7. The action of joining two strings is called _____ .
8. Write a statement that assigns to s1 the end of the string value of s2 starting with the fourth character (i.e., s2[3]).
9. Write statements that take a whole data line as input and display all the uppercase letters in the line.
10. What is the value of the following expression?

```
isdigit(9)
```

# ANSWERS TO QUICK-CHECK EXERCISES

1.

| Function's Purpose | Output Parameter Types | Input Parameter Types | Where Defined |
|---|---|---|---|
| strcpy copies one string into another. | char * (string result) | const char * (input string) | string |
| islower checks whether its argument is the character code for a lowercase character. | none | int | ctype |
| isalpha determines if its argument is the character code for a letter of the alphabet. | none | int | ctype |
| strncpy copies *n* characters of one string into another. | char * (string result) | const char * (source string) int | string |
| strcat concatenates one string on the end of another. | char * (input/output argument — first source string and string result) | const char * (second source string) | string |
| strlen finds the length of its argument, counting the letters that precede the null character. | none | const char * (source string) | string |
| strncat concatenates two arguments by adding up to *n* characters from the second argument to the end of the first argument. | char * (input/output argument — first source string and string result) | const char * (second source string) int (maximum number of characters to copy from second string) | string |

| Function's Purpose | Output Parameter Types | Input Parameter Types | Where Defined |
|---|---|---|---|
| scanline takes one line of input as a string, stores as much as will fit in its output argument, and discards the rest. | char * (string result) | int (space available in result string) | user |
| strcmp compares arguments and returns a negative integer if first is less than second, zero if they are equal, and a positive integer otherwise | none | const char * (2 input strings) | string |

2. Results differ for a, b, e.
3. local variable: str1; parameter: str2
4. The call to scanf may be getting a string too long to fit in s2, and the extra characters could be overwriting memory allocated to s1.
5. char str[9] The longest value ("tungsten") has eight characters, and one more is needed for the null character.
6. "ry Ch"
7. concatenation
8. strcpy(s1, &s2[3]);
9. gets(line);
   for (i = 0; i < strlen(line); ++i)
       if (isupper(line[i]))
           putchar(line[i]);
10. 0 (false). However, isdigit('9') would be true.

# REVIEW QUESTIONS

Refer to these declarations when determining the effect of the statements in Questions 1–4.

```
char s5[5], s10[10], s20[20];
char aday[7] = "Sunday";
char another[9] = "Saturday";
```

1. strncpy(s5, another, 4); s5[4] = '\0';

2. `strcpy(s10, &aday[3]);`
3. `strlen(another)`
4. `strcpy(s20, aday); strcat(s20, another);`
5. Write a function that pads a variable-length string with blanks to its maximum size. For example, if `s10` is a 10-character array currently holding the string `"screen"`, `blank_pad` would add three blanks (one of which would overwrite the null character) and finish the string with the null character. Be sure your function would work if no blank padding were necessary.
6. Write a function that would return a copy of its string argument with the first occurrence of a specified letter deleted.
7. Write functions `isvowel` and `isconsonant` that return true if their type `int` argument is the character code for a vowel (or consonant). *Hint:* Use a `switch` statement in `isvowel`.
8. Which one of the following would call `somefun` only if the string values of character arrays `a` and `b` were equal?

   a. `if (strcmp(a, b))`
       `somefun();`

   b. `if (strcmp(a, b) == 0)`
       `somefun();`

   c. `if (a == b)`
       `somefun();`

   d. `if (a[] == b[])`
       `somefun();`

9. What does this program fragment display?

```
char x[80] = "gorilla";
char y[80] = "giraffe";
strcpy(x, y);
printf("%s %s\n", x, y);
```

   a. `gorilla giraffe`
   b. `giraffegorilla gorilla`
   c. `gorilla gorilla`
   d. `giraffe giraffe`

10. What does this program fragment display?

```
char x[80] = "gorilla";
char y[80] = "giraffe";
strcat(x, y);
printf("%s %s\n", x, y);
```

   a. `gorillagiraffe giraffe`
   b. `giraffegorilla gorilla`
   c. `gorilla gorilla`
   d. `giraffe giraffe`

# PROGRAMMING PROJECTS

1. Write and test a function `deblank` that takes a string output and a string input argument and returns a copy of the input argument with all blanks removed.

2. Write a program that processes a sequence of lines, displaying a count of the total number of words in those lines as well as counts of the number of words with one letter, two letters, and so on.

3. Write and test a function `hydroxide` that returns a 1 for true if its string argument ends in the substring OH.

   Try the function `hydroxide` on the following data:

   KOH   H2O2   NaCl   NaOH   C9H8O4   MgOH

4. Write a program that takes nouns and forms their plurals on the basis of these rules:
   a. If noun ends in "y," remove the "y" and add "ies."
   b. If noun ends in "s," "ch," or "sh," add "es."
   c. In all other cases, just add "s."
   Print each noun and its plural. Try the following data:

   chair   dairy   boss   circus   fly   dog   church   clue   dish

5. Write a program that stores lists of names (the last name first) and ages in parallel arrays and sorts the names into alphabetical order keeping the ages with the correct names. Sample output:

   **Original list**

   ```
   Ryan, Elizabeth      62
   McIntyre, Osborne    84
   DuMond, Kristin      18
   Larson, Lois         35
   Hodge, Jesse         39
   Romero, Robert       56
   ```

   **Alphabetized list**

   ```
   DuMond, Kristin      18
   Hodge, Jesse         39
   Larson, Lois         35
   McIntyre, Osborne    84
   Romero, Robert       56
   Ryan, Elizabeth      62
   ```

6. Write a program that takes data a line at a time and reverses the words of the line. For example,

```
Input: birds and bees
Reversed: bees and birds
```

The data should have one blank between each pair of words.

7. Write and test a function that finds the longest common prefix of two words (e.g., the longest common prefix of "global" and "glossary" is "glo," of "department" and "depart" is "depart," and of "glove" and "dove" is the empty string).

8. Write a program that takes a sequence of lines and displays each line with all four-letter words replaced by asterisks.

# RECURSION

chapter **10**

A function that calls itself is said to be **recursive**. A function f1 is also recursive if it calls a function f2, which under some circumstances calls f1, creating a cycle in the sequence of calls. The ability to invoke itself enables a recursive function to be repeated with different parameter values. You can use recursion as an alternative to iteration (looping). Generally, a recursive solution is less efficient than an iterative solution in terms of computer time due to the overhead for the extra function calls; however, in many instances, the use of recursion enables us to specify a very natural, simple solution to a problem that would otherwise be very difficult to solve. For this reason, recursion is an important and powerful tool in problem solving and programming.

# 10.1 THE NATURE OF RECURSION

Problems that lend themselves to a recursive solution have the following characteristics:

- One or more **simple cases** of the problem have a straightforward, nonrecursive solution.
- The other cases can be redefined in terms of problems that are closer to the simple cases.
- By applying this redefinition process every time the recursive function is called, eventually the problem is reduced entirely to simple cases, which are relatively easy to solve.

The recursive algorithms that we write will generally consist of an if statement with the following form:

*if this is a simple case*
    *solve it*
*else*
    *redefine the problem using recursion*

Figure 10.1 illustrates this approach. Let's assume that for a particular problem of size $n$, we can split the problem into a problem of size 1, which we can solve (a simple case), and a problem of size $n - 1$. We can split the problem of size $n - 1$ into another problem of size 1 and a problem of size $n - 2$, which we can split further. If we split the problem $n - 1$ times, we will end up with $n$ problems of size 1, all of which we can solve.

**Figure 10.1    Splitting a Problem into Smaller Problems**

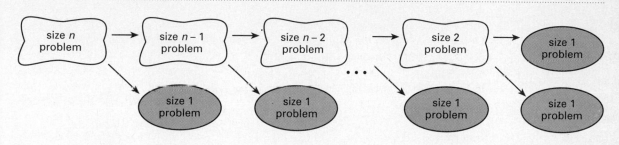

**EXAMPLE 10.1** As a simple example of this approach, let's consider how we might solve the problem of multiplying 6 by 3, assuming we know our addition tables but not our multiplication tables. We do know, however, that any number multiplied by 1 gives us the original number, so if we ever come across this simple case, we'll just solve it. The problem of multiplying 6 by 3 can be split into the two problems:

1. Multiply 6 by 2.
2. Add 6 to the result of problem 1.

Because we know our addition tables, we can solve problem 2 but not problem 1. However, problem 1 is closer to the simple case than the original problem was. We can split problem 1 into the following two problems, 1.1 and 1.2, leaving us three problems to solve, two of which are additions.

1. Multiply 6 by 2.
    1.1    **Multiply 6 by 1.**
    1.2    **Add 6 to the result of problem 1.1.**
2. Add 6 to the result of problem 1.

Problem 1.1 is one of the simple cases we were looking for. By solving problem 1.1 (the answer is 6) and problem 1.2, we get the solution to problem 1 (the answer is 12). Solving problem 2 gives us the final answer (18).

    Figure 10.2 implements this approach to doing multiplication as the recursive C function `multiply` that returns the product m × n of its two arguments. The body of function `multiply` implements the general form of a recursive algorithm shown earlier. The simplest case is reached when the condition n == 1 is true. In this case, the statement

```
ans = m;     /* simple case  */
```

executes, so the answer is m. If n is greater than 1, the statement

```
ans = m + multiply(m, n - 1);   /* recursive step */
```

**Figure 10.2   Recursive Function multiply**

```
/*
 *  Performs integer multiplication using + operator.
 *  Pre:    m and n are defined and n > 0
 *  Post:   returns m * n
 */
int
multiply(int m, int n)
{
      int ans;

      if (n == 1)
            ans = m;        /* simple case */
      else
            ans = m + multiply(m, n - 1);   /* recursive step */

      return (ans);
}
```

executes, splitting the original problem into the two simpler problems:

*   multiply m by n-1
*   add m to the result

The first of these problems is solved by calling multiply again with n-1 as its second argument. If the new second argument is greater than 1, there will be additional calls to function multiply.

At first, it may seem odd that we must rely on the function multiply before we have even finished writing it! However, this approach is the key to developing recursive algorithms. In order to solve a problem recursively, first we must trust our function to solve a simpler version of the problem. Then we build the solution to the whole problem on the result from the simpler version.

For now, you will have to take our word that function multiply performs as desired. We will see how to trace the execution of a recursive function in the next section.

One group of problems for which recursive solutions seem very natural are problems involving varying-length lists. Since a string is a varying-length list of characters, this chapter contains numerous examples of recursive functions that process strings.

**EXAMPLE 10.2**    We need to develop a function to count the number of times a particular character appears in a string. For example,

```
count('s', "Mississippi sassafras")
```

should return the value 8. Of course, we could set up a loop to count the s's, but instead we will look for a recursive solution. Since recursion requires breaking a problem into a combination of simpler problems, our initial reaction to a problem should be something like, "This whole problem is entirely too hard. Maybe I can do a little bit of this problem, but I will definitely need help to do the whole problem." We then need to arrange things so the "help" needed is actually in solving a simpler version of the same problem. When dealing with a list of elements as we are in this problem, a recursive solution usually explicitly processes only the first list element. The recursive problem solver's thought process is illustrated in Fig. 10.3.

Looking back at the `if` statement that is our "generic" recursion algorithm,

*if this is a simple case*
    *solve it*
*else*
    *redefine the problem using recursion*

we see that the thought process shown in Fig. 10.3 fits into our generic `else` clause. We have redefined the problem "Count s's in `Mississippi sassafras`" as "Count s's in `ississippi sassafras` and add one more if the first letter is an s." Our redefinition of the general problem "Count a letter in a string" is recursive, since part of the solution is still to count a letter in a string. What has changed is that the new string is shorter. We still need to identify the simplest case of the problem, which must involve a *very* short string. Although it would be fairly easy to count a certain character in a string with only one character element, we would still need to do a comparison. If the string had *no* characters at all, we would know immediately that there were zero occurrences of the character being counted. Now that we have a simple case and a way to redefine more complex cases using recursion, we can write a

**Figure 10.3
Thought
Process of
Recursive
Algorithm
Developer**

Counting occurrences of 's' in
`Mississippi sassafras`

*If I could just get someone to count the s's in this list*

*...then the number of s's is either that number or 1 more, depending on whether the first letter is an s.*

**Figure 10.4   Recursive Function to Count a Character in a String**

```
/*
 *  Count the number of occurrences of character ch in string str
 */
int
count(char ch, const char *str)
{

    int ans;

    if (str[0] == '\0')                         /*  simple case  */
        ans = 0;
    else                        /*  redefine problem using recursion */
        if (ch == str[0])       /*  first character must be counted  */
            ans = 1 + count(ch, &str[1]);
        else                        /*  first character is not counted    */
            ans = count(ch, &str[1]);

    return (ans);
}
```

recursive function `count`. Because the "rest of the string" to be processed by the recursive call will be examined by `count`, but not modified by it, we do not even need to copy the substring containing all but the first letter of `str`. Our implementation in Fig. 10.4 simply calls `count` with `&str[1]`. ←

In our first example, we saw how a recursive `multiply` function broke a size *n* multiplication problem into *n* size 1 addition problems. Similarly, the effect of our recursive `count` function is to split the problem of analyzing a length *n* string into *n* problems of comparing single characters.

**EXERCISES FOR SECTION 10.1**

Self-Check

1. Using diagrams similar to those in Fig. 10.1, show the specific problems that are generated by the following calls.
   a. `multiply(5, 4)`
   b. `count('d', "dad")`

Programming

1. Write a recursive function `count_digits` that counts all the digits in a string.
2. Write a recursive function `add` that computes the sum of its two integer parameters. Assume `add` does not know general addition tables but does know how to add or subtract 1.

# 10.2 TRACING A RECURSIVE FUNCTION

Hand-tracing an algorithm's execution provides us with valuable insight into how that algorithm works. We can trace the execution of a recursive function, and now we will illustrate how to do this by first studying the execution of a recursive function that returns a value, and then studying the execution of a recursive `void` function.

## Tracing a Recursive Function That Returns a Value

In Section 10.1, we wrote the recursive function `multiply` (see Fig. 10.2). We can trace the execution of the function call

```
multiply(6, 3)
```

**activation frame**
representation of one call to a
function

by drawing an **activation frame** corresponding to each call of the function. An activation frame shows the parameter values for each call and summarizes the execution of the call.

The three activation frames generated to solve the problem of multiplying 6 by 3 are shown in Fig. 10.5. The part of each activation frame that executes before the next recursive call is in color; the part that executes after the return from the next call is in grey. The darker the color of an activation frame, the greater the depth of recursion.

The value returned from each call is shown alongside each black arrow. The return arrow from each call points to the operator + because the addition is performed just after the return.

Figure 10.5 shows three calls to function `multiply`. Parameter m has the value 6 for all three calls; parameter n has the values 3, 2, and, finally, 1. Since n is 1 in the third call, the value of m (6) is assigned to `ans` and is returned as the result of the third and last call. After returning to the second activation frame, the value of m is added to this result, and the sum (12) is returned as the result of the second call. After returning to the first activation frame, the value of m is added to this result, and the sum (18) is returned as the result of the original call to function `multiply`.

**Figure 10.5
Trace of
Function
multiply**

## Tracing a void Function That Is Recursive

Hand-tracing a void function is somewhat simpler than tracing a function that returns a value. For both types of functions, we use activation frames to track each function call.

Function reverse_input_words in Fig. 10.6 is a recursive module that takes n words of input and prints them in reverse order. If this function call statement

reverse_input_words(5)

is executed, the five words entered at the keyboard are printed in reverse order. If the words entered are

the
course
of
human
events

the program output will be

```
events
human
of
course
the
```

**terminating condition**
a condition that is true when a recursive algorithm is processing a simple case

Like most recursive modules, the body of function reverse_input_words consists of an if statement that evaluates a **terminating condition**, n <= 1. When the terminating condition is true, the function is dealing with one of the problem's simple cases—printing in reverse order a list of just one word. Since reversing word order has no effect on a single-word list, for the simple case when n is less than or equal to one, we just get the word using scanf and print it.

**Figure 10.6    Function reverse_input_words**

```
/*
 *  Take n words as input and print them in reverse order on separate lines.
 *  Pre: n > 0
 */
void
reverse_input_words(int n)
{
      char word[WORDSIZ];   /*  local variable for storing one word         */

      if (n <= 1) {    /* simple case: just one word to get and print       */

            scanf("%s", word);
            printf("%s\n", word);

      } else {   /* get this word; get and print the rest of the words in
                    reverse order; then print this word                     */

            scanf("%s", word);
            reverse_input_words(n - 1);
            printf("%s\n", word);
      }
}
```

If the terminating condition is false (n > 1), the recursive step (following else) is executed. This group of statements transfers the current input word into memory, gets "someone" (i.e., reverse_input_words) to take and reverse print the remaining n − 1 words of interest, and then prints the current word.

Figure 10.7 shows a trace of the function call

```
reverse_input_words(3)
```

assuming that the words "bits" "and" "bytes" are entered as data. The trace shows three separate activation frames for function reverse_‐input_words. Each activation frame begins with a list of the initial values of n and word for that frame. The value of n is passed into the function when it is called; the value of the local variable word is initially undefined.

The statements that are executed for each frame are shown next. The statements in color in the activation frames are recursive function calls and result in new activation frames, as indicated by the colored arrows. A void function's return occurs when the closing brace of the function body is encountered, indicated by the word return and a black arrow that points to the statement in the calling frame to which the function returns. Tracing the colored arrows and then the black arrows in Fig. 10.7 gives us the sequence of events listed in Fig. 10.8. To help you understand this list, all the statements for a particular activation frame are indented to the same column.

**Figure 10.7    Trace of reverse_input_words(3) When the Words Entered are "bits" "and" "bytes"**

**Figure 10.8    Sequence of Events for Trace of reverse_input_words(3)**

Call reverse_input_words with n equal to 3.
    Scan the first word ("bits") into word.
    Call reverse_input_words with n equal to 2.
        Scan the second word ("and") into word.
        Call reverse_input_words with n equal to 1.
            Scan the third word ("bytes") into word.
            Display the third word ("bytes").
            Return from third call.
        Display the second word ("and").
        Return from second call.
    Display the first word ("bits").
    Return from original call.

As shown, there are three calls to function reverse_input_words, each with a different parameter value. The function returns always occur in the reverse order of the function calls—that is, we return from the last call first, then we return from the next to last call, and so on. After we return from a particular execution of the function, we display the string that was stored in word just prior to that function call.

## Parameter and Local Variable Stacks

**stack**
a data structure in which the last data item added is the first data item processed

You may be wondering how C keeps track of the values of n and word at any given point. C uses the **stack** data structure that we implemented with an array in Section 8.5 (see Fig. 8.14). In this data structure, we add data items (the push operation) and remove them (the pop operation) from the same end of the list, so the last item stored is the first processed.

When executing a call to reverse_input_words, the system pushes the parameter value associated with the call on top of the parameter stack, and pushes a new undefined cell on top of the stack maintained for the local variable word. A return from reverse_input_words pops each stack, removing the top value.

As an example, let's look at the two stacks as they appear right after the first call to reverse_input_words. One cell is on each stack, as shown.

*After first call to* reverse_input_words

The word `"bits"` is stored in `word` just before the second call to
`reverse_input_words`.

After the second call to `reverse_input_words`, the number 2 is pushed on
the stack for `n`, and the top of the stack for `word` becomes undefined again, as
shown next. The value in color is at the top of each stack.

*After second call to* reverse_input_words

The word `"and"` is scanned and stored in `word` just before the third call to
`reverse_input_words`.

However, `word` becomes undefined again right after the third call.

*After third call to* reverse_input_words

During this execution of the function, the word `"bytes"` is scanned and stored in `word`, and `"bytes"` is echo printed immediately because `n` is 1 (a simple case).

The function return pops both stacks, as shown next.

*After first return*

Because control is returned to a `printf` call, the value of `word` (`"and"`) at the top of the stack is then displayed. Another return occurs, popping the stacks again.

*After second return*

Again, control is returned to a `printf` statement, and the value of `word` (`"bits"`) at the top of the stack is displayed. The third and last return exits the original function call, so there is no longer any memory allocated for `n` and `word`.

A stack is a data structure that you can implement and manipulate yourself using arrays. However, C automatically handles all the stack manipulation associated with function calls, so we can write recursive functions without needing to worry about the stacks.

## Implementation of Parameter Stacks in C

**system stack**
area of memory where parameters and local variables are allocated when a function is called and deallocated when the function returns

For illustrative purposes, we have used separate stacks for each parameter in our discussion; however, the compiler actually maintains a single **system stack**. Each time a call to a function occurs, all its parameters and local variables are pushed onto the stack along with the memory address of the calling statement.

This address gives the computer the return point after execution of the function. Although multiple copies of a function's parameters may be saved on the stack, only one copy of the function body is in memory.

## When and How to Trace Recursive Functions

Doing a trace by hand of multiple calls to a recursive function is helpful in understanding how recursion works but less useful when trying to develop a recursive algorithm. During algorithm development, it is best to trace a specific case simply by trusting any recursive call to return a correct value based on the function purpose. Then the hand trace can check whether this value is manipulated properly to produce a correct function result for the case under consideration.

However, if a recursive function's implementation is flawed, tracing its execution is an essential part of identifying the error. The function can be made to trace itself by inserting debugging print statements showing entry to and exit from the function. Figure 10.9 shows a self-tracing version of function `multiply` as well as output generated by the call

```
multiply(8, 3)
```

**Figure 10.9   Recursive Function multiply with Print Statements to Create Trace and Output from multiply(8, 3)**

```
/*
 *   ***  Includes calls to printf to trace execution ***
 *   Performs integer multiplication using + operator.
 *   Pre:   m and n are defined and n > 0
 *   Post:  returns m * n
 */
int
multiply(int m, int n)
{
      int ans;

   printf("Entering multiply with m = %d, n = %d\n", m, n);

      if (n == 1)
            ans = m;       /* simple case */
      else
            ans = m + multiply(m, n - 1); /* recursive step */
```

*(continued)*

**Figure 10.9**   *(continued)*

```
printf("multiply(%d, %d) returning %d\n", m, n, ans);

    return (ans);
}
```

```
Entering multiply with m = 8, n = 3
Entering multiply with m = 8, n = 2
Entering multiply with m = 8, n = 1
multiply(8, 1) returning 8
multiply(8, 2) returning 16
multiply(8, 3) returning 24
```

**EXERCISES FOR SECTION 10.2**

Self-Check

1. Trace the contents of stack representations of m, n, and ans for the evaluation of `multiply(6,3)` whose activation frames are shown in Fig. 10.5.
2. Draw activation frames showing the evaluation of `count('d',"dad")`, assuming that `count` is defined as shown in Fig. 10.4.

Programming

1. Rewrite function `count` from Fig. 10.4, adding calls to `printf` to make `count` self-tracing. Then show the output produced by the call `count('l', "lull")`.

## 10.3 RECURSIVE MATHEMATICAL FUNCTIONS

Many mathematical functions can be defined recursively. An example is the factorial of a number *n (n!)*, a function that we defined iteratively in Chapter 5.

- 0! is 1
- *n*! is $n \times (n-1)!$, for $n > 0$

Thus 4! is $4 \times 3!$, which means $4 \times 3 \times 2 \times 1$, or 24. Implementing this definition as a recursive function in C is quite straightforward.

### Figure 10.10    Recursive factorial Function

```
/*
 *  Compute n! using a recursive definition
 *  Pre:   n >= 0
 */
int
factorial(int n)
{
      int ans;

      if (n == 0)
            ans = 1;
      else
            ans = n * factorial(n - 1);

      return (ans);
}
```

 **EXAMPLE 10.4** Function `factorial` in Fig. 10.10 computes the factorial of its argument n. The recursive step

```
ans = n * factorial(n - 1);
```

implements the second line of the factorial definition just shown. Thus the result of the current call (argument n) is computed by multiplying by n the result of the call `factorial(n - 1)`.

A trace of

```
fact = factorial(3);
```

is shown in Fig. 10.11. The value returned from the original call, `factorial(3)`, is 6, and this value is assigned to `fact`. Be careful when using the factorial function as its value increases very rapidly and could lead to an integer overflow error (e.g., 8! is 40,320).

Although the recursive implementation of function `factorial` follows naturally from its definition, we saw in Chapter 5 that this function can also be implemented easily using iteration. The iterative version we developed in that chapter is shown in Fig. 10.12.

Note that the iterative version contains a loop as its major control structure, whereas the recursive version contains an `if` statement. In the iterative version, the variable `product` is the target of repeated assignments, each of

**Figure 10.11
Trace of fact =
factorial(3);**

**Figure 10.12  Iterative Function factorial**

```
/*
 * Computes n!
 * Pre: n is greater than or equal to zero
 */
int
factorial(int n)
{
    int i,              /* local variables */
        product = 1;

    /* Compute the product n x (n-1) x (n-2) x ... x 2 x 1 */
    for  (i = n;  i > 1;  --i) {
        product = product * i;
    }

    /* Return function result */
    return (product);
}
```

which brings its value closer to the result value. Compare this use of product to the purpose of the local variable ans in the recursive version. Variable ans holds the answer to the subproblem that is the reason for the current call to the function. ◀

**EXAMPLE 10.5** ▶

The Fibonacci numbers are a sequence of numbers that have many varied uses. They were originally intended to model the growth of a rabbit colony. Although we will not go into the details of the model here, the Fibonacci sequence 1, 1, 2, 3, 5, 8, 13, 21, 34, . . . certainly seems to increase rapidly enough. The fifteenth number in the sequence is 610 (that's a lot of rabbits!). The Fibonacci sequence is defined as

- Fibonacci$_1$ is 1
- Fibonacci$_2$ is 1
- Fibonacci$_n$ is Fibonacci$_{n-2}$ + Fibonacci$_{n-1}$, for $n > 2$.

Verify for yourself that the sequence of numbers just shown is correct.

A recursive function that computes the $n$th Fibonacci number is shown in Fig. 10.13. Although easy to write, this version of fibonacci is not very efficient because each recursive step generates two calls to function fibonacci, and these calls duplicate many computations. Programming Exercise 2 at the end of this section describes an efficient (though more complicated) recursive algorithm for computing Fibonacci numbers. ◀

**Figure 10.13    Recursive Function fibonacci**

```
/*
 *    Computes the nth Fibonacci number
 *    Pre: n > 0
 */
int
fibonacci(int n)
{
     int ans;

     if (n == 1  ||  n == 2)
          ans = 1;
     else
          ans = fibonacci(n - 2)  +  fibonacci(n - 1);

     return (ans);
}
```

**EXAMPLE 10.6** ▶ In a programming exercise for Section 6.5, we presented an iterative algorithm for finding the greatest common divisor of two integers. Euclid's algorithm for finding the gcd can be defined recursively as shown. You recall that the *greatest common divisor* of two integers is the largest integer that divides them both evenly.

- gcd(*m,n*) is *n* if *n* divides *m* evenly
- gcd(*m,n*) is gcd(*n*, remainder of *m* divided by *n*) otherwise

This algorithm states that the gcd is *n* if *n* divides *m* evenly. If *n* does not divide *m* with a zero remainder, the answer is obtained by finding the gcd of *n* and the remainder of *m* divided by *n*. One of the elegant features of this definition is that it does not matter whether *m* or *n* is the larger number. If *m* is greater than *n*, the computation seems to proceed more directly to a solution; if it is not, the first application of the recursive step has the effect of exchanging *m* and *n*. This exchange is a result of the fact that when *m* is less than *n*, the remainder of *m* divided by *n* is *m*. The declaration and use of a recursive gcd function is shown in Fig. 10.14. ◀

**Figure 10.14  Program Using Recursive Function gcd**

```
/*
 *   Displays the greatest common divisor of two integers
 */

#include <stdio.h>

/*
 *   Finds the greatest common divisor of m and n
 *   Pre:  m and n are both > 0
 */
int
gcd(int m, int n)
{
      int ans;

      if (m % n == 0)
            ans = n;
      else
            ans = gcd(n, m % n);

      return (ans);
}
```

*(continued)*

**Figure 10.14** *(continued)*

```
int
main(void)
{
      int n1, n2;

      printf("Enter two positive integers separated by a space> ");
      scanf("%d%d", &n1, &n2);
      printf("Their greatest common divisor is %d\n", gcd(n1, n2));

      return (0);
}


Enter two positive integers separated by a space> 24 84
Their greatest common divisor is 12
```

**EXERCISES FOR SECTION 10.3**

Self-Check

1. Complete the following recursive function that calculates the value of a number (base) raised to a power. Assume that power is a nonnegative integer.

```
int
power_raiser(int base, int power)
{
      int ans;

      if (power == _____)
            ans = _____;
      else
            ans = _____ * _____;

      return (ans);
}
```

2. What is the output of the following program? What does function strange compute when called with a positive integer?

```
#include <stdio.h>

int strange(int n);
```

```
int
main(void)
{
     printf("%d\n", strange(8));
}

int
strange(int n)
{
     int ans;

     if (n == 1)
          ans = 0;
     else
          ans = 1 + strange(n / 2);

     return (ans);
}
```

3. Explain what would happen if the terminating condition for function fibonacci were just (n == 1).

Programming

1. Write a recursive function find_sum that calculates the sum of successive integers starting at 1 and ending at n (i.e., find_sum(n) = (1 + 2 + · · · + (n − 1) + n).
2. Write a recursive function fast_fib to compute a pair of Fibonacci numbers, F($n$ + 1) and F($n$). Function fast_fib should make only one recursive call.

**Algorithm**
if *n* is 1
    The pair to send back is 1, 1.
else
    Use fast_fib to compute F($n$) and F($n$ − 1).
    The pair to send back is [F($n$) + F($n$ − 1)], F($n$).

# 10.4 RECURSIVE FUNCTIONS WITH ARRAY AND STRING PARAMETERS

In this section, we will examine two problems and will implement recursive functions to solve them. Both problems involve processing of some type of array.

## Case Study: Finding Capital Letters in a String

### PROBLEM

Form a string containing all the capital letters found in another string.

### ANALYSIS

Just as in the problem of counting occurrences of a particular letter in a string, recursion will allow us to solve this problem by simply working out what to do with the string's first letter and then combining this processing with a recursive call handling the rest of the string. For instance, if the string in question were `"Franklin Delano Roosevelt"`, finding capital letters in `"ranklin Delano Roosevelt"` would give us the string `"DR"`. It is a simple matter to combine this string with the capital `'F'` to form the full result. Of course, the simplest string in which to look for *anything* is the empty string, so checking for this simple case gives us the necessary terminating condition.

### Data Requirements

**Problem Input**

```
char *str        /* a string from which to extract capital
                    letters                                */
```

**Problem Output**

```
char *caps       /* the capital letters from str    */
```

### DESIGN

**Algorithm**
1. if `str` is the empty string
    2. Store empty string in `caps` (a string with no letters certainly has no caps).
   else

**Figure 10.15    Recursive Function to Extract Capital Letters from a String**

```
/*
 *  Forms a string containing all the capital letters found in the input
 *  parameter str.
 *  Pre:  caps has sufficient space to store all caps in str plus the null
 */
char *
find_caps(char        *caps,  /* output - string of all caps found in str  */
          const char *str)    /* input  - string from which to extract caps  */
{
      char restcaps[STRSIZ]; /* caps from reststr  */

      if (str[0] == '\0')
            caps[0] = '\0';  /* no letters in str => no caps in str        */
      else
            if (isupper(str[0]))
                  sprintf(caps, "%c%s", str[0], find_caps(restcaps, &str[1]));
            else
                  find_caps(caps, &str[1]);

      return (caps);
}
```

3. if initial letter of str is a capital letter
   4. Store in caps this letter and the capital letters from the rest
      of str.
else
   5. Store in caps the capital letters from the rest of str.

Function find_caps in Fig. 10.15 implements the recursive algorithm.

**TESTING**

Given this #define directive and declaration,

```
#define STRSIZ 50
. . .
char caps[STRSIZ];
```

and the statement

```
printf("Capital letters in JoJo are %s\n",
       find_caps(caps, "JoJo"));
```

five calls to `find_caps` will be executed, as shown in Fig. 10.16. The string sent back from each function call is shown to the left of the arrow coming from the `return` statement.

Figure 10.17 shows the sequence of events that results from following first the colored arrows and then the black arrows of Fig. 10.16. There are five

**Figure 10.16   Trace of Call to Recursive Function find_caps**

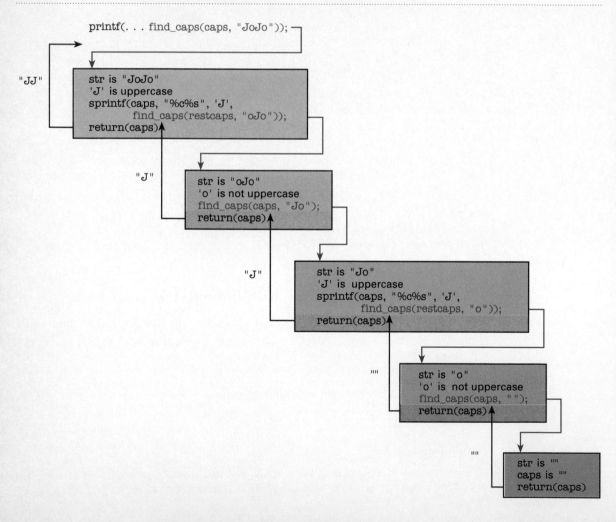

**Figure 10.17   Sequence of Events for Trace of Call to find_caps from printf Statements**

Call `find_caps` with input argument `"JoJo"` to determine value to print.
    Since `'J'` is a capital letter,
    prepare to use `sprintf` to build a string with `'J'`
    and the result of calling `find_caps` with input argument `"oJo"`.
        Since `'o'` is not a capital letter,
        call `find_caps` with input argument `"Jo"`.
            Since `'J'` is a capital letter,
            prepare to use `sprintf` to build a string with `'J'`
            and the result of calling `find_caps` with input argument `"o"`.
                Since `'o'` is not a capital letter,
                call `find_caps` with input argument `""`.
                    Return `""` from fifth call.
                Return `""` from fourth call.
            Complete execution of `sprintf` combining `'J'` and `""`.
            Return `"J"` from third call.
        Return `"J"` from second call.
    Complete execution of `sprintf` combining `'J'` and `"J"`.
    Return `"JJ"` from original call.
Complete call to `printf` to print `Capital letters in JoJo are JJ`.

calls to function `find_caps`, each with a different input argument. The desired string of capital letters is constructed one character at a time as the function returns cause the recursion to unwind.

## Case Study: Recursive Selection Sort

In Chapters 8 and 9, we studied an iterative selection sort algorithm. In this section we develop a recursive version of the algorithm that fills the array from the bottom up.

**PROBLEM**

Sort an array in ascending order using a selection sort.

**ANALYSIS**

To perform a selection sort of an array with $n$ elements (subscripts $0 \ldots n-1$), we locate the largest element in the array and then switch the largest element

**Figure 10.18
Trace of
Selection Sort**

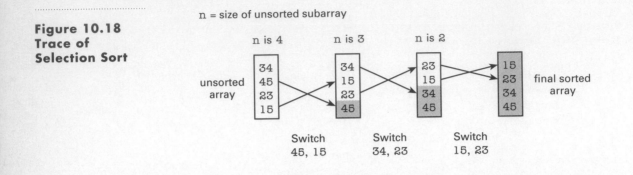

n = size of unsorted subarray

with the element at subscript $n-1$, thereby placing the largest element in the final array position. We then locate the largest element remaining in the subarray with subscripts $0 \ldots n-2$, and switch it with the element at subscript $n-2$, thereby placing the second largest element in the next to last position $n-2$. We continue this process until the whole array is sorted.

Figure 10.18 traces the operation of this version of the selection sort algorithm. The diagram on the left shows the original array. Each subsequent diagram shows the array after the next largest element is moved to its final position in the array. The subarray in the darker color represents the portion of the array that is sorted after each exchange occurs. Note that it will require, at most, $n-1$ exchanges to sort an array with $n$ elements.

### DESIGN

Because the selection sort can be viewed as a sort accomplished by first placing one element and then sorting a subarray, it is a good candidate for a recursive solution.

### Recursive Algorithm for Selection Sort

1. if *n* is 1
    2. The array is sorted.
  else
    3. Place the largest array value in last array element.
    4. Sort the subarray which excludes the last array element
       (`array[0] .. array[n-2]`).

### IMPLEMENTATION

Figure 10.19 shows an implementation of our recursive algorithm that uses a function `place_largest` to perform step 3 and a recursive function `select_sort` that carries out the overall procedure. The recursive function is slightly simpler to understand than the original iterative version because it

**Figure 10.19    Recursive Selection Sort**

```
/*
 *  Finds the largest value in list array[0]..array[n-1] and exchanges it
 *  with the value at array[n-1]
 *  Pre:  n > 0 and first n elements of array are defined
 *  Post: array[n-1] contains largest value
 */
void
place_largest(int array[],    /* input/output - array in which to place
                                   largest                                 */
              int n)          /* input - number of array elements to
                                   consider                                */
{
     int temp,        /* temporary variable for exchange                   */
         j,           /* array subscript and loop control                  */
         max_index;   /* index of largest so far                           */

     /*  Save subscript of largest array value in max_index                */
     max_index = n - 1;      /* assume last value is largest               */
     for  (j = n - 2;  j >= 0;  --j)
         if (array[j] > array[max_index])
               max_index = j;

     /*  Unless largest value is already in last element, exchange
         largest and last elements                                         */
     if (max_index != n - 1) {
          temp = array[n - 1];
          array[n - 1] = array[max_index];
          array[max_index] = temp;
     }
}

/*
 *  Sorts n elements of an array of integers
 *  Pre:  n > 0 and first n elements of array are defined
 *  Post: array elements are in ascending order
 */
void
select_sort(int array[],  /* input/output - array to sort                  */
            int n)        /* input - number of array elements to sort      */
{
```

*(continued)*

**Figure 10.19** *(continued)*

```
if (n > 1) {
        place_largest(array, n);
        select_sort(array, n - 1);
    }
}
```

contains a single if statement rather than a loop. The recursive function typically executes more slowly, however, because of the extra overhead due to the
recursive function calls.

Notice that the logic of the select_sort function does not exactly
match our original algorithm or our generic recursive algorithm. If you look
back at the initial algorithm, you will see that if we are at the simplest case (an
array of one element), no action is necessary. Rather than explicitly making the
test for the simple case and having an empty true branch, we have chosen to
negate the test for the simplest case so that all the actions are on the true branch
of the decision. Notice that if n == 1, the selection sort function returns without
doing anything. This behavior is correct because a one-element array is always
sorted.

**EXERCISES FOR
SECTION 10.4**

Self-Check

1. Using activation frames, hand-trace the execution of the find_caps function on the string "DoD".
2. Trace the execution of both recursive and iterative select_sort functions on an array that has the integers 5, 8, 10, 1 stored in consecutive elements.

Programming

1. Modify the find_caps function to create a find_digits function.

## 10.5 PROBLEM SOLVING WITH RECURSION

Since C does not have a built-in representation of a set data structure, we would
like to develop an implementation of a group of set operations using strings as
our sets.

# Case Study: Operations on Sets

### PROBLEM

Develop a group of functions to perform the ∈ (is an element of), ⊆ (is a subset of), and ∪ (union) operations on sets of characters. Also develop functions to check that a certain set is valid (that is, that it contains no duplicate characters), to check for the empty set, and to print a set in standard set notation.

### ANALYSIS

Character strings provide a fairly natural representation of sets of characters. Like sets, strings can be of varying sizes and can be empty. If a character array that is to hold a set is declared to have one more than the number of characters in the universal set (to allow room for the null character), then set operations should never produce a string that will overflow the array.

### DESIGN

This problem is naturally divided into subproblems, each of which corresponds to a single function. Since these functions are all basic set utilities, their individual algorithms are quite straightforward. We will develop pseudocode for the simplest functions first and will refer to these functions in the more complex solutions. Since one goal of this case study is to demonstrate the use of recursion, we will ignore the existence of looping constructs for the time being.

**Algorithm for `is_empty(set)`**

1. Is initial character `'\0'`?

**Algorithm for `is_element(ele, set)`**

1. if `is_empty(set)`                                    /* simple case 1   */
      2. Answer is false.
   else if initial character of `set` matches `ele`       /* simple case 2   */
      3. Answer is true.
   else
      4. Answer depends on whether `ele`
         is in the rest of `set`.                         /* recursive step  */

**Algorithm for `is_set(set)`**

1. if `is_empty(set)`                                    /* simple case 1   */
      2. Answer is true.
   else if `is_element`(initial set character,
                        rest of `set`)                    /* simple case 2   */

3. Answer is false.

else

4. Answer depends on whether rest of `set` is a
   valid set.                                      /* recursive step    */

### Algorithm for `is_subset(sub, set)`

1. if `is_empty(sub)`                               /* simple case 1    */
   2. Answer is true.
   else if initial character of `sub` is not an element of
   `set`                                            /* simple case 2    */
   3. Answer is false.
   else
      4. Answer depends on whether rest of `sub` is a
         subset of `set`.                           /* recursive step   */

### Algorithm for union of `set1` and `set2`

1. if `is_empty(set1)`                              /* simple case      */
   2. Result is `set2`.
   else if initial character of `set1` is also an element
   of `set2`                                        /* recursive steps */
   3. Result is the union of the rest of `set1` with
      `set2`.                                       /*     case 1       */
   else                                             /*     case 2       */
      4. Result includes initial character of `set1` and the union of the
         rest of `set1` with `set2`.

### Algorithm for `print_set(set)`

1. Output a {.
2. if `set` is not empty, print elements separated by commas.
3. Output a } .

### Algorithm for print_with_commas(set)

1. if `set` has exactly one element
   2. Print it.
   else
      3. Print initial element and a comma.
      4. `print_with_commas` the rest of `set`.

**IMPLEMENTATION**

Every recursive function in the collection of functions we have designed references "the rest of the set" for some set, that is, all but the first letter of the set. In
all of these functions, this "rest of the set" is passed as an input argument only—

the function called looks at it but does not modify it. Since this particular substring includes all the characters of the original string from the substring's starting point right through the original string's null character, we can use &set[1] to reference the rest of the set. Figure 10.20 shows our implementation of all the set operations along with a main program that demonstrates the functions.

You will notice that the name of our function that forms the union of two sets is set_union. We could not use the name union because this is a reserved word in C. In the implementation of set_union, we could not use the variable result as the output argument for both the call to set_union and the call to sprintf because sprintf does not guarantee correct results if there is overlap between its input and output arguments.

**Figure 10.20   Recursive Set Operations on Sets Represented as Character Strings**

```
/*
 *  Functions to perform basic operations on sets of characters
 *  represented as strings. Note: "Rest of set" is represented  as
 *  &set[1], which is indeed the address of the rest of the set excluding
 *  the first element.  This efficient representation, which does not
 *  recopy the rest of the set, is an acceptable substring reference in
 *  these functions only because the "rest of the set" is always passed
 *  strictly as an input argument.
 */

#include <stdio.h>
#include <string.h>
#include <ctype.h>

#define SETSIZ  65   /* 52 uppercase and lowercase letters, 10 digits,
                        {, }, and '\0'                                    */
#define TRUE    1
#define FALSE   0

int is_empty(const char *set);
int is_element(char ele, const char *set);
int is_set(const char *set);
int is_subset(const char *sub, const char *set);
char *set_union(char *result, const char *set1, const char *set2);
void print_with_commas(const char *str);
void print_set(const char *set);
char *get_set(char *set);
```

*(continued)*

**Figure 10.20** *(continued)*

```
/*
 *  Tries out set operation functions.
 */
int
main(void)
{
      char ele, set_one[SETSIZ], set_two[SETSIZ], set_three[SETSIZ];

      printf("A set is entered as a string of up to %d letters\n",
             SETSIZ - 3);
      printf("and digits enclosed in {} ");
      printf("(no duplicate characters)\n");
      printf("For example, {a, b, c} is entered as {abc}\n");

      printf("Enter a set to test validation function> ");
      get_set(set_one);
      putchar('\n');
      print_set(set_one);
      if (is_set(set_one))
            printf(" is a valid set\n");
      else
            printf(" is invalid\n");

      printf("Enter a single character, a space, and a set> ");
      while(isspace(ele = getchar()));   /* gets first character after
                                            white space                */
      get_set(set_one);
      printf("\n%c ", ele);
      if (is_element(ele, set_one))
            printf("is an element of ");
      else
            printf("is not an element of ");
      print_set(set_one);

      printf("\nEnter two sets to test set_union> ");
      get_set(set_one);
      get_set(set_two);
      printf("\nThe union of ");
      print_set(set_one);
      printf(" and ");
      print_set(set_two);
```

*(continued)*

**Figure 10.20**    *(continued)*

```c
        printf(" is ");
        print_set(set_union(set_three, set_one, set_two));
        putchar('\n');

        return (0);
}

/*
 *  Determines if set is empty.  If so, returns 1;  if not, returns 0.
 */
int
is_empty(const char *set)
{
        return (set[0] == '\0');
}

/*
 *  Determines if ele is an element of set.
 */
int
is_element(char       ele,      /* input - element to look for in set   */
           const char *set)     /* input - set in which to look for ele */
{
        int ans;

        if (is_empty(set))
              ans = FALSE;
        else if (set[0] == ele)
              ans = TRUE;
        else
              ans = is_element(ele, &set[1]);

        return (ans);
}

/*
 *  Determines if string value of set represents a valid set (no duplicate
 *  elements)
 */
```

*(continued)*

**Figure 10.20** *(continued)*

```c
int
is_set(const char *set)
{
      int ans;

      if (is_empty(set))
            ans = TRUE;
      else if (is_element(set[0], &set[1]))
            ans = FALSE;
      else
            ans = is_set(&set[1]);
      return (ans);
}

/*
 *  Determines if value of sub is a subset of value of set.
 */
int
is_subset(const char *sub, const char *set)
{
      int ans;

      if (is_empty(sub))
            ans = TRUE;
      else if (!is_element(sub[0], set))
            ans = FALSE;
      else
            ans = is_subset(&sub[1], set);

      return (ans);
}

/*
 *    Finds the union of set1 and set2.
 *    Pre:  size of result array is at least SETSIZ;
 *          set1 and set2 are valid sets of characters and digits
 */
char *
set_union(char         *result,  /* output - space in which to store
                                            string result                */
```

*(continued)*

**Figure 10.20**   *(continued)*

```
            const char *set1,    /* input  - sets whose          */
            const char *set2)    /*           union is being formed   */
{
     char temp[SETSIZ];         /* local variable to hold result of call
                                   to set_union embedded in sprintf call */

     if (is_empty(set1))
          strcpy(result, set2);
     else if (is_element(set1[0], set2))
          set_union(result, &set1[1], set2);
     else
          sprintf(result, "%c%s", set1[0],
                  set_union(temp, &set1[1], set2));

     return (result);
}

/*
 *  Displays a string so that each pair of characters is separated by a
 *  comma and a space.
 */
void
print_with_commas(const char *str)
{
     if (strlen(str) == 1) {
          putchar(str[0]);
     } else {
          printf("%c, ", str[0]);
          print_with_commas(&str[1]);
     }
}

/*
 *  Displays a string in standard set notation.
 *  e.g.  print_set("abc") outputs {a, b, c}
 */
void
print_set(const char *set)
{
```

*(continued)*

**Figure 10.20** **(continued)**

```
        putchar('{');
        if (!is_empty(set))
                print_with_commas(set);
        putchar('}');
}

/*
 *  Gets a set input as a string with brackets (e.g., {abc})
 *  and strips off the brackets.
 */
char *
get_set(char *set)    /* output - set string without brackets {}        */
{
        char inset[SETSIZ];

        scanf("%s", inset);
        strncpy(set, &inset[1], strlen(inset) - 2);
        set[strlen(inset) - 2] = '\0';
        return (set);
}
```

**TESTING**

We have added one function to our group of set functions to make it easier to write a driver function for testing. The function get_set takes an input string representing a set and strips off the brackets { } that the driver program asks the user to place around the set entered. These brackets make it easy for the user to enter the empty set.

When testing this group of functions, choose data that check boundary conditions. For instance, test is_set with valid sets, including the empty set, and with invalid sets that have duplicate letters in various parts of the set string. For is_element, test an element found at the beginning of the set string, an element in the middle, an element at the end, and an element not in the string. Also try the empty set as the second argument. With is_subset, test using empty sets for sub and/or set, and try various orderings of letters in sub. Try a case where the sets are equal as well. When testing set_union, test equal sets, disjoint sets, and partially overlapping sets with various orderings of the elements. In addition, try the empty set as the first argument, then as the second; then call set_union using the empty set for both arguments.

Self-Check

1. Imagine that we add calls to `printf` of the type shown in Fig. 10.9 to functions `is_element` and `is_subset`. Show the tracing output that would be produced for the function call `is_subset("bc", "cebf");`

Programming

1. Define a recursive `intersection` function that computes $set1 \cap set2$. Then, define an iterative version of the same function.
2. Define a very short `set_equal` function that calls the `intersection` function from Programming Exercise 1.

# 10.6  A CLASSIC CASE STUDY IN RECURSION: TOWERS OF HANOI

The Towers of Hanoi problem involves moving a specified number of disks that are all different sizes from one tower (or peg) to another. Legend has it that the world will come to an end when the problem is solved for 64 disks.

**PROBLEM**

Move *n* disks from peg A to peg C using peg B as needed. The following conditions apply:

1. Only one disk at a time may be moved, and this disk must be the top disk on a peg.
2. A larger disk can never be placed on top of a smaller disk.

**ANALYSIS**

The version of the problem shown in Fig. 10.21 has five disks (numbered 1 through 5) and three towers or pegs (lettered A, B, and C). The goal is to move the five disks from peg A to peg C. The simplest cases of the problem involve

**Figure 10.21
Towers of
Hanoi**

**Figure 10.22
Towers of
Hanoi after
Steps 1 and 2**

moving one disk only (e.g., move disk 2 from peg A to peg C). A simpler problem than the original would be to move four disks subject to the conditions given or three disks, and so on. Therefore, we want to split the original five-disk problem into several simpler problems, each of which involves fewer disks. Let's consider splitting the original problem into the following three problems:

1. Move four disks from peg A to peg B.
2. Move disk 5 from peg A to peg C.
3. Move four disks from peg B to peg C.

In Step 1, we move all disks but the largest to peg B, an auxiliary peg not mentioned in the original problem. In Step 2, we move the largest disk to C, the goal peg. Then, in Step 3 we move the remaining disks from B to the goal peg, where they will be placed on top of the largest disk. Let's assume that we will be able to perform Step 1 and Step 2 (a simple case); Fig. 10.22 shows the status of the three pegs after completing these steps. At this point, it should be clear that we will indeed solve the original five-disk problem if we can complete Step 3.

Unfortunately, we still don't know how to perform Step 1 or Step 3. However, both of these steps involve four disks instead of five, so they are easier than the original problem. We should be able to split each of these steps into simpler problems in the same way that we split the original problem. Step 3 involves moving four disks from peg B to peg C, so we can split this step into the following two three-disk problems and one one-disk problem:

3.1 Move three disks from peg B to peg A.
3.2 Move disk 4 from peg B to peg C.
3.3 Move three disks from peg A to peg C.

Figure 10.23 shows the status of the pegs after completing Step 3.1 and Step 3.2. We now have the two largest disks on peg C. Once we complete Step 3.3, all five disks will be on peg C as required.

By splitting each $n$-disk problem into two problems involving $n-1$ disks and a third problem involving only one disk, we will eventually divide our original problem into many one-disk problems. These simple cases are ones we already know how to solve.

**Figure 10.23
Towers of
Hanoi after
Steps 1, 2, 3.1,
and 3.2**

The solution to the Towers of Hanoi problem consists of a printed list of individual disk moves. We need a recursive function that can be used to print instructions for moving any number of disks from one peg to another using the third peg as an auxiliary.

## Data Requirements

### Problem Inputs

```
int n             /* the number of disks to be moved  */
char from_peg     /* the from peg                     */
char to_peg       /* the to peg                       */
char aux_peg      /* the auxiliary peg                */
```

### Problem Outputs

A list of individual disk moves

**DESIGN**

### Algorithm

1. if *n* is 1 then
    2. Move disk 1 from the *from* peg to the *to* peg
   else
    3. Move *n* − 1 disks from the *from* peg to the *auxiliary* peg using the *to* peg.
    4. Move disk *n* from the *from* peg to the *to* peg.
    5. Move *n* − 1 disks from the *auxiliary* peg to the *to* peg using the *from* peg.

If *n* is 1, we have a simple case that we can solve immediately. If *n* is greater than 1, the recursive step (the step following else) splits the original problem into three smaller subproblems, one of which is another simple case. Each simple case displays a move instruction. Verify that the recursive step generates the three problems listed below Fig. 10.22 when *n* is 5, the *from* peg is A, and the *to* peg is C.

The implementation of this algorithm is shown as function `tower` in Fig. 10.24. Function `tower` has four input parameters. The function call statement

```
tower('A', 'C', 'B', 5);
```

solves the problem that was posed earlier of moving five disks from peg A to peg C using B as an auxiliary (see Fig. 10.21).

In Fig. 10.24, when the terminating condition is true, a call to `printf` displays an instruction regarding moving disk 1. Each recursive step consists of two recursive calls to `tower` with a call to `printf` sandwiched between them. The first recursive call solves the problem of moving *n* − 1 disks to the *auxiliary* peg. The call to `printf` displays a message to move the remaining disk to the *to* peg. The second recursive call solves the problem of moving the *n* − 1 disks from the *auxiliary* peg to the *to* peg.

**Figure 10.24    Recursive Function tower**

```
/*
 *  Displays instructions for moving n disks from from_peg to to_peg using
 *  aux_peg as an auxiliary.  Disks are numbered 1 to n (smallest to
 *  largest). Instructions call for moving one disk at a time and never
 *  require placing a larger disk on top of a smaller one.
 */
void
tower(char from_peg,    /* input - characters naming              */
      char to_peg,      /*            the problem's               */
      char aux_peg,     /*            three pegs                   */
      int  n)           /* input - number of disks to move        */
{
      if (n == 1) {
            printf("Move disk 1 from peg %c to peg %c\n", from_peg,
                   to_peg);
      } else {
            tower(from_peg, aux_peg, to_peg, n - 1);
            printf("Move disk %d from peg %c to peg %c\n", n, from_peg,
                   to_peg);
            tower(aux_peg, to_peg, from_peg, n - 1);
      }
}
```

The function call statement

```
tower('A', 'C', 'B', 3);
```

solves a simpler three-disk problem: Move 3 disks from peg A to peg C. Its execution is traced in Fig. 10.25 and the output generated is shown in Fig. 10.26. Verify for yourself that this list of steps does indeed solve the three-disk problem.

**Figure 10.25 Trace of tower('A', 'C', 'B', 3);**

**Figure 10.26
Output
Generated by
tower('A', 'C',
'B', 3);**

| Move disk 1 from A to C |
|---|
| Move disk 2 from A to B |
| Move disk 1 from C to B |
| Move disk 3 from A to C |
| Move disk 1 from B to A |
| Move disk 2 from B to C |
| Move disk 1 from A to C |

## Comparison of Iterative and Recursive Functions

It is interesting to consider that function tower in Fig. 10.26 will solve the Towers of Hanoi problem for any number of disks. The three-disk problem results in a total of seven calls to function tower and is solved by seven disk moves. The five-disk problem would result in a total of 31 calls to function tower and is solved in 31 moves. In general, the number of moves required to solve the $n$-disk problem is $2^n - 1$. Because each function call requires the allocation and initialization of a local data area in memory and the computer time increases exponentially with the problem size, be careful about running this program with a value of n that is larger than 10.

The dramatic increase in processing time for larger numbers of disks is a function of this problem, not a function of recursion. However, in general, if there are recursive and iterative solutions to the same problem, the recursive solution will require more time and space because of the extra function calls.

Although recursion was not really needed to solve the simpler problems in this section, it was extremely useful in formulating an algorithm for Towers of Hanoi. For certain problems, recursion leads naturally to solutions that are much easier to read and understand than their iterative counterparts. To researchers developing solutions to the complex problems that are at the frontiers of their research areas, the benefits gained from increased clarity far outweigh the extra cost in time and memory of running a recursive program.

**EXERCISES FOR
SECTION 10.6**

Self-Check

1. How many moves are needed to solve the six-disk problem?
2. Write a main function that takes a data value for n (the number of disks) and calls function tower to move n disks from A to B.

## 10.7 COMMON PROGRAMMING ERRORS

The most common problem with a recursive function is that it may not terminate properly. For example, if the terminating condition is not correct or is incomplete, the function may call itself indefinitely or until all available memory is used up. Frequently, a run-time error message noting stack overflow or an access violation is an indicator that a recursive function is not terminating. Make sure that you identify all simple cases and provide a terminating condition for each one. Also be sure that each recursive step redefines the problem in terms of arguments that are closer to simple cases so that repeated recursive calls will eventually lead to simple cases only.

In our examples of recursive functions that return a value, we have always used a local variable (or, in the case of string functions, an output parameter) into which the function result is placed by the function's decision structure. Then we have ended the function's code with a `return` statement. Since C permits the use of the `return` statement anywhere in the function code, a module like `is_set` from Fig. 10.20 could also have been written as follows.

```
int
is_set(const char *set)
{
        if (is_empty(set))
                return (TRUE);
        else if (is_element(set[0], &set[1]))
                return (FALSE);
        else
                return (is_set(&set[1]));
}
```

You should be aware that it is critical that every path through a nonvoid function leads to a `return` statement. In particular, the `return` statement to return the value of the recursive call to `is_set` is just as important as the other two `return` statements. However, it is easy to inadvertently omit one of these necessary `return` statements when a multiple `return` style is adopted.

The recopying of large arrays or other data structures can quickly consume all available memory. Such copying should be done inside a recursive function only when absolutely essential for data protection. If only a single copy is necessary, a nonrecursive function can be created that makes the necessary copy, passes the copy and the other arguments to the recursive function, and returns the result computed.

It is also a good idea to introduce a nonrecursive function to handle preliminaries and call the recursive function when there is error checking. Checking for errors inside a recursive function is extremely inefficient if the error is of the type that would be detected on the very first call. In such a situation, repeated checks in recursive calls are a waste of computer time.

Sometimes, it is difficult to observe the output produced when running recursive functions that you have made self-tracing as described in Section 10.2. If each recursive call generates two or more output lines and there are many recursive calls, the output will scroll down the screen more quickly than it can be read. On most systems, pressing a control character sequence (e.g., Control S) will temporarily stop output to the screen. If this is not possible, you can stop your output temporarily by printing a prompting message followed by a call to `getchar`. Your program will resume execution when you enter a data character.

## CHAPTER REVIEW

1. A recursive function either calls itself or initiates a sequence of function calls in which it may be called again.
2. Designing a recursive solution involves identifying simple cases that have straightforward solutions and then redefining more complex cases in terms of problems that are closer to simple cases.
3. Recursive functions depend on the fact, that for each call to a function, space is allocated on the stack for the function's parameters and local variables.

## QUICK-CHECK EXERCISES

1. Explain the use of a stack in recursion.
2. Which is generally more efficient, recursion or iteration?
3. Which control statement do you typically find in a recursive function?
4. How would you improve the efficiency of the following factorial function?

```
int
fact(int n)
{
      int ans;
      if (n < 0  ||  n > 10) {
            printf("\nInvalid argument to fact:  %d\n",
                  n);
            ans = n;
      } else if (n == 0) {
            ans = 1;
      } else {
            ans = n * fact(n - 1);
      }

      return (ans);
}
```

5. When might a programmer conceptualize a problem solution using recursion but implement it using iteration?
6. What problem do you notice in the following recursive function? Show two possible ways to correct the problem.

```
int
silly(int n)
{
      if (n <= 0)
            return (1);
      else if (n % 2 == 0)
            return (n);
      else
            silly(n - 3);
}
```

7. What is a common cause of a stack overflow error?
8. What can you say about a recursive algorithm that has the following form?

   *if condition*
         *Perform recursive step.*

## ANSWERS TO QUICK-CHECK EXERCISES

1. The stack is used to hold all parameter and local variable values along with the return point for each execution of a recursive function.
2. Iteration is generally more efficient than recursion.
3. `if` statement
4. Write as two functions so error checking occurs only once.

```
int
factorial(int n)
{
      int ans;

      if (n == 0)
            ans = 1;
      else
            ans = n * factorial(n - 1);
      return (ans);
}
```

```
int
fact(int n)
{
       int ans;

       if (n < 0  ||  n > 10) {
              printf("\nInvalid argument to fact:  %d\n",
                      n);
              ans = n;
       } else {
              ans = factorial(n);
       }

       return (ans);
}
```

5. When a problem's solution is much easier to conceptualize using recursion but a recursive implementation would be too inefficient.
6. One path through the function does not encounter a `return` statement. Either place a `return` statement in the final `else`

```
return (silly(n - 3));
```

or assign each result to a local variable, and place that variable in a `return` statement at the end of the function.
7. Too many recursive calls
8. Nothing is done when the simplest case is reached.

## REVIEW QUESTIONS

1. Why does recursion make it easier to conceptualize a solution to a problem?
2. Discuss the efficiency of recursive functions.
3. Differentiate between a simple case and a terminating condition.
4. Write a recursive C function that accumulates the sum of the values in an *n*-element array.
5. Write a recursive C function that counts the number of vowels in a string. You may wish to call the `is_element` function defined in Section 10.5.
6. The sequence 2, 6, 18, 54, 162, . . . is *geometric* because each term divided by its predecessor yields the same result, 3. The number 3 is the *common ratio* of the sequence. Write the recursive helper function `check_geo-metric` that assists function `main` in carrying out its purpose.

```
/*
 *   Determines if an input list forms a geometric
 *   sequence, a sequence in which each term is the
 *   product of the previous term and the common
 *   ratio.  Displays the message "List forms a geometric
 *   sequence" if this is the case.  Otherwise, stops
 *   input and prints the messages "Input halted at
 *   <incorrect term value>.  List does not form a
 *   geometric sequence"
 */
int
main(void)
{
      double term1, term2,
             ratio;        /* common ratio of a geometric
                              sequence whose first two
                              terms are term1 and term2  */
      printf("Data:  \n");
      scanf("%lf", &term1);
      printf("%.2f  ", term1);
      scanf("%lf", &term2);
      printf("%.2f  ", term2);

      ratio = term2 / term1;
      check_geometric(ratio, term2);   /* gets and checks
             rest of input list, considering ratios equal
             if they differ by less than .001            */

      return (0);
}
```

7. Write a recursive function that returns the position of the last nonblank character of a string. You may assume that you are working with a disposable copy of the string.

# PROGRAMMING PROJECTS

1. Develop a program to count pixels (picture elements) belonging to an object in a photograph. The data are in a two-dimensional grid of cells, each of which may be empty (value 0) or filled (value 1). The filled cells that are

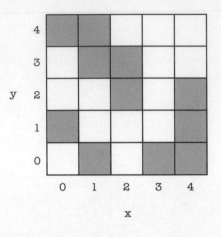

**Figure 10.27
Grid with
Three Blobs**

connected form a blob (an object). Fig. 10.27 shows a grid with three blobs. Include in your program a function `blob_check` that takes as parameters the grid and the *x-y* coordinates of a cell and returns as its value the number of cells in the blob to which the indicated cell belongs.

Function `blob_check` must test whether the cell specified by its arguments is filled. There are two simple cases: The cell (x, y) may not be on the grid, or the cell (x, y) may be empty. In either of these cases, the value returned by `blob_check` is 0. If the cell is on the grid and filled, then the value returned is 1 plus the sizes of the blobs containing each of its eight neighbors. To avoid counting a filled cell more than once, mark a cell as empty once you have counted it

2. A palindrome consists of a word or deblanked, unpunctuated phrase that is spelled exactly the same when the letters are reversed. Write a recursive function that returns a value of 1 if its string argument is a palindrome. Notice that in palindromes such as level, deed, sees, and Madam I'm Adam (madamimadam), the first letter matches the last, the second matches the next-to-last, and so on.

3. Write a recursive function that returns the value of the following recursive definition:

$$f(x, y) = x - y \qquad \text{if } x \text{ or } y < 0$$
$$f(x, y) = f(x{-}1, y) + f(x, y{-}1) \quad \text{otherwise}$$

4. Write a recursive function that lists all of the two-element subsets of a given set of letters. For example, `two_ele_subs("ACEG")` →

```
{A, C}
{A, E}
{A, G}
```

```
{C, E}
{C, G}
{E, G}
```

5. Write a function that accepts an 8 by 8 array of characters that represents a maze. Each position can contain either an X or a blank. Starting at position (0,1), list any path through the maze to get to location (7,7). Only horizontal and vertical moves are allowed. If no path exists, write a message indicating there is no path.

   Moves can be made only to locations that contain a blank. If an X is encountered, that path is blocked and another must be chosen. Use recursion.

6. In Programming Project 9 at the end of Chapter 8, we described an iterative algorithm for searching for a target value in a sorted list. Here again is the introduction to that problem.

   The binary search algorithm that follows may be used to search an array when the elements are in order. This algorithm is analogous to the following approach to finding a name in a telephone book.

   a. Open the book in the middle and look at the middle name on the page.
   b. If the middle name isn't the one you're looking for, decide whether it comes before or after the name you want.
   c. Take the appropriate half of the section of the book you were looking in, and repeat these steps until you land on the name.

### Iterative Algorithm for Binary Search

1. Let bottom be the subscript of the initial array element.
2. Let top be the subscript of the last array element.
3. Let found be false.
4. Repeat as long as bottom isn't greater than top and the target has not been found
   5. Let middle be the subscript of the element halfway between bottom and top
   6. If the element at middle is the target
      7. Set found to true and index to middle.
   else if the element at middle is larger than the target
      8. Let top be middle − 1.
   else
      9. Let bottom be middle + 1.

Develop a recursive binary search algorithm, and write and test a function `binary_srch` that implements the algorithm for an array of integers.

7. Write a recursive function that displays all the binary (base 2) numbers represented by a string of xs, 0s, and 1s. The xs represent digits that can be either 0 or 1. For example, the string 1x0x represents the numbers 1000,

1001, 1100, 1101. The string xx1 represents 001, 011, 101, 111. *Hint:* Write a helper function replace_first_x that builds two strings based on its input argument. In one, the first x is replaced by a 0, and in the other by a 1. The set function is_element may be useful too.

8. The version of the selection sort that we studied in Chapter 8 places the smallest value in the initial array element, the second smallest in the next element, and so on. Implement this version recursively.

# STRUCTURE AND UNION TYPES

chapter **11**

In previous chapters, we have seen how to represent in C numbers, characters, words, other strings, and lists (arrays) of these objects. But surely there is more to the world we live in than words and lists of numbers! Every day the role of computers in this complex universe widens, and a programming language must be able to model not only numbers and names, but also protozoa, people, and planets.

In this chapter, we will study how to broaden the modeling facilities of C by defining our own data types that represent structured collections of data pertaining to particular objects. Unlike an array, a structure can have individual components that contain data of different types. A single variable of a composite type designed for planets can store a planet's name, diameter, number of moons, the number of years to complete one solar orbit, and the number of hours to make one rotation on its axis. Each of these data items is stored in a separate component of the structure and can be referenced by using the component name.

# 11.1 USER-DEFINED STRUCTURE TYPES

**record**
a collection of information
about one data object

A *database* is a collection of information stored in a computer's memory or in a disk file. A database is subdivided into **records**, which normally contain information regarding specific data objects. The structure of the record is determined by the structure of the object's data type.

## Structure Type Definition

Before a structured data object can be created or saved, the format of its components must be defined. Although C provides several ways to define structures, we will explore just one approach—defining a new data type for each category of structured objects.

**EXAMPLE 11.1** ▶

As part of a project for our local observatory, we are developing a database of the planets in our solar system. For each planet, we need to represent information like the following:

Name: Jupiter
Diameter: 142,800 km
Moons: 4
Orbit time: 11.9 yr
Rotation time: 9.925 hr

**structure type**
a data type for a record composed of multiple components

We can define a **structure type** planet_t to use in declaring a variable in which to store this information. There must be five *components* in the structure type, one for each data item. We must specify the name of each component and the type of information stored in each component. We choose the names in the same way we choose all other identifiers: The names describe the nature of the information represented. The contents of each component determine the appropriate data type. For example, the planet's name should be stored in a component that is an array of characters.

The structure type planet_t has five distinct components. One is an array of characters; one is an int. The other three are of type double.

```
#define STRSIZ 10

typedef struct {
    char    name[STRSIZ];
    double diameter;          /* equatorial diameter in
                                   km                  */
    int     moons;            /* number of moons       */
    double orbit_time,        /* years to orbit sun once */
            rotation_time;    /* hours to complete one
                                   revolution on axis  */
} planet_t;
```

*The name of all this ↑*

This type definition is a template that describes the format of a planet structure and the name and type of each component. A name chosen for a component of one structure may be the same as the name of a component of another structure or the same as the name of a variable. We will see that the approach C takes to referencing these components will rule out confusion of matching names used in these different contexts.

The typedef statement itself allocates no memory. A variable declaration is required to allocate storage space for a structured data object. The variables current_planet and previous_planet are declared next, and the variable blank_planet is declared and initialized.

```
{
    planet_t current_planet,
             previous_planet,
             blank_planet = {"", 0, 0, 0, 0};
    . . .
```

The structured variables current_planet, previous_planet, and blank_planet all have the format specified in the definition of type planet_t. Thus the memory allocated for each consists of storage space for five distinct values. The variable `blank_planet` is pictured as it appears after initialization.

Variable blank_planet, a structure of type planet_t

| | |
|---|---|
| .name | \0 ? ? ? ? ? ? ? ? ? |
| .diameter | 0.0 |
| .moons | 0 |
| .orbit_time | 0.0 |
| .rotation_time | 0.0 |

A user-defined type like `planet_t` can be used to declare both simple and array variables and to declare components in other structure types. A structure containing components that are data structures (arrays or `struct`s) is sometimes called a **hierarchical structure**. The following definition of a structure type includes a component that is an array of planets.

**hierarchial structure**
a structure containing components that are structures

```
typedef struct {
      double    diameter;
      planet_t  planets[9];
      char      galaxy[STRSIZ];
} solar_sys_t;
```

---

**Structure Type Definition**

SYNTAX: typedef struct {
           $type_1$ $id\_list_1$;
           $type_2$ $id\_list_2$;
           .
           .
           .
           $type_n$ $id\_list_n$;
       } $struct\_type$;

EXAMPLE: typedef struct { /* complex number structure */
           double real_pt,
               imag_pt;
       } complex_t;

*(continued)*

INTERPRETATION: The identifier *struct_type* is the name of the structure type being defined. Each *id_list*$_i$ is a list of one or more component names separated by commas; the data type of each component in *id_list*$_i$ is specified by *type*$_i$.

NOTE: *type*$_i$ can be any standard or previously specified user-defined data type.

## Manipulating Individual Components of a Structured Data Object

**direct component selection operator**
a period placed between a structure type variable and a component name to create a reference to the component

We can reference a component of a structure by using the **direct component selection operator**, which is a period. The period is preceded by the name of a structure type variable and is followed by the name of a component.

**EXAMPLE 11.2**

Figure 11.1 shows as an example the manipulation of the components of the variable `current_planet` listed at the beginning of Example 11.1. The statements in the figure store in the variable the data pictured earlier.

Once data are stored in a record, they can be manipulated in the same

**Figure 11.1
Assigning
Values to
Components
of Variable
current_planet**

```
strcpy(current_planet.name, "Jupiter");
current_planet.diameter = 142800;
current_planet.moons = 4;
current_planet.orbit_time = 11.9;
current_planet.rotation_time = 9.925;
```

Variable current_planet, a structure of type planet_t

| | |
|---|---|
| .name | J u p i t e r \0 ? ? |
| .diameter | 142800.0 |
| .moons | 4 |
| .orbit_time | 11.9 |
| .rotation_time | 9.925 |

way as other data in memory. For example, the statement

```
printf("%s's equatorial diameter is %.1f km.\n",
        current_planet.name, current_planet.diameter);
```

displays the sentence

```
Jupiter's equatorial diameter is 142800.0 km.
```

← 

## Review of Operator Precedence

With the addition of the direct component selection operator to our repertory of operators, we will take a moment to see how this operator fits into our overall scheme of precedence rules. Table 11.1 not only shows operator precedence answering the question, In an expression with two operators, which is applied first? It also lists operator associativity answering the question, In an expression containing two of these operators in sequence, which is applied first?

In a generic expression containing two of the same operators in sequence,

$$operand_1 \; op \; operand_2 \; op \; operand_3$$

**Table 11.1   Precedence and Associativity of Operators Seen So Far**

| Precedence | Symbols | Operator Names | Associativity |
|---|---|---|---|
| highest | `a[j]  f(...)  .` | Subscripting, function calls, direct component selection | left |
| | `++ --` | Postfix increment and decrement | left |
| | `++ -- !` `- + & *` | Prefix increment and decrement, logical not, unary negation and plus, address of, indirection | right |
| | ( *type name* ) | Casts | right |
| | `* / %` | Multiplicative operators (multiplication, division, remainder) | left |
| | `+ -` | Binary additive operators (addition and subtraction) | left |
| | `< > <= >=` | Relational operators | left |
| | `== !=` | Equality / inequality operators | left |
| | `&&` | Logical and | left |
| | `\|\|` | Logical or | left |
| lowest | `= += -=` `*= /= %=` | Assignment operators | right |

if *op* has left associativity, the expression is evaluated as

(*operand*$_1$  *op*  *operand*$_2$)  *op*  *operand*$_3$

whereas if *op* has right associativity, the implied order of evaluation is:

*operand*$_1$  *op*  (*operand*$_2$  *op*  *operand*$_3$)

## Manipulating Whole Structures

The name of a structure type variable used with no component selection operator refers to the entire structure. A new copy of a structure's value can be made by simply assigning one structure to another as in the following statement:

```
previous_planet = current_planet;
```

We will see other instances of the manipulation of whole structures in the next section when we study the use of structures as input and output parameters of functions and as function result types.

## Program Style   *Naming Convention for Types*

When we write programs that define new types, it is easy to confuse type names and variable names. To help reduce confusion, in this text we choose user-defined type names that use lowercase letters and end in the suffix _t (a practice recommended in some industrial software design environments).

**EXERCISES FOR SECTION 11.1**

Self-Check

1. Define a type named long_lat_t that would be appropriate for storing longitude or latitude values. Include components named degrees (an integer), minutes (an integer), and direction (one of the characters 'N', 'S', 'E', or 'W').
2. The following are a type to represent a geographic location and a variable of this hierarchical structure type. We will assume that STRSIZ means 20.

```
typedef struct {
      char        place[STRSIZ];
      long_lat_t longitude,
                  latitude;
} location_t;

location_t resort;
```

Given that the values shown have been stored in resort, complete the following table to check your understanding of component selection.

Variable resort, a structure of type location_t

| | | | |
|---|---|---|---|
| .place | Fiji\0??... | | |
| .longitude | 178 | 0 | E |
| .latitude | 17 | 50 | S |

| Reference | Data type of reference | Value |
|---|---|---|
| resort.latitude | long_lat_t | 17 50 'S' |
| resort.place | _____ | _____ |
| resort.longitude.direction | _____ | _____ |
| _____ | int | 50 |
| resort.place[3] | _____ | _____ |

3. A catalog listing for a textbook consists of the authors' names, the title, the publisher, and the year of publication. Declare a structure type catalog_entry_t and a variable book, and write statements that store the relevant data for this textbook in book.

## 11.2 STRUCTURE TYPE DATA AS INPUT AND OUTPUT PARAMETERS

When a structured variable is passed as an input argument to a function, all of its component *values* are copied into the components of the function's corresponding formal parameter. When such a variable is used as an output argument, the address-of operator must be applied in the same way that we would pass output arguments of the standard types char, int, and double.

**EXAMPLE 11.3**

Our observatory program from Example 11.1 and Example 11.2 frequently needs to output as a unit all of the descriptive data about a planet. Figure 11.2 shows a function to do this.

To display the value of our structure current_planet, we would use the call statement

```
print_planet(current_planet);
```

**Figure 11.2    Function with a Structured Input Parameter**

```
/*
 * Displays with labels all components of a planet_t structure
 */
void
print_planet(planet_t pl) /* input - one planet structure */
{
      printf("%s\n", pl.name);
      printf("   Equatorial diameter: %.0f km\n", pl.diameter);
      printf("   Number of moons: %d\n", pl.moons);
      printf("   Time to complete one orbit of the sun: %.2f years\n",
             pl.orbit_time);
      printf("   Time to complete one rotation on axis: %.4f hours\n",
             pl.rotation_time);
}
```

Having an output function like print_planet helps us to view the planet object as a concept at a higher level of abstraction rather than as an ad hoc collection of components.

Another function that would help us think of a planet as a data object is a function that would perform an equality comparison of two planets. Although C permits copying of a structure using the assignment operator, the equality and inequality operators cannot be applied to a structured type as a unit. Figure 11.3 shows a planet_equal function that takes two planets as input arguments and returns 1 or 0 depending on whether all components match.

**Figure 11.3    Function Comparing Two Structured Values for Equality**

```
#include <string.h>

/*
 * Determines whether or not the components of planet_1 and planet_2 match
 */
int
planet_equal(planet_t planet_1, /* input - planets to      */
             planet_t planet_2) /*          compare        */
{
```

*(continued)*

**Figure 11.3** *(continued)*

```
        return (strcmp(planet_1.name, planet_2.name) == 0      &&
                planet_1.diameter == planet_2.diameter          &&
                planet_1.moons == planet_2.moons                &&
                planet_1.orbit_time == planet_2.orbit_time      &&
                planet_1.rotation_time == planet_2.rotation_time);
}
```

A planet input function would also help us to process `current_planet` as `planet_t` data. Figure 11.4 shows the function `scan_planet` that resembles `scanf` in that it takes an output argument and returns the value 1 if its single output argument is successfully filled, returns the value 0 if there is an error, and returns the negative value EOF if the end of the file is encountered.        ←

As you can see from this example, manipulating a structured output argument using operators `*` and `.` really requires you to keep C's operator-precedence rules straight. In order to use `scanf` to store a value in one component of the structure whose address is in `plnp`, we must carry out the following steps (in order):

1. Follow the pointer in `plnp` to the structure.
2. Select the component of interest.
3. Unless this component is an array (e.g., component `name` in Fig. 11.4), get its address to pass to `scanf`.

When we check our precedence chart (see Table 11.1), we find that this reference

`&*plnp.diameter`

would attempt Step 2 before Step 1. For this reason, the function in Fig. 11.4 overrides the default operator precedence by parenthesizing the application of the indirect referencing (pointer-following) operator, the unary `*`. Figure 11.5 shows the data areas of functions `main` and `scan_planet` during execution of the following statement in `main`:

`status = scan_planet(&current_planet);`

**indirect component selection operator**
the character sequence -> placed between a pointer variable and a component name creates a reference that follows the pointer to a structure and selects the component

We are assuming that the assignment statement of `scan_planet` calling `scanf` has just finished executing and that it has successfully obtained input values for all components of the output argument structure.

In Table 11.2, we analyze the reference `&(*plnp).diameter` from our function `scan_planet`. C also provides a single operator that combines the functions of the indirection and component selection operators. This **indirect component selection operator** is represented by the character sequence -> (a

**Figure 11.4   Function with a Structured Output Argument**

```
/*
 * Fills a type planet_t structure with input data. Integer returned as
 * function result is success/failure/EOF indicator.
 *      1 => successful input of one planet
 *      0 => error encountered
 *      EOF => insufficient data before end of file
 * In case of error or EOF, value of type planet_t output argument is
 * undefined.
 */
int
scan_planet(planet_t *plnp) /* output - address of planet_t structure
                                        to fill                         */
{
     int result;

     result = scanf("%s%lf%d%lf%lf",  (*plnp).name,
                                      &(*plnp).diameter,
                                      &(*plnp).moons,
                                      &(*plnp).orbit_time,
                                      &(*plnp).rotation_time);

     if (result == 5)
           result = 1;
     else if (result != EOF)
           result = 0;

     return (result);
}
```

*— Array name is a pointer*

minus sign followed by a greater-than symbol). Thus these two expressions are equivalent.

```
(*structp).component              structp->component
```

If we rewrite the `scan_planet` function of Fig. 11.4 using the `->` operator, the assignment to `result` will be

```
result = scanf("%s%lf%d%lf%lf", plnp->name,
                               &plnp->diameter,
                               &plnp->moons,
                               &plnp->orbit_time,
                               &plnp->rotation_time);
```

**Figure 11.5    Data Areas of main and scan_planet during Execution of** `status = scan_planet(&current_planet);`

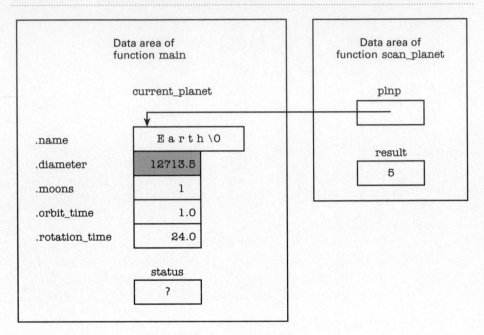

**Table 11.2    Step-by-Step Analysis of Reference &(*plnp).diameter**

| Reference | Type | Value |
|---|---|---|
| `plnp` | `planet_t *` | address of structure that `main` refers to as `current_planet` |
| `*plnp` | `planet_t` | structure that `main` refers to as `current_planet` |
| `(*plnp).diameter` | `double` | `12713.5` |
| `&(*plnp).diameter` | `double *` | address of colored component of structure that `main` refers to as `current_planet` |

In the next section, we see how to write a function that fills up a `planet_t` structure with input data and returns this structure as the function value. This alternative way of approaching input of structures avoids the need for indirect referencing, but it cannot return a status indicator as the function value in the same way `scan_planet` does.

**EXERCISES FOR SECTION 11.2**

Self-Check

1. Write functions `print_long_lat`, `long_lat_equal`, and `scan_long_lat` to perform output, equality comparison, and input of type `long_lat_t` data (see Self-Check Exercise 1 at the end of Section 11.1).

2. Assume that you have a function `verify_location` that manipulates a structured input/output argument of type `location_t` (see Self-Check Exercise 2 at the end of Section 11.1). The figure that follows shows the data areas of functions `main` and `verify_location` during execution of the call

   `code = verify_location(&resort);`

   Complete the table following the figure with references appropriate for use in `verify_location` (if such references were needed).

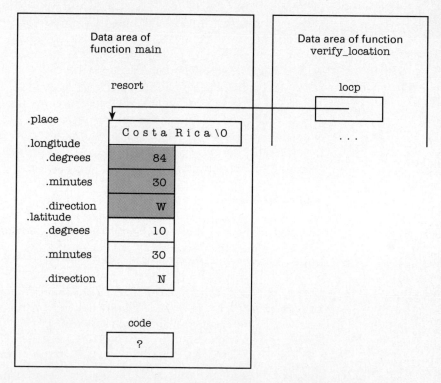

| Reference in verify_location | Type of Reference | Value of Reference |
| --- | --- | --- |
| locp | location_t * | address of the structure that main refers to as resort |
| _____ | _____ | the structure that main refers to as resort |
| _____ | _____ | "Costa Rica" |
| _____ | _____ | address of the colored component of the structure that main refers to as resort |
| _____ | _____ | 84 |

# 11.3 FUNCTIONS WHOSE RESULT VALUES ARE STRUCTURED

In our study so far, we have seen many situations in which user-defined structured data types are treated just like C's own simple types, yet we have seen only one situation in which structures are handled differently, namely, in equality comparisons. In Chapter 8 and Chapter 9, we saw that C's processing of the array data structure differs significantly from its handling of simple data types. One of the many differences is the fact that the values of an entire array cannot be returned as a function result. Rather, functions computing array results typically require the calling module to provide an array output argument in which to store the result and then return this array's address as the function value.

Since arrays and structure types are both data *structures*, one might expect that C would handle them in a similar fashion. In fact, learning C is greatly assisted by doing away with this expectation, because C's approach to processing structure types closely resembles its facilities for working with simple data types, but is very different from its handling of arrays.

A function that computes a structured result can be modeled on a function computing a simple result. A local variable of the structure type can be allocated, filled with the desired data, and returned as the function result. The function does not return the *address* of the structure as it would with an array result; rather it returns the *values* of all components.

**EXAMPLE 11.4** ▶ In Fig. 11.6, we see a function that obtains from the input device values for all components of a planet_t structure and returns the structure as the function result. Like function getchar, our function get_planet requires no arguments. If we assume entry of correct data, the statement

```
current_planet = get_planet();
```

**Figure 11.6    Function get_planet Returning a Structured Result Type**

```
/*
 * Gets and returns a planet_t structure
 */
planet_t
get_planet(void)
{
      planet_t planet;

      scanf("%s%lf%d%lf%lf",  planet.name,
                              &planet.diameter,
                              &planet.moons,
                              &planet.orbit_time,
                              &planet.rotation_time);
      return (planet);
}
```

has the same effect as

```
scan_planet(&current_planet);
```

However, the assumption of correct data entry format is frequently unjustified, so scan_planet with its ability to return an integer error code is the more generally useful function.    ←

**EXAMPLE 11.5** ▶ Before performing a potentially dangerous or costly experiment in the laboratory, we can often use a computer program to simulate the experiment. In computer simulations, we need to keep track of the time of day as the experiment progresses. Normally, the time of day is updated after a certain period has elapsed. Assuming a 24-hour clock, the structure type time_t is defined as follows:

```
typedef struct {
        int hour, minute, second;
} time_t;
```

Function new_time in Fig. 11.7 returns as its value an updated time based on the original time of day and the number of seconds that have elapsed since the

**Figure 11.7** **Function to Compute an Updated Time Value**

```
/*
 * Computes a new time represented as a time_t structure
 * and based on time of day and elapsed seconds.
 */
time_t
new_time(time_t time_of_day,    /* input - time to be
                                     updated                         */
        int     elapsed_secs)  /* input - seconds since last update  */
{
      int new_hr, new_min, new_sec;

      new_sec = time_of_day.second + elapsed_secs;
      time_of_day.second = new_sec % 60;
      new_min = time_of_day.minute + new_sec / 60;
      time_of_day.minute = new_min % 60;
      new_hr = time_of_day.hour + new_min / 60;
      time_of_day.hour = new_hr % 24;

      return (time_of_day);
}
```

previous update. If `time_now` were 21:58:32 and `secs` had the value 97, the result returned by the call

```
new_time(time_now, secs)
```

would be 22:00:09. Because `new_time`'s variable `time_of_day` is strictly an input parameter, the value of `time_now` will not be affected by the call to `new_time`. If the intent is to update `time_now`, an assignment statement is used.

```
time_now = new_time(time_now, secs);
```

Figure 11.8 traces the assignment statement just mentioned showing the structured `time_t` value used as an input argument and the type `time_t` function value.

**Figure 11.8
Structured
Values as a
Function Input
Argument and
as a Function
Result**

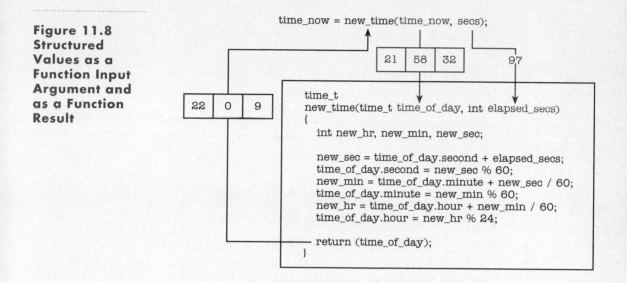

Self-Check

1. Why does function new_time's assignment of new values to the second, minute, and hour components of its formal parameter time_of_day have no effect on the components of actual argument time_now in the call new_time(time_now, secs)?
2. Could you modify function get_planet so that it would still have a type planet_t result but would also indicate input success or failure to the calling function?

Programming

1. Define a structure type to represent a common fraction. Write a program that gets a fraction and displays both the fraction and the fraction reduced to lowest terms using the following code fragment:

```
frac = get_fraction();
print_fraction(frac);
printf(" = ");
print_fraction(reduce_fraction(frac));
```

# 11.4 PROBLEM SOLVING WITH STRUCTURE TYPES

When we solve problems using C's standard data types, we take for granted the fact that C provides us with all the basic operations we need to manipulate our data. However, when we work with a problem whose data objects are more

**Figure 11.9
Data Type
planet_t
and Basic
Operations**

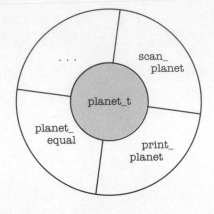

complex, we find that defining our own data types is just the first step in building a tool with which to attack the problem. In order to be able to think about the problem on the basis of our own data types, we must also provide basic operations for manipulating these types.

Combining a user-defined type with a set of basic operations that allow one truly to see the type as a unified concept creates what is called an **abstract data type** (ADT). Figure 11.9 shows one view of our data type planet_t combined with its operations.

**abstract data type (ADT)**
a data type combined with a
set of basic operations

If we take the time to define enough basic operations for a structure type, we then find it possible to think about a related problem at a higher level of abstraction; we are no longer bogged down in the details of manipulating the type's components.

In our next case study, we develop such a group of basic operations for processing complex numbers.

## Case Study: A User-Defined Type for Complex Numbers

**PROBLEM**

We are working on an engineering project that uses complex numbers for modeling of electrical circuits. We need to develop a user-defined structure type and a set of operations that will make complex arithmetic virtually as straightforward as arithmetic on C's built-in numeric types.

**ANALYSIS**

A complex number is a number with a real part and an imaginary part. For example, the complex number $a + bi$ has a real part $a$ and an imaginary part $b$, where the symbol $i$ represents $\sqrt{-1}$. We will need to define functions for complex I/O as well as for the basic arithmetic operations (addition, subtraction, multiplication, and division) and for finding the absolute value of a complex number.

**DESIGN**

The two major aspects of our solution to this problem are defining the structure of the user-defined type and describing the function name, parameters, and purpose of each operation. Each function purpose then forms a subproblem to be solved separately. The details of these subproblems will be of interest to us as we develop our operations. However, once this group of functions is complete, we will be concerned only with *what* each function does, not with *how* it does it. In the same way, when we use C's built-in multiplication operator, we are interested only in the fact that * does multiplication, not caring in the least *how* it manages to accomplish this.

## Specification of Type complex_t and Associated Operations

STRUCTURE: A complex number is an object of type `complex_t` that consists of a pair of type `double` values.

OPERATORS:

```
/*
 * Complex number input function returns standard scanning
 * error code
 */
int
scan_complex(complex_t *c)  /* output - address of complex
                                          variable to fill  */

/*
 * Complex output function displays value as a + bi or a - bi.
 * Displays only a if imaginary part is 0.
 * Displays only bi if real part is 0.
 */
void
print_complex(complex_t c)  /* input - complex number to
                                          display          */

/*
 * Returns sum of complex values c1 and c2
 */
complex_t
add_complex(complex_t c1, complex_t c2)          /* input  */
```

*(continued)*

```
/*
 * Returns difference c1 - c2
 */
complex_t
subtract_complex(complex_t c1, complex_t c2)        /* input */

/*
 * Returns product of complex values c1 and c2
 */
complex_t
multiply_complex(complex_t c1, complex_t c2)        /* input */

/*
 * Returns quotient of complex values (c1 / c2)
 */
complex_t
divide_complex(complex_t c1, complex_t c2)          /* input */

/*
 * Returns absolute value of complex number c
 */
complex_t
abs_complex(complex_t c)                             /* input */
```

As soon as this specification is complete, our co-workers on the circuit modeling project can begin designing algorithms that assume the availability of these operations. Then, when our implementation is complete, our code can either be added to their programs or packaged for inclusion in a way we will describe in Chapter 13.

Figure 11.10 shows a partial implementation of our specification together with a driver function. Functions `multiply_complex` and `divide_complex` have been left as an exercise. Notice that the definition of type `complex_t` is placed immediately after our preprocessor directives so that it is visible throughout the entire program. Function `abs_complex` uses the following formula to compute the absolute value of a complex number:

$$\left| a + bi \right| = \sqrt{(a + bi)(a - bi)} = \sqrt{a^2 + b^2}$$

This result always has an imaginary part of zero, so `print_complex` will display the result as a real number.

**Figure 11.10** **Partial Implementation of Type and Operators for Complex Numbers**

```
/*
 *  Operators to process complex numbers
 */
#include <stdio.h>
#include <math.h>

/*  User-defined complex number type */
typedef struct {
      double real, imag;
} complex_t;

int scan_complex(complex_t *c);
void print_complex(complex_t c);
complex_t add_complex(complex_t c1, complex_t c2);
complex_t subtract_complex(complex_t c1, complex_t c2);
complex_t multiply_complex(complex_t c1, complex_t c2);
complex_t divide_complex(complex_t c1, complex_t c2);
complex_t abs_complex(complex_t c);

/*  Driver                                                              */
int
main(void)
{
      complex_t com1, com2;

      /*  Gets two complex numbers                                      */
      printf("Enter the real and imaginary parts of a complex number\n");
      printf("separated by a space> ");
      scan_complex(&com1);
      printf("Enter a second complex number> ");
      scan_complex(&com2);

      /*  Forms and displays the sum                                    */
      printf("\n");
      print_complex(com1);
      printf("  +  ");
      print_complex(com2);
      printf("  =  ");
      print_complex(add_complex(com1, com2));

      /*  Forms and displays the difference                             */
      printf("\n\n");
```

*(continued)*

**Figure 11.10** *(continued)*

```
     print_complex(com1);
     printf("  -  ");
     print_complex(com2);
     printf("  =  ");
     print_complex(subtract_complex(com1, com2));

     /*  Forms and displays the absolute value of the first number    */
     printf("\n\n|");
     print_complex(com1);
     printf("|  =  ");
     print_complex(abs_complex(com1));
     printf("\n");

     return (0);
}

/*
 *  Complex number input function returns standard scanning error code
 *    1 => valid scan, 0 => error, negative EOF value => end of file
 */
int
scan_complex(complex_t *c) /* output - address of complex variable to
                                        fill                          */
{
     int status;

     status = scanf("%lf%lf", &c->real, &c->imag);
     if (status == 2)
          status = 1;
     else if (status != EOF)
          status = 0;

     return (status);
}

/*
 *  Complex output function displays value as (a + bi) or (a - bi),
 *  dropping a or b if they round to 0 unless both round to 0
 */
```

*(continued)*

**Figure 11.10**   *(continued)*

```
void
print_complex(complex_t c) /* input - complex number to display   */
{
      double a, b;
      char    sign;

      a = c.real;
      b = c.imag;

      printf("(");

      if (fabs(a) < .005  &&  fabs(b) < .005) {
            printf("%.2f", 0.0);
      } else if (fabs(b) < .005) {
            printf("%.2f", a);
      } else if (fabs(a) < .005) {
            printf("%.2fi", b);
      } else {
            if (b < 0)
                  sign = '-';
            else
                  sign = '+';
            printf("%.2f %c %.2fi", a, sign, fabs(b));
      }

      printf(")");
}

/*
 *  Returns sum of complex values c1 and c2
 */
complex_t
add_complex(complex_t c1, complex_t c2) /* input - values to add    */
{
      complex_t csum;

      csum.real = c1.real + c2.real;
      csum.imag = c1.imag + c2.imag;
```

*(continued)*

**Figure 11.10**    *(continued)*

```
        return (csum);
}

/*
 *  Returns difference c1 - c2
 */
complex_t
subtract_complex(complex_t c1, complex_t c2) /* input parameters    */
{
        complex_t cdiff;
        cdiff.real = c1.real - c2.real;
        cdiff.imag = c1.imag - c2.imag;

        return (cdiff);
}

/*  ** Stub **
 *  Returns product of complex values c1 and c2
 */
complex_t
multiply_complex(complex_t c1, complex_t c2) /* input parameters    */
{
        printf("Function multiply_complex returning first argument\n");
        return (c1);
}

/*  ** Stub **
 *  Returns quotient of complex values (c1 / c2)
 */
complex_t
divide_complex(complex_t c1, complex_t c2) /* input parameters    */
{
        printf("Function divide_complex returning first argument\n");
        return (c1);
}

/*
 *  Returns absolute value of complex number c
 */
```

*(continued)*

**Figure 11.10**    *(continued)*

```
complex_t
abs_complex(complex_t c) /* input parameter                          */
{
      complex_t cabs;

      cabs.real = sqrt(c.real * c.real + c.imag * c.imag);
      cabs.imag = 0;

      return (cabs);
}
```

```
Enter the real and imaginary parts of a complex number
separated by a space> 3.5 5.2
Enter a second complex number> 2.5 1.2

(3.50 + 5.20i)   +   (2.50 + 1.20i)   =   (6.00 + 6.40i)

(3.50 + 5.20i)   -   (2.50 + 1.20i)   =   (1.00 + 4.00i)

|(3.50 + 5.20i)|   =   (6.27)
```

**EXERCISES FOR SECTION 11.4**

Self-Check

1. What does the following program segment display if the data entered are 6.5 5.0 3.0 -4.0?

```
complex_t a, b, c;

scan_complex(&a);
scan_complex(&b);

print_complex(a);
printf(" + ");
print_complex(b);
printf(" = ");
print_complex(add_complex(a, b));

c = subtract_complex(a, abs_complex(b));
printf("\n\nSecond result = ");
print_complex(c);
printf("\n");
```

Programming

1. Write functions `multiply_complex` and `divide_complex` to implement the operations of multiplication and division of complex numbers defined as follows:

$$(a + bi) \times (c + di) = (ac - bd) + (ad + bc)i$$

$$\frac{(a + bi)}{(c + di)} = \frac{ac + bd}{c^2 + d^2} + \frac{bc - ad}{c^2 + d^2} \; i$$

## 11.5 PARALLEL ARRAYS AND ARRAYS OF STRUCTURES

Often a data collection contains items of different types or items that, although of the same type, represent quite distinct concepts. For example, the data used to represent a list of students might consist of an integer identification number and

# C IN FOCUS

Creating a Developer-Friendly C Environment

Inspired by the speed of their Turbo Pascal compiler, Borland International spawned Turbo C in response to the overwhelming industry trend toward writing production code in C. Although C was increasingly popular, programming in the C environment was limited by slow, multipass compilers. Turbo C offered C programmers for the first time an integrated development environment (providing an editor and compiler options) and it modified an existing five-pass C compiler into what appeared to be a one-pass compiler. These two developments along with the incorporation of a very fast linker contributed to Turbo C's success.

Projects like Turbo C that introduce new ideas frequently start with a visionary who is in a position to execute his vision.

For Turbo C (and later Turbo C++), Brad Silverberg built a team, gave them goals, and allowed them to innovate. The Turbo C 1.0 team had one member responsible for the compiler, one (in Europe) for the linker, one for the run-time library, one DOS programmer, and Mike Weisert, who was responsible for the user interface. Very late in the project the team added quality assurance and documentation members.

User involvement was and is a routine part of the development process at Borland. All team members interact with beta testers and third-party independent software vendors who give them lots of feedback. In addition, the development team has the added benefit of their own experiences using the tools under construction every day.

a type `double` gpa for each student. The data representing a polygon might be a list of the (*x, y*) coordinates of the polygon's corners.

## Parallel Arrays

In Section 8.1, we learned how to represent such data collections using *parallel arrays* like these:

```
int     id[50];        /* id numbers and               */
double  gpa[50];       /*   gpa's of up to 50 students */
double  x[NUM_PTS],    /* (x,y) coordinates of         */
        y[NUM_PTS];    /*   up to NUM_PTS points       */
```

Arrays `id` and `gpa` are called parallel arrays because the data items with the same subscript (for example, *i*) pertain to the same student (the *i*th student). Similarly, the *i*th elements of arrays x and y are the coordinates of one point. A better way to organize data collections like these is shown next.

The enhancements they make help themselves as well as their customers.

For example, Mike Weisert contributed the message window and message tracking to the Turbo C project. While building Turbo C with another vendor's multipass compiler, he was continually annoyed that the error messages would scroll off the screen. Because it took so long to compile on the 8088s in use then, he frequently went to get a cup of coffee while he waited. Any error messages that appeared would scroll off the screen in his absence. Because it is always the first error message in C that is most useful, he would have to recompile and watch and wait to pause the output at the first sign of error. His decision to buffer all the error messages and display them in a window led to increased satisfaction among Turbo C customers (and himself).

Trends in computing continue to drive the software development process. When the concept of Object Oriented Programming (OOP) was gaining popularity, its promise of reusable code was hampered by the lack of an OOP development environment that was efficient enough for production code. Weisert headed the team at Borland that answered the need with C++.

For Borland C++, the team was a bit larger. Weisert had a team of five (including himself) to build the Integrated Development Environment (IDE). Additional team members worked on the compiler, linker, run-time library, and so on. To make an environment for production code, the team's focus was on size and speed: smaller and faster was better. In the end they were successful; their new development tool influenced both the market and the entire industry.

Today, rapid developments in operating systems for personal computers present new opportunities for Borland. As changes occur, new teams headed by individuals like Mike Weisert will take on the challenge of tailoring programming tools to the new tasks—their customers' and their own.

Many thanks to Michael R. Weisert, Senior Project Manager, Languages C++, of Borland International, Inc., for talking with us about his experiences in developing the successful Borland C and C++ products.

## Declaring an Array of Structures

A more natural and convenient organization of student data or polygon points is to group the information pertaining to one student or to one point in a structure whose type we define. Declarations of arrays whose elements are structures follow.

```
#define MAX_STU 50
#define NUM_PTS 10

typedef struct {
      int     id;
      double gpa;
} student_t;

typedef struct {
      double x, y;
} point_t;

. . .

{
      student_t stulist[MAX_STU];
      point_t   polygon[NUM_PTS];
```

A sample array stulist is shown in Fig. 11.11. The data for the first student are stored in the structure stulist[0]. The individual data items are stulist[0].id and stulist[0].gpa. As shown, stulist[0].gpa is 2.71.

**Figure 11.11**
**An Array of**
**Structures**

| | Array stulist<br>.id | .gpa | |
|---|---|---|---|
| stulist[0] | 609465503 | 2.71 | ← stulist[0].gpa |
| stulist[1] | 512984556 | 3.09 | |
| stulist[2] | 232415569 | 2.98 | |
| . . . | . . . | . . . | |
| stulist[49] | 173745903 | 3.98 | |

If a function `scan_student` is available for scanning a `student_t` structure, the following `for` statement can be used to fill the entire array `stulist` with data.

```
for  (i = 0;  i < MAX_STU;  ++i)
    scan_student(&stulist[i]);
```

This `for` statement would display all the `id` numbers:

```
for  (i = 0;  i < MAX_STU;  ++i)
    printf("%d\n", stulist[i].id);
```

In our next case study, we see how to use an array of descriptive information about units of measurement in order to make possible conversion of any measurement to any other unit of the same category.

## Case Study: Universal Measurement Conversion

In a day when our computer software spell-checks text and looks up synonyms for words, it seems primitive to use printed tables for hand conversion of feet to meters, liters to quarts, and so on.

**PROBLEM**

We would like a program that takes a measurement in one unit (e.g., 4.5 quarts) and converts it to another unit (e.g., liters). For example, this conversion request

```
450 km miles
```

would result in this program output

```
Attempting conversion of 450.0000 km to miles . . .
450.0000km  =  279.6247 miles
```

The program should produce an error message if a conversion between two units of different classes (e.g., liquid volume to distance) is requested. The program should take a database of conversion information from an input file before accepting conversion problems entered interactively by the user. The user should be able to specify units either by name (e.g., kilograms) or by abbreviation (e.g., kg).

**ANALYSIS**

This program's basic data objects are units of measurement. We need to define a structure type that groups all relevant attributes about one unit. We can then store a database of these structures in an array and look up conversion factors as needed. To convert a measurement, the user will need to provide the measurement as a number and a string (e.g., 5 kg or 6.5 inches). The user must also enter the name or abbreviation of the desired units.

The attributes of a unit include its name and abbreviation, its class (mass, distance, and so on), and a representation of the unit in terms of the chosen standard unit for its class. If we allow the actual unit name, class names, and standard units to be determined by the contents of the input file, the program will be usable for any class of measurements and for units in any language based on our character set.

## Data Requirements

### Structured Data Type
```
unit_t
   components:
   name      /* character string such as "milligrams" */
   abbrev    /* shorter character string such as "mg" */
   class     /* character string "liquid_volume",
                  "distance", or "mass"              */
   standard /* number of standard units that are
                  equivalent to this unit            */
```

### Problem Constants
```
NAME_LEN    30  /* storage allocated for a unit name   */
ABBREV_LEN  15  /* storage allocated for a unit
                    abbreviation                       */
CLASS_LEN   20  /* storage allocated for a
                    measurement class                  */
MAX_UNITS   20  /* maximum number of different units
                    handled                            */
```

### Problem Inputs
```
unit_t units[MAX_UNITS]     /* array representing unit
                                conversion factors
                                database             */
double quantity             /* value to convert      */
char old_units[NAME_LEN]    /* name or abbreviation of
                                units to be converted */
char new_units[NAME_LEN]    /* name or abbreviation of
                                units to convert to    */
```

**Problem Output**

message giving conversion

### DESIGN

## Algorithm

1. Load units of measurement database.
2. Get value to convert and old and new unit names.
3. Repeat until data format error encountered
    4. Search for old units in database.
    5. Search for new units in database.
    6. if conversion is impossible
        7. Issue appropriate error message.
    else
        8. Compute and display conversion.
    9. Get value to convert and old and new unit names.

The refinement of Step 1 follows.

1.1  Open database file.
1.2  Initialize subscripting variable i.
1.3  Scan a unit structure from the database file.
1.4  Repeat until EOF, data format error, or attempted overflow of units list
    1.4.1  Store unit structure in units array.
    1.4.2  Update i.
    1.4.3  Scan next unit structure from file.
1.5  Close database file.

We will develop separate functions for Step 1 (load_units), for Step 1.3 and Step 1.4.3 (fscan_unit), for the search used in Step 4 and Step 5, and for the conversion aspect of Step 8. We can base our search function on the linear search algorithm used in Fig. 8.15.

### IMPLEMENTATION

Code that implements our universal conversion program is shown in Fig. 11.12. In the universal conversion program, it makes sense to use two sources of input. The database of units is taken from a file (units.dat) that can be created once and then used for many runs of the program. In contrast, the program expects that the conversion problems will be entered interactively.

**Figure 11.12 Universal Measurement Conversion Program Using an Array of Structures**

```
/*
 *  Converts measurements given in one unit to any other unit of the same
 *  category that is listed in the database file, units.dat.
 *  Handles both names and abbreviations of units.
 */
#include <stdio.h>
#include <string.h>

#define NAME_LEN    30      /* storage allocated for a unit name          */
#define ABBREV_LEN  15      /* storage allocated for a unit abbreviation  */
#define CLASS_LEN   20      /* storage allocated for a measurement class  */
#define NOT_FOUND   -1      /* value indicating unit not found            */
#define MAX_UNITS   20      /* maximum number of different units handled  */

typedef struct {                    /* unit of measurement type            */
        char    name[NAME_LEN];     /* character string such as "milligrams" */
        char    abbrev[ABBREV_LEN];/* shorter character string such as "mg"  */
        char    class[CLASS_LEN];   /* character string such as "pressure",  */
                                    /* "distance", "mass"                     */
        double standard;            /* number of standard units equivalent  */
                                    /* to this unit                          */
} unit_t;

int   fscan_unit(FILE *filep, unit_t *unitp);
void load_units(int unit_max, unit_t units[], int *unit_sizep);
int   search(const unit_t units[], const char *target, int n);
double convert(double quantity, double old_stand, double new_stand);

int
main(void)
{
        unit_t units[MAX_UNITS];    /* units classes and conversion factors*/
        int    num_units;           /* number of elements of units in use  */
        char   old_units[NAME_LEN], /* units to convert (name or abbrev)   */
               new_units[NAME_LEN]; /* units to convert to (name or abbrev)*/
        int    status;              /* input status                        */
        double quantity;            /* value to convert                    */
```

*(continued)*

**Figure 11.12** *(continued)*

```
int     old_index,            /* index of units element where
                                  old_units found                   */
        new_index;            /* index where new_units found        */

/*  Load units of measurement database                              */
load_units(MAX_UNITS, units, &num_units);

/*  Convert quantities to desired units until data format error
    (including error code returned when q is entered to quit)       */
printf("Enter a conversion problem or q to quit.\n");
printf("To convert 25 kilometers to miles, you would enter\n");
printf("> 25 kilometers miles\n");
printf("   or, alternatively,\n");
printf("> 25 km mi\n> ");

for  (status = scanf("%lf%s%s", &quantity, old_units, new_units);
      status == 3;
      status = scanf("%lf%s%s", &quantity, old_units, new_units)) {
   printf("Attempting conversion of %.4f %s to %s . . .\n",
           quantity, old_units, new_units);
   old_index = search(units, old_units, num_units);
   new_index = search(units, new_units, num_units);
   if (old_index == NOT_FOUND)
        printf("Unit %s not in database\n", old_units);
   else if (new_index == NOT_FOUND)
        printf("Unit %s not in database\n", new_units);
   else if (strcmp(units[old_index].class,
                   units[new_index].class) != 0)
        printf("Cannot convert %s (%s) to %s (%s)\n",
                old_units, units[old_index].class,
                new_units, units[new_index].class);
   else
        printf("%.4f%s  =  %.4f %s\n", quantity, old_units,
                convert(quantity, units[old_index].standard,
                        units[new_index].standard),
                new_units);
   printf("\nEnter a conversion problem or q to quit.\n> ");
}

return (0);
}
```

*(continued)*

**Figure 11.12** *(continued)*

```c
/*
 *  Gets data from a file to fill output argument
 *  Returns standard error code:  1 => successful input,  0 => error,
 *                                 negative EOF value => end of file
 */
int
fscan_unit(FILE    *filep,  /*  input - input file pointer        */
           unit_t *unitp)   /*  output - unit_t structure to fill */
{
      int status;

      status = fscanf(filep, "%s%s%s%lf", unitp->name,
                                          unitp->abbrev,
                                          unitp->class,
                                          &unitp->standard);

      if (status == 4)
            status = 1;
      else if (status != EOF)
            status = 0;

      return (status);
}

/*
 *  Opens database file units.dat and gets data to place in units until end
 *  of file is encountered.  Stops input prematurely if there are more than
 *  unit_max data values in the file or if invalid data is encountered.
 */
void
load_units(int        unit_max,   /* input - declared size of units    */
           unit_t     units[],    /* output - array of data            */
           int        *unit_sizep) /* output - number of data values
                                               stored in units          */
{
      FILE  *inp;
      unit_t data;
      int    i, status;
```

*(continued)*

**Figure 11.12** *(continued)*

```
      /*  Gets database of units from file                          */
      inp = fopen("units.dat", "r");
      i = 0;

      for  (status = fscan_unit(inp, &data);
              status == 1  &&  i < unit_max;
              status = fscan_unit(inp, &data)) {
          units[i++] = data;
      }
      fclose(inp);

      /* Issue error message on premature exit                      */
      if (status == 0) {
          printf("\n*** Error in data format ***\n");
          printf("*** Using first %d data values ***\n", i);
      } else if (status != EOF) {
          printf("\n*** Error: too much data in file ***\n");
          printf("*** Using first %d data values ***\n", i);
      }

      /* Send back size of used portion of array                    */
      *unit_sizep = i;
}

/*
 *  Searches for target key in name and abbrev components of first n
 *      elements of array units
 *  Returns index of structure containing target or NOT_FOUND
 */
int
search(const unit_t units[],   /*  array of unit_t structures to search  */
       const char    *target,   /*  key searched for in name and abbrev
                                     components                           */
          int           n)       /*  number of array elements to search    */
{
      int i,
          found = 0,      /*  whether or not target has been found       */
          where;          /*  index where target found or NOT_FOUND      */
```

*(continued)*

**Figure 11.12**   *(continued)*

```
        /*  Compare name and abbrev components of each element to target    */
        i = 0;
        while (!found && i < n) {
            if (strcmp(units[i].name,    target) == 0  ||
                strcmp(units[i].abbrev, target) == 0)
                    found = 1;
            else
                    ++i;
        }
        /* Return index of element containing target or NOT_FOUND           */
        if (found)
                where = i;
        else
                where = NOT_FOUND;
        return (where);
}


/*
 *   Converts one measurement to another given the representation of both
 *   in a standard unit.  For example, to convert 24 feet to yards given a
 *   standard unit of inches:  quantity = 24, old_stand = 12 (there are 12
 *   inches in a foot), new_stand = 36 (there are 36 inches in a yard),
 *   result is 24 * 12 / 36 which equals 8
 */
double
convert(double quantity,     /* value to convert                           */
        double old_stand,    /* number of standard units in one of
                                quantity's original units                  */
        double new_stand)    /* number of standard units in 1 new unit     */
{
        return (quantity * old_stand / new_stand);
}
```

▬▬◣ **TESTING** ◢▬▬

In addition to testing the conversion of units of liquid volume, distance, and mass using values whose conversions are easy to verify, we should also select test cases that exercise each of the error message facilities of the program. Figure 11.13 shows a small data file and one run of the conversion program. The database in this file assumes standard units of meters, liters, and kilograms.

Note that all that is required by the program is that the database consistently use *some* standard units. It does not prescribe *what* units these must be.

## Figure 11.13  Data File and Sample Run of Measurement Conversion Program

*Data file* units.dat:

| miles | mi | distance | 1609.3 |
|---|---|---|---|
| kilometers | km | distance | 1000 |
| yards | yd | distance | 0.9144 |
| meters | m | distance | 1 |
| quarts | qt | liquid_volume | 0.94635 |
| liters | l | liquid_volume | 1 |
| gallons | gal | liquid_volume | 3.7854 |
| milliliters | ml | liquid_volume | 0.001 |
| kilograms | kg | mass | 1 |
| grams | g | mass | 0.001 |
| slugs | slugs | mass | 0.14594 |

*Sample run:*
```
Enter a conversion problem or q to quit.
To convert 25 kilometers to miles, you would enter
> 25 kilometers miles
     or, alternatively,
> 25 km mi
> 450 km miles
Attempting conversion of 450.0000 km to miles . . .
450.0000km  =  279.6247 miles

Enter a conversion problem or q to quit.
> 2.5 qt l
Attempting conversion of 2.5000 qt to l . . .
2.5000qt  =  2.3659 l

Enter a conversion problem or q to quit.
> 100 meters gallons
Attempting conversion of 100.0000 meters to gallons . . .
Cannot convert meters (distance) to gallons (liquid_volume)

Enter a conversion problem or q to quit.
> 1234 mg g
```

*(continued)*

**Figure 11.13**   *(continued)*

```
Attempting conversion of 1234.0000 mg to g . . .
Unit mg not in database

Enter a conversion problem or q to quit.
> q
```

## EXERCISES FOR SECTION 11.5

Self-Check

1. In function `main` of our universal conversion program, we see the statement

   ```
   load_units(MAX_UNITS, units, &num_units);
   ```

   Inside `load_units` we see the function call

   ```
   fscan_unit(inp, &data);
   ```

   Variables `units`, `num_units`, and `data` are all being used as output arguments in these statements. Why is the & applied to `num_units` and `data`, but not to `units`?

2. Write a code fragment that would add `0.2` to all the gpa's in `stulist` (see Fig. 11.11). If the addition of `0.2` would inflate a gpa past `4.0`, just set the gpa to `4.0`.

## 11.6 UNION TYPES (OPTIONAL)

So far, all the variables we have seen of a particular structure type have had exactly the same components. However, sometimes we need structured types in which some components vary depending on the value of another component. For example, if we were to write a program to manipulate a variety of geometric figures, the data we would need to store would vary depending on the type of figure processed. In order to find the area and circumference of a circle, we would need to know the radius; to compute the area and perimeter of a square, we would need to know the length of a side; to figure the area and perimeter of other rectangles, we would need height and width.

**union**
a data structure that overlays components in memory, allowing one chunk of memory to be interpreted in multiple ways

C provides a data structure called a **union** to deal with situations in which one needs a data object that can be interpreted in a variety of ways.

**EXAMPLE 11.6** The following declaration defines a union structure to use as the type of one component of a person's physical description. If the person has hair, we would like to record the hair color. However, if the person is bald, we need to note whether or not this baldness is disguised by a wig.

```
typedef union {
      int   wears_wig;
      char color[20];
} hair_t;
```

As you can see, the format of a union type definition exactly parallels a structure type definition. As before, our `typedef` statement allocates no memory. A later declaration

```
hair_t hair_data;
```

creates a variable `hair_data` built on the template of the type definition. This variable `hair_data` does not contain *both* `wears_wig` *and* `color` components. Rather, it has *either* a `wears_wig` component referenced by `hair_data.wears_wig` *or* a `color` component referenced by `hair_data.color`. When memory is allocated for `hair_data`, the amount of memory is determined by the largest component of the union.

In most cases, it is useful to be able to interpret a chunk of memory in more than one way only if it is possible to determine *which* way is currently the valid interpretation. For this reason, unions are most often used as types of portions of a larger structure, and the larger structure typically contains a component whose value indicates which interpretation of the union is correct at the present time. Such a structure containing a `hair_t` union component is the following:

```
typedef struct {
      int   bald;
      hair_t h;
} hair_info_t;
```

When we write code using a `hair_info_t` structure, we can base our manipulation of the union component h on the value of the `bald` component. This component indicates whether the subject is bald. For bald subjects, the `wears_wig` interpretation of component h is valid. For nonbald subjects, the `color` interpretation is valid and represents the color of the subject's hair. Figure 11.14 shows a function to display `hair_info_t` data.

In Fig. 11.15, we see the two possible interpretations of the h component of parameter hair, one that is conceptually valid when `hair.bald` is true,

**Figure 11.14    Function That Displays a Structure with a Union Type Component**

```
void
print_hair_info(hair_info_t hair) /* input - structure to display      */
{
      if (hair.bald) {
            printf("Subject is bald");
            if (hair.h.wears_wig)
                  printf(", but wears a wig.\n");
            else
                  printf(" and does not wear a wig.\n");
      } else {
            printf("Subject's hair color is %s.\n", hair.h.color);
      }
}
```

**Figure 11.15    Two Interpretations of Parameter hair**

and one that applies when `hair.bald` is false. Referencing the appropriate union component is *always* the programmer's responsibility; C can do no checking of the validity of such a component reference.

**EXAMPLE 11.7**   In Fig. 11.16, we see a partial solution to the problem of finding the area and perimeter (circumference) of a geometric figure, the problem mentioned at the beginning of our discussion of union types. First, we define structure types for each figure of interest including components for the figure's area and perimeter or circumference, as well as components for those dimensions of the figure that are needed in computation of its area and perimeter. Then, we define a union type with a component for each figure type. Finally, we define a structure containing both a component of the union type and a component whose value denotes which is the correct interpretation of the union. Notice that all functions that process `figure_t` data contain `switch` statements to select the valid view of the `fig` component based on the value of the `shape` component. In function `compute_area`, the default case of the `switch` statement prints an error message. This message will never appear as long as the function's pre-conditions are met. ⬅

**Figure 11.16    Program to Compute Area and Perimeter of Geometric Figures**

```
/*
 *   Computes the area and perimeter of a variety of geometric figures.
 */

#include <stdio.h>
#define PI 3.14159

/*  Types defining the components needed to represent each shape.       */
typedef struct {
      double area,
             circumference,
             radius;
} circle_t;

typedef struct {
      double area,
             perimeter,
             width,
             height;
} rectangle_t;

typedef struct {
      double area,
             perimeter,
             side;
} square_t;

/*  Type of a structure that can be interpreted a different way for
      each shape                                                        */
typedef union {
      circle_t    circle;
      rectangle_t rectangle;
      square_t    square;
} figure_data_t;
```

*(continued)*

**Figure 11.16** *(continued)*

```
/*  Type containing a structure with multiple interpretations along with
 *  a component whose value indicates the current valid interpretation  */
typedef struct {
      char          shape;
      figure_data_t fig;
} figure_t;

figure_t get_figure_dimensions(void);
figure_t compute_area(figure_t object);
figure_t compute_perim(figure_t object);
void print_figure(figure_t object);


int
main(void)
{
      figure_t onefig;

      printf("Area and Perimeter Computation Program\n");

      for  (onefig = get_figure_dimensions();
              onefig.shape != 'Q';
              onefig = get_figure_dimensions()) {
          onefig = compute_area(onefig);
          onefig = compute_perim(onefig);
          print_figure(onefig);
      }

      return (0);
}

/*
 *  Prompts for and stores the dimension data necessary to compute a
 *  figure's area and perimeter.  Figure returned contains a 'Q' in the
 *  shape component when signaling end of data.
 */
figure_t
get_figure_dimensions(void)
{
      figure_t object;
```

*(continued)*

**Figure 11.16**    *(continued)*

```
        printf("Enter a letter to indicate the object shape or Q to quit.\n");
        printf("C (circle),  R (rectangle),  or S (square)> ");
        object.shape = getchar();

        switch (object.shape) {
        case 'C':
        case 'c':
             printf("Enter radius> ");
             scanf("%lf", &object.fig.circle.radius);
             break;

        case 'R':
        case 'r':
             printf("Enter height> ");
             scanf("%lf", &object.fig.rectangle.height);
             printf("Enter width> ");
             scanf("%lf", &object.fig.rectangle.width);
             break;

        case 'S':
        case 's':
             printf("Enter length of a side> ");
             scanf("%lf", &object.fig.square.side);
             break;

        default:  /*  Error is treated as a QUIT  */
             object.shape = 'Q';
        }

        return (object);
}

/*
 *  Computes the area of a figure given relevant dimensions.  Returns
 *  figure with area component filled.
 *  Pre:  value of shape component is one of these letters: CcRrSs
 *        necessary dimension components have values
 */
```

*(continued)*

**Figure 11.16** *(continued)*

```
figure_t
compute_area(figure_t object)
{
     switch (object.shape) {
     case 'C':
     case 'c':
          object.fig.circle.area = PI * object.fig.circle.radius *
                                        object.fig.circle.radius;
          break;

     case 'R':
     case 'r':
          object.fig.rectangle.area = object.fig.rectangle.height *
                                           object.fig.rectangle.width;
          break;

     case 'S':
     case 's':
          object.fig.square.area = object.fig.square.side *
                                       object.fig.square.side;
          break;

     default:
          printf("Error in shape code detected in compute_area\n");
     }

     return (object);
}

/*  Code for compute_perim and print_figure goes here  */
```

**EXERCISES FOR SECTION 11.6**

Self-Check

1. Determine how many bytes are needed to store a structure of type hair_info_t, assuming two bytes for an integer and one byte for a character. How much of this space is actually in use when component wears_wig is valid?

Programming

1. Write functions compute_perim and print_figure to complete the program in Fig. 11.16.

# 11.7 COMMON PROGRAMMING ERRORS

When programmers manipulate structure types, their most common error is incorrect use of a component selected for processing. When using the direct selection operator ( . ), always be aware of the type of the component selected, and use the value in a manner consistent with its type. For example, if the component selected is an array, passing it to a function as an output argument does not require application of the address-of operator.

If a structure type output parameter is used in a function, one can avoid the operator precedence problems associated with combining the indirection (*) and direct component selection ( . ) operators by using the indirect component selection operator (->).

C allows the use of structure type values in assignment statements, as function arguments, and as function results, so one can easily forget that expressions of these types cannot be operands of equality comparators nor arguments of `printf` and `scanf`. You can select simple components from a structure to use in these contexts, or you can write your own type-specific equality and I/O functions.

When you use a union type, referencing a component that is not currently valid is easy to do. It is helpful to place the union within another structure that contains a component whose value indicates which interpretation of the union is correct. Then all manipulation of the union can fall within `if` or `switch` statements that reference the union component based on the value of the associated structure component.

# CHAPTER REVIEW

1. C permits the user to define a type composed of multiple named components.
2. A component of a structure is referenced by polacing the direct component selection operator ( . ) between the structure variable name and the component name.
3. A component of a structured output parameter is referenced by placing the indirect component selection operator(->) between the structure variable name and the component name.
4. User-defined structure types can be used in most situations where built-in types are valid: Structured values can be function arguments and function results, and can be copied using the assignment operator; structure types are legitimate in declarations of variables, of structure components, and of arrays.
5. Structured values cannot be compared for equality using the == and != operators.

6. Structure types play an important role in data abstraction: You create an abstract data type (ADT) by implementing as functions all of the type's necessary operators.

7. In a union type variable, structure components are overlaid in memory.

## New C Constructs

| Construct | Effect |
|---|---|
| **Definition of a Structure Type**<br>```typedef struct {```<br>```    char    name[20];```<br>```    int     quantity;```<br>```    double  price;```<br>```} part_t;``` | A structure type `part_t` is defined with components that can store a string and two numbers, one of type `int` and one of type `double`. |
| **Declaration of Variables to Hold One Structure or an Array of Structures**<br>```part_t nuts, bolts, parts_list[40];```<br>```part_t mouse = {"serial mouse", 30,```<br>```               145.00};``` | `nuts`, `bolts`, and `mouse` are structured variables of type `part_t`; `parts_list` is an array of 40 such structures. The three components of `mouse` are initialized in its declaration. |
| **Component Reference**<br>```cost = nuts.quantity * nuts.price;```<br><br>```printf("Part: %s\n",```<br>```       parts_list[i].name);``` | Multiplies two components of type `part_t` variable `nuts`.<br>Displays `name` component of `i`th element of `parts_list`. |
| **Structure Copy**<br>```bolts = nuts;``` | Stores in `bolts` a copy of each component of `nuts`. |
| **Definition of a Union Type**<br>```typedef union {```<br>```    char    str[4];```<br>```    int     intger;```<br>```    double  real;```<br>```} multi_t;``` | A union type `multi_t` is defined allowing three interpretations of the contents of a type `multi_t` variable: the contents may be seen as a four-character string, as an integer, or as a type `double` number. |

*(continued)*

**New C Constructs**  *(continued)*

| Construct | Effect |
|---|---|
| **Definition of a Structure Type with a Union Component**<br><br>```c
typedef struct {
    char    interp;
    multi_t val;
} choose_t;
``` | A structure type `choose_t` is defined with a component `interp` whose value ('S' for string, 'I' for integer, 'D' for double) indicates which interpretation of union component `val` is valid. |

# QUICK-CHECK EXERCISES

1. What is the primary difference between a structure and an array? Which would you use to store the catalog description of a course? To store the names of students in the course?

2. How do you access a component of a structure type variable?

Exercises 3–8 refer to the following type `student_t` and to variables `stu1` and `stu2`.

```c
typedef struct {
    char fst_name[20],
         last_name[20];
    int  score;
    char grade;
} student_t;
. . .
student_t stu1, stu2;
```

3. Identify the following statements as possibly valid or definitely invalid. If invalid, explain why.

   a. `student_t stulist[30];`
   b. `printf("%s", stu1);`
   c. `printf("%d %c", stu1.score, stu1.grade);`
   d. `stu2 = stu1;`
   e. `if (stu2.score == stu1.score)`
        `printf("Equal");`
   f. `if (stu2 == stu1)`
        `printf("Equal structures");`
```

      g. `scan_student(&stu1);`

      h. `stu2.last_name = "Martin";`

4. Write a statement that displays the initials of `stu1` (with periods).
5. How many components does variable `stu2` have?
6. Write functions `scan_student` and `print_student` for type `student_t` variables.
7. Declare an array of 40 `student_t` structures, and write a code segment that displays on separate lines the names (*last name, first name*) of all the students in the list.
8. Identify the type of each of the following references:

    a. `stu1`

    b. `stu2.score`

    c. `stu2.fst_name[3]`

    d. `stu1.grade`

9. When should you use a union type component in a structured variable?

## ANSWERS TO QUICK-CHECK EXERCISES

1. A structure can have components of different types, but an array's elements must all be of the same type. Use a structure for the catalog item and an array of strings for the list of student names.
2. Components of structures are accessed using the direct selection operator followed by a component name.
3. a. Valid

    b. Invalid: `printf` does not accept structured arguments.

    c. Valid

    d. Valid

    e. Valid

    f. Invalid: equality operators cannot be used with structure types.

    g. Valid (assuming parameter type is `student_t *`)

    h. Invalid: cannot copy strings with = except in declaration (this case needs `strcpy`)

4. `printf("%c.%c.",  stu1.fst_name[0], stu1.last_name[0]);`

5. four

6.
```c
int
scan_student(student_t *stup) /* output - student struc-
                                          ture to fill */
{
      int  status,
      char temp[4]; /* temporary storage for grade */
```

```
               status = scanf("%s%s%d%s", stu->fst_name,
                                           stu->last_name,
                                           &stu->score,
                                           temp);
          if (status == 4) {
                status = 1;
                (*stu).grade = tcmp[0];
          } else if (status != EOF) {
                status = 0;
          }

          return (status);
     }


     void
     print_student(student_t stu) /* input - student structure
                                             to display */
     {
          printf("Student: %s, %s\n", stu.last_name,
                 stu.fst_name);
          printf("    Score: %d        Grade: %c\n", stu.score,
                 stu.grade);
     }
```

7. `student_t students[40];`

```
   for  (i = 0;  i < 40;  ++i)
      printf("%s, %s\n", students[i].last_name,
             students[i].fst_name);
```

8. a. `student_t`
   b. `int`
   c. `char`
   d. `char`

9. Use a union type component in a structured variable when the needed structure components vary depending on the value of one component.

# REVIEW QUESTIONS

1. Define a structure type called `subscriber_t` that contains the components name, `street_address`, and `monthly_bill` (i.e., how much the subscriber owes).

2. Write a C program that scans data to fill the variable `competition` declared below and then displays the contents of the structure with suitable labels.

```
#define STR_LENGTH 20

typedef struct {
        char event[STR_LENGTH],
                entrant[STR_LENGTH],
                country[STR_LENGTH];
        int  place;
} olympic_t;
. . .
olympic_t competition;
```

3. How would you call a function `scan_olympic` passing `competition` as an output argument?

4. Identify and correct the errors in the following program:

```
typedef struct
        char   name[15],
                start_date[15],
        double hrs_worked,
summer_help_t;

/* prototype for function scan_sum_hlp goes here */

int
main(void)
{
        struct operator;

        scan_sum_hlp(operator);
        printf("Name: %s\nStarting date: %s\nHours worked:
                %.2f\n", operator);

        return(0);
}
```

5. Define a data structure to store the following student data: gpa, major, address (consisting of street address, city, state, zip), and class schedule (consisting of up to six class records, each of which has description, time, and days components). Define whatever data types are needed.

# PROGRAMMING PROJECTS

1. Define a structure type `auto_t` to represent an automobile. Include components for the make and model (strings), the odometer reading, the manufacture and purchase dates (use another user-defined type called `date_t`), and the gas tank (use a user-defined type `tank_t` with components for tank capacity and current fuel level, giving both in gallons). Write I/O functions `scan_date`, `scan_tank`, `scan_auto`, `print_date`, `print_tank`, and `print_auto`, and also write a driver function that repeatedly fills and displays an auto structure variable until EOF is encountered in the input file.
   Here is a small data set to try:

   ```
   Mercury Sable     99842 1 18 1989 5 30 1991 16     12.5
   Mazda   Navajo    23961 2 20 1993 6 15 1993 19.3 16.7
   ```

2. Define a structure type `element_t` to represent one element from the periodic table of elements. Components should include the atomic number (an integer); the name, chemical symbol, and class (strings); a numeric field for the atomic weight; and a seven-element array of integers for the number of electrons in each shell. The following are the components of an `element_t` structure for sodium.

   ```
   11   Sodium   Na   alkali_metal   22.9898   2 8 1 0 0 0 0
   ```

   Define and test I/O functions `scan_element` and `print_element`.

3. A number expressed in scientific notation is represented by its mantissa (a fraction) and its exponent (an integer). Define a type `sci_not_t` that has separate components for these two parts. Define a function `scan_sci` that takes from the input source a string representing a positive number in scientific notation, and breaks it into components for storage in a `sci_not_t` structure. The mantissa of an input value (m) should satisfy this condition: $0.1 <= m < 1.0$. Also write functions to compute the sum, difference, product, and quotient of two `sci_not_t` values. All these functions should have a result type of `sci_not_t` and should ensure that the result's mantissa is in the prescribed range. Define a `print_sci` function as well. Then, create a driver program to test your functions. Your output should be of this form:

   ```
   Values input:  0.25000e3  0.20000e1
   Sum:  0.25200e3
   Difference:  0.24800e3
   Product:  0.50000e3
   Quotient:  0.12500e3
   ```

4. Numeric addresses for computers on the international network Internet are composed of four parts, separated by periods, of the form

   xx.yy.zz.mm

   where xx, yy, zz, and mm are positive integers. Locally, computers are usually known by a nickname as well. You are designing a program to process a list of Internet addresses, identifying all pairs of computers from the same locality. Create a structure type called address_t with components for the four integers of an Internet address and a fifth component in which to store an associated nickname of 10 characters. Your program should read a list of up to 100 addresses and nicknames terminated by a sentinel address of all zeros and a sentinel nickname.

   Sample data
   ```
   111.22.3.44      platte
   555.66.7.88      wabash
   111.22.5.66      green
   0.0.0.0          none
   ```

   The program should display a list of messages identifying each pair of computers from the same locality, that is, each pair of computers with matching values in the first two components of the address. In the messages, the computers should be identified by their nicknames.

   Example message
   ```
   Machines platte and green are on the same local net-
   work.
   ```

   Follow the messages by a display of the full list of addresses and nicknames. Include in your program a scan_address function, a print_address function, and a local_address function. Function local_address should take two address structures as input parameters and return 1 (for true) if the addresses are on the same local network, and 0 (for false) otherwise.

5. The results of a survey of the households in your township have been made available. Each record contains data for one household, including a four-digit integer identification number, the annual income for the household, and the number of members of the household. You may assume that no more than 25 households were surveyed. Write a program to store the survey results into an array of user-defined structures of type household_t. Then perform the following analyses:

   a.  Print a three-column table displaying the data.
   b.  Calculate the average household income, and list the identification number and income of each household whose income exceeds the average.

c. Determine the percentage of households having incomes below the poverty level. The poverty level income may be computed using the formula

$$P = \$7500.00 + \$950.00 \times (m - 2)$$

where $m$ is the number of members of each household. This formula shows that the poverty level depends on the number of family members $m$ and the poverty level increases as $m$ gets larger.

The following is one data set to use in testing your program.

| Identification Number | Annual Income | Household Members |
|---|---|---|
| 1041 | $12,180 | 4 |
| 1062 | 13,240 | 3 |
| 1327 | 19,800 | 2 |
| 1483 | 24,458 | 8 |
| 1900 | 17,000 | 2 |
| 2112 | 19,125 | 7 |
| 2345 | 17,623 | 2 |
| 3210 | 5,200 | 6 |
| 3600 | 9,500 | 5 |
| 3601 | 11,970 | 2 |
| 4725 | 9,800 | 3 |
| 6217 | 10,000 | 2 |
| 9280 | 8,200 | 1 |

6. Expand the geometric figure program from Fig. 11.16 to handle processing of right triangles. Include components to store the base and height of a right triangle. Some relevant formulas are:

$$area = \frac{1}{2}\, base \times height$$

$$hypotenuse = \sqrt{base^2 + height^2}$$

7. At a grocery store, certain categories of products sold have been established, and this information is to be computerized. Write a function to scan and store information in a structure variable whose data type is one you define— a type that includes a component that has multiple interpretations. Also write an output function and a driver function to use in testing.

The data for each item consists of the item name (a string of less than 20 characters with no blanks), the unit cost in cents (an integer), and a character indicating the product category ('M' for meat, 'P' for produce, 'D' for dairy, 'C' for canned goods, and 'N' for nonfoods). The following additional data will depend on the product category.

| Product Category | Additional Data |
| --- | --- |
| Meats | character indicating meat type 'R' for red meat, 'P' for poultry, 'F' for fish<br>date of packaging<br>expiration date |
| Produce | character 'F' for fruit or 'V' for vegetable<br>date received |
| Dairy | expiration date |
| Canned goods | expiration date (month and year only)<br>aisle number (an integer)<br>aisle side (letter 'A' or 'B') |
| Nonfoods | character indicating category ('C' for cleaning product, 'P' for pharmacy, 'O' for other)<br>aisle number (an integer)<br>aisle side (letter 'A' or 'B') |

A data line for canned corn would be

```
corn   89C   11 95   12B
```

The corn costs 89 cents, expires in November of 1995, and is displayed on aisle 12B.

8. Rewrite the common fraction program from Chapter 6 using a structure type to represent a fraction.

9. In the Self-Check Exercises of Sections 11.1 and 11.2, you defined a data type location_t to represent a geographic location and some functions to process certain components of the type. Write functions print_location, location_equal, and scan_location for processing type location_t data, and develop a driver to use in testing this group of functions.

# TEXT AND BINARY

# FILE PROCESSING

c h a p t e r

This chapter will explore in greater depth the use of standard input, standard output, and program-controlled text files. We also will introduce binary files and compare the advantages and disadvantages of text and binary files.

# 12.1 INPUT/OUTPUT FILES: REVIEW AND FURTHER STUDY

**text file**
a named collection of characters saved in secondary storage

C can process two kinds of files: text files and binary files. We will study text files in this section and binary files later in this chapter. All the files you have created using an editor or word processor have been text files. A **text file** is a named collection of characters saved in secondary storage (e.g., on a disk). A text file has no fixed size. To mark the end of a text file, the computer places a special *end-of-file* character, which we will denote <eof>, after the last character in the file. As you create a text file using an editor program, pressing the <return> or <enter> key causes the newline character (represented by C as '\n') to be placed in the file.

The following lines represent a text file consisting of two lines of letters, blank characters, and the punctuation characters . and ! .

```
This is a text file!<newline>
It has two lines.<newline><eof>
```

Each line ends with the newline character, and the eof character follows the last newline in the file. For convenience in examining the file's contents, we listed each line of the file (through <newline>) as a separate line, although this would not be the case in the actual disk file. The disk file consists of a sequence of characters occupying consecutive storage locations on a track of the disk, as shown here:

```
This is a text file!<newline>It has two lines.<newline><eof>
```

**input (output) stream**
continuous stream of character codes representing textual input (or output) data

The first character of the second line (I) follows directly after the last character of the first line (the newline character). Because all textual input and output data are actually a continuous stream of character codes, we sometimes refer to a data source or destination as an **input stream** or an **output stream**. These general terms can be applied to files, to the terminal keyboard and screen, and to any other sources of input data or destinations of output data.

## The Keyboard and Screen as Text Streams

In interactive programming, C associates system names with the terminal keyboard and screen. The name **stdin** represents the keyboard's input stream. Two system streams, the "normal" output stream **stdout** and the "error" output stream **stderr**, are associated with the screen. All three streams can be treated like text files because their individual components are characters.

Normally at the keyboard, we enter one line of data at a time, pressing <return> or <enter> to indicate the end of a data line. Pressing one of these keys inserts the newline character in system stream stdin. Normally in interactive programming, we use a sentinel value to indicate the end of data rather than attempting to place the eof character in system stream stdin. However, the eof character could be used. No single key represents the eof character, so most systems use the control key followed by a letter. (For example, on computers running the UNIX operating system, the keystrokes <control-d> would be used.)

Writing characters to the streams stdout and stderr causes a display on the screen in an interactive program. We have studied the use of the printf function to write characters to the screen. Using a '\n' in the printf format string causes output of a newline character that moves the cursor to the start of the next line of the screen.

## Newline and EOF

We have seen that C handles the special newline character differently than the eof character, even though they have similar purposes. The <newline> marks the end of a line of text, and the <eof> marks the end of the entire file. The <newline> can be processed like any other character: It can be input using scanf with the %c specifier, it can be compared to '\n' for equality, and it can be output using printf.

However, input of the special eof character is regarded as a failed operation, and the input function responsible returns as its value the negative integer associated with the identifier EOF. Because this special return value gives the calling function an indication that no more data are in the input file, the C run-time support system is under no obligation to provide an error message if the program ignores the warning value and continues to attempt to get input from the stream in question. The following is another example of the input loops that we studied that base their exit condition on the appearance of the EOF return value:

```
for  (status = scanf("%d", &num);
      status != EOF;
      status = scanf("%d", &num))
    process(num);
```

## File Pointer Variables

We saw in Chapter 2 that before using a nonstandard text file for input or output, we must declare a file pointer variable and give it a value, allowing us to access the desired file. The system must prepare the file for input or output before permitting access. This preparation is the purpose of the stdio library function `fopen`. The statements that follow declare and initialize the file pointer variables `infilep` and `outfilep`:

```
FILE *infilep;
FILE *outfilep;

infilep = fopen("b:data.txt", "r");
outfilep = fopen("b:results.txt", "w");
```

Notice that the data type of `infilep` and `outfilep` is `FILE *`. Remember that C is case sensitive, so you must use all capital letters when writing the type name `FILE`. It is possible to declare both `infilep` and `outfilep` in the same statement, but each must be immediately preceded by the asterisk denoting "pointer to," as shown here:

```
FILE *infilep, *outfilep;
```

We use the stdio library function `fopen` to open or create an additional text file. The `"r"` in the first call to `fopen` just shown indicates that we wish to use the text file opened as an input file from which we will read (scan) data. The `"w"` in the second call conveys that our intention is to write to the file, that is, to use it as an output destination. The first argument to `fopen` is a string that is the name of the text file to manipulate. The correct form of such a file name will vary from one operating system to another. The result returned by `fopen` is the file pointer to be used in all further operations on the file. This pointer is the address of a structure of type `FILE` that contains the information necessary to access the file opened by `fopen`. The pointer must be saved in a variable of type `FILE *`. In a program containing the lines just shown, the variable `infilep` will be used to access the input file named `"b:data.txt"`, and the variable `outfilep` will be used to access the newly created output file named `"b:results.txt"`. The identifiers `stdin`, `stdout`, and `stderr` also name variables of type `FILE *`, variables initialized by the system prior to the start of a C program.

If the `fopen` function is unable to accomplish the requested operation, the file pointer that it returns is equal to the value associated with the identifier `NULL` by the stdio library. For example, if execution of this call to `fopen`

```
infilep = fopen("b:data.txt", "r");
```

were unsuccessful due to the nonexistence of a file named `"b:data.txt"`, then execution of the following statement would display an appropriate error message:

```
if (infilep == NULL)
      printf("Cannot open b:data.txt for input\n");
```

**null pointer**
pointer whose value is NULL

A pointer whose value equals `NULL` is called a **null pointer**. Take care not to confuse this concept with the *null character*, whose value is the character `'\0'`.

Using `fopen` with mode `"w"` to open for output a file that already exists usually causes loss of the contents of the existing file. However, if the computer's operating system automatically numbers file versions and creates a new version when it opens an output file, the contents of the existing file will not be lost.

## Functions That Take File Pointer Arguments

Table 12.1 compares calls to `printf` and `scanf` with calls to analogous functions for input from the file accessed by `infilep` and for output to the file accessed by `outfilep`. In this table, we assume that `infilep` and `outfilep` have been initialized as shown earlier.

Line 1 shows input of a single integer value to be stored in `num`. The call to `scanf` obtains this value from the standard input stream, typically the keyboard. The call to `fscanf` obtains the integer value from `"b:data.txt"`, the file accessed through the file pointer `infilep`. Like `scanf`, function `fscanf` returns as its result the number of input values it has successfully stored through its output arguments. Function `fscanf` also returns the negative EOF value when it encounters the end of the file accessed by its file pointer argument.

**Table 12.1    Comparison of I/O with Standard Files and I/O with User-Defined File Pointers**

| Line | Functions That Access stdin and stdout | Functions That Can Access Any Text File |
|---|---|---|
| 1 | `scanf("%d", &num);` | `fscanf(infilep, "%d", &num);` |
| 2 | `printf` `("Number = %d\n", num);` | `fprintf(outfilep,` `"Number = %d\n", num);` |
| 3 | `ch = getchar();` | `ch = getc(infilep);` |
| 4 | `putchar(ch);` | `putc(ch, outfilep);` |

Similarly, the behavior of fprintf, getc, and putc is fully comparable to the behavior of the standard I/O equivalents—printf, getchar, and putchar—except that each takes a file pointer argument through which to access its input source or output destination. Observe carefully that this file pointer is provided as the first argument to fscanf, fprintf, and getc. In contrast, putc takes the file pointer as its second argument.

## Closing a File

When a program has no further use for a file, it should *close* the file by calling the library function fclose with the file pointer. The following statement closes the file accessed through infilep:

```
fclose(infilep);
```

Function fclose disposes of the structure that was created to store file access information and carries out other "cleanup" operations.

If necessary, a program can create an output file and can then rescan the file. The file is first opened in "w" mode, and data are stored using a function such as fprintf. The file is then closed using fclose and reopened in "r" mode, allowing the data to be rescanned with a function such as fscanf.

**EXAMPLE 12.1** For security reasons, having a backup or duplicate copy of a file is a good idea, in case the original is lost. Even though operating systems typically provide a command that will copy a file, we will write our own C program to do this. The program in Fig. 12.1 copies each character in one file to a backup file and allows the user to enter interactively both the name of the file to copy and the name of the backup file.

**Figure 12.1    Program to Make a Backup Copy of a Text File**

```
/*
 *  Makes a backup file.  Repeatedly prompts for the name of a file to
 *  back up until a name is provided that corresponds to an available
 *  file.  Then it prompts for the name of the backup file and creates
 *  the file copy.
 */

#include <stdio.h>
#define  STRSIZ 80
```

*(continued)*

**Figure 12.1    (continued)**

```c
int
main(void)
{
      char  in_name[STRSIZ],   /* strings giving names                */
            out_name[STRSIZ];  /*     of input and backup files       */
      FILE *inp,               /* file pointers for input and         */
           *outp;              /*     backup files                    */
      char ch;                 /* one character of input file         */

      /*  Get the name of the file to back up and open the file for
            input                                                     */
      printf("Enter name of file you want to back up> ");
      for  (scanf("%s", in_name);
            (inp = fopen(in_name, "r")) == NULL;
            scanf("%s", in_name)) {
         printf("Cannot open %s for input\n", in_name);
         printf("Re-enter file name> ");
      }

      /*  Get name to use for backup file and open file for output    */
      printf("Enter name for backup copy> ");
      for  (scanf("%s", out_name);
            (outp = fopen(out_name, "w")) == NULL;
            scanf("%s", out_name)) {
         printf("Cannot open %s for output\n", out_name);
         printf("Re-enter file name> ");
      }

      /*  Make backup copy one character at a time                    */
      for  (ch = getc(inp);  ch != EOF;  ch = getc(inp))
         putc(ch, outp);

      /*  Close files and notify user of backup completion            */
      fclose(inp);
      fclose(outp);
      printf("Copied %s to %s.\n", in_name, out_name);

      return(0);
}
```

The program in Fig. 12.1 begins by displaying a prompting message on the screen using `printf`. Then `scanf` is executed to take the file name typed at the keyboard.

The repetition condition of the first `for` loop is

```
(inp = fopen(in_name, "r")) == NULL
```

The call to function `fopen` causes the system to try to open for input the file whose name is stored in `in_name`. If this attempt is successful, a file pointer is returned and assigned to `inp`. The value of this assignment will equal `NULL` only if the file could not be successfully opened; in this case, the user is asked to reenter the name of the file.

In the next program segment, a similar `for` loop is used to get the name of an output file and to open the file, storing the file pointer in `outp`.

The `for` loop that follows manipulates not the standard I/O streams but rather the input and output files accessed through the file pointers in `inp` and `outp`. Function `getc` is called repeatedly to take one character at a time from the input file, and `putc` echoes these characters to the output file. When the copy is complete, the calls to `fclose` release the two files after writing an `<eof>` on the output file.

Figure 12.2 shows the input and output streams used by the file backup program. ⬅

**Figure 12.2    Input and Output Streams for File Backup Program**

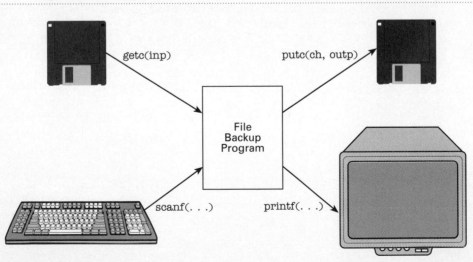

Self-Check

1. Assume these declarations for the problem that follows:

```
double x;
int    n;
char   ch, str[40];
```

Indicate the contents of these variables after each of the following input operations is performed. Assume that the file accessed by indatap consists of the data given and that each lettered group of operations occurs at the beginning of a program, immediately following a statement that opens the file.

123 3.145 xyz<newline>35 z<newline>

a. fscanf(indatap, "%d%lf%s%c", &n, &x, str, &ch);
b. fscanf(indatap, "%d%lf", &n, &x);
   fscanf(indatap, "%s%c", str, &ch);
c. fscanf(indatap, "%lf%d%c%s", &x, &n, &ch, str);
d. fscanf(indatap, "%s%s%s%d%c%c", str, str, str, &n,
         &ch, &ch);
2. List the library functions we have studied that require a file pointer argument.
3. The code for function scan_complex that we used in Chapter 11 to scan one complex number is shown with some blanks added. Fill in the blanks to create fscan_complex, a function that takes a file pointer argument in addition to the complex_t output argument. This function should scan a complex number from the file accessed by the file pointer.

```
/*
 * Complex number _____ input function returns standard
 * scanning error code
 *    1 => valid scan,  0 => error,  negative EOF value =>
 *    end of file
 */
int
fscan_complex(_____
              complex_t *c) /* output - address of complex
                               variable to fill */
{
    int status;
```

```
        status = __scanf(_____,
                         "%lf%lf", &c->real, &c->imag;

        if (status == 2)
              status = 1;
        else if (status != EOF)
              status = 0;

        return (status);
   }
```

Programming

1. Rewrite the file backup program in Fig. 12.1 so it uses a function with file pointer parameters to do the actual file copy.

## 12.2 BINARY FILES

When we use text files for storage of data, a program must expend a significant amount of effort to convert the stream of characters from an input file into the binary integers, type `double` mantissas and exponents, and character strings that are the representation in main memory of the same data. The program must again expend time in converting the internal data format back into a stream of characters for storage in an output file of text. In a C program, these conversions are carried out by functions such as `scanf` and `printf`.

Many programs produce output files that are used as input files for other programs. If there is no need for a human to read the file, it is a waste of computer time for the first program to convert its internal data format to a stream of characters, and then for the second program to have to apply an inverse conversion to extract the intended data from the stream of characters. We can avoid this unnecessary translation by using a binary file rather than a text file.

**binary file**
a file containing binary numbers that are the computer's internal representation of each file component

A **binary file** is a file created by executing a program that stores directly in the file the computer's internal representation of each file component. For example, the code fragment in Fig. 12.3 creates a binary file named `"nums.bin"`, which contains the even integers from 2 to 500.

You see in Fig. 12.3 that a binary file is declared in exactly the same way as a text file. The `fopen` and `fclose` functions are used just as they are for text files, except that the second argument to `fopen` is either `"wb"` (write binary) for output files or `"rb"` (read binary) for input files. However, a different stdio library function is used for copying values into the file: function

### Figure 12.3   Creating a Binary File of Integers

```
FILE *binaryp;
int   i;

binaryp = fopen("nums.bin", "wb");

for  (i = 2;   i <= 500;   i += 2)
    fwrite(&i, sizeof (int), 1, binaryp);

fclose(binaryp);
```

`fwrite`, which has four input parameters. The first parameter is the *address* of the first memory cell whose contents are to be copied to the file. In Fig. 12.3, we want the contents of the variable i copied to the file, so we provide `fwrite` with the address of i (`&i`) as the first argument.

The second parameter of function `fwrite` is the number of bytes to copy to the file for one component. In Chapter 1, we noted that a memory cell is a collection of smaller units called *bytes* and that a byte is the amount of storage needed to represent one character. A C operator **sizeof** can be applied to any data type name to find the number of bytes that the current implementation uses for storage of the data type. For example, these statements will print a sentence indicating how many bytes are being occupied by one integer:

**sizeof**
operator that finds the number of bytes used for storage of a data type

```
printf("An integer requires %d bytes ", sizeof (int));
printf("in this implementation.\n");
```

The `sizeof` operator can be applied to both built-in and user-defined types.

The third parameter of `fwrite` is the number of values to write to the binary file. In our example, we are writing one integer at a time, so we provide the constant 1 as this argument. However, it is possible to save the contents of an entire array using just one call to `fwrite` by providing the array's size as the third argument. The final argument to `fwrite` is a file pointer to the file being created, a file previously opened in mode "wb" using function `fopen`. For example, if array `score` is an array of 10 integers, the statement

```
fwrite(score, sizeof (int), 10, binaryp);
```

writes the entire array to the output file.

Writing the value of an integer variable `i` to a binary file using `fwrite` is faster than writing `i` to a text file. For example, if the value of `i` is `244`, the statement from the `for` loop

```
fwrite(&i, sizeof (int), 1, binaryp);
```

copies the internal binary representation of `i` from memory to the file accessed by `binaryp`. If your computer uses two bytes to store an `int` value, the byte that stores the highest order bits would contain all zeros, and the byte that stores the lowest order bits would contain the binary string `11110100` ($244 = 128 + 64 + 32 + 16 + 4$). Both bytes would be written to disk as the next file component.

Assuming `textp` is a pointer to a text output file, the statement

```
fprintf(textp, "%d ", i);
```

writes the value of `i` to the file using four characters (four bytes). The computer must first convert the binary number in `i` to the character string `"244  "` and then write the binary codes for the characters 2, 4, 4, and blank to the file. Obviously, it takes more time to do the conversion and copy each character than it does to copy the internal binary representation to disk. Also, twice as much disk space is required to store four characters as to store the internal binary representation of the type `int` value (four bytes versus two).

Using a binary file has another advantage. Each time we write a type `double` value to a text file, the computer must convert this value to a character string whose precision is determined by the placeholder in the format string. A loss of precision may result.

There is a negative side to binary file usage, however. A binary file created on one computer is rarely readable on another type of computer. Since a binary file can be read only by a specialized computer program, a person cannot proofread the file by printing it out or by examining it in a word processor. Furthermore, a binary file cannot be created or modified in a word processor, so a program that expects binary file input cannot be tested until the program that produces the needed binary file is complete.

The stdio library includes an input function `fread` that is comparable to `fwrite`. Function `fread` also requires four arguments:

1. Address of first memory cell to fill.
2. Size of one value.
3. Maximum number of elements to copy from the file into memory.
4. File pointer to a binary file opened in mode `"rb"` using function `fopen`.

Function `fread` returns as its value an integer indicating how many elements it successfully copied from the file. This number will be less than the value of the third argument of `fread` if EOF is encountered prematurely.

It is very important not to mix file types. A binary file created (written) using `fwrite` must be read using `fread`. A text file created using `fprintf` must be read using a text file input function such as `fscanf`.

Table 12.2 compares the use of text and binary files for input and output of data of various types. The statements in both columns assume the following constant macros, type definition, and variable declarations.

```
#define STRSIZ  10
#define MAX      40

typedef struct {
     char name[STRSIZ];
     double diameter;        /* equatorial diameter in
                                km                    */
     int    moons;           /* number of moons       */
     double orbit_time ,     /* years to orbit sun once */
            rotation_time;   /* hours to complete one
                                revolution on axis     */
} planet_t;
. . .
double   nums[MAX], data;
planet_t a_planet;
int i, n, status;
FILE *plan_bin_inp, *plan_bin_outp, *plan_txt_inp,
     *plan_txt_outp;
FILE *doub_bin_inp, *doub_bin_outp, *doub_txt_inp,
     *doub_txt_outp;
```

In Example 1 of Table 12.2, we use `fopen` to open our input files, and we store the file pointers returned by `fopen` in variables of type `FILE *`. Notice that the form of the call to `fopen` for opening a binary file differs from the call for opening a text file only in the value of the *mode* (second argument). In fact, even this difference is *optional*. Also notice that the type of the file pointer does not vary. We see a similar situation in the opening of output files in Example 2. One consequence of this similarity is that the ability of the C compiler and run-time support system to detect misuse of a file pointer is severely limited. It is the programmer's responsibility to keep track of which type of file each file pointer accesses and to use the right I/O function at the right time.

In Examples 3 and 4 of Table 12.2, we compare input/output of a user-defined structure type as it is done with text and binary files. In Examples 5 and 6, we see input/output of an array of type `double` values. In the text file code, array elements are scanned or written one at a time in an indexed loop. When we use a binary file, we can fill the array from or copy it to the file using just one call to `fread` or `fwrite`. We see that the calls used to read/write array `nums` provide

**Table 12.2** Data I/O Using Text and Binary Files

| Example | Text File I/O | Binary File I/O | Purpose |
|---|---|---|---|
| 1 | `plan_txt_inp =`<br>`    fopen("planets.txt", "r");`<br><br>`doub_txt_inp =`<br>`    fopen("nums.txt", "r");` | `plan_bin_inp =`<br>`    fopen("planets.bin", "rb");`<br><br>`doub_bin_inp =`<br>`    fopen("nums.bin", "rb");` | Open for input a file of planets and a file of numbers, saving file pointers for use in calls to input functions. |
| 2 | `plan_txt_outp =`<br>`    fopen("pl_out.txt", "w");`<br><br>`doub_txt_outp =`<br>`    fopen("nm_out.txt", "w");` | `plan_bin_outp =`<br>`    fopen("pl_out.bin", "wb");`<br><br>`doub_bin_outp =`<br>`    fopen("nm_out.bin", "wb");` | Open for output a file of planets and a file of numbers, saving file pointers for use in calls to output functions. |
| 3 | `fscanf(plan_txt_inp,`<br>`    "%s%lf%d%lf%lf",`<br>`    a_planet.name,`<br>`    &a_planet.diameter,`<br>`    &a_planet.moons,`<br>`    &a_planet.orbit_time,`<br>`    &a_planet.rotation_time);` | `fread(&a_planet,`<br>`    sizeof (planet_t),`<br>`    1, plan_bin_inp);` | Copy one planet structure into memory from the data file. |
| 4 | `fprintf(plan_txt_outp,`<br>`    "%s %e %d %e %e",`<br>`    a_planet.name,`<br>`    a_planet.diameter,`<br>`    a_planet.moons,`<br>`    a_planet.orbit_time,`<br>`    a_planet.rotation_time);` | `fwrite(&a_planet,`<br>`    sizeof (planet_t),`<br>`    1, plan_bin_outp);` | Write one planet structure to the output file. |

| Example | Text File I/O | Binary File I/O | Purpose |
|---|---|---|---|
| 5 | ```for (i = 0; i < MAX; ++i)
    fscanf(doub_txt_inp,
        "%lf", &nums[i]);``` | ```fread(nums, sizeof (double),
    MAX, doub_bin_inp);``` | Fill array nums with type double values from input file. |
| 6 | ```for (i = 0; i < MAX; ++i)
    fprintf(doub_txt_outp,
        "%e\n", nums[i]);``` | ```fwrite(nums, sizeof (double),
    MAX, doub_bin_outp);``` | Write contents of array nums to output file. |
| 7 | ```n = 0;
for (status =
        fscanf(doub_txt_inp,
            "%lf", &data);
    status != EOF &&
        n < MAX;
    status =
        fscanf(doub_txt_inp,
            "%lf", &data))
    nums[n++] = data;``` | ```n = fread(nums,
        sizeof (double),
        MAX, doub_bin_inp);``` | Fill nums with data until EOF encountered, setting n to the number of values stored. |
| 8 | ```fclose(plan_txt_inp);
fclose(plan_txt_outp);
fclose(doub_txt_inp);
fclose(doub_txt_outp);``` | ```fclose(plan_bin_inp);
fclose(plan_bin_outp);
fclose(doub_bin_inp);
fclose(doub_bin_outp);``` | Close all input and output files. |

the size of one array element as the second argument to `fread` or `fwrite` and the number of array elements to process as the third argument. Example 7 demonstrates partially filling array `nums` and setting n to the number of elements filled. Example 8 shows that all files—binary or text, input or output—are closed in the same way.

Self-Check

Assume the environment shown, and complete the statements that follow so that they are valid:

```
#define NAME_LEN 50
#define SIZE      30

typedef struct {
      char    name[NAME_LEN];
      int     age;
      double income;
} person_t;
. . .
int       num_err[SIZE];
person_t exec;
FILE     *nums_inp, *psn_inp, *psn_outp, *nums_outp;
          /* binary files */
FILE     *nums_txt_inp, *psn_txt_inp, *psn_txt_outp;
          /* text files   */

nums_inp = fopen("nums.bin", "rb");
nums_txt_inp = fopen("nums.txt", "r");
psn_inp = fopen("persons.bin", "rb");
psn_txt_inp = fopen("persons.txt", "r");
psn_outp = fopen("persout.bin", "wb");
psn_txt_outp = fopen("persout.txt", "w");
nums_outp = fopen("numsout.bin", "wb");
```

1. fread(_____, sizeof (person_t), 1,
         _____);
2. fscanf(psn_txt_____, "%s", _____);
3. fwrite(&exec, _____, 1, psn_____);
4. fwrite(num_err, _____, _____,
         nums_outp);

```
5. fread(&num_err[3], _____, _____,
        nums_inp);
6. fprintf(psn_txt_outp, "%s %d %f\n", _____,
        _____, _____);
```

## Programming

1. Write a function `fread_units` that is similar to the `load_units` function from the Universal Measurement Conversion Program (see Fig. 11.12) except it assumes that the unit conversion data have been stored as a binary file. The function should ask the user for the name of a binary file, open the file, and get up to `unit_max` type `unit_t` values to place in array `units`. Be sure to send back to the calling function the size of the used portion of the array.

# 12.3 SEARCHING A DATABASE

Computerized matching of data against a file of records is a common practice. For example, many real estate companies maintain a large file of property listings: A realtor can process the file to locate desirable properties for a client. Similarly, mail-order firms purchase large files of information on potential customers.

**database**
a vast electronic file of information that can be quickly searched using subject headings or keywords

These large files of data are called **databases**. In this section, we will write a program that searches a database to find all records that match a proposed set of requirements.

## Case Study: Database Inquiry

### PROBLEM

Periphs Plus is a mail-order computer supply company that maintains its inventory as a computer file in order to facilitate answering questions regarding that database. Some questions of interest might be

- What printer stands that cost less than $100 are available?
- What product has the code 5241?
- What types of data cartridges are available?

These questions and others can be answered if we know the correct way to ask them.

**ANALYSIS**

A database inquiry program has two phases: setting the search parameters and searching for records that satisfy the parameters. In our program, we will assume that all the structure components can be involved in the search. The program user must enter low and high bounds for each field of interest. Let's illustrate how we might set the search parameters to answer the question, What modems that cost less than $200 are available?

Assuming that the price of any Periphs Plus product does not exceed $1000, we can use the following menu-driven dialogue to set the search parameters.

```
Select by letter a search parameter to set, or enter q to
accept parameters shown.

      Search Parameter                          Current Value
[a]   Low bound for stock number                1111
[b]   High bound for stock number               9999
[c]   Low bound for category                    aaaa
[d]   High bound for category                   zzzz
[e]   Low bound for technical description       aaaa
[f]   High bound for technical description      zzzz
[g]   Low bound for price                       $    0.00
[h]   High bound for price                      $1000.00


Selection> c
New low bound for category> modem


Select by letter a search parameter to set, or enter q to
accept parameters shown.

      Search Parameter                          Current Value
[a]   Low bound for stock number                1111
[b]   High bound for stock number               9999
[c]   Low bound for category                    modem
[d]   High bound for category                   zzzz
[e]   Low bound for technical description       aaaa
[f]   High bound for technical description      zzzz
[g]   Low bound for price                       $    0.00
[h]   High bound for price                      $1000.00


Selection> d
New high bound for category> modem
```

Select by letter a search parameter to set, or enter q to
accept parameters shown.

```
        Search Parameter                      Current Value
[a]   Low bound for stock number              1111
[b]   High bound for stock number             9999
[c]   Low bound for category                  modem
[d]   High bound for category                 modem
[e]   Low bound for technical description     aaaa
[f]   High bound for technical description    zzzz
[g]   Low bound for price                     $   0.00
[h]   High bound for price                    $1000.00

Selection> h
New high bound for price> 199.99
```

Select by letter a search parameter to set, or enter q to
accept parameters shown.

```
        Search Parameter                      Current Value
[a]   Low bound for stock number              1111
[b]   High bound for stock number             9999
[c]   Low bound for category                  modem
[d]   High bound for category                 modem
[e]   Low bound for technical description     aaaa
[f]   High bound for technical description    zzzz
[g]   Low bound for price                     $   0.00
[h]   High bound for price                    $ 199.99

Selection> q
```

## Data Requirements

### Problem Inputs
```
search_params_t params;    /* search parameter
                              bounds                 */
char inv_filename[STR_SIZ] /* name of inventory file */
```

### Problem Outputs
all products that satisfy the search

**Figure 12.4 Structure Chart for Database Inquiry Problem**

---

**DESIGN**

### Initial Algorithm

1. Open inventory file.
2. Get search parameters.
3. Display all products that satisfy the search parameters.

The structure chart for the database inquiry problem is shown in Fig. 12.4. The refinement of this design is distributed through the development of functions `get_params` and `display_match`.

**IMPLEMENTATION**

In Fig. 12.5, we see an outline of the database program's implementation including the full code of function `main`. Our design and implementation of the functions called by `main` and most of their helper functions follow this outline.

**Figure 12.5 Outline and Function main for Database Inquiry Program**

```
/*
 *  Displays all products in the database that satisfy the search
 *  parameters specified by the program user.
 */
#include <stdio.h>
#include <string.h>

#define MIN_STOCK    1111    /* minimum stock number                    */
#define MAX_STOCK    9999    /* maximum stock number                    */
```

*(continued)*

**Figure 12.5**   *(continued)*

```
#define MAX_PRICE    1000.00 /* maximum product price                    */
#define STR_SIZ      80       /* number of characters in a string        */

typedef struct {             /* product structure type                   */
     int    stock_num;              /* stock number                      */
     char   category[STR_SIZ];
     char   tech_descript[STR_SIZ];
     double price;
} product_t;

typedef struct {             /* search parameter bounds type             */
     int    low_stock, high_stock;
     char   low_category[STR_SIZ], high_category[STR_SIZ];
     char   low_tech_descript[STR_SIZ], high_tech_descript[STR_SIZ];
     double low_price, high_price;
} search_params_t;

search_params_t get_params(void);
void display_match(FILE *databasep, search_params_t params);

/* Insert prototypes of functions needed by get_params and display_match */

int
main(void)
{
     char            inv_filename[STR_SIZ]; /* name of inventory file */
     FILE            *inventoryp;            /* inventory file pointer */
     search_params_t params;                /* search parameter
                                               bounds                 */

     /*  Get name of inventory file and open it                     */
     printf("Enter name of inventory file> ");
     scanf("%s", inv_filename);
     inventoryp = fopen(inv_filename, "rb");

     /*  Get the search parameters                                  */
     params = get_params();

     /*  Display all products that satisfy the search parameters    */
     display_match(inventoryp, params);

     return(0);
}
```

*(continued)*

**Figure 12.5** *(continued)*

```
/*
 *  Prompts the user to enter the search parameters
 */
search_params_t
get_params(void)
{
   /* body of get_params to be inserted */
}


/*
 *  Displays records of all products in the inventory that satisfy search
 *  parameters.
 *  Pre:  databasep accesses a binary file of product_t records that has
 *        been opened as an input file, and params is defined
 */
void
display_match(FILE              *databasep, /* input - file pointer to binary
                                                       database file         */
              search_params_t params)    /* input - search parameter
                                                     bounds                  */
{
   /* body of display_match to be inserted */
}


/*  Insert functions needed by get_params and display_match               */
```

### Design of the Function Subprograms

Function `get_params` must first initialize the search parameters to allow the widest search possible and then let the user change some parameters to narrow the search. The local variables and algorithm for `get_params` follow; the structure chart is in Fig. 12.6.

**Local Variables for get_params**

```
search_params_t params;    /* structure whose components
                              must be defined         */
char choice;               /* user's response to menu */
```

**Figure 12.6
Structure Chart
for get_params**

### Algorithm for get_params

1. Initialize `params` to permit widest possible search.
2. Display menu and get response to store in `choice`.
3. Repeat while `choice` is not `'q'`
   4. Select appropriate prompt and get new parameter value.
   5. Display menu and get response to store in `choice`.
6. Return search parameters.

Function `display_match` must examine each file record with a stock number between the low and high bounds for stock numbers. If a record satisfies the search parameters, it is displayed. Function `display_match` will also print a message if no matches are found. The local variables, algorithm, and structure chart for the function follow (see Fig. 12.7).

**Figure 12.7
Structure Chart
for
display_match**

**Local Variables for display_match**

```
product_t next_prod   /*  the current product              */
int no_matches        /*  a flag indicating whether or
                          not there are any matches        */
```

**Algorithm for display_match**

1. Initialize no_matches to true(1).
2. Advance to the first record whose stock number is within range.
3. while the current stock number is still in range repeat
    4. if the search parameters match
        5. Display the product and set no_matches to false(0).
    6. Get the next product record.
7. if there are no matches
    8. Print a no products available message.

**IMPLEMENTATION of the function subprograms**

Figure 12.8 shows the code of functions display_match, menu_choose, and match, along with a stub for function show.

**Figure 12.8    Functions display_match, menu_choose, and match**

```
/*
 *  Displays a lettered menu with the current values of search parameters.
 *  Returns the letter the user enters.  A letter in the range a..h selects
 *  a parameter to change; q quits, accepting search parameters shown.
 *  Post:  first non-whitespace character entered is returned
 */
char
menu_choose(search_params_t params) /* input - current search parameter
                                                 bounds                 */
{
    char choice;

    printf("Select by letter a search parameter to set or enter ");
    printf("q to\naccept parameters shown.\n\n");
    printf("     Search parameter                    ");
    printf("Current value\n\n");
    printf("[a]  Low bound for stock number          %4d\n",
           params.low_stock);
```

*(continued)*

**Figure 12.8**    *(continued)*

```
        printf("[b]  High bound for stock number          %4d\n",
               params.high_stock);
        printf("[c]  Low bound for category               %s\n",
               params.low_category);
        printf("[d]  High bound for category              %s\n",
               params.high_category);
        printf("[e]  Low bound for technical description  %s\n",
               params.low_tech_descript);
        printf("[f]  High bound for technical description %s\n",
               params.high_tech_descript);
        printf("[g]  Low bound for price                  $%7.2f\n",
               params.low_price);
        printf("[h]  High bound for price                 $%7.2f\n\n",
               params.high_price);

        printf("Selection> ");
        scanf(" %c", &choice);

        return (choice);
}

/*
 *  Determines whether record prod satisfies all search parameters
 */
int
match(product_t       prod,     /*  input - record to check       */
      search_params_t params)   /*  input - parameters to satisfy */
{
        return (strcmp(params.low_category, prod.category) <= 0          &&
                strcmp(prod.category, params.high_category) <= 0         &&
                strcmp(params.low_tech_descript, prod.tech_descript) <= 0 &&
                strcmp(prod.tech_descript, params.high_tech_descript) <= 0 &&
                params.low_price <= prod.price                          &&
                prod.price <= params.high_price);
}
/*
 *   *** STUB ***
 *  Displays each field of prod.  Leaves a blank line after the product
 *  display.
 */
```

*(continued)*

**Figure 12.8** *(continued)*

```
void
show(product_t prod)
{
     printf("Function show entered with product number %d\n",
          prod.stock_num);
}

/*
 *  Displays records of all products in the inventory that satisfy search
 *  parameters.
 *  Pre:  databasep accesses a binary file of product_t records that has
 *        been opened as an input file, and params is defined
 */
void
display_match(FILE           *databasep,  /*  file pointer to binary
                                              database file            */
             search_params_t params)     /*  input - search parameter
                                              bounds                   */
{
     product_t next_prod;       /* current product from database      */
     int       no_matches = 1;  /* flag indicating if no matches have
                                   been found                         */
     int       status;          /* input file status                  */

     /*  Advances to first record with a stock number greater than or
         equal to lower bound.                                        */
     for  (status = fread(&next_prod, sizeof (product_t), 1, databasep);
           status == 1  &&  params.low_stock > next_prod.stock_num;
           status = fread(&next_prod, sizeof (product_t), 1, databasep)) {}

     /*  Displays a list of the products which satisfy the search
         parameters                                                   */
     printf("\nProducts satisfying the search parameters:\n");
     while (next_prod.stock_num <= params.high_stock  &&
            status == 1) {
        if (match(next_prod, params)) {
              no_matches = 0;
              show(next_prod);
```

*(continued)*

**Figure 12.8** *(continued)*

```
        }
    status = fread(&next_prod, sizeof (product_t), 1, databasep);
    }

    /*  Displays a message if no products found                          */
    if (no_matches)
        printf("Sorry, no products available\n");
}
```

**EXERCISES FOR SECTION 12.3**

Self-Check

1. What values would you use as search parameter bounds to answer the questions listed at the beginning of this section?
2. Which function in our database search program determines whether a particular record matches the search parameters? Which one displays each matching record?
3. Why does function `match` not need to check a product's `stock_num` field?

Programming

1. Write the functions `get_params` and `show` described in the database inquiry problem. Since `get_params` calls function `menu_choose`, your implementation of algorithm Step 4 for `get_params` must be sure to account for the fact that `menu_choose` does not validate the value the user enters.
2. Write a `void` function `make_product_file` that would convert a text file containing product information to a binary file of `product_t` structures. The function's parameters are file pointers to the text input and binary output files.

# 12.4 COMMON PROGRAMMING ERRORS

File processing in any programming language has many pitfalls; C is no exception. Remember to declare a file pointer variable (type `FILE *`) for each file you want to process. Because C makes no type distinction between file pointers accessing text files and those accessing binary files, it is easy to use the wrong library function with a file pointer. In a program that manipulates both file types, choose names for your file pointers that remind you of the type of file accessed. For example, you could choose names containing "_txt_" for text file pointers and names containing "_bin_" for binary file pointers.

It is also critical that you remember that library functions fscanf, fprintf, getc, and putc must be used for text I/O only; functions fread and fwrite are applied exclusively to binary files. You should have the summary table in this chapter handy for reference when you are using these functions to help you keep straight the order of their arguments. The fact that fprintf, fscanf, and getc take the file pointer as their first argument while putc, fread, and fwrite take it as the last argument is definitely confusing at first.

If you are permitting the program user to enter the name of a file to process, you will have two variables identifying the file—one to hold its name (a character string) and one to hold the pointer for file access. It is essential to remember that the only file operation in which the file *name* is used is the call to fopen. Keep in mind that opening a file for output by calling fopen with a second argument of "w" or "wb" typically results in a loss of any existing file whose name matches the first argument.

It is easy to forget that binary files cannot be created, viewed, or modified using an editor or word processor program. Rather, they must be created and interpreted by a program that reads values into or writes values from variables of the same type as the binary file's elements.

# CHAPTER REVIEW

1. Text files are continuous streams of character codes that can be viewed as broken into lines by the newline character.
2. Processing text files requires the transfer of sequences of characters between main memory and disk storage.
3. In order to be processed as numbers, character strings taken as input from a text file must be converted to a different format such as int or double for storage in memory. Output of numeric values to a text file requires conversion of the internal formats back to a sequence of characters.
4. Binary files permit storage of information using a computer's internal data format: Neither time nor accuracy is lost through conversion of values transferred between main and secondary storage.
5. Binary files cannot be created using a word processor and are not meaningful when displayed on the screen or printed.

## New C Constructs

| Statement | Effect |
|---|---|
| **Declarations** | |
| `char name_txt_in[50],`<br>`    name_bin_out[50];` | Declares two string variables whose names imply that they may be used to hold names of a text file to be used for input and of a binary output file. |
| `FILE *text_inp, *text_outp,`<br>`    *bin_inp, *bin_outp;` | Declares four file pointer variables. |
| **Calls to stdio Library** | |
| `text_inp = fopen(name_txt_in, "r");`<br>`text_outp = fopen("result.txt", "w");`<br>`bin_inp = fopen("data.bin", "rb");`<br>`bin_outp = fopen(name_bin_out, "wb");` | Opens `"data.bin"` and the file whose name is the value of `name_txt_in` as input files; opens `"result.txt"` and the file whose name is the value of `name_bin_out` as output files. Pointers accessing the open files are stored in file pointer variables `text_inp`, `text_outp`, `bin_inp`, and `bin_outp`. |
| `fscanf(text_inp, "%s%d%lf", animal,`<br>`    &age, &weight);` | Copies string, `int`, and `double` values from the *text* input file accessed by file pointer `text_inp`, storing the values in variables `animal`, `age`, and `weight`. |
| `fprintf(text_outp, "(%.2f, %.2f)",`<br>`    x, y);` | Writes to the *text* output file accessed by file pointer `text_outp` a set of parentheses enclosing the values of `x` and `y` rounded to two decimal places. |
| `nextch = getc(text_inp);` | Stores in `nextch` the next character available in the *text* input file accessed by file pointer `text_inp`, or the integer `EOF` value if no characters remain. |
| `putc(ch, text_outp);` | Copies the value of `ch` into the *text* output file accessed by file pointer `text_outp`. |
| `fread(&var, sizeof (double), 1,`<br>`    bin_inp);` | Copies into type `double` variable `var` the next value from the *binary* input file accessed by file pointer `bin_inp`. |
| `fwrite(&insect, sizeof (insect_t), 1,`<br>`    bin_outp);` | Copies the value of type `insect_t` variable `insect` into the *binary* output file accessed by file pointer `bin_outp`. |
| `fclose(text_outp);`<br>`fclose(bin_inp);` | Closes text file accessed by file pointer `text_outp` after writing the `<eof>` character. Closes binary file accessed by `bin_inp` so it is no longer available as an input source. |

## QUICK-CHECK EXERCISES

1. A _____ file consists of a stream of character codes; a _____ file is a sequence of values of any type represented exactly as they would be in main memory.

2. For each of these library functions, indicate whether it is used in processing binary or text files.

   ```
   fread          putc
   fscanf         fwrite
   getc           fprintf
   ```

3. What file pointer name(s) does a C program associate with the keyboard? With the screen?

4. A word processor can be used to create or view a _____ file but not a _____ file.

5. Write a prototype for a function `fprintf_blob` that writes to a text output file the value of a structure of type `blob_t`. The function does *not* open the output file; the function assumes the file is already open.

6. Write a prototype for a function `fwrite_blob` that writes to a binary output file the value of a structure of type `blob_t`. The function does *not* open the output file; the function assumes the file is already open.

7. The _____ character separates a _____ file into lines, and the _____ character appears at the end of a file.

8. Can a file be used for both input and output by the same program?

9. Comment on the correctness of this statement: It is more efficient to use a text file because the computer knows that each component is a single character that can be copied into a single byte of main memory; with a binary file, however, the size of the components may vary.

10. Consider the following code segment, and then choose the correct "next" statement from the two options given. Indicate how you know which is the right choice. If you can't determine which is right, explain what additional information you would need in order to decide.

    ```
    FILE *inp;
    int   n;

    inp = fopen("data.in", "r");
    ```

    "next" option 1
    ```
        fread(&n, sizeof (int), 1, inp);
    ```

    "next" option 2
    ```
        fscanf(inp, "%d", &n);
    ```

## ANSWERS TO QUICK-CHECK EXERCISES

1. text, binary
2. `fread`: binary; `fscanf`: text; `getc`: text; `putc`: text; `fwrite`: binary; `fprintf`: text
3. keyboard: `stdin`; screen: `stdout`, `stderr`
4. text, binary
5. `void fprintf_blob(FILE *filep, blob_t blob);`
6. `void fwrite_blob(FILE *filep, blob_t blob);`
7. newline (or `'\n'`), text, eof
8. Yes, it can be opened in one mode, closed, and then reopened in another mode.
9. The statement is not correct. Because no data conversions are necessary when you use binary files, binary files are more efficient than text files.
10. The code segment shown could be followed by either statement. In order to choose one option, it would be necessary to know whether `data.in` was a text file or a binary file of integers. If one were certain that the code's author always used the mode `"rb"` when opening a binary file, then option 2 would be the expected next statement.

## REVIEW QUESTIONS

1. Where are files stored?
2. How would you modify the program in Fig. 12.1 so the data would be sent to the screen as well as written to the backup file?
3. Consider a file `empstat.txt` that contains employee records. The data for each employee consist of the employee's name (up to 20 characters), social security number (up to 11 characters), gross pay for the week (`double`), taxes deducted (`double`), and the net pay (`double`) for the week. Each record is a separate text line in file `empstat.txt`. Write a program that will create a text file `report.txt` with the heading line

   ```
   NAME            SOC.SEC.NUM   GROSS    TAXES    NET
   ```

   followed by two blank lines and the pertinent information under each column heading. The program should also produce a binary file version of `empstat.txt` named `empstat.bin`.
4. What are the characteristics of a binary file?

5. Write a program that takes as input the file empstat.bin created in Review Question 3 and produces a binary file ssngross.bin containing only social security numbers and gross pay for each employee.

6. What is a file pointer?

7. A sparse matrix is one in which a large number of the elements are zero. Write a void function store_sparse that writes to a binary file a compressed representation of a $50 \times 50$ sparse matrix of type int. The function's parameters are the file pointer and the matrix. The function will store only the nonzero matrix values, writing for each of these a record containing three components: row subscript, column subscript, and value.

8. How would the prototype of function store_sparse be different if its purpose were to write the sparse matrix representation to a text file (see Review Question 7)? Discuss the implications of your answer.

# PROGRAMMING PROJECTS

1. Write a void function that will merge the contents of two text files containing chemical elements sorted by atomic number and will produce a sorted file of binary records. The function's parameters will be three file pointers. Each text file line will contain an integer atomic number followed by the element name, chemical symbol, and atomic weight. Here are two sample lines:

```
11   Sodium     Na   22.99
20   Calcium    Ca   40.08
```

The function can assume that one file does not have two copies of the same element and that the binary output file should have this same property. *Hint:* When one of the input files is exhausted, do not forget to copy the remaining elements of the other input file to the result file.

2. Develop a database inquiry program to search a binary file of aircraft data sorted in descending order by maximum cruise speed. Each aircraft record should include the name (up to 25 characters), maximum cruise speed (in km/h), wing span and length (in m), the character M (for military) or C (for civilian), and a descriptive phrase (up to 80 characters). Your system should implement a menu-driven interface that allows the user to search on all components except the descriptive phrase. Here are three planes to start your database:

```
SR-71 Blackbird                      (name)
3500                                 (max cruise speed)
16.95   32.74   M                    (wing span, length, military/civilian)
high-speed strategic reconnaissance
```

```
EF-111A Raven
2280
19.21   23.16   M
electronic warfare

Concorde
2140
25.61   62.2   C
supersonic airliner
```

3. Each year the state legislature rates the productivity of the faculty of each of the state-supported colleges and universities. The rating is based on reports submitted by the faculty members indicating the average number of hours worked per week during the school year. Each faculty member is rated, and the university receives an overall rating based on the average of the reports from its faculty.

    The faculty productivity ratings are computed as follows:

a. "Highly productive" means reported hours per week are over 55.

b. "Satisfactory" means reported hours per week are between 35 and 55.

c. "Overpaid" means reported hours per week are less than 35.

Take the following data from a text file:

| Name | Hours |
|------|-------|
| Herm | 63 |
| Flo | 37 |
| Jake | 20 |
| Maureen | 55 |
| Saul | 72 |
| Tony | 40 |
| Al | 12 |

Your program should include functions corresponding to the headings shown.

```
/*  Displays table heading  */
void
print_header(void)

/*  Displays name, hours, and productivity rating  */
void
print_productivity(faculty_t fac) /* input */

/*   Gets one faculty member's data from text file returns 1
 *   for successful input, 0 for error, EOF for end of file
 */
```

```
int
scan_faculty(FILE        *text_inp, /* input - file pointer
                                       to data file        */
             faculty_t *fac)        /* output - structure of
                                       faculty data        */
```

4. Write a program that takes words from a text file and prints each one on a separate line of an output file followed by the number of letters (alphabetic characters) in the word. Any leading or trailing punctuation marks should be removed from the word before it is printed. When all the text has been processed, display on the screen a count of the words in the file. Assume that words are groups of nonwhitespace characters separated by one or more whitespace characters.

5. Compute the monthly payment and the total payment for a bank loan. You are given
   a. the amount of the loan
   b. the duration of the loan in months
   c. the interest rate for the loan

   Your program should take from a data file the information for one loan at a time, perform the required computation, and display on the screen the data and the values of the monthly payment and the total payment.

   Create a text file with at least the following data:

   | Loan | Months | Rate |
   | --- | --- | --- |
   | 16000 | 300 | 12.50 |
   | 24000 | 360 | 8.50 |
   | 30000 | 300 | 11.50 |
   | 42000 | 360 | 10.50 |
   | 22000 | 240 | 09.75 |

   *Hint:* The formula for computing monthly payment is

   $$monthpay = \frac{ratem \times expm^{months} \times loan}{expm^{months} - 1.0}$$

   where

   $$ratem = \frac{rate}{1200.00}$$

   $$expm = (1.0 + ratem)$$

6. Use your solution to Project 5 as the basis for writing a program that will write a text file containing a table of the following form:

Loan Amount: $1000.00

| Interest Rate | Duration (years) | Monthly Payment | Total Payment |
|---|---|---|---|
| 10.00 | 20 | _____ | _____ |
| 10.00 | 25 | _____ | _____ |
| 10.00 | 30 | _____ | _____ |
| 10.25 | 20 | _____ | _____ |

The output file produced by your program should contain payment information on a particular loan amount for interest rates from 10% to 14% with increments of 0.25%. The loan durations should be 20, 25, and 30 years.

7. Develop a small airline reservation system. The database of flight information should be kept in a file of structures with the following components:

a. Flight number (including airline code)
b. City of departure
c. Destination
d. Date and time of departure
e. Date and time of arrival
f. Number of first-class seats still available
g. Number of first-class seats sold
h. Number of coach seats still available
i. Number of coach seats sold

Include in your program separate functions for creation, deletion, and update of flight records. Also implement `make_reservation` and `cancel_reservation` functions.

8. Cooking recipes can be stored on a computer and, with the use of files, can be quickly referenced.

a. Write a function that will create a text file of recipes from information entered at the terminal. The format of the data to be stored is
1) recipe type (dessert, meat, etc.)
2) subtype (for dessert, use cake, pie, or cookies)
3) name (e.g., German chocolate)

    4)   number of lines in the recipe to follow

    5)   the actual recipe

Item 3 should be on a separate line.

  b.  Write a function that will accept as parameters a file and a structured record of search parameter bounds. The function should display all recipes satisfying the search parameters.

# PROGRAMMING IN THE LARGE

c h a p t e r

In this chapter, we examine the special difficulties associated with the development of large software systems. We explore how separating our expression of *what* we need to do from *how* we actually plan to accomplish it reduces the complexity of system development and maintenance (upkeep). This chapter introduces C's facilities for formalizing this separation of concerns.

We study how to define flexible macros that help to make a program more readable as well as easier to maintain. This chapter describes the storage classes of variables and functions we have been using along with some additional storage classes that may be useful in large program development. We also investigate how to build a library of reusable code from functions developed for specific contexts. We meet additional preprocessor directives that allow us to format libraries so they are easy to include in any combination.

# 13.1 USING ABSTRACTION TO MANAGE COMPLEXITY

Up to this point in your study of programming, you have been primarily concerned with writing relatively short programs that solve individual problems but otherwise have little general use. In this chapter, we focus on the design and maintenance of large-scale programs. We discuss how to modularize a large project so that individual pieces can be implemented by different programmers at different times. We also see how to write software modules in ways that simplify their reuse in other projects.

## Procedural Abstraction

When a team of programmers is assigned the task of developing a large software system, they must have a rational approach to breaking down the overall problem into solvable chunks. Abstraction is a powerful technique that helps problem solvers deal with complex issues in a piecemeal fashion. The dictionary defines *abstraction* as the process of separating the inherent qualities or properties of something from the actual physical object to which they belong. One example of the use of abstraction is the representation of a program variable (for example, `velocity`) by a storage location in memory. We don't have to know anything about the physical structure of memory in order to use such a variable in programming.

In this text, we have applied aspects of two types of abstraction to program development. First, we practiced **procedural abstraction**, which is the philosophy that function development should separate the concern of *what* is to be achieved by a function from the details of *how* it is to be achieved. In other

**procedural abstraction**
separation of *what* a function does from the details of *how* the function accomplishes its purpose

**622**

words, you can specify what you expect a function to do and then use that function in the design of a problem solution before you know how to implement the function.

For example, in Chapter 12, when we tackled our database inquiry problem, our initial algorithm was one that could lead directly to an outline of a program fragment that identifies three functions representing the major steps of a solution. The following outline defers the details of parameter lists and use of function values.

| Initial Algorithm | Program Outline |
|---|---|
| 1. Open inventory file. | `fopen(...)` |
| 2. Get the search parameters. | `get_params(...)` |
| 3. Display all metals that satisfy the search parameters. | `display_match(...)` |

In this example of procedural abstraction, we see that *what* one of the functions must accomplish (i.e., open a file) corresponds to the purpose of a library function we have studied. Reuse of this existing function means that we *never* have to concern ourselves with the details of *how* this task is accomplished. Clearly, the availability of powerful libraries of functions is of significant benefit in reducing the complexity of large systems. As we have already seen, the use of such libraries is a fundamental feature of the C programming language.

In the example shown, the other two functions identified in this first level of procedural abstraction are excellent candidates for assignment to separate members of a program development team. Once the purpose and parameter lists of each function are spelled out, neither developer will have any need to be concerned about the details of *how* the other member carries out the assigned task.

## Data Abstraction

**data abstraction**
separation of the logical view of a data object (*what* is stored) from the physical view (*how* the information is stored)

**Data abstraction** is another powerful tool we have seen for breaking down a large problem into manageable chunks. When we apply data abstraction to a complex problem, we initially specify the data objects involved and the operations to be performed on these data objects without being overly concerned with how the data objects will be represented and stored in memory. We can describe *what* information is stored in the data object without being specific as to *how* the information is organized and represented. This is the *logical view* of the data object as opposed to its *physical view*, the actual internal representation in memory. Once we understand the logical view, we can use the data object and its operators in our programs; however, we (or someone else) will eventually need to implement the data object and its operators before we can run any program that uses them.

One simple example of data abstraction is our use of the C data type `double`, which is an abstraction for the set of real numbers. The computer hardware limits the range of real numbers that can be represented, and not all real numbers within the specified range can be represented. Different computers use a variety of representation schemes for type `double`. However, we can generally use the data type `double` and its associated operators ($+$, $-$, $*$, $/$, $=$, $==$, $<$, and so on) without being concerned with these details of its implementation. Another example of data abstraction is the definition of a data type and associated operators for complex numbers given in Chapter 11.

## Information Hiding

One advantage of procedural abstraction and data abstraction is that they enable the designer to make implementation decisions in a piecemeal fashion. The designer can postpone making decisions regarding the actual internal representation of the data objects and the implementation of its operators. At the top levels of the design, the designer focuses on how to use a data object and its operators; at the lower levels of design, the designer works out the implementation details. In this way, the designer can hierarchically break down a large problem, controlling and reducing its overall complexity.

If the details of a data object's implementation are not known when a higher-level module is implemented, the higher-level module can access the data object only through its operators. This limitation is actually an advantage: It allows the designer to change his or her mind at a later date and possibly to choose a more efficient method of internal representation or implementation. If the higher-level modules reference a data object only through its operators, a change in the data object's representation will require no change in a higher-level module. The process of protecting the implementation details of a lower-level module from direct access by a higher-level module is called **information hiding**.

**information hiding**
protecting the implementation details of a lower-level module from direct access by a higher-level module

## Reusable Code

One of the keys to productivity in software development is the writing of *reusable code*, code that can be reused in many different applications, preferably without having to be modified or recompiled. One way to facilitate reuse in C is to **encapsulate** a data object together with its operators in a personal library. Then we can use the `#include` preprocessor directive to give functions in a file access to this library.

**encapsulate**
packaging as a unit a data object and its operators

Encapsulation is a powerful concept in everyday life that can be applied very profitably to software design. For example, one encapsulated object that we are all familiar with is an aspirin. Our familiarity is based strictly on *what* the object does (relieves pain and reduces fever) when activated through the standard interface (swallowing). Only its producers and prescribers care *how* an aspirin does what it does (the effect of acetylsalicylic acid on inflammation and blood flow to the skin surface). By applying the principles of procedural and data abstraction, we can package the "bitter" details of a complex problem's solution in equally neat, easy-to-use capsules.

**EXERCISES FOR SECTION 13.1**

Self-Check

1. Describe how each of the following encapsulated objects allows the user to focus on *what* the object does with little or no concern for *how* it does it:

microwave oven      television set      calculator

# 13.2 PERSONAL LIBRARIES: HEADER FILES

We have seen how the availability of C's standard libraries simplifies program development. However, the standard libraries are not extensive enough to handle every programming need. Often we write a function that would be useful in a context other than the one for which it was originally written. Copying the code of functions into other programs to allow reuse is possible but cumbersome, especially when compared to the way we get access to standard libraries. In fact, one can use the C preprocessor directive #include to make available personal libraries as well. Since C permits source code files to be compiled separately and then linked prior to loading and execution, we can provide our personal libraries as object files; programs using our personal libraries need not first compile the functions in them. If we take another look at a diagram first presented in Chapter 1 and now repeated in Fig. 13.1, we are in a better position to understand the bubble that is marked with a colored arrow. Until now, the "other object files" that have been linked to our code have been the standard C libraries. When we learn to make our own library files, these files can also be provided to the linker as part of preparing our program for execution.

## Header Files

**header file**
text file containing the interface information about a library needed by a compiler to translate a program system that uses the library or by a person to understand and use the library

To create a personal library, we must first make a **header file**. A header file is a text file containing all the information about a library needed by the compiler when compiling a program that uses the facilities defined in the library.

**Figure 13.1
Preparing a
Program for
Execution**

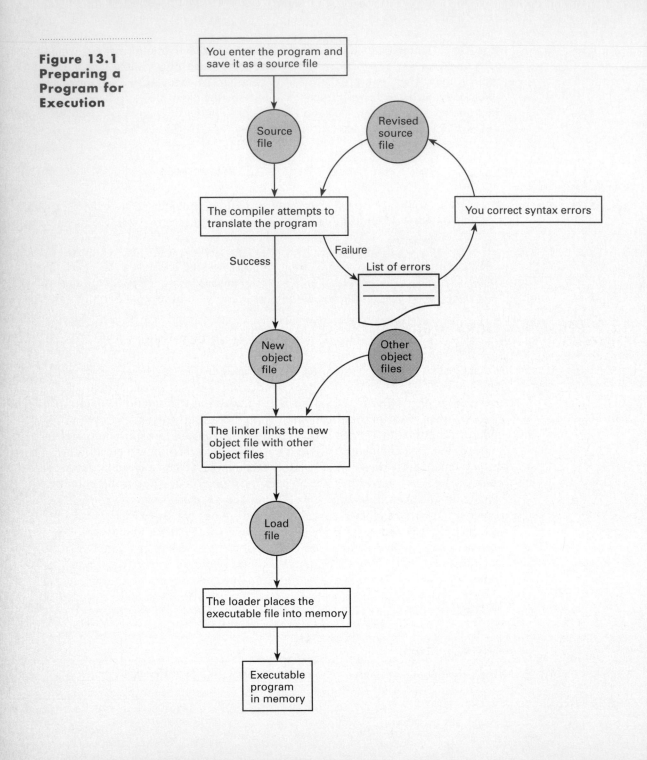

Precisely this type of data is found in system header files such as `stdio.h`, `math.h`, and `string.h`. The form we recommend for a header file also provides all the information that a user of the library needs. Typical contents of a header file include

1. a block comment summarizing the library's purpose
2. `#define` directives naming constant macros
3. type definitions
4. block comments stating the purpose of each library function and declarations of the form

       `extern` *prototype*

The use of the keyword `extern` in a function declaration notifies the compiler that the function's definition will be provided to the linker. Figure 13.2 shows a header file for our planet data type and operators from Chapter 11. In Fig. 13.3, we see the beginning of a source file that has need of facilities from

**Figure 13.2   Header File planet.h for Personal Library with Data Type and Associated Functions**

```
/*   planet.h
 *
 *   abstract data type planet
 *
 *   Type planet_t has these components:
 *       name, diameter, moons, orbit_time, rotation_time
 *
 *   Operators:
 *       print_planet, planet_equal, scan_planet
 */

#define PLANET_STRSIZ  10

typedef struct { /* planet structure */
      char name[PLANET_STRSIZ];
      double diameter;          /* equatorial diameter in km              */
      int    moons;             /* number of moons                        */
      double orbit_time,        /* years to orbit sun once                */
             rotation_time;     /* hours to complete one revolution on
                                          axis                            */
} planet_t;
```

*(continued)*

**Figure 13.2    *(continued)***

```
/*
 *  Displays with labels all components of a planet_t structure
 */
extern void
print_planet(planet_t pl);   /* input - one planet structure            */


/*
 *  Determines whether or not the components of planet_1 and planet_2
 *  match
 */
extern int
planet_equal(planet_t planet_1,   /* input - planets to               */
             planet_t planet_2); /*            compare                */


/*
 *  Fills a type planet_t structure with input data.   Integer returned as
 *  function result is success/failure/EOF indicator.
 *      1 => successful input of planet
 *      0 => error encountered
 *      EOF => insufficient data before end of file
 *  In case of error or EOF, value of type planet_t output argument is
 *  undefined.
 */
extern int
scan_planet(planet_t *plnp); /* output - address of planet_t structure to
                                          fill                         */
```

this library. We are assuming here that the header file is named planet.h, and that it is located in the directory in which the preprocessor first looks for files whose names appear in quotation marks after a #include. This issue is system dependent, but, in many cases, the directory first searched would be the one in which the current source file resides.

In our programming so far, we have used angular brackets (<>), as in

```
#include <stdio.h>
```

to indicate to the preprocessor that a header file is to be found in a system

**Figure 13.3    Portion of Program That Uses Functions from a Personal Library**

```
/*
 *  Beginning of source file in which a personal library and system I/O library
 *  are used.
 */

#include <stdio.h>        /* system's standard I/O functions              */

#include "planet.h"       /* personal library with planet_t data type and
                                         operators                         */
. . .
```

directory. Quotes around the header file name, as in

```
#include "planet.h"
```

mark it as information about a library belonging to the programmer.

When revising a source file, the C preprocessor replaces each #include line by the contents of the header file it references.

In Chapters 3 and 6, when we first met user-defined functions, we emphasized the importance of the block comment placed at the beginning of the function and the importance of the function prototype and the comments on its parameters. When taken together, this prototype and its associated commentary provide the basic information needed by a programmer desiring to call the function: what the function does, what type of value it returns (if any), and what types of arguments it operates on. Notice that this is precisely the information placed in the header file.

An important aspect of dividing any problem into manageable chunks is defining the points at which the chunks of the solution come together to form the complete solution. The common boundary between two separate parts of a solution is called the *interface*. The header file's purpose is to define the interface between a library and any program that uses the library.

## Cautionary Notes for Header File Design

You will notice that in our header file example, the constant macro defined (PLANET_STRSIZ) has a long name that begins with the library name. This naming strategy reduces the likelihood that the name associated with a constant in the header file will conflict with other constant macro names in the program.

In Section 13.3, we will see how to create an implementation file for a personal library. The header (interface) file and the implementation file are the two essential source files in a personal library.

Self-Check

1. How can the C preprocessor determine whether a header file name in an `#include` statement is the name of a system library or of a personal library?
2. A function's _____ and associated _____ are the collection of information that a programmer must know about the function in order to be able to use it.
3. A header (interface) file describes _____ the functions of a library do, not _____ they do it.

Programming

1. Look at the table of math library functions in Chapter 3 (Table 3.1). Define a header file `myops.h` that contains a full description of the interfaces of functions `fabs`, `sqrt`, and `pow`. Then add to this file information about the `factorial` function (see Chapter 5). Would anything about your interface information for `factorial` require your implementation of the function to be iterative? Would anything require the implementation to be recursive?

# 13.3 PERSONAL LIBRARIES: IMPLEMENTATION FILES

In Section 13.2, we saw how to create a library header file containing all the interface information needed by a program and programmer using the library. We created a header file for a planet library and studied a program that uses the `#include` directive in order to make this header a part of the program's code. In this section, we investigate how to create a library **implementation file**. The header file describes *what* the functions of the library do; the implementation file will show *how* the functions do it.

**implementation file**
file containing the C source code of a library's functions and any other information needed for compilation of these functions

A library's implementation file is a C source file that contains both the code of all the library functions and any other information needed for compilation of these functions. The elements of an implementation file are the same as the elements of any program and have many similarities with the elements of the library's header file. These elements are

1. a block comment summarizing the library's purpose

2. #include directives for this library's header file and for other libraries used by the functions in this library
3. #define directives naming constant macros used only inside this library
4. type definitions used only inside this library
5. function definitions including the usual comments

It may seem odd that we #include the header file for the library we are implementing since the prototypes found in it are redundant. We do this to make maintenance and modification of the library more straightforward. Alternatively, we could simply restate the constant macro and type definitions from the header file in the implementation file. However, then a modification of one of these definitions would require changes in *two* files. Using the header file #include as shown, we would simply modify the header file; when the implementation file is recompiled, the change will be taken into account. Figure 13.4 shows an implementation file that might be associated with the header file planet.h.

**Figure 13.4    Implementation File planet.c Containing Library with Planet Data Type and Operators**

```
/*
 *
 *       planet.c
 */
#include <stdio.h>
#include <string.h>
#include "planet.h"
/*
 *  Displays with labels all components of a planet_t structure
 */
void
print_planet(planet_t pl)   /* input - one planet structure */
{
      printf("  Equatorial diameter: %.0f km\n", pl.diameter);
      printf("  Number of moons: %d\n", pl.moons);
      printf("  Time to complete one orbit of the sun: %.2f years\n",
             pl.orbit_time);
      printf("  Time to complete one rotation on axis: %.4f hours\n",
             pl.rotation_time);
}
```

*(continued)*

**Figure 11.4** *(continued)*

```
/*
 *  Determines whether or not the components of planet_1 and planet_2 match
 */
int
planet_equal(planet_t planet_1,   /* input - planets to                     */
             planet_t planet_2)  /*            compare                      */
{
      return (strcmp(planet_1.name, planet_2.name) == 0     &&
              planet_1.diameter == planet_2.diameter        &&
              planet_1.moons == planet_2.moons              &&
              planet_1.orbit_time == planet_2.orbit_time    &&
              planet_1.rotation_time == planet_2.rotation_time);
}


/*
 *  Fills a type planet_t structure with input data.  Integer returned as
 *  function result is success/failure/EOF indicator.
 *      1 => successful input of planet
 *      0 => error encountered
 *      EOF => insufficient data before end of file
 *  In case of error or EOF, value of type planet_t output argument is
 *  undefined.
 */
int
scan_planet(planet_t *plnp) /* output - address of planet_t structure to
                                        fill                               */
{
     int result;

     result = scanf("%s%lf%d%lf%lf",  plnp->name,
                                      &plnp->diameter,
                                      &plnp->moons,
                                      &plnp->orbit_time,
                                      &plnp->rotation_time);

     if (result == 5)
          result = 1;
     else if (result != EOF)
          result = 0;

     return (result);
}
```

## Using a Personal Library

To use a personal library, one must complete these steps:

*Creation*

*C1* Create a header file containing the interface information for a program needing the library.

*C2* Create an implementation file containing the code of the library functions and other details of the implementation that are hidden from the user program.

*C3* Compile the implementation file. This step must be repeated any time either the header file or the implementation file is revised.

*Use*

*U1* Include the library's header file in the user program through an #include directive.

*U2* After compiling the user program, include both its object file and the object file created in C3 in the command that activates the linker.

**EXERCISES FOR SECTION 13.3**

Self-Check

1. Why do we openly define the constant macro PLANET_STRSIZ in the header file "planet.h" rather than protecting this name as one of the implementation details?

2. If you see the following #include directives in a program, what do you assume about libraries red and blue?

```
#include <red.h>
#include "blue.h"
```

Programming

1. Create a library named complex that defines the complex arithmetic operators from Section 11.4.

# 13.4 STORAGE CLASSES

C has five storage classes; so far we have seen three. Formal parameters and local variables of functions are variables that are *auto*matically allocated on the stack when a function is called and *auto*matically deallocated when the function

default storage class of function parameters and local variables: storage is automatically
allocated on the stack at the
time of a function call and
deallocated when the function
returns
extern
storage class of names known
to the linker

returns; they are of storage class **auto**. In Chapter 6, we studied that the *scope* of these names, that is, the program region in which the name is visible, extends from the point of declaration to the end of the function in which the declaration appears.

The names of the functions themselves are of storage class **extern**, meaning that they will be available to the linker. If function prototypes precede any function definition, then these functions may be called by any other function in a program. The compiler needs to know the following vital information about a function in order to translate a call to it: its return type, how many arguments it takes, and the data types of the arguments. Providing this information is the purpose of the

extern *prototype*

statement of which we have seen numerous examples in library header files. This statement *does not create* a function of storage class **extern**; it merely *notifies* the compiler that such a function exists and that the linker will know where to find it. Figure 13.5 shows the two storage classes, auto and extern. Names in color are of storage class auto; those in boldface black are of storage class extern.

**Figure 13.5    Storage Classes auto and extern as Previously Seen**

```
void
fun_one(int arg_one, int arg_two)
{
        int one_local;
        . . .
}


int
fun_two(int a2_one, int a2_two)
{
        int local_var;
        . . .
}
```

*(continued)*

**Figure 13.5** *(continued)*

```
int
main(void)
{
      int num;
      . . .
}
```

The shaded area of Fig. 13.5 marks the program's *top level*. Class `extern` is the default storage class for all names declared at this level.

## Global Variables

We have seen only declarations of functions at the top level of a program. However, it is also possible (though usually inadvisable) to declare variables at the top level. The scope of such a variable name extends from the point of declaration to the end of the source file, except in functions where the same name is declared as a formal parameter or local variable. If we need to reference a top-level variable in the region of its source file that precedes its declaration or in another source file, the compiler can be alerted to the variable's existence by placing a declaration of the variable that begins with the keyword `extern` in the file prior to the first reference. Such a variable can be made accessible to *all* functions in a program and is therefore sometimes called a **global variable**. Figure 13.6 shows the declaration at the top level of `int` variable `global_var_x` of storage class `extern` in file `eg1.c` and an `extern` statement in `eg2.c` that makes the global variable accessible throughout this file as well. Only the *defining declaration*, the one in `eg1.c`, allocates space for `global_var_x`. A declaration beginning with the keyword `extern` allocates no memory; it simply provides information for the compiler.

**global variable**
a variable that may be accessed by many functions in a program

**Figure 13.6
Declaration of a
Global Variable**

```
/* eg1.c */

int global_var_x;

void
afun(int n)
   . . .
```

```
/* eg2.c */

extern int global_var_x;

int
bfun(int p)
   . . .
```

Although there are applications in which global variables are unavoidable, such unrestricted access to a variable is generally regarded as detrimental to a program's readability and maintainability. Global access conflicts with the principle that functions should have access to data on a need-to-know basis only, and then strictly through the documented interface as represented by the function prototype. However, one context in which a global variable can be used without reducing program readability is when the global represents a constant. We have been using globally visible macro constants throughout this text, and they have been a help, not a hindrance, in clarifying the meaning of a program. In Fig. 13.7, we see two global names that represent constant data structures. Because we plan to initialize these memory blocks and never change their values, there is no harm in letting our whole program access them. We include the `const` type qualifier in our declarations that define the globals as well as in the `extern` declarations that give additional functions access to the globals. This qualifier notifies the compiler that the program can look at, but not modify, these locations.

**Figure 13.7
Use of Variables
of Storage Class
extern**

```
/* fileone.c */

typedef struct {
        double real,
                  imag;
} complex_t;

/* Defining declarations of
   global structured constant
   complex_zero and of global
   constant array of month
   names */
const complex_t complex_zero
     = {0, 0};
const char *months[12] =
     {"January", "February",
      "March", "April", "May",
      "June", "July", "August",
      "September", "October",
      "November", "December"};


int
f1_fun1(int n)
{ . . . }

double
f1_fun2(double x)
{ . . . }

char
f1_fun3(char c1, char c2)
{   double months; . . . }
```

```
/* filetwo.c */

/* #define's and typedefs
   including  complex_t */


void
f2_fun1(int x)
{ . . . }

/* Compiler-notifying
   declarations -- no
   storage allocated */
extern const complex_t
     complex_zero;
extern const char
     *months[12];

void
f2_fun2(void)
{ . . . }

int
f2_fun3(int n)
{ . . . }
```

**Table 13.1    Functions in Fig. 13.7 with Global Variable Access and Reasons**

| Function(s) | Can Access Variables of Class extern | Reason |
|---|---|---|
| `f1_fun1` and `f1_fun2` | `complex_zero` and `months` | Their definitions follow in the same source file the top-level defining declarations of `complex_zero` and `months`. The functions have no parameters or local variables by these names. |
| `f1_fun3` | `complex_zero` only | Its definition follows in the same source file the top-level defining declaration of `complex_zero`, and it has no parameter or local variable by this name. |
| `f2_fun1` | none | Its definition precedes the declarations that notify the compiler of the existence of `complex_zero` and `months`. |
| `f2_fun2` and `f2_fun3` | `complex_zero` and `months` | Their definitions follow in the same source file the declarations containing keyword `extern` that notify the compiler of the existence of global names `complex_zero` and `months`. The functions have no parameters or local variables by these names. |

Figure 13.7 also shows the third storage class that we have met before, namely, `typedef`. Including `typedef` in the set of storage classes is merely a notational convenience. As we saw in Chapters 7 and 11, a `typedef` statement does not allocate storage space!

Table 13.1 shows which functions are allowed to access globals `complex_zero` and `months` and why. We assume that any local variable declarations affecting access to the globals are shown.

## Storage Classes static and register

**static**
storage class of variables allocated only once, prior to program execution

C's remaining storage classes are `static` and `register`. Placing the **static** keyword at the beginning of a local variable declaration changes the way the variable is allocated. Let's compare variables `once` and `many` in the following function fragment:

```
int
fun_frag(int n)
{
      static int once = 0;
      int        many = 0;
      . . .
}
```

As a variable of storage class `auto`, `many` is allocated space on the stack each time `fun_frag` is called; for every call `many` is initialized to zero. Every time `fun_frag` returns, `many` is deallocated. In contrast, `static` variable `once` is allocated and initialized *one time*, prior to program execution. It remains allocated until the entire program terminates. If `fun_frag` changes the value of `once`, that value is retained between calls to `fun_frag`.

Using a `static` local variable to retain data from one call to a function to the next is usually a poor programming practice. If the function's behavior depends on these data, then the function is no longer performing a transformation based solely on its input arguments, and the complexity of its purpose from the program reader's perspective is vastly increased.

One situation in which the use of a `static` local variable does not degrade readability is in function `main`, since a return from this function terminates the program. On a system that allocates a relatively small run-time stack, one might wish to declare large arrays as `static` variables in function `main`. Then these arrays will not use up stack space.

**register**
storage class of automatic variables that the programmer would like to have stored in registers

The final storage class, **`register`**, is closely related to storage class `auto` and may be applied only to local variables and parameters. In fact, C implementations are not required to treat `register` variables differently from `auto` variables. Designating that a variable is of storage class `register` simply alerts the compiler to the fact that this memory cell will be referenced more often than most. By choosing storage class `register`, the programmer indicates an expectation that the program would run faster if a *register,* a special high-speed memory location *inside* the central processor, could be used for the variable. Variables serving as subscripts for large arrays are good candidates for this storage class. Here are declarations of variables in storage classes `static` and `register`:

```
static double matrix[50][40];
register int  row, col;
```

## EXERCISES FOR SECTION 13.4

### Self-Check

Reread the program in Fig. 11.12 that converts units of measure.

1. Identify the storage classes of the following names used in the program:

   unit_max (first parameter of `load_units`)
   found (in function `search`)

```
convert
quantity (in function main)
```

2. For which one of the variables in function `search` would it be a good idea to request storage class register?

# 13.5 MODIFYING FUNCTIONS FOR INCLUSION IN A LIBRARY

When building a personal library based on functions originally developed for use in a specific context, usually some modifications are advisable. A library function should be as general as possible, so all constants used should be examined to see whether they could be replaced by input parameters. Any restrictions on the library function's parameters should be carefully defined.

In previous work, our functions have dealt with an error either by returning an error code or by displaying an error message and returning a value that should permit continued execution. In some situations, however, it is better not to permit continued processing. For example, manipulation of a large two-dimensional array can be very time-consuming, and it might be pointless to expend this time on a matrix that contains erroneous data. Similarly, if our `factorial` function is called with a negative number, there is no way it can return a valid answer. Therefore, we might want to print a message and then terminate execution of a program in which this error occurs.

C's `exit` function from the standard library stdlib can be used in these types of situations to terminate execution prematurely. Calling `exit` with the argument 1 indicates that some failure led to the exit. Using the value 0 in an `exit` call implies no such failure, just as a 0 returned from function `main` indicates successful function completion. The `exit` function may also use one of the predefined constants `EXIT_SUCCESS` or `EXIT_FAILURE` as its return value. These constants are an option for use in the `return` statement as well, providing that the standard library stdlib is included. Figure 13.8 shows a library form of function `factorial` that terminates program execution prematurely on a negative input.

**Figure 13.8    Function factorial with Premature Exit on Negative Data**

```
/*
 * Computes n!
 * n is greater than or equal to zero -- premature exit on negative data
```

*(continued)*

**Figure 13.8**   *(continued)*

```
*/
int
factorial(int n)
{
      int i,                /* local variables */
          product = 1;

      if (n < 0) {
            printf("\n***Function factorial reports ");
            printf("ERROR:  %d! is undefined***\n", n);
            exit(1);
      } else {
            /* Compute the product n x (n-1) x (n-2) x ... x 2 x 1 */
            for  (i = n;  i > 1;  --i) {
                product = product * i;
            }

            /* Return function result */
            return (product);
      }
}
```

The following syntax display describes the `exit` function.

**exit Function**

SYNTAX:   `exit(`*return_value*`);`

EXAMPLE:
```
/*
 * Gets next positive number from input
 * stream.  Returns EOF if end of file
 * is encountered. Exits program with error
 * message if erroneous input is encountered.
 */
int
get_positive(void)
{
```

*(continued)*

```
            int n, status
            char ch;

            for  (status = scanf("%d", &n);
                  status == 1  &&  n <= 0;
                  status = scanf("%d", &n)) {}

            if (status == 0) {
                  scanf("%c", &ch);
                  printf("\n***Function get_positive ");
                  printf("reports ERROR in data at ");
                  printf(">>%c<<***\n", ch);
                  exit(1);
            } else if (status == EOF) {
                  return (status);
            } else {
                  return (n);
            }
      }
```

INTERPRETATION: Execution of a call to exit causes program termination from any point in a program. The *return_value* is used to indicate whether termination was brought on by some type of failure. A *return_value* of 0 means normal exit. In general, the use of

```
exit(0);
```

should be avoided in functions other than main since placing "normal" termination of a program in one of its function subprograms tends to diminish the readability of function main. The use of

```
exit(1);
```

should be reserved for terminating execution in cases where error recovery is not possible or not useful.

**EXERCISES FOR SECTION 13.5**

Self-Check

1. Why should you #include the header file of a library in the library's own implementation file?

**Figure 13.11    *(continued)***

```
*      EOF => insufficient data before end of file
*  In case of error or EOF, value of type planet_t output argument is
*  undefined.
*/
extern int
scan_planet(planet_t *plnp); /* output- address of planet_t structure to
                                        fill                             */


#endif
```

**EXERCISES FOR
SECTION 13.6**

Self-Check

1. Use conditional compilation to select an appropriate call to printf. Assume that on a UNIX operating system, the name UNIX will be defined in the C preprocessor; on the VMS operating system, the name VMS will be defined. The desired message on UNIX is

   Enter <ctrl-d> to quit.

   The desired message on VMS is

   Enter <ctrl-z> to quit.

2. Consider the header file shown in Fig. 13.11. Describe what happens (a) when the preprocessor first encounters a #include "planet.h" directive and (b) when the preprocessor encounters a second #include "planet.h" directive.

## 13.7 ARGUMENTS TO FUNCTION main

Up to this point, we have always defined function main with a void parameter list. However, as another possibility, we could use the following prototype that indicates that main has two formal parameters: an integer and an array of pointers to strings:

```
int
main(int   argc,   /* input - argument count (including
                                program name)                    */
       char *argv[]) /* input - argument vector                  */
```

The way you cause your program to run varies from one operating system to another. However, most operating systems provide some way for you to specify values of options when you run a program. For example, on the ULTRIX operating system, one would specify options `opt1`, `opt2`, and `opt3` when running a program named `prog` by typing the command line

```
prog opt1 opt2 opt3
```

The formal parameters `argc` and `argv` provide a mechanism for a C main function to access these **command line arguments**. If the program `prog` just mentioned were the machine code of a C program whose main function prototype had parameters `argc` and `argv`, then the command line

```
prog opt1 opt2 opt3
```

would result in these formal parameter values within `main`:

```
argc    4          argv[0]    "prog"
                       [1]    "opt1"
                       [2]    "opt2"
                       [3]    "opt3"
                       [4]    ""     (empty  string)
```

Figure 13.12 shows a revised version of our program from Chapter 12 to make a backup copy of a text file. Rather than prompting the user for the names of the file to copy and the file to be the backup, the new version expects the user to enter this information on the command line. For example, if the program is named `backup` and the user activates it by typing

```
backup old.txt new.txt
```

the formal parameters of `main` will have these values:

```
argc    3          argv[0]    "backup"
                       [1]    "old.txt"
                       [2]    "new.txt"
                       [3]    ""
```

If the program encounters any difficulty in opening either of the files named by the user, it exits with an appropriate error message. Otherwise, it proceeds with the copy operation.

**Figure 13.12   File Backup Using Arguments to Function main**

```c
/*
 *  Makes a backup of the file whose name is the first command line argument.
 *  The second command line argument is the name of the new file.
 */
#include <stdio.h>
#include <stdlib.h>

int
main(int    argc,    /* input - argument count (including program name) */
     char *argv[]) /* input - argument vector                          */
{
     FILE *inp,     /* file pointers for input     */
          *outp;    /*     and backup files        */
     char  ch;      /* one character of input file */

     /* Open input and backup files if possible                         */
     inp = fopen(argv[1], "r");
     if (inp == NULL) {
          printf("\nCannot open file %s for input\n", argv[1]);
          exit(1);
     }

     outp = fopen(argv[2], "w");
     if (outp == NULL) {
          printf("\nCannot open file %s for output\n", argv[2]);
          exit(1);
     }

     /* Make backup copy one character at a time                        */
     for (ch = getc(inp);  ch != EOF;  ch = getc(inp))
        putc(ch, outp);

     /*  Close files and notify user of backup completion               */
     fclose(inp);
     fclose(outp);
     printf("\nCopied %s to %s\n", argv[1], argv[2]);

     return(0);
}
```

**EXERCISES FOR
SECTION 13.7**

Self-Check

1. How would you modify the program in Fig. 13.12 so that if a user typed a command line with fewer than two file names provided, an appropriate error message would be displayed?

Programming

1. Write a program that takes a single command line argument. The argument should be the name of a text file containing integers, and the program should sum the integers in the file. If any invalid data are encountered, the program should terminate with an error message that includes the file name and the invalid character.

# 13.8 DEFINING MACROS WITH PARAMETERS

**macro**
facility for naming a commonly used statement or operation

We have consistently used the `#define` preprocessor directive we met in Chapter 2 for associating symbolic names with constant values. In Chapter 2, we discussed the fact that C's preprocessor actually revises the text of the source code, replacing each occurrence of a defined name by its meaning before turning the code over to the compiler. In this section, we study how to define **macros** that have formal parameters. The form of such a macro definition is

`#define` *macro_name* (*parameter list*) *macro body*

Like functions, macros allow us to give a name to a commonly used statement or operation. Because macros are handled through textual substitution, however, macro calls execute without the overhead of space allocation and deallocation on the stack that is associated with functions. Of course, since the macro's meaning appears in the program at every call, the object file produced by the compiler typically requires more memory than the same program would require if it used a function rather than a macro.

Figure 13.13 shows a brief program that uses a macro named `LABEL_PRINT_INT` to display the value of an integer variable or expression with a label (a string). Notice that in the directive that defines `LABEL_PRINT_INT`, there is no space between the macro name and the left parenthesis of the parameter list. This detail is critical, for if there were a space, the preprocessor would misinterpret the macro definition and would replace every occurrence of `LABEL_PRINT_INT` by

`(label, num) printf("%s = %d", (label), (num))`

**Figure 13.13    Program Using a Macro with Formal Parameters**

```
/*  Shows the definition and use of a macro                          */

#include <stdio.h>

#define LABEL_PRINT_INT(label, num) printf("%s = %d", (label), (num))

int
main(void)
{
      int r = 5, t = 12;

      LABEL_PRINT_INT("rabbit", r);
      printf("      ");
      LABEL_PRINT_INT("tiger", t + 2);
      printf("\n");

      return(0);
}
rabbit = 5      tiger = 14
```

The process of replacing a macro call such as

    LABEL_PRINT_INT("rabbit", r)

by a copy of the macro body with appropriate parameter substitution,

    printf("%s = %d", ("rabbit"), (r))

**macro expansion**
process of replacing a macro
call by its meaning

is called **macro expansion**. When doing this replacement, the C preprocessor matches each macro parameter name with the corresponding actual argument. Then, in a copy of the macro body, every occurrence of a formal parameter name is replaced by the actual argument. This modified macro body takes the place of the macro call in the text of the program. Figure 13.14 diagrams the process of macro expansion of the last macro call in our sample program. Notice that only the macro name and its argument list are involved in the macro expansion process. The semicolon at the end of the macro call line is unaffected. It would be a mistake to include a semicolon at the end of the printf call in the macro body. If a semicolon were placed there, the statements resulting from macro expansion of our two macro calls would both end in *two* semicolons.

**Figure 13.14    Macro Expansion of Second Macro Call of Program in Fig. 13.13**

```
LABEL_PRINT_INT("tiger", t + 2)
                  ↓        ✓
LABEL_PRINT_INT(label, num)
```

*parameter matching*  →

```
                        "tiger"   t + 2
                           ↓        ↓
            printf("%s = %d", (label), (num))
```

*parameter replacement in body*  →

```
                        printf("%s = %d", ("tiger"), (t + 2))
```

*result of macro expansion*

## Use of Parentheses in Macro Body

You will notice that in the body of LABEL_PRINT_INT, each occurrence of a
formal parameter of the macro is enclosed in parentheses. The use of adequate
parentheses in a macro's body is essential for correct evaluation. In Fig. 13.15,
we see a program fragment that uses a macro to compute $n^2$. We show two versions of the macro definition and the different program outputs that result.

**Figure 13.15    Macro Calls Showing Importance of Parentheses in Macro Body**

         Version 1                                        Version 2

```
#define SQUARE(n)  n * n                  #define SQUARE(n)  ((n) * (n))

                . . .
                double x = 0.5, y = 2.0;
                int    n = 4, m = 12;

                printf("(%.2f + %.2f)squared = %.2f\n\n",
                        x, y, SQUARE(x + y));

                printf("%d squared divided by\n", m);
                printf("%d squared is %d\n", n,
                        SQUARE(m) / SQUARE(n));
```

**Figure 13.15** *(continued)*

```
(0.5 + 2.0)squared = 3.5          (0.5 + 2.0)squared = 6.25

12 squared divided by             12 squared divided by
4 squared is 144                  4 squared is 9
```

Let's look at the different macro expansions that occur in Version 1 and Version 2. Examination of Fig. 13.16 reveals that the incorrect results of Version 1 are a simple consequence of the operator precedence rules.

To avoid the problems illustrated in Figs. 13.15 and 13.16, use parentheses liberally in macro bodies. Specifically, parenthesize each occurrence of a parameter in the macro body, and enclose the entire body in parentheses if it produces a result value. For instance, here is a macro for finding one real root of a quadratic equation:

```
#define ROOT1(a,b,c) ((-(b)+sqrt((b)*(b)-4*(a)*(c)))/(2*(a)))
```

**Figure 13.16** **Macro Expansions of Macro Calls from Fig. 13.5**

| Version 1 | Version 2 |
|---|---|
| `SQUARE(x + y)` | `SQUARE(x + y)` |
|   becomes |   becomes |
| `x + y * x + y` | `((x + y) * (x + y))` |
| *Problem: multiplication done before addition.* | |
| `SQUARE(m) / SQUARE(n)` | `SQUARE(m) / SQUARE(n)` |
|   becomes |   becomes |
| `m * m / n * n` | `((m) * (m)) / ((n) * (n))` |
| *Problem: multiplication and division are of equal precedence; they are performed left to right.* | |

The black parentheses are those normally required for proper evaluation of the expression. The parentheses in color are added in accordance with our guidelines for parenthesizing a macro definition.

One should avoid using operators with side effects in expressions passed as arguments in a macro call, since these expressions may be evaluated multiple times. For example, the statement

```
r = ROOT1(++n1, n2, n3);  /* error: applying ++ in a macro
                                     argument */
```

would be expanded as

```
r = ((-(n2)+sqrt((n2)*(n2)-4*(++n1)*(n3)))/(2*(++n1)));
```

resulting in a statement that violates the principle that the object of an operator with a side effect should not be reused in the expression.

We urge you to use parentheses routinely in macro bodies as described earlier, even if you cannot conceive of any circumstance when a given set of parentheses could matter. One needs only to work with macros a short time to realize how limited is this ability of a programmer to foresee *all* possible situations!

We also encourage you to use all capital letters in your macro names. Remembering that you are calling a macro rather than a function is critical in helping you avoid the use of operators with side effects in your actual arguments.

## Extending a Macro Over Two or More Lines

The preprocessor assumes that a macro definition fits on a single line unless the program indicates otherwise. To extend a macro over multiple lines, all but the last line of the definition must end with the backslash character \. For example, here is a macro that implements the header of a `for` statement to count from the value of `st` up to, but not including, the value of `end`:

```
#define INDEXED_FOR(ct, st, end)   \
     for  ((ct) = (st);   (ct) < (end);   ++(ct))
```

The following code fragment uses `INDEXED_FOR` to display the first `X_MAX` elements of array `x`:

```
INDEXED_FOR(i, 0, X_MAX)
     printf("x[%2d] = %6.2f\n", i, x[i]);
```

After macro expansion, the statement will be

```
for  ((i) = (0);  (i) < (X_MAX);  ++(i))
        printf("x[%2d] = %6.2f\n", i, x[i]);
```

Self-Check

Given these macro definitions, write the macro expansion of each statement that follows. If the expansion seems not to be what the macro definer intended (you may assume the macro names are meaningful), indicate how you would correct the macro definition.

```
#define DOUBLE(x)   (x) + (x)
#define DISCRIMINANT (a,b,c)   ((b) * (b) - 4 * (a) * (c))
#define PRINT_PRODUCT(x, y)\
        printf("%.2f X %.2f = %.2f\n", (x), (y), (x) * (y));
```

1. `y = DOUBLE(a - b)*c;`
2. `y = y - DOUBLE(p);`
3. `if (DISCRIMINANT(a1, b1, c1) == 0)`
   `        r1 = -b1 / (2 * a1);`
4. `PRINT_PRODUCT(a + b, a - b);`

Programming

1. Define a macro named `F_OF_X` that would evaluate the following polynomial for the *x* value passed as its argument. You may assume that the math library has been included.

$$x^5 - 3x^3 + 4$$

2. Define a macro to display its argument preceded by a dollar sign and with two decimal places.

# 13.9 COMMON PROGRAMMING ERRORS

The most common problem in the development of large systems by teams of programmers is a lack of agreement regarding the details of a system's design. If you apply the software development method presented in earlier chapters, you can achieve a rational, stepwise division of a large problem into smaller subproblems that correspond to individual functions. Then you can devise detailed descriptions of *what* each function is to do and *what type*(s) of data it is to manipulate. Only when representatives of all teams are in full agreement about this fundamental interface information is it wise to proceed with a system's implementation.

When developing personal libraries, it is easy to forget the long-range goal of having reusable functions in the rush of completing a current project. An unnecessarily restrictive assumption built into a library function can quickly negate the function's usefulness in another context.

Although macros provide a quick and often quite readable shorthand for the expressions they represent, they are also fertile ground for error growth. It is easy to slip and type a blank after the macro name in the definition of a macro with parameters, causing the preprocessor to misinterpret the definition. Operator precedence mistakes are sure to crop up unless the programmer is absolutely meticulous about parenthesizing every macro body that produces a result value as well as parenthesizing every occurrence of a macro parameter within the body. Following a consistent naming convention for macros can save hours of unnecessary debugging resulting from the programmer's erroneous assumption that a function, not a macro, is being called.

In the history of computing, the inappropriate use of global variables is notorious for corrupting a system's reliability. We cannot overemphasize the importance of maintaining visible interfaces among functions through their parameter lists. Only functions with visible interfaces are good candidates for reuse through inclusion in a library.

# CHAPTER REVIEW

1. C's facility for creating a personal library provides a means of encapsulating an abstract data type.
2. Dividing a library definition into a header file and an implementation file provides a natural separation of the description of *what* the library functions do from *how* they do it.
3. Defining a macro gives a name to a frequently used statement or operation.
4. The `exit` function allows premature termination of program execution.
5. Conditional compilation provides a means of customizing code for different implementations and of creating library header files that protect themselves from duplicate inclusion.
6. Designing function `main` with parameters `argc` and `argv` allows the use of command line arguments.
7. Library functions must have meaningful names, have clearly defined interfaces, and be as independent as possible from globally defined constants.

## New C Constructs

| C Construct | Meaning |
|---|---|

**Header File (with #if...#endif directives)**

```
/*  somelib.h  */
#if !defined (SOMELIB_H_INCL)
#define SOMELIB_H_INCL

#define SOMELIB_MAX 20
typedef struct {
  int   comp;
  char  s[SOMELIB_MAX];
} some_t;

/*  Purpose of function make_some
 */
extern some_t
make_some(int         n,
        const char str[]);

/* other extern prototypes */

#endif
```

somelib.h is a header file to be included (#include "somelib.h") in any program desiring to use its facilities. somelib.h uses conditional compilation (#if...#endif) to protect its contents from duplicate inclusion.

**Implementation File**

```
/* somelib.c */
#include "somelib.h"
#include <string.h>

/*  Purpose of function make_some
 */
some_t
make_some(int         n,
        const char str[])
{
     some_t result;

     result.comp = n;
     strcpy(result.s, str);

     return (result);
}

/*  other function definitions  */
```

somelib.c is the implementation file associated with somelib.h. Its object file must be linked to any other program that includes somelib.h.

*(continued)*

**New C Constructs**    *(continued)*

| C Construct | Meaning |
|---|---|
| **Macro Definition and Call** | |

```
#define AVG(x,y) (((x) + (y)) / 2.0)
. . .

ans = AVG(2*a, b);
```

Preprocessor will replace each call to AVG by its macro expansion. Statement shown becomes
```
    ans = (((2*a) + (b)) / 2.0);
```

**exit Function**

```
/*  Compute decimal equivalent of a
 *  common fraction
 */
double
dec_equiv(int num, int denom)
{
   if (denom == 0) {
      printf("Zero-divide: %d/%d\n",
             num, denom);
      exit(1);
   } else {
      return ((double)num /
              (double)denom);
   }
}
```

Function causes premature program termination if called with an invalid argument.

**Arguments to Function main**

```
int
main(int argc, char *argv[])
{
   if (argc == 3)
      process(argv[1], argv[2]);
   else
      printf
         ("Wrong number of options\n");

   return (0);
}
```

Function main is expecting two command line arguments to pass to function process.

# QUICK-CHECK EXERCISES

1. A system designer who is breaking down a complex problem using _____ _____ will focus first on *what* a function is to do, leaving the details of *how* this is accomplished for later.

2. To use a library function, one must know the function's _____ , _____ , and _____ .
3. Functions that can be used in a variety of applications are examples of _____ code.
4. In C, a(n) _____ file contains information about *what* a library's functions do. The _____ file contains the details of *how* these actions are accomplished.
5. The keyword `extern` in a declaration notifies the _____ that the name declared will be known by the _____ .
6. When defining an implementation file `lib1.c`, why is it advantageous to `#include "lib1.h"`?
7. Given this definition of macro `ABSDF`,

   ```
   #define ABSDF(x, y)  (fabs((x) - (y)))
   ```

   show what this statement will be after macro expansion:

   ```
   if (ABSDF(a + b, c) > ABSDF(b + c, a))
         lgdiff = ABSDF(a + b, c);
   ```

8. Where are variables of storage class `auto` allocated and when? When are they deallocated?
9. When are variables of storage class `static` allocated? When are they deallocated?
10. Which of the following fragments would be followed immediately by the code of function `mangle`?

    ```
    double                        extern double
    mangle(double x, double y)    mangle(double x, double y);
    ```

11. When generalizing a function for inclusion in a library, named constants are often replaced by _____ .
12. What directives could we add to header file `mylib.h` so that no matter how many `#include "mylib.h"` directives were processed, the contents of `mylib.h` would be compiled just once?

# ANSWERS TO QUICK-CHECK EXERCISES

1. procedural abstraction
2. name, purpose, parameter list
3. reusable
4. header, implementation
5. compiler, linker

6. Any necessary macros and data types are defined in just one file, the header file, so modification of a macro or of a data type does not require changes in more than one place.

7. ```
   if ((fabs((a + b) - (c))) > (fabs((b + c) - (a))))
       lgdiff = (fabs((a + b) - (c)));
   ```

8. The variables are allocated on the stack at the time when a function is entered. They are deallocated when the function to which they belong returns.
9. The variables are allocated before program execution. They are deallocated at program termination.
10. The fragment on the left
11. function parameters
12. ```
    #if !defined (MYLIB_H_INCL)
    #define MYLIB_H_INCL
         . . . rest of mylib.h . . .
    #endif
    ```

# REVIEW QUESTIONS

1. Define *procedural abstraction* and *data abstraction*.
2. What feature of C encourages the encapsulation of data objects and their operators?
3. Compare the typical contents of a library header file to the contents of an implementation file. Which of these files defines the interface between a library and a program?
4. How does the C compiler know whether to look for an included file in the system directory or in the program's directory?
5. Compare the execution of the macro call

   ```
   MAC(a, b)
   ```

   to the execution of an analogous function call

   ```
   mac(a, b)
   ```

   Which of the following two calls is sure to be valid and why?

   ```
   mac(++a, b)    or    MAC(++a, b)
   ```

6. When you write the body of a macro definition, where should you use parentheses?

7. What are C's five storage classes? What are the default storage classes for variables declared in each of the following environments?

   declared at the top level
   declared as function parameters
   declared as local variables of a function

8. What is the purpose of storage class `register`?
9. Discuss this statement: If a program has five functions that manipulate an array of data values, it makes more sense to declare this array at the program's top level so that each function does not need to have an array parameter.
10. Why is the argument value 1 used much more often than the argument value 0 in calls to the `exit` function?
11. Describe the purpose of the `defined` operator.
12. When function `main` of a C program has a `nonvoid` parameter list, why is the value of its first parameter never less than 1?

# PROGRAMMING PROJECTS

1. Create a library that defines a data type to represent a common fraction and provides functions for I/O, comparison (less than, equal to), and arithmetic operations (+, −, *, /) on these fractions. Use the library in a program that processes a list of fractions, finding the sum, the mean, the median, and the greatest absolute difference between consecutive elements. All results should be expressed as common fractions in reduced form.

2. Design a library of functions to use when writing a term paper. Define a structure type in which to record bibliographic data about a source along with a summary of the information obtained from the source. Include an enumerated-type component representing the source category (book, encyclopedia, newspaper, periodical, etc.). Allow the bibliographic data stored to vary by source type: Use a multi-field union component for this information. Include a 200-character string in which to record a summary of the information obtained and an `int` component in which the user can note the order in which the sources will be used. Define functions that allow the user to enter a new source, to modify an existing record, to access a source by title or author, and to mark the source as to the order in which it will be used. Also include functions to store and reload the source database as a file, and to display unused sources, used sources in order of selection, and all sources in order by title.

3. Many operational engineering systems require complex scheduling of people, machines, and supplies to provide a service or produce a product. To schedule

a system, one needs to know three things: the resources available to the system, the resources required to provide the desired service, and any constraints on the resources. Many sophisticated algorithms are available to minimize the cost or time required to provide a service. Here we will build a small library of functions useful for solving constrained scheduling problems.

You are head of maintenance scheduling for Brown Bag Airlines. You have three crews, with different qualifications as follows:

| Crew Number | Level | Cost of Crew Per Hour |
|:-----------:|:-----:|:---------------------:|
| 0 | 1 | $200. |
| 1 | 2 | $300. |
| 2 | 3 | $400. |

Crew 2 is certified to do all levels of maintenance work, but costs more per hour than the other crews. Crew 1 can do maintenance work requiring skills 1 and 2, but not skill 3. Crew 0 can do maintenance work only at level 1. You need to schedule the following maintenance:

| Aircraft ID | Level of Maintenance | Number of Hours |
|:-----------:|:--------------------:|:---------------:|
| 7899 | 1 | 8 |
| 3119 | 1 | 6 |
| 7668 | 1 | 4 |
| 2324 | 2 | 4 |
| 1123 | 2 | 8 |
| 7555 | 2 | 4 |
| 6789 | 3 | 2 |
| 7888 | 3 | 10 |

Write the following functions and create a scheduling library from them:

a. A function to scan and store crew data in an appropriate structure.
b. A function to scan and store in an appropriate structure the required maintenance data.
c. A function that checks maintenance level required against the crew abilities and returns the number of the lowest-cost crew that can perform the maintenance.
d. A function that checks the maintenance level required against the crew abilities and current schedule and returns the number of the qualified crew that will be free to perform the maintenance at the earliest time. If more than one crew satisfies the function's constraints, the number of the lowest-cost qualified crew is returned.
e. A function that accumulates hours required for each crew as each maintenance task is scheduled.

Write a main program that calls these functions and any others you feel are needed for scheduling crews to do the listed maintenance jobs. Assume that all three crews can work at the same time and that the crews are paid only when they work. Jobs must be done in their entirety by one crew. Develop one algorithm to find the quickest way to get the maintenance done and another to find the cheapest way to get the work done. How big is the difference between these two solutions in time required to complete the given list of maintenance jobs?

4. You are developing a personal library of functions to assist in solving monthly-installment loan problems where simple interest is charged on the unpaid balance. You will include functions based on various forms of the formula

$$m = \frac{ip}{1 - (i + 1)^{-12y}}$$

where $m$ is the monthly payment, $i$ is the monthly interest rate (as a decimal fraction, not a percentage), $p$ is the principal amount, and $y$ is the number of years of the loan. Your library should have facilities for determining monthly payment (to the next whole dollar—i.e. `ceil(m)`) given $p$, $i$, and $y$, for determining the maximum principal that can be borrowed given a certain interest rate, monthly payment, and loan term, and also for determining the maximum annual interest rate at which a certain principal can be borrowed and repaid in $y$ years with a monthly payment of $m$.

In addition, define a function that will print an amortization table for a loan by displaying in columns the payment number, the payment, the interest paid, the principal paid, and the remaining balance. The last payment must be calculated separately.

5. Write a program that takes a command line argument that is the name of a text file and creates a new text file with a heading line

```
***************** file name ********************
```

and the contents of the original file with line numbers added. If the file's name contains a period, use the part of the name before the period concatenated with `.lis` as the name of the new file. Otherwise, just concatenate `.lis` with the whole file name.

# DYNAMIC DATA STRUCTURES

chapter

a structure that can expand and contract as a program executes

T his chapter discusses **dynamic data structures**, structures that expand and contract as a program executes. C's facilities for creating these structures allow a program to defer until a later time its decision regarding how much space to use in processing a data set. A program that can procrastinate in this way is far more flexible than a comparable program that must make this decision on space earlier. In Chapter 8, we studied how to store a list of data in an array that we declared as a variable. Although we could handle lists of different lengths by only partially filling the array, the maximum list size had to be determined before the program was compiled.

In this chapter, we will study how the use of one dynamic memory allocation function allows us to delay the setting of the maximum list size until the program is already running. Using another function permits us to allocate space separately for each list member, so the program itself *never* actually sets an upper bound on the list size. Since the program can call these functions to request memory at any time, it can use information from the input data as the basis for determining how much space to request and what data types are to be stored in the blocks.

When allocating memory dynamically, a program can use the space to store any of the simple and structured data types and any of the data structures presented in earlier chapters. In addition, it can combine separately allocated structured blocks called **nodes** to form composite structures that expand and contract as the program executes. Such composite dynamic structures are extremely flexible. For example, it is relatively easy to add new information by creating a new node and inserting it between two existing nodes. It is also relatively easy to delete a node.

**nodes**
dynamically allocated structures that are linked together to form a composite structure

In this chapter, we will examine how to create and manipulate a composite data structure called a *linked list* and how to use this structure in forming lists, stacks, and queues of varying lengths.

# 14.1 POINTERS AND THE FUNCTIONS malloc AND calloc

In earlier chapters, we saw two important uses of *pointer* variables, variables whose values are memory addresses. We first met pointer variables in Chapter 6 where we used them as function output parameters. We used the indirection ("pointer-following") operator * to store one of several function results in a variable whose address had been passed as an actual argument:

```
*signp = '+';
```

In Chapter 11, we saw that structured output arguments were also pointers. In Chapter 8 and Chapter 9, we saw that the value of an array name in C is actually the address of (that is, a pointer to) the array's initial element.

In this section, we meet a third context in which C uses pointers—as a means of accessing a memory block allocated in response to an explicit program request. We have seen that declarations such as

```
int      *nump;
char     *letp;
planet_t *planetp;
```

allocate variables of types "pointer to `int`", "pointer to `char`", and "pointer to `planet_t`" where `planet_t` is a user-defined structure type like the one we defined in Chapter 11. If `nump`, `letp`, and `planetp` are local variables of a function, then they are allocated at the time the function block is entered, as shown in Fig. 14.1.

In order to allocate an integer variable, a character variable, and a structured `planet_t` variable dynamically, we call the C memory allocation function `malloc`, which resides in the stdlib library. This function requires a single argument, that is, a number indicating the amount of memory space needed. Applying the `sizeof` operator to the data type we plan to store in the dynamic block gives us precisely the needed number. Thus,

```
malloc(sizeof (int))
```

allocates exactly enough space to hold one type `int` value and returns a pointer to (the address of) the block allocated.

**Figure 14.1
Data Area of a
Function with
Three Pointer-
Type Local
Variables**

Function data area

nump

? 

letp

?

planetp

?

Of course, when we work with pointers in C, we always deal with a "pointer to some specific type," rather than simply a "pointer." Therefore the data type (void *) of the value returned by malloc should always be cast to the specific type we need, such as

```
nump = (int *)malloc(sizeof (int));
letp = (char *)malloc(sizeof (char));
planetp = (planet_t *)malloc(sizeof (planet_t));
```

**heap**
region of memory in which function malloc dynamically allocates blocks of storage
**stack**
region of memory in which function data areas are allocated and reclaimed

The result of these three assignment statements is shown in Fig. 14.2. Notice that the area in which the new memory blocks are allocated is called the **heap**. This storage area is separate from the **stack**, the region of memory in which function data areas are allocated and reclaimed as functions are entered and exited.

Values may be stored in the newly allocated memory using the indirection operator (*), the same operator we used to follow pointers representing function output parameters. The statements

```
*nump = 307;
*letp = 'Q';
*planetp = blank_planet;
```

**Figure 14.2
Dynamic
Allocation of
Variables for
an int, a char,
and a Five-
Component
planet_t
Structure**

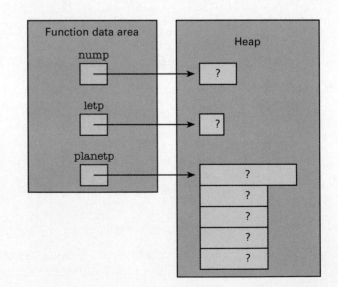

**Figure 14.3
Assignment of
Values to
Dynamically
Allocated
Variables**

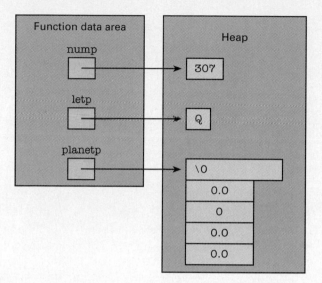

would lead to the memory snapshot in Fig. 14.3 if we assume the following declaration of `blank_planet`:

```
planet_t blank_planet = {"", 0, 0, 0, 0};
```

## Accessing a Component of a Dynamically Allocated Structure

In Chapter 11, we saw that a component of a structure accessed through a pointer could be referenced using a combination of the indirection (`*`) and direct component selection (`.`) operators such as

```
(*planetp).name
```

We also met C's single operator that combines the function of these two operators. This *indirect component selection* operator is represented by the character sequence `->` (a minus sign followed by a greater-than symbol). Thus, these two expressions are equivalent.

```
(*structp).component              structp->component
```

Either notation could be used to access a component of a dynamically allocated structure. We will use the more concise `->`.

**Figure 14.4**   **Referencing Components of a Dynamically Allocated Structure**

```
printf("%s\n", planetp->name);
printf("  Equatorial diameter:  %.0f km\n", planetp->diameter);
printf("  Number of moons: %d\n", planetp->moons);
printf("  Time to complete one orbit of the sun:  %.2f years\n",
       planetp->orbit_time);
printf("  Time to complete one rotation on axis:  %.4f hours\n",
       planetp->rotation_time);
```

In Fig. 14.4 are statements that display our dynamically allocated planet (assuming the `planet_t` definition in Section 11.1).

## Dynamic Array Allocation with calloc

We can use function `malloc` to allocate a single memory block of any built-in or user-defined type. To dynamically create an array of elements of any built-in or user-defined type, we use the contiguous allocation function from stdlib, `calloc`. Function `calloc` takes two arguments: the number of array elements needed and the size of one element. Function `calloc` initializes the array elements to zero. Figure 14.5 allocates and fills three arrays—an array of characters accessed through `string1`, an array of integers accessed through `array_of_nums`, and an array of planets accessed through `array_of_planets`. Figure 14.6 shows memory as we reach the end of the fragment in Fig. 14.5.

**Figure 14.5**   **Allocation of Arrays with calloc**

```
#include <stdlib.h>  /* gives access to calloc */
int scan_planet(planet_t *plnp);

int
main(void)
{
      char     *string1;
      int      *array_of_nums;
      planet_t *array_of_planets;
      int       str_siz, num_nums, num_planets, i;
```

*(continued)*

**Figure 14.5** *(continued)*

```
        printf("Enter string length and string> ");
        scanf("%d", &str_siz);
        string1 = (char *)calloc(str_siz, sizeof (char));
        scanf("%s", string1);

        printf("\nHow many numbers?> ");
        scanf("%d", &num_nums);
        array_of_nums = (int *)calloc(num_nums, sizeof (int));
        array_of_nums[0] = 5;
        for (i = 1;  i < num_nums;  ++i)
                array_of_nums[i] = array_of_nums[i - 1] * i;

        printf("\nEnter number of planets and planet data> ");
        scanf("%d", &num_planets);
        array_of_planets = (planet_t *)calloc(num_planets,
                                        sizeof (planet_t));
        for (i = 0;  i < num_planets;  ++i)
                scan_planet(&array_of_planets[i]);
        . . .
}

Enter string length and string> 9 enormous

How many numbers?> 4

Enter number of planets and planet data> 2
Earth    12713.5 1  1.0 24.0
Jupiter 142800.0 4 11.9  9.925
```

## Returning Cells to the Heap

Execution of a call to the function `free` returns memory cells to the heap so they can be reused later in response to calls to `calloc` and `malloc`. For example,

```
free(letp);
```

**Figure 14.6**
**Stack and Heap**
**after Program**
**Fragment in**
**Fig. 14.5**

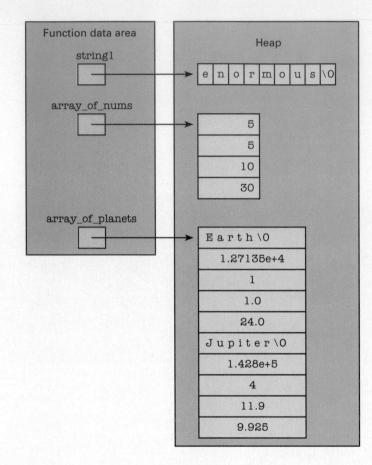

returns to the heap the cell whose address is in `letp`, that is, the cell in which we stored a `'Q'` (see Fig. 14.3);

```
free(planetp);
```

returns the entire structure pointed to by `planetp`.

Often, more than one pointer points to the same memory block. For example, the following statements result in the situation pictured in Fig. 14.7.

```
double *xp, *xcopyp;

xp = (double *)malloc(sizeof (double));
*xp = 49.5;
xcopyp = xp;
free(xp);
. . .
```

**Figure 14.7 Multiple Pointers to a Cell in the Heap**

After the call to free, the cell containing 49.5 may be allocated as part of another structure. Pointer xcopyp should not be used to reference the cell after it is freed, or errors can result. Make sure you have no further need for a particular memory block before you free it.

**EXERCISES FOR SECTION 14.1**

Self-Check

Consider Fig. 14.3. Write statements to accomplish the following:

1. Print the character accessed through letp.
2. Scan a new value into the location whose value is currently 307.
3. Store the value "Uranus" in the name component of the structure.
4. Store in nump the address of a dynamically allocated array of 12 integers, and initialize all the array elements to zero.
5. Store in letp the address of a 30-character dynamically allocated string variable.

# 14.2 LINKED LISTS

**linked list**
a sequence of nodes in which each node but the last contains the address of the next node

A **linked list** is a sequence of nodes in which each node is linked, or connected, to the node following it. Linked lists are like chains of children's "pop beads," where each bead has a hole at one end and a plug at the other (see Fig. 14.8). We can connect the beads in the obvious way to form a chain and easily modify it. We can remove the color bead by disconnecting the two beads at both its ends and reattaching this pair of beads, add a new bead by connecting it to the bead at either end

**Figure 14.8 Children's Pop Beads in a Chain**

Pop bead

Chain of pop beads

of the chain, or break the chain somewhere in the middle (between beads A and B) and insert a new bead by connecting one end to bead A and the other end to bead B. The following is a linked list of three nodes. In all nodes but the last, the linkp component contains the address of the next node in the list.

## Structures with Pointer Components

To construct a dynamic linked list, we will need to use nodes that have pointer components. Because we may not know in advance how many elements will be in our lists, we can allocate storage for each node as needed and use its pointer component to connect it to the next node. A definition of a type appropriate for a node of the linked list pictured earlier is

```
typedef struct node_s {
        char            current[3];
        int             volts;
        struct node_s *linkp;
} node_t;
```

When defining a structure type in C, we have the option of including a *structure tag* such as node_s after the reserved word struct. Then the phrase struct node_s is an alternative name for type node_t. Here we use the type struct node_s * in the declaration of one component to indicate that the linkp component of our node points to another node of the same type. We use struct node_s * rather than node_t * because the compiler has not yet seen the name node_t.

We can allocate and initialize the data components of two nodes as follows:

```
node_t *n1_p, *n2_p, *n3_p;

n1_p = (node_t *)malloc(sizeof (node_t));
strcpy(n1_p->current, "AC");
n1_p->volts = 115;
n2_p = (node_t *)malloc(sizeof (node_t));
strcpy(n2_p->current, "DC");
n2_p->volts = 12;
```

If we then copy the pointer value of n2_p into n3_p,

```
n3_p = n2_p;
```

we will have the memory values shown in Fig. 14.9.

**Figure 14.9**
**Multiple**
**Pointers to**
**the Same**
**Structure**

We can compare two pointer expressions using the equality operators ==
and !=. The following conditions are all true for our node_t * variables
n1_p, n2_p, and n3_p.

n1_p != n2_p          n1_p != n3_p          n2_p == n3_p

## Connecting Nodes

One purpose of using dynamically allocated nodes is to enable us to grow data
structures of varying size. We accomplish this by connecting individual nodes.
If you look at the nodes allocated in the last section, you will see that their
linkp components are undefined. Because the linkp components are of type
node_t *, they can be used to store a memory cell address. The pointer assignment statement

n1_p->linkp = n2_p;

copies the address stored in n2_p into the linkp component of the node
accessed through n1_p, thereby connecting the white and light-colored nodes as
pictured in Fig. 14.10.

**Figure 14.10**
**Linking Two**
**Nodes**

**Table 14.1** **Analyzing the Reference n1_p->linkp->volts**

| Section of Reference | Meaning |
| --- | --- |
| n1_p->linkp | Follow the pointer in n1_p to a structure and select the linkp component. |
| linkp->volts | Follow the pointer in the linkp component to another structure and select the volts component. |

We now have *three* ways to access the 12 in the volts component of the second node: the two references that were also valid in Fig. 14.9,

n2_p->volts

and

n3_p->volts

as well as one through the linkp pointer just assigned

n1_p->linkp->volts

In Table 14.1, we analyze this third reference a section at a time.

The linkp component of our structure with three access paths is still undefined, so we will allocate a third node, storing its pointer in this link. Then we will initialize the new node's data components.

```
n2_p->linkp = (node_t *)malloc(sizeof (node_t));
strcpy(n2_p->linkp->current, "AC");
n2_p->linkp->volts = 220;
```

Now we have the three-node linked list shown in Fig. 14.11.

**Figure 14.11
Three-Node
Linked List
with Undefined
Final Pointer**

**Figure 14.12**
**Three-Element**
**Linked List**
**Accessed**
**through n1_p**

However, we still have an undefined `linkp` component at the end. Clearly, we cannot continue allocating nodes indefinitely. At some point our list must end, and we need a special value to mark the end showing that the linked list of nodes following the current node is empty. In C, the **empty list** is represented by the pointer `NULL`, which we will show in our memory diagrams as a diagonal line through a pointer variable or component. Executing the assignment

**empty list**
a list of no nodes; represented in C by the pointer `NULL` whose value is 0

```
n2_p->linkp->linkp = NULL;
```

marks the end of the data structure pictured in Fig. 14.12, a complete linked list whose length is three. The pointer variable `n1_p` points to the first list element, or **list head**. Any function that knows this address in `n1_p` would have the ability to access every element of the list.

**list head**
the first element in a linked list

## Advantages of Linked Lists

A linked list is an important data structure because it can be modified easily. For example, a new node containing `DC 9` can be inserted between the nodes `DC 12` and `AC 220` by changing only one pointer value (the one from `DC 12`) and setting the pointer from the new node to point to `AC 220`. This means of modifying a linked list works regardless of how many elements are in the list. The list shown in Fig. 14.13 is after the insertion; the new pointer values are shown in color.

Similarly, it is quite easy to delete a list element. Only one pointer value

**Figure 14.13**
**Linked List**
**After an**
**Insertion**

**Figure 14.14   Linked List After a Deletion**

within the list must be changed, specifically, the pointer that currently points to the element being deleted. The linked list is redrawn as is shown in Fig. 14.14 after the node containing DC 12 is deleted by changing the pointer from the node AC 115. The deleted node is effectively disconnected from the list and could be returned to the heap (if we had another pointer through which to access the node). The new list consists of AC 115, DC 9, and AC 220.

**EXERCISES FOR SECTION 14.2**

Self-Check

1. Here is the final linked list created in this section. What is displayed by the code fragment that follows it?

```
n2_p = n1_p->linkp->linkp;
printf(" %s  %s  %s\n", n2_p->current,
        n1_p->linkp->current, n1_p->current);
printf("%3d%4d%4d\n", n1_p->linkp->volts,
        n1_p->volts, n2_p->volts);
```

2. Complete the given code fragment so it will create a linked list containing the musical scale, if the input is

```
do  re  mi  fa  sol  la  ti  do

typedef struct scale_node_s {
    char                note[4];
    struct scale_node_s *linkp;
} scale_node_t;
. . .
```

```
scale_node_t *scalep, *prevp, *newp;
int i;

scalep = (scale_node_t *)malloc(sizeof (scale_node_t));
scanf("%s", scalep->note);
prevp = scalep;
for  (i = 0;  i < 7;  ++i) {

    newp = _____;

    scanf("%s", _____note);

    prevp->linkp = _____;
    prevp = newp;
}


_____ = NULL;
```

## 14.3 LINKED LIST OPERATORS

This section and the ones that follow consider some common list-processing operations and show how to implement them using pointer variables. We assume that the structure of each list node corresponds to type list_node_t, declared as shown. Pointer variable pi_fracp points to the list head.

```
typedef struct list_node_s {
    int                 digit;
    struct list_node_s *restp;
} list_node_t;
. . .
{
    list_node_t *pi_fracp;
```

### Traversing a List

**traversing a list**
processing each node in a linked list in sequence, starting at the list head

In many list-processing operations, we must process each node in the list in sequence; this is called **traversing a list**. To traverse a list, we must start at the list head and follow the list pointers.

One operation that we must perform on any data structure is displaying its contents. To display the contents of a list, we traverse the list and display only the values of the information components, not the pointer fields. Function `print_list` in Fig. 14.15 displays the digit component of each node in the existing list whose list head is passed as an input parameter (of type `list_node_t *`). If `pi_fracp` points to the list

the function call statement

`print_list(pi_fracp);`

displays the output line

`14159`

We have chosen a linked list to store the decimal representation of the fractional part of π because this would permit us to save *many* more digits of this fraction than we could represent in an `int` or a `double`.

   We observed in Chapter 10 that problems involving varying-length lists were well suited to recursive solutions, so we have written a recursive `print_list`. This function takes a typical recursive approach: "If there's anything in this list, I'll be happy to take care of the first element; but somebody else (i.e., another call to the function) will have to deal with the rest of the list."

**tail recursion**
any recursive call that is executed as a function's last step

   Figure 14.16 compares recursive and iterative versions of `print_list`. The type of recursion we see in `print_list` is termed **tail recursion** because

**Figure 14.15   Function print_list**

```
/*
 *  Displays the list pointed to by headp
 */
void
print_list(list_node_t *headp)
{
      if (headp == NULL) {    /* simple case - an empty list          */
          printf("\n");
      } else {                /* recursive step - handles first element */
          printf("%d", headp->digit);  /*       leaves rest to          */
          print_list(headp->restp);    /*       recursion               */
      }
}
```

**Figure 14.16   Comparison of Recursive and Iterative List Printing**

```
                        /* Displays the list pointed to by headp */
                        void
                        print_list(list_node_t *headp)
{                                       | { list_node_t *cur_nodep;
 if (headp == NULL) {/* simple case */  |
    printf("\n");                       |     for  (cur_nodep = headp; /* start at
 } else {         /* recursive step */  |                           beginning */
    printf("%d", headp->digit);         |         cur_nodep != NULL; /* not at
    print_list(headp->restp);           |                           end yet   */
 }                                       |         cur_nodep = cur_nodep->restp)
}                                       |       printf("%d", cur_nodep->digit);
                                        |     printf("\n");
                                        | }
```

the recursive call is executed as the function's *last* step, if it is executed at all. Tail recursion is relatively easy to convert to iteration. Compilers for languages specifically developed for list processing even do such conversions automatically.

Let's examine the header of the iterative version's `for` loop. This header makes traversing every element of a linked list as easy as a counting `for` loop makes processing every element of an array.

We want to begin by examining the linked list's first node, so we initialize our loop control pointer variable `cur_nodep` to the value of `headp`. We want to stay in the loop as long as there remain nodes to process—that is, as long as `cur_nodep` does not contain the `NULL` "end-of-list" pointer. Our loop control update effectively gets us to the next node of the list. Figure 14.17 shows how `cur_nodep` might appear before and after one such update.

**Figure 14.17 Update of List-Traversing Loop Control Variable**

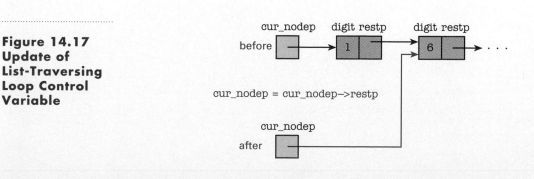

## Getting an Input List

Function `get_list` in Fig. 14.18 creates a linked list from a sequence of integers entered as input. Entry of the sentinel −1 marks the end of the data. The function's recursive algorithm recognizes the sentinel value as an empty data list and returns NULL, which is automatically converted to type `list_node_t *` upon assignment to `ansp`. Function `get_list` views a nonsentinel data item as the first value in the list it is creating, so it allocates a node and places the integer in the digit component. The problem is that the other component, `restp`, should point to the linked list constructed from the rest of the input. Like all good recursive algorithms, this one knows when it's time to call in an expert: It simply trusts that a function whose purpose is to form a linked list from some input data will do its job as advertised, and it calls `get_list` (i.e., itself) to find out the pointer value to store in `restp`.

Figure 14.19 shows an alternative version of `get_list`.

### Figure 14.18   Recursive Function get_list

```
#include <stdlib.h>  /* gives access to malloc */
#define SENT -1
/*
 * Forms a linked list of an input list of integers
 * terminated by SENT
 */
list_node_t *
get_list(void)
{
     int data;
     list_node_t *ansp;

     scanf("%d", &data);
     if (data == SENT) {
          ansp = NULL;
     } else {
          ansp = (list_node_t *)malloc(sizeof (list_node_t));
          ansp->digit = data;
          ansp->restp = get_list();
     }

     return (ansp);
}
```

**Figure 14.19    Iterative Function get_list**

```
/*
 *  Forms a linked list of an input list of integers terminated by SENT
 */
list_node_t *
get_list(void)
{
      int data;
      list_node_t *ansp,
                  *to_fillp, /* pointer to last node in list whose
                                restp component is unfilled        */
                  *newp;      /* pointer to newly allocated node    */

      /* Builds first node, if there is one */
      scanf("%d", &data);
      if (data == SENT) {
            ansp = NULL;
      } else {
            ansp = (list_node_t *)malloc(sizeof (list_node_t));
            ansp->digit = data;
            to_fillp = ansp;

            /* Continues building list by creating a node on each
               iteration and storing its pointer in the restp component
               of the node accessed through to_fillp */
            for  (scanf("%d", &data);
                  data != SENT;
                  scanf("%d", &data)) {
                newp = (list_node_t *)malloc(sizeof (list_node_t));
                newp->digit = data;
                to_fillp->restp = newp;
                to_fillp = newp;
            }

            /* Stores NULL in final node's restp component */
            to_fillp->restp = NULL;
      }
      return (ansp);
}
```

**Figure 14.20** **Function search**

```
/*
 * Searches a list for a specified target value.  Returns a pointer to
 * the first node containing target if found.  Otherwise returns NULL.
 */
list_node_t *
search(list_node_t *headp,  /* input - pointer to head of list  */
       int          target) /* input - value to search for      */
{
     list_node_t *cur_nodep; /* pointer to node currently being checked */

     for  (cur_nodep = headp;
           cur_nodep != NULL  &&  cur_nodep->digit != target;
           cur_nodep = cur_nodep->restp) {}

     return (cur_nodep);
}
```

### Searching a List for a Target

Another common operation is searching for a target value in a list. A list search is similar to an array search in that we must examine the list elements in sequence until we find the value we are seeking or until we examine all list elements without success. The latter is indicated by advancing past the list node whose pointer field is NULL.

Function search in Fig. 14.20 returns a pointer to the first list node that contains the target value. If the target value is missing, search returns a value of NULL.

### Avoid Following a NULL Pointer

Observe carefully that the order of the tests in the loop repetition condition of search is critical. If the order of the tests were reversed and if cur_nodep were NULL,

```
cur_nodep->digit != target  &&  cur_nodep != NULL
```

our program would attempt to follow the NULL pointer, an action that usually causes a run-time error. Because C always does short-circuit evaluation of logical expressions, we can be certain that in the original expression, there will be no attempt to follow cur_nodep if it is found to be NULL.

Self-Check

1. Trace the execution of function `search` for a list that contains the three numbers 4, 1, and 5. Show the value of pointer `cur_nodep` after the update of each iteration of the `for` loop. Do this for the target values 5, 2, and 4.

Programming

1. Write a function that finds the length of a list of `list_node_t` nodes.
2. Write a recursive version of function `search`.

# 14.4 REPRESENTING A STACK WITH A LINKED LIST

**stack**
a list data structure in which elements are inserted in and removed from the same end, the *top* of the stack

**last-in, first-out (LIFO) structure**
a data structure in which the last element stored is the first to be removed

In Chapter 8 we implemented the **stack** data structure as an array. We saw in Chapter 10 how a stack could be used to track multiple parameter and local variable values created by recursive function calls. Stacks are used extensively in computer system software such as compilers and operating systems.

We have seen that in a stack, elements are inserted (pushed) and removed (popped) at the same end of the list, the *top* of the stack. Since the element that is removed first is the one that has been waiting the shortest length of time, a stack is called a **last-in, first-out** list (LIFO).

**EXAMPLE 14.1**

A stack can also be implemented as a linked list in which all insertions and deletions are performed at the list head. List representations of two stacks are shown on the left side of Fig. 14.21. The nodes that hold elements of the stack are

**Figure 14.21   Linked-List Representation of Stacks**

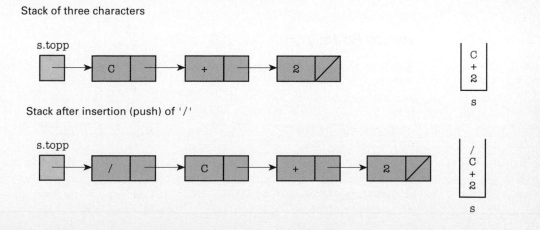

**Figure 14.22   Structure Types for a Linked-List Implementation of a Stack**

```
typedef char stack_element_t;

typedef struct stack_node_s {
      stack_element_t       element;
      struct stack_node_s *restp;
} stack_node_t;

typedef struct {
      stack_node_t *topp;
} stack_t;
```

typical linked-list node structures with an information field plus a pointer field that points to the next node.

The stack s can be represented by a structure with a single pointer component, topp, that points to the top of the stack. The typedefs of Fig. 14.22 define such a stack type.

Figure 14.23 shows implementations of the functions push and pop and a driver program that first builds the stacks illustrated in Fig. 14.21 and then repeatedly pops and prints stack elements until the stack is empty.

Function push allocates a new stack node, storing the pointer to the current stack in the new node's restp component and setting the stack top to point to the new node.

**Figure 14.23   Stack Manipulation with Functions push and pop**

```
/*
 *   Creates and manipulates a stack of characters
 */

#include <stdio.h>
#include <stdlib.h>

/*  Include typedefs from Fig. 14.22 */
void push(stack_t *sp, stack_element_t c);
stack_element_t pop(stack_t *sp);
```

*(continued)*

**Figure 14.23**    *(continued)*

```
int
main(void)
{
      stack_t s = {NULL};  /* stack of characters - initially empty */

      /*  Builds first stack of Fig. 14.21        */
      push(&s, '2');
      push(&s, '+');
      push(&s, 'C');

      /*  Completes second stack of Fig. 14.21    */
      push(&s, '/');

      /*  Empties stack element by element        */
      printf("\nEmptying stack: \n");
      while (s.topp != NULL) {
          printf("%c\n", pop(&s));
      }

      return (0);
}


/*
 *  The value in c is placed on top of the stack accessed through sp
 *  Pre:  the stack is defined
 */
void
push(stack_t        *sp, /* input/output - stack          */
     stack_element_t c)  /* input       - element to add */
{
      stack_node_t *newp;  /* pointer to new stack node */

      /*  Creates and defines new node                  */
      newp = (stack_node_t *)malloc(sizeof (stack_node_t));
      newp->element = c;
      newp->restp = sp->topp;
```

*(continued)*

**Figure 14.23**    *(continued)*

```
      /*  Sets stack pointer to point to new node         */
      sp->topp = newp;
}

/*
 *  Removes and frees top node of stack, returning character value
 *  stored there.
 *  Pre:  the stack is not empty
 */
stack_element_t
pop(stack_t *sp) /* input/output - stack */
{
      stack_node_t    *to_freep;  /* pointer to node removed */
      stack_element_t  ans;       /* value at top of stack   */

      to_freep = sp->topp;            /* saves pointer to node being deleted */
      ans = to_freep->element;        /* retrieves value to return           */
      sp->topp = to_freep->restp;     /* deletes top node                    */
      free(to_freep);                 /* deallocates space                   */

      return (ans);
}

Emptying stack:
/
C
+
2
```

**EXERCISES FOR SECTION 14.4**

Self-Check

1. Draw the stack resulting from execution of the following fragment. Assume you are working with a linked-list implementation of a stack of individual characters, as illustrated in Fig. 14.21.

```
{ stack_t stk = {NULL};

    push(&stk, 'a');
    push(&stk, 'b');
    pop(&stk);
    push(&stk, 'c');
```

# 14.5 REPRESENTING A QUEUE WITH A LINKED LIST

**queue**
a list data structure in which elements are inserted at one end and removed from the other end

**first-in, first-out (FIFO) structure**
a data structure in which the first element stored is the first to be removed

A **queue** is a data abstraction that can be used, for example, to model a line of customers waiting at a check-out counter or a stream of jobs waiting to be printed by a printer in a computer center. In a queue, new elements are inserted at one end (the rear of the queue), and existing elements are removed from the other end (the front of the queue). In this way, the element that has been waiting longest is removed first. A queue is called a **first-in, first-out** list (FIFO).

We can implement a queue using a linked list that grows and shrinks as elements are inserted and deleted. We will need to keep track of both the first node of the linked list, which is the *front* of the queue, and the last node, which is the *rear*, since removing a node from the queue requires access to the front and adding a node requires access to the rear. In addition, we need to be able to find out the size of the queue, preferably without having to traverse the entire list counting nodes. The typedefs in Fig. 14.24 define a queue type with the desired features.

One queue we might wish to model is a line of passengers waiting to be served by a ticket agent. Figure 14.25 shows such a queue. The two primary operations required to maintain a queue are addition and removal of elements. The ability to display the queue is also helpful. Figure 14.26 shows a main function that creates and maintains a queue of passengers based on the user's input. The function's main control structure is a do-while loop to get user choices and an embedded switch statement to process each choice.

**Figure 14.24    Structure Types for a Linked-List Implementation of a Queue**

```
/*  Insert typedef for queue_element_t */


typedef struct queue_node_s {
     queue_element_t      element;
     struct queue_node_s *restp;
} queue_node_t;


typedef struct {
     queue_node_t *frontp,
                  *rearp;
     int          size;
} queue_t;
```

**Figure 14.25
A Queue of
Passengers in
a Ticket Line**

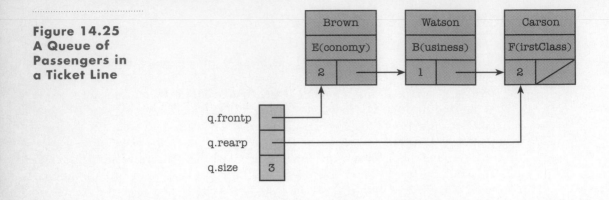

**Figure 14.26   Creating and Maintaining a Queue**

```
/*
 *   Creates and manipulates a queue of passengers.
 */

int scan_passenger(queue_element_t *passp);
void print_passenger(queue_element_t pass);
void add_to_q(queue_t *qp, queue_element_t ele);
queue_element_t remove_from_q(queue_t *qp);
void display_q(queue_t q);

int
main(void)
{
      queue_t pass_q = {NULL, NULL, 0}; /* passenger queue - initialized to
                                           empty state */
      queue_element_t next_pass, fst_pass;
      char choice;   /* user's request */

      /*  Processes requests  */
      do {
          printf("Enter A(dd), R(emove), D(isplay), or Q(uit)> ");
          scanf(" %c", &choice);
          switch (toupper(choice)) {
          case 'A':
                  printf("Enter passenger data> ");
                  scan_passenger(&next_pass);
                  add_to_q(&pass_q, next_pass);
                  break;
```

*(continued)*

**Figure 14.26**   *(continued)*

```
        case 'R':
              if (pass_q.size > 0) {
                    fst_pass = remove_from_q(&pass_q);
                    printf("Passenger removed from queue: \n");
                    print_passenger(fst_pass);
              } else {
                    printf("Queue empty - no-one to delete\n");
              }
              break;

        case 'D':
              if (pass_q.size > 0)
                    display_q(pass_q);
              else
                    printf("Queue is empty\n");
              break;

        case 'Q':
              printf("Leaving passenger queue program with %d \n",
                      pass_q.size);
              printf("passengers in the queue\n");
              break;

        default:
              printf("Invalid choice -- try again\n");
        }
   } while (toupper(choice) != 'Q');

   return (0);
}
```

Figure 14.27 shows functions add_to_q and remove_from_q. Because queue elements are always added at the end of the queue, add_to_q works primarily with the pointer rearp. The pointer frontp would be affected by an addition to the queue only if the queue were previously empty. On the other hand, elements are always removed from the front of a queue, so remove_from_q deals exclusively with the pointer frontp unless the element being removed is the only one remaining. Since queue nodes are dynamically allocated, we must explicitly free their memory when it is no longer needed. Function `remove_from_q` saves a copy of the `frontp` pointer in the variable `to_freep` before placing a new value in `frontp`. Then it uses `to_freep` to free the space allocated for the node being removed.

**Figure 14.27    Functions add_to_q and remove_from_q**

```
/*
 *  Adds ele at the end of queue accessed through qp
 *  Pre:  queue is not empty
 */
void
add_to_q(queue_t          *qp,  /* input/output - queue    */
         queue_element_t  ele)  /* input - element to add */
{
     if (qp->size == 0) {                       /* adds to empty queue      */
          qp->rearp = (queue_node_t *)malloc(sizeof (queue_node_t));
          qp->frontp = qp->rearp;
     } else {                                   /* adds to non-empty queue  */
          qp->rearp->restp =
                  (queue_node_t *)malloc(sizeof (queue_node_t));
          qp->rearp = qp->rearp->restp;
     }
     qp->rearp->element = ele;                  /* defines newly added node */
     qp->rearp->restp = NULL;
     ++(qp->size);
}


/*
 *  Removes and frees first node of queue, returning value stored there.
 *  Pre:  queue is not empty
 */
queue_element_t
remove_from_q(queue_t *qp) /* input/output - queue */
{
     queue_node_t     *to_freep;    /* pointer to node removed             */
     queue_element_t  ans;          /* initial queue value which is to
                                       be returned                         */

     to_freep = qp->frontp;         /* saves pointer to node being
                                       deleted                             */
```

*(continued)*

**Figure 14.27** *(continued)*

```
ans = to_freep->element;         /* retrieves value to return  */
qp->frontp = to_freep->restp;  /* deletes first node          */
free(to_freep);                  /* deallocates space           */
--(qp->size);

if (qp->size == 0)               /* queue's ONLY node was deleted  */
        qp->rearp = NULL;

return (ans);
}
```

Figure 14.28 shows the addition of passenger Carson to a queue that already contains passengers Brown and Watson. The "After" diagram shows the changes in color.

**Figure 14.28
Addition of One
Passenger to a
Queue**

**Figure 14.29
Removal of One
Passenger from
a Queue**

Figure 14.29 shows the removal of passenger Brown from the queue.

Self-Check

1. What does the following segment do to the final queue q, as shown in Fig. 14.29? Draw the result.

```
{
    queue_element_t one_pass = {"Johnson", 'E', 5};
    . . .
```

```
q.rearp->restp =
        (queue_node_t *)malloc(sizeof (queue_node_t));
q.rearp = q.rearp->restp;
q.rearp->element = one_pass;
q.rearp->restp = NULL;
++(q.size);
```

2. Draw the queue resulting from executing

```
one = remove_from_q(&pass_q);
```

if pass_q is

# 14.6 ORDERED LISTS

In queues and stacks, the time when a node was inserted in the list determines the position of the node in the list. The data in a node of an **ordered list** include a *key* component that identifies the structure (for example, an ID number). An ordered list is a list in which each node's position is determined by the value of its key component, so that the key values form an increasing or decreasing sequence as we move down the list.

Maintaining an ordered list is a problem in which linked lists are particularly helpful because of the ease with which one can insert and delete nodes without disturbing the overall list. As you might expect, we can use an ordered list to maintain a list of integers, real numbers, or airline passengers. We could modify the menu-driven program in Fig. 14.26 to maintain an ordered list of passengers instead of placing the passengers in a queue. By using the passenger's name as the key component, we would keep the list in alphabetical order. An advantage of using an ordered list is that we can delete *any* passenger from the list, whereas in a queue only the passenger at the front can be removed. Also, we can easily display the passengers in an ordered list in sequence by key field. Programming Project 1 at the end of this chapter asks you to modify the menu-driven program to use an ordered list of passenger data. We solve a simpler problem next.

## Case Study: Maintaining an Ordered List of Integers

To illustrate some common operations on ordered lists, we will write a program that builds an ordered list of integer values by repeated insertions and then displays the size of and values in the list. The next section of the program deletes values as requested, redisplaying the list after each deletion.

The representation of an ordered list should have a component to represent the list size so that we will not need to traverse all the nodes to count them whenever we need the size. Let's sketch a couple of ordered lists, and then we will specify our data requirements.

A nonempty ordered list would be

An empty ordered list would be

### Data Requirements

**Structure Types**
```
ordered_list_t
    components:
        headp  /* pointer to first of a linked list
                    of nodes                           */
        size   /* number of nodes currently in list    */

list_node_t
    components:
        key    /* integer used to determine node order */
        restp  /* pointer to rest of linked list        */
```

**Problem Constant**
```
SENT  −999    /* sentinel value                              */
```

**Problem Input**
```
int next_key  /* each record key                             */
```

**Problem Output**
```
ordered_list_t my_list    /* the ordered list                */
```

### DESIGN

## Algorithm

1. Create an empty ordered list.
2. for each nonsentinel input key
    3. Insert the key in the ordered list.
4. Display the ordered list and its size.
5. for each nonsentinel input key
    6. Delete node marked by key.
    7. if deletion is successful
        8. Display the ordered list and its size.
      else
        9. Display error message.

### IMPLEMENTATION

The type definitions and main function are shown in Fig. 14.30. Algorithm Step 1 is accomplished through initialization of an ordered list variable at declaration. Step 2 and Step 5 use typical sentinel-controlled `for` loops. Step 6 and Step 7 are combined since we can design function `delete` to return as the function value a flag indicating the success or failure of its attempt to delete a node.

**Figure 14.30   Building an Ordered List through Insertions and Deletions**

```
/*
 *  Program that builds an ordered list through insertions and then modifies
 *  it through deletions.
 */

typedef struct list_node_s {
      int                key;
      struct list_node_s *restp;
} list_node_t;
```

*(continued)*

**Figure 14.30** *(continued)*

```
typedef struct {
      list_node_t *headp;
      int          size;
} ordered_list_t;

list_node_t *insert_in_order(list_node_t *old_listp, int new_key);
void insert(ordered_list_t *listp, int key);
int delete(ordered_list_t *listp, int target);
void print_list(ordered_list_t list);

#define SENT -999

int
main(void)
{
      int             next_key;
      ordered_list_t my_list = {NULL, 0};

      /* Creates list through in-order insertions */
      printf("Enter integer keys--end list with %d\n", SENT);
      for  (scanf("%d", &next_key);
            next_key != SENT;
            scanf("%d", &next_key)) {
          insert(&my_list, next_key);
      }

      /* Displays complete list */
      printf("\nOrdered list before deletions:\n");
      print_list(my_list);

      /* Deletes nodes as requested */
      printf("\nEnter a value to delete or %d to quit> ", SENT);
      for  (scanf("%d", &next_key);
            next_key != SENT;
            scanf("%d", &next_key)) {
          if (delete(&my_list, next_key)) {
                printf("%d deleted.  New list:\n", next_key);
                print_list(my_list);
          } else {
                printf("No deletion.  %d not found\n", next_key);
          }
```

*(continued)*

**Figure 14.30**    *(continued)*

```
      }

      return (0);
}

Enter integer keys--end list with -999
5  8  4  6  -999
Ordered list before deletions:
   size = 4
   list = 4
          5
          6
          8

Enter a value to delete or -999 to quit> 6
6 deleted.  New list:
   size = 3
   list = 4
          5
          8

Enter a value to delete or -999 to quit> 4
4 deleted.  New list:
   size = 2
   list = 5
          8

Enter a value to delete or -999 to quit> -999
```

### Functions insert, delete, and print_list

Function insert is similar to our add_to_queue function in that both the size and pointer components of our ordered list structure will require modification. However, function insert differs from our queue functions in that we must first search our linked list of nodes for the proper place to insert. Finding the right place to insert is quite simple to conceptualize if we use a recursive approach. We use recursion in our design of helper function insert_in_order, the function that handles the linked-list aspect of element insertion. Then function insert can simply increment the list size and update the value of the list head pointer with the value resulting from a call to insert_in_order.

### Algorithm for insert_in_order

1. if the list is empty                             /* simple case 1   */

> 2. The new list is just a new node containing the new key and an empty `restp` component.

    else if the key to insert should precede     /* simple case 2   */
    the list's first node

> 3. The new list is a new node containing the new key and with the old list as the `restp` component.

    else                                                  /* recursive step   */

> 4. The new list starts with the first value of the old list. The `restp` component is the rest of the old list with the new node correctly inserted.

Figure 14.31 illustrates the three possibilities and Fig. 14.32 shows the implementation.

**Figure 14.31
Cases for
Recursive
Function
insert_in_order**

**Figure 14.32    Function insert and Recursive Function insert_in_order**

```
/*
 *  Inserts a new node containing new_key in order in old_list, returning as
 *  the function value a pointer to the first node of the new list
 */
list_node_t *
insert_in_order(list_node_t *old_listp,   /* input/output */
                int          new_key)      /* input        */
{
      list_node_t *new_listp;

      if (old_listp == NULL) {
            new_listp = (list_node_t *)malloc(sizeof (list_node_t));
            new_listp->key = new_key;
            new_listp->restp = NULL;
      } else if (old_listp->key >= new_key) {
            new_listp = (list_node_t *)malloc(sizeof (list_node_t));
            new_listp->key = new_key;
            new_listp->restp = old_listp;
      } else {
            new_listp = old_listp;
            new_listp->restp = insert_in_order(old_listp->restp, new_key);
      }

      return (new_listp);
}


/*
 *  Inserts a node in an ordered list.
 */
void
insert(ordered_list_t *listp, /* input/output - ordered list */
       int             key)    /* input */
{
      ++(listp->size);
      listp->headp = insert_in_order(listp->headp, key);
}
```

For function `delete`, we need to traverse the list until we find the node to delete. Always on the lookout for an opportunity to reuse code previously developed and tested, we might expect that our function `search` from Fig. 14.20 would provide a good starting point. Let's consider the result of applying the algorithm of `search`'s `for` loop to our longest ordered list in search of the value 6 to delete.

```
for  (cur_nodep = headp;
        cur_nodep != NULL  &&  cur_nodep->digit != target;
        cur_nodep = cur_nodep->restp) {}
```

At loop exit, our memory status will be

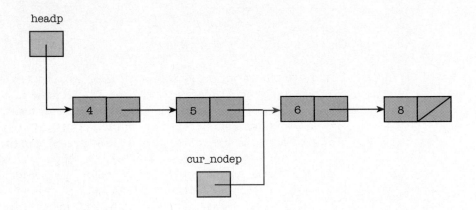

This memory status is a good news/bad news situation. The good news is that we did find the node to delete. The bad news is that we have no way of accessing the node whose `restp` component will need to be changed to carry out the deletion! Clearly, what we really need to search for is not the node we wish to delete, but rather the node that *precedes* the node we wish to delete. This immediately suggests that deleting the list's *first* node is a special case, leading us to the initial algorithm that follows.

**Initial Algorithm for delete**

1. if `target` is found in the list's first node
   2. Copy `headp` into `to_freep`.
   3. Change `headp` to point to rest of list.

    4. Free `to_freep`'s memory block.

    5. Decrement list size.

    6. Set `is_deleted` to 1.

else

    7. Initialize `cur_nodep` to `frontp` and traverse list as long as the node `cur_nodep` accesses is not the last in the list, and the node after it does not contain the target.

    8. if `target` is found

       9. Copy the address of the node to delete into `to_freep`.

      10. Move the `restp` pointer of the node being deleted into the `restp` component of the node accessed by `cur_nodep`.

      11. Free `to_freep`'s memory block.

      12. Decrement list size.

      13. Set `is_deleted` to 1.

    else

      14. Set `is_deleted` to 0.

15. Return `is_deleted`.

    If we trace this algorithm on a few lists, we find that this algorithm is actually a generic "delete from linked list" algorithm that does not take advantage of the fact that our list is ordered. Since the list is ordered, we actually do not always need to search all the way to the end of the list to know that our target is not present. As soon as we encounter a key greater than the target, we can give up. To do this, we need only to modify the last phrase of Step 7 to read "and the node after it does not contain the target or a key greater than the target." In addition, we must add a test that allows us to handle a deletion request for an empty list. Figure 14.33 shows an implementation of this algorithm.

    By the time we handle all the special cases, our simple little search loop has become a fairly complex algorithm. Let's investigate to what extent writing a recursive `delete_ordered_node` helper function would simplify the process. Our `insert_in_order` helper function was quite straightforward, but then we did not have to deal with the possibility that the insertion might fail. We will pattern `delete_ordered_node` after `insert_in_order` with respect to its returning as its value a pointer to the first node of the revised list. We will also need an output parameter that is a flag indicating whether the deletion occurred. Assuming the existence of our helper function makes `delete`'s algorithm very simple, as shown in Fig. 14.34.

**Figure 14.33**   **Iterative Function delete**

```
/*
 *  Deletes first node containing the target key from an ordered list.
 *  Returns 1 if target found and deleted, 0 otherwise.
 */
int
delete(ordered_list_t *listp,       /* input/output - ordered list   */
       int             target)      /* input - key of node to delete */
{
    list_node_t *to_freep,          /* pointer to node to delete                  */
                *cur_nodep;         /* pointer used to traverse list until it
                                       points to node preceding node to delete   */
    int         is_deleted;

    /*  If list is empty, deletion is impossible                      */
    if (listp->size == 0) {
        is_deleted = 0;

    /*  If target is in first node, delete it                         */
    } else if (listp->headp->key == target) {
        to_freep = listp->headp;
        listp->headp = to_freep->restp;
        free(to_freep);
        --(listp->size);
        is_deleted = 1;

    /*  Otherwise, look for node before target node; delete target    */
    } else {
        for  (cur_nodep = listp->headp;
              cur_nodep->restp != NULL  &&  cur_nodep->restp->key < target;
              cur_nodep = cur_nodep->restp) {}
        if (cur_nodep->restp != NULL  &&  cur_nodep->restp->key == target) {
            to_freep = cur_nodep->restp;
            cur_nodep->restp = to_freep->restp;
            free(to_freep);
            --(listp->size);
            is_deleted = 1;
        } else {
            is_deleted = 0;
        }
    }

    return (is_deleted);
}
```

**Figure 14.34    Function delete Using Recursive Helper Function**

```
/*
 *  Deletes first node containing the target key from an ordered list.
 *  Returns 1 if target found and deleted, 0 otherwise.
 */
int
delete(ordered_list_t *listp,   /* input/output - ordered list   */
       int             target) /* input - key of node to delete */
{
      int is_deleted;

      listp->headp = delete_ordered_node(listp->headp, target,
                                          &is_deleted);
      if (is_deleted)
            --(listp->size);

      return (is_deleted);
}
```

We can use the algorithm we developed for our iterative delete as a guide in identifying the cases to handle in function `delete_ordered_node`.

**Algorithm for delete_ordered_node**

1. if `listp` is NULL                        /* simple case 1     */
    2. Set `is_deleted` output parameter to 0.
    3. Set `ansp` to NULL.
else if first node contains target           /* simple case 2     */
    4. Set `is_deleted` output parameter to 1.
    5. Copy `listp` into `to_freep`.
    6. Set `ansp` to `restp` pointer of first node.
    7. Free memory block accessed by `to_freep`.
else if key in first node > target key       /* simple case 3     */
    8. Set `is_deleted` output parameter to 0.
    9. Copy `listp` into `ansp`.
else                                         /* recursive step    */
    10. Copy `listp` into `ansp`.
    11. Use a recursive call to delete target from rest of list and store result in `restp` pointer of first node.
12. Return `ansp`.

Figure 14.35 shows an implementation of this algorithm. We will leave our `print_list` function as an exercise for you to do.

Figure 14.35   Recursive Helper Function delete_ordered_node

```
/*
 *  If possible, deletes node containing target key from list whose first
 *  node is pointed to by listp, returning pointer to modified list and
 *  freeing deleted node.  Sets output parameter flag to indicate whether or
 *  not deletion occurred.
 */
list_node_t *
delete_ordered_node(list_node_t *listp,          /* input/output - list to
                                                                    modify       */
                    int          target,     /* input - key of node to
                                                                  delete          */
                    int         *is_deletedp)/* output - flag indicating
                                                          whether or not target node
                                                          found and deleted       */
{
     list_node_t *to_freep, *ansp;

     /* if list is empty - can't find target node      - simple case 1    */
     if (listp == NULL) {
          *is_deletedp = 0;
          ansp = NULL;

     /* if first node is the target, delete it          - simple case 2    */
     } else if (listp->key == target) {
          *is_deletedp = 1;
          to_freep = listp;
          ansp = listp->restp;
          free(to_freep);

     /* if past the target value, give up               - simple case 3    */
     } else if (listp->key > target) {
          *is_deletedp = 0;
          ansp = listp;

     /* in case target node is farther down the list,   - recursive step
        have recursive call modify rest of list and then return list       */
     } else {
          ansp = listp;
          ansp->restp = delete_ordered_node(listp->restp, target,
                                            is_deletedp);
     }

     return (ansp);
}
```

Self-Check

1. Compare the original call to `delete_ordered_node` (from function `delete`)

   ```
   listp->headp =
       delete_ordered_node(listp->headp, target, &is_deleted);
   ```

   and the recursive call to the same function

   ```
   ansp->restp =
       delete_ordered_node(listp->restp, target,
                           is_deletedp);
   ```

   Why does one call apply the address-of operator to the third argument and the other does not?
2. Modify helper function `insert_in_order` so that it will not insert a duplicate key. Use an output parameter to signal the success or failure of the insertion.

Programming

1. Write the `print_list` function called by the program in Fig. 14.30.
2. Write a function `retrieve_node` that returns a pointer to the node containing a specific key. The function should take a single `ordered_list_t` input parameter. If the desired node is not found, `retrieve_node` should return the `NULL` pointer.

## 14.7 BINARY TREES

We can extend the concept of linked data structures to structures containing nodes with more than one pointer field. One such structure is a *binary tree* (or *tree*) whose nodes contain two pointer fields. Because one or both pointers can have the value `NULL`, each node in a binary tree can have 0, 1, or 2 successor nodes.

Figure 14.36 shows two binary trees. For tree (a), each node stores a three-letter string. The nodes on the bottom of this tree have zero successors and are called **leaf nodes**; all other nodes have two successors. For tree (b), each node stores an integer. The nodes containing 40 and 45 have a single successor; all other nodes have no or two successors. A recursive definition of a binary tree is: A binary tree is either empty (no nodes) or it consists of a node, called the

**leaf node**
a binary tree node with no successors

**Figure 14.36**
**Binary Trees**

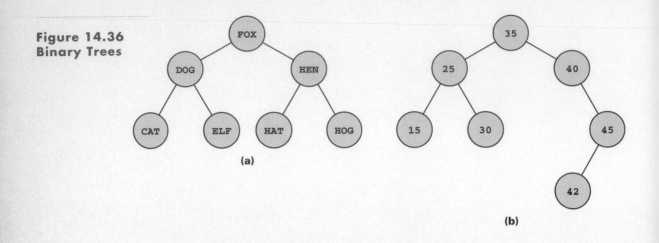

**(a)**

**(b)**

**root**, and two disjoint binary trees called its **left subtree** and **right subtree**, respectively.

In the definition for binary tree, the phrase *disjoint subtrees* means that a node cannot be in both a left and a right subtree of the same root node. For the trees shown in Fig. 14.36, the nodes containing FOX and 35 are the root nodes for each tree. The node containing DOG is the root of the left subtree of the tree whose root is FOX; the node containing CAT is the root of the left subtree of the tree whose root is DOG; the node containing CAT is a leaf node because both its subtrees are empty trees.

A binary tree resembles a family tree and the relationships among its members are described using the same terminology as for a family tree. In Fig. 14.36 the node containing HEN is the *parent* of the nodes containing HAT and HOG. Similarly, the nodes containing HAT and HOG are *siblings*, because they are both *children* of the same parent node. The root of a tree is an *ancestor* of all other nodes in the tree, and they in turn are *descendants* of the root node.

For simplicity, we did not show the pointer fields in Fig. 14.36. Be aware that each node has two pointer fields and that the nodes in (b) containing integers 45 and 42 are stored as follows.

## Binary Search Tree

In the rest of this section, we focus our attention on a particular kind of binary tree called a binary search tree. A binary search tree is a tree structure that stores data in such a way that they can be retrieved very efficiently. Every item stored in a binary search tree has a unique key.

A *binary search tree* is either empty or has the property that the item in its root has a larger key than each item in its left subtree and a smaller key than each item in its right subtree. Also, its left and right subtrees must be binary search trees.

The trees in Fig. 14.36 are examples of binary search trees; each node has a single data field that is its key. For tree (a), the string stored in every node is alphabetically larger than all strings in its left subtree and alphabetically smaller than all strings in its right subtree. For tree (b), the number stored in every node is larger than all numbers in its left subtree and smaller than all numbers in its right subtree. Notice that this must be true for every node in a binary search tree, not just the root node. For example, the number 40 must be smaller than both numbers stored in its right subtree (45, 42).

## Searching a Binary Search Tree

Next we explain how to search for an item in a binary search tree. To find a particular item, say e1, we compare e1's key to the root item's key. If e1's key is smaller, we know that e1 can only be in the left subtree so we search it. If e1's key is larger, we search the root's right subtree. We now write this recursive algorithm in pseudocode; the first two cases are simple cases.

> **Algorithm for Searching a Binary Search Tree**
> 1. if the tree is empty
>       2. The target key is not in the tree.
>    else if the target key is in the root item
>       3. The target key is found in the root item.
>    else if the target key is smaller than the root's key
>       4. Search the left subtree.
>    else
>       5. Search the right subtree.

Figure 14.37 traces the search for 42 in a binary search tree containing integer keys. The pointer labeled Root indicates the root node whose key is being compared to 42 at each step. The colored arrows show the search path. The search proceeds from the top (node 35) down to the node containing 42.

## Building a Binary Search Tree

Before we can retrieve an item from a binary search tree, we must, of course, build the tree. This process requires that we scan a collection of data items that is in no particular order and insert each one individually, making sure that the expanded tree is a binary search tree. A binary search tree builds from the root

**Figure 14.37    Binary Tree Search for 42**

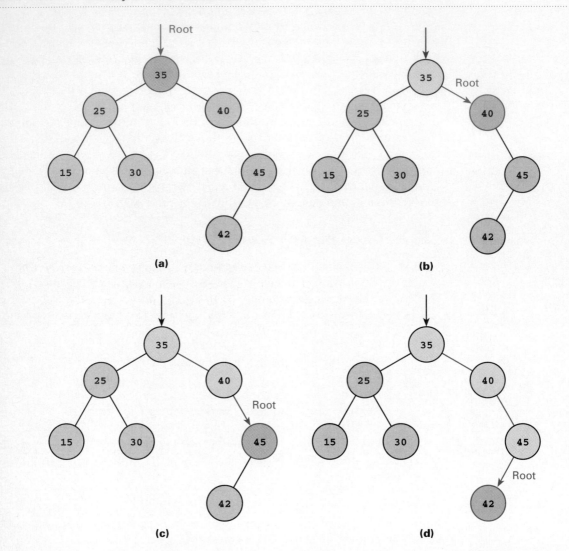

node down, so we must store the first data item in the root node. To store each subsequent data item, we must find the appropriate node to be its parent, attach a new node to the parent, and then store that data item in the new node.

When inserting an item, we must search the existing tree to find that item's key or to locate its parent node. If our search is successful, the item's key is already in the tree, so we will not insert the item. (Duplicate keys are not allowed.) If unsuccessful, the search will terminate at the parent of the item. If the item's key is smaller than its parent's key, we attach a new node as the parent's left subtree and insert the item in this node. If the item's key is larger than its parent's key, we attach a new node as the parent's right subtree and insert the item in this node. The following recursive algorithm maintains the binary search tree property; the first two cases are simple cases.

### Algorithm for Insertion in a Binary Search Tree
1. if the tree is empty
    2.  Insert the new item in the tree's root node.
  else if the root's key matches the new item's key
    3.  Skip insertion—duplicate key.
  else if the new item's key is smaller than the root's key
    4.  Insert the new item in the root's left subtree.
  else
    5.  Insert the new item in the root's right subtree.

Figure 14.38 builds a tree from the list of keys: 40, 20, 10, 50, 65, 45, 30. The search path followed when inserting each key is shown in color.

The last node inserted (bottom-right diagram) contains the key 30 and is inserted in the right subtree of node 20. Let's trace how this happens. Target

### Figure 14.38    Building a Binary Search Tree

key 30 is smaller than 40, so we insert 30 in the left subtree of node 40; this tree has 20 in its root. Target key 30 is greater than 20, so we insert 30 in the right subtree of node 20, an empty tree. Because node 20 has no right subtree, we allocate a new node and insert target 30 in it; the new node becomes the root of 20's right subtree.

Be aware that we would get a very different tree if we changed the order in which we inserted the keys. For example, if we inserted the keys in increasing order (10, 20, 30, . . .), each new key would be inserted in the right subtree of the previous key and all left pointers would be NULL. The resulting tree would resemble a linked list.

In Fig. 14.39 we show an implementation of our algorithm for insertion in a binary tree. The main function repeatedly scans integers and calls tree_insert to insert them in a binary search tree. In this implementation we define a macro that formalizes a standard pattern in dynamic allocation of nodes. If we are allocating a node of type node_t, we always cast the pointer to type node_t *. Using the macro

```
#define TYPED_ALLOC(type) (type *)malloc(sizeof (type))
```

we could give nodep the desired value simply by writing:

```
nodep = TYPED_ALLOC(node_t);
```

Function main displays the resulting ordered list after each insertion by calling function tree_inorder. Next, we study an algorithm that could be the basis of this display function.

**Figure 14.39   Creating a Binary Search Tree**

```
/*
 *  Create and display a binary search tree of integer keys.
 */

#include <stdio.h>
#include <stdlib.h>

#define TYPED_ALLOC(type) (type *)malloc(sizeof (type))
```

*(continued)*

**Figure 14.39** *(continued)*

```
typedef struct tree_node_s {
      int                 key;
      struct tree_node_s *leftp, *rightp;
} tree_node_t;

tree_node_t *tree_insert(tree_node_t *rootp, int new_key);
void tree_inorder(tree_node_t *rootp);

int
main(void)
{
      tree_node_t *bs_treep;   /* binary search tree        */
      int          data_key;   /* input - keys for tree     */
      int          status;     /* status of input operation */

      bs_treep = NULL;   /* Initially, tree is empty */

      /* As long as valid data remains, scan and insert keys,
         displaying tree after each insertion. */
      for  (status = scanf("%d", &data_key);
            status == 1;
            status = scanf("%d", &data_key)) {
         bs_treep = tree_insert(bs_treep, data_key);
         printf("Tree after insertion of %d:\n", data_key);
         tree_inorder(bs_treep);
      }

      if (status == 0) {
            printf("Invalid data >>%c\n", getchar());
      } else {
            printf("Final binary search tree:\n");
            tree_inorder(bs_treep);
      }

      return (0);
}
```

*(continued)*

**Figure 14.39**   **(continued)**

```
/*
 *  Insert a new key in a binary search tree.  If key is a duplicate,
 *  there is no insertion.
 *  Pre:  rootp points to the root node of a binary search tree
 *  Post: Tree returned includes new key and retains binary
 *        search tree properties.
 */
tree_node_t *
tree_insert(tree_node_t *rootp,    /* input/output - root node of
                                      binary search tree    */
            int         new_key) /* input - key to insert */
{
     if (rootp == NULL) {                 /* Simple Case 1 - Empty tree   */
          rootp = TYPED_ALLOC(tree_node_t);
          rootp->key = new_key;
          rootp->leftp = NULL;
          rootp->rightp = NULL;
     } else if (new_key == rootp->key) {          /* Simple Case 2 */
          /* duplicate key - no insertion                         */
     } else if (new_key < rootp->key) {        /* Insert in     */
          rootp->leftp = tree_insert          /* left subtree  */
                     (rootp->leftp, new_key);
     } else {                   /* Insert in right subtree */
          rootp->rightp = tree_insert(rootp->rightp,
                                      new_key);
     }

     return (rootp);
}
```

## Displaying a Binary Search Tree

To display the contents of a binary search tree so that its items are listed in order by key value, use the next recursive algorithm.

**Algorithm for Displaying a Binary Search Tree**
1. if the tree is not empty
   2. Display left subtree.
   3. Display root item.
   4. Display right subtree.

### Table 14.2    Trace of Tree Display Algorithm

Display left subtree of node 40.
    Display left subtree of node 20.
        Display left subtree of node 10.
            Tree is empty—return from displaying left subtree of node 10.
        Display item with key 10.
        Display right subtree of node 10.
            Tree is empty—return from displaying right subtree of node 10.
        Return from displaying left subtree of node 20.
    Display item with key 20.
    Display right subtree of node 20.
        Display left subtree of node 30.
            Tree is empty—return from displaying left subtree of node 30.
        Display item with key 30.
        Display right subtree of node 30.
            Tree is empty—return from displaying right subtree of node 30.
        Return from displaying right subtree of node 20.
    Return from displaying left subtree of node 40.
Display item with key 40.
Display right subtree of node 40.

For each node, the keys in its left subtree are displayed before the key in its root; the keys in its right subtree are displayed after the key in its root. Because the root key value lies between the key values in its left and right subtrees, the algorithm displays the items in order by key value as desired. Because the nodes' data components are displayed in order, this algorithm is also called an **inorder traversal**.

**inorder traversal**
displaying the items in a binary search tree in order by key value

Table 14.2 traces the sequence of calls generated by the display algorithm for the last tree in Fig. 14.38. Completing the sequence of calls for the last step shown, "Display right subtree of node 40.", is left as an exercise at the end of this section. The trace so far displays the item keys in the sequence: 10, 20, 30, 40.

## EXERCISES FOR SECTION 14.7

Self-Check

1. Are the following trees binary search trees? Show the list of keys as they would be displayed by an inorder traversal of each tree. If these trees were

binary search trees, what key values could be stored in the left subtree of the node containing key 50?

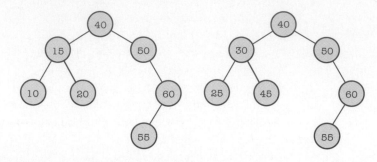

2. Complete the trace started in Table 14.2.

# C IN FOCUS

## Vivo320

### Videoconferencing from Your PC

Videoconferencing has been an accepted concept for several years, but the commonplace video telephone has remained a feature of futuristic movies. Most videoconferencing systems use expensive custom-designed digital signal processors for the repetitive real-time computations necessary to process many frames per second of video, as well as the sound and communications. This design restricts videoconferencing to those who can afford it.

In 1992 Dr. Staffan Ericsson realized that it was possible to perform all the video, audio, and communications processing necessary for videoconferencing in a high-end personal computer such as an Intel Pentium or Motorola PowerPC. This realization led him to found Vivo Software, Inc., to produce standards-based software that would allow personal computers to serve as tools for visual communications.

The videoconferencing project moved from the conceptual to the design phase when Dr. Ericsson, Dr. Bernd Girod, and Oliver Jones started to sort out the implementation issues. Dr. Ericsson bought a 486-based laptop computer and a copy of a highly efficient Watcom 32-bit C compiler, and he and Girod programmed a prototype of the video compression and decompression software in about a month. Drawing on their experience in signal processing, they used the C language as a high-level assembly language, getting the compiler to generate clever sequences of machine instructions to do the computations efficiently. Within a couple of months the design team con-

3. Show the binary search trees that would be created from the following lists of keys. What can you say about the binary search tree formed in parts (a) and (b)? Which of the four trees do you think would be most efficient to search? What can you say about the binary search tree formed in part (d)? How do you think searching it would compare to searching a linked list with the same keys?

a. 25, 45, 15, 10, 60, 55, 12
b. 25, 15, 10, 45, 12, 60, 55
c. 25, 12, 10, 15, 55, 60, 45
d. 10, 12, 15, 25, 45, 55, 60

4. What would be displayed by an inorder traversal of each tree in Question 3?

## Programming

1. Write function `tree_inorder` that is called in Fig. 14.39.

## 14.8 COMMON PROGRAMMING ERRORS

Remember that the indirect selection operator -> is correctly used to reference a component of a structure that is accessed through a pointer, so

```
var->component
```

is valid only if `var` is of a pointer-to-structure type.

There are a number of run-time errors that can occur when you are traversing linked data structures with pointers. The most common error is an attempt to follow a NULL pointer. This error can happen easily when traversing a list in a loop whose repetition condition does not explicitly check for the NULL. Any attempt to follow a pointer in an undefined variable will usually cause a run-time error as well.

Problems with heap management can also cause run-time errors. If your program gets stuck in an infinite loop while you are creating a dynamic data structure, it is possible for your program to consume all memory cells on the storage heap. This situation will lead to a `heap overflow` or `stack overflow` run-time error message.

Make sure your program does not attempt to reference a list node after the node is returned to the heap. Also be careful to return a storage block to the heap before losing all pointers to it.

Because displaying the value of a pointer variable is not very informative, it can be difficult to debug programs that manipulate pointers. To trace the execution of such a program, you must display an information component that uniquely identifies a list element instead of displaying the pointer value itself.

When you are writing driver programs to test and debug list operators, it is often helpful to create a sample linked structure using the technique shown in Section 14.2. Use a sequence of calls to `malloc` and temporary pointer variables to allocate the individual nodes. Next, use assignment statements to define the data and pointer components of the structures.

## CHAPTER REVIEW

1. Function `malloc` from the stdlib library can be used to allocate single elements, or nodes, of a dynamic data structure.
2. Function `calloc` from stdlib dynamically allocates an array.
3. Function `free` from stdlib returns memory cells to the storage heap.

4. A linked list is constructed from nodes containing one or more information components and a pointer component providing access to the next list element. Linked lists can implement stacks, queues, and ordered lists.

5. A stack is a LIFO (last-in, first-out) structure in which all insertions (push operations) and deletions (pop operations) are done at the list head. Stacks have many varied uses in computer science including saving parameter lists for recursive modules and translating arithmetic expressions.

6. A queue is a FIFO (first-in, first-out) structure in which insertions are done at one end and deletions (removals) at the other. Queues are used to save lists of items waiting for the same resource (e.g., a printer).

7. A binary tree is a linked data structure in which each node has two pointer fields leading to the node's left and right subtrees. Each node in the tree belongs to either the left or right subtree of an ancestor node, but it cannot be in both subtrees of an ancestor node.

8. A binary search tree is a binary tree in which each node's key is greater than all keys in its left subtree and smaller than all keys in its right subtree.

## New C Constructs

| Construct | Effect |
|---|---|
| **Pointer declaration** | |
| `typedef struct node_s {`<br>`    int            info;`<br>`    struct node_s *restp;`<br>`} node_t;` | The type name `node_t` is defined as a synonym of the type `struct node_s`, which is a structure containing an integer component and a component that is a pointer to another structure of the same type. |
| `node_t *nodep;` | `nodep` is a pointer variable of type pointer to `node_t`. |
| `int *nums;` | `nums` is a pointer variable of type pointer to `int`. |
| **Dynamic memory allocation** | |
| `nodep = (node_t *)`<br>`    malloc(sizeof (node_t));` | A new structure of type `node_t` is allocated on the heap, and its address is stored in `nodep`. |
| `nodep->info = 5;`<br>`nodep->restp = NULL;` | Values are stored in the new structure like this: <br> |
| `nums = (int *)`<br>`    calloc(10, sizeof (int));` | A new 10-element array of integers is allocated on the heap, and its starting address is stored in `nums`. The elements of the new array are all set to zero. |

*(continued)*

**Memory deallocation**

```
free(nodep);
free(nums);
```
The memory blocks accessed through the pointers nodep and nums are returned to the heap.

**Pointer assignment**

```
nodep = nodep->restp;
```
The pointer nodep is advanced to the next node in the dynamic data structure pointed to by nodep.

# QUICK-CHECK EXERCISES

1. Function _____ allocates storage space for a single data object that is referenced through a _____. Function _____ allocates storage space for an array of objects. Function _____ returns the storage space to the _____.

2. When an element is deleted from a linked list, it is automatically returned to the heap. True or false?

3. All pointers to a node returned to the heap are automatically reset to NULL so they cannot reference the node returned to the heap. True or false?

4. If A, B, and C are inserted into a stack and a queue, what will be the order of removal for the stack? For the queue?

5. Assume the following data type definition and declaration:

```
typedef struct node_s {
      int              num;
      struct node_s *restp;
} node_t;
. . .
node_t *headp, *cur_nodep;
```

Write a for loop header that causes cur_nodep to point in succession to each node of the linked list whose initial pointer is stored in headp. The loop should exit when cur_nodep reaches the end of the list.

6. The process just implemented in Exercise 5 is called _____ a list.

7. If a linked list contains three nodes with values "him", "her", and "its", and hp is a pointer to the list head, what is the effect of the following statements? Assume the data component of node type pro_node_t is pronoun, the link component is nextp, and np and mp are pointer variables.

```
np = hp->nextp;
strcpy(np->pronoun, "she");
```

8. Answer Exercise 7 for the following code fragment:

```
mp = hp->nextp;
np = mp->nextp;
mp->nextp = np->nextp;
free(np);
```

9. Answer Exercise 7 for the following code fragment:

```
np = hp;
hp = (pro_node_t *)malloc(sizeof (pro_node_t));
strcpy(hp->pronoun, "his");
hp->nextp = np;
```

10. Write a `for` loop that would place ones in the even-numbered elements of the following dynamically allocated array.

```
nums_arr = (int *)calloc(20, sizeof (int));
```

11. If a binary search tree has an inorder traversal of 1, 2, 3, 4, 5, 6, and the root node contains 3 and has 5 as the root of its right subtree, what do we know about the order in which numbers were inserted in this tree?
12. What is the relationship between the keys of the left child, the right child, and their parent in a binary search tree? Between the right child and the parent? Between a parent and all descendants in its left subtree?

## ANSWERS TO QUICK-CHECK EXERCISES

1. `malloc`, pointer; `calloc`; `free`, heap
2. false, `free` must be called.
3. false
4. For stack: C, B, A; for queue: A, B, C.

5. ```
   for   (cur_nodep = headp;
             cur_nodep != NULL;
             cur_nodep = cur_nodep->restp)
   ```

6. traversing
7. replaces `"her"` with `"she"`
8. The third list element is deleted.
9. A new node with value `"his"` is inserted at the front of the list.
10. ```
    for   (i = 0;   i < 20;   i += 2)
           nums_arr[i] = 1;
    ```

11. 3 was inserted first, and 5 was inserted before 4 and 6.
12. Left child < parent < right child; all descendants in left subtree < parent

# REVIEW QUESTIONS

1. Differentiate between dynamic and nondynamic data structures.
2. Describe a simple linked list. Indicate how the pointers are utilized to establish a link between nodes. Also indicate any other variables that would be needed to reference the linked list.
3. Give the missing type definitions and variable declarations and show the effect of each of the following statements. What does each do?

```
wp = (word_node_t *)malloc(sizeof (word_node_t));
strcpy(wp->word, "ABC");
wp->next = (word_node_t *)malloc(sizeof (word_node_t));
qp = wp->next;
strcpy(qp->word, "abc");
qp->next = NULL;
```

Assume the following type definitions and variable declarations for Questions 4–9.

```
typedef struct name_node_s {
      char                name[11];
      struct name_node_s *restp;
} name_node_t;

typedef struct {
      name_node_t *headp;
      int          size;
} name_list_t;
. . .
{
      name_list_t  list;
      name_node_t *np, *qp;
```

4. Write a code fragment that places the names Washington, Roosevelt, and Kennedy in successive elements of the linked list referenced by structure list. Define list.size accordingly.
5. Write a code fragment to insert the name Eisenhower between Roosevelt and Kennedy.

6. Write a function called `delete_last` that removes the last element from any list referenced by structure `list`.

7. Write a function `place_first` that places its second parameter value as the first node of the linked list referenced by structure `list`, which is passed as the function's first argument.

8. Write a function called `copy_list` that creates a linked list (the function result) with new nodes that contain the same data as the linked list referenced by the single argument of `copy_list`.

9. Write a function that you could call to delete all nodes with name component `"Smith"` from a linked list referenced by structure `list`. The linked list and the name to delete are the function's two parameters.

10. Often computers allow you to type characters ahead of the program's use of them. Should a stack or a queue be used to store these characters?

11. Discuss the differences between a simple linked list and a binary tree. Compare, for example, the number of pointer fields per node, search techniques, and insertion algorithms.

12. How can you determine whether a binary tree node is a leaf?

## PROGRAMMING PROJECTS

1. Rewrite the passenger list program whose main function is shown in Fig. 14.26 so that it uses an ordered list (alphabetized by passenger name) rather than a queue. Menu selection `'D'` (delete) should prompt for the name of the passenger to delete. In addition to the functions you write to manipulate the ordered list, you will need to write functions `scan_passenger` and `print_passenger`, which are mentioned in Fig. 14.26.

2. Rewrite the passenger list program referred to in Programming Project 1 using a binary search tree rather than an ordered list. When deleting a node, simply change the number of assigned seats to zero, and leave the node in the tree. Do not display such nodes.

3. Create header and implementation files (`"stack.h"` and `"stack.c"`) for a data type `stack_t` and operators for maintaining a stack of single characters. Use functions `push` and `pop`. Also implement function `retrieve` whose header is given here:

```
/*
 * The value at the top of the stack is returned as the
 * function value. The stack is not changed.
 * Pre:  s is not empty
 */
int
retrieve(stack_t s)  /* input */
```

4. Use an adaptation of your stack library from Project 3 to implement the following algorithm for displaying a string in reverse order.

   1. Create an empty stack of characters.
   2. Push each data character onto a stack.
   3. Pop each character and display it.

5. A *postfix expression* is an expression in which each operator follows its operands. Table 14.3 shows several examples of postfix expressions.

   The grouping marks under each expression should help you visualize the operands for each operator. The more familiar *infix expression* corresponding to each postfix expression is also shown.

   The advantage of postfix form is that there is no need to group subexpressions in parentheses or to consider operator precedence. The grouping marks in Table 14.3 are only for our convenience and are not required. You may have used pocket calculators that require entry of expressions in postfix form.

   Use an adaptation of your stack library from Project 3 to write a program that simulates the operation of a calculator by scanning an integer expression in postfix form and displaying its result. Your program should push each integer operand onto the stack. When an operator is encountered, the top two operands are popped, the operation is performed on its operands, and the result is pushed back onto the stack. The final result should be the only value remaining on the stack when the end of the expression is reached.

6. Write a program to monitor the flow of an item into and out of a warehouse. The warehouse will have numerous deliveries and shipments for the item (a widget) during the time period covered. A shipment out is billed at a profit of 50 percent over the cost of a widget. Unfortunately, each shipment received may have a different cost associated with it. The accountants for the firm

**Table 14.3    Examples of Postfix Expressions**

| Example | Infix Expression | Value |
|---------|------------------|-------|
| 5 6 * | 5 * 6 | 30 |
| 5 6 1 + * | 5 * (6 + 1) | 35 |
| 5 6 * 9 − | (5 * 6) − 9 | 21 |
| 4 5 6 * 3 / + | 4 + ((5 * 6) / 3) | 14 |

have instituted a first-in, first-out system for filling orders. This means that the oldest widgets are the first ones sent out to fill an order. This method of inventory can be represented using a queue. Each data record will consist of

S or O: Shipment received or an order to be sent
#: Quantity received or shipped out
Cost: Cost per widget (only for a shipment received)
Vendor: Character string that names company sent to or received from (up to 20 characters)

Write the necessary functions to store the shipments received and to process orders. The output for an order will consist of the quantity and the total cost for all the widgets in the order.

Hint: Each widget price is 50 percent higher than its cost. The widgets used to fill an order may come from multiple shipments with different costs.

7. Each student in the university may take a different number of courses, so the registrar has decided to use a linked list to store each student's class schedule, and to use an array of structures to represent the whole student body. A portion of this data structure follows.

The records show that the first student (array element 0, id 1111) is taking Section 1 of CIS120 for 3 credits and Section 2 of HIS001 for 4 credits; the second student (array element 1, id 1234) is not enrolled, and so on. Define the necessary data types for creating this structure. Provide operators for creating the original array of student ID numbers, inserting a student's initial class schedule, adding a course, and dropping a course. Write a menu-driven main function to use this structure.

8. The *radix sorting algorithm* uses an array of eleven queues to simulate the operation of the old card-sorting machines. The algorithm requires that one pass be made for every digit of the numbers being sorted. For example, a list of three-digit numbers would require three passes through the list. During the first pass, the least significant digit (the ones digit) of each number is examined, and the number is added to the rear of the queue whose array subscript matches the digit. After all numbers have been processed, the elements of each queue beginning with queue[0] are copied one at a time to the end of an 11th queue prior to beginning the next pass. Then, the process is repeated for the next-most significant digit (the tens digit) using the order of the numbers in the 11th queue. Finally, the process is repeated using the hundreds

digit. After the final pass, the 11th queue will contain the numbers in ascending order. Write a program that implements the radix sort.

9. A *dequeue* might be described as a double-ended queue, that is, a structure in which elements can be inserted or removed from either end. Create a personal library (header and implementation files) containing types and functions for creating and maintaining a dequeue. Include functions for inserting and removing elements, for displaying the dequeue, for displaying individual nodes, and for displaying the dequeue in reverse order.

10. Write and test a function that performs an inorder traversal of a binary tree without using recursion. It will be necessary to use a stack.

# Character Sets

The charts in this appendix show the following character sets: ASCII (American Standard Code for Information Interchange), EBCDIC (Extended Binary Coded Decimal Interchange Code), and CDC[†] Scientific. Only printable characters are shown. The integer code for each character is shown in decimal. For example, in ASCII, the code for 'A' is 65, and the code for 'z' is 122. The blank character is denoted by □.

| Left Digit(s) \ Right Digit | 0 | 1 | 2 | 3 | 4 | 5 | 6 | 7 | 8 | 9 |
|---|---|---|---|---|---|---|---|---|---|---|
| **ASCII** | | | | | | | | | | |
| 3 | | | □ | ! | " | # | $ | % | & | ' |
| 4 | ( | ) | * | + | , | – | . | / | 0 | 1 |
| 5 | 2 | 3 | 4 | 5 | 6 | 7 | 8 | 9 | : | ; |
| 6 | < | = | > | ? | @ | A | B | C | D | E |
| 7 | F | G | H | I | J | K | L | M | N | O |
| 8 | P | Q | R | S | T | U | V | W | X | Y |
| 9 | Z | [ | / | ] | ^ | – | ' | a | b | c |
| 10 | d | e | f | g | h | i | j | k | l | m |
| 11 | n | o | p | q | r | s | t | u | v | w |
| 12 | x | y | z | { | | | } | | | | |

Codes 00–31 and 127 are nonprintable control characters.

[†]CDC is a trademark of Control Data Corporation.

| Right Digit → Left Digit(s) | EBCDIC | | | | | | | | | |
|---|---|---|---|---|---|---|---|---|---|---|
| | **0** | **1** | **2** | **3** | **4** | **5** | **6** | **7** | **8** | **9** |
| 6 | | | | | □ | | | | | |
| 7 | | | | | ¢ | . | < | ( | + | \| |
| 8 | & | | | | | | | | | |
| 9 | ! | $ | * | ) | ; | ¬ | _ | / | | |
| 10 | | | | | | | ^ | , | % | — |
| 11 | > | ? | | | | | | | | |
| 12 | | | : | # | @ | ' | = | " | | a |
| 13 | b | c | d | e | f | g | h | i | | |
| 14 | | | | | | j | k | l | m | n |
| 15 | o | p | q | r | | | | | | |
| 16 | | | s | t | u | v | w | x | y | z |
| 17 | | | | | | | | \ | { | } |
| 18 | [ | ] | | | | | | | | |
| 19 | | | | A | B | C | D | E | F | G |
| 20 | H | I | | | | | | | | J |
| 21 | K | L | M | N | O | P | Q | R | | |
| 22 | | | | | | | S | T | U | V |
| 23 | W | X | Y | Z | | | | | | |
| 24 | 0 | 1 | 2 | 3 | 4 | 5 | 6 | 7 | 8 | 9 |

Codes 00–63 and 250–255 are nonprintable control characters.

| Right Digit → Left Digit | CDC | | | | | | | | | |
|---|---|---|---|---|---|---|---|---|---|---|
| | **0** | **1** | **2** | **3** | **4** | **5** | **6** | **7** | **8** | **9** |
| 0 | : | A | B | C | D | E | F | G | H | I |
| 1 | J | K | L | M | N | O | P | Q | R | S |
| 2 | T | U | V | W | X | Y | Z | 0 | 1 | 2 |
| 3 | 3 | 4 | 5 | 6 | 7 | 8 | 9 | + | − | * |
| 4 | / | ( | ) | $ | = | □ | , | . | ≡ | [ |
| 5 | ] | % | ≠ | ⌐ | ∨ | ∧ | ↑ | ↓ | < | > |
| 6 | ≤ | ≥ | ¬ | ; | | | | | | |

# ANSI C Standard Libraries†

## Library Facilities Alphabetized by Name

| Syntax | Header File | Purpose |
|---|---|---|
| `void abort(void);` | `stdlib.h` | Abnormally terminates a program. |
| `int abs(int x);` | `stdlib.h` | Returns the absolute value of an integer. |
| `double acos(double x);` | `math.h` | Returns the arc cosine of the input value (argument must be in the range -1 to 1). |
| `char *asctime`<br>`  (const struct tm *tblock);` | `time.h` | Converts a time stored as a structure in `*tblock` to a 26-character string. |
| `double asin(double x);` | `math.h` | Returns the arc sine of the input value (argument must be in the range -1 to 1). |
| `void assert(int test);` | `assert.h` | If `test` evaluates to zero, `assert` prints a message on `stderr` and aborts the program. |
| `double atan(double x);` | `math.h` | Calculates the arc tangent of the input value. |
| `double atan2(double y,`<br>`  double x);` | `math.h` | Calculates the arc tangent of `y/x`. |
| `int atexit(void (*func)(void));` | `stdlib.h` | Registers a function to be called at normal program termination. |
| `double atof(const char *s);` | `math.h` | Converts a string pointed to by s to `double`. |
| `int atoi(const char *s);` | `stdlib.h` | Converts a string pointed to by s to `int`. |
| `long int atol(const char *s);` | `stdlib.h` | Converts a string pointed to by s to `long int`. |
| `void *bsearch(const void *key,`<br>`  const void *base,`<br>`  size_t nelem, size_t width,`<br>`  int (*fcmp)(const void *,`<br>`          const void *));` | `stdlib.h` | Binary search of the sorted array `base`: returns the address of the first entry in the array that matches the search key using the comparison routine `*fcmp`; if no match is found, returns 0. |

*(continued)*

---

† This table has been adapted from the Borland C++ Library Reference Manual with permission of Borland International, Inc.

## Library Facilities Alphabetized by Name *(continued)*

| Syntax | Header File | Purpose |
|---|---|---|
| `void *calloc(size_t nitems, size_t size);` | `stdlib.h` | Allocates a memory block of size nitems × size, clears the block to zeros, and returns a pointer to the newly allocated block. |
| `double ceil(double x);` | `math.h` | Returns the smallest integer not less than x. |
| `void clearerr(FILE *stream);` | `stdio.h` | Resets stream's error and end-of-file indicators to 0. |
| `clock_t clock(void);` | `time.h` | Returns processor time elapsed since the beginning of program invocation. |
| `double cos(double x);` | `math.h` | Calculates the cosine of a value (angle in radians). |
| `double cosh(double x);` | `math.h` | Calculates the hyperbolic cosine of a value. |
| `char *ctime (const time_t *time);` | `time.h` | Converts date and time value pointed to by time (the value returned by function time) into a 26-character string representing local time. |
| `double difftime (time_t time2, time_t time1);` | `time.h` | Calculates the difference between two times in seconds. |
| `div_t div(int numer, int denom);` | `stdlib.h` | Divides two integers, returning quotient and remainder in a structure whose components are quot and rem. |
| `void exit(int status);` | `stdlib.h` | Terminates program. Before termination, all files are closed, buffered output (waiting to be output) is written, and any registered "exit functions" (posted with atexit) are called; status of 0 indicates normal exit; a nonzero status indicates some error. |
| `double exp(double x);` | `math.h` | Calculates the exponential function $e^x$. |
| `double fabs(double x);` | `math.h` | Calculates the absolute value of a floating-point number. |
| `int fclose(FILE *stream);` | `stdio.h` | Closes the named stream. |
| `int feof(FILE *stream);` | `stdio.h` | Predicate that detects end-of-file on a stream. |
| `int ferror(FILE *stream);` | `stdio.h` | Predicate that detects errors on a stream. |
| `int fflush(FILE *stream);` | `stdio.h` | Flushes a stream: if the stream has buffered output, fflush writes the output for stream to the associated file. |

*(continued)*

## Library Facilities Alphabetized by Name   *(continued)*

| Syntax | Header File | Purpose |
| --- | --- | --- |
| `int fgetc(FILE *stream);` | `stdio.h` | Gets a character from a stream. |
| `int fgetpos(FILE *stream,`<br>`          fpos_t *pos);` | `stdio.h` | Gets the current file pointer and stores it in the location pointed to by `pos`. |
| `char *fgets(char *s, int n,`<br>`  FILE *stream);` | `stdio.h` | Copies characters from `stream` into the string s until it has read `n-1` characters or a newline character, whichever comes first. Marks the end of s with the null character. |
| `double floor(double x);` | `math.h` | Returns the largest whole number not greater than x. |
| `double fmod(double x,`<br>`  double y);` | `math.h` | Calculates x modulo y, the remainder of x divided by y. |
| `FILE *fopen`<br>`  (const char *filename,`<br>`   const char *mode);` | `stdio.h` | Opens file named by `filename` and associates a stream with it. Modes and meanings: `"r"` is read, `"w"` is write, `"a"` is append, `"r+"` is existing file update (reading and writing), `"w+"` is new file update (reading and writing), `"a+"` is update at the end of the file. |
| `int fprintf(FILE *stream,`<br>`  const char *format`<br>`  [, argument, ...]);` | `stdio.h` | Writes formatted output to a stream. |
| `int fputc(int c, FILE *stream);` | `stdio.h` | Outputs a character to a stream. |
| `int fputs(const char *s,`<br>`  FILE *stream);` | `stdio.h` | Outputs a string to a stream. |
| `size_t fread(void *ptr,`<br>`  size_t size, size_t n,`<br>`  FILE *stream);` | `stdio.h` | Reads up to n items of data, each of length `size` bytes, from the given stream into a block pointed to by `ptr`; returns number of items read. |
| `void free(void *block);` | `stdlib.h` | Deallocates a memory block allocated by a previous call to `calloc`, `malloc`, or `realloc`. |
| `FILE *freopen`<br>`  (const char *filename,`<br>`   const char *mode,`<br>`   FILE *stream);` | `stdio.h` | Associates a new file with an open stream; often used for redirecting standard streams. |
| `double frexp(double x,`<br>`  int *exponent);` | `math.h` | Splits a `double` number into mantissa and exponent. |

*(continued)*

## Library Facilities Alphabetized by Name  *(continued)*

| Syntax | Header File | Purpose |
|---|---|---|
| int fscanf(FILE *stream,<br>  const char *format<br>  [, *address*, ...]); | stdio.h | Scans and formats input from a stream. |
| int fseek(FILE *stream,<br>  long int offset, int whence); | stdio.h | Repositions the file pointer associated with stream to a new position that is offset bytes from the file location given by whence. |
| int fsetpos(FILE *stream,<br>  const fpos_t *pos); | stdio.h | Positions the file pointer of a stream to a new position that is the value obtained by a previous call to fgetpos on that stream. |
| long int ftell(FILE *stream); | stdio.h | Returns the current file pointer for stream as the number of bytes from the beginning of the file. |
| size_t fwrite<br>  (const void *ptr,<br>  size_t size, size_t n,<br>  FILE *stream); | stdio.h | Writes n × size bytes to stream from the memory block pointed to by ptr. |
| int getc(FILE *stream); | stdio.h | Gets a character from stream. |
| int getchar(void); | stdio.h | Gets a character from stdin. |
| char *getenv(const char *name); | stdlib.h | Returns the value of a specified variable. |
| char *gets(char *s); | stdio.h | Gets a string (one line) from stdin; discards any newline character. |
| struct tm *gmtime<br>  (const time_t *timer); | time.h | Converts date and time to Greenwich mean time (GMT). |
| int isalnum(int c); | ctype.h | Predicate returning nonzero if c is a letter or a decimal digit. |
| int isalpha(int c); | ctype.h | Predicate returning nonzero if c is a letter. |
| int iscntrl(int c); | ctype.h | Predicate returning nonzero if c is a delete character or an ordinary control character. |
| int isdigit(int c); | ctype.h | Predicate returning nonzero if c is a decimal digit. |
| int isgraph(int c); | ctype.h | Predicate returning nonzero if c is a printing character other than a space. |
| int islower(int c); | ctype.h | Predicate returning nonzero if c is a lowercase letter. |

*(continued)*

## Library Facilities Alphabetized by Name   *(continued)*

| Syntax | Header File | Purpose |
|---|---|---|
| `int isprint(int c);` | `ctype.h` | Predicate returning nonzero if `c` is a printing character. |
| `int ispunct(int c);` | `ctype.h` | Predicate returning nonzero if `c` is a punctuation character. |
| `int isspace(int c);` | `ctype.h` | Predicate returning nonzero if `c` is a space, tab, carriage return, new line, vertical tab, or form feed. |
| `int isupper(int c);` | `ctype.h` | Predicate returning nonzero if `c` is an uppercase letter. |
| `int isxdigit(int c);` | `ctype.h` | Predicate returning nonzero if `c` is a hexadecimal digit (0 to 9, A to F, a to f). |
| `long int labs(long int x);` | `math.h` | Computes the absolute value of the parameter $x$. |
| `double ldexp(double x,`<br>`  int exp);` | `math.h` | Calculates $x \times 2^{exp}$. |
| `ldiv_t ldiv(long int numer,`<br>`  long int denom);` | `stdlib.h` | Divides two `long int`s, returning quotient and remainder in a structure whose components are `quot` and `rem`. |
| `struct lconv *localeconv(void);` | `locale.h` | Sets up country-specific monetary and other numeric formats. |
| `struct tm *localtime`<br>`  (const time_t *timer);` | `time.h` | Accepts the address of a value returned by `time` and returns a pointer to a structure of type `tm` in which the time is corrected for the time zone and possible daylight savings time. |
| `double log(double x);` | `math.h` | Calculates the natural logarithm of $x$. |
| `double log10(double x);` | `math.h` | Calculates $\log_{10}(x)$. |
| `void longjmp(jmp_buf jmpb,`<br>`  int retval);` | `setjmp.h` | Restores the task state captured by the last call to `setjmp` with the argument `jmpb`; then returns in such a way that `setjmp` appears to have returned with the value `retval`. |
| `void *malloc(size_t size);` | `stdlib.h` | Allocates a block of `size` bytes from the memory heap and returns a pointer to the newly allocated block. |

*(continued)*

## Library Facilities Alphabetized by Name    *(continued)*

| Syntax | Header File | Purpose |
|--------|-------------|---------|
| int mblen<br>  (const char *s, size_t n); | stdlib.h | Returns the size in bytes of the multibyte character pointed to by s (n is the maximum size of the character.) |
| int mbtowc(wchar_t *pwc,<br>  const char *s, size_t n); | stdlib.h | Converts the multibyte character accessed by s to a wide character. |
| size_t mbstowcs(wchar_t *pwcs,<br>  const char *s, size_t n); | stdlib.h | Converts up to n multibyte characters from string s to wide characters stored in array pwcs. |
| void *memchr(const void *s,<br>  int c, size_t n); | string.h | Searches the first n bytes of the block pointed to by s for first occurrence of character c. |
| int memcmp(const void *s1,<br>  const void *s2, size_t n); | string.h | Compares two blocks for a length of exactly n bytes; return value < 0 means s1 less than s2, value = 0 means same as, and value > 0 means greater than. |
| void *memcpy(void *dest,<br>  const void *src, size_t n); | string.h | Copies a block of n bytes from src to dest (behavior undefined if src and dest overlap); returns dest. |
| void *memmove(void *dest,<br>  const void *src, size_t n); | string.h | Copies a block of n bytes from src to dest (copy is correct even if src and dest overlap); returns dest. |
| void *memset(void *s, int c,<br>  size_t n); | string.h | Sets the first n bytes of the array s to the character c. |
| time_t mktime(struct tm *t); | time.h | Converts the time in the structure pointed to by t into a calendar time. |
| double modf(double x,<br>  double *ipart); | math.h | Splits a double into integer and fractional parts, both with the same sign as x. |
| void perror(const char *s); | stdio.h | Prints to the stderr stream the system error message for the last library routine that produced the error. |
| double pow(double x, double y); | math.h | Calculates $x^y$. |
| int printf(const char *format<br>  [, *argument*, ...]); | stdio.h | Writes formatted output to stdout. |
| int putc(int c, FILE *stream); | stdio.h | Outputs a character to stream. |
| int putchar(int c); | stdio.h | Outputs a character to stdout. |
| int puts(const char *s); | stdio.h | Outputs a string to stdout; terminates output by a newline character. |

*(continued)*

## Library Facilities Alphabetized by Name *(continued)*

| Syntax | Header File | Purpose |
|---|---|---|
| `void qsort(void *base, size_t nelem, size_t width, int (*fcmp)(const void *, const void *));` | `stdlib.h` | Sorts array `base` using the quicksort algorithm based on the comparison function pointed to by `fcmp`. |
| `int raise(int sig);` | `signal.h` | Sends a signal of type `sig` to the program. If the program has installed a signal handler for the signal type specified by `sig`, that handler will be executed. |
| `int rand(void);` | `stdlib.h` | Returns successive pseudorandom numbers in the range from 0 to RAND_MAX (constant defined in `stdlib.h`). |
| `void *realloc(void *block, size_t size);` | `stdlib.h` | Attempts to shrink or expand the previously allocated block to `size` bytes, copying the contents to a new location if necessary. |
| `int remove (const char *filename);` | `stdio.h` | Deletes the file specified by `filename`. |
| `int rename(const char *oldname, const char *newname);` | `stdio.h` | Changes the name of a file from `oldname` to `newname`. |
| `void rewind(FILE *stream);` | `stdio.h` | Repositions a file pointer to the beginning of a stream. |
| `int scanf(const char *format [, address, ...]);` | `stdio.h` | Scans and formats input from `stdin` stream. |
| `void setbuf(FILE *stream, char *buf);` | `stdio.h` | Causes the buffer `buf` to be used for I/O buffering instead of an automatically allocated buffer. |
| `int setjmp(jmp_buf jmpb);` | `setjmp.h` | Captures the complete task state in `jmpb` and returns 0. |
| `char *setlocale(int category, char *locale);` | `locale.h` | Selects a locale; if selection is successful, returns a string indicating the locale that was in effect prior to invoking the function. |
| `int setvbuf(FILE *stream, char *buf, int type, size_t size);` | `stdio.h` | Causes the buffer `buf` to be used for I/O buffering instead of an automatically allocated buffer. The `type` parameter may be `_IOFBF` (fully buffered), `_IOLBF` (line buffered), or `_IONBF` (unbuffered). |
| `void (*signal(int sig, void (*func)(int sig))) (int);` | `signal.h` | Specifies signal-handling actions. |

*(continued)*

## Library Facilities Alphabetized by Name   *(continued)*

| Syntax | Header File | Purpose |
| --- | --- | --- |
| `double sin(double x);` | `math.h` | Calculates the sine of the input value (angles in radians). |
| `double sinh(double x);` | `math.h` | Calculates hyperbolic sine. |
| `int sprintf(char *buffer,`<br>`   const char *format`<br>`   [, argument, ...]);` | `stdio.h` | Writes formatted output to a string. |
| `double sqrt(double x);` | `math.h` | Calculates the positive square root of a nonnegative input value. |
| `void srand(unsigned int seed);` | `stdlib.h` | Initializes random number generator. |
| `int sscanf(const char *buffer,`<br>`   const char *format`<br>`   [, address, ...]);` | `stdio.h` | Scans and formats input from a string. |
| `char *strcat(char *dest,`<br>`   const char *src);` | `string.h` | Appends a copy of `src` to the end of `dest`; returns `dest`. |
| `char *strchr(const char *s,`<br>`   int c);` | `string.h` | Returns a pointer to the first occurrence of the character `c` in the string `s` (or null). |
| `int strcmp(const char *s1,`<br>`   const char *s2);` | `string.h` | Compares one string to another; return value < 0 means `s1` less than `s2`, value = 0 means same as, and value > 0 means greater than. |
| `int strcoll(const char *s1,`<br>`   const char *s2);` | `string.h` | Compares two strings according to the collating sequence set by `setlocale`; return value < 0 means `s1` less than `s2`, value = 0 means same as, and value > 0 means greater than. |
| `char *strcpy(char *dest,`<br>`   const char *src);` | `string.h` | Copies string `src` to `dest`, stopping after copying the terminating null character; returns `dest`. |
| `size_t strcspn(const char *s1,`<br>`   const char *s2);` | `string.h` | Returns the length of the initial segment of string `s1` that consists entirely of characters *not* from string `s2`. |
| `char *strerror(int errnum);` | `string.h` | Returns a pointer to an error message string associated with `errnum`. |
| `size_t strftime(char *s,`<br>`   size_t maxsize, const char`<br>`   *fmt, const struct tm *t);` | `time.h` | Formats time for output according to the `fmt` specifications; returns the number of characters placed into `s`. |
| `size_t strlen(const char *s);` | `string.h` | Returns the number of characters in `s`, not counting the null terminating character. |

*unsigned long int*

*(continued)*

## Library Facilities Alphabetized by Name    *(continued)*

| Syntax | Header File | Purpose |
| --- | --- | --- |
| `char *strncat(char *dest, const char *src, size_t maxlen);` | string.h | Copies at most `maxlen` characters of `src` to the end of `dest` and appends a null character. |
| `int strncmp(const char *s1, const char *s2, size_t maxlen);` | string.h | Compares a portion (no more than `maxlen` characters) of one string to a portion of another; return value < 0 means portion of `s1` less than portion of `s2`, value = 0 means same as, and value > 0 means greater than. |
| `char *strncpy(char *dest, const char *src, size_t maxlen);` | string.h | Copies up to `maxlen` characters from `src` into `dest`, truncating or null-padding `dest` (which might not be null-terminated). |
| `char *strpbrk(const char *s1, const char *s2);` | string.h | Returns a pointer to the first occurrence in `s1` of any of the characters in `s2` (or returns null). |
| `char *strrchr(const char *s, int c);` | string.h | Returns a pointer to the last occurrence of the character `c` in string `s` (or returns null). |
| `size_t strspn(const char *s1, const char *s2);` | string.h | Returns the length of the initial segment of `s1` that consists entirely of characters from `s2`. |
| `char *strstr(const char *s1, const char *s2);` | string.h | Scans `s1` for the first occurrence of the substring `s2`. |
| `double strtod(const char *s, char **endptr);` | stdlib.h | Converts string `s` to a `double` value; if `endptr` is not null, it sets `*endptr` to point to the character that stopped the scan. |
| `char *strtok(char *s1, const char *s2);` | string.h | Searches `s1` for tokens, which are separated by delimiters defined in `s2`. |
| `long int strtol(const char *s, char **endptr, int radix);` | stdlib.h | Converts a string `s` to a `long int` value in the given radix; if `endptr` is not null, it sets `*endptr` to point to the character that stopped the scan. |
| `unsigned long int strtoul (const char *s, char **endptr, int radix);` | stdlib.h | Converts a string `s` to an `unsigned long int` value in the given radix; if `endptr` is not null, it sets `*endptr` to point to the character that stopped the scan. |
| `size_t strxfrm(char *s1, const char *s2, size_t n);` | string.h | Transforms strings so that `strcmp` of new strings has the same result as `strcoll` of original strings. Changes up to `n` characters of `s1`. |

*(continued)*

## Library Facilities Alphabetized by Name   *(continued)*

| Syntax | Header File | Purpose |
| --- | --- | --- |
| `int system` `(const char *command);` | `stdlib.h` | Executes an operating system command. |
| `double tan(double x);` | `math.h` | Calculates the tangent of an angle specified in radians. |
| `double tanh(double x);` | `math.h` | Calculates the hyperbolic tangent. |
| `time_t time(time_t *timer);` | `time.h` | Gives the current time, in seconds, elapsed since 00:00:00 GMT, January 1, 1970, and stores that value in the location pointed to by `timer`. |
| `FILE *tmpfile(void);` | `stdio.h` | Creates a temporary binary file and opens it for update. |
| `char *tmpnam(char *s);` | `stdio.h` | Creates a unique file name. |
| `int tolower(int ch);` | `ctype.h` | Converts an integer `ch` to its lowercase value. Non-uppercase letter values are returned unchanged. |
| `int toupper(int ch);` | `ctype.h` | Converts an integer `ch` to its uppercase value. Non-lowercase letter values are returned unchanged. |
| `int ungetc(int c,` `FILE *stream);` | `stdio.h` | Pushes a character back into an open input stream. |
| `void va_start(va_list ap,` `lastfix);` `type va_arg(va_list ap, type);` `void va_end(va_list ap);` | `stdarg.h` | Macros for implementing a variable argument list. |
| `int vfprintf(FILE *stream,` `const char *format,` `va_list arglist);` | `stdio.h` | Writes formatted output to a stream: writes the values of a series of arguments, applying the format specifiers from the format string. |
| `int vprintf(const char *format,` `va_list arglist);` | `stdio.h` | Writes formatted output to `stdout`: writes the values of a series of arguments, applying the format specifiers from the format string. |
| `int vsprintf(char *buffer,` `const char *format,` `va_list arglist);` | `stdio.h` | Writes formatted output to a string: writes the values of a series of arguments, applying the format specifiers from the format string. |
| `size_t wcstombs(char *s, const` `wchar_t *pwcs, size_t n);` | `stdlib.h` | Converts a string of wide characters to a string of multibyte characters (changes no more than n bytes of s). |
| `int wctomb(char *s,` `wchar_t wchar);` | `stdlib.h` | Stores in s the multibyte representation of wide character `wchar`. |

## Library Facilities by Header File

**assert.h**
```
void assert(int test);
```

**ctype.h**
```
int isalnum(int c);
int isalpha(int c);
int iscntrl(int c);
int isdigit(int c);
int isgraph(int c);
int islower(int c);
int isprint(int c);
int ispunct(int c);
int isspace(int c);
int isupper(int c);
int isxdigit(int c);
int tolower(int ch);
int toupper(int ch);
```

**locale.h**
```
struct lconv *localeconv(void);
char *setlocale(int category, char *locale);
```

**math.h**
```
double acos(double x);
double asin(double x);
double atan(double x);
double atan2(double y, double x);
double atof(const char *s);
double ceil(double x);
double cos(double x);
double cosh(double x);
double exp(double x);
double fabs(double x);
double floor(double x);
double fmod(double x, double y);
double frexp(double x, int *exponent);
long int labs(long int x);
double ldexp(double x, int exp);
double log(double x);
double log10(double x);
double modf(double x, double *ipart);
double pow(double x, double y);
double sin(double x);
double sinh(double x);
```

*(continued)*

## Library Facilities by Header File *(continued)*

**math.h** *(continued)*
```
double sqrt(double x);
double tan(double x);
double tanh(double x);
```

**setjmp.h**
```
void longjmp(jmp_buf jmpb, int retval);
int setjmp(jmp_buf jmpb);
```

**signal.h**
```
int raise(int sig);
void (*signal(int sig, void (*func)(int sig)))(int)
```

**stdarg.h**
```
void va_start(va_list ap, lastfix);
type va_arg(va_list ap, type);
void va_end(va_list ap);
```

**stdio.h**
```
void clearerr(FILE *stream);
int fclose(FILE *stream);
int feof(FILE *stream);
int ferror(FILE *stream);
int fflush(FILE *stream);
int fgetc(FILE *stream);
int fgetpos(FILE *stream, fpos_t *pos);
char *fgets(char *s, int n, FILE *stream);
FILE *fopen(const char *filename, const char *mode);
int fprintf(FILE *stream, const char *format[, argument, ...]);
int fputc(int c, FILE *stream);
int fputs(const char *s, FILE *stream);
size_t fread(void *ptr, size_t size, size_t n, FILE *stream);
FILE *freopen(const char *filename, const char *mode, FILE *stream);
int fscanf(FILE *stream, const char *format[, address, ...]);
int fseek(FILE *stream, long int offset, int whence);
int fsetpos(FILE *stream, const fpos_t *pos);
long int ftell(FILE *stream);
size_t fwrite(const void *ptr, size_t size, size_t n, FILE *stream);
int getc(FILE *stream);
int getchar(void);
char *gets(char *s);
void perror(const char *s);
int printf(const char *format[, argument, ...]);
int putc(int c, FILE *stream);
int putchar(int c);
```

*(continued)*

## Library Facilities by Header File    *(continued)*

**stdio.h**    *(continued)*
```
int puts(const char *s);
int remove(const char *filename);
int rename(const char *oldname, const char *newname);
void rewind(FILE *stream);
int scanf(const char *format[, address, ...]);
void setbuf(FILE *stream, char *buf);
int setvbuf(FILE *stream, char *buf, int type, size_t size);
int sprintf(char *buffer, const char *format[, argument, ...]);
int sscanf(const char *buffer, const char *format[, address, ...]);
char *strncpy(char *dest, const char *src, size_t maxlen);
FILE *tmpfile(void);
char *tmpnam(char *s);
int ungetc(int c, FILE *stream);
int vfprintf(FILE *stream, const char *format, va_list arglist);
int vprintf(const char *format, va_list arglist);
int vsprintf(char *buffer, const char *format, va_list arglist);
```

**stdlib.h**
```
void abort(void);
int abs(int x);
int atexit(void (*func)(void));
int atoi(const char *s);
long int atol(const char *s);
void *bsearch(const void *key, const void *base, size_t nelem,
  size_t width, int (*fcmp)(const void *, const void *));
void *calloc(size_t nitems, size_t size);
div_t div(int numer, int denom);
void exit(int status);
void free(void *block);
char *getenv(const char *name);
ldiv_t ldiv(long int numer, long int denom);
void *malloc(size_t size);
int mblen (const char *s, size_t n);
int mbtowc(wchar_t *pwc, const char *s, size_t n);
size_t mbstowcs(wchar_t *pwcs, const char *s, size_t n);
void qsort(void *base, size_t nelem, size_t width,
  int (*fcmp)(const void *, const void *));
int rand(void);
void *realloc(void *block, size_t size);
void srand(unsigned int seed);
double strtod(const char *s, char **endptr);
long int strtol(const char *s, char **endptr, int radix);
```

*(continued)*

## Library Facilities by Header File    *(continued)*

**stdlib.h**    *(continued)*
```
unsigned long int strtoul(const char *s, char **endptr, int radix);
int system(const char *command);
size_t wcstombs(char *s, const wchar_t *pwcs, size_t n);
int wctomb(char *s, wchar_t wchar);
```

**string.h**
```
void *memchr(const void *s, int c, size_t n);
int memcmp(const void *s1, const void *s2, size_t n);
void *memcpy(void *dest, const void *src, size_t n);
void *memmove(void *dest, const void *src, size_t n);
void *memset(void *s, int c, size_t n);
char *strcat(char *dest, const char *src);
char *strchr(const char *s, int c);
int strcmp(const char *s1, const char *s2);
int strcoll(const char *s1, const char *s2);
char *strcpy(char *dest, const char *src);
size_t strcspn(const char *s1, const char *s2);
char *strerror(int errnum);
size_t strlen(const char *s);
char *strncat(char *dest, const char *src, size_t maxlen);
int strncmp(const char *s1, const char *s2, size_t maxlen);
char *strpbrk(const char *s1, const char *s2);
char *strrchr(const char *s, int c);
size_t strspn(const char *s1, const char *s2);
char *strstr(const char *s1, const char *s2);
char *strtok(char *s1, const char *s2);
size_t strxfrm(char *s1, const char *s2, size_t n);
```

**time.h**
```
char *ctime(const time_t *time);
char *asctime(const struct tm *tblock);
clock_t clock(void);
double difftime(time_t time2, time_t time1);
struct tm *gmtime(const time_t *timer);
struct tm *localtime(const time_t *timer);
time_t mktime(struct tm *t);
size_t strftime(char *s, size_t maxsize, const char *fmt,
  const struct tm *t);
time_t time(time_t *timer);
```

## Macro Constants, Variables, and Types by Header File

| Construct by Header File | Meaning |
|---|---|
| **errno.h** | |
| EDOM | Error code for math domain error |
| ERANGE | Error code for result out of range |
| errno | Variable whose value is set to indicate type of error when an error in a system call occurs |
| **stddef.h** | |
| NULL | Null pointer value |
| ptrdiff_t | Pointer difference data type |
| size_t | Type used for memory object sizes and repeat counts |
| wchar_t | Wide-character constant type |
| **assert.h** | |
| NDEBUG | If defined, assert is a true function; otherwise, assert is a macro. |
| **locale.h** | |
| | The first argument passed to setlocale specifies which aspect of the locale is changed: |
| LC_ALL | all behavior. |
| LC_COLLATE | behavior of strcoll and strxfrm facilities. |
| LC_CTYPE | character handling functions. |
| LC_MONETARY | monetary information returned by localeconv. |
| LC_NUMERIC | decimal-point and non-monetary information returned by localeconv. |
| LC_TIME | behavior of strftime facility. |
| NULL | When passed as second argument to setlocale, the function returns a pointer to a string that is the name of the current locale for the indicated category. |
| struct lconv | Type used to store strings that represent the settings for the current locale |
| **math.h** | |
| HUGE_VAL | Overflow value for math functions |
| **setjmp.h** | |
| jmp_buf | Type of buffer used to save and restore the program task state |
| **signal.h** | |
| sig_atomic_t | Atomic entity type |
| SIG_DFL | Means that a signal should receive its "default" handling which may cause the program to terminate |
| SIG_IGN | Means that a signal should be ignored, no action |

*(continued)*

## Macro Constants, Variables, and Types by Header File   *(continued)*

| Construct by Header File | Meaning |
| --- | --- |
| **signal.h**   *(continued)* | |
| SIG_ERR | Means that an error code should be returned |
| | Each macro below stands for a standard signal: |
| SIGABRT | abnormal termination |
| SIGFPE | erroneous arithmetic operation |
| SIGILL | illegal computer instruction |
| SIGINT | interrupt or attention signal |
| SIGSEGV | invalid memory access |
| SIGTERM | a termination signal from a user or another program |
| **stdio.h** | |
| | Each macro below expands to values that can be used for parameter type in a call to setvbuf indicating: |
| _IOFBF | fully buffered file |
| _IOLBF | line buffered file |
| _IONBF | unbuffered file |
| BUFSIZE | Default buffer size used by setbuf |
| EOF | Indicates that the end of a file has been reached |
| FILE | Type used to represent file control information |
| FILENAME_MAX | Maximum length for a filename |
| FOPEN_MAX | Number of streams that may be open simultaneously (at least 8) |
| fpos_t | A file position type |
| L_tmpnam | Size of an array large enough to hold a temporary file name string |
| | In a call to fseek, the constants below indicate from which point the offset should be measured: |
| SEEK_CUR | from the current position |
| SEEK_END | from the end of the file |
| SEEK_SET | from the beginning of the file |
| size_t | Type used for memory obect sizes and repeat counts |
| stderr | Standard error output device |
| stdin | Standard input device |
| stdout | Standard output device |
| TMP_MAX | Maximum number of unique file names |
| **stdlib.h** | |
| | Constants defining exit conditions for call to exit function: |
| EXIT_FAILURE | abnormal program termination |
| EXIT_SUCCESS | normal program termination |
| MB_CURR_MAX | Maximum number of bytes used to represent a multibyte character in the current locale |
| RAND_MAX | Maximum value returned by rand function |
| div_t | Integer division return type |
| ldiv_t | Long integer division return type |

*(continued)*

## Macro Constants, Variables, and Types by Header File    *(continued)*

| Construct by Header File | Meaning |
| --- | --- |
| **time.h** | |
| CLOCKS_PER_SEC | The number of time units ("clock ticks") per second |
| clock_t | Type used to represent the processor time |
| time_t | Type used to represent the calendar time |
| struct tm | Structure type defining the broken-down calendar time |

## Table of Implementation Limits

| Constant | Minimum Magnitude |
| --- | --- |
| **limits.h** | |
| CHAR_BIT | 8 |
| CHAR_MAX | UCHAR_MAX or SCHAR_MAX |
| CHAR_MIN | 0 or SCHAR_MIN |
| INT_MAX | +32767 |
| INT_MIN | -32767 |
| LONG_MAX | +2147483647 |
| LONG_MIN | -2147483647 |
| MB_LEN_MAX | 1 |
| SCHAR_MAX | +127 |
| SCHAR_MIN | -127 |
| SHRT_MAX | +32767 |
| SHRT_MIN | -32767 |
| UCHAR_MAX | 255 |
| UINT_MAX | 65535 |
| ULONG_MAX | 4294967295 |
| USHRT_MAX | 65535 |
| **float.h** | |
| DBL_DIG | 10 |
| DBL_MANT_DIG | |
| DBL_MAX_10_EXP | +37 |
| DBL_MAX_EXP | |
| DBL_MIN_10_EXP | -37 |
| DBL_MIN_EXP | |
| FLT_DIG | 6 |
| FLT_MANT_DIG | |
| FLT_MAX_10_EXP | +37 |
| FLT_MAX_EXP | |
| FLT_MIN_10_EXP | -37 |

*(continued)*

**Table of Implementation Limits**   *(continued)*

| Constant | Minimum Magnitude |
|---|---|
| **float.h**   *(continued)* | |
| FLT_MIN_EXP | |
| FLT_RADIX | 2 |
| LDBL_DIG | 10 |
| LDBL_MANT_DIG | |
| LDBL_MAX_10_EXP | +37 |
| LDBL_MAX_EXP | |
| LDBL_MIN_10_EXP | -37 |
| LDBL_MIN_EXP | |
| DBL_MAX | 1E+37 |
| FLT_MAX | 1E+37 |
| LDBL_MAX | 1E+37 |

| Constant | Maximum Value |
|---|---|
| **float.h**   *(continued)* | |
| DBL_EPSILON | 1E-9 |
| DBL_MIN | 1E-37 |
| FLT_EPSILON | 1E-5 |
| FLT_MIN | 1E-37 |
| LDBL_EPSILON | 1E-9 |
| LDBL_MIN | 1E-37 |

# C Operators

Table C.1 shows the precedence and associativity of the full range of C operators. In this table, an ellipsis (. . .) at the beginning of a group of operators indicates that these operators have equal precedence with those on the previous line. The precedence table is followed by a table listing each operator along with its name, the number of operands required, and the section of the text that explains the operator. New operators are marked by lowercase Roman numerals keyed to the descriptions following Table C.2.

**Table C.1    Precedence and Associativity of Operations**

| Precedence | Operation | Associativity |
|---|:---:|---|
| highest | `a[..]`  `f(..)`  `.`  `->` | left |
| (evaluated first) | postfix `++`  postfix `--` | left |
| | prefix `++`  prefix `--`  `sizeof`  `~`  `!` | right |
| | `...` unary `+`  unary `-`  unary `&`  unary `*` | right |
| | casts | right |
| | `*`  `/`  `%` | left |
| | binary `+`  binary `-` | left |
| | `<<`  `>>` | left |
| | `<`  `>`  `<=`  `>=` | left |
| | `==`  `!=` | left |
| | binary `&` | left |
| | binary `^` | left |
| | binary `\|` | left |
| | `&&` | left |
| | `\|\|` | left |
| | `?  :` | right |
| | `=`  `+=`  `-=`  `*=`  `/=`  `%=` | right |
| | `...` `<<=`  `>>=`  `&=`  `^=`  `\|=` | |
| lowest | `,` | left |
| (evaluated last) | | |

**Table C.2   Where To Find Operators in Text**

| Operator | Name | Number of Operands | Where Found |
|----------|------|--------------------|-------------|
| a[..] | subscript | 1 | 8.1 |
| f(..) | function call | varies | 3.2 |
| . | direct selection | 2 | 11.1 |
| -> | indirect selection | 2 | 11.2 |
| ++ | increment | 1 | 5.3 |
| -- | decrement | 1 | 5.3 |
| sizeof | size of memory block | 1 | 12.2 |
| ~ | bitwise negation | 1 | i |
| ! | logical negation | 1 | 4.2 |
| & | address of | 1 | 6.1 |
| * | indirection | 1 | 6.1 |
|   | or multiplication | 2 | 2.5 |
| ( type name ) | cast | 1 | 7.1 |
| / | division | 2 | 2.5 |
| % | remainder | 2 | 2.5 |
| + | unary plus | 1 | 2.5 |
|   | or addition | 2 | 2.5 |
| - | unary minus | 1 | 2.5 |
|   | or subtraction | 2 | 2.5 |
| << | left shift | 2 | ii |
| >> | right shift | 2 | ii |
| < | less than | 2 | 4.2 |
| <= | less than or equal | 2 | 4.2 |
| > | greater than | 2 | 4.2 |
| >= | greater than or equal | 2 | 4.2 |
| == | equality | 2 | 4.2 |
| != | inequality | 2 | 4.2 |
| & | bitwise and | 2 | iii |
| ^ | bitwise xor | 2 | iii |
| \| | bitwise or | 2 | iii |
| && | logical and | 2 | 4.2 |
| \|\| | logical or | 2 | 4.2 |
| ? : | conditional | 3 | iv |
| = | assignment | 2 | 2.3 |
| += -= *= | compound assignment | | |
| /= %= | (arithmetic) | 2 | 5.2 |
| <<= >>= | (shifts) | 2 | ii |
| &= ^= \|= | (bitwise) | 2 | iii |
| , | sequential evaluation | 2 | v |

## Bitwise Operators

In Chapter 7, we studied that positive integers are represented in the computer by standard binary numbers. For example, on a machine where a type int value occupies 16 bits, the statement

n = 13;

would result in the following actual memory configuration:

n  `0 0 0 0 0 0 0 0 0 0 0 0 1 1 0 1`

Ten of the operators given in Table C.1 take operands of any integer type but treat an operand as a collection of bits rather than as a single number. These operations are described below.

   **(i) Bitwise negation**   Application of the ~ operator to an integer produces a value in which each bit of the operand has been replaced by its negation—that is, each 0 is replaced by a 1, and each 1 is replaced by a 0. Using our n value just shown, we compute ~n as follows:

n  `0 0 0 0 0 0 0 0 0 0 0 0 1 1 0 1`

~n `1 1 1 1 1 1 1 1 1 1 1 1 0 0 1 0`

   **(ii) Shift operators**   The shift operators << (left) and >> (right) take two integer operands. The value of the left operand is the number to be shifted and is viewed as a collection of bits that can be moved. To avoid problems with implementation variations, it is best to use left operands that are nonnegative when right shifting. The right operand is a nonnegative number telling how far to move the bits. The << operator shifts bits left, and the >> operator shifts them right. The bits that "fall off the end" are lost, and the "emptied" positions are filled with zeros. Here are some examples:

The compound assignment operators <<= and >>= cause the value resulting from the shift to be stored in the variable supplied as the left operand.

**(iii) Bitwise and, xor, and or**   The bitwise operators & (and), ^ (xor), and | (or) all take two integer operands that are viewed as strings of bits. The operators determine each bit of their result by considering corresponding bits of each operand. For example, if we denote the $i$th bit of operand n by $n_i$ and the $i$th bit of operand m by $m_i$, then the $i$th bit of result r ($r_i$) is defined for each operator as shown in Table C.3.

**Table C.3   Value of Each Bit of Result r for &, ^, and | with Operands n and m**

| Operator | Value of $r_i$ | Explanation |
|----------|----------------|-------------|
| & | $n_i$ & $m_i$ | $r_i$ is 1 only if both corresponding operand bits are 1 |
| ^ | $n_i$ + $m_i$ == 1 | $r_i$ is 1 only if the corresponding operand bits *do not* match |
| \| | $n_i$ \| $m_i$ | $r_i$ is 1 if at least 1 of the corresponding operand bits is 1 |

The following is an example of applying each operator:

| | |
|---|---|
| n | 0 0 0 0 0 0 0 0 0 0 0 0 1 1 0 1 |
| m | 0 0 0 0 0 0 0 0 0 0 1 1 1 1 0 0 |
| n & m | 0 0 0 0 0 0 0 0 0 0 0 0 1 1 0 0 |
| n ^ m | 0 0 0 0 0 0 0 0 0 0 1 1 0 0 0 1 |
| n \| m | 0 0 0 0 0 0 0 0 0 0 1 1 1 1 0 1 |

The compound assignment operators &=, ^=, and |= cause the result value to be stored in the variable supplied as the left operand.

**(iv) Conditional**   The conditional operator ?  : takes three operands:

```
c ? r1 : r2
```

The value of an expression using the conditional is the value of either its second or third operand, depending on the value of the first operand. This evaluation could be expressed in pseudocode as

```
if c
    result value is r1
else
    result value is r2
```

The conditional might be used in defining a macro to find the minimum of two values,

```
#define MIN(x,y)  (((x) <= (y)) ? (x) : (y))
```

   **(v) Sequential evaluation**   The comma operator , evaluates its two operands in sequence, yielding the value of the second operand as the value of the expression. The value of the first operand is discarded. Following are two examples of the comma's use. In the first example, the value of the result of the comma's application is actually used: It is assigned to x. In the second example, the comma is merely a device to allow execution of two assignments in a context where only one expression is permitted.

**EXAMPLE C.1**   The effect of the assignment statement

```
x = (i += 2, a[i]);
```

is the same as the effect of these two statements:

```
i += 2;
x = a[i];
```

Notice that the parentheses around the comma expression in the first version are essential since the precedence of the assignment operator is higher than the precedence of the comma. Here are "before" and "after" snapshots of memory:

| Before | | After | |
|---|---|---|---|
| a[0] | 4.2 | a[0] | 4.2 |
| [1] | 12.1 | [1] | 12.1 |
| [2] | 6.8 | [2] | 6.8 |
| [3] | 10.5 | [3] | 10.5 |
| i | 1 | i | 3 |
| x | ? | x | 10.5 |

**EXAMPLE C.2**

In the code fragment that follows, the two loop control variables are initialized to 0. One of these variables is incremented by 2 at the end of each loop iteration while the second variable is incremented by the new value of the first.

```
for  (i = 0, j = 0;
     i < I_MAX  &&  j < J_MAX;
     i += 2, j += i)
    printf("i - %d,  j = %d\n", i, j);
```

The comma operator should be used sparingly, since frequent use greatly increases the code's complexity from the reader's point of view.

# Pointer Arithmetic

C permits application of the addition and subtraction operators to pointer operands if the pointers reference elements of an array. If p is a pointer to an array element, the value of the expression

p + 1

depends entirely on the size of the memory block occupied by one array element. C guarantees that if p is the address of an array's $n$th element, then p + 1 is the address of element $n + 1$.

An example to illustrate the role of context in the evaluation of a pointer expression follows. In Fig. D.1, our example uses two arrays: p1, which is an

**Figure D.1    Pointer Arithmetic Example**

```
typedef struct {
      char name[STRSIZ];
      double diameter;        /* equatorial diameter in km                  */
      int    moons;           /* number of moons                           */
      double orbit_time,      /* years to orbit sun once                   */
             rotation_time;   /* hours to complete one revolution on axis  */
} planet_t;

. . .

planet_t pl[2] = {{"Earth", 12713.5, 1, 1.0, 24.0},
                  {"Jupiter", 142800.0, 4, 11.9, 9.925}};

int nm[5] = {4, 8, 10, 16, 22};
planet_t *p;
int *np;

p = pl + 1;
np = nm + 1;
```

*(continued)*

**Figure D.1**  *(continued)*

```
printf("sizeof (planet_t) = %d          sizeof (int) = %d\n",
      sizeof (planet_t), sizeof (int));
printf("pl = %d                 nm = %d\n", pl, nm);
printf(" p = %d (pl + %d)        ", p, (int)p - (int)pl);
printf("np = %d (nm + %d)\n", np, (int)np - (int)nm);
printf(" p - pl = %d\n", p - pl);
```

array of planets, and nm, which is an array of integers. Figure D.2 shows the values of pointers p and np after they are assigned 1 more than pl and nm, respectively. In Fig. D.3, we see possible output produced when our example prints the contents of the four pointer variables as integers. We also see the effect of pointer subtraction on two pointers of the same type.

**Figure D.2 Memory Snapshot at Completion of Pointer Arithmetic Example**

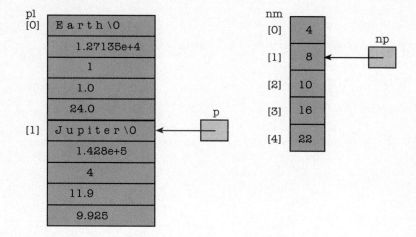

**Figure D.3    Output from Pointer Arithmetic Example**

```
sizeof (planet_t) = 48          sizeof (int) = 4
pl = 2145835092                 nm = 2145835316
 p = 2145835140 (pl + 48)       np = 2145835320 (nm + 4)
 p - pl = 1
```

## ANSI C Reserved Words

| | | | |
|---|---|---|---|
| auto | double | int | struct |
| break | else | long | switch |
| case | enum | register | typedef |
| char | extern | return | union |
| const | float | short | unsigned |
| continue | for | signed | void |
| default | goto | sizeof | volatile |
| do | if | static | while |

# Odd-Numbered Self-Check Exercises

### CHAPTER 1

### Section 1.1

1. Software

### Section 1.2

1. Cell 0: 75.625
   Cell 2: 0.005
   Cell 999: 75.62

3. Bit, byte, memory cell, main memory, secondary storage

### Section 1.3

1. Add values of a, b, and c. Store sum in x.
   Divide y by z. Store result in x.
   Subtract b from c and then add a. Store result in d.
   Add 1 to z. Store result in z.
   Add 273.15 to celsius. Store result in kelvin.

### Section 1.4

1. Source program, compiler, editor (word-processor)

### Section 1.5

1. Problem requirements, analysis, design, implementation, testing and verification, maintenance

### Section 1.6

1. Algorithm with refinements:
   1. Get the distance in kilometers.
   2. Convert the distance to miles,
      2.1 The distance in miles is 0.621 times the distance in kilometers.
   3. Display the distance in miles.

**CHAPTER 2**

## Section 2.1

1. a. `void, double, return`
   b. `printf`
   c. `MAX_ENTRIES, G`
   d. `time, xyz123, this_is_a_long_one`
   e. `Sue's, part#2, "char", #include`

3. The preprocessor; `#define` and `#include`

## Section 2.2

1. a. 0.0103     1234500.0     123450.0
   b. 1.3e+3     1.2345e+2     4.26e−3

3. `double, int, char`

## Section 2.3

1. `Enter two integers> 5 7`
   `m = 10`
   `n = 21`

3. `My name is Jane Doe.`
   `I live in Ann Arbor, MI`
   `and I have 11 years of programming experience.`

## Section 2.4

1. `/* This is a comment? */`
   `/* This one seems like a comment doesn't it */`

## Section 2.5

1. a. `22 / 7 is 3`      `7 / 22 is 0`      `22 % 7 is 1`      `7 % 22 is 7`
   b. `16 / 15 is 1`     `15 / 16 is 0`     `16 % 15 is 1`     `15 % 16 is 15`
   c. `23 / 3 is 7`      `3 / 23 is 0`      `23 % 3 is 2`      `3 % 23 is 3`
   d. `16 / -3 is ??`    `-3 / 16 is ??`    `16 % -3 is ??`    `-3 % 16 is ??`
   (?? means the result varies)

3. a. 3          f. `0.0`        l. 9
   b. ??         g. undefined   m. `-3.14159`
   c. 1          h. undefined   n. `1.0`
   d. `-3.14159` i. ??          o. 1
   e. ??         j. 3           p. undefined
                 k. `-3.0`      q. 3
   (?? means the result varies)

5. a. white is `1.6666...`    c. orange is 0    e. lime is 2
   b. green is `0.6666...`    d. blue is `-3.0`  f. purple is `0.0`
   (?? means the result varies)

## Section 2.6

1. `printf("Salary is %10.2f\n", salary);`

3. `x░is░░12.34░░i░is░100`
   `i░is░100`
   `x░is░12.3`

## Section 2.7

1. Calls to printf to display prompts precede calls to scanf to obtain data. Calls to printf follow calls to scanf when data are echoed. Prompts are used in interactive programs, but not in batch programs. Batch programs should echo input; interactive programs may also echo input.

### CHAPTER 3

## Section 3.1

1.  Problem Inputs
```
double hours              /* number of hours worked */
double rate               /* hourly rate of pay     */
```

Problem Output
```
double gross              /* gross salary */
```

Algorithm
1. Input hours worked and rate of pay.
2. Compute gross salary.
        2.1 Assign hours * rate to gross.
3. Display gross salary.

3.  Problem Inputs
```
double reg_hours          /* number of regular hours worked    */
double ot_hours           /* number of overtime hours worked   */
double rate               /* hourly rate of pay                */
```

Problem Output
```
double gross              /* gross salary                      */
```

Algorithm
1. Input regular (reg_hours) and overtime (ot_hours) hours worked and rate of pay.
2. Compute gross salary.
        2.1 Assign reg_hours * rate to gross.
        2.2 Add ot_hours * 1.5 * rate to the previous gross value.
3. Display gross salary.

## Section 3.2

1.  a. sqrt(u + v) * pow(w, 2)          c. sqrt(pow(x - y, 3))
    b. log(pow(x, y))                    d. fabs(x * y - w / z)

## Section 3.3

1.  The design phase.

## Section 3.4

1. HI MOM is printed vertically in large block letters.

## Section 3.5

1. a. `3141.590000`
   b. `31.415900`
   c.
   ```
   * * * * * * * * * * *
   *               *
   *    31.42    *
   *               *
   * * * * * * * * * * *
   ```
   d. `3.141590`
   e. `3.141590`

3. Function arguments are used to pass information between the separate modules of a program and between the main function and its modules. Arguments make it easier for a function to be reused by other functions or programs. Functions with arguments are building blocks for constructing larger programs.

### CHAPTER 4

## Section 4.2

1. `1 (TRUE)`
   `0 (FALSE)`
   `1 (TRUE)`
   `1 (TRUE)`

3. 
```
x = 3.0      y = 4.0      z = 2.0      flag = 0
 !  (   flag  ||  (  y  +  z  >=  x  -  z  ))
               0        4.0  2.0      3.0  2.0
                        6.0            1.0
                             1
              1
       0
```

5. ans is 2.

## Section 4.3

1. a. `not less`
   b. `greater than`

## Section 4.4

1.
```
if (x > y) {
   x = x + 10.0;
   printf("x Bigger\n");
} else {
   printf("x Smaller\n");
   printf("y is %.2f\n", y);
}
```

3.
```
if (engine_type == 'J') {
      printf("Jet engine");
      speed_category = 1;
} else {
      printf("Propellers");
      speed_category = 2;
}
```

## Section 4.5

1. Additional Program Constant
   ```
   CAP_GALLONS 100   /* maximum number of gallons (in thousands) for basic fee */
   ```

   Additional Program Variable
   ```
   int excess  /* number of gallons over CAP_GALLONS */
   ```

   Revised Algorithm for comp_use_charge:
   ```
   1. used is current - previous
   2. if used > CAP_GALLONS
        excess is used - CAP_GALLONS
        use_charge is CAP_GALLONS * PER_1000_CHG +
           excess * PER_1000_CHG * 2
      else
        use_charge is used * PER_1000_CHG
   ```

## Section 4.7

1.

| Statement Part | salary | tax | Effect |
|---|---|---|---|
| `if (salary < 0.0)` | 23500.00 | ? | 23500.00 < 0.00 is false. |
| `else if (salary < 15000.00)` | | | 23500.00 < 15000.00 is false. |
| `else if (salary < 30000.00)` | | | 23500.00 < 30000.00 is true. |
| `   tax = (salary - 15000.00)` | | | Evaluates to 8500.00. |
| `      * 0.18` | | | Evaluates to 1530.00. |
| `      + 2250.00` | | 3780.00 | Evaluates to 3780.00. |

3.
```
if (pH > 7)
    if (pH < 12)
        printf("Alkaline");
    else
        printf("Very alkaline");
else if (pH == 7)
    printf ("Neutral");
else if (pH > 2)
    printf ("Acidic");
else
    printf ("Very acidic");
```

## Section 4.8

1. ```
   red
   blue
   yellow
   ```
   ```

## Section 5.1

1.  0 10
    1  9
    2  8
    3  7
    4  6
    5  5

## Section 5.2

1.  a. Enter an integer> 5     b. Enter an integer> 6     c. Enter an integer> 7
       5                          6                           7
       25                         36                          49
       125                        216                         343
       625                        1296                        2401

    In general, this loop displays $n$, $n^2$, $n^3$, and $n^4$.

3.  ```
    count = 0;
    sum = 0;
    while (count < 5) {
       printf("Next number> ");
       scanf("%d", &next_num);
       sum += next_num;
       count += 1;
    }
    printf("%d numbers were added; ", count);
    printf("their sum is %d.\n", sum);
    ```

## Section 5.3

1.  For n = 8:

| Statement | odd | sum | Effect |
|---|---|---|---|
| sum = 0; | | 0 | Initialize sum to 0 |
| odd = 1; | 1 | | Initialize odd to 1 |
| odd < n; | | | 1 < 8 is true |
| sum += odd; | | 1 | sum = 0 + 1 |
| odd +=2 | 3 | | odd = 1 + 2 |
| odd < n; | | | 3 < 8 is true |
| sum += odd; | | 4 | sum = 1 + 3 |
| odd +=2 | 5 | | odd = 3 + 2 |
| odd < n; | | | 5 < 8 is true |
| sum += odd; | | 9 | sum = 4 + 5 |
| odd +=2 | 7 | | odd = 5 + 2 |
| odd < n; | | | 7 < 8 is true |
    ```

```
Statement              odd     sum    Effect
sum += odd;                     16     sum = 9 + 7
odd +=2                 9              odd = 7 + 2
odd < n;                               9 < 8 is false
                                       exit loop

printf("Sum of...                      Output: Sum of positive odd numbers less than
                                       8 is 16.
```

3.  The answer to both questions is 0.
5.  ```
    ++i;
    --j;
    n = i * j;
    m = i + j;
    j--;
    p = i + j;
    ```
7.  a. ```
    1   10
    2    8
    3    6
    4    4
    5    2
    ```
    b. ```
    j = 10;
    for (i = 0;  i < 5;  ++i) {
            printf("%d  %d\n", i+1, j);
            j -= 2;
    }
    ```

## Section 5.4

1.  Any initial supply less than 8000 barrels.
3.  ```
    Number of barrels currently in tank> 8350.8
    8350.80 barrels are available.

    Enter number of gallons removed> 7581.0
    After removal of 7581.00 gallons (180.50 barrels),
    8170.30 barrels are available.

    Enter number of gallons removed> 7984.2
    After removal of 7984.20 gallons (190.10 barrels),
    only 7980.20 barrels are left.

    *** WARNING ***
    Available supply is less than 10 percent of tank's 80000.00-barrel capacity.
    ```

## Section 5.5

1.  step a — Initialization of the loop control variable.
    step c — The loop repetition condition.
    step e — The update of the loop control variable.

## Section 5.6

1.  a.  *
        * *
        * * *
        * * * *
        * * * * *
    b.  * * *
        * * *
        * * *
        * * *
        * * *

## Section 5.7

1.  The `while` loop is better because the `do-while` tests the same condition twice on each iteration.

## Section 5.8

```
1.  radiation_lev = init_radiation;
    while (radiation_lev > min_radiation) {
       if (radiation_lev > SAFE_RAD)
            printf(" %3d%5c%9.4f   Unsafe\n", day, ' ', radiation_lev);
       else
            printf(" %3d%5c%9.4f   Safe\n", day, ' ', radiation_lev);
       day += 3;
       radiation_lev /= 2.0;
    }
```

## Section 5.9

```
1.  for (count = 0; count <= n; ++count) {
        printf("DEBUG*** count = %d\n", count);
        sum += count;
        printf("DEBUG*** sum = %d\n", sum);
    }
```

### CHAPTER 6

## Section 6.1

```
1.  void
    sum_n_avg(double  n1, /* input numbers     */
              double  n2,
              double  n3,
              double *sump, /* output -sum of the three numbers */
              double *avgp) /* output -average of the numbers    */
```

3. 

| Reference | Where Legal | Data Type | Value |
|-----------|-------------|-----------|-------|
| &many | main | int * | pointer to gray cell |
| valp | sub | double * | pointer to color-shaded cell |
| code | main | char | 'g' |
| &code | main | char * | pointer to white cell |
| countp | sub | int * | pointer to gray cell |
| *countp | sub | int | 14 |
| *valp | sub | double | 17.1 |
| letp | sub | char * | pointer to white cell |
| &x | main | double * | pointer to color shaded cell |

## Section 6.2

1. 

| Function call | num1 | num2 | num3 |
|---------------|------|------|------|
| | 8 | 12 | 10 |
| order(&num3, &num2); | | | |
| order(&num2, &num1); | 12 | 8 | |
| order(&num3, &num2); | | 10 | 8 |

This sequence of calls to function order puts num1, num2, num3 in descending order (from largest to smallest).

## Section 6.4

1.
```
void
onef(int dat, int *out1p, int *out2p)
{
    int tmp;
    twof(dat, &tmp, out2p);
    . . .
}

void
twof(int indat, int *result1p, int *result2p)
```

## Section 6.5

1. Because multiple values need to be returned and this can only be done by using output parameters.

CHAPTER 7

## Section 7.1

1. Representational error occurs when the number of bits (binary digits) in the mantissa of a type double variable is insufficient to exactly represent a certain fraction. Cancellation error occurs when performing an operation on two numbers that have a very large difference in magnitude, and the smaller number's effect is lost.

3.  | x | y | m | n |
    |---|---|---|---|
    | 10.5 | 7.2 | 5 | 2 |

```
a. x / (double)m          2.1
b. x / m                  2.1
c. (double)(n * m)        10.0
d. (double)(n / m) + y    7.2
e. (double)(n / m)        0.0
```

## Section 7.2

1.  a. 3
    b. 'E'
    c. -1

## Section 7.3

1.  ```
    typedef enum
        {monday, tuesday, wednesday, thursday, friday, saturday, sunday}
    dat_t;
    ```

    a. 0               d. friday
    b. 3               e. wednesday
    c. 0 (FALSE)       f. 1 (TRUE)

## Section 7.4

1.  2.0 . . 3.0 is one such interval.

### CHAPTER 8

## Section 8.1

1.  x3 is a valid variable name. x[3] is a reference to the fourth element of array x.
3.  ```
    double sq_root[11];
    int    cube[11];
    ```

## Section 8.2

1.  Before:

    | x[0] | x[1] | x[2] | x[3] | x[4] | x[5] | x[6] | x[7] |
    |---|---|---|---|---|---|---|---|
    | 16.0 | 12.0 | 6.0 | 8.0 | 2.5 | 12.0 | 14.0 | -54.5 |

    After:

    | x[0] | x[1] | x[2] | x[3] | x[4] | x[5] | x[6] | x[7] |
    |---|---|---|---|---|---|---|---|
    | 16.0 | 12.0 | 6.0 | 8.0 | 12.0 | 14.0 | 14.0 | -54.5 |

**Section 8.3**

1. 
```
#include <math.h>
#define MAX_SIZE 11
...
double cube[MAX_SIZE];
int    sq_root[MAX_SIZE];
int    i;

for  (i = 0;  i < MAX_SIZE;  ++i) {
     sq_root[i] = sqrt((double)i);
     cube[i] = i * i * i;
}
```

**Section 8.4**

1. `seg_len = sqrt(pow(x[i+1] - x[i], 2) + pow(y[i+1] - y[i], 2));`
3. 
```
sum = 0;
for  (i = 0;  i < LIST_SIZE;  i += 2)
     sum += list[i];
```

**Section 8.5**

1. It is better to pass the entire array of data rather than individual elements if several elements of the array are being manipulated by a function.
3. 
```
/*
 * Gets data to place in dbl_arr until value of sentinel
 * is encountered in the input.
 * Returns number of values stored through dbl_sizep.
 * Stops input prematurely if there are more than dbl_max data
 * values before the sentinel or if invalid data is encountered.
 * Pre:  sentinel and dbl_max are defined and dbl_max
 *       is the declared size of dbl_arr
 * Post: returns 1 for no error, and 0 for any error conditions.
 */
int
fill_to_sentinel(int     dbl_max,    /* input - declared size of dbl_arr */
                 double  sentinel,   /* input - end of data value in input
                                               list      */
                 double  dbl_arr[],  /* output - array of data     */
                 int     *dbl_sizep) /* output - number of data values
                                               stored in dbl_arr    */
{
   double data;
   int    i, status;
   int    result = 1;
```

```
        /* Sentinel input loop                                */
        i = 0;
        status = scanf("%lf", &data);
        while (status == 1  &&  data != sentinel  &&  i < dbl_max)
        {
              dbl_arr[i] = data;
              i++;
              status = scanf("%lf", &data);
        }

        /* Issues error message on premature exit              */
        if (status != 1) {
              printf("\n*** Error in data format ***\n");
              printf("*** Using first %d data values ***\n", i);
              result = 0;
        } else if (data != sentinel) {
              printf("\n*** Error: too much data before sentinel ***\n");
              printf("*** Using first %d data values ***\n", i);
              result = 0;
        }

        /* Sends back size of used portion of array, and error status*/
        *dbl_sizep = i;
        return (result);
   }
5. |
   | $
   | $ -
   | $     ch is -.
```

## Section 8.6

1.  a.  n-1 is returned as the position of the match.
    b.  The position of the first match is returned.
3.  To sort in descending order, rewrite the selection-sort algorithm (p. 387) substituting index_of_max for
    each occurrence of index_of_min and replacing all occurrences of "smallest" by "largest."

## Section 8.7

1.  a.
```
int i, j, k;
for  (i = 0;  i < MAXCRS;  ++i) {
     printf("Processing course number %d: \n", i);
     for  (j = 0;  j < 5;  ++j) {
         printf("   Campus %d\n", j);
         for  (k = 0;  k < 4;  ++k)
             printf("     Enter number of ");
```

```
            switch (k) {
            case 0 :
               printf("Freshmen > ");
               break;

            case 1 :
               printf("Sophomores > ");
               break;

            case 2 :
               printf("Juniors > ");
               break;

            case 3 :
               printf("Seniors > ");
               break;
            }
            scanf("%d", &enroll[i][j][k]);
         }
      }
   }
```

b.
```
   int i, j,
       jcnt;   /* Number of juniors. */

   jcnt = 0;
   for (i = 0; i < MAXCRS; ++i)
      for (j = 0; j < 5; ++j)
         jcnt += enroll[i][j][2];
```

c.
```
   /*
    *  Compute the number of students in a course who have a
    *  specific rank.
    *  returns -1 if rank or course is out of range.
    */
   int
   find_students (int enroll[][5][4], int rank, int course)
   {
       int i, cnt = 0;

       if ((rank >= 0 && rank <= 3)
           && (course >= 0 && course < MAXCRS))
         for (i = 0; i < 5; ++i)
            cnt += enroll[course][i][rank];
       else
         cnt = -1;
       return (cnt);
   }
```

To use,

```
printf("Number of sophomores in course 2 is %d\n",
        find_students(enroll, 1, 2);
```

d. int i, j, total, upper;

```
total = 0;
upper = 0;
for (j = 0; j < 5; ++j) {
    for (i = 0; i < MAXCRS; ++i)
        upper += enroll[i][j][2] + enroll[i][j][3];
    printf("Number of upperclass students on campus ");
    printf("%d is %d.\n", j, upper);
    total += upper;
}
printf("Total upperclass students on all campuses is %d.\n",total);
```

## Section 8.8

1.  a. sales[1][fall], sales[1][winter], sales[1][spring],
         sales[1][summer]
    b. sales[0][spring], sales[1][spring], sales[2][spring],
         sales[3][spring], sales[4][spring]
    c. sales[0][fall], sales[1][fall], sales[2][fall],
         sales[3][fall], sales[4][fall]
       sales[0][winter], sales[1][winter], sales[2][winter],
         sales[3][winter], sales[4][winter]
       sales[0][spring], sales[1][spring], sales[2][spring],
         sales[3][spring], sales[4][spring]
       sales[0][summer], sales[1][summer], sales[2][summer],
         sales[3][summer], sales[4][summer]

### CHAPTER 9

## Section 9.1

1.  b
3.
```
                   /*01234567890123456789012345678 90 */
char blanks[]   = "                             ";
        or
char blanks[30] = "                             ";
```

## Section 9.2

1.  Ans: Ad John Quincy Join

## Section 9.3

1. John Adams

## Section 9.4

1. a. 
```
if (strcmp(name1, name2) == 0)
      printf("Names match.\n");
  else
      printf("Names do not match.\n");
```
b. 
```
if (strcmp(w1, w2) < 0)
      strcpy(word, w1);
  else
      strcpy(word, w2);
```

   c. 
```
int i, len;

len = strlen(s1);
i = strlen(s2);
if (i < len)
     len = i;
/* Since len will never be larger than STR_LEN, no need to
   check for overflow of strings. */
for  (i = 0;  i < len && s1[i] == s2[i];  ++i)
    mtch[i] = s1[i];
mtch[i] = '\0';
```

## Section 9.5

1. 
```
/* Orders a list of strings according to the string length —
   shortest to longest */

void order_by_len(char strings[][STRSIZ], /* input/output list of
                                             strings           */
                  int num_str); /* input -number of strings */
void order_by_len(char *strings[], /* input/output list of
                                      strings */
                  int num_str); /* input -number of strings */
```

## Section 9.6

1. The problem is that isupper takes a character argument, not a string.
   Function strncpy returns a string (char *), not a char.

```
if (isupper(str[0]))
     printf("%s begins with a capital letter\n", str);
```

## Section 9.7

1. The & is not needed since dayp, mth_name, yearp are all addresses. Variables dayp and yearp are integer output arguments (type int *), and mth_name is a character array.

**CHAPTER 10**

## Section 10.1

1. a. multiply(5, 4) → multiply(5, 3) → multiply(5, 2) → multiply(5, 1)
      and add 5              and add 5              and add 5
2. b. count('d',"dad") → count('d', "ad") → count('d', "d") → count('d', "")
      and add 1 if              and add 1 if              and add 1 if
      'd' is a 'd'              'a' is a 'd'              'd' is a 'd'

## Section 10.2

1. Stack trace of multiply(6, 3)

   | n | m | ans |
   |---|---|-----|
   | 3 | 6 | ?   |
   |   |   |     |
   | 2 | 6 | ?   |
   | 3 | 6 | ?   |
   |   |   |     |
   | 1 | 6 | 6   |
   | 2 | 6 | ?   |
   | 3 | 6 | ?   |
   |   |   |     |
   | 2 | 6 | 12  |
   | 3 | 6 | ?   |
   |   |   |     |
   | 3 | 6 | 18  |

## Section 10.3

1.
```
int
power_raiser(int base, int power)
{
    int ans;

    if (power = 0)
        ans = 1;
    else
        ans = base * power_raiser(base, power - 1);

    return (ans);
}
```
3. When fibonacci's argument was 2, the else clause assignment statement would generate a call to fibonacci(fibonacci(2 - 2) or fibonacci(0)) whose argument value does not satisfy the precondition.

## Section 10.4

1.　find_caps ("DoD")

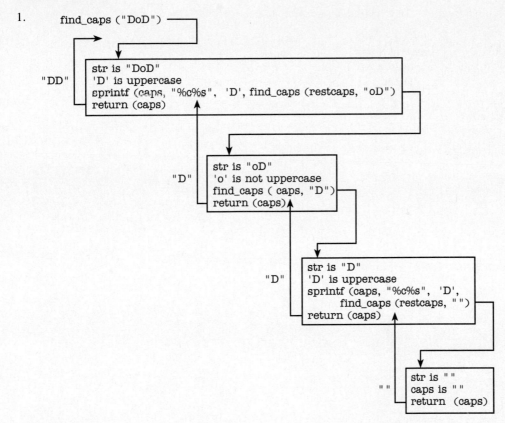

## Section 10.5

1.　Trace of is_element and is_subset on call to is_subset("bc","cebf")
　　Entering is_subset with sub = {b, c} and set = {c, e, b, f}
　　Entering is_element with ele = b and set = {c, e, b, f}
　　Entering is_element with ele = b and set = {e, b, f}
　　Entering is_element with ele = b and set = {b, f}
　　Exiting is_element with ele = b, set = {b, f} and ans = 1
　　Exiting is_element with ele = b, set = {e, b, f} and ans = 1
　　Exiting is_element with ele = b, set = {c, e, b, f} and ans = 1
　　Entering is_subset with sub = {c} and set = {c, e, b, f}
　　Entering is_element with ele = c and set = {c, e, b, f}
　　Exiting is_element with ele = c and set = {c, e, b, f} and ans = 1
　　Entering is_subset with sub = {} and set = {c, e, b, f}
　　Exiting is_subset with sub = {} and set = {c, e, b, f} and ans = 1
　　Exiting is_subset with sub = {c} and set = {c, e, b, f} and ans = 1
　　Exiting is_subset with sub = {b,c} and set = {c, e, b, f} and ans = 1

## Section 10.6

1. By the formula, moves = $2^n - 1$. Thus a six-disk problem would require $2^6 - 1 = 63$ moves.

### CHAPTER 11

## Section 11.1

```
1. typedef struct {
       int   degrees,
             minutes;
       char direction;
   } long_lat_t;
3. typedef struct {
       char authors[50],
             title[50],
             publisher[50];
       int   year;
   } catalog_entry_t;

   catalog_entry_t book;

   strcpy(book.authors,"Hanly, Koffman");
   strcpy(book.title,
          "Problem Solving and Program Design in C");
   strcpy(book.publisher, "Addison-Wesley");
   book.year = 1996;
```

## Section 11.2

```
1. /* Displays with labels all components of a long_lat_t
    * structure
    */
   void
   print_long_lat(long_lat_t pos) /* input - one long_lat
                                              structure */
   {
      printf("  Degrees:   %d deg\n", pos.degrees);
      printf("  Minutes:   %d deg\n", pos.minutes);
      printf("  Direction: %c\n", pos.direction);
   }

   /* Determines whether or not the components of pos_1 and
    * pos_2 match
    */
```

```
int
long_lat_equal(long_lat_t pos_1, /*input - positions to
                                             compare */
               long_lat_t pos_2)
{
    return (pos_1.degrees == pos_2.degrees  &&
            pos_1.minutes == pos_2.minutes  &&
            pos_1.direction == pos_1.direction);
}

/* Fills a type long_lat_t structure with input data.
 * Integer returned as function result is
 * success/failure/EOF indicator.
 *     1   => successful input of pos
 *     0   => error encountered
 *     EOF => insufficient data before end of file
 * In case of error or EOF, value of type long_lat_t
 * output argument is undefined.
 */
int
scan_long_lat(long_lat_t *pos) /* output - address of
                                         long_lat_t
                                         structure to fill */
{
    int result;
    result = scanf("%d%d %c", &pos->degrees,
                   &pos->minutes,
                   &pos->direction);

    if (result == 3)
        result = 1;

    return (result);
}
```

## Section 11.3

1. When time_now is passed as an argument to function new_time, the values of its components are copied into new_time's formal parameter time_of_day. Assignments to these components just change the function's local copy of the structure.

## Section 11.4

1. (6.50 + 5.00i)  +  (3.00 - 4.00i)  =  (9.50 + 1.00i)
   Second result  =  (1.50 + 5.00i)

## Section 11.5

1. The & is not applied to units because units is an array of type unit_t, and an array name with no subscript always represents the address of the array's initial element.

## Section 11.6

1. 22 bytes are allocated for a variable of type hair_info_t, but only four are in use when wear_wig is valid.

### CHAPTER 12

## Section 12.1

1. a. n = 123   x = 3.145 str = "xyz"      ch = \n        3. fscan_complex(FILE *inp
   b. n = 123   x = 3.145 str = "xyz"      ch = \n           ...
   c. n = 3     x = 123.0 str = 145        ch = .            status = fscanf(inp,
   d. n = 35    x = ??    str = xyz        ch = z

## Section 12.2

1. fread(&exec, sizeof (person_t), 1, psn_inp);
3. fwrite(&exec, sizeof (person_t), 1, psn_outp);
5. fread(&num_err[3], sizeof (int), 1, nums_inp);

## Section 12.3

1. a. Low bound for category = "printer stands"
      High bound for category = "printer stands"
      High bound for price = 99.99
   b. Low bound for stock number = 5241
      High bound for stock number = 5241
   c. Low bound for category = "data cartridges"
      High bound for category = "data cartridges"
3. match does not check the number because it is called from within a while loop that calls it only for stock numbers that are in range.

### CHAPTER 13

## Section 13.1

1. a. A microwave oven quickly heats up the objects placed inside of it when the controls are correctly set. It is not necessary to know that the oven is actually emitting energy that is specifically designed to agitate the water molecules in a substance and thus heat up the food.
   b. A television allows one to see various programs simply by turning it on and turning the channels. The user is totally isolated from the electronics used to tune and display the program signal.
   c. A calculator allows the user to compute a myriad of numerical calculations without having any knowledge of the electronics and logic embedded in the calculator.

## Section 13.2

1. A system header file name is surrounded by angular brackets (< >), whereas a personal header file name would be surrounded by quotes (" ").
3. what, how

## Section 13.3

1. This macro is included in the header file so the user will know the string size for the planet structure.

## Section 13.4

```
1. unit_max is auto
   found    is auto
   convert  is extern
   quantity is auto
```

## Section 13.5

1. Having constant macro and type definitions in just one file makes maintenance and modification of the library more straightforward.

## Section 13.6

```
1. #if defined (UNIX)
       printf("Enter <ctrl-d> to quit.")
   #elif defined (VMS)
       printf("Enter <ctrl-z> to quit.")
   #endif
```

## Section 13.7

1. The following code would be added right after the line `int ch;`

```
/* See if arguments were included */
if (argc < 3) {
    printf("\nPlease include input and output file name.\n");
    exit(1);
}
```

## Section 13.8

1. `y = DOUBLE(a - b)` → `y = (a - b) + (a - b)` **OK,**
   but the macro should have been written as `#define DOUBLE(x)  ((x) + (x))`
3. `if  (DISCRIMINANT(a1, b1, c1) == 0)` →
   `if (((b1) * (b1) - 4 * (a1) * (c1)) == 0)`

**CHAPTER 14**

## Section 14.1

```
1. printf("%c", *letp);
3. strcpy(planetp->name, "Uranus");
5. letp = (char *) calloc(30, sizeof (char));
```

## Section 14.2

```
1. AC   DC   AC
    9  115  220
```

## Section 14.3

1. Find 5
   cur_nodep is headp (start)
   cur_nodep is headp->restp (4 checked)
   cur_nodep is headp->restp->restp (1 checked)
   cur_nodep is headp->restp->restp (5 checked and cur_nodep is returned)

   Find 2
   cur_nodep is headp (start)
   cur_nodep is headp->restp (4 checked)
   cur_nodep is headp->restp->restp (1 checked)
   cur_nodep is headp->restp->restp->restp (5 checked)
   cur_nodep is NULL (NULL is returned)

   Find 4
   cur_nodep is headp (start)
   cur_nodep is headp (4 checked and cur_nodep is returned)

## Section 14.4

1. stk.topp

## Section 14.5

1.

## Section 14.6

1.  The call to `delete_ordered_node` does not apply the address-of operator because `is_deletedp` is already a pointer to the integer `is_deleted` flag.

## Section 14.7

1.  a.  The left tree is a binary search tree. The right tree is not a binary search tree because the value 45 is found in its left subtree. This condition violates the requirement that a root have a larger key than each item in its left subtree.
    b.  Inorder traversal of each tree:
        left tree:  10, 15, 20, 40, 50, 55, 60
        right tree:  25, 30, 45, 40, 50, 55, 60
    c.  The key values 41, 42, . . ., 48, 49.

3.  a.

b.

c.

d.

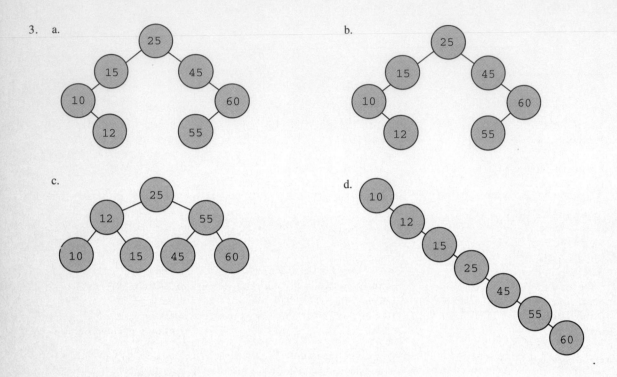

Tree (c) would be the most efficient to search since it has the smallest height.  It will typically require the smallest number of comparisons to determine whether or not a key is in this tree.

The binary search trees formed in parts (a) and (b) are identical in structure. The binary search tree formed in part (d) is the result of worst-case input, with all the data in order.  Searching the binary search tree in part (d) and a linked list with the same keys would be equally costly.

# Reference Guide to ANSI C Constructs

| Construct | Page | Example of Use |
|---|---|---|
| library header inclusion | 28 | `#include <stdio.h>` |
| constant macro definition | 28 | `#define LIMIT 100` |
| macro with parameters | 649 | `#define AVG(x,y) (((x) + (y)) / 2.0)` |
| structure type definition | 533 | `typedef struct {`<br>`        char    name[20];`<br>`        int     quantity;`<br>`        double price;`<br>`} part_t;` |
| linked list node type definition | 672 | `typedef struct node_s {`<br>`        int            data;`<br>`        struct node_s *restp;`<br>`} node_t;` |
| function prototype | 108 | `double next_approx(double previous);` |
| comment | 30 | `/*  C construct examples */` |
| main function heading | 31 | `int`<br>`main(void)` |
| with parameters | 646 | `int`<br>`main(int argc, char *argv[])` |
| variable declaration simple | 35 | `int q, r;`<br>`double x, y;`<br>`char ch;` |
| array | 357 | `int ages[LIMIT];` |
| structure | 533 | `part_t one_part;` |
| pointer | 272 | `double *fracp;`<br>`node_t *listp;` |
| array of pointers | 441 | `char *words[20];` |
| file pointer | 74 | `FILE *infilep, *outfilep;` |
| with initialization | 233 | `int sum = 0;` |
| | 359 | `char hex[16] = {'0','1','2','3','4','5','6',`<br>`        '7','8','9','A','B','C','D','E','F'};` |
| | 447 | `char *greetings[2] = {"Hi", "Bye"};` |